GCSE Edexcel
Combined Science
Higher Level

Here it is, your dream come true! No, not a never-ending pizza buffet, or the secret to eternal youth, it's something much better — it's CGP's Combined Science guide!

It's the ultimate revision triple-threat — everything you need to know for Combined Science Biology, Chemistry and Physics. Plus, there are exam-style questions for every topic, a full set of practice papers, and a free online edition.

You'll also find links to our fantastic online content, with video solutions for practice questions, as well as Retrieval Quizzes to help you nail down all the facts you need to learn.

―――― Unlock your free online extras! ――――

Just go to **cgpbooks.co.uk/extras** and enter this code or scan the QR codes in the book.

0511 2504 9566 9261

By the way, this code only works for one person. If somebody else has used this book before you, they might have already claimed the Online Edition.

Complete
Revision & Practice
Everything you need to pass the exams!

Contents

Working Scientifically

The Scientific Method 2
Models and Communication 3
Issues Created by Science 4
Risk 5
Designing Investigations 6
Processing Data 9
Presenting Data 10
More on Graphs 11
Units and Equations 12
Converting Units 13
Drawing Conclusions 14
Uncertainty 15
Evaluations 16

Section 1 — Key Concepts in Biology

Cells 17
Specialised Cells 19
Microscopy 21
More Microscopy 23
Warm-Up and Exam Questions 25
Enzymes 26
Investigating Enzyme Activity 28
Enzymes in Breakdown and Synthesis 30
Warm-Up and Exam Questions 31
Diffusion and Active Transport 32
Osmosis 33
Warm-Up and Exam Questions 35
Revision Summary for Section 1 36

Section 2 — Cells and Control

Mitosis 37
Cell Division and Growth 39
Percentile Charts 40
Stem Cells 41
Warm-Up and Exam Questions 43
The Nervous System 44
Reflexes 46
Warm-Up and Exam Questions 47

Section 3 — Genetics

Sexual Reproduction 48
Meiosis 49
DNA 50
Warm-Up and Exam Questions 51
Genes and Alleles 52
Genetic Diagrams 53
Warm-Up and Exam Questions 56
Variation 57
Variation and the Human Genome Project 58
The Human Genome Project 59
Warm-Up and Exam Questions 60

Section 4 — Natural Selection and Genetic Modification

Natural Selection and Evidence for Evolution 61
Evidence for Human Evolution 63
Classification 65
Selective Breeding 66
Genetic Engineering 67
Warm-Up and Exam Questions 69

Throughout this book you'll see grade stamps like these:
These grade stamps help to show how difficult the questions are.
Remember — to get a top grade you need to be able to answer **all** the questions, not just the hardest ones.

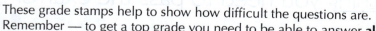

In the real exams, some questions test how well you can structure an answer (as well as your scientific knowledge). In this book, we've marked these questions with an asterisk (*).

Section 5 — Health, Disease and the Development of Medicines

Health and Disease 71
Sexually Transmitted Infections 73
Warm-Up and Exam Questions 74
Fighting Disease 75
Memory Lymphocytes 76
Immunisation 77
Antibiotics and Other Medicines 78
Warm-Up and Exam Questions 79
Non-Communicable Diseases 80
Measures of Obesity 82
Treatments for Cardiovascular Disease 83
Warm-Up and Exam Questions 85
Revision Summary for Sections 2-5 86

Section 6 — Plant Structures and Their Functions

Photosynthesis 87
Investigating Photosynthesis 89
Warm-Up and Exam Questions 90
Transport in Plants 91
Transpiration and Stomata 92
Transpiration Rate 93
Warm-Up and Exam Questions 95

Section 7 — Animal Coordination, Control and Homeostasis

Hormones 96
Comparing Neurones and Hormones 97
Adrenaline and Thyroxine 98
Warm-Up and Exam Questions 99
The Menstrual Cycle 100
Controlling Fertility 102
Warm-Up and Exam Questions 104
Homeostasis 105
Blood Glucose Regulation 106
Diabetes 107
Warm-Up and Exam Questions 108

Section 8 — Exchange and Transport in Animals

Exchange of Materials 109
Exchange Surfaces and the Alveoli 110
Respiration 111
Investigating Respiration 113
Warm-Up and Exam Questions 114
Circulatory System — Blood 115
Circulatory System — Blood Vessels 117
Circulatory System — The Heart 118
Warm-Up and Exam Questions 120

Section 9 — Ecosystems and Material Cycles

Ecosystems and Interactions Between Organisms .. 121
Investigating Ecosystems 123
Warm-Up and Exam Questions 125
Human Impacts on Biodiversity 126
Conservation and Biodiversity 128
Warm-Up and Exam Questions 130
The Carbon Cycle 131
The Water Cycle 132
The Nitrogen Cycle 134
Warm-Up and Exam Questions 136
Revision Summary for Sections 6-9 137

Section 10 — Key Concepts in Chemistry

Chemical Equations 138
Chemical Equations Involving Ions 140
Hazards and Risk 141
Warm-Up and Exam Questions 143
The History of the Atom 144
The Atom 146
Warm-Up and Exam Questions 147
Isotopes and Relative Atomic Masses 148
The Periodic Table 150
Electronic Configurations 152
Warm-Up and Exam Questions 153
Ions 154
Ionic Bonding 155
Ionic Compounds 157

Warm-Up and Exam Questions 159
Covalent Bonding.. 160
Warm-Up and Exam Questions 162
Giant Covalent Structures 163
Fullerenes and Polymers 164
Metallic Bonding... 165
Warm-Up and Exam Questions 166
Conservation of Mass 167
Relative Masses and Chemical Formulas............... 168
Moles and Calculations 169
Warm-Up and Exam Questions 172
Calculating Empirical Formulas 173
Limiting Reactants 174
Balancing Equations Using Masses 176
Warm-Up and Exam Questions 177
Revision Summary for Section 10 178

Section 11 — States of Matter and Mixtures

States of Matter... 179
Warm-Up and Exam Questions 182
Purity... 183
Distillation.. 184
Filtration and Crystallisation 186
Warm-Up and Exam Questions 187
Chromatography... 188
Interpreting Chromatograms 189
Combining Separation Techniques 190
Water Treatment 191
Warm-Up and Exam Questions 192

Section 12 — Chemical Changes

Acids and Bases.. 193
Strong Acids, Weak Acids and their Reactions 194
Warm-Up and Exam Questions 197
Making Insoluble Salts... 198
Making Soluble Salts 199
Warm-Up and Exam Questions 201
Electrolysis 202
Electrochemical Cells 203
Electrolysis of Molten Substances 204
Electrolysis of Aqueous Solutions.......................... 205
Electrolysis of Copper Sulfate................................ 206
Warm-Up and Exam Questions 207

Section 13 — Extracting Metals and Equilibria

The Reactivity Series.. 208
Reactivity of Metals 209
Displacement Reactions 211
Warm-Up and Exam Questions 213
Extracting Metals Using Carbon............................ 214
Extracting Metals Using Electrolysis 215
Biological Methods of Extracting Metals 216
Recycling and Life Cycle Assessments 217
Warm-Up and Exam Questions 220
Dynamic Equilibrium 221
Le Chatelier's Principle 222
Warm-Up and Exam Questions 224
Revision Summary for Sections 11-13................... 225

Section 14 — Groups in the Periodic Table

Group 1 — Alkali Metals..................................... 226
Group 7 — Halogens 228
Halogen Displacement Reactions 230
Group 0 — Noble Gases 232
Warm-Up and Exam Questions 233

Section 15 — Rates of Reaction and Energy Changes

Rates of Reaction... 235
Rate Experiments 237
Calculating Rates... 240
Warm-Up and Exam Questions 241
Collision Theory 243
Catalysts... 245
Warm-Up and Exam Questions 246
Endothermic and Exothermic Reactions................. 247
Bond Energies... 250
Warm-Up and Exam Questions 251

Section 16 — Fuels and Earth Science

Fractional Distillation 252
Hydrocarbons 253
Cracking 255
Warm-Up and Exam Questions 256
Pollutants 257
The Atmosphere 259
Warm-Up and Exam Questions 260
The Greenhouse Effect 261
Climate Change 262
Warm-Up and Exam Questions 264
Revision Summary for Sections 14-16 265

Section 17 — Motion and Forces

Scalars and Vectors 266
Speed 267
Acceleration 268
Distance/Time Graphs 270
Velocity/Time Graphs 271
Warm-Up and Exam Questions 272
Newton's First and Second Laws 273
Inertia and Newton's Third Law 274
Warm-Up and Exam Questions 275
Investigating Motion 276
Weight 278
Warm-Up and Exam Questions 279
Momentum 280
Warm-Up and Exam Questions 283
Reaction Times 284
Stopping Distances 285
Stopping Safely 286
Warm-Up and Exam Questions 287

Section 18 — Conservation of Energy

Energy Stores 288
Energy Stores and Transfers 289
Warm-Up and Exam Questions 291
Unwanted Energy Transfers 292
Efficiency 293
Reducing Unwanted Energy Transfers 294
Warm-Up and Exam Questions 295
Energy Resources 296
More Renewable Energy Resources 297
Non-Renewable Resources 298
Trends in Energy Resource Use 299
Warm-Up and Exam Questions 300

Section 19 — Waves and the Electromagnetic Spectrum

Wave Basics 301
Transverse and Longitudinal Waves 302
Investigating Waves 303
Warm-Up and Exam Questions 305
Wave Behaviour at Boundaries 306
Investigating Refraction 307
Warm-Up and Exam Questions 308
Electromagnetic Waves 309
Uses of EM Waves 310
Dangers of EM Waves 314
Warm-Up and Exam Questions 315

Section 20 — Radioactivity

Developing the Model of the Atom 316
Current Model of the Atom 317
Electron Energy Levels 318
Warm-Up and Exam Questions 319
Isotopes 320
Ionising Radiation 321
Nuclear Equations 322
Warm-Up and Exam Questions 323
Background Radiation and Activity 324
Half-Life 325
Ionisation, Irradiation and Contamination 326
Warm-Up and Exam Questions 327
Revision Summary for Sections 17-20 328

Section 21 — Forces and Energy

Energy Transfers 329
Work Done 330
Power 331
Warm-Up and Exam Questions 332
Forces 333
Resultant Forces 334
Resolving Forces 335
Warm-Up and Exam Questions 336

Section 22 — Electricity and Circuits

Circuit Basics 337
Potential Difference and Resistance 339
Investigating Components 340
Circuit Devices 341
Investigating LDRs and Thermistors 342
Warm-Up and Exam Questions 343
Series Circuits 344
Parallel Circuits 345
Investigating Circuits 346
Warm-Up and Exam Questions 347
Energy in Circuits 348
Heating in Circuits and Power Ratings 349
Power in Circuits 350
Warm-Up and Exam Questions 351
Electricity in the Home 352
Electrical Safety 353
Warm-Up and Exam Questions 355

Section 23 — Magnetic Fields

Magnets and Magnetic Fields 356
Permanent and Induced Magnets 357
Electromagnetism and The Motor Effect 358
The Motor Effect 359
Solenoids 360
Warm-Up and Exam Questions 361
Electromagnetic Induction 362
Transformers and The National Grid 363
Warm-Up and Exam Questions 364

Section 24 — Matter

Density 365
Kinetic Theory and States of Matter 366
Internal Energy and Absolute Zero 367
Gas Pressure 368
Warm-Up and Exam Questions 369
Specific Heat Capacity 370
Specific Latent Heat 371
Investigating Water 372
Warm-Up and Exam Questions 373
Elasticity 374
Investigating Elasticity 376
Warm-Up and Exam Questions 377
Revision Summary for Sections 21-24 378

Practical Skills

Apparatus and Techniques 379
Heating Substances 383
Safety and Experiments 385
Safety and Ethics 386

Practice Exams

Practice Paper 1: Biology 1 387
Practice Paper 2: Biology 2 400
Practice Paper 3: Chemistry 1 412
Practice Paper 4: Chemistry 2 424
Practice Paper 5: Physics 1 436
Practice Paper 6: Physics 2 449

Answers 462
Glossary 489
Index 502
Physics Equation Sheet 506

You'll see **QR codes** throughout the book that you can scan with your smartphone.

A QR code next to a tip box question takes you to a **video** that talks you through solving the question. You can access **all** the videos by scanning this code here.

A QR code on a 'Revision Summary' page takes you to a **Retrieval Quiz** for that topic. You can access **all** the quizzes by scanning this code here.

You can also find the **full set of videos** at cgpbooks.co.uk/GCSEComb-EdexH/Videos and the **full set of quizzes** at cgpbooks.co.uk/GCSEComb-EdexH/Quiz

For useful information about **What to Expect in the Exams** and other exam tips head to cgpbooks.co.uk/GCSEComb-EdexH/Exams

Published by CGP

Editors: Ellen Burton, Emma Clayton, Rob Hayman, Andy Hurst, Paul Jordin, Duncan Lindsay, Jake McGuffie, Sarah Pattison, Charlotte Sheridan and George Wright.

Contributor: Paddy Gannon

From original material by Richard Parsons.

With thanks to Jade Sim for the copyright research.

Percentile growth chart on page 40 reproduced with kind permission of the RCPCH/Harlow Printing.

Definition of health on page 71 reproduced from the WHO website, The Constitution of the World Health Organization. https://www.who.int/about/governance/constitution. Accessed: 3rd October 2022.

Hazard symbols on page 141 are public sector information published by the Health and Safety Executive and licensed under the Open Government Licence. http://www.nationalarchives.gov.uk/doc/open-government-licence/version/3/.

Graphs to show trend in atmospheric CO_2 concentration and global temperature on pages 263 and 264 based on data by EPICA community members 2004 and Siegenthaler et al 2005.

Traffic sign on page 290 © Crown Copyright. Contains public sector information licensed under the Open Government Licence v3.0.

Every effort has been made to locate copyright holders and obtain permission to reproduce sources. For those sources where it has been difficult to trace the originator of the work, we would be grateful for information. If any copyright holder would like us to make an amendment to the acknowledgements, please notify us and we will gladly update the book at the next reprint. Thank you.

ISBN: 978 1 78908 944 8

Printed by Elanders Ltd, Newcastle upon Tyne.
Clipart from Corel®
Illustrations by: Sandy Gardner Artist, email sandy@sandygardner.co.uk

Text, design, layout and original illustrations © Coordination Group Publications Ltd. (CGP) 2022
All rights reserved.

Photocopying more than 5% of this book is not permitted, even if you have a CLA licence.
Extra copies are available from CGP with next day delivery • 0800 1712 712 • www.cgpbooks.co.uk

The Scientific Method

*This section **isn't** about how to 'do' science — but it does show you the way **most scientists** work.*

Scientists Come Up With **Hypotheses** — Then **Test** Them

1) Scientists try to explain things. They start by observing something they don't understand.
2) They then come up with a hypothesis — a possible explanation for what they've observed.
3) The next step is to test whether the hypothesis might be right or not. This involves making a prediction based on the hypothesis and testing it by gathering evidence (i.e. data) from investigations. If evidence from experiments backs up a prediction, you're a step closer to figuring out if the hypothesis is true.

About 100 years ago, scientists hypothesised that atoms looked like this.

Several Scientists Will Test a Hypothesis

1) Normally, scientists share their findings in peer-reviewed journals, or at conferences.
2) Peer-review is where other scientists check results and scientific explanations to make sure they're 'scientific' (e.g. that experiments have been done in a sensible way) before they're published. It helps to detect false claims, but it doesn't mean that findings are correct — just that they're not wrong in any obvious way.
3) Once other scientists have found out about a hypothesis, they'll start basing their own predictions on it and carry out their own experiments. They'll also try to reproduce the original experiments to check the results — and if all the experiments in the world back up the hypothesis, then scientists start to think the hypothesis is true.
4) However, if a scientist does an experiment that doesn't fit with the hypothesis (and other scientists can reproduce the results) then the hypothesis may need to be modified or scrapped altogether.

After more evidence was gathered, scientists changed their hypothesis to this.

If **All** the **Evidence** Supports a Hypothesis, It's **Accepted** — For Now

1) Accepted hypotheses are often referred to as theories. Our currently accepted theories are the ones that have survived this 'trial by evidence' — they've been tested many times over the years and survived.
2) However, theories never become totally indisputable fact. If new evidence comes along that can't be explained using the existing theory, then the hypothesising and testing is likely to start all over again.

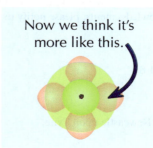

Now we think it's more like this.

Scientific models are constantly being refined...

The scientific method has been developed over time. Aristotle (a Greek philosopher) was the first person to realise that theories need to be based on observations. Muslim scholars then introduced the ideas of creating a hypothesis, testing it, and repeating work to check results.

Models and Communication

*Once scientists have made a **new discovery**, they **don't** just keep it to themselves. Oh no. Time to learn about how scientific discoveries are **communicated**, and the **models** that are used to represent theories.*

Theories Can Involve Different Types of Models

1) A representational model is a simplified description or picture of what's going on in real life. Like all models, it can be used to explain observations and make predictions. E.g. the lock and key model of enzyme action is a simplified way of showing how enzymes work (see p.26). It can be used to explain why enzymes only catalyse particular reactions.

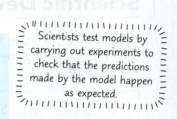
Scientists test models by carrying out experiments to check that the predictions made by the model happen as expected.

2) Computational models use computers to make simulations of complex real-life processes, such as climate change. They're used when there are a lot of different variables (factors that change) to consider, and because you can easily change their design to take into account new data.

3) All models have limitations on what they can explain or predict. E.g. the Bohr model can only be used to make predictions about the electromagnetic radiation emitted by some atoms (like hydrogen).

Scientific Discoveries are Communicated to the General Public

Some scientific discoveries show that people should change their habits, or they might provide ideas that could be developed into new technology. So scientists need to tell the world about their discoveries.

Technologies are being developed that make use of fullerenes (see p.164). These include drug delivery systems for use in medicine. Information about these systems needs to be communicated to doctors so they can use them, and to patients, so they can make informed decisions about their treatment.

Scientific Evidence can be Presented in a Biased Way

1) Scientific discoveries that are reported in the media (e.g. newspapers or television) aren't peer-reviewed.
2) This means that, even though news stories are often based on data that has been peer-reviewed, the data might be presented in a way that is over-simplified or inaccurate, making it open to misinterpretation.
3) People who want to make a point can sometimes present data in a biased way (sometimes without knowing they're doing it). For example, a scientist might overemphasise a relationship in the data, or a newspaper article might describe details of data supporting an idea without giving any evidence against it.

Companies can present biased data to help sell products...
Sometimes a company may only want you to see half of the story so they present the data in a biased way. For example, a pharmaceutical company may want to encourage you to buy their drugs by telling you about all the positives, but not report the results of any unfavourable studies.

Working Scientifically

Issues Created by Science

*Science has helped us **make progress** in loads of areas, from medicine to space travel. But science still has its **issues**. And it **can't answer everything**, as you're about to find out.*

Scientific Developments are Great, but they can Raise Issues

Scientific knowledge is increased by doing experiments. And this knowledge leads to scientific developments, e.g. new technologies or new advice. These developments can create issues though. For example:

> **Economic issues:** Society can't always afford to do things scientists recommend (e.g. investing in alternative energy sources) without cutting back elsewhere.

> **Social issues:** Decisions based on scientific evidence affect people — e.g. should fossil fuels be taxed more highly? Would the effect on people's lifestyles be acceptable?

> **Personal issues:** Some decisions will affect individuals. For example, someone might support alternative energy, but object if a wind farm is built next to their house.

> **Environmental issues:** Human activity often affects the natural environment. For example, building a dam to produce electricity will change the local habitat so some species might be displaced. But it will also reduce our need for fossil fuels, so will help to reduce climate change.

Science Can't Answer Every Question — Especially Ethical Ones

1) We don't understand everything. We're always finding out more, but we'll never know all the answers.
2) In order to answer scientific questions, scientists need data to provide evidence for their hypotheses.
3) Some questions can't be answered yet because the data can't currently be collected, or because there's not enough data to support a theory.
4) Eventually, as we get more evidence, we'll answer some of the questions that currently can't be answered, e.g. what the impact of global warming on sea levels will be. But there will always be the "Should we be doing this at all?"-type questions that experiments can't help us to answer...

> Think about new drugs which can be taken to boost your 'brain power'.
> - Some people think they're good as they could improve concentration or memory. New drugs could let people think in ways beyond the powers of normal brains.
> - Other people say they're bad — they could give some people an unfair advantage in exams. And people might be pressured into taking them so that they could work more effectively, and for longer hours.

There are often issues with new scientific developments...
The trouble is, there's often no clear right answer where these issues are concerned. Different people have different views, depending on their priorities. These issues are full of grey areas.

Working Scientifically

Risk

Scientific discoveries are often great, but they can prove **risky**. With dangers all around, you've got to be aware of hazards — this includes **how likely** they are to **cause harm** and **how serious** the effects may be.

Nothing is Completely Risk-Free

1) A hazard is something that could potentially cause harm.

2) All hazards have a risk attached to them — this is the chance that the hazard will cause harm.

3) The risks of some things seem pretty obvious, or we've known about them for a while, like the risk of causing acid rain by polluting the atmosphere, or of having a car accident when you're travelling in a car.

4) New technology arising from scientific advances can bring new risks, e.g. scientists are unsure whether nanoparticles that are being used in cosmetics and suncream might be harming the cells in our bodies. These risks need to be considered alongside the benefits of the technology, e.g. improved sun protection.

5) You can estimate the size of a risk based on how many times something happens in a big sample (e.g. 100 000 people) over a given period (e.g. a year). For example, you could assess the risk of a driver crashing by recording how many people in a group of 100 000 drivers crashed their cars over a year.

6) To make decisions about activities that involve hazards, we need to take into account the chance of the hazard causing harm, and how serious the consequences would be if it did. If an activity involves a hazard that's very likely to cause harm, with serious consequences if it does, that activity is considered high risk.

People Make Their Own Decisions About Risk

1) Not all risks have the same consequences, e.g. if you chop veg with a sharp knife you risk cutting your finger, but if you go scuba-diving you risk death. You're much more likely to cut your finger during half an hour of chopping than to die during half an hour of scuba-diving. But most people are happier to accept a higher probability of an accident if the consequences are short-lived and fairly minor.

2) People tend to be more willing to accept a risk if they choose to do something (e.g. go scuba diving), compared to having the risk imposed on them (e.g. having a nuclear power station built next door).

3) People's perception of risk (how risky they think something is) isn't always accurate. They tend to view familiar activities as low-risk and unfamiliar activities as high-risk — even if that's not the case. For example, cycling on roads is often high-risk, but many people are happy to do it because it's a familiar activity. Air travel is actually pretty safe, but a lot of people perceive it as high-risk.

4) People may over-estimate the risk of things with long-term or invisible effects, e.g. ionising radiation.

The pros and cons of new technology must be weighed up...
The world's a dangerous place and it's impossible to rule out the chance of an accident altogether. But if you can recognise hazards and take steps to reduce the risks, you're more likely to stay safe.

Working Scientifically

Designing Investigations

*Dig out your lab coat and dust off your badly-scratched safety goggles... it's **investigation time**.*

Evidence Can Support or Disprove a Hypothesis

1) Scientists observe things and come up with hypotheses to explain them (see p.2). You need to be able to do the same. For example:

   > Observation: People with big feet have spots. Hypothesis: Having big feet causes spots.

2) To determine whether or not a hypothesis is right, you need to do an investigation to gather evidence. To do this, you need to use your hypothesis to make a prediction — something you think will happen that you can test. E.g. people who have bigger feet will have more spots.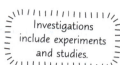
   Investigations include experiments and studies.

3) Investigations are used to see if there are patterns or relationships between two variables, e.g. to see if there's a pattern or relationship between the variables 'number of spots' and 'size of feet'.

Evidence Needs to be Repeatable, Reproducible and Valid

1) Repeatable means that if the same person does an experiment again using the same methods and equipment, they'll get similar results.

2) Reproducible means that if someone else does the experiment, or a different method or piece of equipment is used, the results will still be similar.

3) If data is repeatable and reproducible, it's reliable and scientists are more likely to have confidence in it.

4) Valid results are both repeatable and reproducible AND they answer the original question. They come from experiments that were designed to be a fair test...

Make an Investigation a Fair Test By Controlling the Variables

1) In a lab experiment you usually change one variable and measure how it affects another variable.

2) To make it a fair test, everything else that could affect the results should stay the same — otherwise you can't tell if the thing you're changing is causing the results or not.

3) The variable you CHANGE is called the INDEPENDENT variable.

4) The variable you MEASURE when you change the independent variable is the DEPENDENT variable.

5) The variables that you KEEP THE SAME are called CONTROL variables.

   > You could find how current through a circuit component affects the potential difference (p.d.) across the component by measuring the potential difference at different currents. The independent variable is the current. The dependent variable is the potential difference. Control variables include the temperature of the component, the p.d. of the power supply, etc.

6) Because you can't always control all the variables, you often need to use a control experiment. This is an experiment that's kept under the same conditions as the rest of the investigation, but doesn't have anything done to it. This is so that you can see what happens when you don't change anything at all.

Working Scientifically

Designing Investigations

The Bigger the Sample Size the Better

1) Data based on small samples isn't as good as data based on large samples. A sample should represent the whole population (i.e. it should share as many of the characteristics in the population as possible) — a small sample can't do that as well. It's also harder to spot anomalies if your sample size is too small.

2) The bigger the sample size the better, but scientists have to be realistic when choosing how big. For example, if you were studying how lifestyle affects people's weight it'd be great to study everyone in the UK (a huge sample), but it'd take ages and cost a lot. It's more realistic to study a thousand people, with a mixture of ages, gender and race.

Data Should be Repeatable, Reproducible, Accurate and Precise

1) To check repeatability you need to repeat the readings and check that the results are similar. You need to repeat each reading at least three times.

2) To make sure your results are reproducible you can cross check them by taking a second set of readings with another instrument (or a different observer).

3) Your data also needs to be accurate. Really accurate results are those that are really close to the true answer. The accuracy of your results usually depends on your method — you need to make sure you're measuring the right thing and that you don't miss anything that should be included in the measurements.
E.g. estimating the amount of gas released from a reaction by counting the bubbles isn't very accurate because you might miss some of the bubbles and they might have different volumes. It's more accurate to measure the volume of gas released using a gas syringe (see p.379).

Repeat	Data set 1	Data set 2
1	12	11
2	14	17
3	13	14
Mean	13	14

Data set 1 is more precise than data set 2.

4) Your data also needs to be precise. Precise results are ones where the data is all really close to the mean (average) of your repeated results (i.e. not spread out).

Your Equipment has to be Right for the Job

1) The measuring equipment you use has to be sensitive enough to measure the changes you're looking for. For example, if you need to measure changes of 1 cm^3 you need to use a measuring cylinder or burette that can measure in 1 cm^3 steps — it'd be no good trying with one that only measures 10 cm^3 steps.

2) The smallest change a measuring instrument can detect is called its resolution. E.g. some mass balances have a resolution of 1 g, some have a resolution of 0.1 g, and some are even more sensitive.

3) Also, equipment needs to be calibrated by measuring a known value. If there's a difference between the measured and known value, you can use this to correct the inaccuracy of the equipment.

Working Scientifically

Designing Investigations

You Need to Look out for Errors and Anomalous Results

1) The results of your experiment will always vary a bit because of random errors — unpredictable differences caused by things like human errors in measuring. E.g. the errors you make when you take a reading from a burette are random. You have to estimate or round the level when it's between two marks — so sometimes your figure will be a bit above the real one, and sometimes it will be a bit below.

2) You can reduce the effect of random errors by taking repeat readings and finding the mean. This will make your results more precise.

3) If a measurement is wrong by the same amount every time, it's called a systematic error. For example, if you measured from the very end of your ruler instead of from the 0 cm mark every time, all your measurements would be a bit small. Repeating the experiment in the exact same way and calculating a mean won't correct a systematic error.

If there's no systematic error, then doing repeats and calculating a mean can make your results more accurate.

4) Just to make things more complicated, if a systematic error is caused by using equipment that isn't zeroed properly, it's called a zero error. For example, if a mass balance always reads 1 gram before you put anything on it, all your measurements will be 1 gram too heavy.

5) You can compensate for some systematic errors if you know about them, e.g. if a mass balance always reads 1 gram before you put anything on it, you can subtract 1 gram from all your results.

6) Sometimes you get a result that doesn't fit in with the rest at all. This is called an anomalous result. You should investigate it and try to work out what happened. If you can work out what happened (e.g. you measured something wrong) you can ignore it when processing your results.

Investigations Can be Hazardous

1) Hazards from science experiments might include:

You can find out about potential hazards by looking in textbooks, doing some internet research, or asking your teacher.

- Microorganisms, e.g. some bacteria can make you ill.
- Chemicals, e.g. sulfuric acid can burn your skin and alcohols catch fire easily.
- Fire, e.g. an unattended Bunsen burner is a fire hazard.
- Electricity, e.g. faulty electrical equipment could give you a shock.

2) Part of planning an investigation is making sure that it's safe.

3) You should always make sure that you identify all the hazards that you might encounter. Then you should think of ways of reducing the risks from the hazards you've identified. For example:

- If you're working with springs, always wear safety goggles. This will reduce the risk of the spring hitting your eye if the spring snaps.
- If you're using a Bunsen burner, stand it on a heat proof mat to reduce the risk of starting a fire.

Designing an investigation is an involved process...
Collecting data is what investigations are all about. Designing a good investigation is really important to make sure that any data collected is accurate, precise, repeatable and reproducible.

Processing Data

*Processing your data means doing some **calculations** with it to make it **more useful**.*

Data Needs to be Organised

1) <u>Tables</u> are dead useful for <u>organising data</u>.
2) When you draw a table <u>use a ruler</u> and make sure <u>each column</u> has a <u>heading</u> (including the <u>units</u>).

There are Different Ways of Processing Your Data

1) When you've done repeats of an experiment you should always calculate the <u>mean</u> (average). To do this <u>add together</u> all the data values and <u>divide</u> by the total number of values in the sample.
2) You might also need to calculate the <u>range</u> (how spread out the data is). To do this find the <u>largest</u> number and <u>subtract</u> the <u>smallest</u> number from it.
3) The <u>mode</u> is the <u>most common</u> result in your data set.
4) The <u>median</u> is the '<u>middle</u>' value. You find it by arranging all your data in <u>numerical order</u>, and then seeing which value's in the middle. If there's two, you take the <u>mean</u> of them.

Ignore anomalous results when calculating the mean and the range.

EXAMPLE The results of an experiment to find the mass of gas lost from two reactions are shown below. Calculate the mean and the range for the mass of gas lost in each reaction.

Test tube	Repeat 1 (g)	Repeat 2 (g)	Repeat 3 (g)	Mean (g)	Range (g)
A	28	37	32	(28 + 37 + 32) ÷ 3 = 32	37 − 28 = 9
B	47	51	60	(47 + 51 + 60) ÷ 3 = 53	60 − 47 = 13

Round to the Lowest Number of Significant Figures

The <u>first significant figure</u> of a number is the first digit that's <u>not zero</u>. The second and third significant figures come <u>straight after</u> (even if they're zeros). You should be aware of significant figures in calculations.

1) In <u>any</u> calculation where you need to round, you should round the answer to the <u>lowest number of significant figures</u> (s.f.) given.
2) Remember to write down <u>how many</u> significant figures you've rounded to after your answer.
3) If your calculation has multiple steps, <u>only</u> round the <u>final</u> answer, or it won't be as accurate.

EXAMPLE A plant produces 10.2 cm³ of oxygen in 6.5 minutes whilst photosynthesising. Calculate the rate of photosynthesis.

rate = 10.2 cm³ ÷ 6.5 min = 1.5692... = **1.6 cm³/min (2 s.f.)**

3 s.f. 2 s.f. Final answer should be rounded to 2 s.f.

Don't forget your calculator...

In the exam you could be given some <u>data</u> and be expected to <u>process it</u> in some way. Make sure you keep an eye on <u>significant figures</u> in your answers and <u>always write down your working</u>.

Working Scientifically

Presenting Data

Once you've processed your data, e.g. by calculating the mean, you can present your results in a nice **chart** or **graph**. This will help you to **spot any patterns** in your data.

Bar Charts Can be Used to Show Different Types of Data

Bar charts can be used to display:
1) <u>Categoric</u> data (comes in distinct categories, e.g. flower colour, blood group).
2) <u>Discrete</u> data (the data can be counted in chunks, where there's no in-between value, e.g. number of protons is discrete because you can't have half a proton).
3) <u>Continuous</u> data (numerical data that can have any value in a range, e.g. length or temperature).

There are some <u>golden rules</u> you need to follow for <u>drawing</u> bar charts:

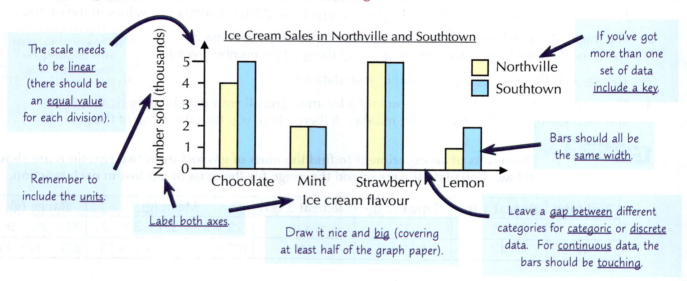

Graphs can be Used to Plot Continuous Data

1) If both variables are <u>continuous</u> you should use a <u>graph</u> to display the data.
2) Here are the <u>rules</u> for plotting points on a graph:

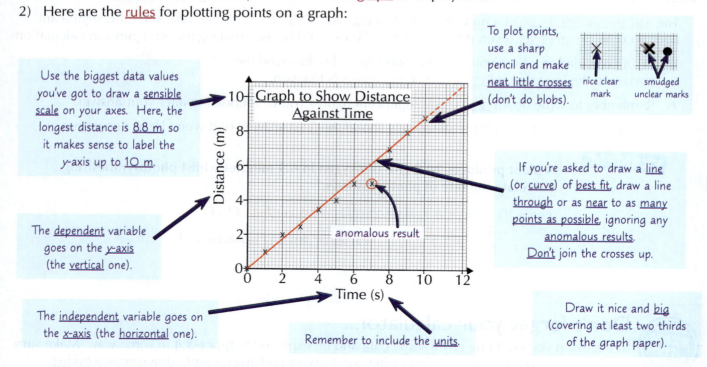

Working Scientifically

More on Graphs

*Graphs aren't just fun to plot, they're also really useful for showing **trends** in your data.*

Graphs Can Give You a Lot of Information About Your Data

1) The gradient (slope) of a graph tells you how quickly the dependent variable changes if you change the independent variable.

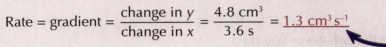

You can use this method to calculate any rates from a graph, not just the rate of a reaction. Just remember that a rate is how much something changes over time, so x needs to be the time.

The graph below shows the volume of gas produced in a reaction against time. The graph is linear (it's a straight line graph), so you can simply calculate the gradient of the line to find out the rate of reaction.

1) To calculate the gradient, pick two points on the line that are easy to read and a good distance apart.

2) Draw a line down from one of the points and a line across from the other to make a triangle. The line drawn down the side of the triangle is the change in y and the line across the bottom is the change in x.

Change in y = 6.8 − 2.0 = 4.8 cm³   Change in x = 5.2 − 1.6 = 3.6 s

Rate = gradient = $\frac{\text{change in } y}{\text{change in } x}$ = $\frac{4.8 \text{ cm}^3}{3.6 \text{ s}}$ = 1.3 cm³ s⁻¹

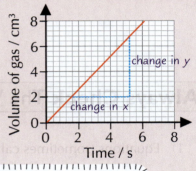

The units of the gradient are (units of y)/(units of x). cm³ s⁻¹ can also be written as cm³/s.

2) If you've got a curved graph, you can find the rate at any point by drawing a tangent — a straight line that touches a single point on a curve. You can then find the gradient of the tangent in the usual way, to give you the rate at that point (see page 240 for more on calculating gradients).

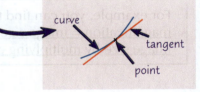

3) The intercept of a graph is where the line of best fit crosses one of the axes. The x-intercept is where the line of best fit crosses the x-axis and the y-intercept is where it crosses the y-axis.

Graphs Show the Relationship Between Two Variables

1) You can get three types of correlation (relationship) between variables:

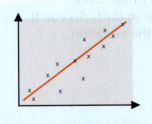

POSITIVE correlation:
as one variable increases
the other increases.

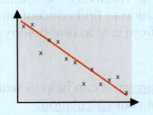

INVERSE (negative) correlation:
as one variable increases the
other decreases.

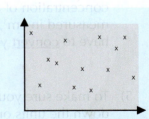

NO correlation:
no relationship between
the two variables.

2) Just because there's correlation, it doesn't mean the change in one variable is causing the change in the other — there might be other factors involved (see page 14).

Working Scientifically

Units and Equations

*Graphs and maths skills are all very well, but the numbers don't mean much if you don't get the **units** right.*

S.I. Units Are Used All Round the World

1) It wouldn't be all that useful if I defined volume in terms of bath tubs, you defined it in terms of egg-cups and my pal Fred defined it in terms of balloons — we'd never be able to compare our data.

2) To stop this happening, scientists have come up with a set of standard units, called S.I. units, that all scientists use to measure their data. Here are some S.I. units that you might see:

Quantity	S.I. Base Unit
mass	kilogram, kg
length	metre, m
time	second, s
temperature	kelvin, K
amount of substance	mole, mol

Always Check The Values Used in Equations Have the Right Units

1) Equations (sometimes called formulas) show relationships between variables.

2) To rearrange an equation, make sure that whatever you do to one side of the equation you also do to the other side.

For example, you can find the magnification of something using the equation: magnification = image size ÷ real size (see p.23). You can rearrange this equation to find the image size by multiplying each side by the real size: image size = magnification × real size.

3) To use an equation, you need to know the values of all but one of the variables. Substitute the values you do know into the formula, and do the calculation to work out the final variable.

4) Always make sure the values you put into an equation have the right units. For example, you might have done a titration experiment to work out the concentration of a solution. The volume of the solution will probably have been measured in cm^3, but the equation to find concentration uses volume in dm^3. So you'll have to convert your volume from cm^3 to dm^3 before you put it into the equation.

5) To make sure your units are correct, it can help to write down the units on each line of your calculation.

S.I. units help scientists to compare data...
You can only really compare things if they're in the same units. E.g. if the rate of blood flow was measured in ml/min in one vein and in l/day in another vein, it'd be hard to know which was faster.

Converting Units

You can **convert units** using **scaling prefixes**. This can save you from having to write a lot of 0's...

Scaling Prefixes Can Be Used for Large and Small Quantities

1) Quantities come in a huge range of sizes. For example, the volume of a swimming pool might be around 2 000 000 000 cm³, while the volume of a cup is around 250 cm³.

2) To make the size of numbers more manageable, larger or smaller units are used. These are the S.I. base units (e.g. metres) with a prefix in front:

Prefix	tera (T)	giga (G)	mega (M)	kilo (k)	deci (d)	centi (c)	milli (m)	micro (µ)	nano (n)
Multiple of Unit	10^{12}	10^9	1 000 000 (10^6)	1000	0.1	0.01	0.001	0.000001 (10^{-6})	10^{-9}

3) These prefixes tell you how much bigger or smaller a unit is than the base unit. So one kilometre is one thousand metres.

4) To swap from one unit to another, all you need to know is what number you have to divide or multiply by to get from the original unit to the new unit — this is called the conversion factor.

The conversion factor is the number of times the smaller unit goes into the larger unit.

- To go from a bigger unit (like m) to a smaller unit (like cm), you multiply by the conversion factor.
- To go from a smaller unit (like g) to a bigger unit (like kg), you divide by the conversion factor.

5) Here are some conversions that'll be useful for GCSE Science:

Length can have lots of units including mm, µm and nm.

mm ⇄ µm ⇄ nm (× 1000 / ÷ 1000)

Mass can have units of kg and g.

kg ⇄ g (× 1000 / ÷ 1000)

Volume can have units of m³, dm³ and cm³.

m³ ⇄ dm³ ⇄ cm³ (× 1000 / ÷ 1000)

Density can have units of kg/m³ and g/cm³.

kg/m³ ⇄ g/cm³ (÷ 1000 / × 1000)

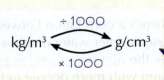
Watch out for conversions involving density — you need to divide when going from kg/m³ to g/cm³, not multiply.

6) Numbers can also be written in standard form, e.g. 1×10^2 m = 100 m. There's more on this on p.24. Make sure you know how to work with standard form on your calculator.

MATHS TIP

To convert from bigger units to smaller units...
...multiply by the conversion factor, and to convert from smaller units to bigger units, divide by the conversion factor. Don't go getting this the wrong way round or you'll get some odd answers.

Drawing Conclusions

*Once you've carried out an experiment and processed your data, it's time to work out **what your data shows**.*

You Can **Only Conclude** What the Data Shows and **No More**

1) Drawing conclusions might seem pretty straightforward — you just look at your data and say what pattern or relationship you see between the dependent and independent variables.

The table on the right shows the rate of a reaction in the presence of two different catalysts:

Catalyst	Rate of Reaction / $cm^3 \, s^{-1}$
A	13.5
B	19.5
No catalyst	5.5

CONCLUSION: Catalyst B makes this reaction go faster than catalyst A.

2) But you've got to be really careful that your conclusion matches the data you've got and doesn't go any further.

You can't conclude that catalyst B increases the rate of any other reaction more than catalyst A — the results might be completely different.

3) You also need to be able to use your results to justify your conclusion (i.e. back up your conclusion with some specific data).

The rate of this reaction was $6 \, cm^3 \, s^{-1}$ faster using catalyst B compared with catalyst A.

4) When writing a conclusion you need to refer back to the original hypothesis and say whether the data supports it or not:

The hypothesis for this experiment might have been that catalyst B would make the reaction go quicker than catalyst A. If so, the data supports the hypothesis.

Correlation **DOES NOT** Mean **Cause**

If two things are correlated (i.e. there's a relationship between them) it doesn't necessarily mean a change in one variable is causing the change in the other — this is REALLY IMPORTANT — DON'T FORGET IT. There are three possible reasons for a correlation:

1) CHANCE: It might seem strange, but two things can show a correlation purely due to chance.

> For example, one study might find a correlation between people's hair colour and how good they are at frisbee. But other scientists don't get a correlation when they investigate it — the results of the first study are just a fluke.

2) LINKED BY A 3RD VARIABLE: A lot of the time it may look as if a change in one variable is causing a change in the other, but it isn't — a third variable links the two things.

> For example, there's a correlation between water temperature and shark attacks. This isn't because warmer water makes sharks crazy. Instead, they're linked by a third variable — the number of people swimming (more people swim when the water's hotter, and with more people in the water you get more shark attacks).

3) CAUSE: Sometimes a change in one variable does cause a change in the other. You can only conclude that a correlation is due to cause when you've controlled all the variables that could affect the result.

> For example, there's a correlation between smoking and lung cancer. This is because chemicals in tobacco smoke cause lung cancer. This conclusion was only made once other variables (such as age and exposure to other things that cause cancer) had been controlled and shown not to affect people's risk of getting lung cancer.

Uncertainty

Uncertainty is how sure you can really be about your data. There's a little bit of maths to do, and also a formula to learn. But don't worry too much — it's no more than a simple bit of subtraction and division.

Uncertainty is the Amount of Error Your Measurements Might Have

1) When you repeat a measurement, you often get a slightly different figure each time you do it due to random error (see page 8). This means that each result has some uncertainty to it.

2) The measurements you make will also have some uncertainty in them due to limits in the resolution of the equipment you use (see page 7).

3) This all means that the mean of a set of results will also have some uncertainty to it. You can calculate the uncertainty of a mean result using the equation:

$$\text{uncertainty} = \frac{\text{range}}{2}$$

The range is the largest value minus the smallest value (see p.9).

4) The larger the range, the less precise your results are and the more uncertainty there will be in your results. Uncertainties are shown using the '±' symbol.

EXAMPLE

The table below shows the results of an experiment to determine the speed of the trolley as it rolls down a ramp. Calculate the uncertainty of the mean.

Repeat	1	2	3	4
Speed (m/s)	2.01	1.98	2.00	2.01

1) First work out the range:

Range = 2.01 − 1.98 = 0.030 m/s

2) Then find the mean:

Mean = (2.01 + 1.98 + 2.00 + 2.01) ÷ 4
= 8.00 ÷ 4 = 2.00

3) Use the range to find the uncertainty:

Uncertainty = range ÷ 2 = 0.030 ÷ 2 = 0.015 m/s

So the uncertainty of the mean = 2.00 ± 0.015 m/s

5) Measuring a greater amount of something helps to reduce uncertainty.

For example, in a rate of reaction experiment, measuring the amount of product formed over a longer period compared to a shorter period will reduce the uncertainty in your results.

The smaller the uncertainty, the more precise your results...

Remember that equation for uncertainty. You never know when you might need it — you could be expected to use it in the exams. You need to make sure all the data is in the same units though. For example, if you had some measurements in metres, and some in centimetres, you'd need to convert them all into either metres or centimetres before you set about calculating uncertainty.

Working Scientifically

Evaluations

*Hurrah! The end of another investigation. Well, now you have to work out all the things you did **wrong**. That's what **evaluations** are all about I'm afraid. Best get cracking with this page...*

Evaluations — Describe How Investigations Could be Improved

An evaluation is a critical analysis of the whole investigation.

1) You should comment on the method — was it valid? Did you control all the other variables to make it a fair test?

2) Comment on the quality of the results — was there enough evidence to reach a valid conclusion? Were the results repeatable, reproducible, accurate and precise?

3) Were there any anomalous results? If there were none then say so. If there were any, try to explain them — were they caused by errors in measurement? Were there any other variables that could have affected the results? You should comment on the level of uncertainty in your results too.

4) All this analysis will allow you to say how confident you are that your conclusion is right.

5) Then you can suggest any changes to the method that would improve the quality of the results, so that you could have more confidence in your conclusion. For example, you might suggest changing the way you controlled a variable, or increasing the number of measurements you took. Taking more measurements at narrower intervals could give you a more accurate result. For example:

> Enzymes have an optimum temperature (a temperature at which they work best). Say you do an experiment to find an enzyme's optimum temperature and take measurements at 10 °C, 20 °C, 30 °C, 40 °C and 50 °C. The results of this experiment tell you the optimum is 40 °C. You could then repeat the experiment, taking more measurements around 40 °C to a get a more accurate value for the optimum.

6) You could also make more predictions based on your conclusion, then further experiments could be carried out to test them.

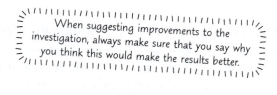
When suggesting improvements to the investigation, always make sure that you say why you think this would make the results better.

Always look for ways to improve your investigations

So there you have it — Working Scientifically. Make sure you know this stuff like the back of your hand. It's not just in the lab, when you're carrying out your groundbreaking investigations, that you'll need to know how to work scientifically. You can be asked about it in the exams as well. So swot up...

Working Scientifically

Section 1 — Key Concepts in Biology

Cells

*When someone first peered down a microscope at a slice of cork and drew the **boxes** they saw, little did they know that they'd seen the **building blocks** of **every organism on the planet**...*

Organisms can be Prokaryotes or Eukaryotes

1) All living things are made of cells.

2) Cells can be either prokaryotic or eukaryotic. Eukaryotic cells are complex and include all animal and plant cells. Prokaryotic cells are smaller and simpler, e.g. bacteria (see next page).

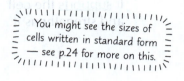
You might see the sizes of cells written in standard form — see p.24 for more on this.

3) Eukaryotes are organisms that are made up of eukaryotic cells.

4) A prokaryote is a prokaryotic cell (it's a single-celled organism).

Plant and Animal Cells have Similarities and Differences

Animal Cells

Subcellular structures are also known as organelles.

The different parts of a cell are called subcellular structures. Most animal cells have the following subcellular structures — make sure you know them all:

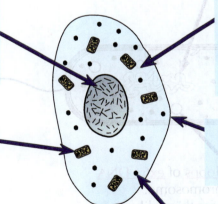

Nucleus — contains genetic material that controls the activities of the cell. Genetic material is arranged into chromosomes.

Mitochondria — these are where most of the reactions for aerobic respiration take place (see page 111). Respiration transfers energy that the cell needs to work.

Cytoplasm — gel-like substance where most of the chemical reactions happen. It contains enzymes (see page 26) that control these chemical reactions.

Cell membrane — holds the cell together and controls what goes in and out.

Ribosomes — these are involved in translation of genetic material in the synthesis of proteins.

Subcellular structures are all the different parts of a cell

Make sure you get to grips with the different subcellular structures that animal cells contain before you move on to the next page. There are more subcellular structures coming up that you need to know...

Cells

Plant Cells

Plant cells usually have all the bits that animal cells have, plus a few extra things that animal cells don't have:

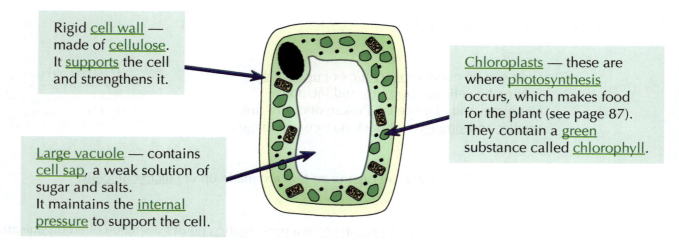

Rigid cell wall — made of cellulose. It supports the cell and strengthens it.

Chloroplasts — these are where photosynthesis occurs, which makes food for the plant (see page 87). They contain a green substance called chlorophyll.

Large vacuole — contains cell sap, a weak solution of sugar and salts. It maintains the internal pressure to support the cell.

Bacterial Cells Have No Nucleus

Bacterial cells are a lot smaller than plant or animal cells and have these subcellular structures:

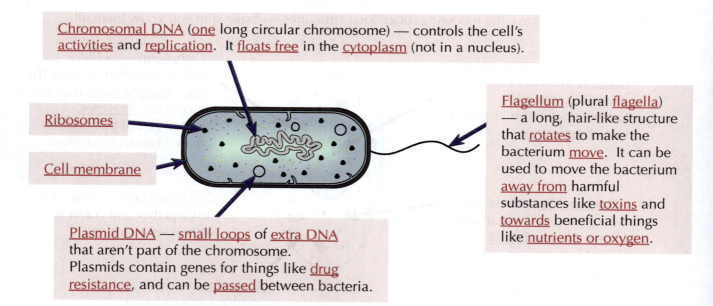

Chromosomal DNA (one long circular chromosome) — controls the cell's activities and replication. It floats free in the cytoplasm (not in a nucleus).

Ribosomes

Cell membrane

Flagellum (plural flagella) — a long, hair-like structure that rotates to make the bacterium move. It can be used to move the bacterium away from harmful substances like toxins and towards beneficial things like nutrients or oxygen.

Plasmid DNA — small loops of extra DNA that aren't part of the chromosome. Plasmids contain genes for things like drug resistance, and can be passed between bacteria.

There's quite a bit to learn in biology — but that's life, I guess...

On these pages are a typical animal cell, plant cell and bacterial cell. Make sure you're familiar with all their structures. A good way to check that you know what all the bits and pieces are is to copy out the diagrams and see if you can remember all the labels. No cheating.

Section 1 — Key Concepts in Biology

Specialised Cells

*The previous pages show the structure of some **typical cells**. However, most cells are **specialised** for a particular function, so their **structure** can vary...*

Different Cells Have Different Functions

1) Multicellular organisms contain lots of different types of cells (i.e. cells with different structures).

2) Cells that have a structure which makes them adapted to their function are called specialised cells.

3) You need to know how egg, sperm and ciliated epithelial cells are adapted to their functions.

Egg Cells and Sperm Cells Are Specialised for Reproduction

1) In sexual reproduction, the nucleus of an egg cell fuses with the nucleus of a sperm cell to create a fertilised egg, which then develops into an embryo. Both the nucleus of an egg cell and of a sperm cell only contain half the number of chromosomes that's in a normal body cell — so they are called 'haploid'.

2) This is important as it means that when an egg and sperm nucleus combine at fertilisation, the resulting cell will have the right number of chromosomes.

There's more about sexual reproduction on page 48.

Egg Cells

The main functions of an egg are to carry the female DNA and to nourish the developing embryo in the early stages. This is how it's adapted to its function:

1) It contains nutrients in the cytoplasm to feed the embryo.

2) It has a haploid nucleus.

3) Straight after fertilisation, its membrane changes structure to stop any more sperm getting in. This makes sure the offspring end up with the right amount of DNA.

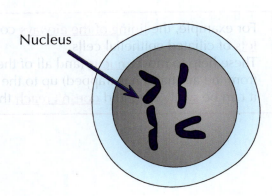

Section 1 — Key Concepts in Biology

Specialised Cells

Sperm Cells

The function of a sperm is to transport the male's DNA to the female's egg.

1) A sperm cell has a long tail so it can swim to the egg.

2) It has lots of mitochondria in the middle section to provide the energy (from respiration) needed to swim this distance.

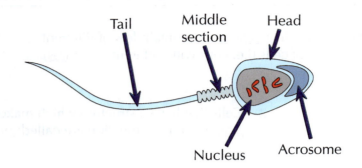

3) It also has an acrosome at the front of the 'head', where it stores enzymes needed to digest its way through the membrane of the egg cell.

4) It also contains a haploid nucleus.

Ciliated Epithelial Cells Are Specialised for Moving Materials

1) Epithelial cells line the surfaces of organs.
2) Some of them have cilia (hair-like structures) on the top surface of the cell.
3) The function of these ciliated epithelial cells is to move substances — the cilia beat to move substances in one direction, along the surface of the tissue.

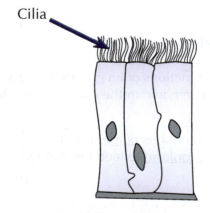

For example, the lining of the airways contains lots of ciliated epithelial cells.
These help to move mucus (and all of the particles from the air that it has trapped) up to the throat so it can be swallowed and doesn't reach the lungs.

Cells have the same basic bits but are specialised for their function

Nearly every cell in your body is specialised to carry out some kind of function, but the ones on these pages — egg cells, sperm cells and ciliated epithelial cells — are the examples you need to learn for your exams.

Section 1 — Key Concepts in Biology

Microscopy

*Without **microscopes** we would never have discovered cells. We can even use them to look **inside** cells.*

Cells are Studied Using Microscopes

Microscopes use lenses to magnify images (make them look bigger). They also increase the resolution of an image. Resolution means how well a microscope distinguishes between two points that are close together. A higher resolution means that the image can be seen more clearly and in more detail.

Light microscopes were invented in the 1590s. They work by passing light through the specimen. They let us see things like nuclei and chloroplasts and we can also use them to study living cells.

Electron microscopes were invented in the 1930s. They use electrons rather than light. Electron microscopes have a higher magnification and resolution than light microscopes, so they let us see much smaller things in more detail like the internal structure of mitochondria and chloroplasts. This has allowed us to have a much greater understanding of how cells work and the role of subcellular structures (although they can't be used to view living cells).

You Can Create a Scientific Drawing of a Specimen

1) Using a sharp pencil, draw outlines of the main features using clear, unbroken lines. Don't include any colouring or shading.

2) Make sure that your drawing takes up at least half of the space available and remember to keep all the parts in proportion.

3) Label the important features of your diagram with straight lines which don't cross over each other, and include the magnification used and a scale.

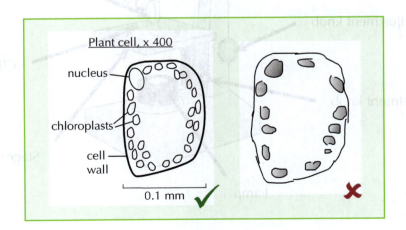

Take your time when you're doing scientific drawings

When you look at a real specimen down a microscope, it often doesn't look exactly like what you'd expect from seeing diagrams in books. But don't be put off — just draw what you can see.

Microscopy

*It's all very well knowing what microscopes **do** — you also have to know how to actually **use** one.*

This is How to View a Specimen Using a Light Microscope:

1) Your specimen needs to let light through it so you'll need to take a thin slice of it to start with.
2) Next, take a clean slide and use a pipette to put one drop of water in the middle of it — this will secure the specimen in place. Then use tweezers to place your specimen on the slide.
3) Add a drop of stain if your specimen is completely transparent or colourless — this makes the specimen easier to see (different stains highlight different structures within cells, e.g. methylene blue stains DNA).
4) Place a cover slip at one end of the specimen, holding it at an angle with a mounted needle and carefully lower it onto the slide. Press it down gently so that no air bubbles are trapped under it. Then clip the slide onto the stage.
5) Select the lowest-powered objective lens.
6) Use the coarse adjustment knob to move the stage up so that the slide is just underneath the objective lens. Then, looking down the eyepiece, move the stage downwards (so you don't accidentally crash it into the lens) until the specimen is nearly in focus.
7) Then adjust the focus with the fine adjustment knob, until you get a clear image. Position a clear ruler on the stage and use it to measure the diameter of the circular area visible — your field of view (FOV).
8) If you need to see your specimen with greater magnification, swap to a higher-powered objective lens, refocus and recalculate your FOV accordingly (e.g. if your FOV was 5 mm then you swap to a lens that is 10 times more powerful, your FOV will now be 5 mm ÷ 10 = 0.5 mm).

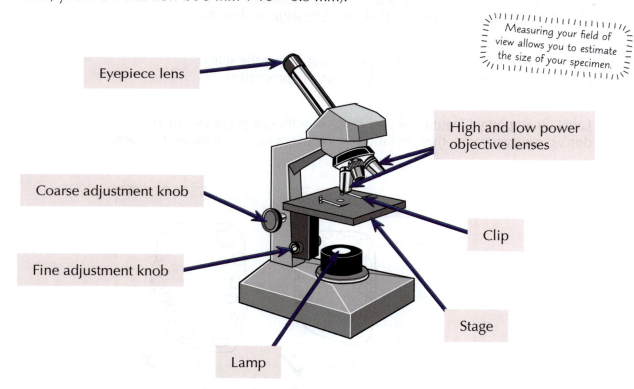

Measuring your field of view allows you to estimate the size of your specimen.

Your microscope might look a bit different

The appearance of light microscopes can vary (e.g. they might have two eyepieces rather than one) but they should have the same basic features shown on this page.

Section 1 — Key Concepts in Biology

More Microscopy

*Sometimes you need to do a bit of **maths** with microscope images.*

Magnification is **How Many Times Bigger** the Image is

1) If you know the power of the lenses used by a microscope to view an image, you can work out the total magnification of the image using this simple formula:

total magnification = eyepiece lens magnification × objective lens magnification

An image is viewed with an eyepiece lens magnification of × 10 and an objective lens magnification of × 40. What is the total magnification?

Total magnification = eyepiece lens magnification × objective lens magnification = 10 × 40 = × 400

2) If you don't know which lenses were used, you can still work out the magnification of an image as long as you can measure the image and know the real size of the specimen. This is the formula you need:

$$\text{magnification} = \frac{\text{image size}}{\text{real size}}$$

Both measurements should have the same units. If they don't, you'll need to convert them first (see next page).

A magnified image is 2 mm wide, and the specimen is 0.02 mm wide. What is the magnification?

$$\text{magnification} = \frac{\text{image size}}{\text{real size}} = \frac{2}{0.02} = \times 100$$

3) If you're working out the image size or the real size of the object, you can rearrange the equation using this formula triangle. Cover up the thing you're trying to find. The parts you can still see are the formula you need to use.

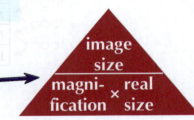

4) Estimating can help you to check that your answer is correct. To estimate an answer, round the numbers so you can do the maths in your head.

The real size of a specimen is 21.5 μm. The size of an image of the specimen is 9800 μm. Estimate the magnification used.

1) First, round both numbers to 1 significant figure.
    21.5 μm = 20 μm to 1 significant figure.
    9800 μm = 10 000 μm to 1 significant figure.

2) Then do the calculation.
    magnification = image size ÷ real size = 10 000 ÷ 20 = × 500

Learn these formulas

You might need to use that formula triangle in the exam, so make sure you know it off by heart. You only really need to remember that image size goes at the top of the triangle, which shouldn't be too tricky, since it comes first when you put the three things in alphabetical order.

Q1   A cheek cell is viewed under a microscope with × 40 magnification. The image of the cell is 2.4 mm wide. Calculate the real width of the cheek cell. Give your answer in μm. [2 marks]

Section 1 — Key Concepts in Biology

More Microscopy

*There's **more maths** coming up on this page — it might look a bit complicated, but really it's just a handy way of writing really small numbers a bit more neatly.*

You Might Need to Work in Standard Form and Convert Units

1) Because microscopes can see such tiny objects, sometimes it's useful to write figures in standard form.

2) This is where you change very big or small numbers with lots of zeros into something more manageable, e.g. 0.017 can be written 1.7×10^{-2}. To do this you just need to move the decimal point left or right.

3) The number of places the decimal point moves is then represented by a power of 10 — this is positive if the decimal point's moved to the left, and negative if it's moved to the right.

4) You can also use different units to express very big or very small numbers. E.g. 0.0007 m could be written as 0.7 mm. The table shows you how to convert between different units. The right hand column of the table shows you how each unit can be expressed as a metre in standard form.

Unit	In standard form:
Millimetre (mm)	$\times 10^{-3}$ m
Micrometre (μm)	$\times 10^{-6}$ m
Nanometre (nm)	$\times 10^{-9}$ m
Picometre (pm)	$\times 10^{-12}$ m

To convert: ×1000, ×1000, ×1000 (down the units); ÷1000, ÷1000, ÷1000 (up the units).

So 1 pm = 0.000000000001 m.

Here's an example of a calculation in standard form:

EXAMPLE

A specimen is 5×10^{-6} m wide. Calculate the width of the image of the specimen under a magnification of × 100. Give your answer in standard form.

1) Rearrange the magnification formula.
   image size = magnification × real size
2) Fill in the values you know.
   image size = 100 × (5×10^{-6} m)
3) Write out the values in full (i.e. don't use standard form).
   = 100 × 0.000005 m
4) Carry out the calculation and then convert back into standard form.
   = 0.0005 m
   = 5×10^{-4} m

0.0005 m could also be written as 0.5 mm or 500 μm.

Make sure you pay close attention to the number of zeros

MATHS TIP If you've got a scientific calculator, you can put standard form numbers into it using the 'EXP' or the '×10^x' button. For example, enter 2.67×10^{15} by pressing 2.67 then 'EXP' or '×10^x', then 15.

Warm-Up and Exam Questions

So, hopefully you've read the last eight pages. But could you cope if a question on cells or microscopes came up in the exam? With amazing new technology we can simulate that very situation...

Warm-Up Questions

1) Name the subcellular structures where aerobic respiration takes place.
2) Give two ways that a sperm cell is adapted to its function.
3) What type of microscope should be used to look at the internal structure of chloroplasts?
4) Write the number 0.00045 μm in standard form.

Exam Questions

1 Which of the following subcellular structures would you not expect to find in a prokaryotic cell?

☐ **A** plasmid ☐ **B** nucleus ☐ **C** cell wall ☐ **D** cell membrane

[1 mark]

2 **Figure 1** shows a typical plant cell.

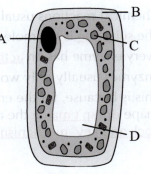

Figure 1

(a) Which label points to a chloroplast?

☐ **A** ☐ **B** ☐ **C** ☐ **D**

[1 mark]

(b) Describe the function of a chloroplast.

[1 mark]

(c) **Figure 1** also shows ribosomes.
Describe the function of a ribosome.

[1 mark]

PRACTICAL

3 A light microscope can be used to observe a layer of onion cells on a slide.

(a)* Describe how you would use a light microscope to view onion cells.
Include how you would prepare the slide.

[6 marks]

(b) When the onion cell is viewed with × 100 magnification, the image of the cell is 7.5 mm wide.
Calculate the real width of the onion cell using the formula:

$$\text{magnification} = \frac{\text{image size}}{\text{real size}}$$

Give your answer in μm.

[3 marks]

Section 1 — Key Concepts in Biology

Enzymes

Chemical reactions are what make you work. And *enzymes* are what make them work.

Enzymes Are Catalysts Produced by Living Things

1) Living things have thousands of different chemical reactions going on inside them all the time.
2) These reactions need to be carefully controlled — to get the right amounts of substances.
3) You can usually make a reaction happen more quickly by raising the temperature. This would speed up the useful reactions but also the unwanted ones too... not good.
4) So... living things produce enzymes which act as biological catalysts. Enzymes reduce the need for high temperatures and we only have enzymes to speed up the useful chemical reactions in the body.

> A CATALYST is a substance which INCREASES the speed of a reaction, without being CHANGED or USED UP in the reaction.

Enzymes Have Special Shapes So They Can Catalyse Reactions

1) Chemical reactions usually involve things either being split apart or joined together.
2) The substrate is the molecule changed in the reaction.
3) Every enzyme has an active site — the part where it joins on to its substrate to catalyse the reaction.
4) Enzymes usually only work with one substrate. They are said to have a high specificity for their substrate.
5) This is because, for the enzyme to work, the substrate has to fit into the active site. If the substrate's shape doesn't match the active site's shape, then the reaction won't be catalysed. This is called the 'lock and key' mechanism, because the substrate fits into the enzyme just like a key fits into a lock.

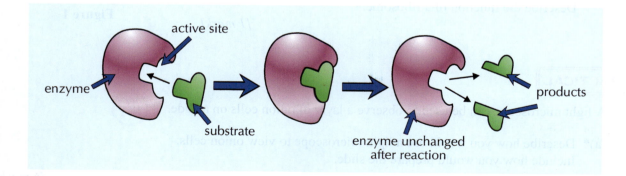

Enzymes speed up chemical reactions

Just like you've got to have the correct key for a lock, you've got to have the right substance for an enzyme. If the substance doesn't fit into the active site, the enzyme won't be able to catalyse the reaction...

Enzymes

*Enzymes are clearly very clever, but they're **not** very versatile. They need just the right **conditions** if they're going to work properly.*

Enzymes Need the Right Temperature...

1) Changing the temperature changes the rate of an enzyme-catalysed reaction.
2) Like with any reaction, a higher temperature increases the rate at first.
3) But if it gets too hot, some of the bonds holding the enzyme together break. This changes the shape of the enzyme's active site, so the substrate won't fit any more. The enzyme is said to be denatured.
4) All enzymes have an optimum temperature that they work best at.

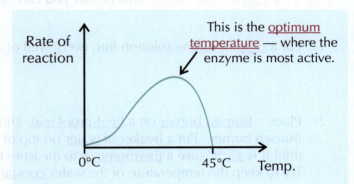

Enzymes denature at different temperatures. Most human enzymes denature at around 45 °C.

... and the Right pH...

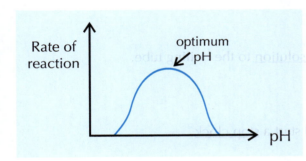

1) The pH also affects enzymes. If it's too high or too low, the pH interferes with the bonds holding the enzyme together.
2) This changes the shape of the active site and denatures the enzyme.
3) All enzymes have an optimum pH that they work best at. It's often neutral pH 7, but not always — e.g. pepsin is an enzyme used to break down proteins in the stomach. It works best at pH 2, which means it's well-suited to the acidic conditions there.

... and the Right Substrate Concentration

1) Substrate concentration also affects the rate of reaction — the higher the substrate concentration, the faster the reaction. This is because it's more likely that the enzyme will meet up and react with a substrate molecule.
2) This is only true up to a point though. After that, there are so many substrate molecules that the enzymes have about as much as they can cope with (all the active sites are full), and adding more makes no difference.

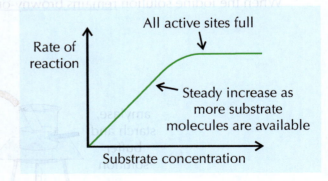

Most enzymes catalyse just one reaction

The optimum temperature for most human enzymes is around normal body temperature.
And stomach enzymes work best at low pH, but the enzymes in your small intestine like a higher pH.

Section 1 — Key Concepts in Biology

Investigating Enzyme Activity

You Can Investigate the Effect of pH on Enzyme Activity — PRACTICAL

The enzyme amylase catalyses the breakdown of starch to maltose. It's easy to detect starch using iodine solution — if starch is present, the iodine solution will change from browny-orange to blue-black. This is how you can investigate how pH affects amylase activity:

1) Put a drop of iodine solution into every well of a spotting tile.

2) Place a Bunsen burner on a heat-proof mat, and a tripod and gauze over the Bunsen burner. Put a beaker of water on top of the tripod and heat the water until it is 35 °C (use a thermometer to measure the temperature). Try to keep the temperature of the water constant throughout the experiment.

You could use an electric water bath, instead of a Bunsen and a beaker of water, to control the temperature.

3) Use a syringe to add 3 cm³ of amylase solution and 1 cm³ of a buffer solution with a pH of 5 to a boiling tube. Using test tube holders, put the tube into the beaker of water and wait for five minutes.

4) Next, use a different syringe to add 3 cm³ of a starch solution to the boiling tube.

5) Immediately mix the contents of the boiling tube and start a stop clock.

6) Use continuous sampling to record how long it takes for the amylase to break down all of the starch. To do this, use a dropping pipette to take a fresh sample from the boiling tube every ten seconds and put a drop into a well. When the iodine solution remains browny-orange, starch is no longer present.

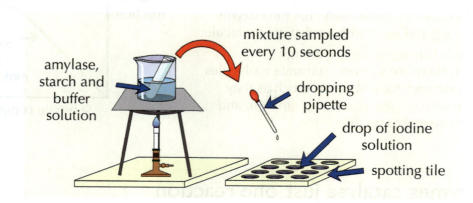

Section 1 — Key Concepts in Biology

Investigating Enzyme Activity

7) Repeat the whole experiment with buffer solutions of different pH values to see how pH affects the time taken for the starch to be broken down.

You could use a pH meter to accurately measure the pH of your solutions.

8) Remember to control any variables each time (e.g. concentration and volume of amylase solution) to make it a fair test.

Here's How to Calculate the Rate of Reaction

1) It's often useful to calculate the rate of reaction after an experiment. Rate is a measure of how much something changes over time.

2) For the experiment above, you can calculate the rate of reaction using this formula:

You could also use the formula '1/time' but '1000/time' will give you a bigger number that's easier to plot on a graph.

$$\text{Rate} = \frac{1000}{\text{time}}$$

E.g. at pH 6, the time taken for amylase to break down all of the starch in a solution was 90 seconds. So the rate of the reaction = $1000 \div 90 = 11 \text{ s}^{-1}$ (2 s.f.)

The units are in s^{-1} since rate is given per unit time.

3) If an experiment measures how much something changes over time, you calculate the rate of reaction by dividing the amount that it has changed by the time taken.

EXAMPLE
The enzyme catalase catalyses the breakdown of hydrogen peroxide into water and oxygen. During an investigation into the activity of catalase, 24 cm³ of oxygen was released in 50 seconds (s). Calculate the rate of the reaction. Write your answer in $cm^3 \, s^{-1}$.

Amount of product formed = change = 24 cm³
Rate of reaction = change ÷ time
  = 24 cm³ ÷ 50 s = **0.48 $cm^3 \, s^{-1}$**

$cm^3 \, s^{-1}$ is another way of writing cm^3/s.

You can investigate other factors too...

You could adapt this experiment to investigate how other factors affect the rate of amylase activity. E.g. you could use a water bath set to different temperatures to investigate the effect of temperature.

Q1   An enzyme-controlled reaction was carried out at pH 4. After 2 minutes, 36 cm³ of product had been released. Calculate the rate of reaction in $cm^3 \, s^{-1}$.   [1 mark]

Q1 Video Solution

Enzymes in Breakdown and Synthesis

*Organisms use **enzymes** to help **break down large molecules** and to **build them back up** again.*

Enzymes Break Down Big Molecules

1) Proteins, lipids and some carbohydrates are big molecules.

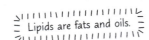
Lipids are fats and oils.

2) It's important that organisms are able to break them down into their smaller components so they can be used for growth and other life processes. For example:

> - Many of the molecules in the food we eat are too big to pass through the walls of our digestive system, so digestive enzymes break them down into smaller, soluble molecules. These can pass easily through the walls of the digestive system, allowing them to be absorbed into the bloodstream. They can then pass into cells to be used by the body.
> - Plants store energy in the form of starch (a carbohydrate). When plants need energy, enzymes break down the starch into smaller molecules (sugars). These can then be respired to transfer energy to be used by the cells (see p.111).

Different Enzymes Break Down Carbohydrates, Proteins and Lipids

Enzymes called carbohydrases convert carbohydrates into simple sugars. E.g. amylase is an example of a carbohydrase. It breaks down starch.

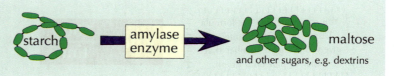

Proteases convert proteins into amino acids.

Lipases convert lipids into glycerol and fatty acids.

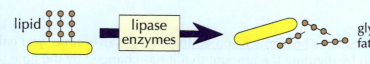

When lipids are broken down, the fatty acids will lower the pH of the solution they are in.

Some Enzymes Join Molecules Together

Organisms need to be able to synthesise carbohydrates, proteins and lipids from their smaller components. Again, enzymes are used in this process.

- Carbohydrates can be synthesised by joining together simple sugars.

> Glycogen synthase is an enzyme that joins together lots of chains of glucose molecules to make glycogen (a molecule used to store energy in animals).

- Proteins are made by joining amino acids together. Enzymes catalyse the reactions needed to do this.
- Lots of enzymes are also involved in the synthesis of lipids from fatty acids and glycerol.

Different types of enzymes act on different molecules

Make sure you know all the smaller components that make up carbohydrates, proteins and lipids and understand that enzymes play a role in both the breakdown and synthesis of these bigger molecules.

Warm-Up and Exam Questions

Doing well in exams isn't just about remembering all the facts, although that's important. You have to get used to the way the questions are phrased and make sure you always read the question carefully.

Warm-Up Questions

1) What is meant by the term 'active site'?
2) What is meant by the optimum pH of an enzyme?
3) Name two other variables that affect the rate of enzyme activity.
4) Which enzyme breaks down: (a) starch   (b) protein   (c) lipids?
5) What are the products of the breakdown of: (a) starch   (b) protein
6) What type of molecule do enzymes join together to synthesise proteins?

Exam Questions

1   **Figure 1** shows the effect of temperature on the action of two different enzymes.

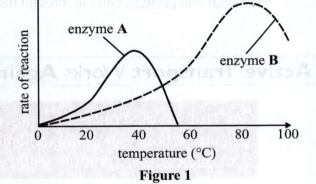
Figure 1

(a) Estimate the optimum temperature for enzyme **A**.

[1 mark]

(b) One of these enzymes was extracted from human liver cells. The other was extracted from bacteria living in hot underwater vents.
Suggest which enzyme came from the bacteria. Give a reason for your answer.

[1 mark]

PRACTICAL

2   A student was investigating the effect of pH on the rate of amylase activity. He used a syringe to put amylase solution and a buffer solution with a pH of 6 into a test tube. He then used a different syringe to add a starch solution to the boiling tube. He mixed the contents and then started a stop clock. Every 30 seconds he took a sample from the boiling tube and tested it for the presence of starch. When there was no starch present he stopped the stop clock. He repeated the experiment three times.

(a) Suggest why he used two different syringes when adding substances to the boiling tube.

[1 mark]

(b) His experiment showed that the average time taken for the starch in the boiling tube to be broken down was 60 seconds. Calculate the rate of the reaction.
Give your answer in s^{-1} to 2 significant figures. Use the formula: $\text{rate} = \dfrac{1000}{\text{time}}$

[1 mark]

(c) Suggest what the student needs to do next in his investigation to determine the effect of pH on the rate of amylase activity.

[1 mark]

Section 1 — Key Concepts in Biology

Diffusion and Active Transport

*Substances can move in and out of cells by **diffusion** and **active transport**...*

Diffusion — Don't be Put Off by the Fancy Word

1) Diffusion is simple. It's just the gradual movement of particles from places where there are lots of them to places where there are fewer of them. That's all it is — just the natural tendency for stuff to spread out. Here's the fancy definition:

> DIFFUSION is the net (overall) movement of particles from an area of higher concentration to an area of lower concentration.

2) Diffusion happens in both liquids and gases — that's because the particles in these substances are free to move about randomly.

3) Only very small molecules can diffuse through cell membranes — things like glucose, amino acids, water and oxygen. Big molecules like starch and proteins can't fit through the membrane.

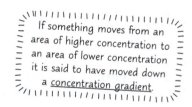

If something moves from an area of higher concentration to an area of lower concentration it is said to have moved down a concentration gradient.

Active Transport Works Against a Concentration Gradient

> ACTIVE TRANSPORT is the movement of particles across a membrane against a concentration gradient (i.e. from an area of lower to an area of higher concentration) using energy transferred during respiration.

1) Active transport is a bit different from diffusion because particles are moved up a concentration gradient rather than down, and the process requires energy (unlike diffusion, which is a passive process).

2) Here's an example of active transport at work in the digestive system:

> When there's a higher concentration of nutrients in the gut than in the blood, the nutrients diffuse naturally into the blood.
> BUT — sometimes there's a lower concentration of nutrients in the gut than in the blood. Active transport allows nutrients to be taken into the blood, despite the fact that the concentration gradient is the wrong way. This is essential to stop us starving.

Both involve movement between different concentrations

Make sure you understand the difference between diffusion and active transport — in one, particles passively move down a concentration gradient, in the other, particles move up a concentration gradient, which requires energy. That's all there is to it. Learn which is which and you'll be golden.

Q1   A sodium ion moves from inside a nerve cell, where there is a low sodium ion concentration, to outside the cell, where the concentration is higher. Name the process by which the ion is moving across the membrane.

[1 mark]

Osmosis

*If you've got your head round **diffusion**, osmosis will be a **breeze**.*
If not, have another look at the previous page...

Osmosis is a Special Case of Diffusion, That's All

OSMOSIS is the net movement of water molecules across a partially permeable membrane from a region of higher water concentration to a region of lower water concentration.

You could also describe osmosis as the net movement of water molecules across a partially permeable membrane from a region of lower solute concentration to a region of higher solute concentration.

1) A partially permeable membrane is just one with very small holes in it. So small, in fact, only tiny molecules (like water) can pass through them, and bigger molecules (e.g. sucrose) can't.

2) The water molecules actually pass both ways through the membrane during osmosis. This happens because water molecules move about randomly all the time.

3) But because there are more water molecules on one side than on the other, there's a steady net flow of water into the region with fewer water molecules, i.e. into the more concentrated solute solution.

4) This means the solute solution gets more dilute. The water acts like it's trying to "even up" the concentration either side of the membrane.

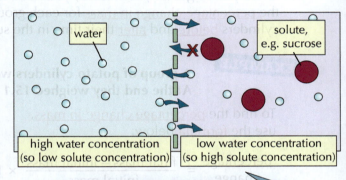

You Can Do an Experiment to Investigate Osmosis   **PRACTICAL**

This experiment involves putting potato cylinders into different concentrations of sucrose solution to see what effect different water concentrations have on them.

The higher the concentration of the sucrose solution, the lower the water concentration.

First You Do the Experiment...

1) Prepare sucrose solutions of different concentrations ranging from pure water to a very concentrated sucrose solution.
2) Use a cork borer to cut a potato into the same sized pieces. (The pieces need to be about 1 cm in diameter and preferably from the same potato.)
3) Divide the cylinders into groups of three and use a mass balance to measure the mass of each group.
4) Place one group in each solution.

'M' is a unit of concentration (you might also see it written as mol dm⁻³). The solution with a concentration of 0.0 M is pure water.

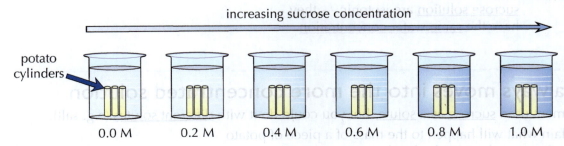

Section 1 — Key Concepts in Biology

 ## Osmosis

5) Leave the cylinders in the solution for at least 40 minutes (making sure that they all get the same amount of time).
6) Remove the cylinders and pat dry gently with a paper towel. This removes excess water from the surface of the cylinders, so you get a more accurate measurement of their final masses.
7) Weigh each group again and record your results.
8) The only thing that you should change in this experiment is the sucrose solution concentration. Everything else (e.g. the volume of solution, the size of the potato cylinders, the type of potatoes used, the amount of drying, etc.) must be kept the same or your results won't be valid.

...Then You Interpret the Results

1) Once you've got all your results, you need to calculate the percentage change in mass for each group of cylinders before and after their time in the sucrose.

Calculating the percentage change allows you to compare the effect of sucrose concentration on cylinders that didn't have the same initial mass.

EXAMPLE A group of potato cylinders weighed 13.2 g at the start of the experiment. At the end they weighed 15.1 g. Calculate the percentage change in mass.

To find the percentage change in mass, use the formula below:

$$\text{percentage change} = \frac{\text{final mass} - \text{initial mass}}{\text{initial mass}} \times 100$$

$$\text{percentage change} = \frac{15.1 - 13.2}{13.2} \times 100 = 14.4\%$$

The positive result tells you the potato cylinders gained mass. If the answer was negative then the potato cylinders lost mass.

2) Then you can plot a graph and analyse your results:

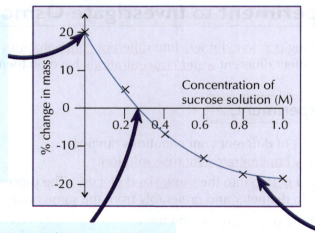

At the points above the x-axis, the water concentration of the sucrose solutions is higher than in the cylinders. The cylinders gain mass as water is drawn in by osmosis.

At the points below the x-axis, the water concentration of the sucrose solutions is lower than in the cylinders. This causes the cylinders to lose water so their mass decreases.

Where there is no change in mass (where the curve crosses the x-axis) the fluid inside the cylinders and the sucrose solution are isotonic — they have the same water concentration.

Water always moves into the more concentrated solution

This experiment used sucrose as a solute, but you could do it with different solutes (e.g. salt).

Q1 Explain what will happen to the mass of a piece of potato added to a concentrated salt solution. [2 marks]

Warm-Up and Exam Questions

Question time again — Warm-Up first, then Exam (or the other way round if you want to be different).

Warm-Up Questions

1) Other than diffusion, by what two processes do substances move across cell membranes?
2) Give two differences between diffusion and active transport.
3) Explain what is meant by a partially permeable membrane.
4) What is the definition of osmosis?

Exam Questions

1   A student adds a drop of ink to a glass of cold water.
    Describe what you would expect to happen to the drop of ink.
    Explain your answer.

    [2 marks]

PRACTICAL

2   In an experiment, four 5 cm long cylinders were cut from a fresh potato.
    The cylinders were then placed in different sugar solutions, as shown in **Figure 1**.
    After 24 hours the potato cylinders were removed and measured.

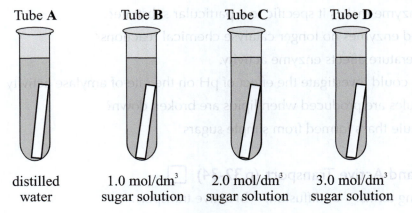

Figure 1

(a) State which potato cylinder you would expect to be shortest after 24 hours.
    Explain your answer.

    [3 marks]

(b) The potato cylinder in tube **A** increased in length during the 24 hours.
    Explain why this happened.

    [2 marks]

Section 1 — Key Concepts in Biology

Revision Summary for Section 1

Make sure you learn all of Section 1 — many of the concepts will crop up again in other sections.
- Try these questions and tick off each one when you get it right.
- When you're completely happy with a topic, tick it off.

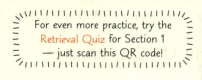
For even more practice, try the Retrieval Quiz for Section 1 — just scan this QR code!

Cells and Specialised Cells (p.17-20) ☐
1) What is the function of the cell membrane?
2) Give three structures found in plant cells but not in animal cells.
3) Name the subcellular structures in plant cells where photosynthesis takes place.
4) Name two structures that are found in both prokaryotic cells and eukaryotic cells.
5) What does the term 'haploid' mean?
6) Give three ways in which an egg cell is adapted to its function.
7) What are cilia?
8) What is the purpose of the ciliated epithelial cells that line the airways?

Microscopy (p.21-24) ☐
9) Give an advantage of electron microscopes over light microscopes.
10) Why is it necessary to use thin samples of tissue when viewing cells using a light microscope?
11) Write the equation you would use to find the size of a specimen using the magnification used and the size of the image seen through a microscope lens.
12) Describe how you would convert a measurement from mm to μm.
13) Which unit can be expressed in standard form as $\times 10^{-12}$ m?

Enzymes (p.26-30) ☐
14) What part of an enzyme makes it specific to a particular substrate?
15) Why can denatured enzymes no longer catalyse chemical reactions?
16) Explain how temperature affects enzyme activity.
17) Describe how you could investigate the effect of pH on the rate of amylase activity.
18) Which two molecules are produced when lipids are broken down?
19) Name a big molecule that's formed from simple sugars.

Diffusion, Osmosis and Active Transport (p.32-34) ☐
20) Define the following terms: a) diffusion, b) active transport.
21) When investigating osmosis using potato cylinders in sucrose solution, why might the mass of a potato cylinder increase?

Section 1 — Key Concepts in Biology

Section 2 — Cells and Control

Mitosis

In order to survive and grow, our cells have got to be able to divide. And that means our DNA as well...

Chromosomes Contain Genetic Information

1) Most cells in your body have a nucleus. The nucleus contains your genetic material in the form of chromosomes. Chromosomes are coiled up lengths of DNA molecules (see p.50 for more on DNA).
2) Body cells normally have two copies of each chromosome — this makes them 'diploid' cells. One chromosome comes from the organism's 'mother', and one comes from its 'father'.
3) When a cell divides by mitosis (see next page) it makes two cells identical to the original cell — the nucleus of each new cell contains the same number of chromosomes as the original cell.

The Cell Cycle Makes New Cells for Growth and Repair

1) Body cells in multicellular organisms divide to produce new cells during a process called the cell cycle. The stage of the cell cycle when the cell divides is called mitosis.

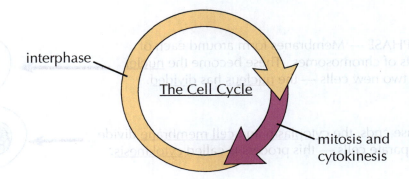

2) Multicellular organisms use mitosis to grow or to replace cells that have been damaged.
3) Some organisms use mitosis to reproduce — this is called asexual reproduction. E.g. strawberry plants form runners by mitosis, which become new plants.
4) You need to know about the main stages of the cell cycle.

Interphase

In a cell that's not dividing, the DNA is all spread out in long strings.

Before it divides, the cell has to grow and increase the amount of subcellular structures such as mitochondria and ribosomes.

It then duplicates its DNA — so there's one copy for each new cell. The DNA is copied and forms X-shaped chromosomes. Each 'arm' of the chromosome is an exact duplicate of the other.

The left arm has the same DNA as the right arm. Each arm is called a chromatid.

Mitosis

Mitosis and Cytokinesis

Once its contents and DNA have been copied, the cell is ready for mitosis. Mitosis is divided into four stages:

1) PROPHASE — The chromosomes condense, getting shorter and fatter. The membrane around the nucleus breaks down and the chromosomes lie free in the cytoplasm.

2) METAPHASE — The chromosomes line up at the centre of the cell.

3) ANAPHASE — Spindle fibres pull the chromosomes apart. Then the chromatids are pulled to opposite ends of the cell.

4) TELOPHASE — Membranes form around each of the sets of chromosomes. These become the nuclei of the two new cells — the nucleus has divided.

Before telophase ends, the cytoplasm and cell membrane divide to form two separate cells — this process is called cytokinesis.

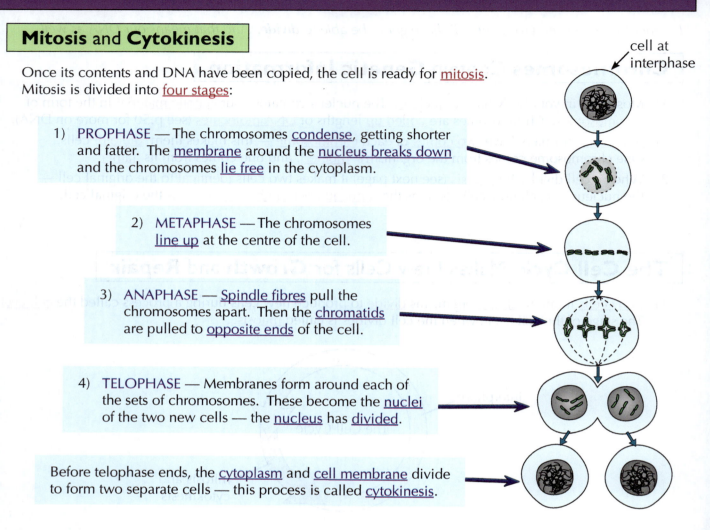

At the end of mitosis, the cell has produced two new daughter cells. Each daughter cell contains exactly the same sets of chromosomes in its nucleus as the other daughter cell — they're genetically identical diploid cells. They're also genetically identical to the parent cell.

You can Calculate the Final Number of Cells

You can calculate the number of cells there'll be after multiple divisions of a cell by mitosis. The formula you need is: number of cells = 2^n, where 'n' is the number of divisions by mitosis.

EXAMPLE   A cell divides by mitosis five times. How many cells are present after this process?

Multiply 2 by itself for the number of divisions to find the number of cells.

$2^5 = 2 \times 2 \times 2 \times 2 \times 2 = 32$ cells

Mitosis produces two identical daughter cells

Mitosis produces identical cells, but there's another type which doesn't... (see page 57).

Q1   A student looks at cells in the tip of a plant root under a microscope. She counts 11 cells that are undergoing mitosis and 62 cells that are not.
     a) Calculate the percentage of cells that are undergoing mitosis.   [1 mark]
     b) Suggest how the student can tell whether a cell is undergoing mitosis or not.   [1 mark]

Cell Division and Growth

Growth — it happens to us all. You need to know the *processes* involved in both *animal* and *plant* growth.

Growth Involves Cell Division, Differentiation and Elongation

Growth is an increase in size or mass. Plants and animals grow and develop due to these processes:

- CELL DIFFERENTIATION — the process by which a cell changes to become specialised for its job. Having specialised cells allows multicellular organisms to work more efficiently.

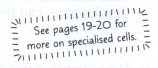
See pages 19-20 for more on specialised cells.

- CELL DIVISION — by mitosis (see pages 37-38).

- Plants also grow by CELL ELONGATION. This is where a plant cell expands, making the cell bigger and so making the plant grow.

Animals

1) All growth in animals happens by cell division.
2) Animals tend to grow while they're young, and then they reach full growth and stop growing.
3) So when you're young, cells divide at a fast rate but once you're an adult, most cell division is for repair — the cells divide to replace old or damaged cells.
4) This also means, in most animals, cell differentiation is lost at an early stage.

Plants

1) In plants, growth in height is mainly due to cell elongation — cell division usually just happens in the tips of the roots and shoots (in areas called meristems — see page 41).
2) But plants often grow continuously — even really old trees will keep putting out new branches. So, plants continue to differentiate to develop new parts, e.g. leaves, roots.

Cancer is a Case of Uncontrolled Cell Division

1) The rate at which cells divide by mitosis is controlled by the chemical instructions (genes) in an organism's DNA.
2) If there's a change in one of the genes that controls cell division, the cell may start dividing uncontrollably.
3) This can result in a mass of abnormal cells called a tumour.
4) If the tumour invades and destroys surrounding tissue it is called cancer.

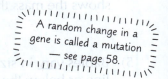
A random change in a gene is called a mutation — see page 58.

Growth is different in plants and animals...

Remember, both plant and animals grow by cell differentiation and cell division, but plants use cell elongation too. Plants continue to grow throughout their lives too, but animals stop growing once they reach full size.

Section 2 — Cells and Control

Percentile Charts

*It's important to **monitor growth** in children — there's a certain type of **graph** that can be used for this...*

Percentile Charts are Used to Monitor Growth

1) Growth charts are used to assess a child's growth over time, so that an overall pattern in development can be seen and any problems highlighted (e.g. obesity, malnutrition, dwarfism).

2) For example, a baby's growth is regularly monitored after birth to make sure it's growing normally. Three measurements are taken — length, mass and head circumference.

3) These results are plotted on growth charts, like the one below.

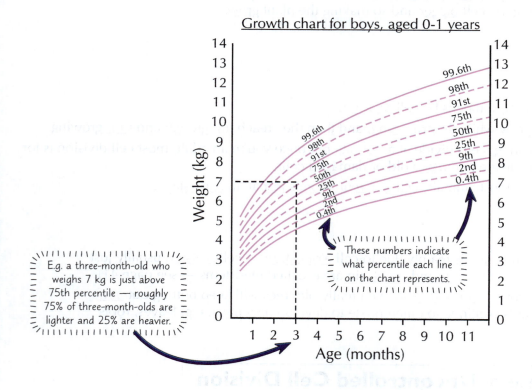

E.g. a three-month-old who weighs 7 kg is just above 75th percentile — roughly 75% of three-month-olds are lighter and 25% are heavier.

These numbers indicate what percentile each line on the chart represents.

4) The chart shows a number of 'percentiles'. E.g. the 50th percentile shows the mass that 50% of babies will have reached at a certain age.

5) Babies vary in size, but doctors are likely to investigate if a baby's size is above the top percentile line or below the bottom percentile line, their size increases or decreases by two or more percentile lines over time, or if there's an inconsistent pattern (e.g. a small baby with a very large head).

Percentile charts show the distribution of sizes in a population

Percentiles tell you where in the data set a data point lies. The value of a percentile tells you what percentage of data has a value equal to or lower than the data points in that percentile.

Section 2 — Cells and Control

Stem Cells

*Your body is made up of **all sorts** of cells — this page tells you where they all **came from**.*

Stem Cells can Differentiate into Different Types of Cells

1) As you saw on page 39, cells differentiate to become specialised cells.

2) Undifferentiated cells are called stem cells.

3) Depending on what instructions they're given, stem cells can divide by mitosis to become new cells, which then differentiate.

4) Stem cells are found in early human embryos. These embryonic stem cells have the potential to divide and produce any kind of cell at all. This makes sense — all the different types of cell found in a human have to come from those few cells in the early embryo.

5) This means stem cells are really important for the growth and development of organisms.

6) Adults also have stem cells, but they're only found in certain places, like bone marrow. These aren't as versatile as embryonic stem cells — they can't produce any cell type at all, only certain ones. In animals, adult stem cells are used to replace damaged cells, e.g. to make new skin or blood cells.

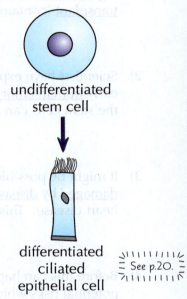

undifferentiated stem cell

differentiated ciliated epithelial cell

See p.20.

Meristems Contain Plant Stem Cells

In plants, the only cells that divide by mitosis are found in plant tissues called meristems.

1) Meristem tissue is found in the areas of a plant that are growing, e.g. the tips of the roots and shoots.
2) Meristems produce unspecialised cells that are able to divide and form any cell type in the plant — they act like embryonic stem cells. But unlike human stem cells, these cells can divide and differentiate to generate any type of cell for as long as the plant lives.
3) The unspecialised cells go on to form specialised tissues like xylem and phloem (see p.91).

Embryonic stem cells can become any type of cell

Unspecialised cells produced by plant meristems can differentiate into any type of cell so that the plant can continue to grow. Because humans stop growing, adult stem cells only differentiate into certain cell types.

Section 2 — Cells and Control

Stem Cells

*Stem cell research has exciting **possibilities**, but it's also pretty **controversial**.*

Stem Cells Can be Used in Medicine

1) Doctors already use adult stem cells to cure some diseases. E.g. sickle cell anaemia can sometimes be cured with a bone marrow transplant (containing adult stem cells which produce new blood cells).

2) Scientists have experimented with extracting stem cells from very early human embryos and growing them. Under certain conditions the stem cells can be stimulated to differentiate into specialised cells.

3) It might be possible to use stem cells to create specialised cells to replace those which have been damaged by disease or injury, e.g. new cardiac muscle cells could be transplanted into someone with heart disease. This potential for new cures is the reason for the huge scientific interest in stem cells.

4) Before this can happen, a lot of research needs to be done. There are many potential risks which scientists need to learn more about. For example:

Rejection
If the transplanted cells aren't grown using the patient's own stem cells, the patient's body may recognise the cells as foreign and trigger an immune response to try to get rid of them. The patient can take drugs to suppress this response, but this makes them susceptible to diseases.

Tumour development
Stem cells divide very quickly. If scientists are unable to control the rate at which the transplanted cells divide inside a patient, a tumour may develop (see page 39).

Disease transmission
Viruses live inside cells. If donor stem cells are infected with a virus and this isn't picked up, the virus could be passed on to the recipient and so make them sicker.

5) Research using embryonic stem cells raises ethical issues. E.g. some people argue that human embryos shouldn't be used for experiments because each one is a potential human life. But others think that the aim of curing patients who are suffering should be more important than the potential life of the embryos.

Stem cells could help cure many diseases in the future
Questions on the issues associated with using stem cells in medicine might crop up in the exam, so make sure you know the potential benefits and the risks associated with using them.

Section 2 — Cells and Control

Warm-Up and Exam Questions

Here's a page of questions — use them to help you brush up your 'cell division and growth' knowledge.

Warm-Up Questions

1) What does cell 'differentiation' mean?
2) True or false? Plants can grow by cell elongation.
3) What does it mean if the weight of a two-month-old baby is at the 25th percentile on a growth chart?
4) Where in the cell are chromosomes found?

Exam Questions

1   **Figure 1** shows how the amount of DNA per cell changes as a cell undergoes two cell divisions by mitosis. Point **C** is the time when the chromosomes first become visible in the cells.

(a) Describe what is happening to the DNA during stage **A**. Suggest why this needs to happen.
  [2 marks]

(b) Suggest what happens at time **B**.
  [1 mark]

(c) State how many cells there are after the first cell division.
  [1 mark]

(d) Cancer is a disease caused by problems in the cell division process. Describe how changes in cells can lead to cancer.
  [2 marks]

2   Adult stem cells have already been used to cure disorders, and it is thought that embryonic stem cells have the potential to treat many more disorders.

(a) Describe how embryonic stem cells could be used to treat disorders.
  [1 mark]

(b) Explain why embryonic stem cells have the potential to treat more disorders than adult stem cells.
  [1 mark]

3   A bacterial cell divides once every 30 minutes. Calculate the number of cells that will be present after 3 hours.
  [2 marks]

The Nervous System

The **nervous system** means that humans can **react to their surroundings** and **coordinate their behaviour**.

The Central Nervous System (CNS) Coordinates a Response

1) The nervous system is made up of neurones (nerve cells) which go to all parts of the body.
2) The body has lots of sensory receptors — groups of cells that can detect a change in your environment (a stimulus). Different receptors detect different stimuli. For example, receptors in your eyes detect light, while receptors in your skin detect touch (pressure) and temperature change.
3) When a stimulus is detected by receptors, the information is converted to a nervous (electrical) impulse and sent along sensory neurones to the CNS (the brain and spinal cord).
4) The CNS coordinates the response (in other words, it decides what to do about the stimulus and tells something to do it). Impulses travel through the CNS along relay neurones.
5) The CNS sends information to an effector (muscle or gland) along a motor neurone. The effector then responds accordingly — e.g. a muscle may contract or a gland may secrete a hormone.

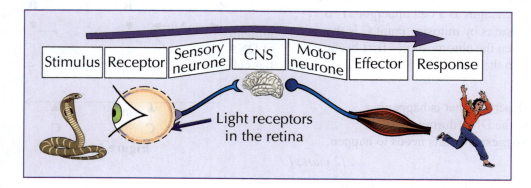

6) The time it takes you to respond to a stimulus is called your reaction time.

Neurones Transmit Information Rapidly as Electrical Impulses

1) All neurones have a cell body with a nucleus (plus cytoplasm and other subcellular structures).
2) The cell body has extensions that connect to other neurones — dendrites and dendrons carry nerve impulses towards the cell body, and axons carry nerve impulses away from the cell body.
3) Some axons are surrounded by a myelin sheath. This acts as an electrical insulator, speeding up the electrical impulse.
4) Neurones can be very long, which also speeds up the impulse (connecting with another neurone slows the impulse down, so one long neurone is much quicker than lots of short ones joined together).

There's more on axons and dendrites on the next page.

 The exam isn't just a test of what you know...
...it's also a test of how well you can apply what you know. For instance, you might have to take what you know about a human's nervous system and apply it to a horse. The key is not to panic — just think carefully about the information that you are given.

Section 2 — Cells and Control

The Nervous System

There are **Different Types** of **Neurones**

You need to know the structure and function of sensory, motor and relay neurones.

Sensory Neurone

1) One long dendron carries nerve impulses from receptor cells to the cell body, which is located in the middle of the neurone.
2) One short axon carries nerve impulses from the cell body to the CNS.

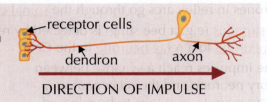

Motor Neurone

1) Many short dendrites carry nerve impulses from the CNS to the cell body.
2) One long axon carries nerve impulses from the cell body to effector cells.

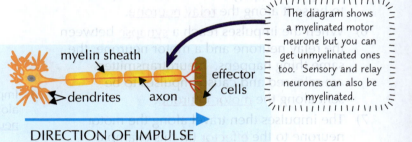

The diagram shows a myelinated motor neurone but you can get unmyelinated ones too. Sensory and relay neurones can also be myelinated.

Relay Neurone

1) Many short dendrites carry nerve impulses from sensory neurones to the cell body.
2) An axon carries nerve impulses from the cell body to motor neurones.

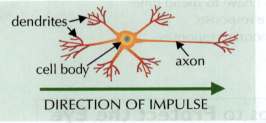

Synapses Connect Neurones

1) The connection between two neurones is called a synapse.
2) The nerve signal is transferred by chemicals called neurotransmitters, which diffuse (move) across the gap.
3) The neurotransmitters then set off a new electrical signal in the next neurone.
4) The transmission of a nervous impulse is very fast, but it is slowed down a bit at the synapse because the diffusion of neurotransmitters across the gap takes time.

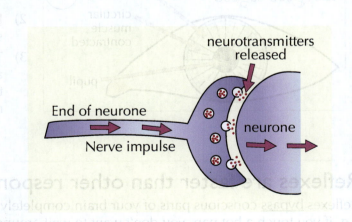

Make sure you know the differences between the neurones
You need to know the structures and functions of the different types of neurones — try drawing out the diagrams yourself and putting annotations on them saying what each part does.

Section 2 — Cells and Control

Reflexes

Sometimes you respond to a stimulus **without thinking** about it — this is a **reflex**.

Reflexes Help Prevent Injury

1) Reflexes are automatic, rapid responses to stimuli — they can reduce the chances of being injured.
2) The passage of information in a reflex (from receptor to effector) is called a reflex arc.
3) The neurones in reflex arcs go through the spinal cord or through an unconscious part of the brain.
4) When a stimulus (e.g. a bee sting) is detected by receptors, impulses are sent along a sensory neurone to a relay neurone in the CNS.
5) When the impulses reach a synapse between the sensory neurone and the relay neurone, they trigger neurotransmitters to be released (see previous page). These cause impulses to be sent along the relay neurone.
6) When the impulses reach a synapse between the relay neurone and a motor neurone, the same thing happens. Neurotransmitters are released and cause impulses to be sent along the motor neurone.
7) The impulses then travel along the motor neurone to the effector (in this example it's a muscle, but it could be a gland).
8) The muscle then contracts and moves your hand away from the bee.
9) Because you don't have to spend time thinking about the response, it's quicker than normal responses.

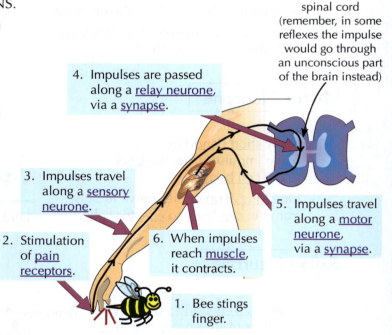

spinal cord (remember, in some reflexes the impulse would go through an unconscious part of the brain instead)

4. Impulses are passed along a relay neurone, via a synapse.
3. Impulses travel along a sensory neurone.
5. Impulses travel along a motor neurone, via a synapse.
2. Stimulation of pain receptors.
6. When impulses reach muscle, it contracts.
1. Bee stings finger.

A Reflex Helps to Protect the Eye

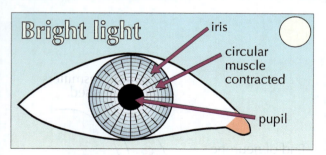

1) Very bright light can damage the eye — so you have a reflex to protect it.
2) Light receptors in the eye detect very bright light and send a message along a sensory neurone to the brain.
3) The message then travels along a relay neurone to a motor neurone, which tells circular muscles in the iris (the coloured part of the eye) to contract, making the pupil smaller.

Reflexes are faster than other responses

Reflexes bypass conscious parts of your brain completely when a super quick response is essential. E.g. if you touch a hot pan, you don't want to wait around deciding to move your hand or not.

Q1 What is a reflex action? [1 mark]

Q2 A chef touches a hot pan. A reflex reaction causes him to immediately move his hand away.
   a) State the effector in this reflex reaction. [1 mark]
   b) Describe the pathway of the reflex from stimulus to effector. [4 marks]

Section 2 — Cells and Control

Warm-Up and Exam Questions

Welcome to some questions. There are quite a few of them, but that's because they're pretty important...

Warm-Up Questions

1) What is meant by the term 'stimulus'?
2) What is the function of an axon?
3) How does a myelin sheath speed up electrical impulses?
4) Name the three types of neurone in a reflex arc.
5) What name is given to the connection between two neurones?

Exam Questions

1 A student is taking part in an experiment to test reaction times. Every time a red triangle appears on the computer screen in front of her, she has to click the mouse.

   (a) Suggest what the stimulus, receptors and effectors are in this experiment.

[3 marks]

   (b) The student took the test three times. Her reaction time in test 1 was 328 ms. Her reaction time in test 2 was 346 ms. Her mean reaction time was 343 ms. Calculate her reaction time for test 3.

[2 marks]

2 Young babies have several reflexes not usually present in adults. For example, if an object is placed in the palm of a newborn baby's hand, the baby will move their fingers to grasp the object. The reflex arc for this reflex is shown in **Figure 1**.

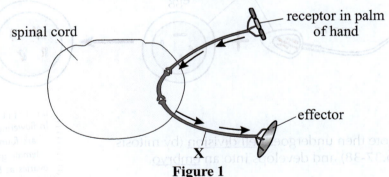

Figure 1

   (a) Name the structure labelled **X** on **Figure 1**.

[1 mark]

   (b) State the type of effector in this response and describe its action.

[2 marks]

   (c) Explain how an electrical impulse in one neurone is able to pass to the next neurone.

[2 marks]

   (d) If an object is placed in the palm of a baby over 6 months old, it can choose whether it wants to grasp hold of the object. Describe **one** way in which the pathway of nervous impulses involved in grasping an object differs between a newborn baby and a baby older than 6 months.

[1 mark]

Section 2 — Cells and Control

Section 3 — Genetics

Sexual Reproduction

*If you've ever wondered why you look **like** your **family members**, but **not exactly the same**, read on...*

Sexual Reproduction Produces Genetically Different Cells

1) Sexual reproduction is where genetic information from two organisms (a father and a mother) is combined to produce offspring which are genetically different to either parent.

2) In sexual reproduction, the father and mother produce gametes (reproductive cells). In animals these are sperm and egg cells.

3) Gametes only contain half the number of chromosomes of normal cells — they are haploid. Normal cells (with the full number of chromosomes) are diploid (see p.37).

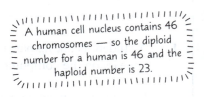

A human cell nucleus contains 46 chromosomes — so the diploid number for a human is 46 and the haploid number is 23.

4) At fertilisation, a male gamete fuses with a female gamete to produce a fertilised egg, also known as a zygote. The zygote ends up with the full set of chromosomes (so it is diploid).

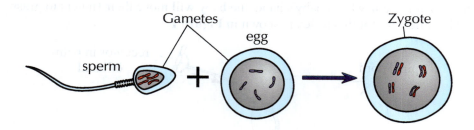

5) The zygote then undergoes cell division (by mitosis — see p.37-38) and develops into an embryo.

In flowering plants, the male gametes are found in the pollen and the female gametes are found in the ovaries at the bottom of the stigma.

6) The embryo inherits characteristics from both parents, as it has received a mixture of chromosomes (and therefore genes) from its mother and its father.

Sexual reproduction combines genetic information from two parents

Make sure you're confident with this page — it will make learning the next few pages much easier.

Meiosis

*This page is all about how gametes end up with **half** the number of **chromosomes** of a normal cell.*

Gametes are Produced by Meiosis

Meiosis is a type of cell division. It's different to mitosis because it doesn't produce identical cells. In humans, meiosis only happens in the reproductive organs (ovaries and testes).

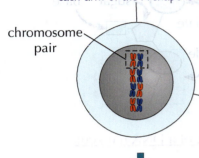

This cell has duplicated each chromosome — each arm of the X-shape is identical.

chromosome pair

Half of the chromosomes in the starting cell were inherited from the organism's father (blue) and half from its mother (red).

DIVISION 1

DIVISION 2

1) Before the cell starts to divide, it duplicates its DNA (so there's enough for each new cell). One arm of each X-shaped chromosome is an exact copy of the other arm.

2) In the first division in meiosis (there are two divisions) the chromosomes line up in pairs in the centre of the cell. One chromosome in each pair came from the organism's mother and one came from its father.

3) The pairs are then pulled apart, so each new cell only has one copy of each chromosome. Some of the father's chromosomes and some of the mother's chromosomes go into each new cell.

4) Each new cell will have a mixture of the mother's and father's chromosomes. Mixing up the genes like this is really important — it creates genetic variation in the offspring.

5) In the second division the chromosomes line up again in the centre of the cell. It's a lot like mitosis. The arms of the chromosomes (called chromatids) are pulled apart.

6) You get four haploid daughter cells — these are the gametes. Each gamete only has a single set of chromosomes. The gametes are all genetically different.

Meiosis is different from Mitosis

Remember — meiosis produces gametes that are genetically different.

Q1 Human body cells contain 46 chromosomes each. The graph on the right shows how the mass of DNA per cell changed as some cells divided by meiosis in a human ovary. How many chromosomes were present in each cell when they reached stage 6?

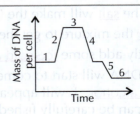

Q1 Video Solution

[1 mark]

Section 3 — Genetics

DNA

*Reproduction is all about **passing on your DNA** to the next generation. This molecule carries all the **instructions** for your characteristics — so it's a big part of what makes you **you**.*

DNA is Made Up of Nucleotides

1) DNA strands are polymers made up of lots of repeating units called nucleotides.
2) Each nucleotide consists of a sugar, a phosphate group and one 'base'.
3) The sugar and phosphate groups in the nucleotides form a 'backbone' to the DNA strands. The sugar and phosphate groups alternate.
4) One of four different bases joins to each sugar. The bases are: A (adenine), T (thymine), C (cytosine) and G (guanine).
5) A DNA molecule has two strands coiled together in the shape of a double helix (a double stranded spiral).
6) Each base links to a base on the opposite strand in the helix.
7) A always pairs with T, and C always pairs with G. This is called complementary base pairing.

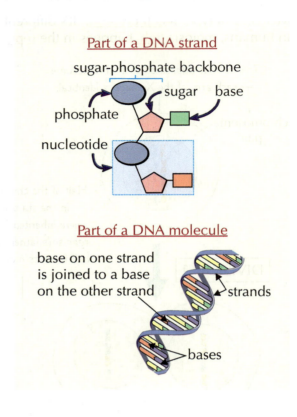

Part of a DNA strand

Part of a DNA molecule — base on one strand is joined to a base on the other strand — strands, bases

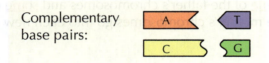

Complementary base pairs: A–T, C–G

8) The complementary base pairs are joined together by weak hydrogen bonds.

DNA is Stored as Chromosomes and Contains Genes

1) Chromosomes are long, coiled up molecules of DNA. They're found in the nucleus of eukaryotic cells.
2) A gene is a section of DNA on a chromosome that codes for a particular protein.
3) All of an organism's DNA makes up its genome.

You Need to Know How to Extract DNA From Fruit Cells

Don't believe that cells contain DNA? Well here's a practical you can do to get it out...

1) Mash some strawberries and then put them in a beaker containing a solution of detergent and salt. Mix well.
   - The detergent will break down the cell membranes to release the DNA.
   - The salt will make the DNA stick together.
2) Filter the mixture to get the froth and big, insoluble bits of cell out.
3) Gently add some ice-cold alcohol to the filtered mixture.
4) The DNA will start to come out of solution as it's not soluble in cold alcohol. It will appear as a stringy white precipitate (a solid) that can be carefully fished out with a glass rod.

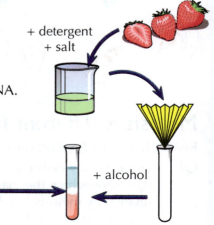

Section 3 — Genetics

Warm-Up and Exam Questions

It's time to see how much you picked up about meiosis, reproduction and DNA.

Warm-Up Questions

1) How many cell divisions take place in meiosis?
2) Which DNA bases pair up according to complementary base pairing?
3) What is a gene?

Exam Questions

1   A student mashes a small sample of kiwi fruit and then adds detergent and salt.
    She filters the solution into a test tube and adds liquid X.
    A stringy white precipitate is formed in the test tube.

    (a) Give an identity for liquid X.

    [1 mark]

    (b) Name the stringy white precipitate that is formed.

    [1 mark]

2   An organism's genetic material is made up of a chemical called DNA.

    (a) Which of the following describes the structure of DNA?

    ☐ A A protein made up of two strands.   ☐ C A polymer made up of two strands.
    ☐ B A protein made up of four strands.   ☐ D A polymer made up of four strands.

    [1 mark]

    (b) Name the type of bond that joins complementary base pairs.

    [1 mark]

    (c) Describe the relationship between DNA and the proteins produced by an organism.

    [3 marks]

3   Mosquitoes have three pairs of chromosomes in their body cells.
    Figure 1 shows a mosquito cell which is about to divide by meiosis.

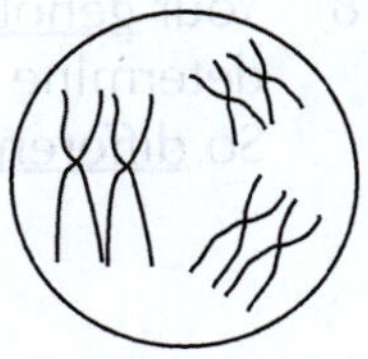

    (a) The cell in **Figure 1** undergoes meiosis.
        State how many chromosomes will be present in each new cell produced.

    [1 mark]

    (b) State the number of cells that will be produced in total when the cell in **Figure 1** undergoes meiosis.

    Figure 1

    [1 mark]

Section 3 — Genetics

Genes and Alleles

*Each pair of **chromosomes** contain the **same genes** in the **same places**. These genes can come in different **versions**, so the **characteristics** you have will depend on which versions you **inherit** from your parents.*

Alleles Are Different Versions of the Same Gene

1) What genes you inherit control what characteristics you develop.

2) Different genes control different characteristics. Some characteristics are controlled by a single gene. However, most characteristics are controlled by several genes interacting.

3) All genes exist in different versions called alleles (which are represented by letters in genetic diagrams).

4) You have two versions (alleles) of every gene in your body — one on each chromosome in a pair.

5) If an organism has two alleles for a particular gene that are the same, then it's homozygous for that trait. If its two alleles for a particular gene are different, then it's heterozygous.

6) Some alleles are dominant (shown with a capital letter, e.g. 'C') and some are recessive (shown by a small letter, e.g. 'c'). Dominant alleles overrule recessive alleles, so if an organism has one dominant and one recessive allele for a gene (e.g. 'Cc'), then the dominant allele will determine what characteristic is present.

7) To display a dominant characteristic, an organism can have either two dominant alleles for a particular gene or one dominant and one recessive allele for that gene. But for an organism to display a recessive characteristic, both its alleles must be recessive.

8) Your genotype is the combination of alleles you have. Your alleles determine what characteristics you have — your phenotype. So different combinations of alleles give rise to different phenotypes.

There are lots of fancy words to learn on this page...
Make sure you fully understand what all the different terms on this page mean (i.e. genes, alleles, homozygous, heterozygous, dominant, recessive, genotype and phenotype). You'll feel much more comfortable going into the exam knowing that these words aren't going to trip you up.

Section 3 — Genetics

Genetic Diagrams

Genetic Diagrams Can Show Inheritance of a Single Characteristic

The inheritance of a single characteristic is called monohybrid inheritance. You can use a monohybrid cross to show how recessive and dominant traits for a single characteristic are inherited.

For example, let's say an allele that causes hamsters to have superpowers is recessive ("b"), and that normal (boring) hamsters don't have superpowers due to a dominant allele ("B"). Here's how you could use a monohybrid cross to show the probability of either the dominant or recessive trait being inherited:

1) The first step is to cross two homozygous hamsters (BB and bb):

'Cross' just means 'breed together'.

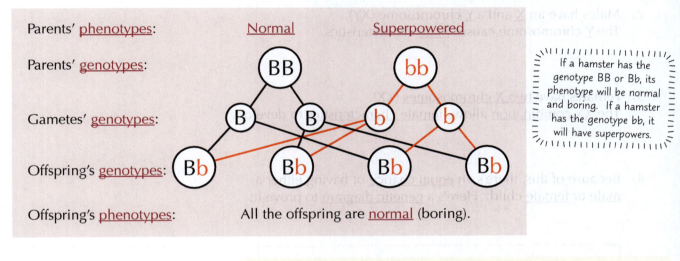

If a hamster has the genotype BB or Bb, its phenotype will be normal and boring. If a hamster has the genotype bb, it will have superpowers.

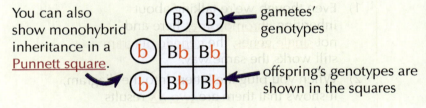

You can also show monohybrid inheritance in a Punnett square.

gametes' genotypes

offspring's genotypes are shown in the squares

2) If two of these offspring now breed, you'll get the next generation:

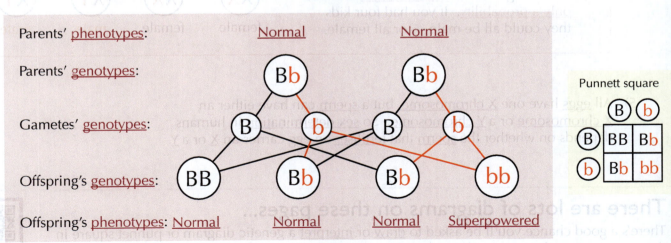

Punnett square

3) In this generation, there's a 3:1 ratio of normal to superpowered offspring. In other words, there's a 3 in 4 (75%) probability of normal hamsters and a 1 in 4 (25%) probability of superpowers.

Genetic Diagrams

You can work out the **probability** of offspring being male or female by using a *genetic diagram*.

A Genetic Diagram Can Show How Sex is Determined in Humans

1) There are 23 matched pairs of chromosomes in every human body cell. The 23rd pair is labelled XX or XY. They're the two chromosomes that decide whether you turn out male or female.

2) Males have an X and a Y chromosome (XY). The Y chromosome causes male characteristics.

3) Females have two X chromosomes (XX). The XX combination allows female characteristics to develop.

4) Because of this, there's an equal chance of having either a male or female child. Here's a genetic diagram to prove it:

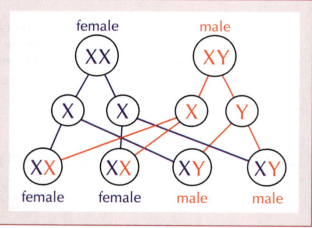

1) Even though we're talking about inheriting chromosomes here and not single genes, the genetic diagram still works the same way.
2) When you plug the letters into the diagram, it shows that there are two XX results and two XY results, so there's the same probability of getting a male or female child.
3) Don't forget that this 50 : 50 ratio is only a probability. If you had four kids they could all be male — or all female.

5) All eggs have one X chromosome, but a sperm can have either an X chromosome or a Y chromosome. So sex determination in humans depends on whether the sperm that fertilises an egg carries an X or a Y.

There are lots of diagrams on these pages...

There's a good chance you'll be asked to draw or interpret a genetic diagram or punnet square in the exam — so make sure you know how to use them.

Q1 Round peas are caused by the dominant allele, R. The allele for wrinkly peas, r, is recessive. Using a Punnett square, predict the ratio of plants with round peas to plants with wrinkly peas for a cross between a heterozygous pea plant and a pea plant that is homozygous recessive.

[3 marks]

Section 3 — Genetics

Genetic Diagrams

Family Pedigrees Can Also Show Monohybrid Inheritance

Knowing how inheritance works helps you to interpret a family pedigree (a family tree of genetic disorders). Here's an example using cystic fibrosis — a genetic disorder of the cell membranes.

Cystic Fibrosis is a Recessive Genetic Disorder

1) The allele which causes cystic fibrosis (CF) is a recessive allele, 'f', carried by about 1 person in 30.
2) Because it's recessive, people with only one copy of the allele won't have the disorder — they're known as carriers.
3) For a child to inherit the disorder, both parents must either have the disorder themselves or be carriers.

This diagram shows a monohybrid cross between two people who are carriers of the cystic fibrosis allele.

You can see from the diagram that there's a 1 in 4 chance of a child having the disorder if both parents are carriers.

The probability of each outcome can also be expressed as a ratio — 1 : 2 : 1 for unaffected : carrier : disorder.

4) You can show information about how alleles are passed through families on a family pedigree diagram. The lines on the pedigree link the parents to each other (horizontal) and to their children (vertical).
5) The example below shows a family pedigree for a family that includes carriers of cystic fibrosis:

- You can tell from the pedigree that the allele for cystic fibrosis isn't dominant because plenty of family members carry the allele but don't have the disorder.
- There is a 1 in 4 (25%) chance that the new baby will have cystic fibrosis and a 1 in 2 (50%) chance that it will be a carrier (because both of its parents are carriers).
- In fact, the case of the new baby is the same as in the monohybrid cross diagram above — they could be unaffected (FF), be a carrier (Ff) or have the disorder (ff).

A carrier is someone with only one copy of the recessive allele

In the exam, you might get a family pedigree showing the inheritance of a dominant allele — in this case, there won't be any carriers (everyone with the allele has that phenotype).

Q1 Cystic fibrosis is caused by a recessive allele, f. The dominant allele is F. The family pedigree on the right shows the inheritance of cystic fibrosis. What is Tamsin's genotype? Use the key above to help you. [1 mark]

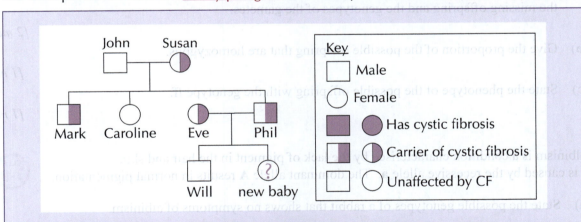

Section 3 — Genetics

Warm-Up and Exam Questions

Take a deep breath and go through these Warm-Up Questions one by one. Then on to the Exam Questions. Don't panic if you get something wrong — as they say, practice makes perfect...

Warm-Up Questions

1) What are alleles?
2) What does phenotype mean?
3) For a certain type of mouse, having the genotype bb results in white fur. Having the genotype Bb or BB, results in brown fur. Which characteristic, white fur or brown fur is recessive? Explain your answer.
4) What combination of sex chromosomes do human females have?

Exam Questions

1   Cystic fibrosis is a genetic disorder caused by a recessive allele.

   F = normal allele   **f** = faulty allele that leads to cystic fibrosis

   Figure 1 is an incomplete Punnett square showing the possible inheritance of cystic fibrosis from one couple.

   (a) Complete the Punnett square to show the genotype of the missing offspring and the genotypes of the gametes.

   [2 marks]

   (b) Give the proportion of the possible offspring that are homozygous.

   [1 mark]

   (c) State the phenotype of the possible offspring with the genotype ff.

   [1 mark]

2   Albinism is a condition characterised by the lack of pigment in the hair and skin. It is caused by the recessive allele **a**. The dominant allele **A** results in normal pigmentation.

   (a) State the possible genotypes of a rabbit that shows no symptoms of albinism.

   [1 mark]

   A rabbit with albinism mated with a rabbit that showed no symptoms of the condition. 56% of the offspring had albinism.

   (b) Deduce the genotypes of the parent rabbits and the possible genotypes of their offspring. Use a genetic diagram to explain your answer.

   [3 marks]

   (c) Using your genetic diagram, give the percentage of offspring that are likely to have albinism.

   [1 mark]

   (d) Suggest why the percentage of offspring which were born with albinism was not exactly the same as that suggested by your genetic diagram.

   [1 mark]

Variation

You'll probably have noticed that not all people are **identical**. There are reasons for this.

Organisms of the Same Species Have Differences

1) Different species look different.

2) But even organisms of the same species will usually look at least slightly different. E.g. all dogs are the same species, but a Dalmatian looks quite different to a Pug.

3) These differences are called the variation within a species. It can be genetic or environmental.

4) Genetic variation within a species is caused by organisms having different alleles (versions of genes) which can lead to differences in phenotype (the characteristics an organism displays).

5) Genetic variation can be caused by new alleles arising through mutations (see next page). Sexual reproduction also causes genetic variation since it results in alleles being combined in lots of different ways in offspring.

> Sexual reproduction means no two members of a species are genetically identical (apart from identical twins).

6) There tends to be a lot of genetic variation within a population of a species. This is mostly due to neutral mutations (see next page).

7) Variation within a species can also be caused by the environment (the conditions in which organisms live). For example:

 A plant grown on a nice sunny windowsill could grow luscious and green. The same plant grown in darkness would grow tall and spindly and its leaves would turn yellow.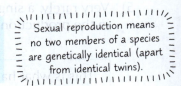

These environmental variations in phenotype are also known as acquired characteristics. They're characteristics that organisms acquire (get) during their lifetimes.

8) Most variation in phenotype is determined by a mixture of genetic and environmental factors.

> For example, the maximum height that an animal or plant could grow to is determined by its genes. But whether it actually grows that tall depends on its environment (e.g. how much food it gets).

You can't blame all of your faults on your parents...

Although the genes that you inherit from your parents are really important at determining what characteristics you have, the conditions in which you live usually play a role too.

Section 3 — Genetics

Variation and the Human Genome Project

Alleles Arise Due to Genetic Mutations

1) Mutations are changes to the base sequence of DNA.

2) When they occur within a gene they result in an allele, or a different version of the gene.

3) They don't always have a big effect on the phenotype of an organism. In fact, most mutations don't have any effect — in other words they are neutral.

4) But some mutations do have a small effect on the phenotype — they alter an individual's characteristics, but only very slightly. E.g. a mutation might give a hamster long hair instead of short hair.

5) Very rarely, a single mutation will have a big effect on phenotype. For example, it might result in the production of a protein that is so different that it can no longer carry out its function.

> This is what happens in cystic fibrosis (see page 55). A mutation causes a protein that controls the movement of salt and water into and out of cells to stop working properly. This leads to the production of thick, sticky mucus in the lungs and the digestive system, which can make it difficult to breathe and digest food.

6) New combinations of alleles may also interact with each other to produce new phenotypes.

Over 20 000 Genes Were Mapped in the Human Genome Project

1) Thousands of scientists from all over the world collaborated (worked together) on the Human Genome Project. The big idea was to find every single human gene.

2) The project officially started in 1990 and a complete map of the human genome, including the locations of around 20 500 genes, was completed in 2003.

3) Now that the genes have all been found, scientists are trying to figure out what they all do.

4) So far, the project has helped to identify about 1800 genes related to disease, which has huge potential benefits for medicine (see next page).

The Human Genome Project

*Here's a bit more about the **Human Genome Project** — including how we might use the data it produced.*

There are Lots of Medical Applications for the Project's Research

Prediction and prevention of diseases

Many common diseases like cancers and heart disease are caused by the interaction of different genes, as well as lifestyle factors. If doctors knew what genes predisposed people to what diseases, we could all get individually tailored advice on the best diet and lifestyle to avoid our likely problems. Doctors could also check us regularly to ensure early treatment if we do develop the diseases we're susceptible to.

Testing and treatment for inherited disorders

1) Inherited disorders (e.g. cystic fibrosis) are caused by the presence of one or more faulty alleles in a person's genome.
2) Thanks to the Human Genome Project, scientists are now able to identify the genes and alleles that are suspected of causing an inherited disorder much more quickly than they could do in the past.
3) Once an allele that causes an inherited disorder has been identified, people can be tested for it and it may be possible to develop better treatments or even (eventually) a cure for the disease.

New and better medicines

1) Genome research has highlighted some common genetic variations between people. Some variations affect how our individual bodies will react to certain diseases and to the possible treatments for them.
2) Scientists can use this knowledge to design new drugs that are specifically tailored to people with a particular genetic variation. They can also determine how well an existing drug will work for an individual. Tests can already identify whether or not someone with breast cancer will respond to a particular drug, and what dosage is most appropriate for certain drugs in different patients.
3) More generally, knowing how a disease affects us on a molecular level should make it possible to design more effective treatments with fewer side-effects.

But There Could Also be Drawbacks

1) Increased stress — for example, if someone knew from an early age that they're susceptible to a nasty brain disease, they could panic every time they get a headache (even if they never get the disease).
2) Gene-ism — people with genetic problems could come under pressure not to have children.
3) Discrimination by employers and insurers — life insurance could become impossible to get (or expensive at least) if you have any genetic likelihood of serious disease. And employers might discriminate against people who are genetically likely to get a disease.

Scientists can learn a lot about diseases from the human genome

Working out the human genome was a massive project — it involved scientists from many different parts of the world and took more than ten years to complete. Still, if scientists can use the information to help us understand more about diseases and how to fight them, then I reckon it was well worth all the effort.

Section 3 — Genetics

Warm-Up and Exam Questions

By doing these questions, you'll soon find out if you've got the basic facts straight.

Warm-Up Questions

1) Explain what is meant by environmental variation.
2) Amy and Beth are sisters. Amy's hair is curly and Beth's hair is straight. Suggest one way that this difference could be caused by a) a genetic factor, b) an environmental factor.
3) True or False? Genetic mutations in an organism's DNA always have an effect on the organism's phenotype.

Exam Questions

1 Helen and Stephanie are identical twins. This means they have identical DNA. *(Grade 4-6)*

   (a) Which of the following characteristics can you be certain that Helen and Stephanie will share?

   ☐ A   They will speak the same language.

   ☐ B   They will be the same height.

   ☐ C   They will both be fast runners.

   ☐ D   They will have the same blood group.

   [1 mark]

   (b) Helen weighs 7 kg more than Stephanie.
   Explain whether this is due to genes, environmental factors or both.

   [2 marks]

   (c) Stephanie has a birthmark on her shoulder. Helen doesn't.
   State whether this type of birthmark is caused by genes and explain your answer.

   [1 mark]

2 A group of scientists used data from the Human Genome Project to identify an allele that puts people who carry it at high risk of developing colorectal cancer. Eshan has a family history of colorectal cancer. He is offered a genetic test that will tell him if he is carries the allele or not. *(Grade 6-7)*

   (a) Suggest **one** advantage to Eshan of having this genetic test.

   [1 marks]

   (b) Suggest **one** disadvantage to Eshan of having this genetic test.

   [1 mark]

3 Genetic variation in a population arises partly due to mutations. *(Grade 6-7)*

   (a) Explain how mutations can increase variation in a species.

   [3 marks]

   (b) Some mutations are neutral, having no effect on an organism, but some do have an impact.
   Suggest how a single mutation could have a large impact on phenotype.

   [2 marks]

Section 3 — Genetics

Section 4 — Natural Selection and Genetic Modification

Natural Selection and Evidence for Evolution

Evolution is the **slow and continuous change** of organisms from one generation to the next. **Charles Darwin** came up with the theory of **natural selection** to explain how **evolution** occurs.

Natural Selection Means "Survival of the Fittest"

1) Individuals in a population show genetic variation because of differences in their alleles (see page 57). New alleles arise through mutations.

   Alleles are versions of genes — see page 52.

2) Things like predation, competition for resources (e.g. food, water, mates, etc.) and disease act as selection pressures. This means they affect an organism's chance of surviving and reproducing.

3) Those individuals with characteristics that make them better adapted to the selection pressures in their environment have a better chance of survival and so are more likely to breed successfully.

4) This means the alleles that are responsible for the useful characteristics are more likely to be passed on to the next generation.

5) However, some individuals will be less well adapted to the selection pressures in their environment and may be less able to compete. These individuals are less likely to survive and reproduce.

   A species that can't compete is likely to go extinct.

6) The beneficial characteristics become more common in the population over time.

Fossils Provide Evidence for Evolution

1) A fossil is any trace of an animal or plant that lived a long time ago (e.g. over a thousand years). They are most commonly found in rocks. Generally, the deeper the rock, the older the fossil.

2) By arranging fossils in chronological (date) order, gradual changes in organisms can be observed. This provides evidence for evolution, because it shows how species have changed and developed over billions of years. Fossils that provide evidence for human evolution are covered on page 63.

Natural selection — the fittest pass on their alleles...

Natural selection's all about the organisms with the best characteristics surviving to pass on their alleles, so that the whole species ends up adapted to its environment. It doesn't happen overnight.

Q1 The sugary nectar in some orchid flowers is found at the end of a long tube behind the flower. There are moth species with long tongues that can reach the nectar. Explain how natural selection could have led to the moths developing long tongues. [4 marks]

Natural Selection and Evidence for Evolution

*It's not just fossils from many, many years ago that provide **evidence for evolution** — we can observe the process of **natural selection** happening in real-time in **bacteria**...*

Bacteria Provide Evidence for Evolution

1) Like all organisms, bacteria sometimes develop random mutations in their DNA. These can create new alleles, which can change the bacteria's characteristics — e.g. a bacterium could become less affected by a particular antibiotic (a drug designed to kill bacteria or prevent them from reproducing).

2) For the bacterium, the ability to resist this antibiotic is a big advantage. In a host who's being treated to get rid of the infection, a resistant bacterium is better able to survive than a non-resistant bacterium — and so it lives for longer and reproduces many more times.

3) This leads to the allele for antibiotic resistance being passed on to lots of offspring — it's just natural selection. This is how it spreads and becomes more common in a population of bacteria over time.

It's easy to see evolution happening in bacteria because they reproduce so rapidly.

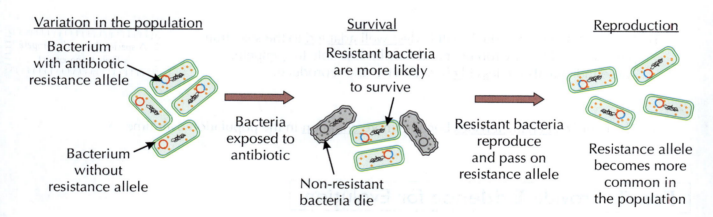

4) Antibiotic resistance provides evidence for evolution because it makes the bacteria better adapted to an environment in which antibiotics (a selection pressure) are present. And as a result, antibiotic resistance becomes more common in the population over time.

5) The emergence of other resistant organisms (e.g. rats resistant to the poison warfarin) also provides evidence for evolution.

Don't become resistant to revision...

Evolution by natural selection is a theory — an accepted hypothesis. Evidence is really important when it comes to accepting or rejecting scientific hypotheses — if there's no evidence to support a hypothesis, it won't become a theory.

Evidence for Human Evolution

*There's a lot of **fossil evidence** that suggests that humans evolved from a **common ancestor** with other **apes**.*

Fossils Give Us Clues About What Human Ancestors Were Like

1) Evidence from fossils suggests that humans and chimpanzees evolved from a common ancestor that existed around 6 million years ago.

2) Human beings and their ancestors are known as hominids. Fossils of several different hominid species have been found.

3) These fossils have characteristics that are between apes and humans — by looking at hominid fossils you can see how humans have evolved over time.

'Ardi' is a Fossil Hominid 4.4 Million Years Old

Ardi is a fossil of the species *Ardipithecus ramidus*. She was found in Ethiopia and is 4.4 million years old. Ardi's features are a mixture of those found in humans and in apes:

1) The structure of her feet suggests she climbed trees — she had an ape-like big toe to grasp branches.
2) She also had long arms and short legs (more like an ape than a human).
3) Her brain size was about the same as a chimpanzee's.
4) But the structure of her legs suggests that she walked upright. Her hand bone structure also suggests she didn't use her hands to help her walk (like apes do).

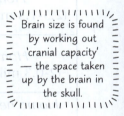
Brain size is found by working out 'cranial capacity' — the space taken up by the brain in the skull.

'Lucy' is a Fossil Hominid 3.2 Million Years Old

Lucy is a fossil of the species *Australopithecus afarensis*. She was found in Ethiopia and is 3.2 million years old. Lucy also has a mixture of human and ape features, but she is more human-like than Ardi.

1) Lucy had arched feet, more adapted to walking than climbing, and no ape-like big toe.
2) The size of her arms and legs was between what you would expect to find in apes and humans.
3) Her brain was slightly larger than Ardi's but still similar in size to a chimp's brain.
4) The structure of Lucy's leg bones and feet suggest she walked upright, but more efficiently than Ardi.

Leakey and His Team Found Fossil Hominids 1.6 Million Years Old

In 1984 scientist Richard Leakey organised an expedition to Kenya to look for hominid fossils. He and his team discovered many important fossils of different *Australopithecus* and *Homo* species.

1) One find was Turkana Boy — a 1.6 million year old fossil skeleton of the species *Homo erectus*. He has a mixture of human and ape-like features, but is more human-like than Lucy.
2) His short arms and long legs are much more like a human than an ape, and his brain size was much larger than Lucy's — similar to human brain size.
3) The structure of his legs and feet suggest he was even better adapted to walking upright than Lucy.

Section 4 — Natural Selection and Genetic Modification

Evidence for Human Evolution

You Can Show Human Evolution on a Timeline

So you know that the Ardipithecus and Australopithecus species were more ape-like, compared to the Homo species, which are human-like. They can all be put on a timeline, showing how humans have evolved:

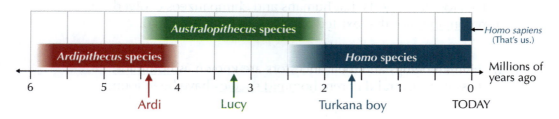

Stone Tools Provide More Evidence for Human Evolution

The different Homo species continued to evolve. You can tell this because they started using stone tools and these gradually became more complex (so their brains must have been getting larger):

Homo species	Tool use
Homo habilis (2.5-1.5 million years ago)	Made simple stone tools called pebble tools by hitting rocks together to make sharp flakes. These could be used to scrape meat from bones or crack bones open.
Homo erectus (2-0.3 million years ago)	Sculpted rocks into shapes to produce more complex tools like simple hand-axes. These could be used to hunt, dig, chop and scrape meat from bones.
Homo neanderthalensis (300 000-25 000 years ago)	More complex tools. Evidence of flint tools, pointed tools and wooden spears.
Homo sapiens (200 000 years ago-present)	Flint tools widely used. Pointed tools including arrowheads, fish hooks and needles appeared around 50 000 years ago.

Stone Tools and Fossils Can be Dated

When an ancient stone tool or hominid fossil (see previous page) is found, there are several different ways scientists can work out how old it is. These include:

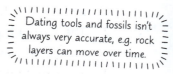
Dating tools and fossils isn't always very accurate, e.g. rock layers can move over time.

1) Looking at the structural features of the tool or fossil. For example, simpler tools are likely to be older than more complex tools.

2) Using stratigraphy — the study of rock layers. Older rock layers are normally found below younger layers, so tools or fossils in deeper layers are usually older.

3) Stone tools are sometimes found with carbon-containing material, for instance a wooden handle. Carbon-14 dating can be used to date this material.

Don't get bogged down by all this information...

It's a bit mind-boggling really how fossils can still exist even millions of years after the organism died. They really are fascinating things, and scientists have learned a whole lot from studying them in detail.

Section 4 — Natural Selection and Genetic Modification

Classification

*It seems to be a basic human urge to want to **classify** things — that's the case in biology anyway...*

Classification is Organising Living Organisms into Groups

1) Traditionally, organisms were classified according to similarities and differences in their observable characteristics, i.e. things you can see (like how many legs something has). As technology improved, this included things you can see with a microscope, e.g. cell structure.
2) These characteristics were used to classify organisms in the five kingdom classification system. In this system, living things are first divided into five groups called kingdoms. These are:

- Animals — fish, mammals, reptiles, etc.
- Plants — grasses, trees, etc.
- Fungi — mushrooms and toadstools, yeasts, mould.
- Prokaryotes — all single-celled organisms without a nucleus.
- Protists — eukaryotic single-celled organisms, e.g. algae.

There's more on prokaryotes and eukaryotes on p.17.

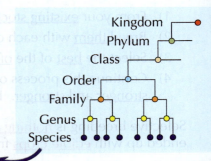

3) The kingdoms are then subdivided into smaller and smaller groups that have common features — phylum, class, order, family, genus, species.

Classification Systems Change Over Time

1) The five kingdom classification system is still used, but it's now a bit out of date.
2) Over time, technology has developed further and our understanding of things like biochemical processes and genetics has increased. For example, we are now able to determine the sequence of DNA bases in different organisms' genes and compare them — the more similar the sequence of a gene, the more closely related the organisms.
3) This led to a bit of a rethink about the way organisms are classified and to the proposal of the three domain system of classification by a scientist called Carl Woese.
4) Using genetic analysis, Woese found that some members of the Prokaryote kingdom were not as closely related as first thought. He proposed that this kingdom should be split into two groups called Archaea and Bacteria.
5) In fact, Woese suggested that all organisms should first be divided into three large groups called domains. Archaea and Bacteria are two of these domains, and the third domain is Eukarya.

There's more on DNA on page 50.

> ARCHAEA — Organisms in this domain look similar to bacteria but are actually quite different — as differences in their genetic sequences show. They were first found in extreme places such as hot springs and salt lakes.
>
> BACTERIA — This domain contains true bacteria like *E. coli* and *Staphylococcus*.
>
> EUKARYA — This domain includes a broad range of organisms including fungi, plants, animals and protists.

6) The three domains are then subdivided into smaller groups used in the five kingdom system (beginning with kingdom and finishing with species).

Section 4 — Natural Selection and Genetic Modification

Selective Breeding

'Selective breeding' is breeding together the **best** plants or animals to get the best possible **offspring**. That's it.

Selective Breeding is Very Simple

Selective breeding is when humans artificially select the plants or animals that are going to breed so that the genes for particular characteristics remain in the population. Organisms are selectively bred to develop features that are useful or attractive. For example:

- Animals that produce more meat or milk.
- Crops with disease resistance.
- Dogs with a good, gentle temperament.
- Plants that produce bigger fruit.

This is the basic process involved in selective breeding:

1) From your existing stock, select the ones which have the characteristics you're after.
2) Breed them with each other.
3) Select the best of the offspring, and breed them together.
4) Continue this process over several generations, and the desirable trait gets stronger and stronger. Eventually, all the offspring will have the characteristic.

Selective breeding is also known as 'artificial selection'.

Selective breeding is nothing new — people have been doing it for thousands of years. It's how we ended up with edible crops from wild plants and how we got domesticated animals like cows and dogs.

Selective Breeding is Useful...

Selective breeding is important in agriculture and medical research. For example:

In agriculture

Genetic variation means some cattle will have better characteristics for producing meat than others (e.g. a larger size). To improve meat yields, a farmer could select cows and bulls with these characteristics and breed them together. After doing this, and selecting the best of the offspring for several generations, the farmer would get cows with a very high meat yield.

In medical research

In several studies investigating the reasons behind alcoholism, rats have been bred with either a strong preference for alcohol or a weak preference for alcohol.
This has allowed researchers to compare the differences between the two different types of rats, including differences in their behaviour and in the way that their brains work.

...but Also Has Disadvantages

1) The main problem with selective breeding is that it reduces the gene pool — the number of different alleles (forms of a gene) in a population. This is because the "best" animals or plants are always used for breeding — and they are all closely related. This is known as inbreeding.
2) Inbreeding can cause health problems because there's more chance of the organisms inheriting harmful genetic defects when the gene pool is limited. Some dog breeds are susceptible to certain defects because of inbreeding, e.g. heart disease in boxer dogs. This leads to ethical considerations — particularly if animals are deliberately bred to have negative characteristics for medical research.
3) There can also be serious problems if a new disease appears. There's not much variation in the population, so there's less chance of resistance alleles being present. All the stock are closely related to each other, so if one is going to be killed by a new disease, the others are also likely to succumb to it.

Selective breeding — breeding from specific individuals

Different breeds of dog came from selective breeding. For example, somebody thought 'I like this small, yappy wolf — I'll breed it with this other one'. After thousands of generations, we got poodles.

Q1 Explain how you could selectively breed for floppy ears in rabbits. [4 marks]

Section 4 — Natural Selection and Genetic Modification

Genetic Engineering

Genetic engineering is a relatively new area of science (well, it began in the 1970s). We've already put the technology to **good use** and it has many more **exciting possibilities** too...

Genetic Engineering is Useful in Agriculture and Medicine

Genetic engineering involves modifying an organism's genome (its DNA) to introduce desirable characteristics. For example:

In agriculture, crops can be genetically modified to be resistant to herbicides (chemicals that kill plants). Making crops herbicide-resistant means farmers can spray their crops to kill weeds, without affecting the crop itself. This can also increase crop yield.

In medicine, bacteria can be genetically engineered to produce human insulin, (see next page).

Researchers have managed to transfer human genes that produce useful proteins into sheep and cows. E.g. human antibodies used in therapy for illnesses like arthritis, some types of cancer and multiple sclerosis. These proteins can then be extracted from the animal, e.g. from their milk.

It's possible that animals with organs suitable for organ transplantation into humans might also be produced in the future.

Genetic Engineering Comes With Risks

1) Genetic engineering has risks as well as benefits.

2) There are concerns about growing genetically modified crops. One is that transplanted genes may get out into the environment. E.g. a herbicide resistance gene may be picked up by weeds, creating a new 'superweed' variety. Another concern is that genetically modified crops could adversely affect food chains — or even human health.

3) There are also concerns about the genetic engineering of animals. It can be hard to predict what effect modifying its genome will have on the organism — many genetically modified embryos don't survive and some genetically modified animals suffer from health problems later in life.

Genetic engineering has huge potential benefits...

Scientists have used genetic engineering to produce organisms that benefit humans in all sorts of ways — from bacteria that can make medicines for us, to food crops that contain extra vitamins. But, as with any new technology, we need to be aware of the risks that it carries too.

Section 4 — Natural Selection and Genetic Modification

Genetic Engineering

*The process of **transferring** a **new gene** into another **organism's** genome requires **enzymes** and **vectors**.*

Enzymes Can Cut Up DNA or Join DNA Pieces Together

1) Restriction enzymes recognise specific sequences of DNA and cut the DNA at these points — the pieces of DNA are left with sticky ends where they have been cut.
2) Ligase enzymes are used to join two pieces of DNA together at their sticky ends.
3) Two different bits of DNA stuck together are known as recombinant DNA.

Vectors Can Be Used To Insert DNA Into Other Organisms

A vector is something that's used to transfer DNA into a cell. There are two sorts — plasmids and viruses:

1) Plasmids are small, circular molecules of DNA that can be transferred between bacteria.
2) Viruses insert DNA into the organisms they infect.

Here's how genetic engineering works:

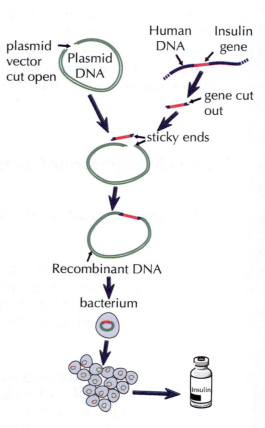

1) The DNA you want to insert (e.g. the gene for human insulin) is cut out with a restriction enzyme. The vector DNA is then cut open using the same restriction enzyme.

2) The vector DNA and the DNA you're inserting are left with sticky ends. They are mixed together with ligase enzymes.

3) The ligases join the pieces of DNA together to make recombinant DNA.

4) The recombinant DNA (i.e. the vector containing new DNA) is inserted into other cells, e.g. bacteria.

5) These cells can now use the gene you inserted to make the protein you want. E.g. bacteria containing the gene for human insulin can be grown in huge numbers in a fermenter to produce insulin for people with diabetes.

It looks hard, but it's a fancy cut and paste...

Make sure you've got everything on this page firmly in your noggin. You need to understand the lot.

Q1   Rennin is an enzyme used to make cheese. It is naturally produced by stomach cells in cows, which contain the rennin gene. Suggest how a bacterial cell could be genetically engineered to produce rennin.   [4 marks]

Section 4 — Natural Selection and Genetic Modification

Warm-Up and Exam Questions

There's only one way to do well in the exam — learn the facts and practise, practise, practise. We couldn't have made it much easier for you — so have a go.

Warm-Up Questions

1) Why is a beneficial characteristic likely to become more common in a population over time?
2) What is a fossil?
3) Give one example of how advances in technology allowed scientists to distinguish between Archaea and Bacteria.
4) Name two types of enzyme needed for the process of genetic engineering.

Exam Questions

1   Most populations of organisms show a lot of variation due to differences in their alleles.

   (a) State how new alleles arise in a population.

   [1 mark]

   A selection pressure is a change in an environment which can affect the chance of an organism surviving and reproducing.

   (b) (i) Give **two** examples of a selection pressure in an environment.

   [2 marks]

   (ii) Explain why some organisms may not be able to survive if a new selection pressure is introduced to the environment.

   [2 marks]

2   The characteristics of two varieties of wheat plants are shown in **Figure 1**.

Variety	Grain yield	Resistance to bad weather
Tall stems	High	Low
Dwarf stems	Low	High

   Figure 1

   (a) Describe how selective breeding could be used to create a wheat plant with a high grain yield and high resistance to bad weather.

   [3 marks]

   (b) Explain why selectively breeding the wheat plants could cause problems if the selectively bred wheat plants are exposed to a new wheat disease.

   [3 marks]

Section 4 — Natural Selection and Genetic Modification

Exam Questions

3 Scientists can carry out genetic analysis of DNA to determine the evolutionary relationships between organisms.

Figure 2 shows the percentage similarities between the DNA sequences of humans and four other organisms.

Organism	A	B	C	D
% DNA sequence similarity to humans	18	44	92	54

Figure 2

(a) Suggest which of the organisms, A-D, is most closely related to humans. Explain your answer.

[2 marks]

(b) Genetic analysis led the scientist Carl Woese to propose the three domain classification system. Name the three domains in this system.

[3 marks]

4 *Clostridium difficile* is a bacterium that causes diarrhoea when it infects the bowel.

Infections by *Clostridium difficile* are becoming increasingly difficult to treat as some strains of the bacterium have developed resistance to a number of antibiotics.

Explain how a population of *Clostridium difficile* bacteria could have developed resistance to an antibiotic.

[4 marks]

5* Figure 3 shows a type of stingray. The stingray's appearance mimics a flat rock. It spends most of its time on a rocky sea bed.

Figure 3

Explain how the stingray might have evolved to look like this.

[6 marks]

Section 4 — Natural Selection and Genetic Modification

Section 5 — Health, Disease and the Development of Medicines

Health and Disease

*Try as we might, it's unlikely that we'll be in tip-top condition for all of our lives — **disease** tends to get us all at some point. There are lots of **different types** of diseases we could get...*

You Need to Know How 'Health' is Defined

1) It might surprise you to know that being healthy is about more than just not being sick.
2) The World Health Organisation (the WHO) defines health as "a state of complete physical, mental and social well-being, and not merely the absence of disease or infirmity".
3) This means that even if someone is very physically fit, they still might be unhealthy if, e.g. they have mental health issues or are socially isolated.

Infirmity means weakness or frailness, commonly due to old age.

Diseases Can be Communicable or Non-Communicable

1) A disease is a condition where part of an organism doesn't function properly. There are two sorts of disease — communicable and non-communicable.
2) Communicable diseases are diseases that can be spread between individuals.
3) Non-communicable diseases can't be transmitted between individuals. They include things like cancer and heart disease. There's more on these on pages 80-81.
4) If you are affected by one disease, it could make you more susceptible to others — your body may become weakened by the disease, so it's less able to fight off others.

Being susceptible to a disease, means that you have an increased chance of getting it.

Communicable Diseases are Caused by Pathogens

Pathogens are organisms such as viruses, bacteria, fungi and protists (see p.65) that cause communicable diseases. Here are some examples of communicable diseases that you need to know about for your exam:

Chalara Ash Dieback is a Fungal Disease

1) Chalara ash dieback is caused by a fungus that infects ash trees.
2) Symptoms include leaf loss and bark lesions (wounds).
3) The fungus is carried through the air by the wind. (It also spreads when diseased ash trees are moved between areas.)
4) Transmission can be reduced by removing young, infected ash trees and replanting with different species or by restricting the import or movement of ash trees.

Health and Disease

Malaria is a Disease Caused by a Protist

1) The pathogen that causes malaria is a protist.
2) The effects of malaria include damage to red blood cells and, in severe cases, to the liver.
3) Mosquitoes act as animal vectors (carriers) — they pass on the protist to humans but don't get the disease themselves.
4) Mosquito nets and insect repellent can be used to prevent mosquitoes carrying the pathogen from biting people.

Cholera is a Bacterial Disease

1) Cholera is a disease caused by a bacterium called *Vibrio cholerae*.
2) It causes diarrhoea.
3) Cholera spreads via contaminated water sources.
4) Transmission can be reduced by making sure that people have access to clean water supplies.

Tuberculosis is a Bacterial Disease

1) Tuberculosis is caused by a bacterium called *Mycobacterium tuberculosis*.
2) It causes coughing and lung damage.
3) The bacteria are spread through the air when infected individuals cough.
4) Infected people should avoid crowded public spaces, practise good hygiene and sleep alone. Their homes should also be well-ventilated.

Communicable diseases spread from one individual to another

In the exam, you could be asked how to prevent the transmission of a disease. Remember, preventing the spread of a disease is linked to how it spreads. For example, if a disease is transmitted through contaminated water sources, then its spread can be prevented by making sure that individuals have access to clean water supplies.

Sexually Transmitted Infections

*Some communicable diseases are transmitted **sexually**.*

STIs are Sexually Transmitted Infections

STIs are infections that are spread through sexual contact, including sexual intercourse. Here are two STIs that you need to know about:

Some STIs, including Chlamydia, are spread by genital contact, not just sexual intercourse.

Chlamydia

1) *Chlamydia* is a kind of bacterium, but it behaves in a similar way to a virus because it can only reproduce inside host cells.

2) Although it doesn't always cause symptoms, it can result in infertility.

3) The spread of *Chlamydia* can be reduced by wearing a condom when having sex, screening individuals so they can be treated for the infection or avoiding sexual contact.

HIV

1) HIV is the Human Immunodeficiency Virus — it kills white blood cells, which are really important in the immune response.

2) HIV infection eventually leads to AIDS (Acquired Immune Deficiency Syndrome).

3) This is when the infected person's immune system deteriorates and eventually fails — because of this, the person becomes very vulnerable to opportunistic infections by other pathogens.

4) HIV is spread via infected bodily fluids (e.g. blood, semen, vaginal fluids). One of the main ways to prevent its spread is to use a condom when having sex. Drug users should also avoid sharing needles. Medication can reduce the risk of an infected individual passing the virus on to others during sex (or of a mother passing the virus to her baby during pregnancy) so screening and proper treatment are also important.

Watch yourself, there are a lot of nasties out there...

Try drawing out a table with columns for 'disease', 'pathogen', 'symptom / effects', 'how it's spread' and 'how to reduce/prevent transmission', then fill it in for all the diseases on the previous three pages. See how much you can write down without looking back at the pages.

Section 5 — Health, Disease and the Development of Medicines

Warm-Up and Exam Questions

Have a go at these questions to test what you've picked up about diseases — their symptoms, how they are transmitted and how their spread can be limited. You can go back over anything you struggle with.

Warm-Up Questions

1) How does the World Health Organisation (WHO) define the term 'health'?
2) What does it mean if a disease is 'communicable'?
3) Name two diseases caused by bacteria.
4) How is HIV spread through sexual contact?
5) Give one way to reduce the spread of *Chlamydia*.

Exam Questions

1   Chalara ash dieback is caused by a pathogen that infects ash trees. *(Grade 4-6)*

(a) Give the definition of the term 'pathogen'.

[1 mark]

(b) What type of pathogen causes Chalara ash dieback?

☐ **A** A bacterium

☐ **B** A virus

☐ **C** A protist

☐ **D** A fungus

[1 mark]

(c) Outline **one** way that Chalara ash dieback spreads.

[1 mark]

2   The methods used to prevent the spread of a disease depend on how the disease is transmitted. *(Grade 6-7)*

(a) Explain why hand washing may not be helpful in limiting the spread of malaria.

[2 marks]

(b) Suggest and explain **one** reason why efforts to limit the spread of malaria often focus on the mosquito.

[1 mark]

Typhoid fever is a bacterial disease that infects humans. Typhoid fever is spread by eating or drinking food or water contaminated with the faeces of an infected person.

(c) Suggest **one** way that the spread of typhoid fever could be reduced.

[1 mark]

Section 5 — Health, Disease and the Development of Medicines

Fighting Disease

The human body has some pretty neat features when it comes to **fighting disease**.

Physical and Chemical Barriers Stop Pathogens Entering the Body

The human body has physical and chemical defences against pathogen entry.

Physical barriers

1) The skin acts as a barrier to pathogens, and, if it gets damaged, blood clots quickly seal cuts and keep microorganisms out.
2) Hairs and mucus in your nose trap particles that could contain pathogens.
3) Cells in your trachea and bronchi (airways in the lungs) also produce mucus, which traps pathogens. Other cells that line the trachea and bronchi have cilia. These are hair-like structures which waft the mucus up to the back of the throat where it can be swallowed.

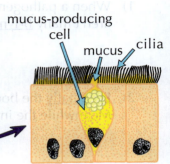

Chemical barriers

1) The stomach produces hydrochloric acid. This kills most pathogens that are swallowed.
2) The eyes produce a chemical called lysozyme (in tears) which kills bacteria on the surface of the eye.

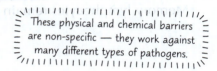

These physical and chemical barriers are non-specific — they work against many different types of pathogens.

Your Immune System Can Attack Pathogens

1) If pathogens do make it into your body, your immune system kicks in to destroy them.
2) The most important part of your immune system is the white blood cells. They travel around in your blood and crawl into every part of you, patrolling for pathogens.
3) B-lymphocytes are a type of white blood cell that are involved in the specific immune response — this is the immune response to a specific pathogen. Here's how it works:

   1) Every pathogen has unique molecules (e.g. proteins) on its surface called antigens.
   2) When your B-lymphocytes come across an antigen on a pathogen, they start to produce proteins called antibodies. Antibodies bind (lock on) to the new invading pathogen, so it can be found and destroyed by other white blood cells. The antibodies produced are specific to that pathogen — they won't lock on to any other pathogens.
   3) The antibodies are then produced rapidly and flow all round the body to find all similar pathogens.

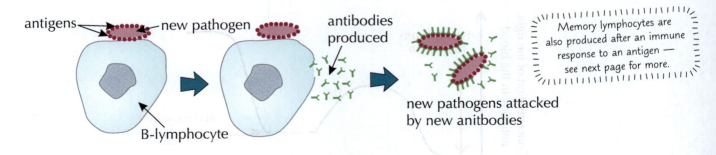

Memory lymphocytes are also produced after an immune response to an antigen — see next page for more.

Antigens on the surfaces of pathogens trigger an immune response

If you have a low level of white blood cells, you'll be more susceptible to infections. HIV attacks white blood cells and weakens the immune system, making it easier for other pathogens to invade.

Memory Lymphocytes

*Our **immune system** contains **special cells** which can **remember** what **pathogens** have invaded our bodies in the past. This means our bodies can **respond faster** if they invade **again**.*

Memory Lymphocytes Give Immunity To Later Infection

1) When a pathogen enters the body for the <u>first time</u> the response is <u>slow</u> because there aren't many <u>B-lymphocytes</u> that can make the <u>antibody</u> needed to <u>lock on to the antigen</u>.

2) <u>Eventually</u> the body will produce <u>enough</u> of the right antibody to <u>overcome</u> the infection. Meanwhile the infected person will show <u>symptoms</u> of the disease.

3) As well as antibodies, <u>memory lymphocytes</u> are also produced in response to a foreign antigen. Memory lymphocytes remain in the body for a <u>long time</u>, and '<u>remember</u>' a <u>specific</u> antigen.

4) The person is now <u>immune</u> — their immune system has the ability to <u>respond quickly</u> to a <u>second</u> infection.

5) If the <u>same pathogen</u> enters the body again, there are more cells that will recognise it and produce antibodies against it. This <u>secondary immune response</u> is <u>faster</u> and <u>stronger</u>.

6) The <u>secondary response</u> often <u>gets rid</u> of the pathogen <u>before</u> you begin to show any symptoms.

7) This can all be shown in a <u>graph</u> like the one here:

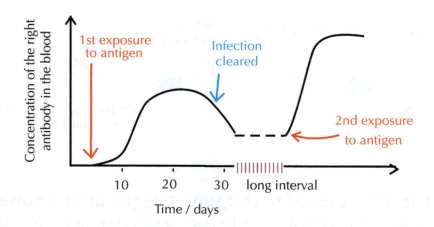

Immunisation

*Immunisation has changed the way we fight disease. We don't always have to deal with the problem once it's happened — we can **prevent** it happening in the first place.*

Immunisation Can Stop You Getting Infections

1) To make it less likely that you'll get ill, you can be immunised against some diseases, e.g. measles.

2) Immunisation usually involves injecting dead or inactive pathogens into the body. These are antigenic (they carry antigens), so even though they're harmless your body makes antibodies to help destroy them.

3) The antigens also trigger the production of memory lymphocytes.

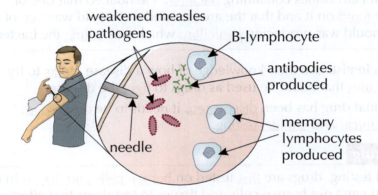

4) So, if live pathogens of the same type get into the body, there will already be memory lymphocytes that can cause a fast secondary immune response. This means that you're less likely to get the disease.

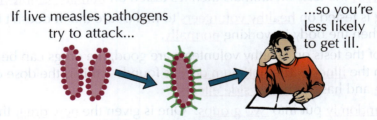

Memory lymphocytes 'remember' a specific antigen

Immunisation has helped to save millions of lives — it's all because of antibodies and memory cells.

Q1 Basia is immunised against flu and Cassian isn't. They are both exposed to a flu virus. Cassian falls ill whereas Basia doesn't. Explain why. [2 marks]

Section 5 — Health, Disease and the Development of Medicines

Antibiotics and Other Medicines

*New medicines are constantly being **developed**. This page tells you all about how that happens.*

Antibiotics Are Used to Treat Bacterial Infections

1) Antibiotics work by inhibiting processes in bacterial cells, but not in the host organism. For example, some antibiotics inhibit the building of bacterial cell walls — this prevents the bacteria from dividing, and eventually kills them, but has no effect on cells in the human host (which don't have cell walls).
2) Different antibiotics kill different types of bacteria, so it's important to be treated with the right one.
3) But antibiotics don't destroy viruses (e.g. flu or cold viruses). Viruses reproduce using your body cells, which makes it very difficult to develop drugs that destroy just the virus without killing the body's cells.

There Are Several Stages in the Development of New Drugs

1) First a drug has to be discovered. This can happen in lots of different ways — for example:

> Penicillin is an antibiotic. It was discovered by Alexander Fleming when he was clearing out Petri dishes containing bacteria. He noticed that one of the dishes had mould on it and that the area around the mould was free of bacteria. The mould was producing penicillin, which was killing the bacteria.

2) Nowadays, most scientists use their knowledge of how a disease works to try and identify molecules that could be used as drugs to fight the disease.
3) Once a new potential drug has been discovered, it needs to be developed. This involves preclinical and clinical testing.

Preclinical testing

1) In preclinical testing, drugs are first tested on human cells and tissues in the lab. However, you can't use human cells and tissues to test drugs that affect whole or multiple body systems, e.g. a drug for blood pressure must be tested on a whole animal.
2) The next step is to test the drug on live animals. This is to test that the drug works (produces the effect you're looking for), to find out how toxic (harmful) it is and to find the best dosage.

Clinical testing

1) If the drug passes the tests on animals then it's tested on human volunteers in a clinical trial.
2) First, the drug is tested on healthy volunteers to make sure that it doesn't have any harmful side effects when the body is working normally.
3) If the results of the tests on healthy volunteers are good, the drugs can be tested on people suffering from the illness. The optimum dose is found — this is the dose of drug that is the most effective and has the fewest side effects.
4) Patients are randomly put into two groups. One is given the new drug, the other is given a placebo (a substance that looks like the drug being tested but doesn't do anything, e.g. a sugar pill). This is to allow for the placebo effect (when the patient expects the treatment to work and so feels better, even though the treatment isn't doing anything).
5) Clinical trials are blind — the patient in the study doesn't know whether they're getting the drug or the placebo. In fact, they're often double-blind — neither the patient nor the doctor knows until all the results have been gathered. This is so the doctors monitoring the patients and analysing the results aren't subconsciously influenced by their knowledge.

4) When a drug has finally passed all of these tests, it still needs to be approved by a medical agency before it can be used to treat patients. All of this means that drugs are as effective and safe as possible.

Section 5 — Health, Disease and the Development of Medicines

Warm-Up and Exam Questions

It's that time again — time to test just how much of the previous pages you really remember...

Warm-Up Questions

1) How is the skin adapted to defend against the entry of pathogens?
2) What is the role of the specific immune system?
3) What type of white blood cell produces antibodies?
4) True or false? Antibiotics kill viruses.
5) What is a placebo?

Exam Questions

1   There are many different lines of defence in the human body that help to prevent pathogens from entering the blood. *Grade 4-6*

   (a) Give the role of mucus in the nose.
   [1 mark]

   (b) Describe how the cilia in the trachea and bronchi help to defend the body.
   [1 mark]

   (c) Name the substance produced by the stomach to kill pathogens.
   [1 mark]

   (d) Name the chemical produced to kill bacteria on the surface of the eyes.
   [1 mark]

2   A scientist is carrying out a clinical trial. *Grade 6-7*

   (a) What is a drug tested on in a clinical trial?

   ☐ A   human cells
   ☐ B   human volunteers
   ☐ C   live animals
   ☐ D   human tissue
   [1 mark]

   (b) The clinical trial is double blind. Explain what this means.
   [2 marks]

   When testing the drug on living organisms, the scientist has to find out how toxic the drug is by seeing whether it causes any harm.

   (c) Apart from the toxicity of the drug, suggest **two** other factors that scientists research during drug testing.
   [2 marks]

Section 5 — Health, Disease and the Development of Medicines

Non-Communicable Diseases

*Non-communicable diseases **aren't caused by pathogens**. Instead, there are **risk factors** associated with them.*

Lifestyle Factors May Increase the Risk of Disease

1) Risk factors are things that are linked to an increase in the likelihood that a person will develop a certain disease during their lifetime. They don't guarantee that someone will get the disease.

2) Risk factors can be unavoidable, e.g. a person's age or gender may make them more likely to get a disease. But some are lifestyle factors that people can change. For example:

> Smoking is a major risk factor associated with cardiovascular disease — any disease associated with the heart or blood vessels, e.g. a heart attack or stroke (see p.83). This is because:
> - Nicotine in cigarette smoke increases heart rate, which increases blood pressure.
> - High blood pressure damages artery walls, which contributes to the build up of fatty deposits in the arteries. These deposits restrict blood flow and increase the risk of a heart attack or stroke.
> - Smoking increases the risk of blood clots forming in arteries, which can restrict or block blood flow, leading to a heart attack or stroke.

3) Other lifestyle factors are associated with different diseases. E.g.

> A diet with too many or too few nutrients can lead to malnutrition (and diseases associated with malnutrition, e.g. scurvy — a vitamin C deficiency disease.)

Malnutrition doesn't just mean not getting enough nutrients. Getting too many nutrients is also a form of malnutrition, and it can lead to obesity.

> Not getting enough exercise and having a diet high in fat and sugar are risk factors for obesity.

> Drinking too much alcohol is a major risk factor for the development of liver disease, e.g. cirrhosis (scarring of the liver). This is because alcohol is broken down by enzymes in the liver and some of the products are toxic. Drinking too much over a long period of time can cause permanent liver damage.

Non-communicable diseases don't spread between people

In the exam, you might need to read data related to disease risk factors from a table, graph or chart, or explain what the data is showing. Remember to always check any units or graph scales carefully before answering any questions.

Section 5 — Health, Disease and the Development of Medicines

Non-Communicable Diseases

You need to know about the **effect** *of* ***lifestyle factors*** *on non-communicable diseases at different* ***levels****.*

Non-Communicable Diseases Have Many Risk Factors

1) As well as smoking, there are lots of other risk factors associated with cardiovascular disease, including: drinking too much alcohol, lack of exercise, and a diet high in saturated fat.

2) In fact, many non-communicable diseases are caused by several different risk factors interacting with each other, rather than one factor alone, including cancer, liver and lung diseases and obesity. Obesity is also a risk factor for other non-communicable diseases, e.g. type 2 diabetes (see p.107) and cardiovascular disease.

Non-Communicable Diseases Can Have Wide-Ranging Effects

1) Non-communicable diseases can have knock-on effects for local areas. For example, in areas where there are high levels of obesity, smoking or excess alcohol consumption, there's likely to be a high occurrence of certain non-communicable diseases, e.g. cardiovascular or liver disease. This can put pressure on the resources (money, beds, staff, etc.) of local hospitals.

2) Non-communicable diseases are also costly at a national level because the National Health Service provides the resources for the treatment of patients all over the UK. And sometimes, people suffering from a non-communicable disease may not be able to work. A reduction in the number of people able to work can affect a country's economy.

3) As well as being costly, non-communicable diseases are very common, e.g. cardiovascular disease is the number one cause of death worldwide. In developing countries, malnutrition is also a big problem because people are not able to access enough food. The high cost and occurrence of these diseases can hold back the development of a country — so they have an effect at a global level.

It's hard to avoid all risk factors of disease...
...but risk factors don't mean you'll definitely get the disease — they just increase the chance of getting it.

Measures of Obesity

You can't just say that anyone **over a particular weight** is **obese** — you have to use **indices** and **ratios**.

A **Body Mass Index** Indicates If You're **Under-** or **Overweight**

1) The Body Mass Index (BMI) is used as a guide to help decide whether someone is underweight, of healthy weight, overweight or obese. It's calculated from their height and mass. This is the formula:

$$BMI = \frac{mass\ (kg)}{(height\ (m))^2}$$

2) Once you have a value for a person's BMI, you can refer to a table that shows how the different values are classified. The thresholds used depend on the person's ethnicity.

	Underweight	Healthy Weight	Overweight	Obese
People of white heritage	BMI of below 18.5	BMI of 18.5 - 24.9	BMI of 25 - 29.9	BMI of 30 or over
People in black, Asian or certain other minority ethnic groups	BMI of below 18.5	BMI of 18.5 - 22.9	BMI of 23 - 27.4	BMI of 27.5 or over

People in black, Asian or certain other minority ethnic groups are at a higher risk of obesity-related health problems at a lower BMI.

EXAMPLE Calculate the BMI of a person of white heritage who has a mass of 63.0 kg and is 1.70 m tall. Is this person overweight?

$$BMI = \frac{mass\ (kg)}{(height\ (m))^2} = 63.0\ kg \div 1.70\ m^2 = 21.8\ kg\ m^{-2}$$

This person is not overweight — their BMI lies between 18.5 and 24.9 (the healthy weight range).

3) If you eat a high fat, high sugar diet and you don't do enough exercise, you're likely to take in more energy than you use. The excess energy is stored as fat, so you're more likely to have a high BMI and be obese.

4) BMI isn't always a reliable measure of obesity. For example, athletes have lots of muscle, which has a higher mass than fat, so they can come out with a high BMI even though they're not overweight.

A **Waist-to-Hip Ratio** Can Also Be Used

1) By measuring the circumference of a person's waist and hips, you can use the following formula to figure out their waist-to-hip ratio.

$$waist\text{-}to\text{-}hip\ ratio = \frac{waist\ circumference}{hip\ circumference}$$ (e.g. in cm)

The circumference of a person's waist or hips is the distance the whole way around their body at that point.

2) The higher your waist-to-hip ratio, the more weight you're likely to be carrying around your middle.

3) A ratio above 1.0 for males and above 0.85 for females indicates you're carrying too much weight around your middle — this is known as abdominal obesity. It puts you at a greater risk of developing obesity-related health problems, such as type 2 diabetes (see p.107).

EXAMPLE A woman has a waist measurement of 29 cm and a hip measurement of 36 cm. Find her waist-to-hip ratio.

$$waist\text{-}to\text{-}hip\ ratio = \frac{waist\ circumference\ (cm)}{hip\ circumference\ (cm)} = 29 \div 36 = 0.81$$

These measures of obesity aren't perfect...

However, they do provide a good guide for helping people know when it's time to lose weight.

Q1 A person of Asian ethnicity has a mass of 76.0 kg and has a height of 1.62 m.
   a) Calculate the person's BMI. [1 mark]
   b) Use the table above to find the weight description of the person. [1 mark]

Q1 Video Solution

Treatments for Cardiovascular Disease

Cardiovascular disease is a **big, big problem** in the UK. The good news is there are lots of ways to **treat** it.

Cardiovascular Disease Affects Your Heart and Blood Vessels

Cardiovascular disease (CVD) is any disease associated with your heart and blood vessels.

1) Arteries are blood vessels that carry blood away from the heart.

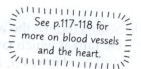
See p.117-118 for more on blood vessels and the heart.

2) Cholesterol is a fatty substance that the body needs to make things like cell membranes. But too much cholesterol in the blood can cause fatty deposits to build up in arteries, restricting blood flow.

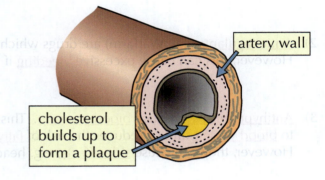
artery wall
cholesterol builds up to form a plaque

3) Deposits occur in areas where the artery wall has been damaged, e.g. by high blood pressure.

4) The fatty deposits can also trigger blood clots to form, which can block blood flow completely. If this happens in an artery supplying the heart muscle, the heart muscle will be deprived of oxygen. This causes a heart attack. A blockage in the brain deprives the brain of oxygen and can cause a stroke.

Lifestyle Changes Can be Used to Treat CVD

1) Making changes to your lifestyle can reduce your risk of developing CVD. If you already have CVD, these changes can form part of the treatment, helping to reduce the risk of a further heart attack or stroke.

2) People with (or at risk of) CVD may be encouraged to eat a healthy, balanced diet, which is low in saturated fat (as saturated fat can increase blood cholesterol level). They may also be encouraged to exercise regularly, lose weight if necessary and stop smoking.

3) Lifestyle changes are often recommended first because they don't really have any downsides.

Cardiovascular disease is associated with blood flow

Other factors, such as age, gender and family history can also increase the risk of developing CVD. These factors can't be changed, but it is possible to control and modify lifestyle-related risk factors.

Section 5 — Health, Disease and the Development of Medicines

Treatments for Cardiovascular Disease

Lifestyle changes can help stop CVD from getting worse, but sometimes drugs or surgery are needed too...

Some Drugs Can Reduce the Risk of a Heart Attack or Stroke

Lifestyle changes aren't always enough to treat CVD. Sometimes medicines are needed too. Some people may need to take these medicines for the rest of their lives.

1) Statins reduce the amount of cholesterol in the bloodstream. This slows down the rate at which fatty deposits form — reducing the risk of heart attacks and strokes. However, they can sometimes cause negative side effects, e.g. aching muscles. Some of these side effects can be serious, e.g. liver damage.

2) Anticoagulants (e.g. Warfarin) are drugs which make blood clots less likely to form. However, this can cause excessive bleeding if the person is hurt in an accident.

3) Antihypertensives reduce blood pressure. This helps to prevent damage to blood vessels and so reduces the risk of fatty deposits forming. However, they can cause side effects, e.g. headaches and fainting.

Surgical Procedures are Sometimes Necessary to Repair Damage

1) Stents are tubes that are inserted inside arteries. They keep them open, making sure blood can pass through to the heart muscles, lowering the risk of a heart attack. But over time, the artery can narrow again as stents can irritate the artery and make scar tissue grow. The patient also has to take drugs to stop blood clotting on the stent.

2) If part of a blood vessel is blocked, a piece of healthy vessel taken from elsewhere can be used to bypass the blocked section. This is known as coronary bypass surgery.

3) The whole heart can be replaced with a donor heart. However, the new heart does not always start pumping properly and drugs have to be taken to stop the body rejecting it. These drugs can have side effects, e.g. making you more vulnerable to infections.

Any heart surgery is a major procedure and there is risk of bleeding, clots and infection.

Don't lose heart...
You could be asked to evaluate treatments for cardiovascular disease. Don't panic — just use any information you're given and your own knowledge to weigh up the advantages and disadvantages. Make sure your answer doesn't just focus on one side — e.g. don't just talk about the advantages and ignore the disadvantages — and don't forget to include a justified conclusion.

Section 5 — Health, Disease and the Development of Medicines

Warm-Up and Exam Questions

It's time for some more questions — don't just assume that you've remembered everything you read on the past few pages. Give these a go, and then go back over anything that you struggled with.

Warm-Up Questions

1) Give one way that smoking can increase a person's risk of developing CVD.
2) How might excessive alcohol consumption contribute towards liver disease?
3) Give an example of a national cost associated with non-communicable diseases in the UK.
4) Give one disadvantage of the body mass index (BMI) as a measure of obesity.
5) Give one advantage of making lifestyle changes as treatment for CVD.

Exam Questions

1   Many non-communicable diseases are associated with certain lifestyle factors.

   (a) Give **one** lifestyle factor associated with liver disease.

   [1 mark]

   (b) Give **one** example of a cost to the local area associated with liver disease.

   [1 mark]

2   Person A has a waist circumference of 31 cm and a hip circumference of 33 cm.

   (a) Calculate the waist-to-hip ratio of person A. Give your answer to two significant figures.

   [1 mark]

   (b) Waist-to-hip ratio can be used to determine whether someone has abdominal obesity.
        State the other piece of information that is needed to determine whether Person A has abdominal obesity.

   [1 mark]

   (c) Body Mass Index (BMI) can also be used to determine whether a person is obese.
        State the two pieces of information that are required in order to calculate a person's BMI.

   [1 mark]

3   Cardiovascular disease is non-communicable.

   (a) Describe what is meant by the term 'non-communicable disease'.

   [1 mark]

   (b) Explain how smoking increases a person's risk of cardiovascular disease.

   [4 marks]

Section 5 — Health, Disease and the Development of Medicines

Revision Summary for Sections 2-5

Well, that's Sections 2-5 finished. Time to test what you've learned...
- Try these questions and tick off each one when you get it right.
- When you're completely happy with a section, tick it off.

For even more practice, try the Retrieval Quizzes for Sections 2-5 — just scan the QR codes!

Section 2 — Cells and Control (p.37-47) ☐
1) What is the cell cycle?
2) Name the four stages of mitosis. Describe what happens in each one.
3) What major illness can result from uncontrolled cell division?
4) How are embryonic stem cells different to adult stem cells?
5) Give three potential risks associated with using stem cells in medicine.
6) Draw and label a motor neurone.
7) Describe the role of neurotransmitters in the transmission of nervous impulses.
8) What is a reflex arc?

Section 3 — Genetics (p.48-60) ☐
9) Name the gametes in humans.
10) What happens to the DNA in a cell before the first division in meiosis?
11) What is meant by the term 'double helix'?
12) What is monohybrid inheritance?
13) A couple have a child. What's the probability that the child will have the XX combination of sex chromosomes?
14) What causes genetic variation in a species?
15) Write down three applications of the knowledge gained from the Human Genome Project.

Section 4 — Natural Selection and Genetic Modification (p.61-70) ☐
16) Describe how organisms evolve by the process of natural selection.
17) What are hominids?
18) What is stratigraphy? How might it be used to date stone tools?
19) What classification system was proposed by Carl Woese and what led him to propose it?
20) Describe one way in which selective breeding can be useful outside of agriculture.
21) Why does selective breeding reduce gene pools?
22) What are restriction enzymes used for in genetic engineering?

Section 5 — Health, Disease and the Development of Medicines (p.71-85) ☐
23) Explain why being healthy doesn't just mean not being sick.
24) Why does HIV eventually lead to AIDS?
25) Give two types of chemical defence that prevent pathogens from infecting humans.
26) What is an antigen?
27) How do vaccines prepare the immune system against infection by a particular pathogen?
28) Which type of pathogen can antibiotics be used to kill?
29) Give two risk factors related to lifestyle associated with obesity.
30) Give three examples of lifestyle changes that can help to prevent cardiovascular disease.

Section 6 — Plant Structures and Their Functions

Photosynthesis

Photosynthesis is where **energy** enters most of the **food chains** on Earth. **Organisms** that can carry out photosynthesis have crucial positions at the **start** of those food chains.

Plants are Able to Make Their Own Food by Photosynthesis

1) During photosynthesis, photosynthetic organisms, such as green plants and algae, use energy from the Sun to make glucose.

2) Some of the glucose is used to make larger, complex molecules that the plants or algae need to grow. These make up the organism's biomass — the mass of living material.

3) The energy stored in the organisms' biomass then works its way through the food chain as animals eat them and each other. So photosynthetic organisms are the main producers of food for nearly all life on Earth.

4) Photosynthesis happens inside chloroplasts — they contain chlorophyll which absorbs light. Energy is transferred to the chloroplasts by light. This is the equation for photosynthesis:

$$\text{carbon dioxide} + \text{water} \xrightarrow[\text{chlorophyll}]{\text{light}} \text{glucose} + \text{oxygen}$$
$$6CO_2 + 6H_2O \xrightarrow[\text{chlorophyll}]{\text{light}} C_6H_{12}O_6 + 6O_2$$

5) Photosynthesis is an endothermic reaction — energy is taken in during the reaction.

6) The rate of photosynthesis is affected by the light intensity, the concentration of CO_2 and the temperature. Any of these three factors can become the limiting factor. This just means that it's stopping photosynthesis from happening any faster.

The TEMPERATURE has to be Just Right for Photosynthesis

Temperature affects the rate of photosynthesis because it affects the enzymes involved.

1) Usually, if the temperature is the limiting factor it's because it's too low — the enzymes needed for photosynthesis work more slowly at low temperatures.

2) But if the plant gets too hot, the enzymes it needs for photosynthesis and its other reactions will be denatured (see page 27).

3) This happens at about 45 °C (which is pretty hot for outdoors, although greenhouses can get that hot if you're not careful).

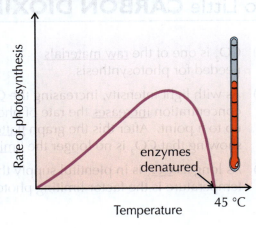

Photosynthesis

Not Enough LIGHT Slows Down the Rate of Photosynthesis

1) Light transfers the energy needed for photosynthesis.
2) At first, as the light level is raised, the rate of photosynthesis increases steadily (the rate is directly proportional to light intensity). But this is only true up to a certain point.
3) Beyond that, it won't make any difference — it'll be either the temperature or the CO_2 level which is the limiting factor.
4) In the lab you can investigate light intensity by moving a lamp closer to or further away from your plant (see next page).
5) But if you just plot the rate of photosynthesis against "distance of lamp from the plant", you get a weird-shaped graph. To get a graph like the one above you either need to measure the light intensity at the plant using a light meter or do a bit of maths with your results. Here's why:

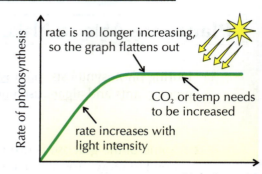

The square of the distance from the lamp and the light intensity are inversely proportional to each other — this means as the distance increases, the light intensity decreases. However, light intensity decreases in proportion to the square of the distance. This is called the inverse square law and is written like this:

$\propto$ is the 'proportional to' symbol.

$$\text{light intensity} \propto \frac{1}{\text{distance (d)}^2}$$

6) The inverse square law means that if you halve the distance, the light intensity will be four times greater. And if you double the distance, the light intensity will be four times smaller. (Trebling the distance would make it nine times smaller.) You can use $1/d^2$ as a measure of light intensity:

EXAMPLE Using the inverse square law, calculate the light intensity at both 20 cm and 10 cm from a lamp.

1) Use the formula for calculating light intensity.
2) For each of the distances, put the value into the formula, then calculate the answer.

$$\text{light intensity} = \frac{1}{d^2}$$

At 20 cm: light intensity $= \frac{1}{20^2} = \frac{1}{400} = 0.0025$ a.u

At 10 cm: light intensity $= \frac{1}{10^2} = \frac{1}{100} = 0.0100$ a.u.

'a.u.' stands for 'arbitrary units'.

Halving the distance has made the light intensity four times greater.

Too Little CARBON DIOXIDE Slows Photosynthesis Down

1) CO_2 is one of the raw materials needed for photosynthesis.
2) As with light intensity, increasing the CO_2 concentration increases the rate of photosynthesis up to a point. After this the graph flattens out, showing that CO_2 is no longer the limiting factor.
3) As long as CO_2 is in plentiful supply then light or temperature is the factor limiting photosynthesis.

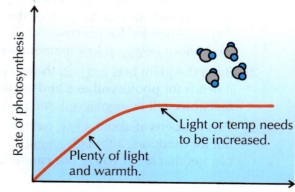

Investigating Photosynthesis

*It's practical time again. This one lets you see how changing **light intensity** affects the **rate of photosynthesis**.*

You Can Investigate the Rate of Photosynthesis

Canadian pondweed (an aquatic plant) can be used to measure the effect of light intensity on the rate of photosynthesis. The rate at which the pondweed produces oxygen corresponds to the rate at which it's photosynthesising — the faster the rate of oxygen production, the faster the rate of photosynthesis. Here's how the experiment works:

1) The apparatus is set up as shown in the diagram below. The gas syringe should be empty to start with. Sodium hydrogencarbonate may be added to the water to make sure the plant has enough carbon dioxide (sodium hydrogencarbonate releases CO_2 in solution).

2) A source of white light is placed at a specific distance from the pondweed.

3) The pondweed is left to photosynthesise for a set amount of time.

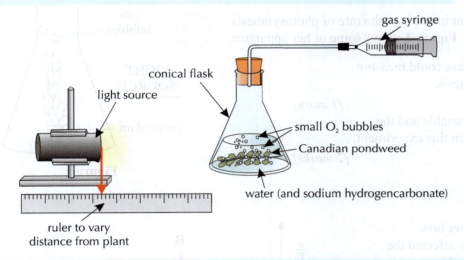

This experiment can be modified to test the effect of temperature or carbon dioxide concentration too — just remember to only change one variable at a time.

You can also investigate the rate of photosynthesis using algal balls, instead of pondweed. These are little balls of jelly which contain algae.

4) As it photosynthesises, the oxygen released will collect in the gas syringe. This allows you to accurately measure the volume of oxygen produced.

5) The whole experiment is repeated with the light source at different distances from the pondweed. The rate of oxygen production at each distance can then be calculated (volume produced ÷ time taken).

You could measure how much oxygen is produced by counting the number of bubbles given off in a certain time instead — but this is less accurate.

6) For this experiment, any variables that could affect the results should be controlled, e.g. the temperature (which can be controlled by putting the conical flask in a water bath) and the carbon dioxide concentration (which can be controlled by adding a set amount of sodium hydrogencarbonate to a set volume of water).

Faster photosynthesis means faster oxygen production

Q1 An experiment was carried out to find out the effect of temperature on the rate of photosynthesis. Name two variables that should have been controlled in this experiment.
[2 marks]

Q2 A plant is moved from 15 cm away from its light source to 5 cm away from its light source. Using the inverse square law, show that the light intensity becomes nine times greater.
[3 marks]

Section 6 — Plant Structures and Their Functions

Warm-Up and Exam Questions

Time for a break in the section and some questions. Do them now, whilst all that learning is fresh in your mind. Using that knowledge will help you to remember it all, and that's what this game is all about.

Warm-Up Questions

1) True or false? Photosynthesis is an exothermic reaction.
2) What is meant by a limiting factor for the rate of photosynthesis?
3) Explain why the rate of photosynthesis decreases if the temperature is too high.
4) Write down the inverse square law for light intensity.

Exam Questions

PRACTICAL

1 A student did an experiment to see how the rate of photosynthesis depends on light intensity. **Figure 1** shows some of her apparatus.

(a) Suggest how the student could measure the rate of photosynthesis.
   [1 mark]

(b) State the dependent variable and the independent variable in this experiment.
   [2 marks]

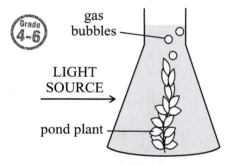

Figure 1

2 The graph in **Figure 2** shows how changing the light intensity affected the rate of photosynthesis of a plant.

During the experiment, the plant was kept at a constant temperature and a constant concentration of carbon dioxide.

(a) State what factor was limiting the rate of photosynthesis of the plant between points **A** and **B** on the graph. Explain your answer.
   [2 marks]

(b) Explain why the graph flattens off after point **B**.
   [2 marks]

3 A student is investigating the effect of light intensity on the rate of photosynthesis by placing a lamp at various distances from a plant and measuring the rate of photosynthesis.

Use the inverse square law to calculate the light intensity when the lamp is 7.5 cm from the plant. Give your answer in arbitrary units (a.u.) to 2 significant figures.
   [2 marks]

Transport in Plants

Plants need to get stuff from **A to B**. Flowering plants have **two types** of **transport vessel** — **xylem** and **phloem**. Both types of vessel go to **every part** of the plant, but they are totally **separate**.

Root Hairs Take In Minerals and Water

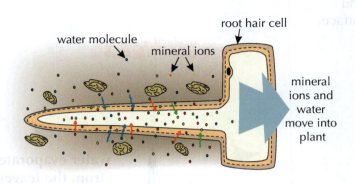

1) The cells on the surface of plant roots grow into "hairs", which stick out into the soil.
2) Each branch of a root will be covered in millions of these microscopic hairs.
3) This gives the plant a large surface area for absorbing water and mineral ions from the soil.
4) The concentration of mineral ions is usually higher in the root hair cells than in the soil around them, so mineral ions are absorbed by active transport (see page 32).
5) Water is absorbed by osmosis.

Phloem Tubes Transport Food

1) Phloem tubes are made of columns of elongated living cells with small pores in the end walls to allow stuff to flow through.
2) They transport food substances (mainly sucrose) made in the leaves to the rest of the plant for immediate use (e.g. in growing regions) or for storage.
3) This process is called translocation and it requires energy from respiration (see page 111). The transport goes in both directions.

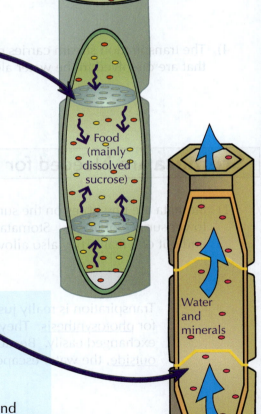

Xylem Tubes Take Water UP

1) Xylem tubes are made of dead cells joined end to end with no end walls between them and a hole down the middle. They're strengthened with a material called lignin.
2) They carry water and mineral ions from the roots to the stem and leaves.
3) The movement of water from the roots, through the xylem and out of the leaves is called the transpiration stream (see next page).

Xylem vessels carry water, phloem vessels carry sucrose

Make sure you don't get your phloem mixed up with your xylem. To help you to learn which is which, you could remember that phl**o**em transports substances in b**o**th directions, but xylem only transports things upwards — x**y** to the sky. It might just bag you a mark or two on exam day...

Section 6 — Plant Structures and Their Functions

Transpiration and Stomata

Plants need *water* and *gases* such as carbon dioxide and oxygen.

Transpiration is the Loss of Water from the Plant

1) Transpiration is caused by the evaporation and diffusion (see p.32) of water from a plant's surface. Most transpiration happens at the leaves.

2) The loss of water creates a slight shortage of water in the leaf, and so more water is drawn up from the rest of the plant through the xylem vessels to replace it.

3) This in turn means more water is drawn up from the roots, and so there's a constant transpiration stream of water through the plant.

4) The transpiration stream carries mineral ions that are dissolved in the water along with it.

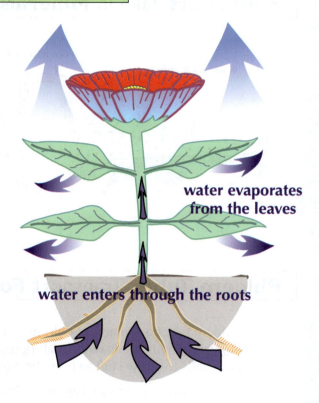

water evaporates from the leaves

water enters through the roots

Stomata are Needed for Gas Exchange

1) Stomata are tiny pores on the surface of a plant. They're mostly found on the lower surface of leaves. Stomata allow CO_2 and oxygen to diffuse directly in and out of a leaf. They also allow water vapour to escape during transpiration.

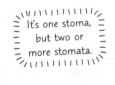
It's one stoma, but two or more stomata.

2) Transpiration is really just a side-effect of the way leaves are adapted for photosynthesis. They have to have stomata so that gases can be exchanged easily. Because there's more water inside the plant than in the air outside, the water escapes from the leaves through the stomata by diffusion.

3) Stomata are surrounded by guard cells, which change shape to control the size of the pore — when the guard cells are turgid (swollen with water) the stomata are open and when the guard cells are flaccid (low on water and limp) the stomata are closed.

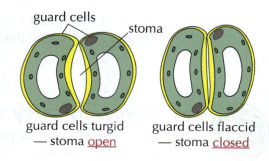

guard cells turgid — stoma open   guard cells flaccid — stoma closed

Section 6 — Plant Structures and Their Functions

Transpiration Rate

*The **rate of transpiration** varies according to the **environmental conditions**.*

Transpiration Rate is Affected by Environmental Factors

Light Intensity

1) The brighter the light, the greater the transpiration rate.
2) Stomata begin to close as it gets darker. Photosynthesis can't happen in the dark, so they don't need to be open to let CO_2 in. When the stomata are closed, very little water can escape.

Temperature

1) The warmer it is, the faster transpiration happens.
2) When it's warm the water particles have more energy to evaporate and diffuse out of the stomata.

The faster the transpiration rate, the faster the water uptake by the plant.

Air Flow

1) The better the air flow around a leaf (e.g. stronger wind), the greater the transpiration rate.
2) If air flow around a leaf is poor, the water vapour just surrounds the leaf and doesn't move away. This means there's a high concentration of water particles outside the leaf as well as inside it, so diffusion doesn't happen as quickly.
3) If there's good air flow, the water vapour is swept away, maintaining a low concentration of water in the air outside the leaf. Diffusion then happens quickly, from an area of higher concentration to an area of lower concentration.

The opening and closing of stomata is important for plants to survive

Plants need stomata for gas exchange but they let out a lot of water too. A big tree can lose about a thousand litres of water from its leaves every single day. That's a lot of water, which is why closing the stomata in certain conditions (e.g at night) is really important to stop too much water being lost.

Transpiration Rate

*Sorry, more on **transpiration**, but at least this page is about a **practical**.*

You Can Estimate Transpiration Rate

You can use a special piece of apparatus called a potometer to estimate transpiration rate. It actually measures water uptake by a plant, but it's assumed that water uptake by the plant is directly related to water loss from the leaves (transpiration). Here's what you do:

1) Set up the apparatus as in the diagram, and then record the starting position of the air bubble.
2) Start a stopwatch and record the distance moved by the bubble per unit time, e.g. per hour. Calculating the speed of air bubble movement gives an estimate of the transpiration rate.

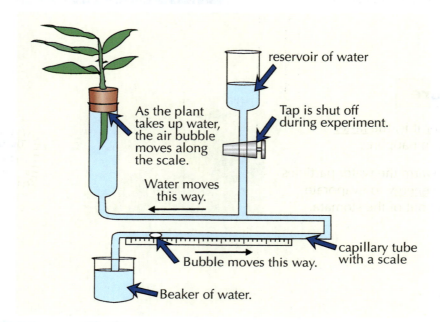

EXAMPLE

A potometer was used to estimate the transpiration rate of a plant cutting. The bubble moved 25 mm in 10 minutes. Estimate the transpiration rate.

To estimate the rate of transpiration, divide the distance the bubble moved by the time taken.

$$\frac{\text{distance moved}}{\text{time taken}} = \frac{25 \text{ mm}}{10 \text{ min}} = 2.5 \text{ mm min}^{-1}$$

mm min^{-1} is the same as mm/min.

You can use a potometer to estimate how light intensity, temperature or air flow around the plant affect the transpiration rate. Just remember to only change one variable at a time and control the rest.

Make sure you know how to work out transpiration rate

You need to know how to calculate the rate of transpiration using measurements taken in a practical like the one above. Watch out for the units — you might be asked to use different ones in the exam. Don't panic though, just make sure your units match all the way through the calculation.

Section 6 — Plant Structures and Their Functions

Warm-Up and Exam Questions

There's a fair few diagrams on the previous pages. Make sure you familiarise yourself with the labels and content of each one, don't just look at the pretty colours... Anyway you know what's next by now...

Warm-Up Questions

1) Where are most of a plant's stomata located?
2) True or false? Substances pass in both directions through xylem vessels.
3) State the three main factors that affect the rate of transpiration in plants.

Exam Questions

1   Plants absorb water and mineral ions through their root hair cells.

   (a) Name the vessels that transport water and mineral ions from the roots of a plant to the leaves.
   [1 mark]

   (b) Describe the structure of the vessels you named in **1(a)**.
   [3 marks]

   (c) Name the process by which water is transported through and lost from a plant.
   [1 mark]

2   Aphids are insects. They feed on liquid which they extract from a plant's transport vessels, using their sharp mouthparts to pierce the stem. This liquid contains dissolved sucrose.

   (a) Name the type of transport vessel that the aphids extract their liquid food from.
   [1 mark]

   (b) Describe and explain how the structure of this type of transport vessel is adapted to its function.
   [4 marks]

3   A student investigated the effect of temperature and air flow on transpiration in basil plants. She put groups of three plants in four different conditions. She weighed the plants before and after the experiment and calculated the % loss in mass for each plant. Her results are shown in **Figure 1**.

plant	% loss in mass			
	Group A: 20 °C Still Room	Group B: 20 °C Next to a Fan	Group C: 25 °C Still Room	Group D: 25 °C Next to a Fan
1	5	8	10	13
2	5	9	11	15
3	4	11	9	13
mean	4.7	9.3		13.6

Figure 1

   (a) Calculate the mean % loss in mass for the three plants in Group **C**.
   [2 marks]

   (b)* Explain why keeping the plants in Group **D** at 25 °C and placing them next to a fan meant that they lost more mass than the plants in Group **A**.
   [6 marks]

Section 7 — Animal Coordination, Control and Homeostasis

Hormones

Way back in Section 2 you learnt how information is passed around the body via **neurones**. Well the body also uses **hormones** as a way to communicate, which is what this page is all about.

Hormones Are Chemical Messengers Sent in the Blood

1) Hormones are chemical molecules released directly into the blood.
2) They are carried in the blood to other parts of the body, but only affect particular cells in particular organs (called target organs).
3) Hormones control things in organs and cells that need constant adjustment.
4) Hormones are produced in (and secreted by) various glands, called endocrine glands. These glands make up your endocrine system.

Endocrine Glands Are Found in Different Places in the Body

PITUITARY GLAND
1) The pituitary gland produces many hormones that regulate body conditions.
2) It is sometimes called the 'master gland' because these hormones act on other glands, directing them to release hormones that bring about change.

THYROID
This produces thyroxine, which is involved in regulating things like the rate of metabolism, heart rate and temperature (see page 98).

ADRENAL GLAND
This produces adrenaline, which is used to prepare the body for a 'fight or flight' response (see page 98).

OVARIES (females only)
Produce oestrogen, which is involved in the menstrual cycle (see pages 100-101).

PANCREAS
This produces insulin, which is used to regulate the blood glucose level (see page 106).

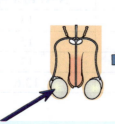

TESTES (males only)

Produce testosterone, which controls puberty and sperm production in males.

Comparing Neurones and Hormones

*Now you know that there are **two** ways information can be sent round the body — via the **nervous** or **hormonal** systems — here's a page comparing the differences between them...*

Hormones and Nerves Carry Messages in Different Ways

Hormones and nerves do similar jobs — they both carry information and instructions around the body. But there are some important differences between them:

Nerves	Hormones
Very FAST action.	SLOWER action.
Act for a very SHORT TIME.	Act for a LONG TIME.
Act on a very PRECISE AREA.	Act in a more GENERAL way.

If you're not sure whether a response is nervous or hormonal, have a think about the speed of the reaction and how long it lasts.

If the Response is Really Quick, It's Probably Nervous

1) Some information needs to be passed to effectors really quickly. For example:

   - Signals telling you that a part of your body is feeling pain (so you can take action quickly to avoid your body being damaged).
   - Information from your eyes telling you there's something dangerous heading your way.

2) It's no good using hormones to carry messages like these — they would be too slow.

If a Response Lasts For a Long Time, It's Probably Hormonal

Hormonal responses tend to carry on having an effect for a longer time than nervous responses.

For example, when you get a shock, a hormone called adrenaline is released into the body (causing the fight or flight response, where your body is hyped up ready for action). You can tell it's a hormonal response (even though it kicks in pretty quickly) because you feel a bit wobbly for a while afterwards.

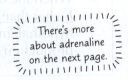
There's more about adrenaline on the next page.

Nerves, hormones — no wonder revision makes me tense...

Hormones control various organs and cells in the body, though they tend to control things that aren't immediately life-threatening (so things like sexual development, blood sugar level, water content, etc.).

Adrenaline and Thyroxine

On the previous two pages you learnt what **hormones** are. Now it's time to look at a **couple of examples**...

Adrenaline Prepares You for 'Fight or Flight'

1) Adrenaline is a hormone released by the adrenal glands (which are located just above the kidneys — see page 96).
2) Adrenaline prepares the body for 'fight or flight' — in other words, standing your ground in the face of a threat (e.g. a predator) or bravely running away. It does this by activating processes that increase the supply of oxygen and glucose to cells. For example:

   - Adrenaline binds to specific receptors in the heart. This causes the heart muscle to contract more frequently and with more force, so heart rate and blood pressure increase.
   - This increases blood flow to the muscles, so the cells receive more oxygen and glucose for increased respiration.
   - Adrenaline also binds to receptors in the liver. This causes the liver to break down its glycogen stores (see p.106) to release glucose.
   - This increases the blood glucose level, so there's more glucose in the blood to be transported to the cells.

3) When your brain detects a stressful situation, it sends nervous impulses to the adrenal glands, which respond by secreting adrenaline. This gets the body ready for action.

Hormone Release can be Affected by Negative Feedback

Your body can control the levels of hormones (and other substances) in the blood using negative feedback systems. When the body detects that the level of a substance has gone above or below the normal level, it triggers a response to bring the level back to normal again. Here's an example of just that:

Thyroxine Regulates Metabolism

1) Thyroxine is a hormone released by the thyroid gland.
2) It plays an important role in regulating metabolic rate — the speed at which chemical reactions in the body occur.
3) A negative feedback system keeps the amount of thyroxine in the blood at the right level:

An underactive thyroid gland can cause weight gain. Less thyroxine is produced, so your metabolic rate drops. This means that less of the glucose you take in gets broken down in respiration, so more is stored as fat.

- When the blood thyroxine level is lower than normal, the hypothalamus (a structure in the brain) is stimulated to release thyrotropin releasing hormone (TRH).
- TRH stimulates the pituitary gland to release thyroid stimulating hormone (TSH).
- TSH stimulates the thyroid gland to release thyroxine, so the blood thyroxine level rises back towards normal.
- When the blood thyroxine level becomes higher than normal, the release of TRH from the hypothalamus is inhibited, which reduces the production of TSH, so the blood thyroxine level falls.

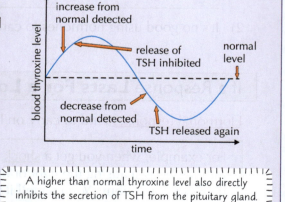

A higher than normal thyroxine level also directly inhibits the secretion of TSH from the pituitary gland.

Negative feedback works a bit like a thermostat...

...if the temperature is too low, the thermostat turns the heating on. If it's too high, it turns it off.

Q1 Graves' disease is a condition where the immune system produces an antibody that has the same effect as TSH. Explain why this could lead to an abnormally high blood thyroxine level.

[3 marks]

Q1 Video Solution

Section 7 — Animal Coordination, Control and Homeostasis

Warm-Up and Exam Questions

Yep, that's right, this section is no different from the last — there are still plenty of questions for you to get practising what you've learnt. Don't worry, the warm-up questions will ease you in gently.

Warm-Up Questions

1) What term is used to describe an organ whose cells are affected by a particular hormone?
2) a) Name five endocrine glands found in the male human body.
   b) Name one type of endocrine gland found in the female human body that is not found in the male human body.
3) Name the glands that produce adrenaline.
4) Name the gland that produces thyroxine.

Exam Questions

1   **Figure 1** shows thyroxine undergoing regulation in the human body. Changes from the normal thyroxine level trigger a response that returns the level to normal.

   (a) Name the type of system that regulates the level of a hormone, such as thyroxine, in the blood.
   [1 mark]

   (b) Which of these things is happening at point **X** in **Figure 1**?

   ☐ A   TRH release is stimulated.
   ☐ B   TSH production is increased.
   ☐ C   TSH release is inhibited.
   ☐ D   Thyroxine release is stimulated.
   [1 mark]

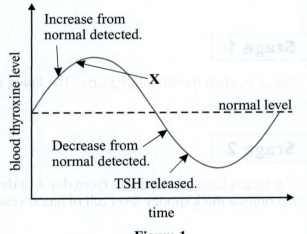

Figure 1

2   Hypopituitarism is a condition in which the pituitary gland doesn't secrete enough of one or more of the pituitary hormones.

   People with hypopituitarism may experience tiredness and weight gain. These symptoms are linked to low thyroid hormone levels.

   Suggest why someone with hypopituitarism may experience these symptoms.
   [3 marks]

3* A dog suddenly runs towards a cat across the street, which frightens the cat.

   Describe how a hormonal response would affect the cat's heart rate and blood glucose level when it sees the dog. Explain why these effects are beneficial.
   [6 marks]

Section 7 — Animal Coordination, Control and Homeostasis

The Menstrual Cycle

The monthly **release of an egg** from the ovaries is part of the **menstrual cycle**.

The Menstrual Cycle Has Four Stages

The menstrual cycle is the monthly sequence of events in which the female body releases an egg and prepares the uterus (womb) in case the egg is fertilised. This is what happens at each stage:

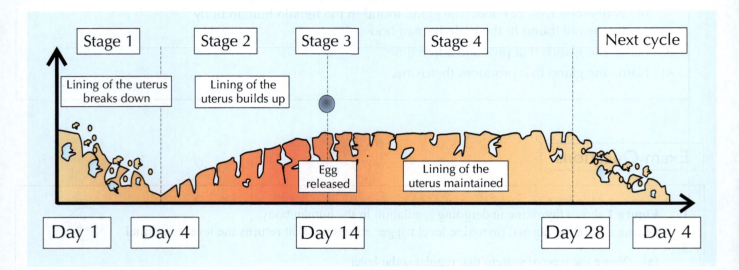

Stage 1

Day 1 is when menstruation starts. The lining of the uterus breaks down and is released.

The lining of the uterus is also called the 'endometrium'.

Stage 2

The uterus lining is repaired. From day 4 to day 14, the uterus lining builds up again until it becomes a thick spongy layer full of blood vessels, ready for a fertilised egg to implant there.

Stage 3

An egg develops and is released from the ovary (ovulation) at about day 14.

Stage 4

The lining is then maintained for about 14 days, until day 28. If no fertilised egg has landed on the uterus wall by day 28, the spongy lining starts to break down again, and the whole cycle starts over.

Examiners love a good menstrual cycle graph...

Make sure you have a good handle on the different stages of the menstrual cycle before moving on to the next page to learn about the hormones that control those stages — examiners like asking about it.

The Menstrual Cycle

The Menstrual Cycle is Controlled by Four Hormones

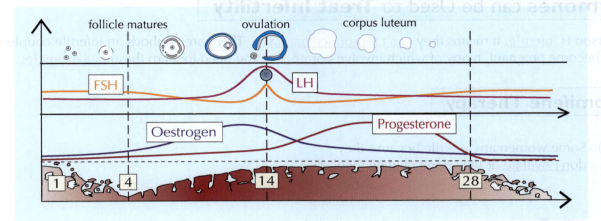

1. FSH (Follicle-Stimulating Hormone)

1) Released by the pituitary gland.
2) Causes a follicle (an egg and its surrounding cells) to mature in one of the ovaries.
3) Stimulates oestrogen production.

2. Oestrogen

1) Released by the ovaries.
2) Causes the lining of the uterus to thicken and grow.
3) A high level stimulates an LH surge (a rapid increase).

3. LH (Luteinising Hormone)

1) Released by the pituitary gland.
2) The LH surge stimulates ovulation at day 14 — the follicle ruptures and the egg is released.
3) Stimulates the remains of the follicle to develop into a structure called a corpus luteum — which secretes progesterone.

4. Progesterone

1) Released by the corpus luteum after ovulation.
2) Maintains the lining of the uterus.
3) Inhibits the release of FSH and LH.
4) When the progesterone level falls, and there's a low oestrogen level, the uterus lining breaks down.
5) A low progesterone level allows FSH to increase and then the whole cycle starts again.

If a fertilised egg implants in the uterus (i.e. the woman becomes pregnant) then the level of progesterone will stay high to maintain the lining of the uterus during pregnancy.

Section 7 — Animal Coordination, Control and Homeostasis

Controlling Fertility

*Hormones can be used **artificially** to help **infertile** women have babies.*

Hormones can be Used to Treat Infertility

If a person is infertile, it means they can't reproduce naturally. There are methods an infertile couple can use to become pregnant, many of which involve hormones. You need to learn these two examples:

Clomifene Therapy

1) Some women are infertile because they don't ovulate or they don't ovulate regularly.

2) These women can take a drug called clomifene. This works by causing more FSH and LH to be released by the body, which stimulates egg maturation and ovulation — see previous page.

3) By knowing when the woman will be ovulating, the couple can have intercourse during this time period to improve the chance of becoming pregnant.

IVF ("*in vitro* fertilisation")

1) IVF involves collecting eggs from the woman's ovaries and fertilising them in a lab using the man's sperm. These are then grown into embryos.

2) Once the embryos are tiny balls of cells, one or two of them are transferred to the woman's uterus to improve the chance of pregnancy.

3) FSH and LH are given before egg collection to stimulate egg production (so more than one egg can be collected).

4) IVF is an example of Assisted Reproductive Technology (ART) — a fertility treatment that involves eggs being handled (and usually fertilised) outside of the body.

Understanding how hormones work helps put them to use artificially

Knowing the effects that LH and FSH have on the menstrual cycle allows us the use the hormones to manipulate the menstrual cycle when treating infertility. In clomifene therapy and IVF, FSH and LH are really important because they both stimulate egg production, maturation and ovulation.

Controlling Fertility

Pregnancy can happen if sperm reaches the ovulated egg. *Contraception* tries to *stop* this happening.

Contraceptives are Used to Prevent Pregnancy

1) Hormones can also be used as contraceptives. For example, oestrogen can be used to prevent the release of an egg. This may seem kind of strange (since naturally oestrogen helps stimulate the release of eggs). But if oestrogen is taken every day to keep the level of it permanently high, it inhibits the production of FSH, and after a while egg development and production stop and stay stopped.

2) Progesterone can also be used to reduce fertility. It works in several different ways — one of which is by stimulating the production of thick cervical mucus, which prevents any sperm getting through the entrance to the uterus (the cervix) and reaching an egg.

3) Some hormonal contraceptives contain both oestrogen and progesterone — for example, the combined pill (which is an oral contraceptive) and the contraceptive patch (which is worn on the skin).

4) The mini-pill (another oral contraceptive) and the contraceptive injection both contain progesterone only.

5) Pregnancy can also be prevented by barrier methods of contraception — these put a barrier between the sperm and egg so they don't meet. Examples include condoms (both male and female) and diaphragms (flexible, dome-shaped devices that fit over the opening of the uterus and are inserted before sex).

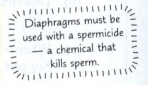
Diaphragms must be used with a spermicide — a chemical that kills sperm.

Hormonal and Barrier Contraceptive Methods Have Pros and Cons

1) Generally, when used correctly, hormonal methods are more effective at preventing pregnancy than barrier methods. Also, hormonal methods mean the couple don't have to stop and think about contraception each time they have intercourse (as they would if they relied on barrier methods).

2) However, hormonal methods can have unpleasant side-effects, such as headaches, acne and mood changes. Also, hormonal methods don't protect against sexually transmitted infections — condoms are the only form of contraception that do this.

People have a choice to make when picking a contraceptive
You might be asked to evaluate different methods of contraception in your exam. If you are, remember: you need to weigh up and write about both the pros and the cons of each method and write a sensible conclusion too. That's how you get your hands on those top marks.

Section 7 — Animal Coordination, Control and Homeostasis

Warm-Up and Exam Questions

Right then, another lot of pages down. Now there's just the small matter of answering some questions...

Warm-Up Questions

1) Name the hormone that stimulates an egg to mature in the ovary.
2) Name the only form of contraception that protects against sexually transmitted infections.
3) What is Assisted Reproductive Technology (ART)?
4) What effect does the drug clomifene have on the release of FSH and LH?

Exam Questions

1 The menstrual cycle is controlled by several different hormones.

(a) Describe the effect of progesterone on the release of FSH.

[1 mark]

(b) Name the hormone responsible for stimulating the formation of the corpus luteum.

[1 mark]

(c) State the day of the menstrual cycle on which the egg is released.

[1 mark]

Towards the end of the menstrual cycle, oestrogen levels are low and progesterone levels begin to fall.

(d) Describe the effect that this will have on the uterus lining.

[1 mark]

(e) When a fertilised egg implants in the uterus, the level of progesterone remains high.
Suggest why this happens.

[1 mark]

2 A couple are researching which form of contraceptive to use. One option is the combined oral contraceptive pill. The pill contains both oestrogen and progesterone and is taken everyday.

(a) Explain how taking oestrogen every day will stop the woman getting pregnant.

[2 marks]

(b) State and explain **one** way in which taking a contraceptive pill containing progesterone could stop a woman getting pregnant.

[2 marks]

(c) The couple are also considering using barrier contraceptives to prevent pregnancy.
Describe how barrier contraceptives prevent pregnancies.

[1 mark]

(d) State **one** advantage and **one** disadvantage for the couple if they choose to use a barrier contraceptive instead of a hormonal contraceptive.

[2 marks]

Section 7 — Animal Coordination, Control and Homeostasis

Homeostasis

Homeostasis means **maintaining** the right **conditions** inside your body, so that everything **works properly**. Luckily there are some clever **systems** in place to keep things plodding along steadily.

Homeostasis is Maintaining a Constant Internal Environment

1) Conditions in your body need to be kept steady — this is really important because your cells need the right conditions in order to function properly, including the right conditions for enzyme action (see p.27). It can be dangerous for your health if conditions vary too much from normal levels.

2) To maintain a constant internal environment, your body needs to respond to both internal and external changes, whilst balancing inputs (stuff going into your body) with outputs (stuff leaving).

3) Examples of homeostasis in action include:

   Blood glucose regulation — you need to make sure the amount of glucose in your blood doesn't get too high or too low (see next page).

   Thermoregulation (regulating body temperature) — you need to reduce your body temperature when you're hot, but increase it when the environment is cold.

   Osmoregulation (regulating water content) — you need to keep a balance between the water you gain (in drink, food, and from respiration) and the water you pee, sweat and breathe out.

4) Negative feedback systems (see p.98) help to keep conditions in your body steady. This means that if a condition changes away from the normal level, a response is triggered that counteracts the change. E.g. a rise in blood glucose level causes a response that lowers blood glucose level (and vice versa).

Homeostasis is really important to keep your body "normal"

Without negative feedback systems, changes in your body conditions would go unregulated. This would be really bad because your body wouldn't function properly. So we need homeostasis to keep things in check.

Blood Glucose Regulation

Insulin and *glucagon* are *hormones* that control how much *glucose* there is in your *blood*.

Insulin and Glucagon Control Blood Glucose Concentration

1) Eating foods containing carbohydrate puts glucose into the blood from the small intestine.
2) The normal metabolism of cells removes glucose from the blood.
3) Vigorous exercise removes much more glucose from the blood.
4) Excess glucose can be stored as glycogen in the liver and in the muscles.
5) When these stores are full then the excess glucose is stored as lipid (fat) in the tissues.
6) Changes in blood glucose are monitored and controlled by the pancreas, using the hormones insulin and glucagon, as shown:

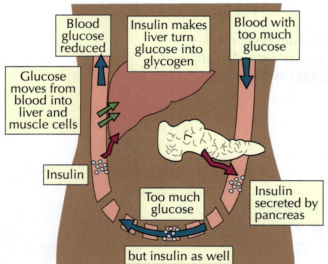

Blood glucose concentration too HIGH — INSULIN is added.

So insulin removes glucose from the blood.

Blood glucose concentration too LOW — GLUCAGON is added.

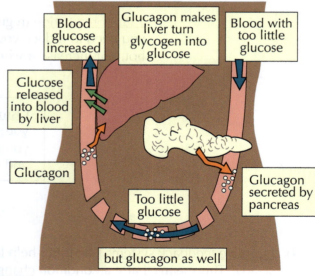

And people used to think the pancreas was just a cushion...

This stuff can seem a bit confusing at first, but you could have a go at remembering it like this:
If blood glucose is increasing, insulin's added.
If blood glucose is almost gone, glucagon's added.

Q1 The graph shows the relative secretion rates of insulin and glucagon as the blood glucose level increases. Which curve represents glucagon? Explain your answer.

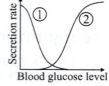

[2 marks]

Section 7 — Animal Coordination, Control and Homeostasis

Diabetes

Diabetes is an example of when homeostasis **doesn't work**. Make sure you fully understand how **insulin** affects **blood glucose concentration** (on the previous page) before you try getting your head around diabetes.

Type 1 Diabetes — Caused by a Lack of Insulin

1) Type 1 diabetes is a condition where the pancreas produces very little or no insulin. The result is that a person's blood glucose can rise to a level that can kill them.

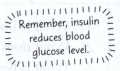
Remember, insulin reduces blood glucose level.

2) A person with type 1 diabetes will need to be treated with insulin therapy — this usually involves injecting insulin into the subcutaneous tissue (fatty tissue just under the skin), from where it will enter the bloodstream. This is often done at mealtimes to make sure that the glucose is removed from the blood quickly once the food has been digested. This stops the level of glucose in the blood from getting too high and is a very effective treatment. The amount of insulin that needs to be injected depends on the person's diet and how active they are.

Injecting too much insulin could result in a dangerously low blood glucose level.

Type 2 Diabetes — a Person is Resistant to Insulin

1) Type 2 diabetes is a condition where the pancreas doesn't produce enough insulin or when a person becomes resistant to insulin (their body's cells don't respond properly to the hormone). In both of these cases, blood glucose level rises.

2) There is a correlation (see p.14) between obesity and type 2 diabetes — this means that obese people have an increased risk of developing type 2 diabetes. People can be classified as obese by looking at their body mass index (BMI). BMI is worked out using this formula:

$$\text{BMI} = \frac{\text{mass (kg)}}{(\text{height (m)})^2}$$

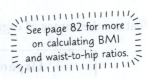
See page 82 for more on calculating BMI and waist-to-hip ratios.

3) Where the body stores excess fat is also important — storing a lot of fat around the abdomen (tummy area) is associated with an increased risk of developing type 2 diabetes. Calculating a person's waist-to-hip ratio gives an indication of how fat is stored. This is the formula you need:

$$\text{Waist-to-hip ratio} = \frac{\text{waist circumference (cm)}}{\text{hip circumference (cm)}}$$

4) A ratio above 1.0 for males and above 0.85 for females is associated with an increased risk of type 2 diabetes because it indicates that a lot of fat is being stored around the abdomen.

5) Type 2 diabetes can be controlled by eating a healthy diet, getting regular exercise and losing weight if needed. Some people with type 2 diabetes also have medication or insulin injections.

Section 7 — Animal Coordination, Control and Homeostasis

Warm-Up and Exam Questions

Welcome to some more questions. There are quite a few of them, but that's because they're pretty important.

Warm-Up Questions

1) What is homeostasis?
2) What does insulin do?
3) What is type 2 diabetes?
4) Name one factor that increases your risk of developing type 2 diabetes.

Exam Questions

1   **Figure 1** shows how the blood glucose level is regulated in humans.

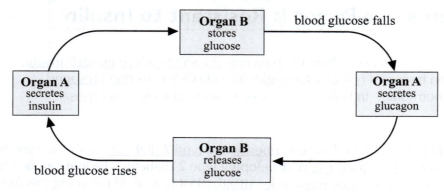

Figure 1

(a) What are the names of organs **A** and **B** in **Figure 1**?

	Organ A	Organ B
☐ A	pancreas	kidney
☐ B	liver	pancreas
☐ C	kidney	liver
☐ D	pancreas	liver

[1 mark]

(b) Apart from organ **B** releasing glucose, suggest **one** reason why a person's blood glucose level might rise.

[1 mark]

(c) With reference to **Figure 1**, explain what goes wrong with the regulation of blood glucose level in people with type 1 diabetes.

[3 marks]

(d) Describe what the hormone glucagon does.

[1 mark]

Section 8 — Exchange and Transport in Animals

Exchange of Materials

Like all organisms, animals need to exchange things with their environment — but being multicellular makes things a little bit complicated...

Organisms Exchange Substances with their Environment

1) All organisms must take in substances that they need from the environment and get rid of any waste products. For example:

   Cells need oxygen for aerobic respiration (see page 111), which produces carbon dioxide as a waste product. These two gases move between cells and the environment by diffusion (see next page).

   Water is taken up by cells by osmosis. In animals, dissolved food molecules (the products of digestion, e.g. glucose, amino acids) and mineral ions diffuse along with it.

   Urea (a waste product produced by animals from proteins) diffuses from cells to the blood plasma for removal from the body by the kidneys.

   There's more on diffusion and osmosis on pages 32-33.

2) How easy it is for an organism to exchange substances with its environment depends on the organism's surface area to volume ratio (SA : V).

You Can Compare Surface Area to Volume Ratios

A ratio shows how big one value is compared to another. The larger an organism is, the smaller its surface area is compared to its volume. You can show this by calculating surface area to volume ratios:

A hippo can be represented by a 2 cm × 4 cm × 4 cm block.

The area of a surface is found by the equation: LENGTH × WIDTH
So the hippo's total surface area is:

(4 × 4) × 2 (top and bottom surfaces of block)
+ (4 × 2) × 4 (four sides of the block)
= 64 cm^2.

The volume of a block is found by the equation: LENGTH × WIDTH × HEIGHT
So the hippo's volume is 4 × 4 × 2 = 32 cm^3.
The surface area to volume ratio of the hippo can be written as 64 : 32.
To simplify the ratio, divide both sides of the ratio by the volume.
So the surface area to volume ratio of the hippo is 2 : 1.

A mouse can be represented by a 1 cm × 1 cm × 1 cm block.
Its surface area is (1 × 1) × 6 = 6 cm^2.
Its volume is 1 × 1 × 1 = 1 cm^3.
So the surface area to volume ratio of the mouse is 6 : 1.

The block mouse's surface area is six times its volume, but the block hippo's surface area is only twice its volume. So the mouse has a larger surface area compared to its volume.

Larger organisms have smaller surface area to volume ratios

Try this question to make sure you understand how to calculate surface area to volume ratios.

Q1 A bacterial cell can be represented by a 2 μm × 2 μm × 1 μm block.
    Calculate the cell's surface area to volume ratio.   [3 marks]

Q1 Video Solution

Exchange Surfaces and the Alveoli

The alveoli are an **exchange surface** found in the lungs of mammals. They're **well-adapted** for the **efficient exchange** of two important **gases** — oxygen and carbon dioxide.

Multicellular Organisms Need Exchange Surfaces

1) In single-celled organisms, gases and dissolved substances can diffuse directly into (or out of) the cell across the cell membrane — it's because they have a large surface area compared to their volume, so enough substances can be exchanged across the membrane to supply the volume of the cell.
2) Multicellular organisms (such as animals) have a smaller surface area compared to their volume. This makes it difficult to exchange enough substances to supply their entire volume across their outside surface alone. So they need some sort of exchange surface for efficient diffusion and a mass transport system to move substances between the exchange surface and the rest of the body.
3) The exchange surfaces have to allow enough of the necessary substances to pass through, so they are adapted to maximise effectiveness.

Gas Exchange in Mammals Happens in the Alveoli

1) The job of the lungs is to transfer oxygen (O_2) to the blood and to remove waste carbon dioxide (CO_2) from it.

2) To do this, the lungs contain millions of little air sacs called alveoli where gas exchange takes place.

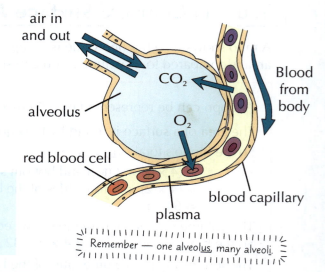

Remember — one alveol*us*, many alveol*i*.

3) Blood arriving at the alveoli has just returned to the lungs from the rest of the body, so it contains lots of CO_2 and not much O_2. This maximises the concentration gradient for the diffusion of both gases.

4) O_2 diffuses out of the air in the alveoli (where the concentration of O_2 is high) and into the blood (where the concentration of O_2 is low). CO_2 diffuses in the opposite direction to be breathed out.

5) The alveoli are specialised to maximise the diffusion of O_2 and CO_2. They have:
 - A moist lining for dissolving gases.
 - A good blood supply to maintain the concentration gradients of O_2 and CO_2.
 - Very thin walls — minimising the distance that gases have to move.
 - An enormous surface area (about 75 m² in humans).

O_2 and CO_2 diffuse across the membranes of the cells that make up the walls of the capillary and alveolus. These membranes are partially permeable — see page 33.

Humans need alveoli for gas exchange...

You might well get asked to explain how the adaptations of the alveoli help gas exchange, so make sure you know what those adaptations are and why they maximise the diffusion of O_2 and CO_2.

Respiration

*You need **energy** to keep your body going. Energy comes from **food**, and it's **released** by **respiration**.*

Cellular Respiration Releases Energy

1) Respiration is <u>NOT</u> breathing in and breathing out.

2) <u>Respiration</u> actually goes on in <u>every cell</u> of all living organisms — and it happens <u>continuously</u>.

3) It's the process of <u>transferring</u> (releasing) <u>energy</u> from the breakdown of <u>organic compounds</u> (usually <u>glucose</u>). The <u>energy</u> is then used for things like:

Organic compounds are compounds containing carbon. They include carbohydrates, lipids and proteins.

- <u>metabolic processes</u> — such as making larger molecules from smaller ones (e.g. proteins from amino acids),
- <u>contracting muscles</u> (in animals),
- <u>maintaining</u> a steady <u>body temperature</u> (in mammals and birds).

4) Because energy is transferred <u>to the environment</u>, respiration is an <u>exothermic reaction</u>. Some of this energy is transferred by <u>heating</u>.

5) There are <u>two types</u> of respiration, <u>aerobic</u> and <u>anaerobic</u>.

Aerobic Respiration Needs Plenty of Oxygen

1) <u>Aerobic respiration</u> is what happens when there's <u>plenty of oxygen</u> available.
2) <u>Aerobic</u> just means "<u>with oxygen</u>" and it's the most efficient way to transfer <u>energy</u> from <u>glucose</u>.
3) This type of respiration goes on <u>all the time</u> in <u>plants</u> and <u>animals</u>. Here's the <u>equation</u>:

glucose + oxygen ⟶ carbon dioxide + water

$$C_6H_{12}O_6 + 6O_2 \longrightarrow 6CO_2 + 6H_2O$$

This is the reverse of the photosynthesis equation (see page 87).

Section 8 — Exchange and Transport in Animals

Respiration

Anaerobic Respiration Doesn't Use Oxygen At All

1) When you do really <u>vigorous exercise</u> your body can't supply enough <u>oxygen</u> to your muscles for aerobic respiration — even though your <u>heart rate</u> and <u>breathing rate</u> increase as much as they can. Your muscles have to start <u>respiring anaerobically</u> as well.

2) <u>An</u>aerobic just means "<u>without</u> oxygen". It transfers much <u>less energy</u> than aerobic respiration so it's much less <u>efficient</u>. In anaerobic respiration, the glucose is only <u>partially</u> broken down, and <u>lactic acid</u> is also produced.

3) The <u>lactic acid</u> builds up in the muscles — it gets <u>painful</u> and leads to <u>cramp</u>.

4) This is the <u>word equation</u> for anaerobic respiration in <u>animals</u>:

$$\text{glucose} \longrightarrow \text{lactic acid}$$

Anaerobic Respiration in Plants is Slightly Different

1) <u>Plants</u> can respire <u>without oxygen</u> too, but they produce <u>ethanol</u> (alcohol) and CO_2 <u>instead</u> of lactic acid.

2) This is the <u>word equation</u> for anaerobic respiration in <u>plants</u>:

Fungi such as yeast also do anaerobic respiration like this.

$$\text{glucose} \longrightarrow \text{ethanol} + \text{carbon dioxide}$$

Respiration releases energy from glucose

Remember, anaerobic respiration has <u>different products</u> to aerobic respiration and transfers much <u>less energy</u>, as well as taking place without oxygen. Both aerobic and anaerobic respiration are <u>exothermic</u> though — don't forget that. You may need to compare the two in your exam.

Q1   A scientist measured the concentration of lactic acid in her blood after walking for 5 minutes. She also measured the concentration of lactic acid in her blood after running for 5 minutes. Suggest why the concentration of lactic acid in her blood was higher after running than after walking.   [3 marks]

Q1 Video Solution

Investigating Respiration

The rate at which an organism respires will change depending on different factors. You can do experiments to see how these factors affect the rate of respiration.

You Can Measure the Rate of Respiration Using a Respirometer

In aerobic respiration, organisms use up oxygen from the air. By measuring the amount of oxygen consumed by organisms in a given time, you can calculate their rate of respiration.

Here's an experiment which uses woodlice, a water bath and a piece of equipment called a respirometer. It allows you to measure the effect of temperature on the rate of respiration of the woodlice. (You could use germinating peas or beans instead of woodlice. Germinating seeds respire to provide energy for growth.)

1) Some soda lime granules are added to two test tubes. The soda lime absorbs the CO_2 produced by the respiring woodlice in the experiment. (You could use cotton wool soaked in a few drops of potassium hydroxide solution to absorb the CO_2 produced by the woodlice instead.)

Soda lime is corrosive. Safety goggles and gloves are worn when handling it to protect the eyes and skin.

2) A ball of cotton wool is placed above the soda lime in each tube. Woodlice are placed on top of the cotton wool in one tube. Glass beads with the same mass as the woodlice are used in the control tube. (There's more on controls on page 6.)

3) The respirometer is then set up as shown in the diagram.

4) The syringe is used to set the fluid in the manometer to a known level.

5) The apparatus is then left for a set period of time in a water bath set to 15 °C.

6) During this time, there'll be a decrease in the volume of the air in the test tube containing the woodlice. This is because the woodlice use up oxygen in the tube as they respire. (The CO_2 they produce is absorbed by the soda lime so it doesn't affect the experiment.)

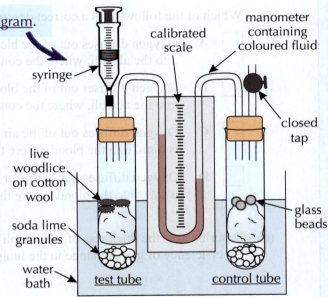

7) The decrease in volume reduces the pressure in the tube, causing the coloured liquid in the manometer to move towards the test tube containing the woodlice.

8) The distance moved by the liquid in a given time is measured. From this you can calculate the volume of oxygen taken in by the woodlice per minute — this is the rate of respiration in, e.g. $cm^3\ min^{-1}$.

9) Repeat steps 1-8 with the water bath set at different temperatures, e.g. 20 °C and 25 °C. This will allow you to see how changing the temperature affects the rate of respiration.

Any live animals you use in this experiment should be treated ethically (e.g. it's important not to leave woodlice in a respirometer for too long, or they may run out of oxygen and die). There's more about treating organisms ethically on page 386.

You should make sure that the woodlice can't come into contact with the soda lime too.

Section 8 — Exchange and Transport in Animals

Warm-Up and Exam Questions

There's no better way to practise exam questions than doing... err... practice exam questions. Hang on, what's this I see...

Warm-Up Questions

1) Why do multicellular organisms need specialised exchange surfaces?
2) Give two examples of how animals use the energy transferred by respiration.
3) Name two substances that diffuse out from cells into the bloodstream.
4) What are the reactants of aerobic respiration?
5) Name a piece of scientific equipment that can be used to measure the rate of respiration in living organisms.

Exam Questions

1   The lungs contain millions of air sacs, called alveoli, which are adapted for the efficient exchange of oxygen and carbon dioxide in respiration. *(Grade 4-6)*

  (a) Which of the following is a correct description of the diffusion of oxygen in gas exchange?

     ☐ A Oxygen diffuses out of the blood, where the concentration of oxygen is high, into the alveoli, where the concentration of oxygen is low.

     ☐ B Oxygen diffuses out of the blood, where the concentration of oxygen is low, into the alveoli, where the concentration of oxygen is high

     ☐ C Oxygen diffuses out of the air in the alveoli, where the concentration of oxygen is high, into the blood, where the concentration of oxygen is low.

     ☐ D Oxygen diffuses out of the air in the alveoli, where the concentration of oxygen is low, into the blood, where the concentration of oxygen is high.

[1 mark]

  (b) Describe how the thickness of the alveoli walls improves the efficiency of gas exchange in the lungs.

[2 marks]

2   Respiration is a process carried out by all living cells. It can take place aerobically or anaerobically. *(Grade 4-6)*

  (a) State the purpose of respiration.

[1 mark]

  (b) Give **two** differences between aerobic and anaerobic respiration.

[2 marks]

  (c) Write the word equation for anaerobic respiration in humans.

[2 marks]

Section 8 — Exchange and Transport in Animals

Circulatory System — Blood

Blood is a **tissue**. One of its jobs is to act as a huge **transport** system. There are four main things in blood...

Red Blood Cells Carry Oxygen

1) The job of red blood cells (also called erythrocytes) is to carry oxygen from the lungs to all the cells in the body.

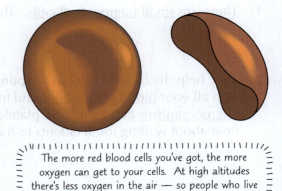

2) They have a biconcave disc shape (in other words, they look a bit like a jam doughnut that's being pressed in at the top and bottom) to give a large surface area for absorbing oxygen.

The more red blood cells you've got, the more oxygen can get to your cells. At high altitudes there's less oxygen in the air — so people who live there produce more red blood cells to compensate.

3) They don't have a nucleus — this allows more room to carry oxygen.

4) They contain a red pigment called haemoglobin, which contains iron.

5) In the lungs, haemoglobin binds to oxygen to become oxyhaemoglobin. In body tissues, the reverse happens — oxyhaemoglobin splits up into haemoglobin and oxygen, to release oxygen to the cells.

White Blood Cells Defend Against Infection

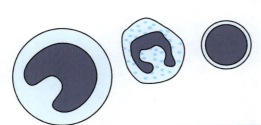

1) Phagocytes are white blood cells that can change shape to engulf (gobble up) unwelcome microorganisms — this is called phagocytosis.

Unlike red blood cells, white blood cells do have a nucleus.

2) Lymphocytes are white blood cells that produce antibodies against microorganisms (see p.75). Some also produce antitoxins to neutralise any toxins produced by the microorganisms.

3) When you have an infection, your white blood cells multiply to fight it off — so a blood test will show a high white blood cell count.

Section 8 — Exchange and Transport in Animals

Circulatory System — Blood

Platelets Help Blood Clot

1) These are small fragments of cells. They have no nucleus.

2) They help the blood to clot at a wound — to stop all your blood pouring out and to stop microorganisms getting in. (So platelets basically float about waiting for accidents to happen.)

3) Lack of platelets can cause excessive bleeding and bruising.

Plasma is the Liquid That Carries Everything in Blood

This is a pale, straw-coloured liquid which carries just about everything:

1) Red and white blood cells and platelets.

2) Nutrients like glucose and amino acids. These are the soluble products of digestion which are absorbed from the gut and taken to the cells of the body.

3) Carbon dioxide from the organs to the lungs.

4) Urea, from the liver to the kidneys.

5) Hormones.

6) Proteins.

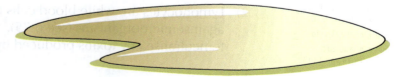

7) Antibodies and antitoxins produced by the white blood cells.

Circulatory System — Blood Vessels

Blood needs a good set of 'tubes' to carry it round the body. Here's a page on the different types:

Blood Vessels are Designed for Their Function

There are three different types of blood vessel:
1) ARTERIES — these carry the blood away from the heart.
2) CAPILLARIES — these are involved in the exchange of materials at the tissues.
3) VEINS — these carry the blood to the heart.

Arteries Carry Blood Under Pressure

1) The heart pumps the blood out at high pressure so the artery walls are strong and elastic.
2) The walls are thick compared to the size of the hole down the middle (the "lumen").
3) They contain thick layers of muscle to make them strong, and elastic fibres to allow them to stretch and spring back.

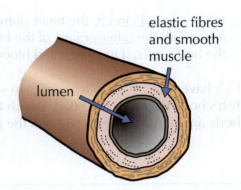
elastic fibres and smooth muscle
lumen

Capillaries are Really Small

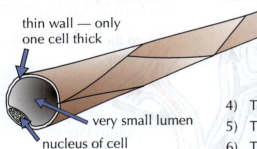
thin wall — only one cell thick
very small lumen
nucleus of cell

1) Arteries branch into capillaries.
2) Capillaries are really tiny — too small to see.
3) They are very narrow, so they can squeeze into the gaps between cells. This means they can carry the blood really close to every cell in the body to exchange substances with them.
4) They have permeable walls, so substances can diffuse in and out.
5) They supply food and oxygen, and take away waste like CO_2.
6) Their walls are usually only one cell thick. This increases the rate of diffusion by decreasing the distance over which it occurs.

Veins Take Blood Back to the Heart

1) Capillaries eventually join up to form veins.
2) The blood is at lower pressure in the veins so the walls don't need to be as thick as artery walls.
3) They have a bigger lumen than arteries to help the blood flow despite the lower pressure.
4) They also have valves to help keep the blood flowing in the right direction.

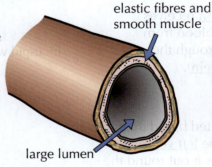
elastic fibres and smooth muscle
large lumen

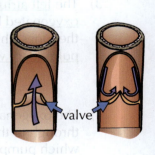
valve

REVISION TIP

Blood vessels carry blood around the body...
It's easy to forget which vessels carry blood where. Remember, arteries carry the blood away from the heart, veins carry the blood back into the heart and capillaries carry blood close to cells.

Section 8 — Exchange and Transport in Animals

Circulatory System — The Heart

The **heart** plays a major role in the circulatory system. It is needed to **pump the blood** through the blood vessels so that material can be **transported** to and from the cells.

Mammals Have a Double Circulatory System

1) This means that the heart pumps blood around the body in two circuits.

   In the first circuit, the heart pumps deoxygenated blood to the lungs to take in oxygen. Oxygenated blood then returns to the heart.

   In the second circuit, the heart pumps oxygenated blood around all the other organs of the body to deliver oxygen to the body cells. Deoxygenated blood then returns to the heart.

2) Fish have a single circulatory system — deoxygenated blood from the fish's body travels to the heart, which then pumps it right round the body again in a single circuit (via the gills where it picks up oxygen).

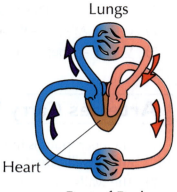

The Heart Pumps Blood Through the Blood Vessels

The mammalian heart has four chambers and four major blood vessels.

A fish's heart only has two chambers.

1) The right atrium of the heart receives deoxygenated blood from the body (through the vena cava).

2) The deoxygenated blood moves through to the right ventricle, which pumps it to the lungs (via the pulmonary artery).

3) The left atrium receives oxygenated blood from the lungs (through the pulmonary vein).

4) The oxygenated blood then moves through to the left ventricle, which pumps it out round the whole body (via the aorta).

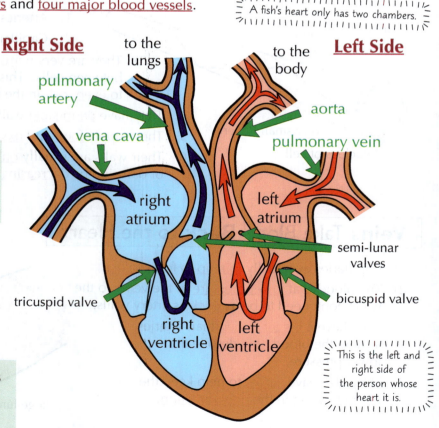

Blue = deoxygenated blood. Red = oxygenated blood.

This is the left and right side of the person whose heart it is.

The left ventricle has a much thicker wall than the right ventricle. It needs more muscle because it has to pump blood around the whole body at high pressure, whereas the right ventricle only has to pump it to the lungs. Valves prevent the backflow of blood in the heart.

Circulatory System — The Heart

You Can Calculate How Much Blood is Pumped Every Minute

1) Cardiac output is the total volume of blood pumped by a ventricle every minute.

2) You can calculate it using this equation:

> cardiac output = heart rate × stroke volume
>
> in $cm^3\ min^{-1}$ — in beats per minute (bpm) — in cm^3

3) The heart rate is the number of beats per minute (bpm).

4) The stroke volume is the volume of blood pumped by one ventricle each time it contracts.

5) You might be asked to find the stroke volume or the heart rate in the exam instead of the cardiac output — if so, you can just rearrange the equation above. You can use this formula triangle to help you:

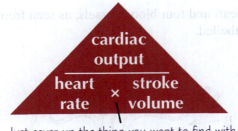

Just cover up the thing you want to find with your finger and write down what's left showing.

EXAMPLE

What is the heart rate of a person with an average stroke volume of 72 cm^3 and a cardiac output of 5420 $cm^3\ min^{-1}$?

1) Rearrange the formula to find heart rate.

   Heart rate (bpm) = cardiac output ($cm^3\ min^{-1}$) ÷ stroke volume (cm^3)

2) Fill in the values and work out the answer.

   Heart rate (bpm) = 5420 ÷ 72
   = 75.27...
   = **75 bpm (2 s.f.)**

   For more on rounding to significant figures, see page 9.

Make sure you learn the equation...

If you know the volume of blood pumped during each ventricle contraction (stroke volume), and how many contractions there are a minute (heart rate), you can multiply them to find the total volume of blood pumped each minute (cardiac output).

Q1 Calculate the stroke volume for a heart rate of 67 bpm and a cardiac output of 4221 $cm^3\ min^{-1}$.

[2 marks]

Q1 Video Solution

Warm-Up and Exam Questions

Who knew the circulatory system had so many different parts, with so many different functions? Time to check you remember them all...

Warm-Up Questions

1) What do veins do?
2) Describe the purpose of platelets in blood.
3) Give three things that are carried in blood plasma.
4) Give the equation for calculating cardiac output.

Exam Questions

1   Blood is a tissue which transports important components, such as red blood cells, around the body.

(a) Name the other main type of blood cell, and state its function.

[2 marks]

(b) Blood cells are carried in the bloodstream inside blood vessels.
Capillaries are one type of blood vessel.

State and explain **two** ways that the structure of a capillary enables it to carry out its function.

[4 marks]

2   **Figure 1** shows the human heart and four blood vessels, as seen from the front. The left ventricle has been labelled.

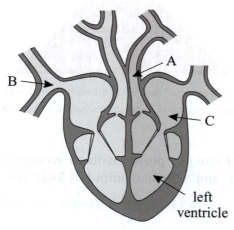

Figure 1

(a) Name the parts labelled A, B and C.

[1 mark]

(b) Describe the function of the left ventricle.

[1 mark]

(c) Give the function of the valves in the heart.

[1 mark]

(d) Describe the passage of deoxygenated blood from the body through the heart to reach the lungs.

[4 marks]

Section 8 — Exchange and Transport in Animals

Section 9 — Ecosystems and Material Cycles

Ecosystems and Interactions Between Organisms

Organisms live together in **ecosystems**. They depend on other **organisms** in their **ecosystem** for **survival**.

Ecosystems are Organised into Different Levels

Ecosystems have different levels of organisation:

Level	Definition
Individual	A single organism.
Population	All the organisms of one species in a habitat.
Community	All the organisms of different species living in a habitat.
Ecosystem	A community of organisms along with all the non-living (abiotic) conditions (see next page).

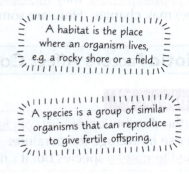

A habitat is the place where an organism lives, e.g. a rocky shore or a field.

A species is a group of similar organisms that can reproduce to give fertile offspring.

Organisms in a Community Are Interdependent

1) Organisms depend on each other for things like food and shelter in order to survive and reproduce. This is known as interdependence. It means that a change in the population of one species can have huge knock on effects for other species in the same community.

2) Mutualism is a relationship between two organisms, from which both organisms benefit. E.g. bees and flowering plants have a mutualistic relationship. When bees visit flowers to get nectar, pollen is transferred to their bodies. The bees then spread the pollen to other plants when they land on their flowers. The bees get food and the plants get help reproducing. Everyone's a winner.

3) Parasites live very closely with a host species (e.g. in or on them). The parasite takes what it needs to survive, but the host doesn't benefit. E.g. fleas are parasites of mammals such as dogs. Fleas feed on their host's blood, but don't offer anything in return.

Interdependence is the key to communities

Because all organisms in a community share the same habitat, different species are often dependent on each other. Some species rely on each other so much that one couldn't survive without the other.

Ecosystems and Interactions Between Organisms

The environment in which organisms live **changes** all the time. The things that change are either *abiotic* (non-living) or *biotic* (living) factors. These can have a big **effect** on a community...

Environmental Changes **Affect Communities** in **Different Ways**

The environment in which plants and animals live changes all the time. These changes are caused by abiotic (non-living) and biotic (living) factors. They will affect communities in different ways — for some species population size may increase, for others it may decrease, or the distribution of populations (where they live) may change. Here are some examples of the effects of changes in abiotic and biotic factors:

Abiotic Factors Affect Communities...

Temperature

E.g. the distribution of bird species in Germany is probably changing because of a rise in average temperature. For instance, the European Bee-Eater bird is a Mediterranean species but it's now present in parts of Germany.

Amount of Water

E.g. daisies grow best in soils that are slightly damp. If the soil becomes waterlogged or too dry, the population of daisies will decrease.

Light Intensity

E.g. as trees grow and provide more shade, grasses may be replaced by fungi (or mosses, etc.) which are better able to cope with the lower light intensity.

Levels of Pollutants

E.g. lichen are unable to survive if the concentration of sulfur dioxide (an air pollutant) is too high.

...and so do **Biotic** Factors

Competition

Organisms compete with other species (and members of their own species) for the same resources. E.g. red and grey squirrels live in the same habitat and eat the same food. Competition with the grey squirrels for these resources in some areas means there's not enough food for the reds — the population of red squirrels is decreasing, partly as a result of this.

Predation

E.g. if the number of lions (predators) decreases then the number of gazelles (their prey) might increase because fewer of them will be eaten by the lions.

Investigating Ecosystems — PRACTICAL

*This is where the **fun** starts. Studying **ecosystems** gives you the chance to **rummage around** in bushes, get your hands **dirty** and look at some **real organisms**, living in the **wild**.*

Use Quadrats to Study the Distribution of Small Organisms

A quadrat is a square frame enclosing a known area, e.g. 1 m². To compare how common an organism is in two sample areas just follow these simple steps:

1) Place a 1 m² quadrat on the ground at a random point within the first sample area. You could do this by dividing the sample area into a grid and using a random number generator to pick coordinates to place your quadrats at. This will help to make sure the results you get are representative of the whole sample area.
2) Count all the organisms you're interested in within the quadrat.
3) Repeat steps 1 and 2 lots of times.
4) Work out the mean number of organisms per quadrat within the first sample area — this is the total number of organisms you counted divided by the number of quadrats you placed.

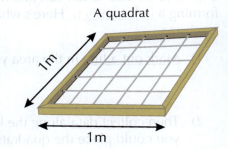

A quadrat

EXAMPLE

Anna counted the number of daisies in 7 quadrats that she placed at random in her first sample area. She recorded the following results: 18, 20, 22, 23, 23, 23, 25.

Here the MEAN is: $\dfrac{\text{TOTAL number of organisms}}{\text{NUMBER of quadrats}} = \dfrac{154}{7} =$ **22 daisies per quadrat**

5) Repeat steps 1 to 4 in the second sample area.
6) Finally, compare the two means. E.g. you might find a mean of 2 daisies per m² in one area, and 22 daisies per m² (lots more) in another area.

You Can Also Estimate the Population Size of an Organism in an Area

1) To work out the population size of an organism in a sample area, first you need to use a quadrat to find the mean number of organisms per m². (If you use a quadrat with an area of 1 m², this is the same as the mean number of organisms per quadrat, as shown above.)
2) Then just multiply the mean by the total area of your sample area:

EXAMPLE

Students used quadrats, each with an area of 0.5 m², to randomly sample daisies in a field. They found a mean of 10 daisies per quadrat. The area of the field was 800 m². Estimate the population of daisies in the field.

1) Work out the mean number of organisms per m².
   $1 \div 0.5 = 2$
   $2 \times 10 = 20$ daisies per m²

   Because the quadrat is only 0.5 m², first you need to work out how many quadrats make up 1 m².

2) Then multiply the mean by the total area (in m²) of the habitat.
   20×800
   = **16 000 daisies on the field**

It's key that you put your quadrat down in a random place...

...that way you won't influence your results, and they'll be representative of the whole area.

Q1 A 1200 m² field was randomly sampled for buttercups using a quadrat with an area of 0.25 m². A mean of 0.75 buttercups were found per quadrat. Estimate the total population of buttercups. [2 marks]

Q1 Video Solution

 **Investigating Ecosystems**

*So, now you think you've learnt **all about** quadrats. Well **hold on** — there's more **fun** to be had.*

Use Belt Transects to Study Distribution Along a Gradient

Sometimes abiotic factors will change across a habitat. The change is known as a gradient. You can use quadrats to help find out how organisms (like plants) are distributed along a gradient. For example, how a species becomes more or less common as you move from an area of shade (near a hedge at the edge of a field) to an area of full sun (the middle of the field). The quadrats are laid out along a line, forming a belt transect. Here's what you do:

1) Mark out a line in the area you want to study, e.g. from the hedge to the middle of the field.

2) Then collect data along the line using quadrats placed next to each other. If your transect is long, you could place the quadrats at regular intervals (e.g. every 2 metres) instead. Collect data by counting all the organisms of the species you're interested in, or by estimating percentage cover. This means estimating the percentage area of a quadrat covered by a particular type of organism.

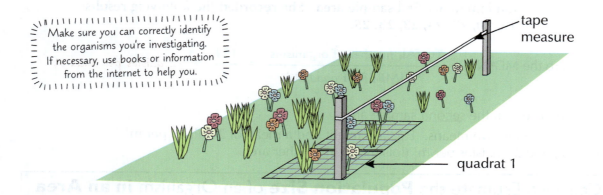

3) You could also record other data, such as the mean height of the plants you're counting or the abiotic factors in each quadrat (e.g. you could use a light meter to measure the light intensity).

4) Repeat steps 1 and 2 several times, then find the mean number of organisms or mean percentage cover for each quadrat.

5) Plot graphs to see if the changing abiotic factor is correlated with a change in the distribution of the species you're studying.

Organisms have a relationship with their environment

You could be asked to interpret some data showing the relationship between the distribution of a species and an abiotic factor. But remember, just because two things are correlated, it doesn't always mean a change in one is causing the change in the other. There might be other factors involved.

Section 9 — Ecosystems and Material Cycles

Warm-Up and Exam Questions

This Ecosystems and Material Cycles section's a long one — so make sure you've got these first few pages stuck in your head before moving on and learning the rest. These questions should help you.

Warm-Up Questions

1) What is the correct scientific term for all the organisms of different species living in a habitat?
2) What is an ecosystem?
3) Give four examples of abiotic factors that could affect communities.

Exam Questions

PRACTICAL

1   Some students investigated the distribution of poppies across a field next to a wood. A sketch of the area is shown in **Figure 1**.

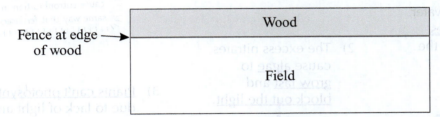

Figure 1

The students' results are shown in **Figure 2**.

Number of poppies per m²	5	9	14	19	26
Distance from wood (m)	2	4	6	8	10

Figure 2

(a) Describe how the students could have used quadrats to obtain the results in **Figure 2**.

[3 marks]

(b) Describe the trend in the results in **Figure 2**.

[1 mark]

2   Cutthroat trout are present in lakes in Yellowstone National Park. In the last few decades, lake trout have been introduced to the lakes. However, lake trout have emerged as predators and have been eating the cutthroat trout.

(a) Suggest and explain how the introduction of the lake trout might cause the population sizes of both species of fish to fluctuate over time.

[4 marks]

(b) Give **one** other biotic factor that could affect the size of the cutthroat trout population.

[1 mark]

Section 9 — Ecosystems and Material Cycles

Human Impacts on Biodiversity

However you look at it, **humans** have a **big impact** on the environment, including on **biodiversity**.

Human Activities Affect Biodiversity

1) Biodiversity is the variety of living organisms in an ecosystem.
2) Human interactions within ecosystems often affect biodiversity.
3) Sometimes we have a positive impact on biodiversity (e.g. by carrying out conservation schemes or reforestation, see page 128), but we often have a negative effect. Here are some examples:

Fertilisers can Leach into Water and Cause Eutrophication

Nitrates are put onto fields as fertilisers (see p.135). If too much fertiliser is applied and it rains afterwards, nitrates easily find their way into rivers and lakes. The result is eutrophication — an excess of nutrients in water — which can lead to the death of many of the species present in the water, reducing the biodiversity of the habitat. Here's how it happens:

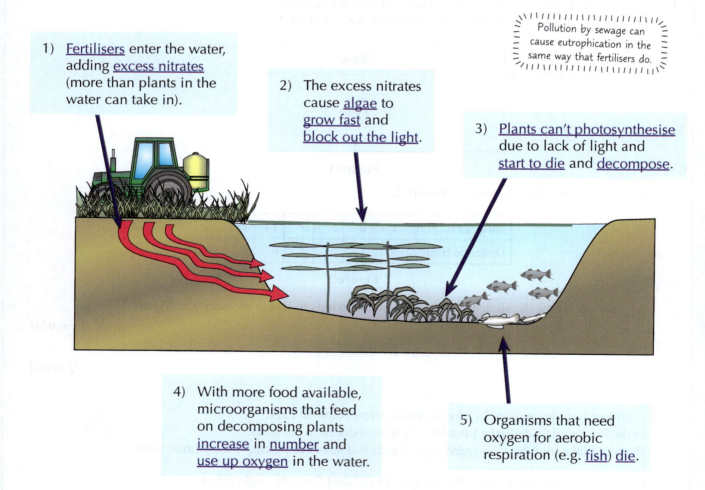

Pollution by sewage can cause eutrophication in the same way that fertilisers do.

1) Fertilisers enter the water, adding excess nitrates (more than plants in the water can take in).
2) The excess nitrates cause algae to grow fast and block out the light.
3) Plants can't photosynthesise due to lack of light and start to die and decompose.
4) With more food available, microorganisms that feed on decomposing plants increase in number and use up oxygen in the water.
5) Organisms that need oxygen for aerobic respiration (e.g. fish) die.

Fertilisers need to be used responsibly

Unfortunately, it's difficult to stop using fertilisers altogether because farmers worldwide are under pressure to produce enough food — and using fertilisers helps them improve their crop yields. As you'll see on the next page our demand for fish is also affecting the biodiversity of our lakes and seas.

Human Impacts on Biodiversity

Fish can be Farmed in Holding Nets in Open Water

Fish farms in areas of open water (e.g. lakes or the sea) can reduce biodiversity in the surrounding area. It can happen like this:

1) Food is added to the nets to feed the fish, which produce huge amounts of waste. Both the food and the waste can leak into the open water, causing eutrophication and the death of wild species.
2) Fish farms in open water often act as a breeding ground for large numbers of parasites. These parasites can get out of the farm and infect wild animals, sometimes killing them.
3) Predators (e.g. sea lions) are attracted to the nets and can become trapped in them and die.
4) Sometimes farmed fish can escape into the wild, which can cause problems for wild populations of indigenous species (see below).

Sometimes fish are farmed in large tanks rather than in open water nets. These farms are low in biodiversity because often only one species is farmed, the tanks are often kept free of plants and predators, and any parasites and microorganisms are usually killed.

The Introduction of Non-Indigenous Species Can Reduce Biodiversity

1) A non-indigenous species is one that doesn't naturally occur in an area. They can be introduced intentionally (e.g. for food or hunting) or unintentionally (e.g. as a stowaway in international cargo). The introduction of a non-indigenous species may cause problems for indigenous (native) species.

2) Non-indigenous species compete with indigenous species for resources like food and shelter. Sometimes, they are better at getting these resources and out-compete the indigenous species, which decrease in number and eventually die out. For example, signal crayfish were introduced to the UK for food, but they prey on and out-compete many indigenous river species, reducing biodiversity.

3) Non-indigenous species sometimes also bring new diseases to a habitat. These often infect and kill lots of indigenous species, reducing the habitat's biodiversity.

Adding a new species to a habitat can reduce biodiversity

You'd think that introducing a new species into an ecosystem would increase biodiversity. But when they out-compete the indigenous species, the numbers of their competitors decline. And since many organisms in an ecosystem are interdependent (see p.121), this can have big knock-on effects in the community.

Section 9 — Ecosystems and Material Cycles

Conservation and Biodiversity

*Trying to conserve biodiversity can be **tricky**, given all the **challenges** that face different ecosystems (many of which are a result of human activities). There are **benefits** of doing this though, so it's **pretty worthwhile**...*

There Are Lots of Ways to Conserve and Maintain Biodiversity

Lots of human activities can reduce biodiversity (see the previous two pages). However, there are plenty of things that we can do to increase biodiversity. Here are a couple of examples...

Reforestation Can Increase Biodiversity in Deforested Areas

1) Reforestation is when land where a forest previously stood is replanted to form a new forest.

2) Forests generally have a high biodiversity because they contain a wide variety of trees and other plants, and these provide food and shelter for lots of different animal species.

3) Deforestation reduces this biodiversity by removing the trees (either by chopping them down or burning them). Reforestation helps to restore it.

4) Reforestation programmes need to be carefully planned to maximise positive effects and minimise negative ones. For example, replanting a forest with a variety of tree species will result in a higher biodiversity than replanting using only a single type of tree.

Conservation Schemes Protect At-Risk Species

1) Conservation schemes can help to protect biodiversity by preventing species from dying out.
2) Conservation methods include:

   1) Protecting a species' natural habitat (so that individuals have a place to live).
   2) Protecting species in safe areas outside of their natural habitat (e.g. animals can be protected in zoos) and introducing captive breeding programmes to increase numbers.
   3) The use of seed banks to store and distribute the seeds of rare and endangered plants.

It's not all lost — biodiversity can be increased

There are ways in which we can improve the biodiversity of an area — but the scale of efforts to maintain or increase biodiversity often isn't large enough to combat the huge negative impact of other human activities.

Section 9 — Ecosystems and Material Cycles

Conservation and Biodiversity

*The last few pages have been all about what **biodiversity** is, how humans **affect biodiversity** and how we might go about **maintaining** it. But why is it **important** for us to maintain biodiversity? Read on...*

Maintaining Biodiversity Has Many Benefits

There are lots of benefits to both wildlife and humans of maintaining biodiversity on a local and global scale.

1) Protecting the human food supply — over-fishing has greatly reduced fish stocks in the world's oceans. Conservation programmes can ensure that future generations will have fish to eat.

2) Ensuring minimal damage to food chains — if one species becomes extinct it will affect all the organisms that feed on and are eaten by that species, so the whole food chain is affected. This means conserving one species may help others to survive.

3) Providing future medicines — many of the medicines we use today come from plants. Undiscovered plant species may contain new medicinal chemicals. If these plants are allowed to become extinct, e.g. through rainforest destruction, we could miss out on valuable medicines.

4) Cultural aspects — individual species may be important in a nation's or an area's cultural heritage, e.g. the bald eagle is being conserved in the USA as it is regarded as a national symbol.

5) Ecotourism — people are drawn to visit beautiful, unspoilt landscapes with a variety of animal and plant species. Ecotourism (environmentally-friendly tourism) helps bring money into biodiverse areas where conservation work is taking place.

6) Providing new jobs — things such as ecotourism, conservation schemes and reforestation schemes provide employment opportunities for local people.

Biodiversity is important for us all

In some way or another the loss of biodiversity affects everyone — after all we are part of the biodiversity on earth. Make sure you know and can explain the benefits of maintaining biodiversity.

Section 9 — Ecosystems and Material Cycles

Warm-Up and Exam Questions

You can't just stare at these pages and expect all of the information to go in. Do these questions to see how well you really know the stuff. If you get stuck you can always go back to the page for a quick recap.

Warm-Up Questions

1) What is biodiversity?
2) Explain how excess nitrates in water systems can lead to the death of fish living in the water.
3) How do conservation schemes affect biodiversity? Explain your answer.
4) Describe two ways that an open water fish farm can reduce the biodiversity of an area.

Exam Questions

1   Black rats were accidentally introduced into an island habitat by a tourist boat which visited the island. Local biologists are worried that the introduction of the non-indigenous rat species will have a negative impact on biodiversity.

Suggest and explain **two** ways that the introduction of black rats to the island could reduce biodiversity.

[4 marks]

2   A group of conservationists are working to replant the trees in an area of forest which has been badly damaged by a forest fire.

(a) There is a suggestion that the whole area should be replanted with white spruce, a tree species which will be cheap to plant.
Explain why only planting white spruce will result in low biodiversity.

[2 marks]

(b) Several years after the area was successfully reforested, the conservationists found a few individuals of an endangered small mammal species living in the forest. The conservationists want to protect the species. Suggest **one** way they could do this.

[1 mark]

3* Human activity has reduced the rainforest cover in Ecuador significantly. Deforestation has reduced biodiversity and endangered certain animal and plant species that are only found in Ecuador.

Some conservation schemes have been set up which employ local people to protect at-risk species found in the rainforest.

Discuss why conservation schemes like this may be beneficial.
In your answer you should include ideas about the potential benefits to plants and animals in the ecosystem, the people of Ecuador and people from other countries.

[6 marks]

Section 9 — Ecosystems and Material Cycles

The Carbon Cycle

Recycling may be a buzz word for us but it's old school for nature. All the **nutrients** in our environment are constantly being **recycled** — there's a nice balance between what **goes in** and what **goes out** again.

Materials are Constantly Recycled in an Ecosystem

1) An ecosystem is all the organisms living in an area, as well as all the non-living conditions, e.g. soil quality, availability of water, temperature.
2) Materials are recycled through both the living (biotic) and non-living (abiotic) components of ecosystems:

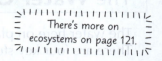
There's more on ecosystems on page 121.

1) Living things are made of elements they take from the environment, e.g. plants take in carbon and oxygen from the air and nitrogen from the soil.
2) They turn these elements into the complex compounds (carbohydrates, proteins and fats) that make up living organisms. Elements are passed along food chains when animals eat the plants and each other.
3) The elements are recycled — waste products and dead organisms are broken down by decomposers (usually microorganisms) and the elements in them are returned to the soil or air, ready to be taken in by new plants and put back into the food chain.

The Carbon Cycle Shows How Carbon is Recycled

Carbon is an important element in the materials that living things are made from. But there's only a fixed amount of carbon in the world. This means it's constantly recycled:

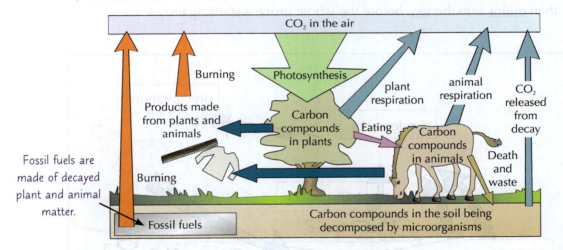

CO_2 is carbon dioxide.

This diagram isn't half as bad as it looks. Learn these important points:

1) There's only one arrow going down from CO_2 in the air. The whole thing is 'powered' by photosynthesis. Green plants use the carbon from CO_2 to make carbohydrates, fats and proteins.
2) Eating passes the carbon compounds in the plants along to animals in a food chain.
3) Both plant and animal respiration while the organisms are alive releases CO_2 back into the air.
4) Plants and animals eventually die and decompose, or are killed and turned into useful products.
5) When plants and animals decompose they're broken down by microorganisms, like bacteria and fungi. These decomposers release CO_2 into the air by respiration, as they break down the material.
6) Some useful plant and animal products, e.g. wood and fossil fuels, are burned (combustion). This process also releases CO_2 back into the air.
7) Decomposition of materials means that habitats can be maintained for the organisms that live there, e.g. nutrients are returned to the soil, and waste material, such as dead leaves, doesn't just pile up.

Section 9 — Ecosystems and Material Cycles

The Water Cycle

The **amount** of water on Earth is pretty much **constant** — but **where** it is changes.
Water moves between **rivers**, **lakes**, **oceans** and the **atmosphere** in what's known as the **water cycle**.

The Water Cycle Means Water is Endlessly Recycled

The water here on planet Earth is constantly recycled.
There are four key steps you should understand:

1) Energy from the Sun makes water evaporate from the land and sea, turning it into water vapour. Water also evaporates from plants — this is known as transpiration (see p.92).

As warm water vapour rises, it cools down and forms clouds.

2) The warm water vapour is carried upwards (as warm air rises). When it gets higher up it cools and condenses to form clouds.

3) Water falls from the clouds as precipitation (usually rain, but sometimes snow or hail) onto land, where it provides fresh water for plants and animals.

4) It then drains into the sea, before the whole process starts again.

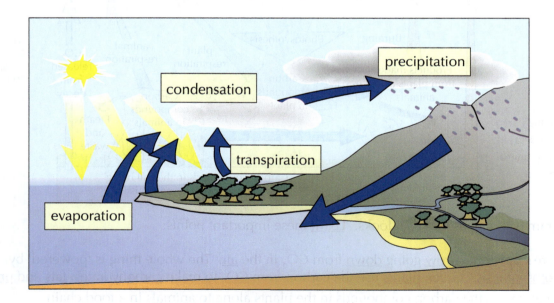

If it wasn't for the water cycle constantly recycling water, we'd quickly run out of the stuff. That would be really bad news because all living things on our planet need water to survive.

Evaporation, transpiration, condensation, precipitation

The water cycle is pretty straightforward, so there's absolutely no excuse not to learn it inside out. It's important to remember that it's a cycle — a continuous process with no beginning or end.

Q1   Explain how water from the sea can eventually fall as rain.   [4 marks]

The Water Cycle

A **Drought** Occurs When There **Isn't Enough Precipitation**

Droughts can cause big problems, partly because we rely on precipitation to get fresh water for drinking (sea water is too salty). Luckily, in times of drought, there are methods we can use to produce potable water (water that's suitable for drinking). One of these methods is called desalination.

Desalination Can Be Used to Produce **Potable Water** From **Salt Water**

Desalination removes salts (mineral ions) from salt water (e.g. sea water). There are a few different methods of desalination. One really simple method is thermal desalination:

1) Salt water is boiled in a large enclosed vessel, so that the water evaporates.
2) The steam rises to the top of the vessel, but the salts stay at the bottom.
3) The steam then travels down a pipe from the top of the vessel and cools and condenses back into pure water.

Reverse Osmosis is a Widely Used Modern Method of **Desalination**

1) Osmosis is the net movement of water across a partially permeable membrane, from an area of HIGHER water concentration to an area of LOWER water concentration (see page 33).
2) The higher the salt concentration in a solution, the lower the water concentration, so you could also say that osmosis is the net movement of water from an area of LOWER salt concentration to an area of HIGHER salt concentration.
3) Reverse osmosis reverses this process to get rid of impurities in water. Here's how:

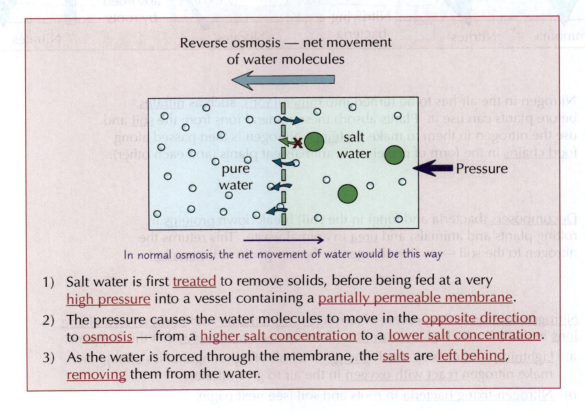

1) Salt water is first treated to remove solids, before being fed at a very high pressure into a vessel containing a partially permeable membrane.
2) The pressure causes the water molecules to move in the opposite direction to osmosis — from a higher salt concentration to a lower salt concentration.
3) As the water is forced through the membrane, the salts are left behind, removing them from the water.

Section 9 — Ecosystems and Material Cycles

The Nitrogen Cycle

*Just like carbon and water, nitrogen is constantly being **recycled**.*

Nitrogen is Recycled in the Nitrogen Cycle

1) The <u>atmosphere</u> contains <u>78% nitrogen gas</u>, N_2. This is <u>very unreactive</u> and so it can't be used <u>directly</u> by plants or animals. <u>Nitrogen</u> is <u>needed</u> for making <u>proteins</u> for growth, so living organisms have to get it somehow.

2) <u>Nitrogen</u> is passed back and forth between the air, living organisms and the soil in the <u>nitrogen cycle</u>. Here's a diagram showing how it works. (Don't worry, it's all explained in more detail below.)

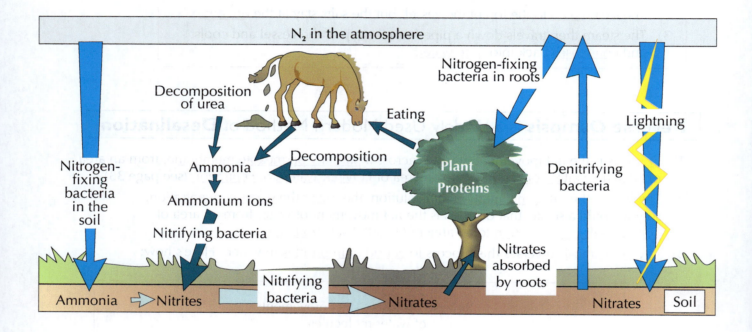

3) Nitrogen in the air has to be turned into <u>mineral ions</u>, such as <u>nitrates</u>, before plants can use it. Plants absorb these mineral ions from the <u>soil</u> and use the nitrogen in them to make <u>proteins</u>. Nitrogen is then passed along <u>food chains</u> in the form of proteins, as animals eat plants (and each other).

4) <u>Decomposers</u> (bacteria and fungi in the soil) break down <u>proteins</u> in rotting plants and animals, and <u>urea</u> in animal waste. This returns the nitrogen to the soil — so the nitrogen in these organisms is <u>recycled</u>.

5) <u>Nitrogen fixation</u> is the process of turning N_2 <u>from the air</u> into <u>nitrogen-containing ions</u> in the soil which <u>plants can use</u>. There are <u>two main ways</u> that this happens:
   a) <u>Lightning</u> — there's so much <u>energy</u> in a bolt of lightning that it's enough to make nitrogen <u>react with oxygen</u> in the air to give nitrates.
   b) <u>Nitrogen-fixing bacteria</u> in roots and soil (see next page).

Section 9 — Ecosystems and Material Cycles

The Nitrogen Cycle

6) There are <u>four</u> different types of <u>bacteria</u> involved in the nitrogen cycle:

> 1) <u>DECOMPOSERS</u> — decompose <u>proteins</u> and <u>urea</u> and turn them into <u>ammonia</u>. Ammonia forms <u>ammonium ions</u> in solution that plants can use.
> 2) <u>NITRIFYING BACTERIA</u> — turn <u>ammonia</u> in decaying matter into <u>nitrites</u> and then into <u>nitrates</u>. Different species of nitrifying bacteria are responsible for producing nitrites and nitrates.
> 3) <u>NITROGEN-FIXING BACTERIA</u> — turn <u>atmospheric N_2</u> into <u>ammonia</u>, which forms <u>ammonium ions</u>.
> 4) <u>DENITRIFYING BACTERIA</u> — turn <u>nitrates</u> back into <u>N_2 gas</u>. This is of no benefit to living organisms. Denitrifying bacteria are often found in <u>waterlogged soils</u>.

7) Some <u>nitrogen-fixing bacteria</u> live in the <u>soil</u>. Others live in <u>nodules</u> on the roots of <u>legume plants</u> (e.g. peas and beans). When these plants <u>decompose</u>, the nitrogen <u>stored</u> in them and in their <u>nodules</u> is returned to the soil. Nitrogen-containing ions can also <u>leak out</u> of the nodules <u>during plant growth</u>. The plants have a <u>mutualistic relationship</u> (see page 121) with the bacteria — the bacteria get <u>food</u> (sugars) from the plant, and the plant gets <u>nitrogen-containing ions</u> from the bacteria to make into <u>proteins</u>.

Farmers Can Increase the Amount of Nitrates in the Soil

1) Like all plants, crops take up <u>nitrates</u> from the soil as they grow.
2) But crops are <u>harvested</u>, rather than being left to <u>die</u> and <u>decompose</u>, so the nitrogen they contain <u>isn't returned</u> to the soil.
3) Over time, the nitrogen content of the soil <u>decreases</u>, leading to <u>poor crop growth</u> and <u>deficiency diseases</u>.
4) So farmers have ways of increasing the amount of nitrates in the soil to help their crops <u>grow better</u>:

Crop Rotation

This is where, instead of growing the same crop in a field year after year, <u>different crops</u> are grown each year in a <u>cycle</u>. The cycle usually includes a <u>nitrogen-fixing</u> crop (e.g. peas or beans), which helps to put nitrates back into the soil for another crop to use the following year.

Fertilisers

Spreading <u>animal manure</u> or <u>compost</u> on fields <u>recycles</u> the nutrients left in plant and animal waste and returns them to the soil through <u>decomposition</u>. <u>Artificial fertilisers</u> containing <u>nitrates</u> (and other mineral ions needed by plants) can also be used, but these can be <u>expensive</u> and can cause <u>environmental problems</u> (see page 126).

Bacteria do a lot of the hard work in the nitrogen cycle

Different types of <u>bacteria</u> play <u>different roles</u> at <u>different points</u> in the <u>nitrogen cycle</u>. You definitely need to get your head around which type of bacteria does what.

Q1 Describe how the nitrogen compounds in dead leaves are turned into nitrates in the soil. [3 marks]

Warm-Up and Exam Questions

You know the drill, first some warm-up questions to ease you in, then the slightly trickier exam questions.

Warm-Up Questions

1) How is the carbon that is stored in fossil fuels returned to the atmosphere?
2) How are clouds formed in the water cycle?
3) Describe the role of nitrifying bacteria in the nitrogen cycle.
4) Explain why using nitrogen-containing fertilisers can be beneficial to farmers.

Exam Questions

1 Figure 1 shows a simplified version of part of the nitrogen cycle.

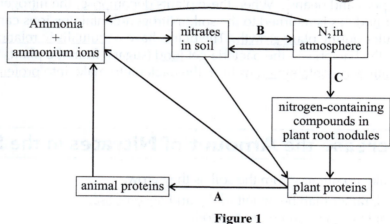

Figure 1

(a) Describe what is happening at stage **A**.

[1 mark]

(b) Name the type of bacteria responsible for stage **B**.

[1 mark]

(c) Name the type of bacteria responsible for stage **C**.

[1 mark]

2 Desalination can be used to produce drinking water from salt water.
Describe one method of desalination.

[4 marks]

3* An area of woodland is cleared to build a house. The tree trunks are taken away to be dried and used in furniture making. The smaller tree branches are used for firewood.
The green plants are piled up at the edge of the building site and left there.

Describe how carbon stored in the vegetation that has been cleared could be returned to the atmosphere.

[6 marks]

Section 9 — Ecosystems and Material Cycles

Revision Summary for Sections 6-9

Congratulations, you've made it to the end of Sections 6-9 — now it's time to test how much you've taken in...
- Try these questions and tick off each one when you get it right.
- When you're completely happy with a section, tick it off.

For even more practice, try the Retrieval Quizzes for Sections 6-9 — just scan these QR codes!

Section 6 — Plant Structures and Their Functions (p.87-95)

1) In what part of a cell does photosynthesis take place?
2) Describe how you could investigate the effect of light intensity on the rate of photosynthesis.
3) How are root hair cells adapted to their function?
4) By what process do phloem tubes transport sucrose around a plant?
5) a) What are stomata?
   b) What is the role of stomata in transpiration?
6) How does light intensity affect the rate of transpiration?

Section 7 — Animal Coordination, Control and Homeostasis (p.96-108)

7) How do hormones travel to target organs?
8) Name the gland where each of the following hormones is produced:
   a) oestrogen,   b) testosterone,   c) insulin.
9) Describe how a negative feedback system works in the body.
10) Draw and label a timeline of the 28 day menstrual cycle.
11) Describe two effects of oestrogen on the body.
12) Write down two pros and two cons of hormonal contraceptives.
13) Explain how type 1 and type 2 diabetes can be treated.

Section 8 — Exchange and Transport in Animals (p.109-120)

14) Name three substances that animals have to exchange with their environment.
15) Explain the movement of oxygen between the alveoli and the blood.
16) What are the products of aerobic respiration?
17) Under what circumstances do muscles perform anaerobic respiration?
18) What is the name of the pigment contained within red blood cells and what does it do?
19) What is the function of blood plasma?
20) How are arteries adapted for carrying blood at high pressure?
21) What is the equation for cardiac output?

Section 9 — Ecosystems and Material Cycles (p.121-136)

22) Define the following terms: a) population,   b) community.
23) Give two biotic factors and explain how each one could affect a community.
24) Briefly describe how you could use quadrats to investigate the population size of a species.
25) Explain how having an open water fish farm in a water system can cause eutrophication.
26) Give three benefits of maintaining biodiversity.
27) Name two processes that put carbon dioxide back into the air in the carbon cycle.
28) Produce a labelled diagram of the water cycle.
29) Describe the role of nitrogen-fixing bacteria in the nitrogen cycle.

Section 10 — Key Concepts in Chemistry

Chemical Equations

Chemical equations are used to show what is happening to substances involved in **chemical reactions**. They tell us what **atoms** are involved and how the substances change during a reaction.

Chemical Changes are Shown Using Chemical Equations

One way to show a chemical reaction is to write a word equation. It's not as quick as using chemical symbols and you can't tell straight away what's happened to each of the atoms, but it's dead easy.

> Here's an example — you're told that methane burns in oxygen giving carbon dioxide and water:
>
> methane + oxygen → carbon dioxide + water
>
> The molecules on the left-hand side of the equation are called the reactants (because they react with each other).
> The molecules on the right-hand side are called the products (because they've been produced from the reactants).

Symbol Equations Show the Atoms on Both Sides

Chemical changes can be shown in a kind of shorthand using symbol equations. Symbol equations just show the symbols or formulas of the reactants and products...

magnesium + oxygen → magnesium oxide
$2Mg + O_2$ → $2MgO$

You'll have spotted that there's a '2' in front of the Mg and the MgO. The reason for this is explained on the next page.

Symbol Equations Need to be Balanced

1) There must always be the same number of atoms on both sides — they can't just disappear.
2) You balance the equation by putting numbers in front of the formulas where needed.
3) Take this equation for reacting sulfuric acid (H_2SO_4) with sodium hydroxide (NaOH) to get sodium sulfate (Na_2SO_4) and water (H_2O):

$$H_2SO_4 + NaOH \rightarrow Na_2SO_4 + H_2O$$

The formulas for all of the compounds are correct but the numbers of some atoms don't match up on both sides. E.g. there are 3 Hs on the left, but only 2 on the right. You can't change formulas like H_2SO_4 to H_2SO_5. You can only put numbers in front of them.

4) The equation needs balancing — this is covered on the next page.

Chemical equations form the basis of chemistry...

... so you're going to come across them an awful lot in this book. Remember, the reactants on the left-hand side of the equation react to form the products shown on the right-hand side. What's more, atoms can't be created or destroyed, so there needs to be the same number of each type on the left and right.

Chemical Equations

Here's how to Balance an Equation

The more you practise, the quicker you get, but all you do is this:

- Find an element that doesn't balance and pencil in a number to try and sort it out.
- See where it gets you. It may create another imbalance, but if so, pencil in another number and see where that gets you.
- Carry on chasing unbalanced elements and it'll sort itself out pretty quickly.

EXAMPLE

In the equation on the previous page there aren't enough H atoms on the RHS (Right-Hand Side).

1) The only thing you can do about that is make it $2H_2O$ instead of just H_2O:

$$H_2SO_4 + NaOH \rightarrow Na_2SO_4 + 2H_2O$$

2) But that now causes too many H atoms and O atoms on the RHS, so to balance that up you could try putting 2NaOH on the LHS (Left-Hand Side):

$$H_2SO_4 + 2NaOH \rightarrow Na_2SO_4 + 2H_2O$$

3) And suddenly there it is. Everything balances. And you'll notice the Na just sorted itself out.

State Symbols Tell You the State of a Substance in an Equation

You saw on the previous page how a chemical reaction can be shown using a word equation or symbol equation. Symbol equations can also include state symbols next to each substance — they tell you what physical state the reactants and products are in:

(s) — solid   (l) — liquid   (g) — gas   (aq) — aqueous

'Aqueous' means 'dissolved in water'.

Here are a couple of examples:

Aqueous hydrogen chloride reacts with solid calcium carbonate to form aqueous calcium chloride, liquid water and carbon dioxide gas:

$$2HCl_{(aq)} + CaCO_{3(s)} \rightarrow CaCl_{2(aq)} + H_2O_{(l)} + CO_{2(g)}$$

Chlorine gas reacts with aqueous potassium iodide to form aqueous potassium chloride and solid iodine:

$$Cl_{2(g)} + 2KI_{(aq)} \rightarrow 2KCl_{(aq)} + I_{2(s)}$$

Getting good at balancing equations takes patience and practice

Remember, a number in front of a formula applies to the entire formula — so $3Na_2SO_4$ means three lots of Na_2SO_4. The little numbers within or at the end of a formula only apply to the atom or brackets immediately before. So the 4 in Na_2SO_4 means there are 4 Os, but there's just 1 S, not 4.

Q2 Video Solution

Q1 Balance the equation: $Fe + Cl_2 \rightarrow FeCl_3$ [1 mark]

Q2 Hydrogen and oxygen molecules are formed in a reaction where water splits apart. For this reaction: a) State the word equation. b) Give a balanced symbol equation. [3 marks]

Section 10 — Key Concepts in Chemistry

Chemical Equations Involving Ions

Chemical reactions can also involve *ions* — *charged* atoms or molecules.

Learn the Formulas of Some Simple Compounds and Ions

1) Here are the chemical formulas of some common molecules. They crop up all the time.

- Water — H_2O
- Ammonia — NH_3
- Carbon dioxide — CO_2
- Hydrogen — H_2
- Chlorine — Cl_2
- Oxygen — O_2

2) You also need to be able to recall the formulas of <u>certain ions</u>.
3) For <u>single atoms</u>, you can use the periodic table to work out what <u>charges</u> their ions will form (see page 154).
4) For ions made up of groups of atoms, it's not so simple. You just have to <u>learn</u> these ones.

Ions form when atoms, or groups of atoms, gain or lose electrons to form charged particles (see page 154).

- Ammonium — NH_4^+
- Hydroxide — OH^-
- Nitrate — NO_3^-
- Carbonate — CO_3^{2-}
- Sulfate — SO_4^{2-}

Ionic Equations Show Just the Useful Bits of Reactions

1) You can also write an <u>ionic equation</u> for any reaction involving ions that happens in solution.
2) In an ionic equation, only the <u>reacting particles</u> (and the products they form) are included.
3) To write an ionic equation, all you need to do is look at the balanced symbol equation and take out any <u>aqueous ions</u> that are present on <u>both sides</u> of the equation.

EXAMPLE Write the ionic equation for the following reaction:
$$CaCl_{2\,(aq)} + 2NaOH_{(aq)} \rightarrow Ca(OH)_{2\,(s)} + 2NaCl_{(aq)}$$

1) Anything that's <u>ionic</u> (i.e. made of ions — see page 157) and <u>aqueous</u> will break up into its ions in solution. So, write out the equation showing all the <u>aqueous ions</u> separately.

$$Ca^{2+}_{(aq)} + 2Cl^-_{(aq)} + 2Na^+_{(aq)} + 2OH^-_{(aq)} \rightarrow Ca(OH)_{2\,(s)} + 2Na^+_{(aq)} + 2Cl^-_{(aq)}$$

You should make sure your symbol equation is balanced before you start trying to write the ionic equation (see the previous page for more on how to balance symbol equations).

2) To get to the ionic equation, <u>cross out</u> anything that's the <u>same on both sides</u> of the equation — here, that's the Na^+ and Cl^- ions.

$$Ca^{2+}_{(aq)} + \cancel{2Cl^-_{(aq)}} + \cancel{2Na^+_{(aq)}} + 2OH^-_{(aq)} \rightarrow Ca(OH)_{2\,(s)} + \cancel{2Na^+_{(aq)}} + \cancel{2Cl^-_{(aq)}}$$

$$Ca^{2+}_{(aq)} + 2OH^-_{(aq)} \rightarrow Ca(OH)_{2\,(s)}$$

The overall charge should be the same on both sides. Here, charge on RHS = 0 and charge on LHS = (2+) + (2 × 1−) = 0.

Ionic equations show ionic substances reacting in a solution...

Make sure you learn all the <u>molecules</u> and <u>ions</u> on this page — it'll come in handy when you need to figure out how to <u>write</u> or <u>balance</u> equations. It's really important that you know what <u>charges</u> the different ions have too, as this will affect how they bond with <u>other ions</u>.

Section 10 — Key Concepts in Chemistry

Hazards and Risk

*Chemistry's a **risky business** — you'll sometimes have to handle some really **dangerous** chemicals...*

You Need to Learn the Common Hazard Symbols

1) A hazard is anything that has the potential to cause harm or damage. The risk associated with that hazard is the probability of someone (or something) being harmed if they are exposed to the hazard.
2) Lots of the chemicals you'll meet in chemistry can be bad for you or dangerous in some way. That's why the chemical containers will normally have symbols on them to tell you what the dangers are.
3) Understanding these symbols means you'll be able to use suitable safe-working procedures in the lab.

Oxidising
Provides oxygen which allows other materials to burn more fiercely.
Example: Liquid oxygen.

Environmental Hazard
Harmful to organisms and to the environment.
Example: Mercury.

Toxic
Can cause death by, e.g., being swallowed, breathed in, absorbed through the skin.
Example: Hydrogen cyanide.

Harmful
Can cause irritation, reddening or blistering of the skin.
Example: Bleach.

Highly Flammable
Catches fire easily.
Example: Petrol.

Corrosive
Destroys materials, including living tissues (e.g. eyes and skin).
Example: Concentrated sulfuric acid.

You must pay attention to the hazard symbols on chemicals...
Hazard symbols are there for a reason — to make you aware of the dangers associated with the chemicals you're handling so you can take sensible precautions when using them. Make sure you know what each symbol means, so that you're prepared if you come across them in a practical.

Section 10 — Key Concepts in Chemistry

Hazards and Risk

Experiments Involve **Risks** and **Hazards**

1) Many chemistry experiments have risks associated with them. These can include:

   - Risks associated with the equipment you're using (e.g. the risk of burning from an electric heater).
   - Risks associated with chemicals (see previous page).

2) When you plan an experiment, you need to identify all the hazards and what the risk is from each hazard. This includes:

   - Working out how likely it is that something could go wrong.
   - How serious it would be if it did.

3) You then need to think of ways to reduce these risks. This procedure is called a risk assessment.

   1) Example:
   A student is going to react a solution of sodium hydroxide with hydrochloric acid to form a metal salt and water. Identify any hazards in this experiment, and suggest how the student could reduce the risk.

   2) Hazards:
   Sodium hydroxide and hydrochloric acid are harmful at low concentrations and corrosive at high concentrations. Harmful substances can cause blistering or reddening of the skin, but corrosive substances are much more dangerous if they come into contact with your skin or eyes.

   3) Suggestions to reduce the risk:
   To reduce the risks posed by these hazards, the student should try to use low concentrations of the substances if possible, and wear gloves, a lab coat and goggles when handling the chemicals.

Risk assessments help to keep you safe during an experiment

There are two parts to a risk assessment — identifying all of the hazards, and finding ways to reduce the risks. As well as thinking about how the chemicals that you're using might be hazardous, you also have to think of other things that might be risky during an experiment, e.g. a Bunsen burner or glass equipment.

Warm-Up and Exam Questions

Right, that's enough learning for a bit. Time to test your knowledge with some questions.

Warm-Up Questions

1) Balance the equation: $Al + Cl_2 \rightarrow AlCl_3$
2) Write the ionic equation for the following reaction: $HNO_{3\,(aq)} + NaOH_{(aq)} \rightarrow NaNO_{3\,(aq)} + H_2O_{(l)}$
3) A student is carrying out an experiment using two chemicals. Chemical A is corrosive while chemical B is highly flammable. Suggest appropriate safety precautions the student could take to minimise the risks associated with the chemicals.

Exam Questions

1 Sodium hydroxide reacts with hydrochloric acid to make sodium chloride and water.

(a) Write a word equation for this reaction.

[1 mark]

(b) The sodium hydroxide is in solution. Which state symbol would be used in a chemical equation to indicate that a substance is in solution?

[1 mark]

2 Methane (CH_4) burns in oxygen to make carbon dioxide and water.

(a) State the names of the reactants in this reaction.

[1 mark]

(b) State the names of the products in this reaction.

[1 mark]

(c) Complete and balance the symbol equation for the reaction below.

.........CH_4 + ... $\rightarrow$ ....CO_2 + ...H_2O

[2 marks]

3 Sulfuric acid (H_2SO_4) reacts with ammonia to form ammonium sulfate, $(NH_4)_2SO_4$.

(a) Complete and balance the symbol equation below.

........H_2SO_4 + ... $\rightarrow$ ....$(NH_4)_2SO_4$

[2 marks]

(b) In the balanced equation, how many atoms are there in the reactants?

[1 mark]

(c) How many hydrogen atoms are present in ammonium sulfate?

[1 mark]

The History of the Atom

Atoms are the **tiny particles** of matter (stuff that has a mass) which makes up **everything** in the universe. The next couple of pages are all about how **scientists** came to understand the atom as we do today.

The Theory of Atomic Structure Has Changed Over Time

At the start of the 19th century John Dalton described atoms as solid spheres, and said that different spheres made up the different elements.

In 1897 J J Thomson concluded from his experiments that atoms weren't solid spheres. His measurements of charge and mass showed that an atom must contain even smaller, negatively charged particles — electrons.

The 'solid sphere' idea of atomic structure had to be changed. The new theory was known as the 'plum pudding model'.

The plum pudding model showed the atom as a ball of positive charge with electrons stuck in it.

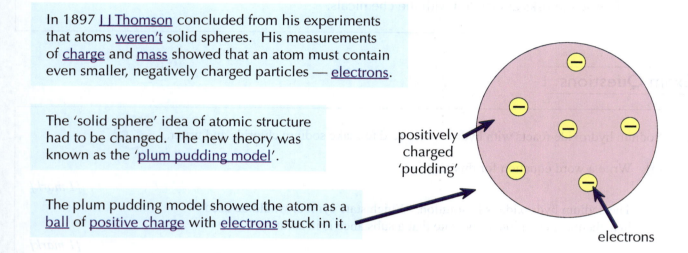

Rutherford Showed that the Plum Pudding Model Was Wrong

1) In 1909, Ernest Rutherford and his students, Hans Geiger and Ernest Marsden, conducted the famous gold foil experiment. They fired positively charged alpha particles at an extremely thin sheet of gold.

2) From the plum pudding model, they were expecting the particles to pass straight through the sheet or be slightly deflected at most. This was because the positive charge of each atom was thought to be very spread out through the 'pudding' of the atom. But, whilst most of the particles did go straight through the gold sheet, some were deflected more than expected, and a small number were deflected backwards. So the plum pudding model couldn't be right.

3) Rutherford came up with an idea to explain this new evidence — the nuclear model of the atom. In this, there's a tiny, positively charged nucleus at the centre, where most of the mass is concentrated. A 'cloud' of negative electrons surrounds this nucleus — so most of the atom is empty space. When alpha particles came near the concentrated, positive charge of the nucleus, they were deflected. If they were fired directly at the nucleus, they were deflected backwards. Otherwise, they passed through the empty space.

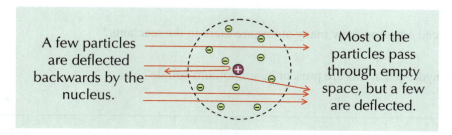

Section 10 — Key Concepts in Chemistry

The History of the Atom

The Refined Bohr Model Explains a Lot

1) Scientists realised that electrons in a 'cloud' around the nucleus of an atom, as Rutherford described, would be attracted to the nucleus, causing the atom to collapse.

2) Niels Bohr proposed a new model of the atom where all the electrons were contained in shells.

3) Bohr proposed that electrons orbit the nucleus in fixed shells and aren't anywhere in between. Each shell is a fixed distance from the nucleus and has a fixed energy.

4) Bohr's theory of atomic structure was supported by many experiments and it helped to explain lots of other scientists' observations at the time.

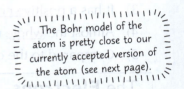

The Bohr model of the atom is pretty close to our currently accepted version of the atom (see next page).

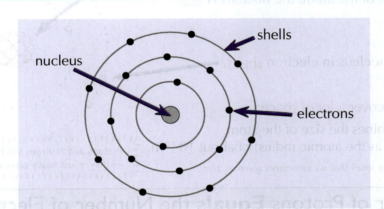

Scientific Theories Have to be Backed Up by Evidence

1) So, our current model of the atom is completely different to what people thought the atom looked like in the past. These different ideas were accepted because they fitted the evidence available at the time.

2) As scientists did more experiments, new evidence was found and our theory of the structure of the atom was modified to fit it. This is nearly always the way scientific knowledge develops — new evidence prompts people to come up with new, improved ideas. These ideas can be used to make predictions which, if proved correct, are a pretty good indication that the ideas are right.

3) Scientists also put their ideas and research up for peer review. This means everyone gets a chance to see the new ideas and check for errors, and then other scientists can use it to help develop their own work.

The theory of atomic structure has changed over time...

Our understanding of the atom has gone through many stages thanks to other people's work being built upon with new evidence and new predictions made. A fine example of the scientific method.

Section 10 — Key Concepts in Chemistry

The Atom

*All substances are made of **atoms**. They're really **tiny** — too small to see, even with a microscope.*

Atoms Contain Protons, Neutrons and Electrons

The atom is made up of three subatomic particles — protons, neutrons and electrons.
- Protons are heavy and positively charged.
- Neutrons are heavy and neutral.
- Electrons have hardly any mass and are negatively charged.

Particle	Relative Mass	Relative Charge
Proton	1	+1
Neutron	1	0
Electron	0.0005	−1

Relative mass (measured in atomic mass units) measures mass on a scale where the mass of a proton or neutron is 1.

The Nucleus

1) It's in the middle of the atom.
2) It contains protons and neutrons.
3) It has a positive charge because of the protons.
4) Almost the whole mass of the atom is concentrated in the nucleus.
5) Compared to the overall size of the atom, the nucleus is tiny.

The Electrons

1) Electrons move around the nucleus in electron shells.
2) They're negatively charged.
3) They're tiny, but their shells cover a lot of space.
4) The size of their shells determines the size of the atom. Atoms have a radius (known as the atomic radius) of about 10^{-10} m.
5) Electrons have a tiny mass (so small that it's sometimes given as zero).

Protons and neutrons still have a tiny mass — they're just heavy compared to electrons.

In an Atom the Number of Protons Equals the Number of Electrons

1) Atoms are neutral — they have no charge overall (unlike ions).
2) This is because they have the same number of protons as electrons.
3) The charge on the electrons is the same size as the charge on the protons, but opposite — so the charges cancel out.
4) In an ion, the number of protons doesn't equal the number of electrons. This means it has an overall charge. For example, an ion with a 2− charge has two more electrons than protons.

An ion is an atom or group of atoms that has lost or gained electrons.

Atomic Number and Mass Number Describe an Atom

1) The nuclear symbol of an atom tells you its atomic (proton) number and mass number.
2) The atomic number tells you how many protons an atom has. Every atom of an element has the same number of protons.
3) For a neutral atom, the number of protons equals the number of electrons, so the number of electrons equals the atomic number.
4) The mass number tells you the total number of protons and neutrons in the atom.
5) To work out the number of neutrons in an atom, just subtract the atomic number from the mass number.

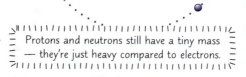

Nuclear symbol for sodium: Mass number → 23, Atomic number → 11, Na (Element symbol)

Electrons orbit around a nucleus containing protons and neutrons

Make sure you learn the relative masses and relative charges of the different parts of the atom.

Q1 An atom of gallium has an atomic number of 31 and a mass number of 70. Give the number of electrons, protons and neutrons in the atom. *[3 marks]*

Q1 Video Solution

Warm-Up and Exam Questions

Right, time to test whether you know more about the atom than Niels Bohr himself.
Yes, that's right, it's question time...

Warm-Up Questions

1) Draw and label a diagram to show the Bohr model of the atom.
2) State the relative charge and relative mass of an electron.
3) What does the mass number tell you about an atom?
4) A certain neutral atom of potassium has an atomic number of 19 and a mass number of 39. Give the number of electrons, protons and neutrons in the atom.

Exam Questions

1   This question is about atomic structure.

(a) Use your knowledge to complete **Figure 1**.

Name of particle	Relative charge
Proton	....
Neutron	....

Figure 1

[2 marks]

(b) Where are protons and neutrons found in an atom?

[1 mark]

(c) An atom has 8 electrons. How many protons does the atom have?

[1 mark]

(d) What is the relative mass of a proton?

[1 mark]

2   **Figure 2** gives some information about nitrogen.

Element	Number of protons	Mass number
nitrogen	7	14

Figure 2

(a) How many neutrons does nitrogen have?

[1 mark]

(b) Describe how the information in **Figure 2** can be used to work out the atomic number of nitrogen.

[1 mark]

3* Describe how the theory of atomic structure has changed throughout history. Your answer should include the models of the atom proposed by John Dalton, J J Thomson, Ernest Rutherford and Niels Bohr, and the current accepted model.

[6 marks]

Section 10 — Key Concepts in Chemistry

Isotopes and Relative Atomic Masses

Atoms were reasonably straightforward, weren't they? Think again. Here come **isotopes** to confuse everything.

Isotopes are the Same Except for Extra Neutrons

1) Isotopes are defined as:

> Different forms of the same element, which have the SAME number of PROTONS but a DIFFERENT number of NEUTRONS.

2) So isotopes have the same atomic number but different mass numbers.
3) A very popular example of a pair of isotopes are carbon-12 and carbon-13.

Remember that the number of protons in an atom is unique to each element. For example, every carbon atom will have 6 protons.

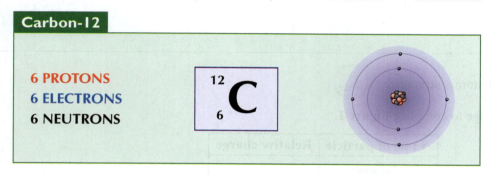

Carbon-12
- 6 PROTONS
- 6 ELECTRONS
- 6 NEUTRONS

$^{12}_{6}C$

Remember — the number of neutrons is just the mass number minus the atomic number.

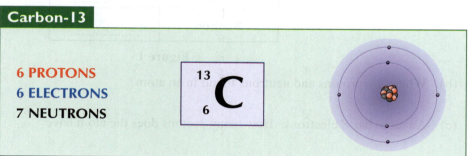

Carbon-13
- 6 PROTONS
- 6 ELECTRONS
- 7 NEUTRONS

$^{13}_{6}C$

Relative Atomic Mass Takes Isotopes into Account

1) In the periodic table, the elements all have two numbers next to them. The bigger one is the relative atomic mass (A_r) of the element.

> The relative atomic mass of an element is the average mass of one atom of the element, compared to $1/12$ of the mass of one atom of carbon-12.

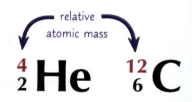

relative atomic mass

$^{4}_{2}He$ $^{12}_{6}C$

2) If an element only has one isotope, its A_r will be the same as its mass number (see page 146).
3) If an element has more than one isotope, its A_r is the average of the mass numbers of all the different isotopes, taking into account how much there is of each one. So, it might not be a whole number.

> For example, chlorine has two stable isotopes, chlorine-35 and chlorine-37. There's quite a lot of chlorine-35 around and not so much chlorine-37 — so chlorine's A_r works out as 35.5.

Section 10 — Key Concepts in Chemistry

Isotopes and Relative Atomic Masses

A_r Can Be Worked Out from Isotopic Abundances

1) Different isotopes of an element occur in different quantities, or <u>isotopic abundances</u>.
2) You need to know how to <u>calculate</u> the <u>relative atomic mass</u> of an element from its <u>isotopic abundances</u>.
3) To work out the relative atomic mass of an element, you need to find the <u>average mass</u> of <u>all its atoms</u>. Here's the formula...

$$\text{Relative atomic mass } (A_r) = \frac{\text{sum of (isotope abundance} \times \text{isotope mass number)}}{\text{sum of abundances of all the isotopes}} \times 100$$

Boron has two isotopes, boron-10 and boron-11.
Given that the relative abundances of boron-10 and boron-11 are 4 and 16 respectively, work out the relative atomic mass of boron.

$$\text{Relative atomic mass} = \frac{(4 \times 10) + (16 \times 11)}{4 + 16} = \frac{40 + 176}{20} = \frac{216}{20} = 10.8$$

Copper has two stable isotopes, copper-63 and copper-65.
Cu-63 has an abundance of 69.2% and Cu-65 has an abundance of 30.8%.
Calculate the relative atomic mass of copper to 1 decimal place.

$$\text{Relative atomic mass} = \frac{(69.2 \times 63) + (30.8 \times 65)}{69.2 + 30.8} = \frac{6361.6}{100} = 63.616 = 63.6 \text{ (to 1 d.p.)}$$

Magnesium has three stable isotopes, Mg-24, Mg-25 and Mg-26.
Mg-24 has an abundance of 79%, Mg-25 has an abundance of 10% and Mg-26 has an abundance of 11%.
Calculate the relative atomic mass of magnesium to 1 decimal place.

$$\text{Relative atomic mass} = \frac{(79 \times 24) + (10 \times 25) + (11 \times 26)}{79 + 10 + 11} = \frac{2432}{100} = 24.32 = 24.3 \text{ (to 1 d.p.)}$$

Relative atomic mass is the average atomic mass of an element

Relative atomic mass takes into account all isotopes of an element — this is <u>different</u> to the <u>mass number</u>, which is the <u>mass</u> of a <u>specific isotope</u> of an element. It's easy to confuse them, but just remember that relative atomic mass has the symbol <u>A_r</u> and is an <u>average</u> mass.

Q1 Silicon, Si, has three stable isotopes. Si-28 has an abundance of 92.2%, Si-29 has an abundance of 4.7% and Si-30 has an abundance of 3.1%. Calculate silicon's relative atomic mass to 1 decimal place. [2 marks]

Section 10 — Key Concepts in Chemistry

The Periodic Table

We haven't always known as much about chemistry as we do now. Early chemists looked to try and understand **patterns** in the elements' properties to get a bit of understanding.

Dmitri Mendeleev Made the First Proper Periodic Table

1) In 1869, Dmitri Mendeleev arranged the 50 or so elements known at the time into a Table of Elements.

Mendeleev's Table of the Elements

```
H
Li Be                                    B  C  N  O  F
Na Mg                                    Al Si P  S  Cl
K  Ca *  Ti V  Cr Mn Fe Co Ni Cu Zn *  * As Se Br
Rb Sr Y  Zr Nb Mo *  Ru Rh Pd Ag Cd In Sn Sb Te I
Cs Ba *  *  Ta W  *  Os Ir Pt Au Hg Tl Pb Bi
```

2) He began by sorting the elements into groups, based on their properties (and the properties of their compounds).

3) As he did this, he realised that if he put the elements in order of atomic mass, a pattern appeared — he could put elements with similar chemical properties in columns.

4) A few elements, however, seemed to end up in the wrong columns. In some cases this was because the atomic mass Mendeleev had was wrong (due to the presence of isotopes) — but some elements just didn't quite fit the pattern. Wherever this happened, he switched the order of the elements to keep those with the same properties in the same columns.

5) To keep elements with similar properties together, Mendeleev also had to leave some gaps (shown by the *s in the table above). He used the properties of the other elements in the columns with the gaps to predict the properties of undiscovered elements. When they were found and they fitted the pattern, it helped to confirm his ideas. For example, Mendeleev predicted the chemical and physical properties of an element he called ekasilicon, which we know today as germanium.

Mendeleev used chemical properties to sort the elements...

...and this meant that he was able to put them into groups and then into columns according to their atomic mass. His arrangement wasn't perfect, but the basic idea wasn't too far away from the periodic table we know today (see next page) which was made possible by sorting elements by their atomic number.

The Periodic Table

*Mendeleev got fairly close to producing something that you might **recognise** as a periodic table. The big breakthrough came when the **structure** of the **atom** was understood a bit better.*

The Periodic Table Helps you to See Patterns in Properties

1) Once protons and electrons were discovered, the atomic number (see p.146) of each element could be found, based on the number of protons in its nucleus. The modern periodic table (see below) shows the elements in order of ascending atomic number — and they fit the same patterns that Mendeleev worked out.

Remember, Mendeleev tried to order elements according to their atomic mass (not atomic number), which is why he sometimes had to swap them around to make them fit the patterns.

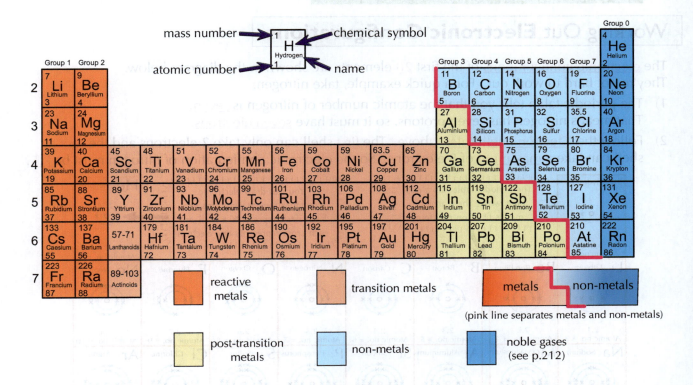

2) The periodic table is laid out so elements with similar chemical properties form columns called groups.

3) The group to which the element belongs corresponds to the number of electrons it has in its outer shell. E.g. Group 1 elements have 1 outer shell electron, Group 7 elements have 7, etc. Group 0 elements are the exception — they have full outer shells of 8 electrons (or 2 in the case of helium).

4) The rows are called periods. Each new period represents another full shell of electrons (see next page).

5) The period to which the element belongs corresponds to the number of shells of electrons it has.

The modern periodic table is vital for understanding chemistry

WORKING SCIENTIFICALLY This is a good example of how science progresses. A scientist has a basically good (though incomplete) hypothesis (see page 2), and other scientists question it and bring more evidence to the table. The hypothesis may be modified or even scrapped to take account of available evidence. Only when all of the available evidence supports a hypothesis will it be accepted.

Section 10 — Key Concepts in Chemistry

Electronic Configurations

The way in which electrons occupy 'shells' around the nucleus is responsible for lots of aspects of chemistry.

Electron Shell Rules:

1) Electrons always occupy shells (sometimes called energy levels).
2) The lowest energy levels are always filled first — these are the ones closest to the nucleus.
3) Only a certain number of electrons are allowed in each shell:

   1st shell: 2   2nd shell: 8   3rd shell: 8

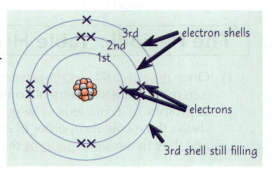

Working Out Electronic Configurations

The electronic configurations of the first 20 elements are shown in the diagram below. They're not hard to work out. For a quick example, take nitrogen:

1) The periodic table tells you that the atomic number of nitrogen is seven. That means nitrogen has seven protons, so it must have seven electrons.
2) Follow the 'Electron Shell Rules' above. The first shell can only take 2 electrons and the second shell can take a maximum of 8 electrons. So the electronic configuration of nitrogen must be 2.5.

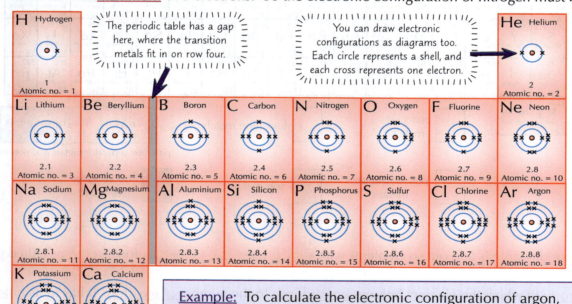

Example: To calculate the electronic configuration of argon, follow the rules. It's got 18 protons, so it must have 18 electrons. The first shell must have 2 electrons, the second shell must have 8, and so the third shell must have 8 as well. It's as easy as 2.8.8.

3) You can also work out the electronic configuration of an element from its period and group:
   - The number of shells which contain electrons is the same as the period of the element.
   - The group number tells you how many electrons occupy the outer shell of the element.

   Example: Sodium is in period 3, so it has 3 shells occupied. The first two shells must be full (2.8). It's in Group 1, so it has 1 electron in its outer shell. So its electronic configuration is 2.8.1.

Electron shells — one of the most important ideas in chemistry

Electronic configurations may seem a bit complicated but once you learn the rules, it's simple.

Q1 Give the electronic configuration of aluminium (atomic number = 13). [1 mark]

Warm-Up and Exam Questions

Well, that's a lot of information to take in... now it's time to see how much you can remember.

Warm-Up Questions

1) Define the relative atomic mass of an element.
2) a) How were elements generally ordered in Mendeleev's table of elements?
   b) How are the elements arranged in the modern periodic table?
3) How many electrons can be held in the following shells of an atom:
   a) the first
   b) the second
   c) the third
4) Give the electronic configuration of chlorine (atomic number = 17).

Exam Questions

1   Sodium has an atomic number of 11.

(a) Complete the dot and cross diagram to show the electron configuration of sodium.

[1 mark]

(b) Sodium is in Group 1.
Name another element that would have the same number of outer shell electrons.

[1 mark]

(c) How many electrons does sodium need to lose so that it has a full outer shell?

[1 mark]

2   Carbon has several isotopes. These include carbon-12 and carbon-13.
Details about the carbon-13 isotope are shown on the right.

(a) Explain what an isotope is.

[3 marks]

(b) Give the number of protons, neutrons and electrons that carbon-13 contains.

[3 marks]

(c) Details of element **X** are shown on the right.
Explain how you can tell that element **X** is not an isotope of carbon.

[1 mark]

(d) There are two isotopes of element **X**. One isotope has a mass number of 13 and a percentage abundance of 79%. The other isotope has a mass number of 14 and a percentage abundance of 21%. Use this information to calculate the relative atomic mass of element **X**. Give your answer to 1 d.p.

[3 marks]

Section 10 — Key Concepts in Chemistry

Ions

*Some atoms are keen on getting rid of some of their **electrons**. Others want more. That's **ions** for you...*

Simple Ions Form When Atoms Lose or Gain Electrons

1) Ions are charged particles — they can be single atoms (e.g. Na^+) or groups of atoms (e.g. NO_3^-).
2) When atoms lose or gain electrons to form ions, all they're trying to do is get a full outer shell (also called a "stable electronic structure"). Atoms like full outer shells — it's atom heaven.
3) Negative ions (anions) form when atoms gain electrons — they have more electrons than protons.
   Positive ions (cations) form when atoms lose electrons — they have more protons than electrons.
4) The number of electrons lost or gained is the same as the charge on the ion. E.g. If 2 electrons are lost the charge is 2+.
   If 3 electrons are gained the charge is 3–.

You calculate the number of protons and neutrons in an ion in the same way as for an atom (see page 146).

- F^- has a single negative charge, so it must have one more electron than protons.
  F has an atomic number of 9, so it has 9 protons. So F^- must have 9 + 1 = 10 electrons.
- Fe^{2+} has a 2+ charge, so it must have two more protons than electrons.
  Fe has an atomic number of 26, so it has 26 protons. So Fe^{2+} must have 26 – 2 = 24 electrons.

Groups 1 & 2 and 6 & 7 are the Most Likely to Form Ions

1) The elements that most readily form ions are those in Groups 1, 2, 6 and 7.
2) Group 1 and 2 elements are metals and they lose electrons to form positive ions (cations).
3) Group 6 and 7 elements are non-metals. They gain electrons to form negative ions (anions).
4) Elements in the same group all have the same number of outer electrons. So they have to lose or gain the same number to get a full outer shell. And this means that they form ions with the same charges.

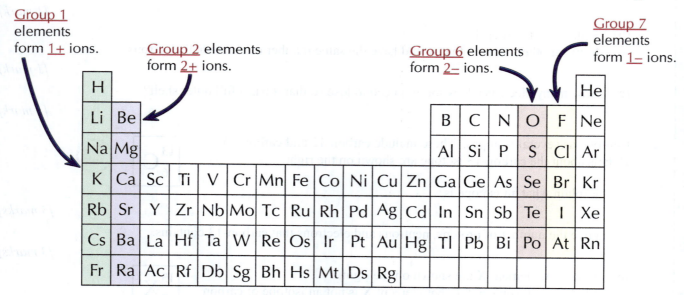

Ions are formed from the loss or gain of electrons...

Here's a way to remember what anions are: anions are negatively charged and are formed by gaining electrons. Then you just have to remember that cations are the opposite of anions — i.e. they're positively charged and formed by losing electrons.

Section 10 — Key Concepts in Chemistry

Ionic Bonding

*Time to find out how particles bond together to form compounds (bet you can't wait). There are **three** types of bonding you need to know about — **ionic**, **covalent** and **metallic**. First up, it's **ionic bonds**.*

Ionic Bonding — Transfer of Electrons

1) When a metal and a non-metal react together, the metal atom loses electrons to form a positive ion (cation) and the non-metal gains these electrons to form a negative ion (anion).
2) These oppositely charged ions are strongly attracted to one another by electrostatic forces.
3) This attraction is called an ionic bond.

Dot and Cross Diagrams Show How Ionic Compounds Form

Dot and cross diagrams show the arrangement of electrons in an atom or ion. Each electron is represented by a dot or a cross. So these diagrams can show which atom the electrons in an ion originally came from.

Sodium Chloride (NaCl)

1) The sodium atom gives up its outer electron, becoming an Na^+ ion.
2) The chlorine atom picks up the electron, becoming a Cl^- (chloride) ion.

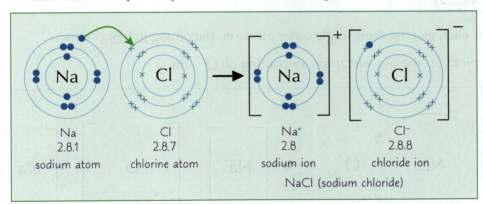

Remember, you can work out how many electrons an atom will gain or lose from its group number.

Here, the dots represent the Na electrons and the crosses represent the Cl electrons. All electrons are really identical, but this is a good way of following their movement.

Magnesium Oxide (MgO)

1) The magnesium atom gives up its two outer electrons, becoming an Mg^{2+} ion.
2) The oxygen atom picks up the electrons, becoming an O^{2-} (oxide) ion.

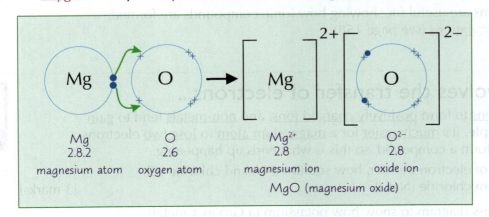

Here we've only shown the outer shell of electrons on the dot and cross diagram — it makes it much simpler to see what's going on.

Ionic Bonding

Magnesium Chloride (MgCl₂)

1) The magnesium atom gives up its two outer electrons, becoming an Mg^{2+} ion.
2) The two chlorine atoms pick up one electron each, becoming two Cl^- (chloride) ions.

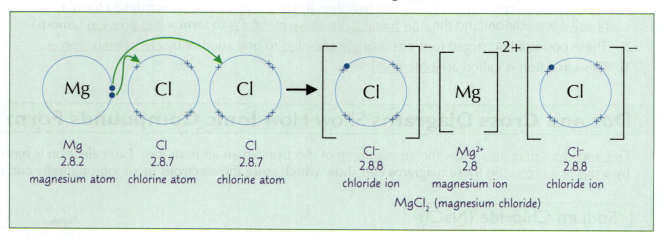

Sodium Oxide (Na₂O)

1) Two sodium atoms each give up their single outer electron, becoming two Na^+ ions.
2) The oxygen atom picks up the two electrons, becoming an O^{2-} ion.

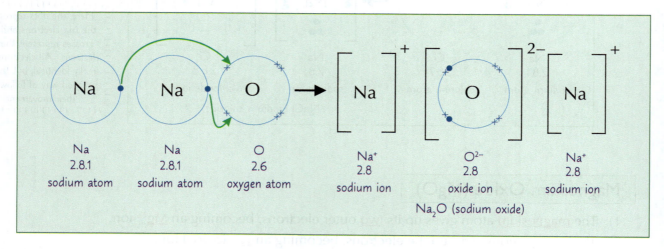

Dot and cross diagrams are useful for showing how ionic compounds are formed, but they have some limitations (see page 158).

Ionic bonding involves the transfer of electrons...

Metals tend to lose electrons to form positively charged ions, and non-metals tend to gain these electrons. For example, it's much easier for a magnesium atom to lose two electrons than gain six electrons to form a compound, so this is what ends up happening.

Q1   Describe, in terms of electron transfer, how sodium (Na) and chlorine (Cl) react to form sodium chloride (NaCl). [3 marks]

Q2   Draw a dot and cross diagram to show how potassium (a Group 1 metal) and bromine (a Group 7 non-metal) form potassium bromide (KBr). [3 marks]

Section 10 — Key Concepts in Chemistry

Ionic Compounds

An **ionic compound** is any compound that only contains **ionic bonds**...

Ionic Compounds Have a Regular Lattice Structure

1) Ionic compounds have a structure called a giant ionic lattice.
2) The ions form a closely packed regular lattice arrangement and there are very strong electrostatic forces of attraction between oppositely charged ions, in all directions in the lattice.

The electrostatic attraction between the oppositely charged ions is ionic bonding.

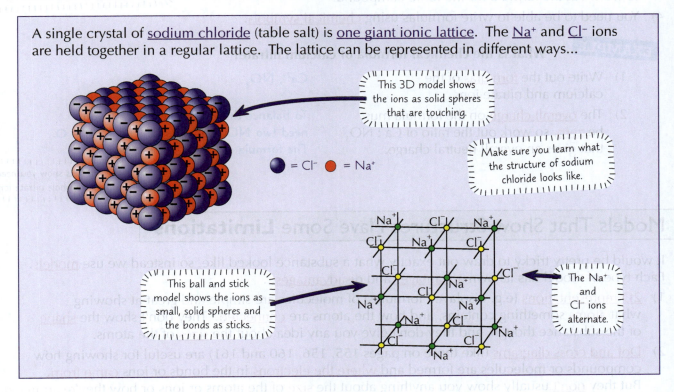

A single crystal of sodium chloride (table salt) is one giant ionic lattice. The Na^+ and Cl^- ions are held together in a regular lattice. The lattice can be represented in different ways...

This 3D model shows the ions as solid spheres that are touching.

● = Cl^- ● = Na^+

Make sure you learn what the structure of sodium chloride looks like.

This ball and stick model shows the ions as small, solid spheres and the bonds as sticks.

The Na^+ and Cl^- ions alternate.

Ionic Compounds All Have Similar Properties

1) They all have high melting points and high boiling points due to the many strong bonds between the ions. It takes lots of energy to overcome this attraction.
2) When they're solid, the ions are held in place, so the compounds can't conduct electricity.
3) When ionic compounds melt, the ions are free to move and they'll carry electric charge.
4) Some ionic compounds dissolve in water. The ions separate and are all free to move in the solution, so they'll carry electric charge.

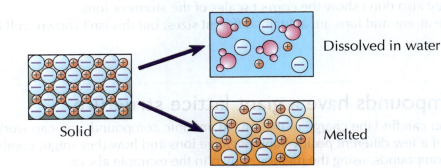

Solid   Dissolved in water   Melted

Section 10 — Key Concepts in Chemistry

Ionic Compounds

You Can Work Out the Formula of an Ionic Compound

1) Ionic compounds (see page 157) are made up of a positively charged part and a negatively charged part.
2) The overall charge of any ionic compound is zero. So all the negative charges in the compound must balance all the positive charges.
3) You can use the charges on the individual ions present to work out the formula for the ionic compound.
4) You need to be able to write formulas using chemical symbols.

Ions with names ending in -ate (e.g. nitrate) are negative ions containing oxygen and at least one other element. Ions with names ending in -ide (e.g. chloride) are negative ions containing only one element (apart from hydroxide ions which are OH⁻).

EXAMPLE What is the chemical formula of calcium nitrate?

1) Write out the formulas of the calcium and nitrate ions.
   Ca^{2+}, NO_3^-

2) The overall charge on the formula must be zero, so work out the ratio of Ca : NO_3 that gives an overall neutral charge.
   To balance the 2+ charge on Ca^{2+}, you need two NO_3^- ions: $(+2) + (2 \times -1) = 0$.
   The formula is $Ca(NO_3)_2$

The brackets show you need two of the whole nitrate ion.

Models That Show Structures Have Some Limitations

It would be pretty tricky to draw out exactly what a substance looked like, so instead we use models. Each type of model has its own advantages and disadvantages...

1) 2D representations (e.g. displayed formulas) of molecules are simple and great at showing what atoms something contains, and how the atoms are connected. They don't show the shape of the substance though, and they don't give you any idea about the sizes of the atoms.
2) Dot and cross diagrams (like those on pages 155, 156, 160 and 161) are useful for showing how compounds or molecules are formed and where the electrons in the bonds or ions came from. But they don't usually show you anything about the size of the atoms or ions or how they're arranged.
3) 3D models of ionic solids show the arrangement of ions, but only show the outer layer of the substance.

Ball and stick models (like the one for NaCl on the previous page) show how the atoms in a substance are connected. You can draw them, or make them with plastic molecular model kits, or as computer models.

- They're great for helping to visualise structures, as they show the shape of the lattice or molecule in 3D.
- They're more realistic than 2D drawings, but they're still a bit misleading. They make it look like there are big gaps between the atoms — in reality this is where the electron clouds interact.
- They also don't show the correct scales of the atoms or ions. The atoms and ions are actually different sizes, but this isn't shown well by ball and stick models.

It's easiest to make ball and stick models of small molecules. Here's one of ethanol (C_2H_5OH).

Ionic compounds have a giant lattice structure

As long as you can find the charge of the ions in an ionic compound, you can work out the formula. Try thinking of a few different positive and negative ions and how they might combine together to make ionic compounds, using the method shown in the example above.

Q1 What is the formula of the ionic compound, lithium oxide? [1 mark]

Warm-Up and Exam Questions

That's all things ionic wrapped up (for now at least). Try your hand at these questions to make sure you've understood everything that's been covered over the last few pages.

Warm-Up Questions

1) What is an ion?
2) What is the charge on an ion formed from a Group 2 element?
3) Sodium chloride has a giant ionic structure. Explain why it has a high melting and boiling point.
4) Some ionic compounds conduct electricity when dissolved in water. Explain why.
5) What is the formula of the compound containing Al^{3+} and OH^- ions only?

Exam Questions

1 **Figure 1** shows the electronic structures of sodium and fluorine.

Figure 1

(a) Describe what will happen when sodium and fluorine react, in terms of electrons.

[2 marks]

(b) When sodium and fluorine react they form an ionic compound.
Describe the structure of an ionic compound.

[3 marks]

2 When lithium reacts with oxygen it forms the ionic compound Li_2O.

(a) Name the compound formed.

[1 mark]

(b) Complete **Figure 2** below using arrows to show how the electrons are transferred when Li_2O is formed. Show the electron arrangements and the charges on the ions formed.

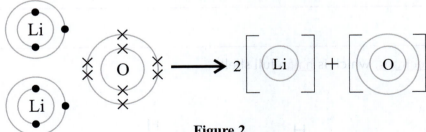

Figure 2

[3 marks]

(c) Explain why Li_2O conducts electricity when molten.

[2 marks]

(d) Lithium forms an ionic compound with chlorine.
What is the formula of this compound? Explain why this is.

[2 marks]

Section 10 — Key Concepts in Chemistry

Covalent Bonding

*These molecules might be **simple**, but you've still got to know about them...*

Learn These Examples of Simple Molecular Substances

1) A covalent bond is a strong bond that forms when a pair of electrons is shared between two atoms.
2) Simple molecular substances are made up of molecules containing a few atoms joined together by covalent bonds. These dot and cross diagrams show six examples that you need to know about.

A covalent bond helps both of the atoms to make a full outer shell of electrons.

Hydrogen, H_2

Hydrogen atoms have just one electron. They only need one more to complete the first shell...

...so they often form single covalent bonds, either with other hydrogen atoms or with other elements, to achieve this.

Hydrogen chloride, HCl

This is very similar to H_2...

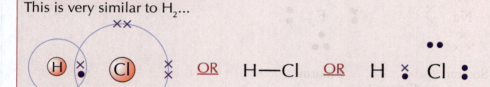

...again, both atoms only need one more electron to complete their outer shells.

Water, H_2O

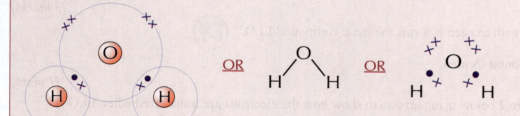

In water molecules, the oxygen shares a pair of electrons with two H atoms to form two single covalent bonds.

Methane, CH_4

Carbon has four outer electrons, which is half a full shell.

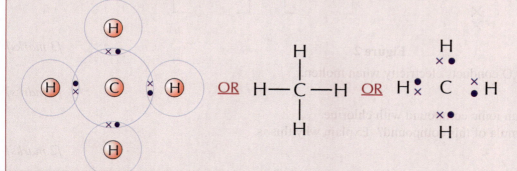

It can form four covalent bonds with hydrogen atoms to fill up its outer shell.

Section 10 — Key Concepts in Chemistry

Covalent Bonding

Oxygen, O_2

An oxygen atom needs <u>two more electrons</u> to complete its outer shell.

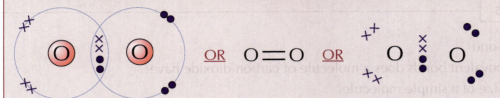

In <u>oxygen gas</u> each <u>oxygen atom</u> forms a <u>double covalent bond</u> (a bond made of <u>two shared electron pairs</u>) with another oxygen atom.

Carbon dioxide, CO_2

In <u>CO_2 molecules</u>, the carbon atom shares two pairs of electrons with two oxygen atoms to form two <u>double covalent bonds</u>.

3) Simple molecules are tiny — they generally have sizes around 10^{-10} m. The bonds that form between these molecules are generally about 10^{-10} m too.

Properties of **Simple Molecular** Substances

1) Substances containing <u>covalent bonds</u> usually have <u>simple molecular structures</u>, like the examples shown above and on the previous page.

2) The atoms within the molecules are held together by <u>very strong covalent bonds</u>. By contrast, the forces of attraction <u>between</u> these molecules are <u>very weak</u>.

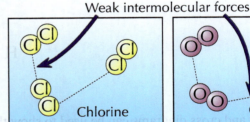

Weak intermolecular forces

Chlorine   Oxygen

3) To melt or boil a simple molecular compound, you only need to break these <u>feeble intermolecular forces</u> and <u>not</u> the covalent bonds. So the melting and boiling points are <u>very low</u>, because the molecules are <u>easily parted</u> from each other.

4) Most molecular substances are <u>gases or liquids</u> at room temperature.

5) As molecules get <u>bigger</u>, the strength of the intermolecular forces <u>increases</u>, so <u>more energy</u> is needed to break them, and the melting and boiling points <u>increase</u>.

6) Molecular compounds <u>don't conduct electricity</u>, simply because they <u>aren't charged</u>, so there are <u>no free electrons</u> or ions.

7) There's no easy rule about solubility in water for simple molecules — some <u>are soluble</u> and some <u>aren't</u>.

EXAM TIP

Covalent bonding involves sharing electrons

You might be asked to draw a <u>dot and cross diagram</u> for a simple molecule in the exam. The ones shown on the previous couple of pages are good ones to learn.

Warm-Up and Exam Questions

The questions on this page are all about covalent bonding. Go through them and if you have any problems, make sure you look back at the relevant pages until you've got to grips with it all.

Warm-Up Questions

1) What is a covalent bond?
2) How many double covalent bonds does a molecule of carbon dioxide have?
3) What is the typical size of a simple molecule?
4) In which states are most simple molecular substances at room temperature?
5) Which forces are stronger in simple molecular substances
   — covalent bonds or intermolecular forces?
6) What forces need to be overcome to boil a simple molecular compound?

Exam Questions

1   Methane is a covalently bonded molecule with the formula CH_4.
Complete the dot and cross diagram for the methane molecule.
Show only the outer electrons.

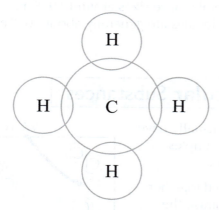

[2 marks]

2   Dot and cross diagrams can be used to show the position of electrons in covalent molecules.

   (a) Draw a dot and cross diagram for hydrogen chloride (HCl). Only show the outer electrons.

[2 marks]

   (b) Oxygen is in Group 6 of the periodic table.
       How many single bonds does it need to make to gain a full outer shell?

[1 mark]

3   Hydrogen chloride is a simple molecular substance.

   (a) Explain why hydrogen chloride has poor electrical conductivity.

[1 mark]

   (b) A molecule of hydrogen chloride has a stronger bond than a molecule of chlorine (Cl_2).
       However, hydrogen chloride boils at –85 °C, whereas chlorine boils at –34 °C.
       Suggest and explain why chlorine has a higher boiling point than hydrogen chloride.

[3 marks]

Section 10 — Key Concepts in Chemistry

Giant Covalent Structures

Simple molecular substances aren't the only compounds held together by covalent bonds.
Giant covalent structures are too. Here are some you need to know about for the exam.

Most Giant Covalent Structures Have Certain Properties

1) In giant covalent structures, <u>all</u> the atoms are <u>bonded</u> to <u>each other</u> by <u>strong</u> covalent bonds.
2) They have <u>very high</u> melting and boiling points as lots of energy is needed to break the covalent bonds.
3) They generally <u>don't</u> contain charged particles, so they <u>don't conduct electricity</u>. — Apart from graphite and graphene.
4) They <u>aren't</u> soluble in water.
5) The following examples are all <u>carbon-based giant covalent structures</u>.

Diamond is Very Hard

1) Diamond is made up of a network of carbon atoms that each form <u>four covalent bonds</u>.
2) The <u>strong covalent bonds</u> take lots of energy to break, so diamond has a <u>high melting point</u>.
3) The strong covalent bonds also hold the atoms in a <u>rigid lattice structure</u>, making diamond <u>really hard</u> — it's used to <u>strengthen cutting tools</u> (e.g. saw teeth and drill bits).
4) It <u>doesn't conduct electricity</u> because it has <u>no free electrons</u> or <u>ions</u>.

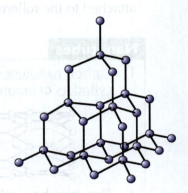

Graphite Contains Sheets of Hexagons

1) In graphite, each carbon atom only forms <u>three covalent bonds</u>, creating <u>sheets</u> of <u>carbon atoms</u> arranged in <u>hexagons</u>.
2) There <u>aren't</u> any covalent bonds <u>between</u> the layers — they're only held together <u>weakly</u>, so they're free to move over each other. This makes graphite <u>soft</u> and <u>slippery</u>, so it's ideal as a <u>lubricating material</u>.
3) Graphite's got a <u>high melting point</u> — the covalent bonds in the layers need <u>loads of energy</u> to break.
4) Only <u>three</u> out of each carbon's four outer electrons are used in bonds, so each carbon atom has <u>one</u> electron that's <u>delocalised</u> (free) and can move. So graphite <u>conducts electricity</u> and is often used to make <u>electrodes</u>.

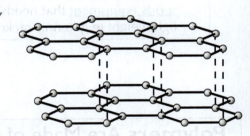

Graphene is One Layer of Graphite

1) Graphene (a type of fullerene — see next page) is one layer of graphite.
2) It's a <u>sheet</u> of carbon atoms joined together in <u>hexagons</u>.
3) The sheet is just <u>one atom</u> thick, making it a <u>two-dimensional</u> substance.

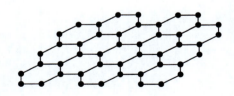

Pay close attention to the different properties of each structure

You'll need to be able to <u>describe</u> and <u>explain</u> the properties of these giant covalent structures.

Q1   Describe the structure and bonding of graphite.   [4 marks]

Fullerenes and Polymers

Fullerenes and *polymers* are also made up of *lots* of covalently bonded atoms...

Fullerenes Form Spheres and Tubes

1) Fullerenes are molecules of carbon, shaped like closed tubes or hollow balls.
2) They're mainly made up of carbon atoms arranged in hexagons, but can also contain pentagons (rings of five carbons) or heptagons (rings of seven carbons).
3) Fullerenes can be used to 'cage' other molecules. The fullerene structure forms around another atom or molecule, which is then trapped inside. This could be used to deliver a drug directly to cells in the body.
4) Fullerenes have a huge surface area, so they could help make great industrial catalysts — individual catalyst molecules could be attached to the fullerenes (the bigger the surface area the better).

Catalysts speed up the rates of reactions without being used up (see page 245).

Nanotubes

1) Carbon nanotubes are fullerenes. They're tiny cylinders of graphene — so they conduct electricity.

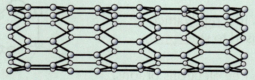

2) They also have a high tensile strength (they don't break when they're stretched), so can be used to strengthen materials without adding much weight.
3) For example, they can be used to strengthen sports equipment that needs to be strong but also lightweight (e.g. tennis rackets).

Buckminsterfullerene

Buckminsterfullerene has the molecular formula C_{60} and forms a hollow sphere made up of 20 hexagons and 12 pentagons. It's a stable molecule that forms soft brownish-black crystals.

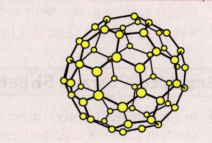

Polymers Are Made of Covalently Bonded Carbon Chains

1) Polymers are molecules made up of long chains of covalently bonded carbon atoms. A famous example is poly(ethene).
2) They're formed when lots of small molecules called monomers join together.

Poly(ethene)

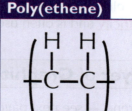

This is known as the repeat unit. The n shows that there are loads of these units joined, one after another.

Diamond, graphite and fullerenes contain exactly the same atoms

Apart from polymers, all of the giant covalent structures on the last two pages are made purely from carbon. The difference in properties between these structures is all down to the way the atoms are held together.

Section 10 — Key Concepts in Chemistry

Metallic Bonding

Ever wondered what gives a metal its properties? It all comes down to bonding...

Metallic Bonding Involves Delocalised Electrons

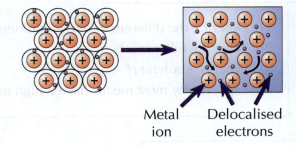

Metal ion   Delocalised electrons

1) Metals also consist of a giant structure.
2) The electrons in the outer shell of the metal atoms are delocalised (free to move around). There are strong forces of electrostatic attraction between the positive metal ions and the shared negative electrons.
3) These forces of attraction hold the atoms together in a regular structure and are known as metallic bonding. Metallic bonding is very strong.
4) Substances that are held together by metallic bonding include metallic elements and alloys.
5) It's the delocalised electrons in the metallic bonds which produce all the properties of metals.

Metals Have Certain Physical Properties

1) The electrostatic forces between the metal ions and the delocalised sea of electrons are very strong, so need lots of energy to be broken.
2) This means that most compounds with metallic bonds have very high melting and boiling points, so they're generally shiny solids at room temperature. They aren't soluble in water either.
3) Metals are also generally more dense than non-metals as the ions in the metallic structure are packed close together.
4) The layers of atoms in a pure metal can slide over each other, making metals malleable — this means that they can be hammered or rolled into flat sheets.
5) The delocalised electrons carry electrical charge through the material, so metals are good conductors of electricity.

Metals and Non-Metals Have Different Physical Properties

1) All metals have metallic bonding which causes them to have similar basic physical properties.
2) As non-metals don't have metallic bonding, they don't tend to exhibit the same properties as metals.
3) Non-metals form a variety of different structures so have a range of chemical and physical properties.
4) They tend to be dull looking, more brittle, have lower boiling points (they're not generally solids at room temperature), don't generally conduct electricity and often have a lower density.
5) Metals and non-metals also have different chemical properties. Non-metals tend to gain electrons to form full outer shells — they are found on the top and right-hand side of the periodic table (see p.151) and their outer shells are generally over half-filled. Metals lose electrons to gain full outer shells — they're found at the bottom and left-hand side of the periodic table and their outer shells are generally under half-filled.

The blue boxes show the metals in the periodic table (see p.151).

The white boxes show non-metals.

Metallic bonding is all about the delocalised electrons...

Delocalised electrons allow metals to be good conductors of electricity and have high melting and boiling points. You'll need to be able to explain why this is the case too...

Section 10 — Key Concepts in Chemistry

Warm-Up and Exam Questions

You know the drill by now — have a crack at the questions on this page to see how much you really know. If you're struggling, take a look back over the last few pages and give it another read through...

Warm-Up Questions

1) Describe the differences in the hardness and electrical conductivity of diamond and graphite.
2) What are fullerenes?
3) What is a polymer?
4) Explain why most metals have a high melting point.

Exam Questions

1   Silicon carbide has a giant covalent structure and is a solid at room temperature.

   (a)   Explain, in terms of its bonding and structure, why silicon carbide has a high melting point.

[2 marks]

   (b)   Give **one** other example of a substance with a giant covalent structure.

[1 mark]

2   Copper is a metallic element. It can be used to make the wires in electrical circuits.

   (a)   State a property of copper that makes it suitable for use in electrical circuits, and explain why it has this property.

[2 marks]

   (b)   Explain why copper is also malleable.

[1 mark]

3   Graphite, diamond and fullerenes are entirely made from carbon but have different properties.

   (a)   Explain why the structure of graphite makes it a useful lubricant.

[2 marks]

   (b)   Explain why graphite is able to conduct electricity.

[1 mark]

   (c)   Using your knowledge of the structure of diamond, suggest why it is useful as a cutting tool.

[2 marks]

   (d)   **Figure 1** shows a fullerene.

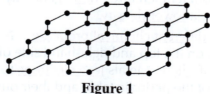

Figure 1

      (i)   Name the type of fullerene shown in **Figure 1**.

[1 mark]

      (ii)   Describe **one** property of fullerenes that makes them suitable for use in catalysts.

[1 mark]

Conservation of Mass

Conservation of mass is a really important concept in **all of chemistry** — so **pay attention** to this page...

In a Chemical Reaction, Mass is Always Conserved

1) During a chemical reaction no atoms are destroyed and no atoms are created.
2) This means there are the same number and types of atoms on each side of a reaction equation.
3) You can see this in action if you do a reaction in a closed system (this is a system where nothing can get in or out). The total mass of the system before and after doesn't change.
4) A good way of showing this is to do a precipitation reaction.

A precipitation reaction happens when two solutions react and an insoluble solid, called a precipitate, forms in the solution.

Example: Copper sulfate solution reacts with sodium hydroxide to form insoluble copper hydroxide and soluble sodium sulfate:

$$CuSO_{4(aq)} + 2NaOH_{(aq)} \rightarrow Cu(OH)_{2(s)} + Na_2SO_{4(aq)}$$

As no reactants or products can escape, the scales will read the same throughout the experiment.

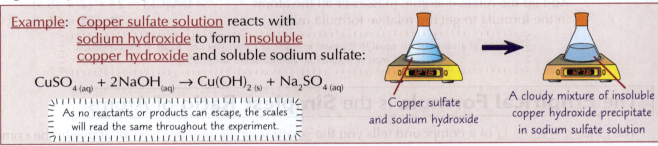

Copper sulfate and sodium hydroxide → A cloudy mixture of insoluble copper hydroxide precipitate in sodium sulfate solution

If the Mass Seems to Change, There's Usually a Gas Involved

In some experiments, you might observe a change of mass in an unsealed reaction vessel during a reaction. There are two reasons why this might happen:

1
- If the mass increases, it's probably because at least one of the reactants is a gas that's found in air (e.g. oxygen) and the products are solids, liquids or aqueous.
- Before the reaction, the gas is floating around in the air. It's there, but it's not contained in the reaction vessel, so you can't measure its mass.
- When the gas reacts to form part of the product, it becomes contained inside the reaction vessel.
- So the total mass of the stuff inside the reaction vessel increases.
- For example, when a metal in an unsealed container reacts with oxygen from the air, the mass inside the container increases. The mass of the metal oxide produced equals the total mass of the metal and the oxygen that reacted from the air.

$$metal_{(s)} + oxygen_{(g)} \rightarrow metal\ oxide_{(s)}$$

2
- If the mass decreases, it's probably because some, or all, of the reactants are solids, liquids or aqueous and at least one of the products is a gas.
- Before the reaction, any solid, liquid or aqueous reactants are contained in the reaction vessel.
- If the vessel isn't enclosed, then the gas can escape from the reaction vessel as it's formed. It's no longer contained in the reaction vessel, so you can't measure its mass.
- So the total mass of the stuff inside the reaction vessel decreases.
- For example, when a metal carbonate thermally decomposes in an unsealed container to form a metal oxide and carbon dioxide gas, the mass of the container will appear to decrease as the carbon dioxide escapes. But in reality, the mass of the metal oxide and the carbon dioxide produced will equal the mass of the metal carbonate that reacted.

$$metal\ carbonate_{(s)} \rightarrow metal\ oxide_{(s)} + carbon\ dioxide_{(g)}$$

A gas will expand to fill any container it's in. So if the reaction vessel isn't sealed the gas expands out from the vessel, and escapes into the air around. There's more about this on page 179.

The total mass of reactants = the total mass of products

Q1 The following reaction occurs in an unsealed container: $2Cu_{(s)} + O_{2(g)} \rightarrow 2CuO_{(s)}$
    Predict how the mass of the reaction container will change over the reaction.
    Explain your answer. [3 marks]

Section 10 — Key Concepts in Chemistry

Relative Masses and Chemical Formulas

Here's how to work out **relative formula mass**, **empirical** and **molecular formulas**, and **percentage mass**...

Relative Formula Mass, M_r

The relative formula mass, M_r, of a compound is the relative atomic masses (A_r) of all the atoms in its formula added together.

> You can find the relative atomic mass (A_r) of an element from the periodic table (see p.151). You'll be given the periodic table in the exam too, so there's no need to worry about remembering all the numbers.

EXAMPLE Find the relative formula mass of magnesium chloride, $MgCl_2$.

Use the periodic table to find the relative atomic masses of magnesium and chlorine.
Add up the relative atomic masses of all the atoms in the formula to get the relative formula mass.

$A_r(Mg) = 24$ $A_r(Cl) = 35.5$

$M_r(MgCl_2) = 24 + (2 \times 35.5)$
$= 24 + 71 = 95$

> The M_r of a compound is equal to the mass in grams of 1 mole (see next page) of the compound. So, 1 mole of magnesium chloride would weigh 95 g.

The Empirical Formula is the Simplest Ratio of Atoms

The empirical formula of a compound tells you the smallest whole number ratio of atoms in the compound.

EXAMPLE Find the empirical formula of glucose, $C_6H_{12}O_6$.

The numbers in the molecular formula of glucose are 6, 12 and 6.
To simplify the ratio, divide them by the largest number that goes into 6, 12 and 6 exactly — that's 6.

C: $6 \div 6 = 1$
H: $12 \div 6 = 2$
O: $6 \div 6 = 1$

The empirical formula of glucose is CH_2O.

You can use the empirical formula of a compound, together with its M_r, to find its molecular formula.

EXAMPLE Compound X has the empirical formula C_2H_6N. The M_r of compound X is 88. Find the molecular formula of compound X.

1) Start by finding the M_r of the empirical formula. The A_r of carbon is 12, the A_r of hydrogen is 1 and the A_r of nitrogen is 14.

$M_r(C_2H_6N) = (2 \times A_r(C)) + (6 \times A_r(H)) + A_r(N)$
$= (2 \times 12) + (6 \times 1) + 14$
$= 24 + 6 + 14 = 44$

2) Divide the M_r of the compound by the M_r of the empirical formula.

$88 \div 44 = 2$

3) Now just multiply everything in the empirical formula by the result — in this case, by 2.

C: $2 \times 2 = 4$ H: $6 \times 2 = 12$ N: $1 \times 2 = 2$

The molecular formula of compound X is $C_4H_{12}N_2$.

You Can Calculate the % Mass of an Element in a Compound

$$\text{Percentage mass of an element in a compound} = \frac{A_r \times \text{number of atoms of that element}}{M_r \text{ of the compound}} \times 100$$

EXAMPLE Find the percentage mass of sodium in sodium carbonate, Na_2CO_3.

A_r of sodium = 23, A_r of carbon = 12, A_r of oxygen = 16

M_r of $Na_2CO_3 = (2 \times 23) + 12 + (3 \times 16) = 106$

Percentage mass of sodium = $\frac{A_r \times \text{number of atoms of that element}}{M_r \text{ of the compound}} \times 100 = \frac{23 \times 2}{106} \times 100 = 43\%$

Section 10 — Key Concepts in Chemistry

Moles and Calculations

The mole seems like a strange old concept — it's difficult to see the relevance of the word "mole" to anything but a small burrowing animal. They're **really important** though, so make sure you're concentrating...

"The Mole" is the Name Given to a Certain Number of Particles

1) Just like a million is this many: 1 000 000, or a billion is this many: 1 000 000 000, a mole is an amount of particles (e.g. atoms, molecules or ions) equal to a number called Avogadro's constant, and it's this many: 602 000 000 000 000 000 000 000 or 6.02×10^{23}.

2) But why is Avogadro's constant useful? The answer is that when you get that number of atoms or molecules, of any element or compound, then, conveniently, they weigh exactly the same number of grams as the relative atomic mass, A_r, (or relative formula mass, M_r) of the element or compound.

> One mole of atoms or molecules of any substance will have a mass in grams equal to the relative particle mass (A_r or M_r) for that substance.

3) Here are some examples:

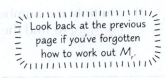
Look back at the previous page if you've forgotten how to work out M_r.

Carbon has an A_r of 12.
So one mole of carbon weighs exactly 12 g.

Nitrogen gas, N_2, has an M_r of 28 (2×14).
So one mole of N_2 weighs exactly 28 g.

Hexane, C_6H_{14}, has an M_r of 86 ($[6 \times 12] + [14 \times 1]$).
So one mole of C_6H_{14} weighs exactly 86 g.

4) So 12 g of carbon, 28 g of nitrogen gas and 86 g of hexane all contain the same number of particles, namely one mole or 6.02×10^{23} particles.

A mole of a substance is 6.02×10^{23} particles of that substance

You'll need to make sure that you're crystal clear on moles before moving on, so you may need to read through this page a few times. Truth is, once you've got it, you've got it — it's a bit like riding a bike...

Section 10 — Key Concepts in Chemistry

Moles and Calculations

Avogadro's Constant is Used to Calculate Numbers of Particles

You need to be able to work out the number of molecules, atoms or ions in a certain number of moles.

EXAMPLE How many atoms are there in 5 moles of oxygen gas?

1) Multiply Avogadro's constant by the number of moles you have to find the number of particles.
   $6.02 \times 10^{23} \times 5 = 3.01 \times 10^{24}$

2) There are two atoms in each molecule of oxygen gas, so multiply your answer by 2.
   $3.01 \times 10^{24} \times 2 = 6.02 \times 10^{24}$

Give your answer in standard form (in terms of × 10ˣ) to save you having to write out lots of 0's.

If you're asked for the number of particles in a given mass, you need to do some converting first. There's a formula you can use to find the number of moles in a certain mass of something.

$$\text{Number of Moles} = \frac{\text{Mass in g (of element or compound)}}{M_r \text{ (of compound) or } A_r \text{ (of element)}}$$

EXAMPLE How many magnesium atoms are there in 60 g of magnesium? (A_r of Mg = 24)

1) Convert mass into moles using the equation.
   moles = mass ÷ A_r
   = 60 ÷ 24 = 2.5 moles

2) Multiply the number of moles by Avogadro's constant to find the number of atoms.
   $6.02 \times 10^{23} \times 2.5$
   = 1.505×10^{24}

If you need to get from a number of particles to a number of moles, you divide by 6.02×10^{23} instead.

You Need to be Able to Rearrange the Equation for Moles

1) Just being able to plug numbers into the equation moles = mass ÷ M_r isn't going to cut it in the exams. You need to be able to rearrange the formula to find out other unknowns, e.g. to find a mass if you've been given moles and M_r.

2) Putting an equation into a formula triangle makes rearranging equations straightforward. Here's the formula triangle that links moles, mass and relative formula mass.

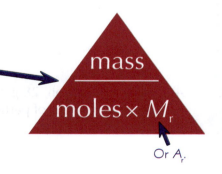

Or A_r.

3) To use a formula triangle, just cover the thing you want to find, and you're left with the expression you need to calculate it. The line through the triangle stands for division.

To find the number of moles, you need the mass and the M_r

Q1 Calculate the number of moles in 90 g of water. M_r of water = 18. [1 mark]
Q2 How many molecules of ammonia are present in 3.5 moles of ammonia gas? [1 mark]
Q3 How many atoms are present in 81.4 g of calcium hydroxide, Ca(OH)₂?
    M_r of Ca(OH)₂ = 74. [3 marks]

Q3 Video Solution

Section 10 — Key Concepts in Chemistry

Moles and Calculations

EXAMPLE

How many moles are there in 66 g of carbon dioxide?

M_r of carbon dioxide (CO_2) = 12 + (16 × 2) = 44

moles = mass ÷ M_r = 66 ÷ 44 = **1.5 moles**

EXAMPLE

What mass of carbon is there in 4 moles of carbon dioxide?

mass = moles × $A_r(C)$
= 4 × 12 = **48 g**

Concentration is a Measure of How Crowded Things Are

1) The more solute (the solid you're dissolving) you dissolve in a given volume, the more crowded the particles are and the more concentrated the solution.
2) Concentration can be measured in grams per dm^3 ($g\,dm^{-3}$) — so 1 gram of stuff dissolved in 1 dm^3 of solution has a concentration of 1 $g\,dm^{-3}$.
3) Here's the formula for finding concentration from the mass of solute:

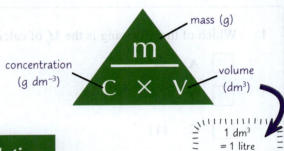

Concentration = Mass of solute ÷ Volume of solution

EXAMPLE

25 g of copper sulfate is dissolved in 500 cm^3 of water. What's the concentration in $g\,dm^{-3}$?

1) Make sure the values are in the right units. The mass is already in g, but you need to convert the volume to dm^3.

   1000 cm^3 = 1 dm^3, so
   500 cm^3 = (500 ÷ 1000) dm^3 = 0.5 dm^3

2) Now just substitute the values into the formula:

   concentration = 25 ÷ 0.5 = **50 $g\,dm^{-3}$**

EXAMPLE

What mass of sodium chloride is in 300 cm^3 of solution with a concentration of 12 $g\,dm^{-3}$?

1) Rearrange the formula so that mass is by itself.

   mass = concentration × volume

2) Put the volume into the right units.

   300 cm^3 = (300 ÷ 1000) dm^3 = 0.30 dm^3

3) Substitute the values into the rearranged formula.

   mass = 12 × 0.30 = **3.6 g**

Learn the formula triangles — they're really handy

Make sure you pay close attention to the units for any questions involving the formulas above. You might have to convert the units first. E.g. if you need to give a concentration in $g\,dm^{-3}$, make sure your mass value is in grams and your volume in dm^3 before doing the calculation.

Q1 Calculate the concentration, in $g\,dm^{-3}$, of a solution that contains 0.60 g of salt in 15 cm^3 of solvent.

[2 marks]

Warm-Up and Exam Questions

Phew... that was heavy going. All that stands between you and a huge sigh of relief are these questions. Make sure you've understood everything on the last few pages though, or you may be in for a bumpy ride.

Warm-Up Questions

1) What is meant by the relative formula mass of a compound?
2) What is the empirical formula of a compound with the molecular formula $C_4H_8Cl_2$?
3) Write down the definition of a mole.
4) Calculate the number of moles in 184 g of nitrogen dioxide. M_r of nitrogen dioxide = 46.
5) 0.500 moles of substance X has a mass of 87.0 g. What is the relative formula mass of X?
6) What mass of sodium hydroxide is contained in 200 cm³ of a 55 g dm⁻³ solution?

Exam Questions

1 Which of the following is the M_r of calcium chloride ($CaCl_2$)?

☐ **A** 54

☐ **B** 75.5

☐ **C** 111

☐ **D** 71

[1 mark]

2 A student carries out the following reaction in an unsealed container:

$$2HCl_{(aq)} + MgCO_{3(s)} \rightarrow MgCl_{2(aq)} + H_2O_{(l)} + CO_{2(g)}$$

(a) Calculate the relative formula mass of $MgCO_3$.

[1 mark]

(b) Predict how the mass of the reaction vessel and its contents will change over the reaction. Explain your answer.

[3 marks]

3 A teacher decides to carry out the following reaction between solutions of potassium hydroxide and copper sulfate:

$$2KOH_{(aq)} + CuSO_{4(aq)} \rightarrow Cu(OH)_{2(s)} + K_2SO_{4(aq)}$$

(a) The teacher uses 140 g of potassium hydroxide (KOH) in the reaction. Calculate, in grams, how much more KOH the teacher needs to have a 4 mole sample.

[3 marks]

(b) 1.25 moles of K_2SO_4 are produced in the experiment. Calculate the mass of K_2SO_4 produced.

[2 marks]

(c) The teacher makes up a solution for another experiment by dissolving copper sulfate in 1500 ml of water. The concentration of copper ions in the solution is 12 g dm⁻³. Calculate the number of copper ions present in the solution.

[4 marks]

Section 10 — Key Concepts in Chemistry

Calculating Empirical Formulas

You first met **empirical formulas** back on page 168, but now **they're back** and they mean business.

Empirical Formulas can be Calculated from Masses

You can work out the empirical formula of a compound from the masses of the elements it contains.

EXAMPLE A sample of a hydrocarbon contains 36 g of carbon and 6 g of hydrogen. Work out the empirical formula of the hydrocarbon.

1) First work out how many moles of each element you have.

   $A_r(C) = 12$ moles of C = 36 ÷ 12 = 3 moles
   $A_r(H) = 1$ moles of H = 6 ÷ 1 = 6 moles

2) Work out the smallest whole number ratio between the moles of C and H atoms to get the empirical formula.

   Ratio C:H = 3:6. Now divide both numbers by the smallest — here it's 3. So, the ratio C:H = 1:2. The empirical formula must be CH_2.

Remember — moles = mass ÷ A_r.

You can also find the empirical formula of a compound from the percentage of each element it contains (its percentage composition). The method for doing this is the same as the one above, but you divide the percentage (rather than the mass) of each element by its A_r.

You can Use Experiments to Find Empirical Formulas

Here's an experiment you could use to calculate the empirical formula of a metal oxide, e.g. magnesium oxide.

1) Get a **crucible** and heat it until it's red hot. (This will make sure it's **clean** and that there are no traces of **oil or water** lying around from a previous experiment.)
2) Leave the crucible to **cool**, then **weigh** it, along with its lid.
3) Add some clean **magnesium ribbon** to the crucible. **Reweigh** the crucible, lid and magnesium ribbon. The **mass of magnesium** you're using is this reading minus the initial reading for the mass of the crucible and lid.
4) **Heat** the crucible containing the magnesium. Put the lid on the crucible so as to **stop** any bits of solid from **escaping**, but leave a **small gap** to allow **oxygen** to enter the crucible.
5) Heat the crucible strongly for around **10 minutes**, or until all the magnesium ribbon has turned **white**.
6) Allow the crucible to **cool** and **reweigh** the crucible with the lid and its contents. The **mass** of **magnesium oxide** you have is this reading, minus the initial reading for the mass of the crucible and lid.

[Diagram: crucible containing magnesium ribbon on gauze, tripod, with lid, being heated]

EXAMPLE A student heats 1.08 g of magnesium ribbon in a crucible so it completely reacts to form magnesium oxide. The total mass of magnesium oxide formed was 1.80 g. Calculate the empirical formula of magnesium oxide.

1) The extra mass in the magnesium oxide must have come from oxygen, so you can work out the **mass of oxygen**.

   mass of O = 1.80 − 1.08 = 0.72 g

2) Work out the **number of moles** of **magnesium** and **oxygen atoms** involved in the reaction.

   moles of Mg = 1.08 ÷ 24 = 0.045 moles
   moles of O = 0.72 ÷ 16 = 0.045 moles

3) Work out the **lowest whole number ratio** between Mg and O by dividing the moles of both by the **smallest number**.

   Mg = 0.045 ÷ 0.045 = 1
   O = 0.045 ÷ 0.045 = 1

This shows that the ratio between O and Mg in the formula is 1:1, so the empirical formula of the magnesium oxide must be **MgO**.

You can work out empirical formulas using experiments

Q1 A 45.6 g sample of an oxide of nitrogen contains 13.9 g of nitrogen. What is the empirical formula of the nitrogen oxide?   [3 marks]

Section 10 — Key Concepts in Chemistry

Limiting Reactants

*Reactions don't go on forever — you need stuff in the reaction flask that can react. Sooner or later one of the reactants **runs out** and the reaction **stops**.*

Reactions Stop When One Reactant is Used Up

1) A reaction stops when all of one of the reactants is used up. Any other reactants are said to be in excess.

2) The reactant that's used up in a reaction is called the limiting reactant (because it limits the amount of product that's formed).

3) The amount of product formed is directly proportional to the amount of the limiting reactant used.

4) This is because if you add more of the limiting reactant there will be more reactant particles to take part in the reaction, which means more product particles are made (as long as the other reactants are in excess).

You can Calculate the Amount of Product from the Limiting Reactant

You can use a balanced chemical equation to work out the mass of product formed from a given mass of a limiting reactant. Here's how...

1) Write out the balanced equation.
2) Work out relative formula masses (M_r) of the reactant and product you're interested in.
3) Find out how many moles there are of the substance you know the mass of.
4) Use the balanced equation to work out how many moles there'll be of the other substance (i.e. how many moles of product will be made by this many moles of reactant).
5) Use the number of moles to calculate the mass.

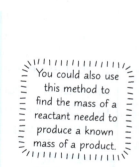

You could also use this method to find the mass of a reactant needed to produce a known mass of a product.

EXAMPLE Calculate the mass of aluminium oxide, Al_2O_3, formed when 135 g of aluminium is burned in air.

1) Write out the balanced equation:

   $4Al + 3O_2 \rightarrow 2Al_2O_3$

2) Calculate the relative formula masses of the reactants and products you're interested in.

   Al: 27 Al_2O_3: $(2 \times 27) + (3 \times 16) = 102$

3) Calculate the number of moles of aluminium in 135 g:

   moles = mass ÷ M_r = 135 ÷ 27 = 5

4) Look at the ratio of moles in the equation:

   4 moles of Al react to produce 2 moles of Al_2O_3 — half the number of moles are produced. So 5 moles of Al will react to produce 2.5 moles of Al_2O_3.

5) Calculate the mass of 2.5 moles of aluminium oxide:

   mass = moles × M_r = 2.5 × 102 = **255 g**

See the next page for another example on how to calculate masses using the chemical equation for a reaction.

Section 10 — Key Concepts in Chemistry

Limiting Reactants

EXAMPLE Magnesium oxide, MgO, can be made by burning magnesium in air.
What mass of magnesium is needed to make 100 g of magnesium oxide?

1) Write out the balanced equation. $2Mg + O_2 \rightarrow 2MgO$

2) Work out the relative formula masses of the reactants and products you're interested in.   Mg: 24   MgO: 24 + 16 = 40

3) Calculate the number of moles of magnesium oxide in 100 g: moles = mass ÷ M_r = 100 ÷ 40 = 2.5

4) Look at the ratio of moles in the equation: 2 moles of MgO are made from 2 moles of Mg. So 2.5 moles of MgO will be formed from 2.5 moles of Mg.

5) Calculate the mass of 2.5 moles of Mg.   mass = moles × M_r = 2.5 × 24 = **60 g**

You Can Also Work Out Limiting Reactants

You can use a balanced chemical equation to work out the limiting reactant in a reaction.

EXAMPLE 8.1 g of zinc oxide (ZnO) were put in a crucible with 0.30 g of carbon and heated until they reacted. Given that the balanced chemical equation for this reaction is:
$2ZnO + C \rightarrow CO_2 + 2Zn$, work out the limiting reactant in this reaction.

1) Divide the mass of each substance by its M_r or A_r to find how many moles of each substance were reacted:

   ZnO: $\frac{8.1}{81}$ = 0.10 mol

   C: $\frac{0.30}{12}$ = 0.025 mol

   This calculation uses a similar method to the one shown on the next page.

2) Divide by the smallest number of moles, which is 0.025:

   ZnO: $\frac{0.10}{0.025}$ = 4.0

   C: $\frac{0.025}{0.025}$ = 1.0

   This is a neat way of making the smallest number of moles equal 1 — it often makes the other numbers a lot nicer too...

3) Compare the ratios between the moles of products with the balanced chemical equation.

   In the balanced equation, ZnO and C react in a ratio of 2 : 1. Using the masses, there is a 4 : 1 ratio of ZnO to C. So, ZnO is in excess, and **C must be the limiting reactant.**

Practice makes perfect with these calculations...

The best thing to do is to learn the method for answering each type of question. Then you can follow the same process every time you answer one, and it'll become second nature in no time at all.

Q1 The balanced equation for the reaction between chlorine and potassium bromide is:
$$Cl_2 + 2KBr \rightarrow Br_2 + 2KCl$$
Calculate the mass of potassium chloride produced when 23.8 g of potassium bromide reacts in an excess of chlorine. $A_r(K) = 39$, $A_r(Br) = 80$, $A_r(Cl) = 35.5$.   [4 marks]

Q1 Video Solution

Balancing Equations Using Masses

You've already seen how to **balance equations** back on page 139. But, sometimes, you may have to balance equations given the **masses** of the reactants and products. Your good old friend the **mole** will come in handy.

You Can Balance Equations Using Reacting Masses

If you know the masses of the reactants and products that took part in a reaction, you can work out the balanced symbol equation for the reaction. Here are the steps you should take:

1) Divide the mass of each substance by its relative formula mass to find the number of moles. *You may need to work out some unknown masses first (see below).*
2) Divide the number of moles of each substance by the smallest number of moles in the reaction.
3) If needed, multiply all the numbers by the same amount to make them all whole numbers.
4) Write the balanced symbol equation for the reaction by putting these numbers in front of the formulas.

EXAMPLE

Paula burns a metal, X, in oxygen. There is a single product, an oxide of the metal. Given that 25.4 g of X burns in 3.2 g of oxygen, write a balanced equation for this reaction. A_r of X = 63.5 and M_r of X oxide = 143.0.

1) Work out the mass of metal oxide produced. Because it's the only product, the mass of metal oxide produced must equal the total mass of reactants. *This is because mass is always conserved in a chemical reaction (see p.167).*

    25.4 + 3.2 = 28.6 g of X oxide

2) Divide the mass of each substance by its M_r or A_r to calculate how many moles of each substance reacted or were produced:

    X: $\frac{25.4}{63.5}$ = 0.40 mol O_2: $\frac{3.2}{32.0}$ = 0.10 mol   X oxide: $\frac{28.6}{143.0}$ = 0.20 mol

3) Divide by the smallest number of moles, which is 0.10:

    X: $\frac{0.40}{0.10}$ = 4.0 O_2: $\frac{0.10}{0.10}$ = 1.0   X oxide: $\frac{0.20}{0.10}$ = 2.0

    Remember, this step is used to make the smallest number of moles equal 1.

4) The numbers are all whole numbers, so you can write out the balanced symbol equation straight away.

    $4X + O_2 \rightarrow 2(X\ oxide)$

5) The oxide of X must have a chemical formula containing X and O atoms. In order for the equation to balance, each molecule of X oxide must contain one O atom and 2 X atoms.

    $4X + O_2 \rightarrow 2X_2O$

Another handy method for balancing equations...

Moles are a measure of the number of particles of a substance, but mass depends on the M_r or A_r of each particle. Converting mass to moles allows you to directly compare the ratios of particles.

Q1 84 g of N_2 reacts completely with 18 g of H_2 to produce 102 g of NH_3. $M_r(N_2) = 28$, $M_r(H_2) = 2$, $M_r(NH_3) = 17$.
 a) Calculate how many moles of each substance reacted or was produced. [3 marks]
 b) Use your answer to part a) to write a balanced symbol equation for this reaction. [2 marks]

Q1 Video Solution

Warm-Up and Exam Questions

It's nearly the end of Section 10 but it's not quite done with yet. Before you start celebrating have a go at the questions on the last few pages of stuff. Don't skip over them — doing them now will help it all stick.

Warm-Up Questions

1) A compound of boron and fluorine contains 5.5 g of boron and 28.5 g of fluorine. What is the empirical formula of the compound? $A_r(B) = 11$, $A_r(F) = 19$
2) Describe what a limiting reactant is.
3) In a reaction, suggest what happens to the amount of product formed if the amount of limiting reactant is halved?

Exam Questions

1   3.5 g of a metal, X, reacts completely with 4.0 g of oxygen to form 7.5 g of an oxide of the metal. A_r(metal X) = 7, M_r(oxygen) = 32, M_r(metal oxide) = 30.

(a) Calculate how many moles of each substance reacted or was produced.

[2 marks]

(b) Use your answer to part (a) to write a balanced symbol equation for this reaction.

[2 marks]

2   Sulfuric acid reacts with sodium hydrogen carbonate to produce aqueous sodium sulfate, water and carbon dioxide. The balanced equation for this reaction is:

$$H_2SO_{4(aq)} + 2NaHCO_{3(s)} \rightarrow Na_2SO_{4(aq)} + 2H_2O_{(l)} + 2CO_{2(g)}$$

A student reacted 6.0 g of solid $NaHCO_3$ with an excess of sulfuric acid (H_2SO_4).

(a) (i) Calculate the moles of Na_2SO_4 produced in this reaction.

[3 marks]

(ii) Calculate the mass of Na_2SO_4 produced in this reaction.

[2 marks]

(b) The student repeated the experiment using double the amount of H_2SO_4. Explain why the mass of Na_2SO_4 produced in the reaction remained the same.

[1 mark]

3   A student heats 2.4 g of iron oxide (Fe_2O_3) with 0.36 g of carbon until they reacted. The balanced chemical equation for the reaction is:

$$2Fe_2O_3 + 3C \rightarrow 4Fe + 3CO_2$$

(a) Deduce which reactant was **not** in excess in this reaction.

[4 marks]

(b) During a different experiment, the student heats some iron, Fe, in the presence of an unknown gas, Y_2. A single product forms, which is an ionic compound containing Fe and Y only.
Given that during the reaction, the student heated 17.92 g of iron, and 52.00 g of product were formed, write a balanced equation for the reaction.
A_r(Fe) = 56, M_r(product) = 162.5 and $M_r(Y_2)$ = 71

[4 marks]

Section 10 — Key Concepts in Chemistry

Revision Summary for Section 10

There was a lot of information crammed into Section 10 — use the questions below to see how much you've remembered.
- Try these questions and tick off each one when you get it right.
- When you're completely happy with a topic, tick it off.

For even more practice, try the Retrieval Quiz for Section 10 — just scan this QR code!

Chemical Equations, Risks and Hazards (p.138-142) ☐

1) What are the chemicals on the left-hand side of a chemical equation called?
2) Write out the four state symbols used in chemical equations, and state what each one means.
3) Write out the formulas, complete with charges, of the carbonate and sulfate ions.
4) Sketch the following hazard symbols: a) toxic b) harmful.

Atoms, Isotopes and Electronic Configurations (p.144-152) ☐

5) Describe the main features of the plum pudding model of the atom.
6) Name the three subatomic particles found in an atom, and state the relative mass of each.
7) What can you say about the number of protons and electrons in a neutral atom?
8) State what isotopes are, using an example to explain your answer.
9) Describe why Dmitri Mendeleev had gaps in his version of the periodic table.
10) What can you say about the number of electron shells in elements in the same period?
11) What does the group number of an element in the periodic table tell you about its electronic structure?

Types of Bonding and Structures (p.154-165) ☐

12) What charge will the ion of a Group 6 element have?
13) Describe how ionic bonding occurs.
14) Draw a dot and cross diagram to show how magnesium chloride forms.
15) Outline the limitations associated with ball and stick models of molecules and compounds.
16) Draw a dot and cross diagram to show the bonding in a molecule of:
    a) hydrogen   b) water
17) Do simple molecular substances have high or low boiling points?
18) Explain why hydrogen, H_2, doesn't conduct electricity.
19) Describe the structures of the following substances:
    a) diamond   b) buckminsterfullerene
20) Give three general properties of metals.

Calculations and Moles (p.167-176) ☐

21) Why does the mass of a sealed system stay the same during a chemical reaction?
22) State Avogadro's constant.
23) What is the empirical formula of a compound?
24) What equation links the number of moles with the mass and M_r of a substance?
25) What equation links the concentration of a solution with its volume and the mass of solute used?
26) What is the concentration, in g dm^{-3}, of a solution that contains 4 g of solute in 2 dm^3 of solvent?
27) Outline an experiment you could use to work out the empirical formula of magnesium oxide.
28) Describe how to balance an equation using the masses of the reactants and products in a reaction.

Section 10 — Key Concepts in Chemistry

Section 11 — States of Matter and Mixtures

States of Matter

*All stuff is made of **particles** (molecules, ions or atoms). The **forces** between these particles can be weak or strong, depending on whether it's a **solid**, a **liquid** or a **gas**. Want to find out more? Then read on...*

States of Matter Depend on the Forces Between Particles

1) There are <u>three states of matter</u> that you need to know about — <u>solids</u>, <u>liquids</u> and <u>gases</u>. You can model these three different states using the <u>particle model</u>.
2) In the particle model, each particle (it could be a molecule, an ion or an atom) is represented by a <u>solid sphere</u>.
3) The <u>properties</u> of each state of matter depend on the <u>forces</u> between the particles.
4) The forces between the particles can be <u>weak</u> or <u>strong</u>, depending on whether the substance is a solid, a liquid or a gas.

Solids

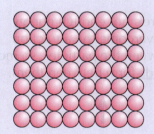

1) There are <u>strong forces</u> of attraction between particles, which hold them in <u>fixed positions</u> in a regular <u>lattice arrangement</u>.
2) The particles <u>don't move</u> from their positions, so all solids keep a <u>definite shape</u> and <u>volume</u>.
3) The particles in a solid <u>don't</u> have much <u>energy</u>.
4) They hardly move at all — in fact, they can only <u>vibrate</u> about their fixed positions. The <u>hotter</u> the solid becomes, the <u>more</u> they vibrate (causing solids to <u>expand</u> slightly when heated).

Liquids

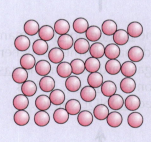

1) There is <u>some force</u> of attraction between the particles. They're <u>free</u> to <u>move</u> past each other, but they do tend to <u>stick together</u>.
2) Liquids <u>don't</u> keep a <u>definite shape</u> and will flow to fill the bottom of a container. But they do keep the <u>same volume</u>.
3) For any given substance, in the <u>liquid state</u> its particles will have <u>more energy</u> than in the <u>solid state</u> (but <u>less</u> energy than in the <u>gas state</u>).
4) The particles are <u>constantly</u> moving with <u>random motion</u>. The <u>hotter</u> the liquid gets, the <u>faster</u> they move. This causes liquids to <u>expand</u> slightly when heated.

Gases

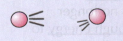
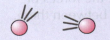

1) There's next to <u>no force</u> of attraction between the particles — they're <u>free</u> to <u>move</u>. They travel in <u>straight lines</u> and only interact when they <u>collide</u>.
2) Gases <u>don't</u> keep a definite <u>shape</u> or <u>volume</u> and will always <u>fill</u> any container. When particles bounce off the walls of a container they exert a <u>pressure</u> on the walls. *This means a gas will escape from a container if it isn't airtight.*
3) For any given substance, in the <u>gas state</u> its particles will have more energy that in the <u>solid state</u> or the <u>liquid state</u>.
4) The particles move <u>constantly</u> with <u>random motion</u>. The <u>hotter</u> the gas gets, the <u>faster</u> they move. Gases either <u>expand</u> when heated, or their <u>pressure increases</u>.

States of Matter

*By **adding** or **taking away energy** from a substance, you can **convert** it from one **physical state** to another.*

Heating or Cooling a Substance can Change its State

When a substance changes from one state of matter to another, it's a physical change. Physical changes are pretty easy to undo by heating or cooling.

The red arrows show heat being added. The blue arrows show heat being given out.

1) When a solid is heated, its particles gain more energy.

2) This makes the particles vibrate more, which weakens the forces that hold the solid together. This makes the solid expand.

3) At a certain temperature, called the melting point, the particles have enough energy to break free from their positions. This is called MELTING and the solid turns into a liquid.

4) When a liquid is heated, the particles get even more energy.

5) This energy makes the particles move faster, which weakens and breaks the bonds holding the liquid together.

6) At a certain temperature, called the boiling point, the particles have enough energy to break their bonds. This is BOILING (or evaporating). The liquid becomes a gas.

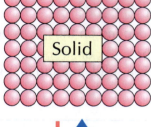
Solid

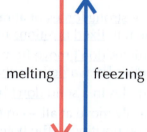
Liquid

melting | freezing

boiling (or evaporating) | condensing

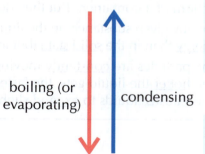
Gas

12) At the melting point, so many bonds have formed between the particles that they're held in place. The liquid becomes a solid. This is FREEZING.

11) There's not enough energy to overcome the attraction between the particles, so more bonds form between them.

10) When a liquid cools, the particles have less energy, so move around less.

9) At the boiling point, so many bonds have formed between the gas particles that the gas becomes a liquid. This is called CONDENSING.

8) Bonds form between the particles.

7) As a gas cools, the particles no longer have enough energy to overcome the forces of attraction between them.

Solids can also change directly into a gas — this is called subliming.

Section 11 — States of Matter and Mixtures

States of Matter

Atoms are **Rearranged** During **Chemical Reactions**

1) Chemical changes are different to physical changes.

2) Chemical changes happen during chemical reactions, when bonds between atoms break and the atoms change places.

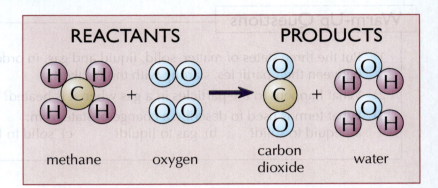

REACTANTS → PRODUCTS

methane + oxygen → carbon dioxide + water

3) The atoms from the substances you start off with (the reactants) are rearranged to form different substances (the products).

4) Compared to physical changes, chemical changes are often hard to reverse.

You Can Make **Predictions** about Substances from their **Properties**

You might be asked to use data to work out what state substances will be in under certain conditions.

EXAMPLE

The table on the right gives information about the properties of four different substances.

Predict the state of substance D at 1000 °C.

Substance	Melting point / °C	Boiling point / °C
A	−218.4	−183.0
B	1535	2750
C	1410	2355
D	801	1413

1) The melting point of D is 801 °C and its boiling point is 1413 °C.
2) That means it's a solid below 801 °C, a gas above 1413 °C, and a liquid in between.
3) 1000 °C is between 801 °C and 1413 °C, so... **D is a liquid at 1000 °C.**

Physical changes are reversible, chemical changes are less so...

Make sure you can describe what happens to particles, and the forces between them, as a substance is heated and cooled. Don't forget to learn the technical terms for each state change too.

Q1 Ethanol melts at −114 °C and boils at 78 °C. Predict the state that ethanol is in at:
   a) −150 °C   b) 0 °C   c) 25 °C   d) 100 °C   [4 marks]

Q1 Video Solution

Warm-Up and Exam Questions

Reckon you know all there is to know about this section so far? Have a go at these questions and see how you get on. If you get stuck on something, just flick back and give it another read through.

Warm-Up Questions

1) Put the three states of matter, solid, liquid and gas, in order of the strength of the forces between their particles, starting with the weakest.
2) What happens to the particles in a gas when it is heated?
3) What term is used to describe a change of state from:
   a) liquid to solid?   b) gas to liquid?   c) solid to liquid?   d) solid to gas?

Exam Questions

1   **Figure 1** shows a vessel in a distillery.
    The walls of the vessel are solid copper.

    (a) Describe the arrangement of particles
        in the solid copper walls of the vessel.

    [1 mark]

    (b) Inside the vessel, liquid ethanol is turned into ethanol gas.
        Explain the changes in arrangement, movement and energy of the
        ethanol particles when the liquid ethanol is heated to become a gas.

    [3 marks]

Figure 1

2   **Table 1** shows the melting and boiling points of three molecular substances.

Substance	Melting point (°C)	Boiling point (°C)
oxygen	−219	−183
chlorine	−101	−34
bromine	−7	59

Table 1

(a) Predict the state of bromine at room temperature (25 °C).

[1 mark]

(b) Predict the state of chlorine at −29 °C.

[1 mark]

3   This question is on states of matter.

(a) Use your knowledge of how particles move to explain why gases fill their containers.

[2 marks]

(b) Use your knowledge of how particles move to explain why a liquid is able to flow but a solid is not.

[2 marks]

Section 11 — States of Matter and Mixtures

Purity

*Substances are often not **100% pure** — they might have **other stuff** that you can't see mixed in with them. The purity of a substance might need to be **checked** before, say, a drug is made from it.*

Pure Substances Contain Only One Thing

1) In everyday life, the word 'pure' is often used to mean 'clean' or 'natural'.
2) In chemistry, it's got a more specific meaning — a substance is pure if it's completely made up of a single element or compound.
3) If you've got more than one compound present, or different elements that aren't all part of a single compound, then you've got a mixture.
4) So, for example, fresh air might be thought of as nice and 'pure', but it's chemically impure, because it's a mixture of nitrogen, oxygen, argon, carbon dioxide, water vapour and various other gases.
5) Lots of mixtures are really useful — alloys (e.g. steel) are a great example. But sometimes chemists need to obtain a pure sample of a substance.

You Can Test for Purity Using Melting Points

1) Every pure substance has a specific, sharp melting point and boiling point. For example, pure ice melts at 0 °C, and pure water boils at 100 °C.
2) You can use this to test the purity of a sample of a substance, by comparing the actual melting point of the sample to the expected value.
3) If a substance is a mixture then it will melt gradually over a range of temperatures, rather than having a sharp melting point, like a pure substance.
4) Impure substances will melt over a range of temperatures, because they are effectively mixtures.
5) To measure the melting point of a substance, you can use melting point apparatus. This is a piece of kit that allows you to heat up a small sample of a solid very slowly, so you can observe and record the exact temperature that it melts at.

If you don't have melting point apparatus, you could use a water bath and a thermometer instead — but it's harder to control the temperature as exactly as when using this apparatus.

Example: Adil's teacher gives him samples of four powdered solids, labelled A, B, C and D. He uses melting point apparatus to determine the melting point of each of the solids. Adil's results are shown in the table below.

Solid	A	B	C	D
Melting point (°C)	82	72-79	101	63

Which of the four solids, A, B, C or D, was a mixture?

Answer: B — Adil's results show that solid B must be a mixture, because it melted over a range of temperatures (rather than melting at a specific temperature, as the other three solids did).

Pure substances are only made up of one element or compound...

...so their melting and boiling points are specific. There are many ways to extract a pure substance from a mixture. You'll learn about some of these techniques over the next few pages. Right, let's get cracking then.

Section 11 — States of Matter and Mixtures

Distillation

Distillation is used to separate mixtures which contain **liquids**. This first page looks at **simple** distillation.

Simple Distillation Separates Out Solutions

Simple distillation is used for separating out a liquid from a solution. Here's how to use simple distillation to get pure water from seawater:

1) Pour your sample of seawater into the distillation flask.
2) Set up the apparatus as shown in the diagram below. Connect the bottom end of the condenser to a cold tap using rubber tubing. Run cold water through the condenser to keep it cool.
3) Gradually heat the distillation flask. The part of the solution that has the lowest boiling point will evaporate — in this case, that's the water.
4) The water vapour passes into the condenser where it cools and condenses (turns back into a liquid). It then flows into the beaker where it is collected.
5) Eventually you'll end up with just the salt left in the flask.

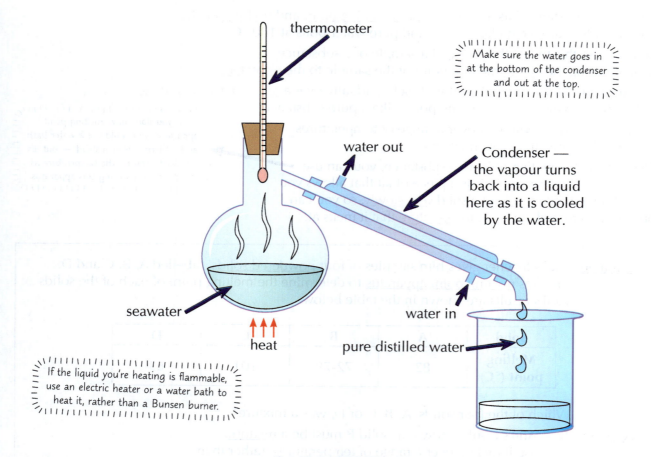

Make sure the water goes in at the bottom of the condenser and out at the top.

If the liquid you're heating is flammable, use an electric heater or a water bath to heat it, rather than a Bunsen burner.

The problem with simple distillation is that you can only use it to separate things with very different boiling points.

If you have a mixture of liquids with similar boiling points, you need another method to separate them out — like fractional distillation...

Section 11 — States of Matter and Mixtures

Distillation

*Another type of distillation is **fractional distillation**. This is more complicated to carry out than simple distillation but it can separate out **mixtures of liquids** even if their **boiling points** are close together.*

Fractional Distillation is Used to Separate a Mixture of Liquids

Here's a lab demonstration that can be used to model fractional distillation of crude oil at a refinery:

1) Put your mixture in a flask.
2) Attach a fractionating column and condenser above the flask as shown below.
3) Gradually heat the flask. The different liquids will all have different boiling points — so they will evaporate at different temperatures.
4) The liquid with the lowest boiling point evaporates first. When the temperature on the thermometer matches the boiling point of this liquid, it will reach the top of the column.
5) Liquids with higher boiling points might also start to evaporate. But the column is cooler towards the top, so they will only get part of the way up before condensing and running back down towards the flask.
6) When the first liquid has been collected, raise the temperature until the next one reaches the top.

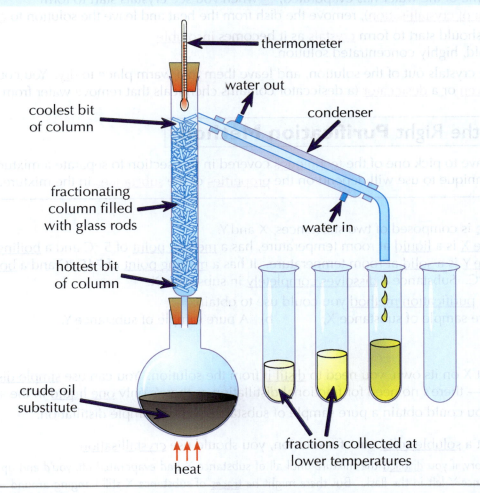

Fractional distillation is used in the lab and industry...

The industrial method for fractional distillation of crude oil isn't quite as simple as the one shown here. If you're desperate to find out what goes on in oil refineries, have a look at page 252.

Q1 Propan-1-ol, methanol and ethanol have boiling points of 97 °C, 65 °C and 78 °C respectively. A student uses fractional distillation to separate a mixture of these compounds. State which liquid will be collected in the second fraction and explain why. [2 marks]

Section 11 — States of Matter and Mixtures

Filtration and Crystallisation

*If you've mixed a **solid** with a **liquid**, it should be pretty easy to **separate** them out again. Which **method** you'll need to use depends on whether or not the solid can **dissolve** in the liquid.*

Filtration is Used to Separate an Insoluble Solid from a Liquid

1) If the product of a reaction is an insoluble solid, you can use filtration to separate it out from the liquid reaction mixture.
2) It can be used in purification as well. For example, solid impurities can be separated out from a reaction mixture using filtration.
3) All you do is pop some filter paper into a funnel and pour your mixture into it. The liquid part of the mixture runs through the paper, leaving behind a solid residue.

Filter paper folded into a cone shape.
The solid is left in the filter paper.

Crystallisation Separates a Soluble Solid from a Solution

Here's how you crystallise a product...

1) Pour the solution into an evaporating dish and gently heat the solution. Some of the water will evaporate and the solution will get more concentrated.
2) Once some of the water has evaporated, or when you see crystals start to form (the point of crystallisation), remove the dish from the heat and leave the solution to cool.
3) The salt should start to form crystals as it becomes insoluble in the cold, highly concentrated solution.
4) Filter the crystals out of the solution, and leave them in a warm place to dry. You could also use a drying oven or a desiccator (a desiccator contains chemicals that remove water from the surroundings).

evaporating dish

Choose the Right Purification Method

You might have to pick one of the techniques covered in this section to separate a mixture. The best technique to use will depend on the properties of the substances in the mixture.

> Example:
> A mixture is composed of two substances, X and Y.
> Substance X is a liquid at room temperature, has a melting point of 5 °C and a boiling point of 60 °C.
> Substance Y is a solid at room temperature. It has a melting point of 745 °C and a boiling point of 1218 °C. Substance Y dissolves completely in substance X.
> Suggest a purification method you could use to obtain:
> a) A pure sample of substance X,   b) A pure sample of substance Y.
>
> Answer:
> a) To get X on its own, you need to distil it from the solution. You can use simple distillation here — there's no need for fractional distillation as there's only one liquid in the solution.
> So, you could obtain a pure sample of substance X using simple distillation.
>
> b) To get a soluble solid out of a solution, you should use crystallisation.
> In theory, if you distilled the mixture until all of substance X had evaporated off, you'd end up with just substance Y left in the flask. But there might be traces of substance X still hanging around — crystallisation's a better way of getting a pure sample of a solid from a solution.
> So, you could obtain a pure sample of substance Y using crystallisation.

Crystallisation is for soluble solids...
REVISION TIP — ... and filtration is for insoluble solids in a mixture. It's important to remember the difference.

Section 11 — States of Matter and Mixtures

Warm-Up and Exam Questions

So the last few pages have all been about mixtures and how to separate them.
Here are some questions to test whether you know your filtration from your distillation...

Warm-Up Questions

1) What is meant by a pure substance in chemistry?
2) What effect will impurities in a substance have on its boiling point?
3) Which technique could you use to separate a mixture of liquids with similar boiling points?
4) Name a separation technique that could be used to separate a soluble solid from a solution.

Exam Questions

1   A scientist analysed a compound to identify if it was pure.
    When heated slowly, the compound completely melted at 65 °C.
    What does this suggest about the compound's purity? Explain your answer.

    [2 marks]

2   Lawn sand is a mixture of insoluble sharp sand and soluble ammonium sulfate fertiliser.

    (a) Describe how you would obtain pure, dry samples of the two components of lawn sand in the lab.
    [3 marks]

    (b) A student separated 51.4 g of lawn sand into sharp sand and ammonium sulfate.
    After separation, the total mass of the two products was 52.6 g.
    Suggest a reason for the difference in mass.
    [1 mark]

3   Table 1 gives the boiling points of three liquids.

    (a) State why simple distillation cannot be used to separate water from a solution of water and methanoic acid.
    [1 mark]

Liquid	Boiling point (°C)
Methanoic acid	101
Propanone	56
Water	100

Table 1

   (b) The apparatus in Figure 1 was used to separate
       a mixture of propanone and water.
       Complete the table using the options below.

   no liquid   water   propanone   both liquids

Temperature on thermometer	Contents of the flask	Contents of the beaker
30 °C	....	....
65 °C	....	....
110 °C	....	....

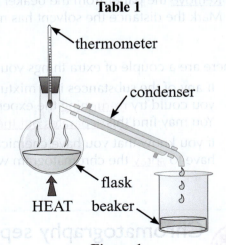

Figure 1

[3 marks]

Chromatography

Chromatography is a method used to **separate** a mixture of soluble substances and **identify** them.

Chromatography uses Two Phases

There are lots of different types of chromatography — but they all have two 'phases':

- A mobile phase — where the molecules can move. This is always a liquid or a gas.
- A stationary phase — where the molecules can't move. This can be a solid or a really thick liquid.

1) The components in the mixture separate out as the mobile phase moves over the stationary phase — they all end up in different places in the stationary phase.
2) This happens because each of the chemicals in a mixture will spend different amounts of time dissolved in the mobile phase and stuck to the stationary phase.
3) How fast a chemical moves through the stationary phase depends on how it 'distributes' itself between the two phases.

For each component in your mixture, you'll end up with one spot on your chromatogram (see next page for more on chromatograms).

In Paper Chromatography the Mobile Phase is a Solvent

In paper chromatography, the stationary phase is a piece of filter paper and the mobile phase is a solvent (e.g. water or ethanol). Here's the method for setting it up:

PRACTICAL

1) Draw a line near the bottom of the paper — this is the baseline.
   (Use a pencil to do this — pencil marks are insoluble and won't move with the solvent as ink might.) Put a spot of the mixture to be separated on the line.
2) Put some of the solvent into a beaker.
   Dip the bottom of the paper (but not the spot) into the solvent.
3) Put a watch glass on the top of the beaker to stop any solvent from evaporating away.
4) The solvent will start to move up the paper. When the chemicals in the mixture dissolve in the solvent, they will move up the paper too.
5) You will see the different chemicals in the sample separate out, forming spots at different places on the paper.
   (If one of your components is insoluble in the mobile phase, it won't move — it'll stay as a spot on the baseline.)
6) Remove the paper from the beaker before the solvent reaches the top.
   Mark the distance the solvent has moved (the solvent front) in pencil.

Diagram labels: watch glass, solvent front, paper, spot of unknown substance, point of origin, solvent

There are a couple of extra things you should bear in mind too:

1) If any of the substances in a mixture are insoluble in one solvent (e.g. stay on the baseline), you could try re-running the experiment with the same mixture, but using a different solvent. You may find this separates out the components, allowing you to find their R_f values (see next page).
2) If you know that you have chemicals in your mixture that are colourless (e.g. amino acids), you might have to spray the chromatogram with a chemical called a locating agent to show where the spots are.

Chromatography separates the different dyes in inks

Make sure you use a pencil to draw your baseline. If you use a pen, all the components of the ink in the pen will get separated, along with the substance you're analysing, which will make your results very confusing. There's more on how you can analyse your results on the next page.

Section 11 — States of Matter and Mixtures

Interpreting Chromatograms

*So, what use is **chromatography**, apart from making a pretty pattern of spots? Let's find out...*

You can Calculate the R_f Value for Each Chemical

1) In paper chromatography, the piece of paper that you end up with is called a chromatogram.
2) You need to know how to work out the R_f values for the spots on a chromatogram.
3) An R_f value is the ratio between the distance travelled by the dissolved substance (the solute) and the distance travelled by the solvent.
4) You can find R_f values using the formula:

$$R_f = \frac{\text{distance travelled by substance}}{\text{distance travelled by solvent}}$$

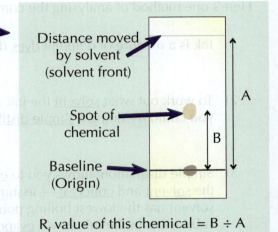

R_f value of this chemical = B ÷ A

5) To find the distance travelled by the solute, measure from the baseline to the centre of the spot.

Different Substances Have Different R_f Values

1) The R_f value is controlled by the amount of time the molecules spend in each phase. This depends on two things:
   - How soluble they are in the solvent.
   - How attracted they are to the stationary phase.

2) Molecules with a higher solubility in the solvent (and which are less attracted to the paper) will spend more time in the mobile phase than the stationary phase — so they'll be carried further up the paper.
3) As a result, different substances will separate out on a chromatogram and have different R_f values.

There are Several Ways to Interpret a Chromatogram

1) Chromatography is often carried out to see if a certain substance is present in a mixture. You run a pure sample of a substance that you think might be in your mixture alongside a sample of the mixture itself. If the sample has the same R_f values as one of the spots, they're likely to be the same.
2) Chemists sometimes run samples of pure substances called standard reference materials (SRMs) next to a mixture to check the identities of its components. SRMs have controlled concentrations and purities.
3) You can also use chromatography to do a purity test. A pure substance won't be separated by chromatography — it'll move as one blob (while a mixture should give you multiple blobs).

You need to learn the formula for R_f

R_f values always lie between 0 and 1, as the solvent always travels further than any of the substances in the mixture. If you work out an R_f value to be outside this range, you know you've gone wrong somewhere (e.g. you may have written the fraction in the formula upside-down).

Q1 A spot on a chromatogram moved 6.3 cm from the baseline. The solvent front moved 8.4 cm. Calculate the R_f value. [1 mark]

Q1 Video Solution

Section 11 — States of Matter and Mixtures

Combining Separation Techniques

You can **combine** separation techniques to analyse mixtures. Here's an example:

You can Use **Simple Distillation** and **Chromatography** to Analyse **Ink**

Here's one method of analysing the composition of an ink:

1) Ink is a mixture of different dyes dissolved in a solvent.

2) To work out what solvent the ink contains, you could try doing a simple distillation.

3) Simple distillation allows you to evaporate off the solvent and collect it — assuming that the solvent has the lowest boiling point of all the substances in the ink, it will evaporate first.

4) The thermometer in the distillation set-up will read the boiling point of the solvent when it's evaporating (and therefore when it's being collected).

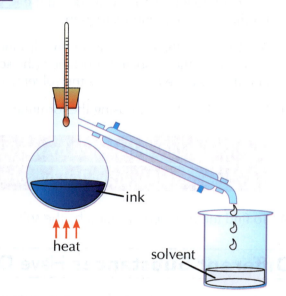

5) You can use the boiling point of the solvent to try and determine what it is. For example, if the solvent in a certain ink evaporates at 100 °C, it's quite likely to be water.

6) You could then carry out paper chromatography on a sample of the ink — this will separate out the different dyes in the ink, so that you can see how many there are.

7) You can compare the R_f values of the different spots on the chromatogram produced with reference values (or run further chromatography experiments with pure substances) to work out what dyes are in the ink.

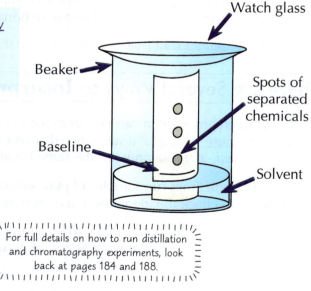

For full details on how to run distillation and chromatography experiments, look back at pages 184 and 188.

You're not just limited to using one separation technique...

Some mixtures are made up of several components, so you might need to use a combination of the methods covered in this section to get all the different components out. Make sure you understand each step of the experiment above — you may be tested on it in the exam.

Section 11 — States of Matter and Mixtures

Water Treatment

Water often needs to be *purified* to make it *safe to drink*...

There are a Variety of Limited Water Resources in the UK

In the UK, there are a number of sources of water which can be purified to provide us with potable water (water that is fit to drink). We get our water from:

1) SURFACE WATER: from lakes, rivers and reservoirs. In much of England and Wales, these sources start to run dry during the summer months.
2) GROUND WATER: from aquifers (rocks that trap water underground). In parts of south-east England, where surface water is very limited, as much as 70% of the domestic water supply comes from ground water.
3) WASTE WATER: from water that's been contaminated by a human process, e.g. as a by-product from some industrial processes. Treating waste water to make it potable is preferable to disposing of the water, which can be polluting. How easy waste water is to treat depends on the levels of contaminants in it.

Water is Purified in Water Treatment Plants

The water that comes out of your taps doesn't just come straight from the source — first it has to be purified. How much purification it needs will depend on the source. Ground water from aquifers is usually quite pure, but waste water and surface water needs a lot of treatment. But, wherever it comes from, before we can drink it most water will be purified using the following processes:

1) Filtration — a wire mesh screens out large twigs etc., and then gravel and sand beds filter out any other solid bits.
2) Sedimentation — iron sulfate or aluminium sulfate is added to the water, which makes fine particles clump together and settle at the bottom.
3) Chlorination — chlorine gas is bubbled through to kill harmful bacteria and other microbes.

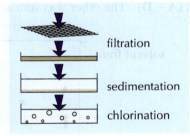

Some soluble impurities that are dissolved in the water are not removed as they can't be filtered out — these include the minerals which cause water hardness.

You Can Get Potable Water by Distilling Sea Water

1) In some very dry countries, e.g. Kuwait, sea water is distilled (see p.184) to produce drinking water.
2) Distillation needs loads of energy, so it's really expensive, especially if you're trying to produce large quantities of fresh water. So, we don't tend to use this method of producing potable water in the UK.

Water Used in Chemical Analysis must be Pure

1) Lots of chemistry involves carrying out experiments to work out what something is, or how it will react.
2) For experiments that involve mixing or dissolving something in water, you should use deionised water.
3) Deionised water is water that has had the ions (such as calcium, iron and copper ions) that are present in normal tap water removed.
4) These ions, although present in small amounts and harmless in tap water, can interfere with reactions. Using normal water could give your experiment a false result.

So purified water isn't completely pure...

Don't forget that even drinking water isn't pure enough to use in lab experiments.

Q1 Describe the steps used to treat waste water to make it potable. [3 marks]

Warm-Up and Exam Questions

Look, a chromatography question — those things are fun. Get your investigative hat on and get stuck in...

Warm-Up Questions

1) In paper chromatography, what is the stationary phase?
2) Why is a pencil used to draw the baseline on a chromatogram?
3) A mixture of two chemicals, A and B, is separated using paper chromatography. Chemical A is more soluble in the solvent than B is. Which chemical, A or B, will end up closer to the solvent front?
4) Name the process used to convert sea water to potable water.

Exam Questions

1   A student is making a solution to use in an experiment by dissolving pure, solid sodium iodide in water. Suggest why the student should not use tap water. State what he should use instead.

[2 marks]

PRACTICAL

2   A scientist used chromatography to analyse the composition of five inks. Four of the inks were unknown (**A – D**). The other was sunrise yellow. The results are shown in **Figure 1**.

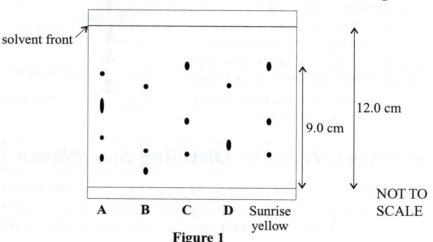

Figure 1

(a) Explain how **Figure 1** shows that none of the inks are pure substances.

[1 mark]

(b) Which ink definitely contains at least four different compounds?

[1 mark]

(c) Which of the inks, **A-D**, could be the same as sunrise yellow? Explain your answer.

[2 marks]

(d) Calculate the R_f value for the spot of chemical in sunrise yellow which is furthest up the chromatogram.

[2 marks]

(e) State **one** technique you could use to identify the solvent in each of the inks.

[1 mark]

Section 11 — States of Matter and Mixtures

Section 12 — Chemical Changes

Acids and Bases

You can test the pH of a solution using an **indicator** — and that means pretty **colours**...

The pH Scale Goes From 0 to 14

1) The pH scale is a measure of how acidic or alkaline a solution is. A neutral substance has pH 7.
2) An acid is a substance with a pH of less than 7. Acids form H^+ ions in water.
3) The higher the concentration of hydrogen ions in a solution, the more acidic it is, so the lower its pH will be. In other words, as the concentration of hydrogen ions increases, the pH decreases.
4) A base is a substance that reacts with an acid to produce a salt and water.
5) An alkali is a base that is soluble in water. All alkalis have a pH of more than 7 and they form OH^- ions (otherwise known as hydroxide ions) in water.
6) In alkaline solutions, the higher the concentration of OH^- ions, the higher the pH.

You Can Measure the pH of a Solution

1) An indicator is a dye that changes colour depending on whether it's above or below a certain pH.
2) Indicators are simple to use — add a few drops to the solution you're testing, then compare the colour the solution goes to a pH chart for that indicator. E.g. here's the pH chart for Universal indicator.

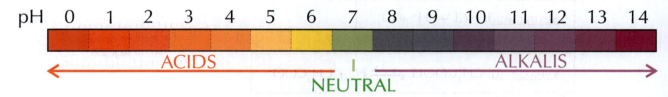

Some indicators that you need to know about are:
- litmus — is red in acidic solutions, purple in neutral solutions and blue in alkaline solutions.
- methyl orange — is red in acidic solutions and yellow in neutral and alkaline solutions.
- phenolphthalein — is colourless in acidic or neutral solutions and pink in alkaline solutions.

Acids and Bases Neutralise Each Other

1) The reaction between an acid and a base is called neutralisation. It produces a salt and water.

$$\text{acid} + \text{base} \rightarrow \text{salt} + \text{water}$$

e.g. $HCl + NaOH \rightarrow NaCl + H_2O$
(acid) (base) (salt) (water)

2) Neutralisation reactions in aqueous solution can also be shown as an ionic equation (see p.140) in terms of H^+ and OH^- ions:

$$H^+_{(aq)} + OH^-_{(aq)} \rightarrow H_2O_{(l)}$$

3) When an acid neutralises a base (or vice versa), the products are neutral, i.e. they have a pH of 7. At pH 7, the concentration of hydrogen ions is equal to the concentration of hydroxide ions.

Interesting fact — your skin is slightly acidic (pH 5.5)

It's important to use the right indicator with acids and alkalis. You can't use phenolphthalein to distinguish between acidic and neutral solutions, but litmus or methyl orange would be good choices.

Q1 Explain how water is produced in a neutralisation reaction. [2 marks]

Strong Acids, Weak Acids and their Reactions

*Right then. More on **acids**. Brace yourself...*

Acids Produce Hydrogen Ions in Water

All acids can ionise (or dissociate) in solution — that means splitting up to produce a hydrogen ion, H^+, and another ion. For example,

$$HCl \rightarrow H^+ + Cl^-$$
$$HNO_3 \rightarrow H^+ + NO_3^-$$

HCl and HNO_3 don't produce hydrogen ions until they meet water.

Acids Can be Strong or Weak

1) Strong acids (e.g. sulfuric, hydrochloric and nitric acids) ionise almost completely in water — a large proportion of the acid molecules dissociate to release H^+ ions. They tend to have low pHs (pH 0-2).
2) Weak acids (e.g. ethanoic, citric and carbonic acids) do not fully ionise in solution — only a small proportion of the acid molecules dissociate to release H^+ ions. Their pHs tend to be around 2-6.
3) The ionisation of a weak acid is a reversible reaction, which sets up an equilibrium. Since only a few of the acid particles release H^+ ions, the equilibrium lies well to the left.

Strong acid: $HCl \rightarrow H^+ + Cl^-$

Weak acid: $CH_3COOH \rightleftharpoons H^+ + CH_3COO^-$

For more on equilibria turn to page 221.

Don't Confuse Strong Acids with Concentrated Acids

1) Acid strength (i.e. strong or weak) tells you what proportion of the acid molecules ionise in water.

2) The concentration of an acid is different. Concentration measures how much acid there is in a litre (1 dm^3) of water. Concentration is basically how watered down your acid is.

3) An acid with a large number of acid molecules compared to the volume of water is said to be concentrated. An acid with a small number of acid molecules compared to the volume of water is said to be dilute.

Concentration is measured in $g\ dm^{-3}$ or $mol\ dm^{-3}$.

4) Note that concentration describes the total number of dissolved acid molecules — not the number of molecules that produce hydrogen ions.

5) The more grams (or moles) of acid per dm^3, the more concentrated the acid is.

6) So you can have a dilute strong acid, or a concentrated weak acid.

Section 12 — Chemical Changes

Strong Acids, Weak Acids and their Reactions

Changing the Concentration of an Acid Affects its pH

1) If the concentration of H⁺ ions increases by a factor of 10, the pH decreases by 1.
2) So if the H⁺ ion concentration increases by a factor of 100 (= 10 × 10), the pH decreases by 2 (= 1 + 1), and so on.
3) Decreasing the H⁺ ion concentration has the opposite effect — a decrease by a factor of 10 in the H⁺ concentration means an increase of 1 on the pH scale.

A solution with a hydrogen ion concentration of 0.001 mol dm⁻³ has a pH of 3. What would happen to the pH if you increased the hydrogen ion concentration to 0.01 mol dm⁻³?

The H⁺ concentration has increased by a factor of 10, so the pH would decrease by 1. So the new pH would be 3 − 1 = 2.

Acids React With Metals or Metal Carbonates to Form Salts

1) Salts are ionic compounds.
2) In general, hydrochloric acid produces chloride salts, sulfuric acid produces sulfate salts and nitric acid produces nitrate salts.
3) You need to know what happens when you react an acid with a metal or a metal carbonate:

Acid + Metal → Salt + Hydrogen

Examples: $2HCl + Mg \rightarrow MgCl_2 + H_2$ (Magnesium chloride)
$H_2SO_4 + Mg \rightarrow MgSO_4 + H_2$ (Magnesium sulfate)

The reaction of nitric acid with metals can be more complicated — you get a nitrate salt, but instead of hydrogen gas, the other products are usually a mixture of water, NO and NO_2.

1) You can test for hydrogen using a lighted splint.
2) Hydrogen makes a "squeaky pop" with a lighted splint.
3) The noise comes from the hydrogen burning with the oxygen in the air to form water.

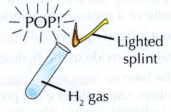

Acid + Metal Carbonate → Salt + Water + Carbon Dioxide

Examples:
$2HCl + Na_2CO_3 \rightarrow 2NaCl + H_2O + CO_2$ (Sodium chloride)
$H_2SO_4 + K_2CO_3 \rightarrow K_2SO_4 + H_2O + CO_2$ (Potassium sulfate)
$2HNO_3 + ZnCO_3 \rightarrow Zn(NO_3)_2 + H_2O + CO_2$ (Zinc nitrate)

1) You can test to see if a gas is carbon dioxide by bubbling it through limewater.
2) If the gas is carbon dioxide, the limewater will turn cloudy.

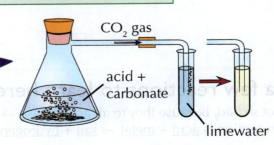

Section 12 — Chemical Changes

Strong Acids, Weak Acids and their Reactions

Salts Also Form When Acids React with Bases

1) A salt is formed during a neutralisation reaction (a reaction between an acid and a base).
2) You need to be able to remember what happens when you add acids to various bases...

Acid + Metal Hydroxide → Salt + Water

Examples:
$HCl + NaOH \rightarrow NaCl + H_2O$ (Sodium chloride)
$H_2SO_4 + Zn(OH)_2 \rightarrow ZnSO_4 + 2H_2O$ (Zinc sulfate)
$HNO_3 + KOH \rightarrow KNO_3 + H_2O$ (Potassium nitrate)

These are the same as the acid/base neutralisation reaction you met on page 193.

Acid + Metal Oxide → Salt + Water

Examples:
$2HCl + CuO \rightarrow CuCl_2 + H_2O$ (Copper chloride)
$H_2SO_4 + ZnO \rightarrow ZnSO_4 + H_2O$ (Zinc sulfate)
$2HNO_3 + MgO \rightarrow Mg(NO_3)_2 + H_2O$ (Magnesium nitrate)

You Can Investigate How pH Changes in Neutralisation Reactions

Here's how to investigate the neutralisation reaction between calcium oxide (a base) and dilute hydrochloric acid.

You can do this experiment with calcium hydroxide too.

1) Start by measuring out a set volume of dilute hydrochloric acid into a conical flask. Use a pipette or a measuring cylinder for this (see page 379).
2) Measure out a fixed mass of calcium oxide using a mass balance.
3) Add the calcium oxide to the hydrochloric acid.
4) Wait for the base to completely react, then record the pH of the solution, using either a pH probe (see page 380) or Universal indicator paper. (You can use a glass rod to spot samples of the solution to the paper.)
5) Repeat steps 2 to 4 until all the acid has reacted. You'll know you've reached this point when you get unreacted calcium oxide sitting at the bottom of the flask.
6) You can then plot a graph to see how the pH changes with the mass of base added. You should find it looks a bit like this.

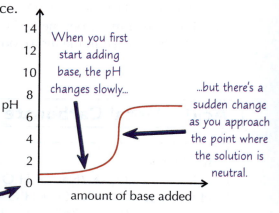

When you first start adding base, the pH changes slowly... ...but there's a sudden change as you approach the point where the solution is neutral.

Quite a few reactions to learn here...

...but it's not so bad, because they're all acid + base → salt + water (and sometimes carbon dioxide). The only exception is acid + metal → salt + hydrogen. Keep that in mind and you'll be laughing.

Warm-Up and Exam Questions

So you think you know everything there is to know about acids? Time to put yourself to the test.

Warm-Up Questions

1) What is a base?
2) What range of values can pH take?
3) What term is used to describe a solution with a pH of 7?
4) What's the difference between:
   a) a strong acid and a weak acid?   b) a dilute acid and a concentrated acid?
5) Name the two substances formed when hydrochloric acid reacts with sodium.
6) Write a balanced chemical equation for the reaction of sulfuric acid with calcium carbonate.
7) Describe the chemical test for carbon dioxide.

Exam Questions

1 A student had a sample of acid in a test tube. He gradually added some alkali to the acid. *(Grade 4-6)*

(a) Name the type of ion that acids produce in aqueous solutions.
[1 mark]

(b) What type of reaction took place in the student's experiment?

☐ thermal decomposition   ☐ neutralisation   ☐ redox   ☐ combustion
[1 mark]

PRACTICAL

2 Calcium hydroxide was added to a solution of dilute hydrochloric acid. *(Grade 6-7)*

(a) Complete and balance the symbol equation given below for the reaction of hydrochloric acid with calcium hydroxide.

$$2HCl + Ca(OH)_2 \rightarrow \text{..................} + \text{..................}$$
[2 marks]

(b) Universal indicator was used to indicate when the reaction was complete.
Dilute hydrochloric acid has a pH of around 1.
Describe the colour change you would expect to see as the acidic solution approached a neutral pH.
[2 marks]

In another experiment, the pH of the acid solution rose from 2 to 5 when the calcium hydroxide was added.

(c) What factor would the hydrogen ion concentration of the solution have decreased by?
[1 mark]

(d) Explain why the concentration of hydrogen ions decreases during the reaction.
[1 mark]

(e) Calcium hydroxide is insoluble in water. What name is given to a soluble base?
[1 mark]

Making Insoluble Salts

Now it's time to learn which salts are **soluble** and which ones **are insoluble**.

The Rules of Solubility

Soluble things dissolve in water. Insoluble things don't.

1) How you make a salt depends on whether it's soluble or insoluble.
2) You may need to work out if, when two solutions are mixed, a salt will form as a precipitate (i.e. it's an insoluble salt), or whether it will just form in solution (i.e. it's a soluble salt).
3) This table is a pretty fail-safe way of working out whether a substance is soluble in water or not.

Substance	Soluble or Insoluble?
common salts of sodium, potassium and ammonium	soluble
nitrates	soluble
common chlorides	soluble (except silver chloride and lead chloride)
common sulfates	soluble (except lead, barium and calcium sulfate)
common carbonates and hydroxides	insoluble (except for sodium, potassium and ammonium ones)

Making Insoluble Salts — Precipitation Reactions

1) To make a pure, dry sample of an insoluble salt, you can use a precipitation reaction. You just need to pick the right two soluble salts and react them together to get your insoluble salt.
2) E.g. to make lead chloride (insoluble), mix lead nitrate and sodium chloride (both soluble).

lead nitrate + sodium chloride → lead chloride + sodium nitrate

$$Pb(NO_3)_{2\,(aq)} + 2NaCl_{(aq)} \rightarrow PbCl_{2\,(s)} + 2NaNO_{3\,(aq)}$$

Method

1) Add 1 spatula of lead nitrate to a test tube. Add water to dissolve it. You should use deionised water to make sure there are no other ions about. Shake it thoroughly to ensure that all the lead nitrate has dissolved. Then, in a separate test tube, do the same with 1 spatula of sodium chloride.
2) Tip the two solutions into a small beaker, and give it a good stir to make sure it's all mixed together. The lead chloride should precipitate out.

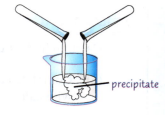
precipitate

filter paper
filter funnel

3) Put a folded piece of filter paper into a filter funnel, and stick the funnel into a conical flask.
4) Pour the contents of the beaker into the middle of the filter paper. Make sure that the solution doesn't go above the filter paper — otherwise some of the solid could dribble down the side.
5) Swill out the beaker with more deionised water, and tip this into the filter paper — to make sure you get all the precipitate from the beaker.
6) Rinse the contents of the filter paper with deionised water to make sure that all the soluble sodium nitrate has been washed away.
7) Then just scrape the lead chloride onto fresh filter paper and leave it to dry in an oven or a desiccator.

lead chloride

Solubility rules tell you which salts dissolve and which don't

You'll need to know the solubility rules for different salts, so make sure you learn the table above.

Q1 Suggest two reactants you could use to form barium sulfate in a precipitation reaction. [2 marks]

Q1 Video Solution

Making Soluble Salts

You met the technique for making **insoluble salts** on the previous page. Time to cover **soluble salts** now...

Making **Soluble Salts** — Use an **Acid** and an **Insoluble Base**

You can make a soluble salt by reacting an acid that contains one of the ions you want in the salt with an insoluble base that contains the other ion you need (often a metal oxide or metal hydroxide).

For some salts, you can use a metal instead of the base.

Method

1) Start by heating the acid in a water bath (see p.383) — this speeds up the reaction between the acid and the insoluble base. Do this in a fume cupboard to avoid releasing acid fumes into the room.

2) Then add the base to the acid — the base and acid will react to produce a soluble salt (and water). You will know when the base is in excess and all the acid has been neutralised because the excess solid will just sink to the bottom of the flask.

3) Filter off the excess solid to get a solution containing only the salt and water.

4) Heat the solution gently, using a Bunsen burner, to slowly evaporate off some of the water.

5) Leave the solution to cool and allow the salt to crystallise (see p.186).

6) Filter off the solid salt and leave it to dry.

Example: You can add copper oxide to warm sulfuric acid to make a solution of copper sulfate:

$$CuO_{(s)} + H_2SO_{4\,(aq)} \rightarrow CuSO_{4\,(aq)} + H_2O_{(l)}$$

If you evaporate off some of the water and leave this solution to crystallise, you should get lovely blue crystals of hydrated copper sulfate, which you can filter off and dry.

Acid + insoluble base → soluble salt + water

It's important that you make sure the base is in excess in this experiment, so that you don't have any leftover acid in your product. That way, the final solution is simply a soluble salt and water.

Section 12 — Chemical Changes

Making Soluble Salts

You can Make Soluble Salts Using Acid/Alkali Reactions

1) Soluble salts (salts that dissolve in water) can be made by reacting an acid with an alkali.
2) But you can't tell whether the reaction has finished — there's no signal that all the acid has been neutralised. You also can't just add an excess of alkali to the acid, because the salt is soluble and would be contaminated with the excess alkali.
3) Instead, you need to work out exactly the right amount of alkali to neutralise the acid. For this, you need to do a titration using an indicator. Here's what you do...

Method

1) Measure out a set amount of acid into a conical flask using a pipette.

2) Add a few drops of indicator. For a titration, you should use an indicator with a single, clear colour change (like phenolphthalein or methyl orange). Universal indicator is no good as its colour change is too gradual.

3) Slowly add alkali to the acid, using a burette, until you reach the end point — this is when the acid's been exactly neutralised and the indicator changes colour.

4) Then, carry out the reaction using exactly the same volumes of alkali and acid but with no indicator, so the salt won't be contaminated with indicator.

5) The solution that remains when the reaction is complete contains only the salt and water.

6) Slowly evaporate off some of the water and then leave the solution to crystallise (see page 186 for more on crystallisation). Filter off the solid and dry it — you'll be left with a pure, dry salt.

Titrations can be used to make sure the alkali isn't in excess

Alkalis are soluble in water, so it's hard to stop them from contaminating the soluble salt produced in the reaction. Fortunately, titrations can help you out — they allow you to calculate the exact amount of acid and alkali you need to add to complete the reaction without either of them being in excess. Splendid.

Section 12 — Chemical Changes

Warm-Up and Exam Questions

Salt, glorious salt. There were a lot of experimental methods crammed into the previous few pages, so make sure you can remember each of the steps and why they're important before tackling these questions.

Warm-Up Questions

1) State whether the following salts are soluble or insoluble:
   a) potassium chloride   b) copper carbonate   c) lead sulfate   d) ammonium hydroxide
2) Explain why a titration must be used to make a soluble salt by reacting an acid and an alkali.

Exam Questions

1   Lead nitrate and potassium chloride are both soluble salts.

Name the **two** products of the reaction between a solution of lead nitrate and a solution of potassium chloride. For each product, state whether it is soluble or insoluble in water.

[2 marks]

2   A student mixes calcium chloride and magnesium sulfate solutions in a beaker.
The two solutions undergo the following reaction.

$$CaCl_{2\,(aq)} + MgSO_{4\,(aq)} \rightarrow CaSO_{4\,(s)} + MgCl_{2\,(aq)}$$

Describe a method that could be used to obtain a pure, dry sample of calcium sulfate ($CaSO_4$) from the products of the reaction.

[3 marks]

PRACTICAL

3   Copper sulfate is a soluble salt. It can be made by adding an excess of insoluble copper oxide to sulfuric acid until no further reaction occurs.

(a)   Give **one** observation that would indicate that the reaction is complete.
[1 mark]

(b)   Once the reaction is complete, the excess copper oxide can be separated from the copper sulfate solution using the apparatus shown in **Figure 1**. What is this method of separation called?
[1 mark]

(c)   Describe how you could produce solid copper sulfate from a solution of copper sulfate.

Figure 1

[3 marks]

4*   Sodium hydroxide solution and hydrochloric acid react to produce sodium chloride (a soluble salt).

Describe how you could produce a sample of pure, dry sodium chloride from sodium hydroxide solution and hydrochloric acid.

[6 marks]

Section 12 — Chemical Changes

Electrolysis

Now I hope you're sitting comfortably. We're about to embark on five pages on electrolysis.

Electrolysis Involves Oxidation and Reduction

1) Electrolysis is the breaking down of a substance using electricity. An electric current is passed through an electrolyte (a molten or dissolved ionic compound), causing it to decompose.

2) In electrolysis, oxidation (loss of electrons) and reduction (gain of electrons) occur.

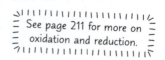
See page 211 for more on oxidation and reduction.

3) The positive ions (cations) in the electrolyte move towards the cathode (negative electrode) and are reduced (gain electrons).

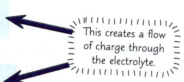
This creates a flow of charge through the electrolyte.

4) The negative ions (anions) in the electrolyte move towards the anode (positive electrode) and are oxidised (lose electrons).

5) As ions gain or lose electrons they form the uncharged substances and are discharged from the electrolyte.

Half Equations Show How Electrons are Transferred During Reactions

Half equations are really useful for showing what happens at each electrode during electrolysis. To write a half equation:

1) Put one of the things being oxidised or reduced on one side of an arrow, and the thing it gets oxidised or reduced to on the other.
2) Balance up the numbers of atoms just like in a normal equation.
3) Then add electrons (written e⁻) on to one side to balance up the charges.

Examples: Sodium is losing one electron to become a sodium ion: $Na \rightarrow Na^+ + e^-$

Hydrogen ions are gaining electrons to become hydrogen: $2H^+ + 2e^- \rightarrow H_2$

The charges on each side of the equation should balance.

Electrolysis means splitting up an electrolyte with electricity

An electrolyte must be an ionic compound that is either molten or in solution. This is so that the ions are free to move towards the oppositely-charged electrode — the cathode for cations, and the anode for anions.

Section 12 — Chemical Changes

Electrochemical Cells

*Right, now that you know what electrolysis is, it's time to find out how you **set it all up**.*

Here's How to **Set Up** an **Electrochemical Cell**

1) An electrochemical cell is a circuit made up of the anode, cathode, electrolyte, a power source and the wires that connect the two electrodes.

2) You need to know how to set up an electrochemical cell. The method used depends on whether your electrolyte is a solution or a molten ionic substance.

You could put an ammeter or bulb in series with your circuit to check you've set it up correctly.

If Your **Electrolyte** is a **Solution**...

1) Get two inert (unreactive) electrodes, e.g. graphite or platinum electrodes.

2) Clean the surfaces of the electrodes using some emery paper (or sandpaper).

3) From this point on, be careful not to touch the surfaces of the electrodes with your hands — you could transfer grease back onto the strips.

4) Place both electrodes into a beaker filled with your electrolyte.

5) Connect the electrodes to a power supply using crocodile clips and wires. When you turn the power supply on, a current will flow through the cell.

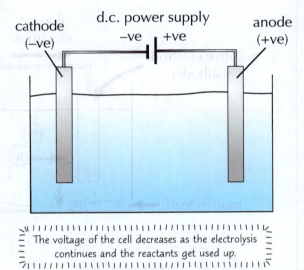

The voltage of the cell decreases as the electrolysis continues and the reactants get used up.

If Your **Electrolyte** is a **Molten Ionic Substance**...

1) Put your solid ionic substance (which will become your electrolyte) in a crucible.

2) Heat the crucible with a Bunsen burner until the solid's molten. You should do this in a fume cupboard to avoid releasing any toxic fumes into the room.

3) Once the solid's molten, dip two clean, inert electrodes into the electrolyte.

4) Then, connect the electrodes to a power supply using wires and clips — you should get a current flowing through the cell when you turn the power on.

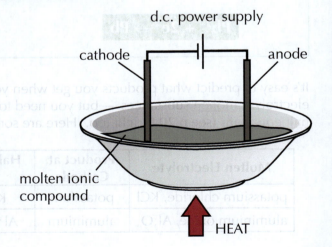

The electrodes should be clean before they're used in electrolysis

You can also do electrolysis with non-inert electrodes. Have a look at page 206 for more about this.

Section 12 — Chemical Changes

Electrolysis of Molten Substances

*Time to cover what's **going on** at the **electrodes** themselves. First up, it's **molten ionic substances**...*

Electrolysis of Molten Ionic Compounds Forms Elements

1) An ionic solid can't be electrolysed because the ions are in fixed positions and can't move.
2) Molten ionic compounds can be electrolysed because the ions can move freely and conduct electricity.
3) Positive metal ions are reduced to metal atoms at the cathode.
4) Negative ions are oxidised to atoms or molecules at the anode.
5) Molten ionic compounds are always broken up into their elements.

Example: Electrolysis of Molten Lead Bromide ($PbBr_2$)

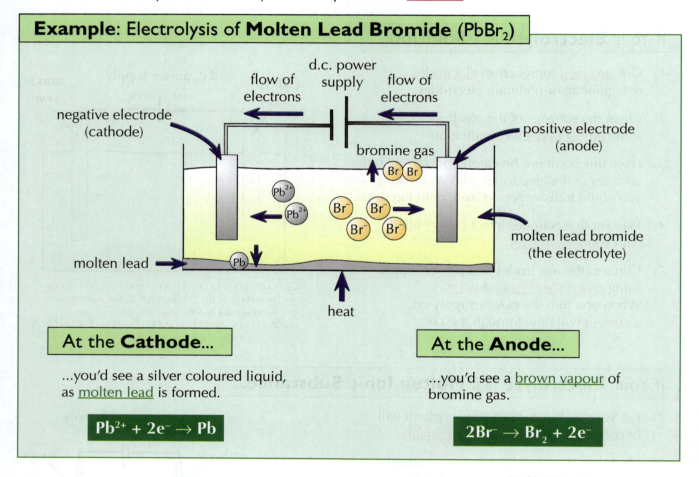

At the Cathode...
...you'd see a silver coloured liquid, as molten lead is formed.

$$Pb^{2+} + 2e^- \rightarrow Pb$$

At the Anode...
...you'd see a brown vapour of bromine gas.

$$2Br^- \rightarrow Br_2 + 2e^-$$

It's easy to predict what products you get when you electrolyse molten substances — but you need to get the half equations (see p.202) right too. Here are some examples:

See page 154 for predicting what ions different metals and non-metals form.

Molten Electrolyte	Product at Cathode	Half equation at Cathode	Product at Anode	Half equation at Anode
potassium chloride, KCl	potassium	$K^+ + e^- \rightarrow K$	chlorine	$2Cl^- \rightarrow Cl_2 + 2e^-$
aluminium oxide, Al_2O_3	aluminium	$Al^{3+} + 3e^- \rightarrow Al$	oxygen	$2O^{2-} \rightarrow O_2 + 4e^-$

Molten ionic compounds only have one source of ions

The only ions you need to worry about are those in the ionic compound. The next page about electrolysis of aqueous solutions is a bit harder, so make sure you fully understand this page first.

Q1 A student carries out electrolysis on molten calcium chloride. What is produced at:
a) the anode?   b) the cathode?
[2 marks]

Electrolysis of Aqueous Solutions

When carrying out **electrolysis** on an **aqueous solution** you have to factor in the ions in **water**.

Electrolysis of Aqueous Solutions is a Bit More Complicated

In aqueous solutions, as well as the ions from the ionic compound, there will be hydrogen ions (H^+) and hydroxide ions (OH^-) from the water: $H_2O_{(l)} \rightleftharpoons H^+_{(aq)} + OH^-_{(aq)}$

Cathode
1) At the cathode, if H^+ ions and metal ions are present, hydrogen gas will be produced if the metal is more reactive than hydrogen (e.g. sodium).
2) If the metal is less reactive than hydrogen (e.g. copper or silver), then a solid layer of the pure metal will be produced instead.

Anode
1) At the anode, if OH^- and halide ions (Cl^-, Br^-, I^-) are present, molecules of chlorine, bromine or iodine will be formed.
2) If no halide ions are present, then oxygen will be formed.

You can use reactivity series to find out which metals are more or less reactive than hydrogen (see page 208).

Example: Electrolysis of Sodium Chloride (NaCl) Solution

1) A solution of sodium chloride (NaCl) contains four different ions: Na^+, Cl^-, OH^- and H^+.

2) Sodium metal is more reactive than hydrogen. So at the cathode, hydrogen gas is produced.

$$2H^+ + 2e^- \rightarrow H_2$$

3) Chloride ions are present in the solution. So at the anode chlorine gas is produced.

$$2Cl^- \rightarrow Cl_2 + 2e^-$$

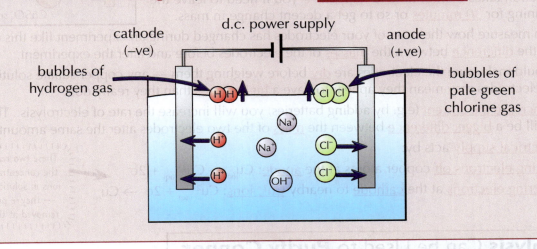

Here are some more examples of aqueous electrolytes and the products of their electrolysis:

Aqueous Electrolyte	Product at Cathode	Half equation at Cathode	Product at Anode	Half equation at Anode
copper chloride, $CuCl_2$	copper	$Cu^{2+} + 2e^- \rightarrow Cu$	chlorine	$2Cl^- \rightarrow Cl_2 + 2e^-$
sodium sulfate, Na_2SO_4	hydrogen	$2H^+ + 2e^- \rightarrow H_2$	oxygen	$4OH^- \rightarrow O_2 + 2H_2O + 4e^-$
water acidified with sulfuric acid, H_2O/H_2SO_4	hydrogen	$2H^+ + 2e^- \rightarrow H_2$	oxygen	$4OH^- \rightarrow O_2 + 2H_2O + 4e^-$

There are lots of ions to think about here...

EXAM TIP: In the exam, it might be a good idea to write out all of the ions in the solution, and then circle the ones that react at the electrodes. That way, you're less likely to forget any of the ions present.

Section 12 — Chemical Changes

PRACTICAL: Electrolysis of Copper Sulfate

Electrolysis of Copper Sulfate with Inert Electrodes Produces Oxygen

1) A solution of copper sulfate ($CuSO_4$) contains four different ions: Cu^{2+}, SO_4^{2-}, H^+ and OH^-.
2) When you electrolyse copper sulfate solution with inert electrodes:

The method used to set up this electrochemical cell is on page 203.

- Copper is less reactive than hydrogen, so copper metal is produced at the cathode (you see a coating of copper on the electrode).

$$Cu^{2+} + 2e^- \rightarrow Cu$$

- There aren't any halide ions present, so oxygen and water are produced at the anode (you see bubbles of oxygen gas forming).

$$4OH^- \rightarrow O_2 + 2H_2O + 4e^-$$

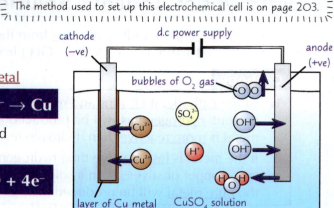

Non-Inert Electrodes Take Part in Electrolysis Reactions

1) If you set up an electrochemical cell in the same way as the one above, but using copper electrodes in a solution of copper sulfate instead of inert electrodes, the result is different.
2) As the reaction continues, the mass of the anode will decrease and the mass of the cathode will increase. This is because copper is transferred from the anode to the cathode.
3) The reaction takes a bit of time to happen — you'll need to leave the cell running for 30 minutes or so to get a decent change in mass.
4) You can measure how the mass of your electrodes has changed during an experiment like this one by finding the difference between the masses of the electrodes before and after the experiment.
5) You should make sure the electrodes are dry before weighing them — any copper sulfate solution on the electrodes may mean they appear to have a higher mass than they really do...
6) If you increase the current (e.g. by adding batteries) you will increase the rate of electrolysis. This means there will be a bigger difference between the mass of the two electrodes after the same amount of time.
7) The electrical supply acts by:
   - Pulling electrons off copper atoms at the anode: $Cu_{(s)} \rightarrow Cu^{2+}_{(aq)} + 2e^-$
   - Offering electrons at the cathode to nearby Cu^{2+} ions: $Cu^{2+}_{(aq)} + 2e^- \rightarrow Cu_{(s)}$

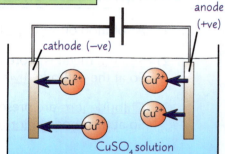

These two reactions mean the concentration of Cu^{2+} ions in solution is constant — they're produced and removed at the same rate.

Electrolysis Can be Used to Purify Copper

Copper can be extracted from its ore by reduction with carbon (see p.214), but copper made in this way is impure. Electrolysis is used to purify it — this method uses an electrochemical cell with copper electrodes:

When copper is purified using electrolysis, the anode starts off as a big lump of impure copper, the electrolyte is copper(II) sulfate solution (which contains Cu^{2+} ions) and the cathode starts off as a thin piece of pure copper. Here's what happens during the process:

1) The impure copper anode is oxidised, dissolving into the electrolyte to form copper ions:

$$Cu \rightarrow Cu^{2+} + 2e^-$$

2) The copper ions are reduced at the pure copper cathode, and add to it as a layer of pure copper:

$$Cu^{2+} + 2e^- \rightarrow Cu$$

3) Any impurities from the impure copper anode sink to the bottom of the cell, forming a sludge.

Warm-Up and Exam Questions

Time to test your mettle. Try and get through the following questions. If there's anything you're not quite sure about, have a look at the pages again until you can answer the questions without batting an eyelid.

Warm-Up Questions

1) a) Explain what is meant by "oxidation" in terms of the transfer of electrons.
   b) At which electrode does oxidation happen during electrolysis?
2) Describe how you would carry out an electrolysis where the electrolyte is a solution.
3) What products are made when molten zinc chloride is electrolysed?
4) What is formed at the anode during the electrolysis of an aqueous solution of sodium sulfate?
5) When you electrolyse copper sulfate solution with inert electrodes, what forms at the cathode?

Exam Questions

1   Aluminium is extracted by electrolysis of molten aluminium oxide (Al_2O_3).

   (a) Complete the half equation below for the reaction that occurs at the negative electrode.

   .... + 3e⁻ → ....

   [1 mark]

   (b) Complete the half equation below for the reaction that occurs at the positive electrode.

   .... → .... + 4e⁻

   [1 mark]

   (c) The positive electrode is made of carbon. Carbon is non-inert.
   Suggest why the positive electrode will need to be replaced over time.

   [2 marks]

2   When sodium chloride solution is electrolysed, a gas is produced at each electrode.

   (a) Name the gas produced at the negative electrode.

   [1 mark]

   (b) Give the half equation for the reaction at the negative electrode.

   [1 mark]

   (c) Name the gas produced at the positive electrode.

   [1 mark]

   (d) Give the half equation for the reaction at the positive electrode.

   [1 mark]

   (e) Explain why sodium hydroxide is left in solution at the end of the reaction.

   [2 marks]

   (f) If copper chloride solution is electrolysed, copper metal is produced at the negative electrode, instead of the gas named in part **(a)**. Explain why.

   [1 mark]

Section 12 — Chemical Changes

Section 13 — Extracting Metals and Equilibria

The Reactivity Series

Reactivity series are lists of **metals** (sometimes with some **carbon** or **hydrogen** thrown in). But they're not just any old lists in any old order. As the name suggests, they tell you all about **reactivities**.

If Something Gains Oxygen it's Oxidised

Oxidation can mean the reaction with, or addition of oxygen. Reduction can be the removal of oxygen.

E.g. $Fe_2O_3 + 3CO \rightarrow 2Fe + 3CO_2$

- Iron oxide is reduced to iron (as oxygen is removed).
- Carbon monoxide is oxidised to carbon dioxide (as oxygen is added).

Reduction and oxidation can also be to do with electrons (see page 211).

Combustion reactions involve oxidation. They're always exothermic (see page 247).

E.g. $CH_4 + 2O_2 \rightarrow CO_2 + 2H_2O$

- Both the carbon and hydrogen are oxidised — they gain oxygen.
- The oxygen molecules are reduced as the oxygen atoms get split up by the reaction.

The Reactivity Series Shows How Easily Metals Are Oxidised

1) A reactivity series is a table that lists metals in order of their reactivity.
2) As well as the metals, carbon is often included in reactivity series — a metal's position in the reactivity series compared to carbon dictates how it's extracted from its ore (see pages 214-215).
3) Hydrogen can be included in the reactivity series too — this shows the reactivity of metals with dilute acids (see next page).
4) Here's an example of a reactivity series:

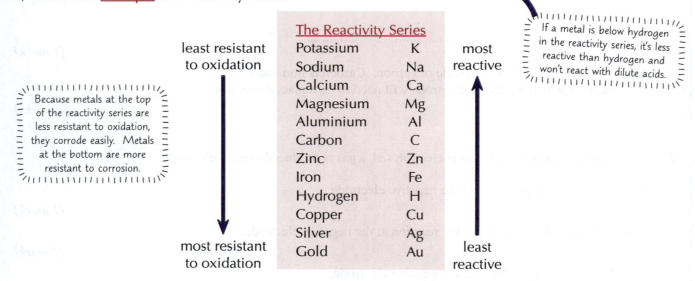

If a metal is below hydrogen in the reactivity series, it's less reactive than hydrogen and won't react with dilute acids.

Because metals at the top of the reactivity series are less resistant to oxidation, they corrode easily. Metals at the bottom are more resistant to corrosion.

The Reactivity Series
Potassium	K
Sodium	Na
Calcium	Ca
Magnesium	Mg
Aluminium	Al
Carbon	C
Zinc	Zn
Iron	Fe
Hydrogen	H
Copper	Cu
Silver	Ag
Gold	Au

least resistant to oxidation → most resistant to oxidation
most reactive → least reactive

5) The metals at the top of the reactivity series are the most reactive — they easily lose their electrons to form cations (positive ions). They're also oxidised easily.
6) The metals at the bottom of the reactivity series are less reactive — they don't give up their electrons to form cations as easily. They're more resistant to oxidation than the metals higher up the reactivity series.
7) You can determine a metal's position in the reactivity series by reacting it with water and dilute acids (see p.209-210).

Metals at the top of a reactivity series are more reactive

Don't worry if you come across different reactivity series to the one shown above — they all work the same. The more reactive elements are at the top of the series and the less reactive ones are at the bottom.

Reactivity of Metals

Reactive metals tend to fizz around a bit when you drop them into acid.

How Metals React With Acids Tells You About Their Reactivity

1) The more easily a metal atom loses its outer electrons and forms a <u>positive ion</u>, the <u>more reactive</u> it will be.

2) Here's a classic experiment that you can do to show that some metals are <u>more reactive</u> than others. All you do is to place little pieces of various <u>metals</u> into <u>dilute hydrochloric acid</u>:

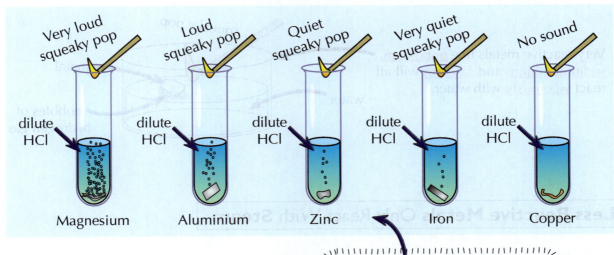

3) The more <u>reactive</u> the metal is, the <u>faster</u> the reaction with the acid will go (see page 195 for more on the reactions of metals with acids).

It's worth making sure the pieces of metal are a similar size and shape so as you can compare your results. Powdered metals will react much faster than lumps of metal as they've got larger surface areas (see page 244).

4) Very reactive metals (e.g. <u>magnesium</u>) will <u>fizz vigorously</u>, less reactive metals (e.g. <u>zinc</u>) will <u>bubble a bit</u>, and unreactive metals (e.g. <u>copper</u>) will <u>not</u> react with dilute acids <u>at all</u>.

5) You can show that <u>hydrogen</u> is forming using the <u>burning splint test</u> (see page 195). The <u>louder</u> the squeaky pop, the more hydrogen has been made in the time period and the <u>more reactive</u> the metal is.

6) The <u>speed</u> of reaction is also indicated by the <u>rate</u> at which the <u>bubbles</u> of hydrogen are given off — the faster the bubbles form, the faster the reaction and the more reactive the metal.

You could also follow the rate of the reaction by using a gas syringe to measure the volume of gas given off at regular time intervals (see p.236) or using a thermometer to measure by how much the temperature changes (as the reaction of acids with metals is exothermic — see p.247).

PRACTICAL TIP

Always take care when carrying out experiments

It's a good idea to think about how you could <u>minimise</u> the <u>risks</u> before doing any practical work. For example, when carrying out the reaction above, you should wear <u>goggles</u> to protect yourself from any acid that might spit out of the test tube when you add the metal.

Section 13 — Extracting Metals and Equilibria

Reactivity of Metals

Some Metals React With Water

1) In a similar way to their reactions with acids, the reactions of metals with water also show the reactivity of metals.

2) This is the basic reaction:

> metal + water → metal hydroxide + hydrogen

3) Very reactive metals like potassium, sodium, lithium and calcium will all react vigorously with water.

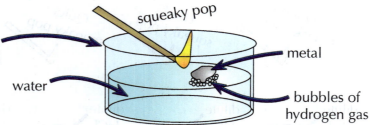

Less Reactive Metals Only React With Steam

1) Less reactive metals like magnesium, zinc and iron won't react much with cold water, but they will react with steam.

> less reactive metal + steam → metal oxide + hydrogen

2) You could show this in the lab using this experiment:

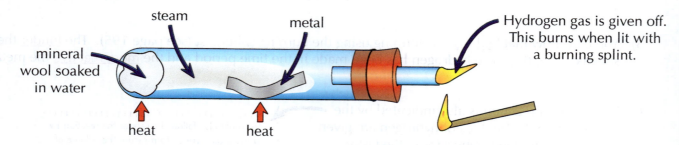

3) Copper is so unreactive that it won't react with either water or steam.

Less reactive metals need a bit of encouragement to react with H_2O

Some metals lower down the reactivity series aren't reactive enough to react with liquid water — they'll only react if you give the water a bit more energy by heating it to form steam. Splendid.

Section 13 — Extracting Metals and Equilibria

Displacement Reactions

*As well as by reacting metals with **dilute acids** and **water**, you can directly compare the reactivity of metals using **displacement reactions**. This involves reacting metals with **metal salt solutions**. Exciting stuff.*

Displacement Reactions are Redox Reactions

1) As well as talking about reduction and oxidation in terms of the loss and gain of oxygen (as on page 208), you can also talk about them in terms of electrons (as in electrolysis).

2) Oxidation can be the loss of electrons, and reduction can be the gain of electrons.

> When dealing with electrons:
> Oxidation Is Loss, Reduction Is Gain.

Remember it as OIL RIG.

3) Reduction and oxidation happen simultaneously — hence the name redox reactions.

4) Displacement reactions are examples of redox reactions.

5) In displacement reactions, a more reactive element reacts to take the place of a less reactive element in a compound. In metal displacement reactions, the more reactive metal loses electrons and the less reactive metal gains electrons.

6) So, during a displacement reaction, the more reactive metal is oxidised, and the less reactive metal is reduced. For example:

calcium + zinc sulfate → calcium sulfate + zinc

zinc is reduced

$Ca + ZnSO_4 \rightarrow CaSO_4 + Zn$

calcium is oxidised

aluminium + copper oxide → aluminium oxide + copper

copper is reduced

$2Al + 3CuO \rightarrow Al_2O_3 + 3Cu$

aluminium is oxidised

Remember OIL RIG — 'Oxidation is Loss, Reduction is Gain'

OIL RIG is a pretty handy way to remind yourself what goes on during a redox reaction. Make sure that you don't forget that redox reactions are all about the transfer of electrons.

Displacement Reactions

More Reactive Metals Displace Less Reactive Ones

1) If you put a reactive metal into a solution of a less reactive metal salt, the reactive metal will replace the less reactive metal in the salt.

> Example: if you put an iron nail in a solution of copper sulfate, the more reactive iron will "kick out" the less reactive copper from the salt. You end up with iron sulfate solution and copper metal.
>
> copper sulfate + iron → iron sulfate + copper
> $CuSO_4$ + Fe → $FeSO_4$ + Cu

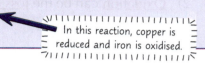
In this reaction, copper is reduced and iron is oxidised.

2) If you put a less reactive metal into a solution of a more reactive metal salt, nothing will happen.

> Example: if you put a small piece of silver metal into a solution of copper sulfate, nothing will happen. The more reactive metal (copper) is already in the salt.

3) You can use displacement reactions to work out where in the reactivity series a metal should go.

> Example: A student adds some metals to metal salt solutions and records whether any reactions happen. Use the table of results, below, to work out an order of reactivity for the metals.
>
> | | copper nitrate | magnesium chloride | zinc sulfate |
> |---|---|---|---|
> | **copper** | no reaction | no reaction | no reaction |
> | **magnesium** | magnesium nitrate and copper formed | no reaction | magnesium sulfate and zinc formed |
> | **zinc** | zinc nitrate and copper formed | no reaction | no reaction |
>
> - Magnesium displaces both copper and zinc, so it must be more reactive than both.
> - Copper is displaced by both magnesium and zinc, so it must be less reactive than both.
> - Zinc can displace copper, but not magnesium, so it must go between them.
> - The order of reactivity, from most to least, is: magnesium, zinc, copper.

A displacement reaction is a type of redox reaction

In the exam, you could be given the results of some displacement reactions and asked to use them to work out the order of reactivity of the metals involved. It's worth getting to grips with how displacement reactions work — if you know your stuff it, could be easy marks in the exam.

Section 13 — Extracting Metals and Equilibria

Warm-Up and Exam Questions

Hoping to test your knowledge with some questions? You're in luck...

Warm-Up Questions

1) What determines the reactivity of a metal?
2) Gold is below magnesium in the reactivity series. Is gold more or less easily oxidised than magnesium?
3) Write the word equation for the reaction of a metal with water.
4) What is meant by the term reduction? Give your answer in terms of electrons.
5) State which species is being oxidised in this reaction: $Zn_{(s)} + CuCl_{2(aq)} \rightarrow ZnCl_{2(aq)} + Cu_{(s)}$

Exam Questions

1 **Figure 1** shows part of the reactivity series of metals. Hydrogen has also been included in this reactivity series.

Potassium K
Sodium Na
Calcium Ca
Magnesium Mg
Zinc Zn
Iron Fe
HYDROGEN H
Copper Cu

Figure 1

(a) Name **one** metal from **Figure 1** that is more reactive than magnesium.

[1 mark]

(b) Name **one** metal from **Figure 1** which would not react with dilute acid.

[1 mark]

(c) A student adds a small piece of zinc to dilute acid.
 (i) Name the gas produced during the reaction.

[1 mark]

 (ii) The reaction produces bubbles of gas fairly slowly. Use this information to predict what would happen if the student repeated the experiment using iron.

[2 marks]

2 A student adds a piece of copper to some iron sulfate solution and a piece of iron to some copper sulfate solution. **Figure 2** shows what the test tubes looked like just after she added the metals.

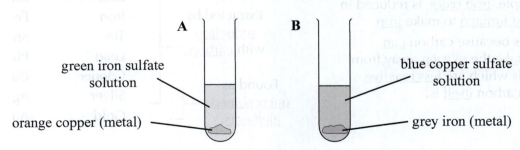

Figure 2

Predict the appearance of the solutions in tubes **A** and **B** after 2 hours. Explain your answer.

[4 marks]

Section 13 — Extracting Metals and Equilibria

Extracting Metals Using Carbon

We get most of our metals by **extracting** them **from rocks** — read on to find out how...

Ores Contain Enough Metal to Make Extraction Worthwhile

1) A metal ore is a rock which contains enough metal to make it economically worthwhile extracting the metal from it. In many cases the ore is an oxide of the metal.

> Example: the main aluminium ore is called bauxite — it's aluminium oxide (Al_2O_3).

2) Most of the metals that we use are found in their ores in the Earth's crust. The ores are mined and the metals can then be extracted from the ores.

3) Some unreactive metals, such as gold and platinum, are present in the Earth's crust as uncombined elements. These metals can be mined straight out of the ground, but they usually need to be refined before they can be used.

Some Metals can be Extracted by Reduction with Carbon

1) A metal can be extracted from its ore chemically by reduction using carbon.
2) When an ore is reduced, oxygen is removed from it. For example:

$$2Fe_2O_3 + 3C \rightarrow 4Fe + 3CO_2$$
iron oxide + carbon → iron + carbon dioxide

Most of the time, you actually get a mixture of carbon dioxide (CO_2) and carbon monoxide (CO) when you reduce metal oxides with carbon.

See page 208 for more on the reactivity series.

3) The position of the metal in the reactivity series determines whether it can be extracted by reduction with carbon.

- Metals higher than carbon in the reactivity series have to be extracted using electrolysis (see next page) which is expensive.
- Metals below carbon in the reactivity series can be extracted by reduction using carbon. For example, iron oxide is reduced in a blast furnace to make iron.
- This is because carbon can only take the oxygen away from metals which are less reactive than carbon itself is.

The Reactivity Series

Potassium	K	more reactive
Sodium	Na	
Calcium	Ca	
Magnesium	Mg	
Aluminium	Al	
CARBON	**C**	
Zinc	Zn	
Iron	Fe	
Tin	Sn	
Lead	Pb	
Copper	Cu	
Silver	Ag	less reactive
Gold	Au	

Extracted by using electrolysis.

Extracted by reduction with carbon.

Found as uncombined elements.

Carbon can't reduce things that are above it in the reactivity series

How a metal is extracted from its ore is dependent on where it's positioned in the reactivity series. Less reactive metals are positioned at the bottom and more reactive ones are at the top.

Q1 Write a balanced equation for the reduction of lead oxide, PbO, by carbon, C. [2 marks]
Q2 How would you extract tin from its metal ore? Explain your answer. [2 marks]

Q1 Video Solution

Extracting Metals Using Electrolysis

*Not all metals can be **extracted** from their ores by **reduction** with **carbon** — for some **electrolysis** is used.*

Some Metals have to be Extracted by Electrolysis

1) Metals that are <u>more reactive</u> than carbon (see previous page) are extracted using electrolysis of <u>molten compounds</u> (see page 204 for more on this).

2) Once the metal ore is melted, an electric current is passed through it. The metal is discharged at the <u>cathode</u> and the non-metal at the <u>anode</u>.

The compounds have to be molten (i.e. liquid) so that the ions are free to move.

> Example: <u>Aluminium</u> is extracted from its ore using electrolysis with carbon electrodes. Aluminium oxide (Al_2O_3) has a high melting point, so the ore is first <u>dissolved</u> in molten cryolite (an aluminium compound with a lower melting point than Al_2O_3) to lower the melting point. The ions in this molten mixture are <u>free to move</u>.
>
> During electrolysis, <u>aluminium</u> is formed at the <u>cathode</u>:
>
> $$Al^{3+} + 3e^- \rightarrow Al$$
>
> *Aluminium metal sinks to the bottom of the cell and is siphoned off.*
>
> Oxygen forms at the <u>anode</u>:
>
> $$2O^{2-} \rightarrow O_2 + 4e^-$$
>
> The <u>overall equation</u> is:
>
> $$2Al_2O_{3(l)} \rightarrow 4Al_{(l)} + 3O_{2(g)}$$

Electrolysis is a More Expensive Process than Reduction with Carbon

1) In order to run electrolysis to extract metals from their ores, you need <u>large amounts</u> of <u>electricity</u>. <u>Electricity</u> is <u>expensive</u>, making electrolysis a pretty pricey process. There are also <u>costs</u> associated with <u>melting</u> or <u>dissolving</u> the metal ore so it can conduct electricity.

2) In comparison, extracting metals using <u>reduction with carbon</u> is much <u>cheaper</u>. Carbon is cheap, and also acts as a fuel to provide the heat needed for the reduction reaction to happen.

> This means that, in general, metals <u>lower down the reactivity series</u> (less reactive metals) are <u>cheaper to extract</u> than those higher up the reactivity series (more reactive metals).

Electrolysis is used to extract reactive metals from their ores

Extracting aluminium by electrolysis does have some <u>downsides</u>. In industry, the mixture of aluminium oxide and cryolite is heated to around 960 °C. This requires large amounts of <u>energy</u>, which often comes from <u>burning fossil fuels</u> and contributes to <u>global warming</u> (see p.263 for more.)

Q1 Use the reactivity series to predict whether aluminium or iron would be more expensive to extract from its ore. Explain your answer. [3 marks]

Q1 Video Solution

Biological Methods of Extracting Metals

*So, metals can be extracted by reducing them with carbon, or by electrolysis. That's not all though — there are some pretty nifty **biological methods** that can be used for extraction too.*

There are Biological Methods to Extract Metals

1) The supply of some metal rich ores, e.g. copper ore, is limited.

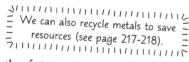
We can also recycle metals to save resources (see page 217-218).

2) The demand for lots of metals is growing and this may lead to shortages in the future.

3) Scientists are looking into new ways of extracting metals from low-grade ores (ores that only contain small amounts of the metal) or from the waste that is currently produced when metals are extracted.

4) Examples of new methods to extract metals from their ores are bioleaching and phytoextraction. These are biological methods as they use living organisms.

Bioleaching

1) This uses bacteria to separate metals from their ores, e.g. copper can be separated from copper sulfide this way.
2) The bacteria get energy from the bonds between the atoms in the ore, separating out the metal from the ore in the process.
3) The leachate (the solution produced by the process) contains metal ions, which can be extracted, e.g. by electrolysis or displacement (see pages 211-212) with a more reactive metal.

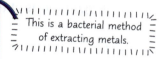
This is a bacterial method of extracting metals.

Phytoextraction

1) This involves growing plants in soil that contains metal compounds.
2) The plants can't use or get rid of the metals so they gradually build up in the leaves.
3) The plants can be harvested, dried and burned in a furnace.
4) The ash contains metal compounds from which the metal can be extracted by electrolysis or displacement reactions.

5) Traditional methods of mining are pretty damaging to the environment (see page 218). These new methods of extraction have a much smaller impact, but the disadvantage is that they're slow.

EXAM TIP

Bioleaching and phytoextraction are biological methods

In the exam, you might be asked to evaluate the use of biological methods of extracting metals, as an alternative to traditional methods of extraction. In general, biological methods are better for the environment than traditional methods, but they take a lot longer to extract the desired metal.

Section 13 — Extracting Metals and Equilibria

Recycling and Life Cycle Assessments

Recycling's a hot topic. We don't have an ***infinite amount*** of materials, e.g. metals, to keep on making things from, so recycling's really important to make sure we ***don't run out*** of lots of important raw materials.

Recycling Conserves Resources and Energy

1) Extracting raw materials can take large amounts of energy, lots of which comes from burning fossil fuels.

2) Fossil fuels are running out (they're a non-renewable resource) so it's important to conserve them. Not only this, but burning them contributes to acid rain and climate change (see pages 257 and 262-263).

3) Recycling materials saves energy as this process often only uses a small fraction of the energy needed to extract and refine the material from scratch.

4) As there's a finite amount of many raw materials, e.g. metals, on Earth, recycling conserves these resources too. Metals, like fossil fuels, are non-renewable.

5) It's particularly important to recycle materials that are rare.

Recycling Has Important Economic Benefits

1) As you saw above, extracting materials often requires more energy than just recycling them, and energy doesn't come cheap. So recycling saves money.

2) It is particularly beneficial to the economy to recycle metals that are expensive to extract or buy.

3) Recycling is also a massive industry and creates lots of jobs. The materials to be recycled need to be transported to and processed at recycling centres. They then need to be reprocessed into new products which can be sold.

4) Jobs are created at every stage of this process — far more than are created by simply disposing of waste by dumping it into landfill.

It's important to recycle — some resources are starting to run out...

If we increase the amount of products that we recycle, it'll reduce the amount of raw materials that need to be extracted. Recycling also saves money, as it generally uses less energy to recycle materials than to dig them up and process them etc. That's the theory, at least. It's often harder to put into practice...

Section 13 — Extracting Metals and Equilibria

Recycling and Life Cycle Assessments

Recycling Protects the Environment

1) Extracting metals also impacts on the environment. Mines are damaging to the environment and destroy habitats — not to mention the fact that they're a bit of an eyesore. Recycling more metals means that we don't need so many mines.

2) Recycling materials also cuts down on the amount of rubbish that gets sent to landfill. Landfill takes up space and pollutes the surroundings.

Example: Recycling Aluminium

1) If you didn't recycle aluminium, you'd have to mine more aluminium ore — 4 tonnes for every 1 tonne of aluminium you need.

2) But mining makes a mess of the landscape (and these mines are often in rainforests).

3) The ore then needs to be transported, and the aluminium extracted (which uses loads of electricity).

4) It is also expensive to send the used aluminium to landfill.

5) So it's a complex calculation, but for every 1 kg of aluminium cans you recycle, you save:
- 95% or so of the energy needed to mine and extract 'fresh' aluminium,
- 4 kg of aluminium ore,
- a lot of waste.

In fact, aluminium's about the most cost-effective metal to recycle.

Life Cycle Assessments Show Total Environmental Costs

A life cycle assessment (LCA) looks at each stage of the life of a product — from making the material from natural raw materials, to making the product from the material, using the product and disposing of the product. It works out the potential environmental impact of each stage.

There's more on LCAs on the next page.

Recycling's great — it's useful in so many different ways...

The examiners might ask you to evaluate the benefits of metal recycling. Remember that recycling doesn't just reduce the use of raw materials, it reduces the amount of energy used, the amount of damage to the environment and the amount of waste produced. It also has economic benefits.

Section 13 — Extracting Metals and Equilibria

Recycling and Life Cycle Assessments

Life Cycle Assessments can be Split in to Different Stages

There are four main stages in a product's life that should be considered when carrying out an LCA.

Choice of material
1) Metals have to be mined and extracted from their ores. These processes need a lot of energy and cause a lot of pollution.
2) Raw materials for chemical manufacture often come from crude oil. Crude oil is a non-renewable resource, and supplies are decreasing. Also, obtaining crude oil from the ground and refining it into useful raw materials requires a lot of energy and generates pollution.

Manufacture
1) Manufacturing products uses a lot of energy and other resources.
2) It can also cause a lot of pollution, e.g. harmful fumes such as CO or HCl.
3) You also need to think about any waste products and how to dispose of them.
4) Some waste can be recycled and turned into other useful chemicals, reducing the amount that ends up polluting the environment.
5) Most chemical manufacture needs water. Businesses have to make sure they don't put polluted water back into the environment at the end of the process.

Product Use
Using the product can also damage the environment. For example:
1) Paint gives off toxic fumes.
2) Burning fuels releases greenhouse gases and other harmful substances.
3) Fertilisers can leach into streams and rivers and cause damage to ecosystems.

Disposal
1) Products are often disposed of in a landfill site at the end of their life.
2) This takes up space and can pollute land and water.
3) Products might be incinerated (burnt), which causes air pollution.

Some products can be disposed of by being recycled (see p.217-218).

EXAMPLE

A company is carrying out a life cycle assessment to work out which car, A, B or C, it should make. Using the data in the table, explain which car the company should produce to minimise the environmental impact.

Car	CO_2 emissions (tonnes)	Waste solid produced (kg)	Water used (m^3)	Expected product lifespan (years)
A	17	10 720	8.2	11
B	21	5900	6.0	17
C	34	15 010	9.5	12

- Car A produces the least CO_2, but produces the second highest amount of waste solids and uses the second highest amount of water. It also has the shortest life span.
- Car B produces more CO_2 than car A, but produces by far the least waste solid, uses the least water and also has the longest life span. On balance, this looks a better choice than car A.
- Car C produces the most CO_2, the most waste solid, uses the most water, and has almost as short a life span as car A. This looks like the worst choice.

So, on balance, car B looks like the one that will have the least environmental impact.

LCAs look at the environmental impact of a product's entire life

Doing an LCA for a product is time consuming and expensive — there's a lot to take into account.

Section 13 — Extracting Metals and Equilibria

Warm-Up and Exam Questions

Time to have a go at some questions. If there's anything you're not quite sure about, have a look back at the relevant pages until you can answer the questions without batting an eyelid.

Warm-Up Questions

1) Explain why carbon can't be used to extract metals above it in the reactivity series.
2) List the main steps in the process of phytoextraction.
3) Give two economic benefits of recycling metals.
4) What are the four stages that need to be considered when conducting a life cycle assessment?

Exam Questions

1 Iron can be extracted by the reduction of iron(III) oxide (Fe_2O_3) with carbon (C), to produce iron and carbon dioxide.

(a) Write a balanced symbol equation for this reaction.

[2 marks]

(b) Explain why the iron(III) oxide is described as being reduced during this reaction.

[1 mark]

2 Aluminium is extracted by electrolysis of molten aluminium oxide (Al_2O_3).

(a) The aluminium oxide is dissolved in molten cryolite. State why.

[1 mark]

(b) Complete the half equation below for the reaction that occurs at the negative electrode.

.... + 3e⁻ → ....

[1 mark]

3 Copper needs to be extracted from its ore before it can be used.

(a) Copper can be extracted biologically from low-grade ores using bacteria. Explain how the process works.

[3 marks]

(b) Give **one** advantage and **one** disadvantage of using bioleaching rather than traditional methods of mining metals.

[2 marks]

4* **Figure 1** gives information about two types of carrier bag.

Use the information in **Figure 1** and your own knowledge to evaluate which type of bag has the smallest environmental impact over its lifetime.

[6 marks]

	Plastic Poly(ethene) Bag	Paper Bag
Raw Materials	Crude oil	Timber
Manufacture	The compounds needed to make the plastic are obtained from crude oil by fractional distillation, cracking and polymerisation.	Processing pulped timber uses lots of energy. Lots of waste is made.
Using the Product	Reusable, can be used for other things as well as shopping.	Usually single-use
Product Disposal	Recyclable but not biodegradable and will take up space in landfill and pollute land.	Biodegradable, non-toxic and can be recycled.

Figure 1

Section 13 — Extracting Metals and Equilibria

Dynamic Equilibrium

*In a **reversible reaction**, both the forward and the backward reactions are happening **at the same time**.*

Reversible Reactions can go Forwards and Backwards

A reversible reaction is one where the products can react with each other to produce the original reactants. In other words, it can go both ways.

$$A + B \rightleftharpoons C + D$$

The '$\rightleftharpoons$' shows that the reaction goes both ways.

The Haber process is an example of a reversible reaction.
1) During the Haber process, nitrogen and hydrogen react to form ammonia: $N_2 + 3H_2 \rightleftharpoons 2NH_3$
   - The nitrogen (N_2) is obtained easily from the air, which is about 78% nitrogen.
   - The hydrogen (H_2) can be extracted from hydrocarbons from sources like natural gas and crude oil.
2) The Haber process is carried out at 450 °C, with a pressure of 200 atmospheres and an iron catalyst.

Reversible Reactions Will Reach Equilibrium

1) As the reactants (A and B) react, their concentrations fall — so the forward reaction will slow down. But as more and more of the products (C and D) are made and their concentrations rise, the backward reaction will speed up.
2) After a while the forward reaction will be going at exactly the same rate as the backward one — this is equilibrium.

See page 223 for more on concentrations and rate.

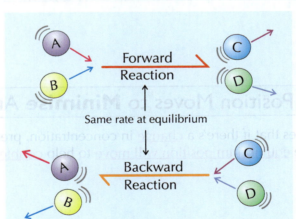

3) At equilibrium both reactions are still happening, but there's no overall effect.
4) This is a dynamic equilibrium — the forward and backward reactions are both happening at the same time and at the same rate, and the concentrations of reactants and products have reached a balance and won't change.
5) Equilibrium can only be reached if the reversible reaction takes place in a 'closed system'. A closed system just means that none of the reactants or products can escape.

Dynamic equilibrium — lots of activity, but no overall effect

The idea of dynamic equilibrium is something that you need to get to grips with, as things will get more complicated over the next couple of pages. Have another read and make sure you've got the basics sorted.

Section 13 — Extracting Metals and Equilibria

Le Chatelier's Principle

This stuff might feel a bit complicated to start with, but it all comes down to one simple rule — whatever you do to a **reversible reaction**, the **system** will **respond** to try to **undo** your change. How contrary.

The Position of Equilibrium Can be on the Right or the Left

1) When a reaction's at equilibrium it doesn't mean that the amounts of reactants and products are equal.
2) Sometimes the equilibrium will lie to the right — this basically means "lots of the products and not much of the reactants" (i.e. the concentration of products is greater than the concentration of reactants).
3) Sometimes the equilibrium will lie to the left — this basically means "lots of the reactants but not much of the products" (the concentration of reactants is greater than the concentration of products).
4) The exact position of equilibrium depends on the conditions (as well as the reaction itself).

Three Things Can Change the Position of Equilibrium

1) Three things can change the position of equilibrium (which changes the amounts of products and reactants present at equilibrium).
2) These are temperature, pressure (for equilibria involving gases) and concentrations (of reactants or products).

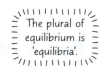
The plural of equilibrium is 'equilibria'.

> Example: ammonium chloride ⇌ ammonia + hydrogen chloride
> Heating this reaction moves the equilibrium to the right (more ammonia and hydrogen chloride) and cooling it moves it to the left (more ammonium chloride).

The Equilibrium Position Moves to Minimise Any Changes You Make

Le Chatelier's principle states that if there's a change in concentration, pressure or temperature in a reversible reaction, the equilibrium position will move to help counteract that change.

Temperature

All reactions are exothermic in one direction and endothermic in the other (see page 247).

1) If you decrease the temperature, the equilibrium will move in the exothermic direction to produce more heat.
2) If you increase the temperature, the equilibrium will move in the endothermic direction to absorb the extra heat.

> For example:
> $N_2 + 3H_2 \rightleftharpoons 2NH_3$
>
> This reaction is exothermic in the forward direction. If you decrease the temperature, the equilibrium will shift to the right (so you'll make more product).

Section 13 — Extracting Metals and Equilibria

Le Chatelier's Principle

Pressure

Changing pressure only affects equilibria involving gases.

1) If you increase the pressure, the equilibrium will move towards the side that has fewer molecules of gas to reduce pressure.
2) If you decrease the pressure, the equilibrium will move towards the side that has more molecules of gas to increase pressure.

> For example:
> $N_2 + 3H_2 \rightleftharpoons 2NH_3$
> This reaction has 4 molecules of gas on the left and 2 on the right. If you increase the pressure, the equilibrium will shift to the right (so you'll make more product).

Concentration

1) If you increase the concentration of the reactants, the equilibrium will move to the right to use up the reactants (making more products).
2) If you increase the concentration of the products, the equilibrium will move to the left to use up the products (making more reactants).
3) Decreasing the concentration will have the opposite effect.

> For example:
> $N_2 + 3H_2 \rightleftharpoons 2NH_3$
> If you increase the concentration of N_2 or H_2, the equilibrium will shift to the right to use up the extra reactants (so you'll make more product).

You Can Predict How the Position of Equilibrium Will Change

1) You can apply the rules above to any reversible reaction to work out how changing the conditions will affect the equilibrium position.
2) This has useful applications in industry — you can increase yield (how much product you get) by changing the conditions to shift the equilibrium position to the right (towards the products).

> **EXAMPLE**
> The compound PCl_5 can be made using this reaction: $PCl_{3(g)} + Cl_{2(g)} \rightleftharpoons PCl_{5(g)}$
> Explain what would happen to the equilibrium position and to the yield of PCl_5 if you increased the pressure that the reaction was being performed at.
>
> According to Le Chatelier's Principle, if you increase the pressure, the position of equilibrium will move towards the side with fewer molecules of gas to reduce the pressure. In this reaction there are 2 molecules of gas in the reactants and 1 in the products.
> The position of equilibrium will move to the right, since that is the side with fewer molecules of gas. This shifts the equilibrium towards the products, so the yield of PCl_5 will increase.

So, you do one thing, and the reaction does the other...

The best way to get your head around all this is to practise it. So have a go at the question below.

Q1   For each of the following reactions, state the effect of an increase in pressure on the amount of products at equilibrium.
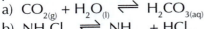
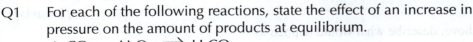
a) $CO_{2(g)} + H_2O_{(l)} \rightleftharpoons H_2CO_{3(aq)}$ [1 mark]
b) $NH_4Cl_{(s)} \rightleftharpoons NH_{3(g)} + HCl_{(g)}$ [1 mark]
c) $2CO_{(g)} + O_{2(g)} \rightleftharpoons 2CO_{2(g)}$ [1 mark]

Section 13 — Extracting Metals and Equilibria

Warm-Up and Exam Questions

Not long now 'til this section's over, but first there are some questions for you to tackle.

Warm-Up Questions

1) What can you say about forward and backward reaction rates at equilibrium?
2) Equilibrium can only be reached if the reaction takes place in a closed system. What is meant by a 'closed system'?
3) For the reaction, $N_{2(g)} + O_{2(g)} \rightleftharpoons 2NO_{(g)}$, how would changing the gas pressure affect the position of equilibrium?
4) For a reversible reaction, what is the effect on equilibrium of removing some of the reactants from the reaction mixture?

Exam Questions

1   In the reaction below, substances A and B react to form substances C and D.

$$2A + B \rightleftharpoons 2C + D$$

(a) State what the symbol $\rightleftharpoons$ indicates about the reaction of A and B.

[1 mark]

(b) State what is meant by the term **dynamic equilibrium**.

[1 mark]

2   This question is about how pressure affects the position of equilibrium.

Reaction 1: $N_2O_{4(g)} \rightleftharpoons 2NO_{2(g)}$

Reaction 2: $ClNO_{2(g)} + NO_{(g)} \rightleftharpoons NO_{2(g)} + ClNO_{(g)}$

(a) For Reaction 1, explain the effect of an **increase** in pressure on the amount of products at equilibrium.

[2 marks]

(b) For Reaction 2, explain the effect of a **decrease** in pressure on the amount of products at equilibrium.

[2 marks]

3   When calcium carbonate is heated to a high temperature in a closed system, an equilibrium is reached:

$$CaCO_{3(s)} \rightleftharpoons CaO_{(s)} + CO_{2(g)}$$

The forward reaction is endothermic.

(a) Explain whether the reverse reaction takes in or gives out energy.

[2 marks]

(b) Explain why changing the temperature of a reversible reaction always affects the position of the equilibrium.

[2 marks]

(c) For the reaction shown above, describe what would happen to the equilibrium position if the temperature was raised.

[1 mark]

Section 13 — Extracting Metals and Equilibria

Revision Summary for Sections 11-13

That's it for Sections 11-13 — there's just a page of questions standing between you and the end of these sections.
- Try these questions and tick off each one when you get it right.
- When you're completely happy with a section, tick it off.

For even more practice, try the Retrieval Quizzes for Sections 11-13 — just scan these QR codes!

Section 11 — States of Matter and Mixtures (p.179-192)

1) Describe the arrangement of particles, and the forces between them, in a liquid.
2) What states of matter are you moving from and to if you are condensing a substance?
3) Explain why air isn't considered a pure substance, according to the scientific definition of pure.
4) Draw the apparatus you would use to carry out a simple distillation.
5) Describe how to carry out crystallisation.
6) What causes different substances to separate out during a chromatography experiment?
7) Write out the formula you would use to work out the R_f value of a substance.
8) Name three different sources of water that can be made potable.

Section 12 — Chemical Changes (p.193-207)

9) What pH value would a neutral substance have?
10) Write an equation to show how ethanoic acid (CH_3COOH) acts as a weak acid.
11) If you increase the hydrogen ion concentration of a solution by a factor of 10, what will happen to the pH of the solution?
12) Write a chemical equation to show how hydrochloric acid reacts with copper oxide.
13) List three insoluble sulfates.
14) Describe how you could make a pure sample of a soluble salt from an acid and an alkali.
15) Towards which electrode do the anions in an electrolyte move?
16) Write a half equation to show what happens at the cathode in the electrolysis of copper chloride solution, $CuCl_2$.
17) Explain how electrolysis is used to purify copper.

Section 13 — Extracting Metals and Equilibria (p.208-225)

18) Describe oxidation and reduction in terms of the addition and removal of oxygen.
19) In a reactivity series, where do you find the least reactive elements?
20) You are given samples of four mystery metals and some dilute hydrochloric acid. Briefly describe how you could use these things to work out a reactivity series for the four metals.
21) What is a redox reaction?
22) Describe what happens during a displacement reaction.
23) Describe how metals less reactive than carbon are usually extracted from their ores.
24) Name two biological methods that can be used to extract metals from low-grade ores.
25) Explain how recycling metals helps to conserve energy.
26) What is a life cycle assessment?
27) If the position of equilibrium for a reversible reaction lies to the right, what does that tell you about the relative amounts of reactants and products present?
28) Describe what would happen to the equilibrium position of a reversible reaction if you increased the concentration of the reactants.

Section 14 — Groups in the Periodic Table

Group 1 — Alkali Metals

You can predict how different elements will **react** from their position in the **periodic table** — elements in the **same group** will react in **similar ways**. Time to take a look at some of the groups, starting with **Group 1**...

Group 1 Metals are Known as the 'Alkali Metals'

The Group 1 metals are lithium, sodium, potassium, rubidium, caesium and francium.

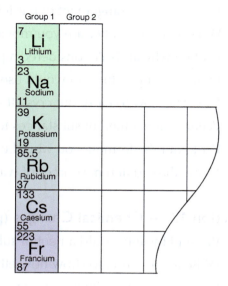

1) The alkali metals all have <u>one outer electron</u> — so they have <u>similar chemical properties</u>.

2) They all have the following <u>physical properties</u>:
   - <u>Low melting points</u> and <u>boiling points</u> (compared with other metals).
   - <u>Very soft</u> — they can be cut with a knife.

3) The alkali metals form <u>ionic</u> compounds. They lose their single outer electron <u>so easily</u> that sharing it is out of the question, so they <u>don't</u> form covalent bonds.

Group 1 Metals are Very Reactive

1) The Group 1 metals readily <u>lose</u> their single <u>outer electron</u> to form a <u>1+ ion</u> with a <u>stable electronic structure</u>.

2) The <u>more readily</u> a metal loses its outer electrons, the <u>more reactive</u> it is — so the Group 1 metals are very reactive.

3) As you go <u>down</u> Group 1, the alkali metals get <u>more reactive</u>. The <u>outer electron</u> is more easily <u>lost</u> because it's further from the nucleus (the <u>atomic radius</u> is <u>larger</u>) — so it's less strongly attracted to the nucleus and <u>less energy</u> is needed to remove it.

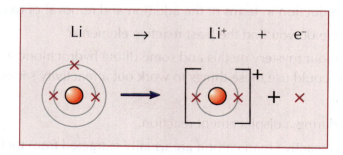

Alkali metals get more reactive as you go down the group

Remember, an alkali metal's <u>reactivity</u> comes from its ability to easily <u>give up</u> its outer shell electron — the <u>more easily</u> it does this, the <u>more reactive</u> it is. This explains why alkali metals at the <u>bottom</u> of the group are the <u>most reactive</u> — they lose their electrons much more easily than the metals at the top of the group.

Group 1 — Alkali Metals

You saw on the last page how the **reactivity** of the alkali metals **increases** as you move **down the group**. This **trend** is clearly shown in the reactions of the alkali metals with **water**. Read on to find out more.

Reactions with **Cold Water** Produce a **Hydroxide** and **Hydrogen**

1) When the alkali metals are put in water, they react vigorously.

2) The reaction produces hydrogen gas and a hydroxide of the metal (an alkali — see page 193). For example, here's the overall equation for the reaction of sodium with water:

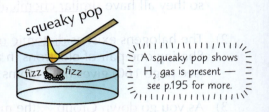

A squeaky pop shows H$_2$ gas is present — see p.195 for more.

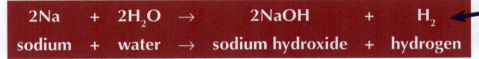

$$2Na + 2H_2O \rightarrow 2NaOH + H_2$$
sodium + water → sodium hydroxide + hydrogen

The same reaction happens with all of the alkali metals — make sure you can write balanced equations for them all.

You Can Make **Predictions** About the **Reactions** of Alkali Metals

1) The reactivity of Group 1 metals with water (and dilute acid) increases down the group because the outer electron is lost more easily in the reaction (see previous page). This results in the reaction becoming more violent:

- Lithium will move around the surface, fizzing furiously.
- Sodium and potassium do the same, but they also melt in the heat of the reaction. Potassium even gets hot enough to ignite the hydrogen gas being produced.

2) Because you know the reactivity trend in Group 1 (the elements get more reactive as you go down the group), you can make predictions about the reactions of elements further down the group.

Example: You may predict that the reactions of rubidium and caesium with water will be more violent than the reaction of potassium and water. And sure enough, rubidium and caesium react violently with water and tend to explode when they get wet...

All alkali metals react in similar ways

...so you can use the reactivity of one alkali metal to predict how another is likely to react.

Q1 Write a word equation for the reaction between lithium and water. [1 mark]

Section 14 — Groups in the Periodic Table

Group 7 — Halogens

*Here's a page on another periodic table group that you need to be familiar with — **the halogens**.*

Group 7 Elements are Known as the 'Halogens'

Group 7 is made up of the elements fluorine, chlorine, bromine, iodine and astatine.

1) All Group 7 elements have 7 electrons in their outer shell so they all have similar chemical properties.

2) The halogens exist as diatomic molecules (e.g. Cl_2, Br_2, I_2). Sharing one pair of electrons in a covalent bond (see page 160) gives both atoms a full outer shell.

3) As you go down Group 7, the melting points and boiling points of the halogens increase. This means that at room temperature:

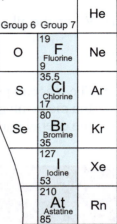

Chlorine (Cl_2) is a fairly reactive, poisonous, green gas.

Bromine (Br_2) is a poisonous, red-brown liquid which gives off an orange vapour.

Iodine (I_2) is a dark grey crystalline solid which gives off a purple vapour when heated.

You Can Make Predictions About the Properties of Halogens

You can use the trends in physical properties from chlorine to iodine to predict the properties of halogens further down the group.

> For example, you can see that the melting points increase down the group, and the colours of the halogens get darker, so you could predict that astatine (which comes below iodine) would be a dark-coloured solid at room temperature.

Test for Chlorine Using Damp Blue Litmus Paper

You can test to see if a gas is chlorine by holding a piece of damp blue litmus paper over it. Chlorine will bleach the litmus paper, turning it white. It may also turn red for a moment first — that's because a solution of chlorine is acidic (see p.193-196 for more on acids).

damp blue litmus paper

Halogens — one electron short of a full outer shell...

Halogens have seven electrons in their outer shell, so they need one more to complete it. That's why they all exist as diatomic molecules — they share one pair of their electrons to get a full outer shell.

Section 14 — Groups in the Periodic Table

Group 7 — Halogens

You need to know all about how the halogens *react*, so get reading this page...

Reactivity Decreases Going Down Group 7

1) A halogen atom only needs to gain one electron to form a 1– ion with a stable electronic structure.

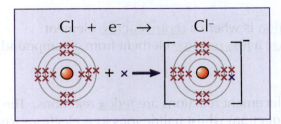

2) The easier it is for a halogen atom to attract an electron, the more reactive the halogen will be.
3) As you go down Group 7, the halogens become less reactive — it gets harder to attract the extra electron to fill the outer shell when it's further away from the nucleus (the atomic radius is larger).

The Halogens Can React With Metals and Hydrogen

1) The halogens will react vigorously with some metals to form salts called 'metal halides'.

2Na	+	Cl_2	→	2NaCl
sodium	+	chlorine	→	sodium chloride

Metals lose electrons and form positive ions when they react.

2) Halogens higher up in Group 7 are more reactive because they can attract the outer electron of the metal more easily.

3) Halogens can also react with hydrogen to form hydrogen halides.

H_2	+	Cl_2	→	2HCl
hydrogen	+	chlorine	→	hydrogen chloride

4) Hydrogen halides are soluble, and they can dissolve in water to form acidic solutions. For example, HCl forms hydrochloric acid in water.

5) Since all halogens have the same number of electrons in their outer shells, they all have similar reactions. So you can use the reactions of chlorine, bromine and iodine to predict how fluorine and astatine will react.

Remember — halogens at the top of the group are the most reactive

The reactivity of a halogen depends on how easily it can attract an electron to get a full outer shell. Halogens at the top of the group are smaller, so can attract electrons more easily than those at the bottom.

Halogen Displacement Reactions

*The halogens are competitive — the **more reactive** ones will push the **less reactive** ones out of a compound.*

A More Reactive Halogen Will **Displace** a Less Reactive One

1) The elements in Group 7 take part in displacement reactions.

2) A displacement reaction is where a more reactive element 'pushes out' (displaces) a less reactive element from a compound.

3) The halogen displacement reactions are redox reactions. The halogens gain electrons (reduction) whilst halide ions lose electrons (oxidation).

Example: **Chlorine** Can **Displace Bromine**

Chlorine is more reactive than bromine (it's higher up Group 7). If you add chlorine water (an aqueous solution of Cl_2) to potassium bromide solution, the chlorine will displace the bromine from the salt solution.

1) The chlorine is reduced to chloride ions, so the salt solution becomes potassium chloride.

2) The bromide ions are oxidised to bromine, which turns the solution orange.

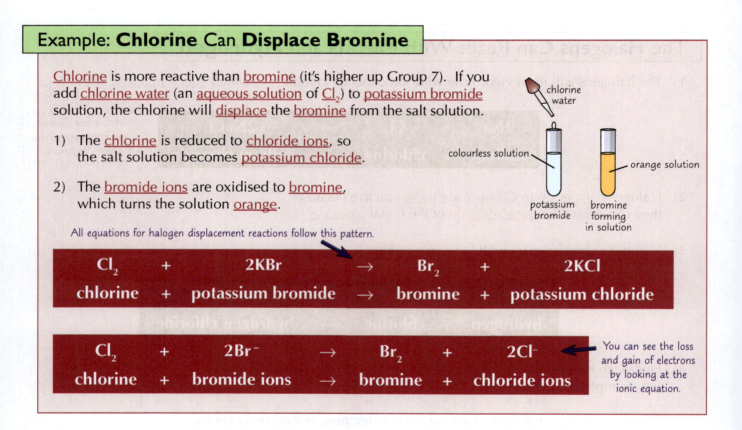

All equations for halogen displacement reactions follow this pattern.

$$Cl_2 + 2KBr \rightarrow Br_2 + 2KCl$$
chlorine + potassium bromide → bromine + potassium chloride

$$Cl_2 + 2Br^- \rightarrow Br_2 + 2Cl^-$$
chlorine + bromide ions → bromine + chloride ions

You can see the loss and gain of electrons by looking at the ionic equation.

Halogens higher up the group will displace the ones lower down

You need to be able to write balanced symbol and ionic equations for halogen displacement reactions. Luckily, since they all follow the same pattern, if you learn them for one reaction, you've learnt them all.

Halogen Displacement Reactions

*A halide salt is made up of a **halide** and a **positive ion** (normally a **metal** or **hydrogen**). By adding halide salts to **halogens** and seeing which halogens **displace** the others, you can find out the halogens' **relative reactivities**.*

Displacement Reactions Show Reactivity Trends

You can use displacement reactions to show the reactivity trend of the halogens.

1) Start by measuring out a small amount of a halide salt solution in a test tube.

2) Add a few drops of a halogen solution to it and shake the tube gently.

A halide salt that contains a metal can also be called a metal halide (see page 229).

3) If you see a colour change, then a reaction has happened — the halogen has displaced the halide ions from the salt. If no reaction happens, there won't be a colour change — the halogen is less reactive than the halide and so can't displace it.

4) Repeat the process using different combinations of halide salt and halogen.

5) The table below shows what should happen when you mix different combinations of chlorine, bromine and iodine water with solutions of the salts potassium chloride, potassium bromide and potassium iodide.

Start with:	Potassium chloride solution $KCl_{(aq)}$ — colourless	Potassium bromide solution $KBr_{(aq)}$ — colourless	Potassium iodide solution $KI_{(aq)}$ — colourless
Add chlorine water $Cl_{2\,(aq)}$ — colourless	no reaction	orange solution (Br_2) formed	brown solution (I_2) formed
Add bromine water $Br_{2\,(aq)}$ — orange	no reaction	no reaction	brown solution (I_2) formed
Add iodine water $I_{2\,(aq)}$ — brown	no reaction	no reaction	no reaction

6) Chlorine displaces both bromine and iodine from salt solutions.
   Bromine can't displace chlorine, but it does displace iodine.
   Iodine can't displace chlorine or bromine.

7) This shows the reactivity trend — the halogens get less reactive as you go down the group.

8) You can use this trend to predict how astatine might react. Since astatine is the least reactive halogen, you'd predict it wouldn't displace any other halogens from their salt solutions.

Chlorine can displace bromine and iodine...

...because it's more reactive than both of them. If you remember that halogens get less reactive as you go down the group, you can work out what will happen when you mix any halogen with any halide salt.

Section 14 — Groups in the Periodic Table

Group 0 — Noble Gases

The elements in **Group 0** of the periodic table are known as the **noble gases**. 'Noble' here is just being used in the old chemistry sense of being **unreactive** — nothing to do with them being honourable or good.

Group 0 Elements are All Inert, Colourless Gases

Group 0 elements are called the noble gases. Group 0 is made up of the elements helium, neon, argon, krypton, xenon and radon.

1) All of the Group 0 elements are colourless gases at room temperature.
2) The noble gases are all monatomic — that just means that their gases are made up of single atoms (not molecules).
3) They're also more or less inert — this means they don't react with much at all. The reason for this is that they have a full outer shell of electrons. This means they don't easily give up or gain electrons.
4) As the noble gases are inert, they're non-flammable — they won't set on fire.
5) These properties make the gases pretty hard to observe — it took a long time for them to be discovered.

The Noble Gases have Many Everyday Uses...

1) Noble gases can be used to provide an inert atmosphere.
2) Argon does this in filament lamps (light bulbs). Since it's non-flammable, it stops the very hot filament from burning away. Flash photography uses the same principle — argon, krypton and xenon are used to stop the flash filament from burning up during the high temperature flashes.
3) Argon and helium can also be used to protect metals that are being welded. The inert atmosphere stops the hot metal reacting with oxygen.
4) Helium is used in airships and party balloons. Helium has a lower density than air — so it makes balloons float. It is also non-flammable, which makes it safer to use than hydrogen gas.

There are Patterns in the Properties of the Noble Gases

1) As with the other groups in the periodic table, there are also trends in the properties of the noble gases.
2) For example, boiling point, melting point and density all increase as you go down Group 0.
3) You could be given information about a particular property of the noble gases (or Group 7) and asked to use it to estimate the value of this property for a certain element. For example:

EXAMPLE

Use the densities of helium (0.2 kg m^{-3}) and argon (1.8 kg m^{-3}) to predict the density of neon.

Neon comes between helium and argon in the group, so you can predict that its density will be roughly halfway between their densities:
(0.2 + 1.8) ÷ 2 = 2.0 ÷ 2 = 1.0
Neon should have a density of about 1.0 kg m^{-3}.

There are other methods you could use for these types of question, but don't worry — you'd get marks for any sensible answer.

4) You could be asked about how an element reacts too, so remember — elements in the same group react in similar ways because they all have the same number of electrons in their outer shells. And, to find out which group an element is in, all you need to do is look at the periodic table. Simple.

The noble gases are unreactive and colourless

You might be asked to explain why a Group 0 element is suited to a particular use. The answer will almost always be related to their inertness, their non-flammability or their low density.

Warm-Up and Exam Questions

These questions are all about the groups 1, 7 and 0 of the periodic table.
Treat the exam questions like the real thing — don't look back through the book until you've finished.

Warm-Up Questions

1) How many electrons do alkali metals have in their outer shells?
2) Do alkali metals get more or less reactive as you go down the group?
3) What happens to the boiling point of the halogens as you go down Group 7?
4) What is the product of a reaction between chlorine and sodium?
5) What is a displacement reaction?
6) Do halide ions have a positive or a negative charge?
7) In which group of the periodic table are the noble gases?

Exam Questions

1 **Figure 1** shows some of the physical properties of four of the halogens.

Halogen	Properties			
	Atomic number	Colour	Physical state at room temperature	Reactivity
Fluorine	9	yellow	gas	....
Chlorine	17	green	gas	....
Bromine	35	red-brown	liquid	....
Iodine	53	dark grey	solid	....

Figure 1

(a) **Figure 1** has a column for reactivity. Write an **X** in the row of the halogen with the **highest** reactivity and a **Y** in the row of the halogen with the **lowest** reactivity.

[2 marks]

(b) State the halogen in **Figure 1** with the highest melting point.

[1 mark]

2 The electronic configuration of a sodium atom is shown in **Figure 2**.

(a) State which group of the periodic table sodium belongs to.

[1 mark]

(b) Sodium chloride (NaCl) is an ionic compound formed from sodium cations and chloride anions.

Draw a diagram to show the electronic configuration of a sodium ion in sodium chloride. Clearly show the charge on the ion.

[2 marks]

Figure 2

Section 14 — Groups in the Periodic Table

Exam Questions

3   Chlorine is a Group 7 element.
    Its electronic configuration is shown in **Figure 3**.

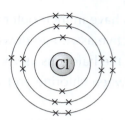

Figure 3

(a) Describe a method of testing chlorine gas to confirm its identity.
    Include in your answer the result you would expect to see if chlorine was present.

[2 marks]

When chlorine is bubbled through potassium iodide solution a reaction occurs.
The equation below shows the reaction.

$$Cl_{2(g)} + 2KI_{(aq)} \rightarrow I_{2(aq)} + 2KCl_{(aq)}$$

(b) State what type of reaction this is.

[1 mark]

(c) State the less reactive halogen in this reaction. Explain your answer.

[2 marks]

(d) Chlorine gas can also react with potassium bromide.
    Using your knowledge of Group 7 elements, predict the products of this reaction and their states.
    Give an explanation for your answer.

[4 marks]

(e) None of the elements in Group 0 will react with potassium iodide or potassium bromide.
    Using your knowledge of the electronic structure of the Group 0 elements,
    explain why no reaction occurs.

[2 marks]

4   Group 1 elements are metals.
    They include lithium, sodium and potassium.

(a) Explain why the Group 1 elements react vigorously with water.

[1 mark]

(b) The Group 1 elements all react with water at a different rate. Explain why this is.

[3 marks]

(c) (i) Name the **two** products formed when potassium reacts with water.

[2 marks]

(ii) Write a balanced symbol equation for the reaction of potassium with water.

[2 marks]

Section 15 — Rates of Reaction and Energy Changes

Rates of Reaction

*Reactions can be **fast** or **slow**. The following pages show a few ways you can **measure** the **rate of a reaction**.*

The Rate of Reaction is How Fast the Reaction Happens

1) The rate of a reaction is how quickly a reaction happens.
2) It can be observed either by measuring how quickly the reactants are used up or how quickly the products are formed.
3) The average rate of a reaction can be calculated using the following formula:

It's usually a lot easier to measure products forming.

$$\text{Average Rate of Reaction} = \frac{\text{amount of reactant used or amount of product formed}}{\text{time}}$$

You Can Do Experiments to Follow Reaction Rates

There are different ways that the rate of a reaction can be measured. Here's one example, and there are another two on the next page:

Precipitation

1) This method works for any reaction where mixing two see-through solutions produces a precipitate, which clouds the solution.

2) You mix the two reactant solutions and put the flask on a piece of paper that has a mark on it.

3) Observe the mark through the mixture and measure how long it takes for the mark to be obscured. The faster it disappears, the faster the reaction.

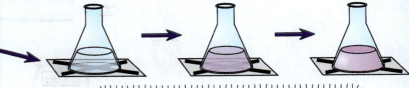

You can use this method to investigate how temperature affects the rate of the reaction between sodium thiosulfate and hydrochloric acid. See page 239.

4) The result is subjective — different people might not agree on exactly when the mark 'disappears'.

Make sure you use a method appropriate to your reaction

The method shown on this page only works if there's a really obvious change in the solution. If there's only a small change in colour, it might not be possible to observe and time the change.

Q1 A reaction takes 200 s. 6.0 g of reactant are used up. What is the average rate of the reaction in g s⁻¹? Give your answer to one significant figure. **[2 marks]**

Q1 Video Solution

Rates of Reaction

Change in Mass (Usually Gas Given Off)

1) You can measure the rate of a reaction that <u>produces a gas</u> using a <u>mass balance</u>.
2) As the gas is released, the <u>lost mass</u> is easily measured on the balance. The <u>quicker</u> the reading on the balance <u>drops</u>, the <u>faster</u> the reaction.
3) You know the reaction has <u>finished</u> when the reading on the balance <u>stops changing</u>.
4) You can use your results to plot a <u>graph</u> of <u>change in mass</u> against <u>time</u>.
5) This method does release the gas produced straight into the room — so if the gas is <u>harmful</u>, you must take <u>safety precautions</u>, e.g. do the experiment in a <u>fume cupboard</u>.

The cotton wool lets gases through but stops any solid, liquid or aqueous reactants flying out during the reaction.

The Volume of Gas Given Off

1) This involves the use of a <u>gas syringe</u> to measure the <u>volume</u> of gas given off.
2) The <u>more</u> gas given off during a set <u>time interval</u>, the <u>faster</u> the reaction.
3) You can tell the reaction has <u>finished</u> when <u>no more gas</u> is produced.
4) You can use your results to plot a graph of <u>gas volume</u> against <u>time elapsed</u>.
5) You need to be careful that you're using the <u>right size</u> gas syringe for your experiment though — if the reaction is too <u>vigorous</u>, you can blow the plunger out of the end of the syringe.

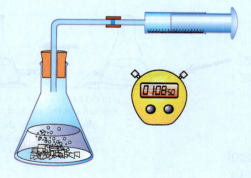

Each of these three methods has pros and cons

The mass balance method is only accurate as long as the flask isn't <u>too hot</u>, otherwise the loss in mass that you see might be partly due to <u>evaporation</u> of liquid as well as being due to the loss of gas formed during the reaction. The first method (on the previous page) is <u>subjective</u> so it isn't very accurate, but if you're not producing a gas you can't use either of the other two.

Section 15 — Rates of Reaction and Energy Changes

Rate Experiments **PRACTICAL**

You can use the three methods on the previous pages to measure the effects of different **factors** (**surface area**, **concentration** and **temperature**) on the rate of a reaction. The next few pages look at how.

You can Measure how Surface Area Affects Rate

Here's how you can carry out an experiment to measure the effect of surface area on rate, using marble chips and hydrochloric acid.

1) Set the apparatus up as shown in the diagram on the right.
2) Measure the volume of gas produced using a gas syringe. Take readings at regular time intervals and record the results in a table.
3) You can plot a graph of your results — time goes on the x-axis and volume goes on the y-axis.
4) Repeat the experiment with exactly the same volume and concentration of acid, and exactly the same mass of marble chips, but with the marble more crunched up.
5) Then repeat with the same mass of powdered chalk.

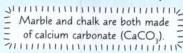
Marble and chalk are both made of calcium carbonate ($CaCO_3$).

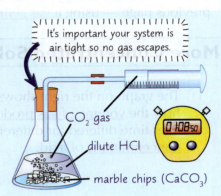
It's important your system is air tight so no gas escapes.
CO_2 gas
dilute HCl
marble chips ($CaCO_3$)

Finer Particles of Solid Mean a Higher Rate

1) The sooner a reaction finishes, the faster the reaction.
2) The steeper the gradient of the graph, the faster the rate of reaction. When the line becomes flat, no more gas is being produced and the reaction has finished.
3) Using finer particles means that the marble has a larger surface area.
4) Lines 1 to 3 on the graph on the right show that the finer the particles are (and the greater the surface area of the solid reactants), the sooner the reaction finishes and so the faster the reaction.
5) Line 4 shows the reaction if a greater mass of small marble chips is added. The extra surface area gives a faster reaction and there is also more gas evolved overall.

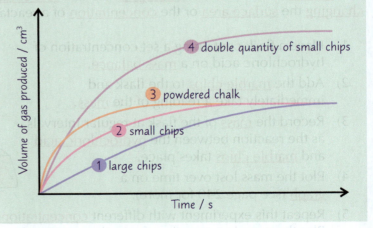
Volume of gas produced / cm^3
4 double quantity of small chips
3 powdered chalk
2 small chips
1 large chips
Time / s

MATHS TIP

Increasing a reactant's surface area increases the reaction rate
The graph above shows how to compare rates of reactions when using solid reactants with different surface areas, but if you want to calculate a numerical value for the rate, you need to use a calculation. Take a look at p.240 for how to find the rate of reaction from a graph.

Section 15 — Rates of Reaction and Energy Changes

 **Rate Experiments**

*Another important experiment — this time, how the **concentration** of a reactant can affect the **rate**.*

Changing the **Concentration** of Acid Affects the **Rate** too

1) The reaction between marble chips and hydrochloric acid is also good for measuring how changing the reactant concentration affects reaction rate.
2) You can measure the rate of this reaction using the method shown on the previous page — using a gas syringe to measure the volume of gas released.

More Concentrated Solutions Mean a Higher Rate

1) The graph on the right shows how the volume of gas produced over time differed for different concentrations of acid.

2) Lines 1 to 3 on the graph show that a higher concentration gives a faster reaction, with the reaction finishing sooner.

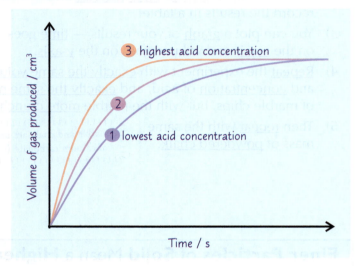

You Can Also Measure the **Change in Mass** During the Reaction

This method can be used to investigate how the rate of reaction is affected by changing the surface area or the concentration of a reactant.

1) Place a flask containing a set concentration of hydrochloric acid on a mass balance.
2) Add the marble chips to the flask and immediately take a reading of the mass.
3) Record the mass of the flask at regular intervals as the reaction between the hydrochloric acid and marble chips takes place.
4) Plot the mass lost over time on a graph (see page 240 for more).
5) Repeat this experiment with different concentrations of hydrochloric acid. Plot the mass lost over time for each concentration on the same graph, to allow comparison of the rates of each reaction.

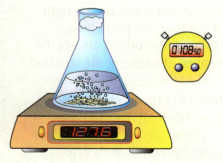

 The rate of the reaction is shown by how steep the slope is...
The steeper the slope, the greater the volume of gas produced in a set time, so the faster the reaction rate. Don't forget that you can also use the method involving a mass balance — then the graph would show the mass lost over time, instead of the volume of gas released.

Rate Experiments

*That's right — another page, another **reaction rate experiment** to learn. This one's a **precipitation** reaction, which means using the method covered back on page 235. Have a flick back if you need to.*

Reaction Rate is Also Affected by Temperature

1) You can see how temperature affects reaction rate by looking at the reaction between sodium thiosulfate and hydrochloric acid.
2) Sodium thiosulfate and hydrochloric acid are both clear, colourless solutions. They react together to form a yellow precipitate of sulfur.
3) You can use the amount of time that it takes for the coloured precipitate to form as a measure of the rate of this reaction.
4) You use a method like the one on page 235 to carry out this experiment.

You can find out how temperature affects the reaction rate on page 243.

- Measure out fixed volumes of sodium thiosulfate and hydrochloric acid, using a measuring cylinder.
- Use a water bath to gently heat both solutions to the desired temperature before you mix them.
- Mix the solutions in a conical flask. Place the flask over a black mark on a piece of paper which can be seen through the solution. Watch the black mark disappear through the cloudy, yellow sulfur and time how long it takes to go.

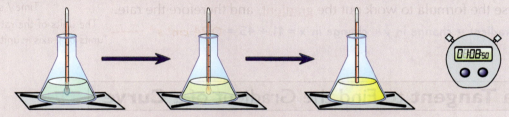

- The reaction can be repeated for solutions at different temperatures.
- The depth and volumes of liquid must be kept the same each time. The concentrations of the solutions must also be kept the same.
- You can use your results to measure what effect changing the temperature has on the rate of the reaction. The shorter the length of time taken for the mark to be obscured, the faster the rate.

Higher Temperatures Mean a Higher Rate

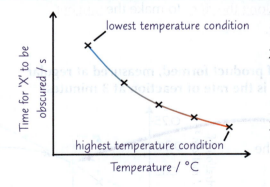

1) You can plot the time taken for the mark to disappear against the temperature of the reacting solutions.
2) If you look at the graph, you can see that the reactions that happened at lower temperatures took longer to obscure the mark, whereas the reactions happening at higher temperatures finished sooner.
3) So increasing the temperature increases the rate of the reaction.

How temperature, concentration and pressure affect the rate of a reaction can be explained using collision theory — see p.243-244.

Hotter mixtures have more energy and so react faster...

With all of these experiments, you need to make sure you're only changing one thing for each repeat. So for this one, you need to make sure only temperature is changed, and not, e.g. the concentration of HCl. That way you'll know that it's definitely the temperature affecting the rate.

Section 15 — Rates of Reaction and Energy Changes

Calculating Rates

*You can work out rates of reaction using **graphs** — to do that, you need to know how to measure **gradients**...*

Faster Rates of Reaction are Shown by Steeper Gradients

If you have a graph of amount of product formed (or reactant used up) against time, then the gradient (slope) of the graph will be equal to the rate of the reaction — the steeper the slope, the faster the rate. The gradient of a straight line is given by the equation:

gradient = change in y ÷ change in x

EXAMPLE
Calculate the rate of the reaction shown on the graph below.

1) Find two points on the line that are easy to read the x and y values of (ones that pass through grid lines).
2) Draw a line straight down from the higher point and straight across from the lower one to make a triangle.
3) The height of your triangle = change in y
   The base of your triangle = change in x
   Change in y = 16 − 5 = 11
   Change in x = 65 − 20 = 45
4) Use the formula to work out the gradient, and therefore the rate.
   Gradient = change in y ÷ change in x = 11 ÷ 45 = **0.24 cm³ s⁻¹**

The units of the rate are just "units of y-axis ÷ units of x-axis".

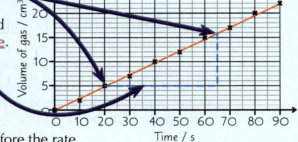

Draw a Tangent to Find the Gradient of a Curve

1) If your graph (or part of it) is a curve, the gradient, and therefore rate, is different at different points along the curve.
2) To find the gradient of the graph at a certain point, you'll have to draw a tangent at that point.
3) A tangent is just a line that touches the curve and has the same gradient as the line at that point.
4) To draw a tangent, place a ruler on the line of best fit at the point you're interested in, so you can see the whole curve. Adjust the ruler so the space between the ruler and the curve is the same on both sides of the point. Draw a line along the ruler to make the tangent.
5) The rate at that point is then just the gradient of the tangent.

EXAMPLE
The graph below shows the concentration of product formed, measured at regular intervals, during a chemical reaction. What is the rate of reaction at 3 minutes?

1) Position a ruler on the graph at the point where you want to know the rate — here it's 3 minutes.
2) Adjust the ruler until the space between the ruler and the curve is equal on both sides of the point.
3) Draw a line along the ruler to make the tangent. Extend the line right across the graph.
4) Pick two points on the line that are easy to read. Use them to calculate the gradient of the tangent in order to find the rate:
   gradient = change in y ÷ change in x
   = (0.22 − 0.14) ÷ (5.0 − 2.0)
   = 0.08 ÷ 3.0 = 0.027

   So, the rate of reaction at 3 minutes was **0.027 mol dm⁻³ min⁻¹**.

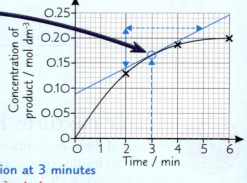

Section 15 — Rates of Reaction and Energy Changes

Warm-Up and Exam Questions

Make sure you take some time to do these questions before moving on — they'll help you pull together all of that information you've just learned about rate experiments, so that it really sticks.

Warm-Up Questions

1) What is meant by the rate of a reaction?
2) Reaction A forms more product than Reaction B over 30 seconds. Which reaction, A or B, has a higher rate?
3) What effect does increasing the concentration of a reactant have on the rate of a reaction?
4) What is the equation for calculating the gradient of a straight line on a graph?

Exam Questions

PRACTICAL

1 Figure 1 shows one method of measuring the rate of a reaction which produces a gas.

(a) What piece of apparatus necessary for measuring the rate of this reaction is missing from **Figure 1**?

[1 mark]

(b) Name the piece of apparatus in **Figure 1** labelled **X**.

[1 mark]

(c) Describe **one** other method of measuring the rate of a reaction which produces a gas.

[2 marks]

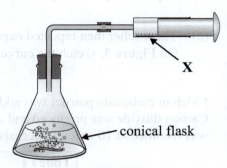

Figure 1

PRACTICAL

2 Set volumes of sodium thiosulfate and hydrochloric acid were reacted at different temperatures. The time taken for a black cross to be obscured by the sulfur precipitate was measured at each temperature. The results are shown in **Figure 2**.

(a) Give **two** variables that should be kept constant in this experiment.

[2 marks]

(b) Plot the results on a graph (with time on the *x*-axis) and draw a line of best fit.

[4 marks]

(c) Describe the relationship illustrated by your graph.

[1 mark]

Temperature / °C	Time / s
55	6
36	11
24	17
16	27
9	40
5	51

Figure 2

(d) Describe how the results would change if the experiment was repeated with a **lower** concentration of sodium thiosulfate.

[1 mark]

(e) Suggest how you could assess if the results of the experiment are repeatable.

[2 marks]

Exam Questions

3 A teacher demonstrated an experiment to investigate the effect of concentration on the rate of a reaction. The teacher added 0.5 mol dm^{-3} hydrochloric acid (HCl) to 50 g of marble chips and measured the volume of gas produced at regular time intervals. The teacher then repeated the experiment using 1 mol dm^{-3} HCl and the same mass of marble chips of the same size. The results are shown in **Figure 3**.

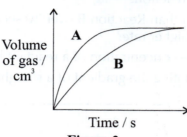

Figure 3

(a) Identify which curve on **Figure 3**, **A** or **B**, shows the result of the experiment using 1 mol dm^{-3} HCl.

[1 mark]

(b) The teacher made sure that the temperature of the reactants was the same in each repeat. Explain why the temperature needed to be controlled.

[1 mark]

(c) The teacher then repeated experiment **A**, but with 50 g of powdered chalk instead of marble chips. On **Figure 3**, sketch the curve you would expect to see from this experiment. Label it **C**.

[1 mark]

4 Calcium carbonate powder was added to a conical flask containing dilute hydrochloric acid. Carbon dioxide was produced and collected in a gas syringe. The volume of gas released was recorded at 10 second intervals in **Figure 4**:

Time / s	0	10	20	30	40	50	60
Volume of CO$_2$ / cm^3	0	24	32	36	38	39	40

Figure 4

(a) Calculate the rate of reaction between 0 and 60 seconds. Give your answer in cm^3 s^{-1}.

[1 mark]

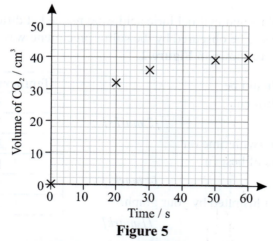

Figure 5

(b) Two of the results listed in **Figure 4** are missing from **Figure 5**. Plot these missing points and draw a line of best fit on **Figure 5**.

[2 marks]

(c) Use your graph to find the rate of the reaction 25 seconds after starting the experiment. Give your answer in cm^3 s^{-1}.

[4 marks]

Collision Theory

The rate of a reaction depends on: **temperature**, **concentration** (or **pressure** for gases) and the **size of the particles** (for solids). This is because these factors affect how particles in a reaction **collide** with each other.

Particles Must Collide with Enough Energy in Order to React

Reaction rates are explained by collision theory. It's simple really.

The rate of a chemical reaction depends on:
- The collision frequency of reacting particles (how often they collide). The more successful collisions there are, the faster the reaction is.
- The energy transferred during a collision. The minimum energy that particles need to react when they collide is called the activation energy. Particles need to collide with at least the activation energy for the collision to be successful.

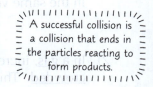
A successful collision is a collision that ends in the particles reacting to form products.

The More Collisions, the Higher the Rate of Reaction

1) Reactions happen if particles collide with enough energy to react.
2) So, if you increase the number of collisions or the energy with which the particles collide, the reaction happens more quickly (i.e. the rate increases).
3) Temperature, concentration (or pressure) and surface area all affect the rate of a reaction. First up is the effect of temperature on rate...

Increasing the Temperature Increases Rate

1) When the temperature is increased the particles move faster. If they move faster, they're going to have more frequent collisions.
2) Higher temperatures also increase the energy of the collisions, since the particles are moving faster. Reactions only happen if the particles collide with enough energy.
3) This means that at higher temperatures there will be more successful collisions (more particles will collide with enough energy to react). So increasing the temperature increases the rate of reaction.

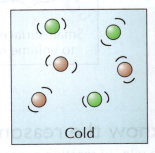
Cold

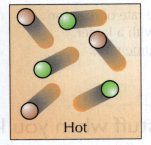
Hot

Just colliding isn't enough — there needs to be enough energy too...

Collision theory is the key to understanding how lots of factors can affect the reaction rate. Just think of how changing a particular factor might affect the particles in a reaction mixture and how they bump into each other. Then you can figure out whether the rate of the reaction is likely to be increased or decreased.

Section 15 — Rates of Reaction and Energy Changes

Collision Theory

*Now for another **two factors** that affect the rate of a reaction — **concentration** (or **pressure**) and **surface area**.*

Increasing Concentration (or Pressure) Increases Rate

1) If a <u>solution</u> is made more <u>concentrated</u> it means there are more particles of <u>reactant</u> in the same volume. This makes collisions <u>more likely</u>, so the reaction rate <u>increases</u>.

2) In a <u>gas</u>, increasing the <u>pressure</u> means that the particles are <u>more crowded</u>. This means that the frequency of <u>collisions</u> between particles will <u>increase</u> — so the rate of reaction will also <u>increase</u>.

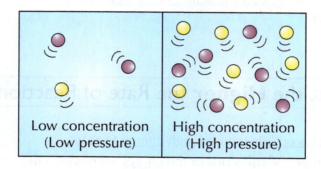

Low concentration (Low pressure) | High concentration (High pressure)

Smaller Solid Particles (or More Surface Area) Means a Higher Rate

1) If one reactant is a <u>solid</u>, breaking it into <u>smaller</u> pieces will <u>increase its surface area to volume ratio</u> (i.e. more of the solid will be exposed, compared to its overall volume).

2) The particles around it will have <u>more area to work on</u>, so the frequency of collisions will <u>increase</u>.

3) This means that the rate of reaction is faster for solids with a larger <u>surface area to volume</u> ratio.

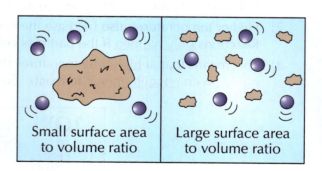

Small surface area to volume ratio | Large surface area to volume ratio

---

It's easier to learn stuff when you know the reasons for it

Once you've learnt everything off these two pages, the <u>rates of reaction</u> pages should start making <u>a lot more sense</u> to you. The concept's fairly simple — the <u>more often</u> particles bump into each other, and the <u>harder</u> they hit when they do, the <u>faster</u> the reaction happens.

Q2 Video Solution

Q1   Explain how increasing the temperature of a reaction mixture affects the number of collisions that occur between particles in a given time period.   [2 marks]

Q2   Explain why breaking a solid reactant into smaller pieces increases the rate of a reaction.   [3 marks]

Catalysts

Catalysts are very important for *commercial reasons* — they *increase reaction rate* and *reduce energy costs* in industrial reactions. They're also important in *living things* — read on to find out more...

A **Catalyst Increases** the **Rate** of a Reaction

1) A catalyst is a substance which increases the rate of a reaction, without being chemically changed or used up in the reaction.
2) Using a catalyst won't change the products of the reaction — so the reaction equation will stay the same.
3) Because it isn't used up, you only need a tiny bit to catalyse large amounts of reactants.
4) Catalysts tend to be very fussy about which reactions they catalyse though — you can't just stick any old catalyst in a reaction and expect it to work.
5) Catalysts work by decreasing the activation energy (see page 243) needed for a reaction to occur.
6) They do this by providing an alternative reaction pathway that has a lower activation energy.
7) As a result, more of the particles have at least the minimum amount of energy needed for a reaction to occur when the particles collide.
8) You can see this if you look at a reaction profile.

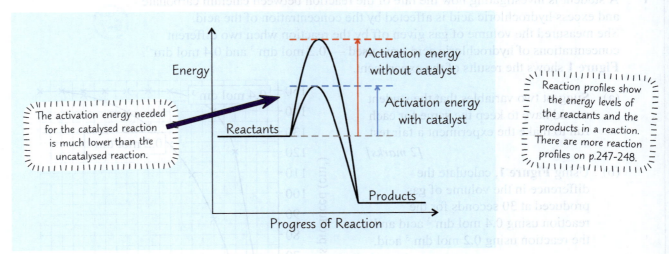

The activation energy needed for the catalysed reaction is much lower than the uncatalysed reaction.

Reaction profiles show the energy levels of the reactants and the products in a reaction. There are more reaction profiles on p.247-248.

Enzymes Control **Cell Reactions**

1) Enzymes are biological catalysts.
2) This means that they catalyse (speed up) the chemical reactions in living cells.
3) Reactions catalysed by enzymes include respiration, photosynthesis and protein synthesis.

> - Enzymes from yeast cells are used in the fermentation process which is used to make alcoholic drinks.
> - They catalyse the reaction that converts sugars (such as glucose) into ethanol and carbon dioxide.

Enzymes make sure reactions happen fast enough for us to stay alive

Some reactions take a very long time to happen by themselves, which isn't good for industrial reactions. Catalysts help to produce an acceptable amount of product in an acceptable length of time.

Section 15 — Rates of Reaction and Energy Changes

Warm-Up and Exam Questions

It's easy to think that you've understood something when you've just read through it. These questions should test whether you really understand the previous few pages, and get you ready for the next bit.

Warm-Up Questions

1) According to collision theory, what must happen in order for two particles to react?
2) Explain why increasing the temperature of a reaction can affect the rate of the reaction.
3) True or False? A catalyst is unchanged chemically during a reaction.
4) Explain why enzymes are considered biological catalysts.

Exam Questions

1   A student is investigating how the rate of the reaction between calcium carbonate and excess hydrochloric acid is affected by the concentration of the acid. She measured the volume of gas given off by the reaction when two different concentrations of hydrochloric acid were used — 0.2 mol dm^{-3} and 0.4 mol dm^{-3}. **Figure 1** shows the results of the experiment.

(a) Suggest two variables that the student would have to keep the same for each run to make the experiment a fair test.
[2 marks]

(b) Using **Figure 1**, calculate the difference in the volume of gas produced at 30 seconds for the reaction using 0.4 mol dm^{-3} acid and the reaction using 0.2 mol dm^{-3} acid.
[1 mark]

(c) Using your knowledge of collision theory, explain the difference between the two curves shown in **Figure 1**.
[3 marks]

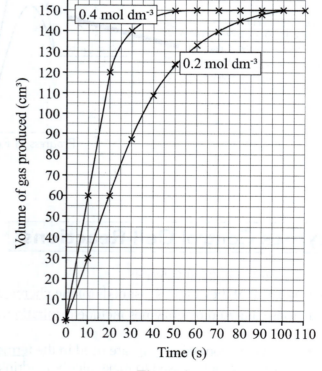

Figure 1

2* Hydrogen gas and ethene gas react to form ethane. Nickel can be used as a catalyst for this reaction.

Using your knowledge of collision theory, explain how the rate of this reaction can be increased.

[6 marks]

Section 15 — Rates of Reaction and Energy Changes

Endothermic and Exothermic Reactions

Endothermic and *exothermic reactions* are all about taking in and giving out energy to the **surroundings**.

Reactions are **Exothermic** or **Endothermic**

An <u>EXOTHERMIC reaction</u> is one which <u>gives out energy</u> to the surroundings, usually in the form of <u>heat</u> and usually shown by a <u>rise in temperature</u> of the surroundings.

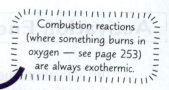

Combustion reactions (where something burns in oxygen — see page 253) are always exothermic.

An <u>ENDOTHERMIC reaction</u> is one which <u>takes in energy</u> from the surroundings, usually in the form of <u>heat</u> and usually shown by a <u>fall in temperature</u> of the surroundings.

Reaction Profiles Show if a Reaction's **Exo-** or **Endothermic**

<u>Reaction profiles</u> show the energy levels of the <u>reactants</u> and the <u>products</u> in a reaction. You can use them to work out if energy is <u>released</u> (exothermic) or <u>taken in</u> (endothermic).

1) This shows an <u>exothermic reaction</u> — the products are at a <u>lower energy</u> than the reactants.
2) The <u>difference in height</u> represents the <u>energy given out</u> in the reaction.

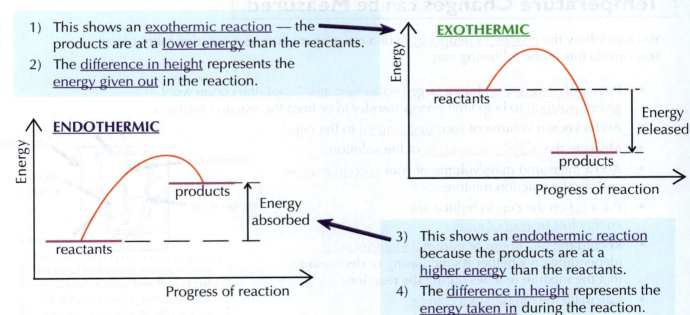

3) This shows an <u>endothermic reaction</u> because the products are at a <u>higher energy</u> than the reactants.
4) The <u>difference in height</u> represents the <u>energy taken in</u> during the reaction.

A reaction profile shows the energy levels during a reaction

Remember, "<u>exo-</u>" = <u>exit</u>, so an exothermic reaction is one that <u>gives out energy</u> — and endothermic just means the opposite. The diagrams above might seem a bit confusing — remember, it's the energy in the <u>chemicals</u>, not in their surroundings, which is being measured.

Q1 Video Solution

Q1 Here is the equation for the combustion of methane in air: $CH_{4(g)} + 2O_{2(g)} \rightarrow CO_{2(g)} + 2H_2O_{(g)}$
Draw a reaction profile for this reaction. [3 marks]

Section 15 — Rates of Reaction and Energy Changes

Endothermic and Exothermic Reactions

Sometimes it's not enough to just know if a reaction is **endothermic** or **exothermic**. You may also need to know **how much** energy is absorbed or released — you can do experiments to find this out.

Activation Energy is the Energy Needed to Start a Reaction

1) The activation energy is the minimum amount of energy needed for bonds to break (see page 250) and a reaction to start.
2) On a reaction profile, it's the energy difference between the reactants and the highest point on the curve.
3) It's a bit like having to climb up one side of a hill before you can ski/snowboard/sledge/fall down the other side.
4) If the energy input is less than the activation energy there won't be enough energy to start the reaction — so nothing will happen.

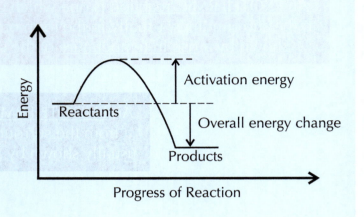

Temperature Changes can be Measured

You can follow the change in temperature of a reaction mixture as a reaction takes place. You can do this in the following way:

- Put a polystyrene cup into a large beaker of cotton wool (the cotton wool gives insulation to help limit energy transfer to or from the reaction mixture).
- Add a known volume of your first reagent to the cup.
- Measure the initial temperature of the solution.
- Add a measured mass/volume of your second reagent and stir the reaction mixture.
- Put a lid on the cup to reduce any energy lost by evaporation.
- Record the maximum or minimum temperature (depending on whether it's increasing or decreasing) that the mixture reaches during the reaction.
- Calculate the temperature change.

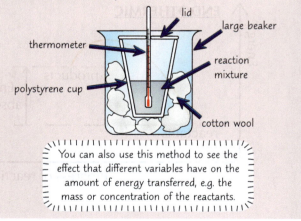

You can also use this method to see the effect that different variables have on the amount of energy transferred, e.g. the mass or concentration of the reactants.

Activation energy — the energy needed to get a reaction going

It's really important that the reaction mixture is well insulated in the method shown above. Without insulation, energy might escape or be transferred to the reaction mixture. This will affect what temperature change the thermometer records — insulation ensures that just the temperature change in the reaction itself is measured.

Endothermic and Exothermic Reactions

*For certain types of reaction you can sometimes **predict** whether energy will be **released** or **taken in**. This page covers a few different **types** of reaction you should know about.*

The Change in Temperature Depends on the Reagents Used

You can measure the temperature change for different types of reaction. Whether there's an increase or decrease in temperature depends on which reagents take part in the reaction.

Dissolving Salts in Water

1) You can measure the temperature change when dissolving salts in water by adding the salt to a polystyrene cup of water and measuring the change in temperature when the salt has dissolved.
2) Dissolving ammonium chloride decreases the temperature of the reaction mixture — it's endothermic.
3) Dissolving calcium chloride causes the temperature of the solution to rise — it's exothermic.

Neutralisation Reactions

1) In a neutralisation reaction (see page 193), an acid and a base react to form a salt and water. Most neutralisation reactions are exothermic, e.g. HCl + NaOH → NaCl + H$_2$O
2) However, the neutralisation reaction between ethanoic acid and sodium carbonate is endothermic.

Displacement Reactions

1) In a displacement reaction (see page 211), a more reactive element displaces a less reactive element in a compound. These types of reactions are accompanied by a release of energy — they're exothermic.
2) Zinc powder and copper sulfate react in a displacement reaction forming zinc sulfate and copper.

Precipitation Reactions

1) Precipitates are insoluble solids which can sometimes form when two solutions are mixed together.
2) Precipitation reactions are exothermic. For example, the reaction between lead(II) nitrate solution and potassium iodide forming a lead iodide precipitate would result in an increase in the temperature of the surroundings.

You need to know about each type of reaction here...

Certain types of reaction, e.g. precipitation or displacement reactions, are always exothermic. For other types, e.g. dissolving salts, you need to be a bit more careful as it depends on the reagents used.

Section 15 — Rates of Reaction and Energy Changes

Bond Energies

Energy transfer in chemical reactions is all to do with **making and breaking bonds**.

There's more on energy transfer on page 247.

Energy Must Always be Supplied to Break Bonds

1) During a chemical reaction, old bonds are broken and new bonds are formed.
2) Energy must be supplied to break existing bonds — so bond breaking is an endothermic process.
3) Energy is released when new bonds are formed — so bond formation is an exothermic process.

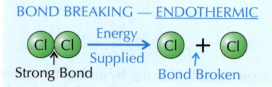

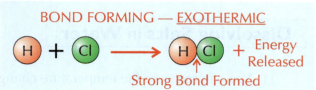

4) In endothermic reactions, the energy used to break bonds is greater than the energy released by forming them.
5) In exothermic reactions, the energy released by forming bonds is greater than the energy used to break 'em.

Bond Energy Calculations — Need to be Practised

1) Every chemical bond has a particular bond energy associated with it. This bond energy varies slightly depending on the compound the bond occurs in.
2) You can use these known bond energies to calculate the overall energy change for a reaction.

Overall Energy Change = Energy required to break bonds − Energy released by forming bonds

3) A positive energy change means an endothermic reaction and a negative energy change means an exothermic reaction.
4) You need to practise a few of these, but the basic idea is really very simple...

EXAMPLE Using the bond energy values below, calculate the energy change for the following reaction, where hydrogen and chlorine react to produce hydrogen chloride:

H—H + Cl—Cl → 2H—Cl

H—H: 436 kJ mol^{-1} Cl—Cl: 242 kJ mol^{-1} H—Cl: 431 kJ mol^{-1}

1) Work out the energy required to break the original bonds in the reactants.
(1 × H—H) + (1 × Cl—Cl) = 436 + 242 = 678 kJ mol^{-1}

2) Work out the energy released by forming the new bonds in the products.
(2 × H—Cl) = 2 × 431 = 862 kJ mol^{-1}

3) Work out the overall change.

In this reaction, the energy released by forming bonds is greater than the energy used to break them so the reaction is exothermic.

overall energy change = energy required to break bonds − energy released by forming bonds
= 678 − 862 = −184 kJ mol^{-1}

It's useful to draw the molecules in full for these calculations...

... then you can count all the different types of bonds more easily. This might look hard now, but with a bit of practice, it'll win you easy marks if you understand all the theory behind it.

Q1 During the Haber Process, N_2 reacts with H_2 in the following reaction: $N_2 + 3H_2 \rightleftharpoons 2NH_3$
The bond energies for these molecules are:
N≡N: 941 kJ mol^{-1}
H–H: 436 kJ mol^{-1}
N–H: 391 kJ mol^{-1}

N≡N + H—H + H—H + H—H → H–N(H)(H) + H–N(H)(H)

Calculate the overall energy change for the forward reaction. [3 marks]

Q1 Video Solution

Warm-Up and Exam Questions

Funny diagrams, a whole bunch of reactions, bond energy calculations — there's a lot to get your head around on the last few pages. Here are some questions so that you can check how you're getting on.

Warm-Up Questions

1) What is an exothermic reaction?
2) What is an endothermic reaction?
3) What is meant by the activation energy of a reaction?
4) Lead(II) nitrate reacts with potassium iodide to form a lead iodide precipitate. State the temperature change that this reaction results in.
5) Is energy released when bonds are formed or when bonds are broken?

Exam Questions

1   The diagrams in **Figure 1** represent the energy changes in four different chemical reactions.

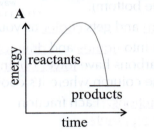
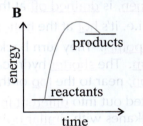
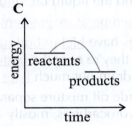
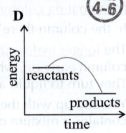

Figure 1

Write the letter of **one** diagram, **A**, **B**, **C** or **D**, which illustrates an endothermic reaction.

[1 mark]

2   A student places two beakers of ethanoic acid and dilute potassium hydroxide into a water bath until they are both 25 °C. He adds the ethanoic acid and then the potassium hydroxide to a polystyrene cup. After 1 minute the temperature of the mixture is 28.5 °C.

(a) Is this reaction endothermic or exothermic? Explain your answer.

[2 marks]

(b) The student put a lid on the polystyrene cup during the experiment. Suggest why this was done.

[1 mark]

3   When methane burns in air it produces carbon dioxide and water, as shown in **Figure 2**. The bond energies for each bond in the molecules involved are shown in **Figure 3**.

Figure 2

	Bond energies / kJ mol^{-1}
C – H	414
O = O	494
C = O	800
O – H	459

Figure 3

(a) Which **two** types of bond are broken during the reaction shown in **Figure 2**?

[1 mark]

(b) Calculate the overall energy change for the reaction shown in **Figure 2**.

[4 marks]

Section 16 — Fuels and Earth Science

Fractional Distillation

Fossil fuels like *coal*, *oil* and *gas* are called *non-renewable fuels* — they take so long to make that they're being used up much faster than they're being formed. They're finite resources — one day they'll run out.

Crude Oil is Separated into Different Hydrocarbon Fractions

1) Crude oil is our main source of hydrocarbons and is used as a raw material (sometimes called a feedstock) to create lots of useful substances used in the petrochemical industry.
2) It's formed underground, over millions of years (at high temperatures and pressures), from the buried remains of plants and animals. It's a non-renewable (finite) resource, so one day it will run out.
3) Crude oil is a complex mixture of lots of different hydrocarbons — compounds which contain just carbon and hydrogen. The hydrocarbons found in crude oil have their carbon atoms arranged in either chains or rings and are mostly alkanes (hydrocarbons with the general formula C_nH_{2n+2}).
4) Crude oil can be separated out into fractions — simpler, more useful mixtures containing groups of hydrocarbons of similar lengths (i.e. they have similar numbers of carbon and hydrogen atoms). The fractions from crude oil, e.g. petrol, kerosene and diesel, are examples of non-renewable fossil fuels. (Methane, the main component of natural gas, is another non-renewable fossil fuel.)
5) The different fractions in crude oil are separated by fractional distillation. The oil is heated until most of it has turned into gas. The gases enter a fractionating column (and the liquid bit, bitumen, is drained off at the bottom).
6) In the column there's a temperature gradient (i.e. it's hot at the bottom and gets cooler as you go up).
7) The longer hydrocarbons have higher boiling points. They turn back into liquids and drain out of the column early on, when they're near the bottom. The shorter hydrocarbons have lower boiling points. They turn to liquid and drain out much later on, near to the top of the column where it's cooler.
8) You end up with the crude oil mixture separated out into different fractions. Each fraction contains a mixture of hydrocarbons, mostly alkanes with similar boiling points.

Natural gas is a mixture of gases which forms underground in a similar way to crude oil.

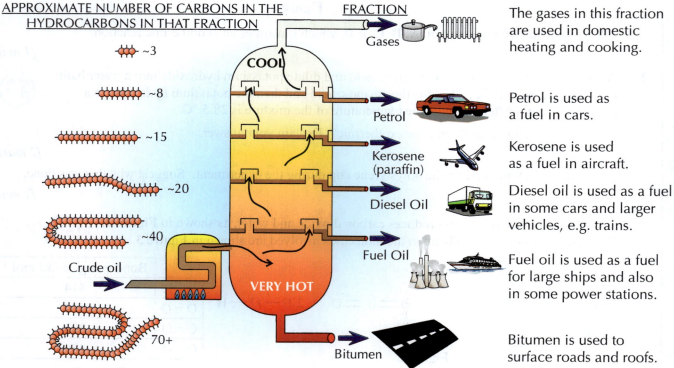

Each fraction has molecules of similar lengths and boiling points

Q1 Petrol drains out of a fractionating column further up than diesel.
Use the diagram of the fractionating column to explain
why the boiling point of petrol is lower than that of diesel. [1 mark]

Hydrocarbons

Time to look at **hydrocarbons** in more detail. First on the agenda — why hydrocarbons make **good fuels**.

Fuels Release Energy in Combustion Reactions

1) As you saw on the previous page, many hydrocarbons are used as fuels.

2) This is because the combustion reactions that happen when you burn them in oxygen give out lots of energy — the reactions are very exothermic (see page 247).

3) When you burn hydrocarbons in plenty of oxygen, the only products are carbon dioxide and water — this is called complete combustion.

> Hydrocarbon + oxygen → carbon dioxide + water
> E.g. $C_3H_8 + 5O_2 \rightarrow 3CO_2 + 4H_2O$

4) Incomplete combustion occurs when a hydrocarbon burns in a limited supply of oxygen (see page 257).

There are Different Homologous Series of Hydrocarbons

1) A homologous series is a family of molecules which have the same general formula and share similar chemical properties.

2) The molecular formulas of neighbouring compounds in a homologous series differ by a CH_2 unit.

3) The physical properties of compounds in a homologous series vary between the different molecules. For example, the bigger a molecule is, the higher the boiling point will be (see next page).

Alkane	Molecular formula	Boiling point (°C)	Fraction in crude oil
Methane	CH_4	−162	Gases
Ethane	C_2H_6	−89	Gases
Dodecane	$C_{12}H_{26}$	216	Kerosene
Icosane	$C_{20}H_{42}$	343	Diesel Oil
Tetracontane	$C_{40}H_{82}$	524	Fuel Oil

4) Alkanes and alkenes are two different homologous series of hydrocarbons.

Combustion of hydrocarbons releases lots of energy

Complete combustion of hydrocarbons only produces carbon dioxide and water, but incomplete combustion will also produce pollutants, as you'll see on page 257.

Q1 Write a balanced symbol equation for the complete combustion of ethane, C_2H_6. [2 marks]

Q1 Video Solution

Section 16 — Fuels and Earth Science

Hydrocarbons

The **physical properties** of crude oil fractions all depend on how **big** the hydrocarbons in that fraction are.

Intermolecular Forces are Stronger Between Bigger Molecules

1) The size of a hydrocarbon determines which fraction of crude oil it will separate into (see page 252).
2) Each fraction contains hydrocarbons (mostly alkanes) with similar numbers of carbon atoms, so all of the molecules in a fraction will have similar properties and behave in similar ways.
3) The physical properties are determined by the intermolecular forces that hold the chains together.

Boiling Point

- The intermolecular forces of attraction break a lot more easily in small molecules than they do in bigger molecules. That's because the forces are much stronger between big molecules than they are between small molecules.
- It makes sense if you think about it — even if a big molecule can overcome the forces attracting it to another molecule at a few points along its length, it's still got lots of other places where the force is still strong enough to hold it in place.
- That's why big molecules have higher boiling points than small molecules do.

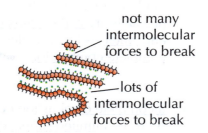

not many intermolecular forces to break

lots of intermolecular forces to break

Ease of Ignition

- Shorter hydrocarbons are easy to ignite because they have lower boiling points, so tend to be gases at room temperature.
- These gas molecules mix with oxygen in the air to produce a gas mixture which bursts into flames if it comes into contact with a spark.
- Longer hydrocarbons are usually liquids at room temperature. They have higher boiling points and are much harder to ignite.

Viscosity

- Viscosity measures how easily a substance flows.
- The stronger the force is between hydrocarbon molecules, the harder it is for the liquid to flow.
- Fractions containing longer hydrocarbons have a higher viscosity — they're thick like treacle.
- Fractions made up of shorter hydrocarbons have a lower viscosity and are much runnier.

The size of a hydrocarbon determines its properties

Intermolecular forces are stronger between longer chain hydrocarbons than shorter chain ones. You can remember the effects of this with the three Hs — longer chain hydrocarbons have **h**igher boiling points and **h**igher viscosity and are **h**arder to ignite than shorter chain hydrocarbons.

Cracking

*Crude oil fractions from fractional distillation are split into **smaller molecules** — this is called **cracking**. It's dead important — otherwise we might not have enough fuel for cars and planes and things.*

Cracking is Splitting Up Long-Chain Hydrocarbons

1) Cracking turns long saturated (alkane) molecules into smaller unsaturated (alkene) and alkane molecules (which are much more useful).
2) It's a form of thermal decomposition, which is when one substance breaks down into at least two new ones when you heat it. This means breaking strong covalent bonds, so you need lots of energy. A catalyst is often added to speed things up.
3) A lot of the longer molecules produced from fractional distillation are cracked into smaller ones because there's more demand for products like petrol and diesel than for bitumen and fuel oil.
4) Cracking also produces lots of alkene molecules, which can be used to make polymers (mostly plastics).

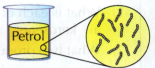

Cracking Involves Heat, Moderate Pressures and a Catalyst

1) Vaporised hydrocarbons are passed over powdered catalyst at about 400 °C–700 °C and 70 atm.
2) Aluminium oxide is the catalyst used. The long-chain molecules split apart or "crack" on the surface of the bits of catalyst.

You don't need to remember the conditions used for cracking.

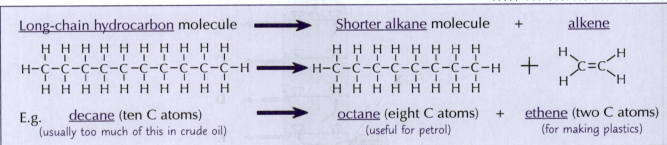

3) You can use the apparatus shown below to crack alkanes in the lab. During this reaction, the alkane is heated until it is vaporised. It then breaks down when it comes into contact with the catalyst, producing a mixture of short-chain alkanes and alkenes.

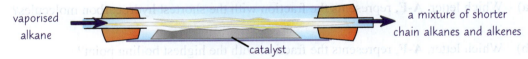

Cracking Helps Match Supply and Demand

The examiner might give you a table like the one below to show the supply and demand for various fractions obtained from crude oil. You could be asked which fraction is more likely to be cracked to provide us with petrol and diesel oil (demand for petrol and diesel oil is greater than the amount in crude oil).

Fraction	Approx % in crude oil	Approx % demand
Gases	2	4
Petrol	16	27
Kerosene	13	8
Diesel Oil	19	23
Fuel Oil and Bitumen	50	38

OK, you could use the kerosene fraction to supply the extra petrol and the fuel oil and bitumen fraction to supply the extra diesel oil.

Or you could crack the fuel oil and bitumen to supply both the extra petrol and the extra diesel oil. This might be cleverer, as there's a lot more fuel oil/bitumen than kerosene.

Section 16 — Fuels and Earth Science

Warm-Up and Exam Questions

Hydrocarbons contain only hydrogen and carbon atoms. This page contains only Warm-Up and Exam Questions. Time to get thinking.

Warm-Up Questions

1) What is each of the following used for?
   a) kerosene   b) diesel oil   c) bitumen
2) What two products are made by the complete combustion of a hydrocarbon?
3) Give an example of a homologous series found in crude oil.
4) Describe the relationship between the length of the molecules in a hydrocarbon and the ease with which it ignites.

Exam Question

1   Crude oil can be separated into a number of different compounds in a fractional distillation column. **Figure 1** shows a fractional distillation column.

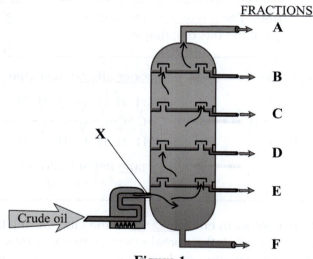

Figure 1

(a) Which letter, **A–F**, represents the fraction with the shortest hydrocarbon molecules?

[1 mark]

(b) Which letter, **A–F**, represents the fraction with the highest boiling point?

[1 mark]

(c) Gaseous crude oil enters near the bottom of the fractional distillation column (point **X** in **Figure 1**). Explain why different fractions exit the column at different points and how this relates to their structure.

[3 marks]

Cracking is a process used to break longer chain molecules in crude oil down to shorter ones.

(d) Why is cracking an important process in the petrochemical industry?

[1 mark]

(e) Octane (C_8H_{18}) can be cracked to form two products. Complete the equation below for this reaction:

$$C_8H_{18} \rightarrow \text{............} + 2C_3H_6$$

[1 mark]

Section 16 — Fuels and Earth Science

Pollutants

*You get lots of nasties like **carbon monoxide**, **oxides of nitrogen** and **sulfur dioxide** when you burn fossil fuels.*

Incomplete Combustion Produces Carbon Monoxide and Soot

1) Complete combustion reactions of hydrocarbons produce only carbon dioxide and water (see page 253).

2) If there's not enough oxygen around for complete combustion, you get incomplete combustion. This can happen in some appliances, e.g. boilers, that use carbon compounds as fuels.

3) The products of incomplete combustion contain less oxygen than carbon dioxide.

4) As well as carbon dioxide and water, incomplete combustion produces carbon monoxide (CO), a toxic gas, and carbon in the form of soot.

- Carbon monoxide can combine with red blood cells and stop your blood from doing its proper job of carrying oxygen around the body.
- A lack of oxygen in the blood supply to the brain can lead to fainting, a coma or even death.

- During incomplete combustion, tiny particles of carbon can be released into the atmosphere. When they fall back to the ground, they deposit themselves as the horrible black dust we call soot.
- Soot makes buildings look dirty, reduces air quality and can cause or worsen respiratory problems.

Sulfur Dioxide Causes Acid Rain

1) When fossil fuels are burned, they release mostly CO_2 (a big cause of global warming, see page 263).

2) But they also release other harmful gases — especially sulfur dioxide and various nitrogen oxides.

3) The sulfur dioxide (SO_2) comes from sulfur impurities in the fossil fuels.

4) When sulfur dioxide mixes with clouds, it forms dilute sulfuric acid. This then falls as acid rain.

5) Acid rain causes lakes to become acidic and many plants and animals die as a result.

6) Acid rain kills trees, damages limestone buildings and stone statues, and can also make metal corrode.

Section 16 — Fuels and Earth Science

Pollutants

Oxides of Nitrogen Are Also Pollutants

1) Nitrogen oxides are created from a reaction between the nitrogen and oxygen in the air, caused by the energy released by combustion reactions, for example, in the internal combustion engines of cars.

2) Nitrogen oxides are harmful pollutants — they can contribute to acid rain and, at ground level, can cause photochemical smog.

3) Photochemical smog is a type of air pollution that can cause breathing difficulties, headaches and tiredness.

Hydrogen can be Used as a Clean, Renewable Fuel

Hydrogen gas can also be used to power vehicles. It's often used as a fuel in fuel cells.

Pros

1) Hydrogen is a very clean fuel. In a hydrogen fuel cell, hydrogen combines with oxygen to produce energy, and the only waste product is water — no nasty pollutants like carbon dioxide, toxic carbon monoxide or soot (which are produced when fossil fuels are burnt).
2) Hydrogen is obtained from water, which is a renewable resource, so it's not going to run out (unlike fossil fuels). Hydrogen can even be obtained from the water produced by the cell when it's used in fuel cells.

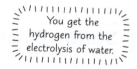
You get the hydrogen from the electrolysis of water.

Cons

1) You need a special, expensive engine.
2) Hydrogen gas needs to be manufactured, which is expensive and often uses energy from another source — this energy often comes from burning fossil fuels, which produces pollutants.
3) Hydrogen is hard to store and not widely available.

Fossil fuels are bad news — but we depend on them for many things

Make sure you know the different pollutants that are given out when fossil fuels are burnt, along with the negative effects that each of the pollutants has on us and the environment.

The Atmosphere

*Scientists have looked at **evidence** from rocks, air bubbles in ice and fossils to see how our **atmosphere** has **changed** over many, many years. Here's one theory about how our atmosphere might have evolved.*

Phase 1 — Volcanoes Gave Out Steam and CO₂

1) The Earth's surface was originally molten for many millions of years. There was almost no atmosphere.
2) Eventually the Earth's surface cooled and a thin crust formed, but volcanoes kept erupting, releasing gases from inside the Earth. This 'degassing' released mainly carbon dioxide, but also steam, methane and ammonia.
3) When things eventually settled down, the early atmosphere was mostly CO_2 and water vapour. There was very little oxygen.
4) The water vapour later condensed to form the oceans.

Phase 2 — Green Plants Evolved and Produced Oxygen

1) A lot of the early CO_2 dissolved into the oceans.
2) Nitrogen gas (N_2) was then put into the atmosphere in two ways — it was formed by ammonia reacting with oxygen, and was released by denitrifying bacteria.
3) N_2 isn't very reactive. So the amount of N_2 in the atmosphere increased, because it was being made but not broken down.
4) Next, green plants evolved over most of the Earth. As they photosynthesised, they removed CO_2 and produced O_2.
5) Thanks to the plants, the amount of O_2 in the air gradually built up and much of the CO_2 eventually got locked up in fossil fuels and sedimentary rocks.

Phase 3 — Ozone Layer Allows Evolution of Complex Animals

1) The build-up of oxygen in the atmosphere killed off early organisms that couldn't tolerate it.
2) But it did allow the evolution of more complex organisms that made use of the oxygen.
3) The oxygen also created the ozone layer (O_3), which blocked harmful rays from the Sun and enabled even more complex organisms to evolve.
4) There is virtually no CO_2 left now, compared to how much there used to be.

Today's Atmosphere is Mainly Nitrogen and Oxygen

The atmosphere today is made up of:
- approximately 78% nitrogen and approximately 21% oxygen,
- small amounts of other gases (each making up less than 1% of the atmosphere), mainly carbon dioxide, noble gases and water vapour.

There's more about today's atmosphere on p.261-263.

Test for Oxygen Using a Glowing Splint

You can test for oxygen by checking if the gas will relight a glowing splint.

Before volcanic activity, the Earth didn't even have an atmosphere

One way scientists can get information about what Earth's atmosphere was like in the past is from Antarctic ice cores. Each year a layer of ice forms with tiny bubbles of air trapped in it. The deeper you go in the ice, the older the air. So analysing bubbles from different layers shows you how the atmosphere has changed.

Section 16 — Fuels and Earth Science

Warm-Up and Exam Questions

There's lots of important information in this section on air pollution and the Earth's atmosphere. Answer these questions to see what you can remember and what you need to go over again.

Warm-Up Questions

1) What is meant by the incomplete combustion of hydrocarbons?
2) a) Name two pollutants that could be released as a result of the incomplete combustion of hydrocarbons, that wouldn't be released as a result of complete combustion.
   b) For each pollutant you named in part a), state one way in which it could affect human health.
3) State one advantage and one disadvantage of using hydrogen gas to fuel cars.

Exam Questions

1   Which of the following statements about nitrogen oxides is correct?

☐ A   Nitrogen oxides are produced by car batteries.

☐ B   Nitrogen oxides are produced in the internal combustion engines of cars.

☐ C   Using hydrogen as a fuel increases the amount of nitrogen oxides in the atmosphere.

☐ D   Nitrogen oxides react with carbon dioxide in the air to produce acid rain.

[1 mark]

2   Burning fossil fuels can produce pollutants like sulfur dioxide.
    Sulfur dioxide can cause acid rain.

(a) Explain why sulfur dioxide is produced when some fossil fuels are burned.

[1 mark]

(b) Describe how sulfur dioxide can cause acid rain.

[2 marks]

(c) Give **one** environmental problem caused by acid rain.

[1 mark]

3* Some information about the amounts of oxygen, carbon dioxide and water vapour in the Earth's atmosphere is shown in **Figure 1**.

Gas	Amount in atmosphere today (%)
Oxygen	21
Carbon dioxide	0.04
Water vapour	0.25

Figure 1

Describe the composition of the Earth's early atmosphere and explain the main changes that are thought to have occurred over the past 4 billion years to result in the amounts of oxygen, carbon dioxide and water vapour shown in **Figure 1**.

[6 marks]

Section 16 — Fuels and Earth Science

The Greenhouse Effect

*Some of the gases in the **atmosphere** are **greenhouse gases** — they help to **trap** the **Sun's energy**, which keeps the Earth nice and **warm**. Without them, the **average global temperature** would be over **30 °C cooler**. Brrr...*

The Greenhouse Effect Helps to Keep the Earth Warm

1) Greenhouse gases, such as carbon dioxide, methane and water vapour, are present in small amounts in the Earth's atmosphere.
2) They act like an insulating layer, keeping the Earth warm — this is the greenhouse effect. Here's how it works...

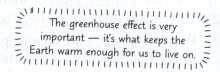
The greenhouse effect is very important — it's what keeps the Earth warm enough for us to live on.

1) The Sun emits short wavelength electromagnetic radiation, which passes through the Earth's atmosphere as it isn't absorbed by greenhouse gases.

2) The short wavelength radiation reaches the Earth's surface, is absorbed, and then is re-emitted as long wavelength, infrared (IR) radiation.

3) This radiation is absorbed by greenhouse gases in the atmosphere.

4) The greenhouse gases then re-radiate it in all directions — including back towards Earth.

5) The IR radiation is thermal radiation, so it warms the surface of the Earth.

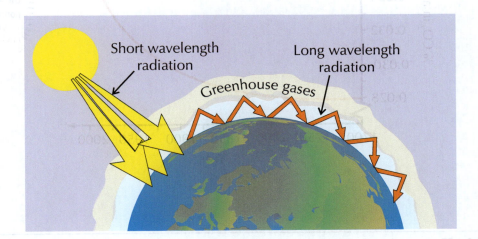

If the concentration of greenhouse gases in the atmosphere increases, you get an enhanced greenhouse effect, which causes the Earth to get warmer.

Atmospheric greenhouse gases make the Earth a warmer place

Make sure that you can name the three greenhouse gases given above.
You will also need to be able to explain how they affect the Earth's climate.

Q1 Describe the greenhouse effect and how it affects global temperature. [4 marks]

Q1 Video Solution

Section 16 — Fuels and Earth Science

Climate Change

*The amount of **greenhouse gases** in the atmosphere is **increasing** — and it's mainly down to **human activity**.*

Human Activity Affects the Atmospheric Carbon Dioxide Level

1) Over the last 150 years or so, the human population has rapidly increased.
2) This means that more energy is needed for lighting, heating, cooking, transport and so on.
3) People's lifestyles are changing too. More and more countries are becoming industrialised and well-off. This means the average energy demand per person is also increasing (since people have more electrical gadgets, more people have cars or travel on planes, etc.).
4) This increased energy consumption comes mainly from the burning of fossil fuels, which releases more CO_2.
5) More people also means more land is needed to build houses and grow food. This space is often made by chopping down trees — this is called deforestation. But plants are the main things taking carbon dioxide out of the atmosphere (as they photosynthesise) — so fewer plants means less carbon dioxide is taken out of the atmosphere.
6) The graph shows how CO_2 levels in the atmosphere have risen over the last 300 years.

As the consumption of fossil fuels increases, so does the concentration of CO_2 in the atmosphere.

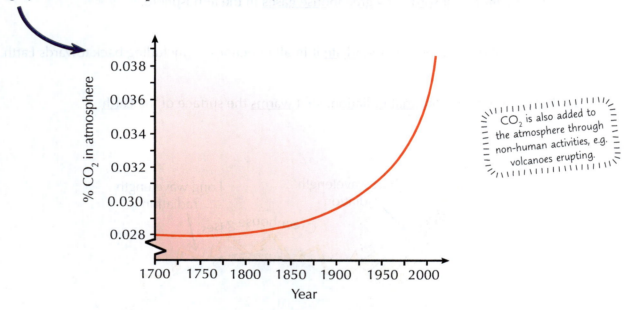

CO_2 is also added to the atmosphere through non-human activities, e.g. volcanoes erupting.

Livestock Farming Affects the Atmospheric Methane Level

1) The level of carbon dioxide in the atmosphere is increasing, but that's not the whole story...
2) The greenhouse gas methane is also causing problems. The concentration of methane has risen lots in recent years due to increased human activity.
3) Methane is produced in the digestive processes of certain livestock (e.g. cattle, goats and camels). So, the more livestock we farm, the more methane is produced.
4) Though it's currently only present in tiny amounts in our atmosphere, the increasing concentration of methane is an issue as it's a super-effective greenhouse gas.

Climate Change

Increasing Levels of Greenhouse Gases Cause Climate Change

1) Historically, temperature change at the Earth's surface is correlated to the level of carbon dioxide in the atmosphere. Recently, the average temperature at the Earth's surface has been increasing as the level of carbon dioxide has increased.
2) There's a scientific consensus that extra greenhouse gases from human activity have caused the average temperature of the Earth to increase, due to the enhanced greenhouse effect — see page 261. This effect is known as global warming.
3) Global warming is a type of climate change and causes other types of climate change, e.g. changing rainfall patterns. It could also cause severe flooding due to the polar ice caps melting. It's a BIG problem that could affect the whole world, so we need to deal with it seriously.
4) Global warming can be described as anthropogenic — this means 'caused by humans'.

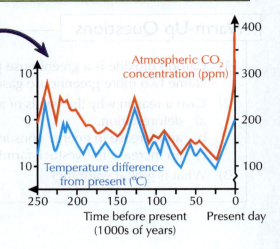

Historical Data is Much Less Accurate Than Current Records

1) Current global temperature and carbon dioxide levels can be worked out pretty accurately as they're based on measurements taken all over the world.
2) Historical data is less accurate — less data was taken over fewer locations and the methods used to collect the data were less accurate. If you go back far enough, there are no records of global temperature and carbon dioxide levels at all...
3) But there are ways to estimate past data. For example, you can analyse fossils, tree rings or gas bubbles trapped in ice sheets to estimate past levels of atmospheric carbon dioxide.
4) The problem with using these kinds of measurements is that they're much less precise than current measurements made using instrumental sampling. They're also much less representative of global levels.

We Can Try to Use Less Fossil Fuels

1) In order to prevent or slow down climate change, we need to cut down on the amount of greenhouse gases we're releasing into the atmosphere.
2) To reduce carbon dioxide emissions, we can try to limit our own use of fossil fuels. This could be by doing things on a personal level, like walking or cycling instead of driving or turning your central heating down.
3) On a larger scale, the UK government has formed plans to encourage the public and industry to become more energy efficient, to create financial incentives to reduce CO_2 emissions, to use more renewable energy and to increase research into new energy sources.

People can get quite hot under the collar talking about all this...

That's because climate change could have a massive impact on many people's lives across the world. It's really important that we understand what causes it, as well as how to prevent any damaging consequences.

Section 16 — Fuels and Earth Science

Warm-Up and Exam Questions

We're approaching the end of another section. All that's standing between you and a well-earned break are a few questions on the greenhouse effect and climate change. Time to see how much you remember.

Warm-Up Questions

1) Carbon dioxide is a greenhouse gas.
   Name two more greenhouse gases present in the atmosphere.
2) Give a reason why the levels of atmospheric greenhouse gases will increase as a result of:
   a) deforestation,
   b) an increase in energy consumption,
   c) an increase in livestock farming.
3) What is global warming?

Exam Questions

1 **Figure 1** shows an estimate of how the atmospheric CO_2 concentration and the Earth's surface temperature have changed over the last 250 000 years.

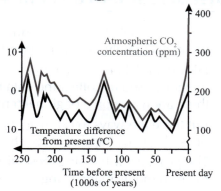

Figure 1

(a) Give **one** reason why historical data may be less accurate than data collected more recently.

[1 mark]

(b) In 1960, the atmospheric CO_2 concentration was 317 ppm. In 2010, it was 22.7% higher than in 1960.
Calculate the atmospheric CO_2 concentration in 2010.
Give your answer to three significant figures.

[2 marks]

(c) Give **one** conclusion that can be drawn from **Figure 1**.

[1 mark]

2 Carbon dioxide is a greenhouse gas.

(a) Explain how carbon dioxide contributes to the greenhouse effect.

[2 marks]

The level of atmospheric carbon dioxide is increasing, which has enhanced the greenhouse effect. This has led to global warming.

(b) State **two** effects that an increase in global temperature could have on the environment.

[2 marks]

(c) (i) Give **one** measure an individual could take to reduce their carbon dioxide emissions on a personal level.

[1 mark]

(ii) Give **one** way that governments can act to encourage reductions in carbon dioxide emissions.

[1 mark]

Section 16 — Fuels and Earth Science

Revision Summary for Sections 14-16

That wraps up Sections 14, 15 and 16 — time to put yourself to the test and find out how much you really know.
- Try these questions and tick off each one when you get it right.
- When you're completely happy with a section, tick it off.

For even more practice, try the Retrieval Quizzes for Sections 14-16 — just scan these QR codes!

Section 14 — Groups in the Periodic Table (p.226-234)

1) Give two properties of the Group 1 metals.
2) Explain why Group 1 metals are so reactive.
3) How many electrons do halogens have in their outer shells?
4) Why can halogen displacement reactions be described as redox reactions?
5) If chlorine water is added to potassium bromide solution, what colour will the solution turn?
6) Write a balanced symbol equation for the reaction between bromine (Br_2) and sodium (Na).
7) Does the boiling point of Group 0 elements increase or decrease going down the group?

Section 15 — Rates of Reaction and Energy Changes (p.235-251)

8) State the formula for calculating the rate of reaction.
9) A student carries out a reaction which produces carbon dioxide gas. He collects the carbon dioxide in a gas syringe. How will he know when the reaction has finished?
10) Draw a diagram of equipment you could use to measure the rate of reaction between hydrochloric acid and marble chips.
11) How does the rate of a reaction change with concentration of reactants?
12) Describe how you would find the rate of a reaction from a curve on a graph.
13) What is the term for the minimum energy needed in a collision between reacting particles in order for a reaction to occur?
14) In a gaseous reaction, why would a decrease in pressure result in a slower rate of reaction?
15) What effect does a catalyst have on the activation energy needed for a reaction to take place?
16) What change in temperature would you expect to observe in an exothermic reaction?
17) Describe the temperature change that would take place in a displacement reaction.
18) What is the equation for calculating the overall energy change for a reaction?

Section 16 — Fuels and Earth Science (p.252-265)

19) Which elements are hydrocarbons made from?
20) What is the purpose of fractional distillation?
21) What is the gas fraction used for?
22) Give the word equation for the complete combustion of hydrocarbons.
23) What is the definition of a homologous series?
24) Are longer or shorter hydrocarbons associated with a low viscosity?
25) What is cracking?
26) Why is carbon monoxide bad for human health?
27) Give three problems associated with acid rain.
28) How did the formation of the oceans affect the level of carbon dioxide in the Earth's atmosphere?
29) How could you test an unknown gas to see if it was oxygen?
30) Give two reasons why the increasing human population has affected the level of atmospheric CO_2.

Section 16 — Fuels and Earth Science

Section 17 — Motion and Forces

Scalars and Vectors

There are a lot of very similar variables on this page, but they're different in some very important ways, so prepare to pay extra close attention. It's down to whether they're a vector or a scalar quantity.

Vectors Have Magnitude and Direction

1) Vector quantities have a magnitude (size) and a direction.
2) Lots of physical quantities are vector quantities:

   Vector quantities: force, velocity, displacement, weight, acceleration, momentum, etc.

3) Some physical quantities only have magnitude and no direction. These are called scalar quantities:

   Scalar quantities: speed, distance, mass, energy, temperature, time, etc.

> Velocity is a vector, but speed is a scalar quantity.
> Both bikes are travelling at the same speed, v.
> They have different velocities because they are travelling in different directions.

Distance is Scalar, Displacement is a Vector

1) Distance is just how far an object has moved. It's a scalar quantity so it doesn't involve direction.
2) Displacement is a vector quantity. It measures the distance and direction in a straight line from an object's starting point to its finishing point — e.g. the plane flew 5 metres north. The direction could be relative to a point, e.g. towards the school, or a bearing (a three-digit angle from north, e.g. 035°).
3) If you walk 5 m north, then 5 m south, your displacement is 0 m but the distance travelled is 10 m.

Speed and Velocity are Both How Fast You're Going

1) Speed and velocity both measure how fast you're going, but speed is a scalar and velocity is a vector:

   > Speed is just how fast you're going (e.g. 30 mph or 20 m/s) with no regard to the direction.
   > Velocity is speed in a given direction, e.g. 30 mph north or 20 m/s, 060°.

2) This means you can have objects travelling at a constant speed with a changing velocity. This happens when the object is changing direction whilst staying at the same speed.

When it comes to vectors the sign is important...

If you're working on a question which involves vectors that point in opposite directions, pick one direction to have a positive sign and the other negative. For example, if you decide to make all velocities pointing to the left positive, be sure that you give those pointing to the right a negative sign.

Speed

Speed tells you the **distance** an object travels in a **given time**. You're typically going to deal with speeds in metres per second — so you need to be able to **estimate** some everyday speeds in these units.

You Need to Know Some **Typical** Everyday **Speeds**

1) For an object travelling at a constant speed, distance, (average) speed and time are related by the formula:

   distance travelled (m) = (average) speed (m/s) × time (s)

2) Objects rarely travel at a constant speed. E.g. when you walk, run or travel in a car, your speed is always changing. Make sure you have an idea of the typical speeds for different transport methods:

   Walking — 1.4 m/s (5 km/h)
   Running — 3 m/s (11 km/h)
   Cycling — 5.5 m/s (20 km/h)

   Cars in a built-up area — 13 m/s (47 km/h)
   Cars on a motorway — 31 m/s (112 km/h)
   Aeroplanes — 250 m/s (900 km/h)
   Trains — up to 55 m/s (200 km/h)
   Ferries — 15 m/s (54 km/h)

   Wind speed — 5 – 20 m/s
   Speed of sound in air — 340 m/s

You can use **Different Equipment** to Measure **Distance** and **Time**

To calculate speed you'll need measurements of distance and time. For distances less than 1 m and times greater than 5 s, you'll probably use a stopwatch and a metre ruler, but there are many different ways to take distance and time measurements:

1) Light gates (p.382) are often the best option for short time intervals. They get rid of the human error caused by reaction times (p.284).

2) For finding something like a person's walking speed, the distances and times you'll look at are quite large. You can use a rolling tape measure (one of those clicky wheel things) and markers to measure and mark out distances.

3) If you're feeling a bit high-tech, you could also record a video of the moving object and look at how far it travels each frame. If you know how many frames per second the camera records, you can find the distance travelled by the object in a given number of frames and the time that it takes to do so.

Speed is distance over time — learn it and remember it...

This all seems basic, but it's vital you understand it if you want to get through the rest of this topic.

Q1 A sprinter runs 200 m in 25 s. Calculate his average speed. [2 marks]

Acceleration

Acceleration is the *rate of change* of *velocity*. You need to be able estimate some day to day accelerations. This might take you a while at first, but over time you should get *faster*.

Acceleration is How Quickly You're Speeding Up

1) Acceleration is definitely <u>not</u> the same as <u>velocity</u> or <u>speed</u>.

2) Acceleration is the <u>change in velocity</u> in a certain amount of <u>time</u>.

3) You can find the <u>average acceleration</u> of an object using:

$$a = \frac{(v - u)}{t}$$

- Acceleration (m/s²)
- Change in velocity (m/s) where u is the initial velocity in m/s and v is the final velocity in m/s
- Time (s)

4) <u>Initial velocity</u> is just the <u>starting velocity</u> of the object.

5) <u>Negative</u> acceleration is <u>deceleration</u> (if something <u>slows down</u>, the change in velocity is <u>negative</u>).

You Need to be Able to Estimate Accelerations

You might have to <u>estimate</u> the <u>acceleration</u> (or <u>deceleration</u>) of an object:

EXAMPLE

A car is travelling at 15 m/s, when it collides with a tree and comes to a stop. Estimate the deceleration of the car.

1) <u>Estimate</u> how long it would take the car to <u>stop</u>. The car comes to a stop in ~1 s.

2) Put these numbers into the <u>acceleration equation</u>.
$a = (v − u) ÷ t$
$= (0 − 15) ÷ 1$
$= −15$ m/s²

3) As the car has slowed down, the <u>change in velocity</u> and so the acceleration is <u>negative</u> — the car is <u>decelerating</u>.

So the deceleration is about 15 m/s²

The ~ symbol just means it's an approximate value (or answer).

From the deceleration, you can estimate the <u>forces</u> involved too — more about that on page 286.

Acceleration doesn't always have to mean getting faster or slower...

<u>Acceleration</u> measures how quickly <u>velocity changes</u>. Speeding up or slowing down is one way in which velocity can change — but not the only way. Velocity can also <u>change in direction</u>. So, although it might seem weird, a car driving round a roundabout at constant speed is actually experiencing acceleration.

Acceleration

*For cases of **constant acceleration**, which includes pretty much anything that's falling, there's a really useful **equation** you can use to calculate all sorts of **variables** of **motion**.*

Uniform Acceleration Means a Constant Acceleration

1) Constant acceleration is sometimes called uniform acceleration.

2) Acceleration due to gravity (g) is uniform for objects in free fall. It's roughly equal to 10 m/s² near the Earth's surface and has the same value as gravitational field strength (p.278).

3) You can use this equation for uniform acceleration:

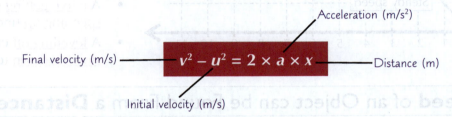

$$v^2 - u^2 = 2 \times a \times x$$

Final velocity (m/s) — Initial velocity (m/s) — Acceleration (m/s²) — Distance (m)

EXAMPLE

A van travelling at 23 m/s starts decelerating uniformly at 2.0 m/s² as it heads towards a built-up area 112 m away.
What will its speed be when it reaches the built-up area?

1) First, rearrange the equation so v^2 is on one side. $v^2 = u^2 + (2 \times a \times x)$
2) Now put the numbers in — remember a is $v^2 = 23^2 + (2 \times -2.0 \times 112)$
   negative because it's a deceleration. $= 81$
3) Finally, square root the whole thing. $v = \sqrt{81}$ = **9 m/s**

EXAMPLE

A ball is launched from the ground, directly upwards, at an initial speed of 14 m/s.
What is the maximum height the ball will reach? (You may ignore air resistance.)

1) This time you'll need to rearrange the equation so x is on one side. $x = (v^2 - u^2) \div (2 \times a)$
2) Again, put the numbers in — this is a little $x = (0^2 - 14^2) \div (2 \times (-10))$
   trickier. Remember a is negative as the ball $x = (-196) \div (-20)$
   is decelerating. Also the final velocity, at the x = **9.8 m**
   instant the ball peaks, will be 0 m/s.

Acceleration due to gravity is 10 m/s² in an ideal world...

You might think 'acceleration due to gravity can't have the same value, g, for all objects — I know a bowling ball falls faster than a feather'. This is because air resistance has a much bigger effect on the feather's motion. If gravity were the only force acting, they really would accelerate at the same rate.

Q1 Video Solution

Q1 A ball is dropped from a height, h, above the ground.
    The speed of the ball just before it hits the ground is 5 m/s.
    Calculate the height the ball is dropped from. (acceleration due to gravity ≈ 10 m/s²) **[2 marks]**

Distance/Time Graphs

It's time for some exciting **graphs**. **Distance/time graphs** contain a lot of **information**, but they can look a bit complicated. Read on to get to grips with the **rules** of the graphs, and all will become clear.

Distance/Time Graphs Tell You How Far Something has Travelled

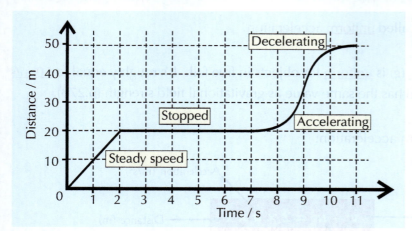

The different parts of a distance/time graph describe the motion of an object:
- The gradient (slope) at any point gives the speed of the object.
- Flat sections are where it's stopped.
- A steeper graph means it's going faster.
- Curves represent acceleration.
- A curve getting steeper means it's speeding up (increasing gradient).
- A levelling off curve means it's slowing down (decreasing gradient).

The Speed of an Object can be Found From a Distance/Time Graph

You can find the speed at any time on a distance/time graph:

1) If the graph is a straight line, the speed at any point along that line is equal to the gradient of the line.
   For example, in the graph above, the speed at any time between 0 s and 2 s is:
   $$\text{Speed} = \text{gradient} = \frac{\text{change in the vertical}}{\text{change in the horizontal}} = \frac{20}{2} = 10 \text{ m/s}$$

2) If the graph is curved, to find the speed at a certain time you need to draw a tangent to the curve at that point, and then find the gradient of the tangent.

3) You can also calculate the average speed of an object when it has non-uniform motion (i.e. it's accelerating) by dividing the total distance travelled by the time it takes to travel that distance.

A tangent is a line that is parallel to the curve at that point.

EXAMPLE

The graph shows the distance/time graph for a cyclist on his bike.
Calculate:
a) the speed of the bike 25 s into the journey.
b) the average speed of the cyclist from 0 to 30 s.

1) Draw the tangent to the curve at 25 s (red line).
2) Then calculate the gradient of the tangent (blue lines).
   $$\text{gradient} = \frac{\text{change in the vertical}}{\text{change in the horizontal}} = \frac{80}{10} = 8 \text{ m/s}$$
   So, the speed of the bike 25 s into the journey is **8 m/s**.
3) Use the formula from page 267 to find the average speed of the bike.
   average speed = distance ÷ time = 150 ÷ 30 = **5 m/s**

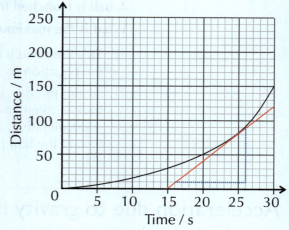

Draw a few distance/time graphs to get a feel for them.

Q1 Sketch the distance-time graph for an object that accelerates, then travels at a steady speed, and then comes to a stop. [3 marks]

Q1 Video Solution

Section 17 — Motion and Forces

Velocity/Time Graphs

*Even more graphs — **velocity/time graphs** this time. These look a lot like the **distance/time graphs** on page 270, so make sure you check the labels on the axes really carefully. You don't want to mix them up.*

Velocity/Time Graphs can have a Positive or Negative Gradient

How an object's velocity changes over time can be plotted on a velocity/time (or *v/t*) graph.

1) Gradient = acceleration, since acceleration = change in velocity ÷ time.
2) Flat sections represent a steady speed.
3) The steeper the graph, the greater the acceleration or deceleration.
4) Uphill sections (/) are acceleration.
5) Downhill sections (\) are deceleration.
6) A curve means changing acceleration.

If the graph is curved, you can use a tangent to the curve (p.270) at a point to find the acceleration at that point.

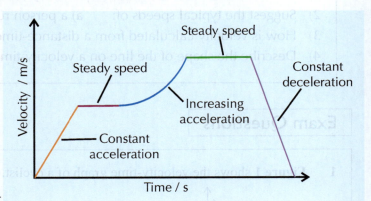

The Distance Travelled is the Area Under the Graph

1) The area under any section of the graph (or all of it) is equal to the distance travelled in that time interval.
2) For bits of the graph where the acceleration's constant, you can split the area into rectangles and triangles to work it out.
3) You can also find the area under the graph by counting the squares under the line and multiplying the number by the value of one square.

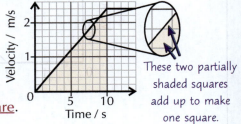

These two partially shaded squares add up to make one square.

EXAMPLE

The velocity/time graph of a car's journey is plotted.
a) **Calculate the acceleration of the car over the first 10 s.**
b) **How far does the car travel in the first 15 s of the journey?**

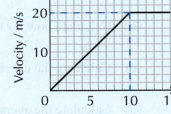

a) This is just the gradient of the line: $a = (v - u) \div t$
   $= (20 - 0) \div 10 = 2$ m/s^2

b) Split the area into a triangle and a rectangle, then add together their areas — remember the area of a triangle is ½ × base × height.

   Area = (½ × 10 × 20) + (5 × 20)
   = 200 m

OR b) Find the value of one square, count the total number of squares under the line, and then multiply these two values together.

   1 square = 2 m/s × 1 s = 2 m
   Area = 100 squares
   = 100 × 2 = 200 m

They look similar to distance/time graphs, but don't be fooled...

Make sure you are familiar with the differences between distance/time and velocity/time graphs.

Q1 A stationary car starts accelerating increasingly for 10 s until it reaches a speed of 20 m/s. It travels at this speed for 20 s until the driver sees a hazard and brakes. He decelerates uniformly, coming to a stop 4 s after braking. Draw the velocity-time graph for this journey. [3 marks]

Warm-Up and Exam Questions

Slow down, it's not time to move on to the next topic just yet. First it's time to check that all the stuff you've just read is still running around your brain. Dive into these questions.

Warm-Up Questions

1) What is the difference between speed and velocity?
2) Suggest the typical speeds of: a) a person running,   b) an aeroplane,   c) sound in air.
3) How is velocity calculated from a distance-time graph?
4) Describe the shape of the line on a velocity-time graph for an object travelling at a steady speed.

Exam Questions

1   **Figure 1** shows the velocity-time graph of a cyclist. *Grade 4-6*

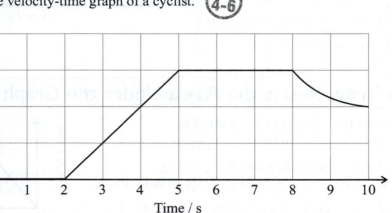

Figure 1

(a) Describe the motion of the cyclist between 5 and 10 seconds.

[2 marks]

(b) Calculate how far the cyclist travelled between 2 and 5 seconds.

[2 marks]

(c) Calculate the acceleration of the cyclist between 2 and 5 seconds.

[2 marks]

(d) Calculate the average deceleration of the cyclist between 8 and 10 seconds.

[3 marks]

2   A car travelling down the motorway has to perform an emergency stop. *Grade 6-7*

(a) Estimate the original speed of the car in metres per second.

[1 mark]

(b) After pressing the brake pedal, the car decelerates uniformly for 5 seconds until reaching a complete stop.

    (i) Calculate the deceleration the car experiences.

[2 marks]

    (ii) Calculate the distance travelled by the car in this time.
       Use the correct equation from the Physics Equation Sheet on page 506.

[3 marks]

Section 17 — Motion and Forces

Newton's First and Second Laws

Way back in the 1660s, some clever chap named **Isaac Newton** worked out some **Laws of Motion**...

A Force is Needed to Change Motion

This may seem simple, but it's important. Newton's First Law says that a resultant force (p.334) is needed to make something start moving, speed up or slow down:

> If the resultant force on a stationary object is zero, the object will remain stationary. If the resultant force on a moving object is zero, it'll just carry on moving at the same velocity (same speed and direction).

stationary bus

So, when a train or car or bus or anything else is moving at a constant velocity, the resistive and driving forces on it must all be balanced. The velocity will only change if there's a non-zero resultant force acting on the object.

bus with constant velocity

1) A non-zero resultant force will always produce acceleration (or deceleration) in the direction of the force.

2) This "acceleration" can take five different forms: starting, stopping, speeding up, slowing down and changing direction.

accelerating bus

Newton's First Law Helps to Describe Circular Motion

1) Velocity is both the speed and direction of an object (p.266).
2) If an object is travelling in a circular orbit (at a constant speed) it is constantly changing direction, so it is constantly changing velocity. This means it's accelerating.
3) From Newton's First Law, this means there must be a resultant force (p.334) acting on it.
4) This force acts towards the centre of the circle.
5) This force that keeps something moving in a circle is called a centripetal force.

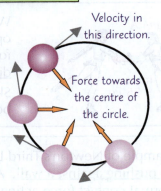

Acceleration is Proportional to the Resultant Force

1) The larger the resultant force acting on an object, the more the object accelerates — the force and the acceleration are directly proportional. You can write this as $F \propto a$.

2) Acceleration is also inversely proportional to the mass of the object — so an object with a larger mass will accelerate less than one with a smaller mass (for a fixed resultant force).

3) There's an incredibly useful formula that describes Newton's Second Law:

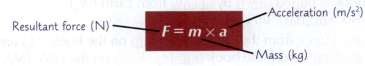

$$F = m \times a$$

Resultant force (N), Acceleration (m/s²), Mass (kg)

If there's no net force, then there's no acceleration...

So an object moving at a steady speed doesn't need a net force to keep moving.

Q1 Find the force needed for an 80 kg man on a 10 kg bike to accelerate at 0.25 m/s². **[2 marks]**

Inertia and Newton's Third Law

Newton's Third Law and *inertia* sound pretty straightforward, but things can quickly get confusing...

Inertia is the Tendency for Motion to Remain Unchanged

1) Until acted on by a resultant force, objects at rest stay at rest and objects moving at a constant velocity will stay moving at that velocity (Newton's First Law).
2) This tendency to keep moving with the same velocity is called inertia.
3) An object's inertial mass measures how difficult it is to change the velocity of an object.
4) Inertial mass can be found using Newton's Second Law of $F = m \times a$ (p.273). Rearranging this gives $m = F \div a$, so inertial mass is just the ratio of force over acceleration.

Newton's Third Law — Interaction Pairs are Equal and Opposite

Newton's Third Law says:

> When two objects interact, the forces they exert on each other are equal and opposite.

1) If you push something, say a shopping trolley, the trolley will push back against you, just as hard.
2) And as soon as you stop pushing, so does the trolley. Kinda clever really.
3) So far so good. The slightly tricky thing to get your head round is this — if the forces are always equal, how does anything ever go anywhere? The important thing to remember is that the two forces are acting on different objects.

When skater A pushes on skater B, she feels an equal and opposite force from skater B's hand (the 'normal contact' force). Both skaters feel the same sized force, in opposite directions, and so accelerate away from each other.

Skater A will be accelerated more than skater B, though, because she has a smaller mass — remember $a = F \div m$.

An example of Newton's Third Law in an equilibrium situation is a man pushing against a wall. As the man pushes the wall, there is a normal contact force acting back on him. These two forces are the same size. As the man applies a force and pushes the wall, the wall 'pushes back' on him with an equal force.

It can be easy to get confused with Newton's Third Law when an object is in equilibrium. E.g. a book resting on a table is in equilibrium. The weight of the book is equal to the normal contact force. The weight of the book pulls it down, and the normal contact force from the table pushes it up. This is NOT Newton's Third Law. These forces are different types and they're both acting on the book.

The pairs of forces due to Newton's Third Law in this case are:

1) The weight of book is pulled down by gravity from Earth (W_B) and the book also pulls back up on the Earth (W_E).
2) The normal contact force from the table pushing up on the book (N_B) and the normal contact force from the book pushing down on the table (N_T).

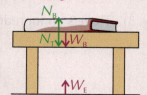

Know your interaction pairs, especially for objects in equilibrium.

Q1 A car moves at a constant velocity along a road, so that it is in equilibrium. Give an example of a pair of forces that demonstrate Newton's Third Law in this situation. [1 mark]

Warm-Up and Exam Questions

Now you've gotten yourself on the right side of the law(s) of motion), it's time to put your knowledge on trial. Have a go at cross-examining these questions.

Warm-Up Questions

1) What is the resultant force on an object moving at a constant velocity?
2) Write down the formula that links mass, force and acceleration.
3) True or false? An object travelling at a constant speed around a circular path is not accelerating.
4) Boulders A and B are accelerated from 0 m/s to 5 m/s in 10 s. Boulder A required a force of 70 N, and Boulder B required a force of 95 N. Which boulder has the greater inertial mass?
5) True or false? Two interacting objects exert equal and opposite forces on each other.

Exam Questions

1   A student has a cricket bat with a mass of 1.2 kg.
    She uses it to hit a ball with a mass of 160 g forwards with a force of 500 N.

   (a) State the force that the ball exerts on the bat. Explain your answer.

   [2 marks]

   (b) State and explain whether the acceleration of the ball is greater or smaller than the acceleration of the bat.

   [2 marks]

2   A camper van has a mass of 2500 kg. It is driven along a straight, level road
    at a constant speed of 90.0 kilometres per hour, as shown in **Figure 1**.

Figure 1

   (a) A headwind begins to blow, so that the resultant force acting on the van is 200 N in the opposite direction to the van's motion. This causes the van to slow down. Calculate the van's deceleration.

   [3 marks]

   The van begins travelling at a constant speed before colliding with a stationary 4.50 kg traffic cone. The traffic cone accelerates in the direction of the van's motion with an acceleration of 28.0 m/s².

   (b) Calculate the force applied to the traffic cone by the van.

   [2 marks]

   (c) Calculate the deceleration of the van, due to the force of the cone, during the collision.

   [3 marks]

Section 17 — Motion and Forces

Investigating Motion

Here comes a **Core Practical**. This one's all about testing **Newton's Second Law**. It uses some nifty bits of kit that you may not have seen before, so make sure you follow the instructions closely.

You can Investigate the Motion of a Trolley on a Ramp

It's time for an experiment that tests Newton's 2nd Law, $F = m \times a$ (p.273).

1) Measure the mass of the trolley, the unit masses and the hanging hook. Measure the length of the piece of card which will interrupt the light gate beams. Then set up your apparatus as shown in the diagram below, but don't attach the string to the trolley.

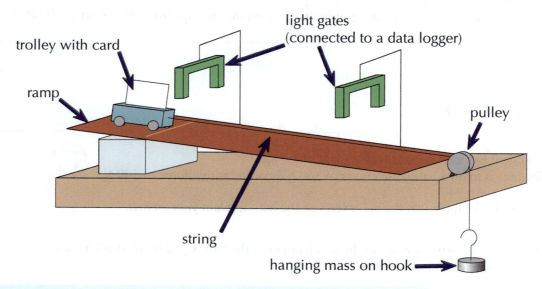

2) Adjust the height of the ramp until the trolley just starts to move. This means that the force due to gravity acting on the hanging mass will be the main cause of the trolley accelerating as it travels down the ramp.

3) Mark a line on the ramp just before the first light gate, so the trolley travels the same distance every time. The light gate will record the initial speed of the trolley as it begins to move.

4) Attach the trolley to the hanging mass by the string. Hold the trolley still at the start line, and then let go of it so that it starts to roll down the slope.

5) The weight of the hook and any masses attached to it will provide the accelerating force, equal to the mass of the hook (m) × acceleration due to gravity (g). The weight of the hook and masses accelerates both the trolley and the masses, so you are investigating the acceleration of the system (the trolley and the masses together).

6) Each light gate will record the time when the trolley passes through it and the speed of the trolley at that time. The acceleration of the trolley can then be found using acceleration = change in speed ÷ time, with the following values:
   - the initial speed of the trolley as it passes through the first light gate (it'll be roughly 0 m/s),
   - the final speed of the trolley, as it passes through the second light gate,
   - the time it takes the trolley to travel between the two light gates.

7) Repeat the experiment at least three times and calculate an average acceleration from the results.

Investigating Motion

*Now you've set up the **equipment**, and you're used to how it works, it's time to start **adjusting** your **variables**. Take care with the **method** here — there are some important points you don't want to miss.*

Varying Mass and Force

1) To investigate how the mass of the system affects its acceleration, add masses one at a time to the trolley.
2) Don't add masses to the hook, as this will change the force acting on the system.
3) Each time you add a mass to the trolley, take a measurement of the system's average acceleration using the method described in points 2-7 on the previous page.

1) To investigate how the force acting on the system affects its acceleration, you need to keep the total mass of the system the same, but change the mass on the hook.
2) To do this, start with all the masses loaded onto the trolley, and transfer the masses to the hook one at a time, to increase the accelerating force (the weight of the hanging masses).
3) The mass of the system stays the same as you're only transferring the masses from one part of the system (the trolley) to another (the hook).
4) Each time you transfer a mass from the trolley to the hook, take a measurement of the system's average acceleration using the method described in points 2-7 on the previous page.

Newton's Second Law Can Explain the Results

1) Newton's Second Law can be written as $F = m \times a$. Here, F = weight of the hanging masses, m = mass of the whole system and a = acceleration of the system.

2) By adding masses to the trolley, the mass of the whole system increases, but the force applied to the system stays the same. This should lead to a decrease in the acceleration of the trolley, so a is inversely proportional to m ($a = F \div m$).

3) By transferring masses to the hook, you are increasing the accelerating force without changing the mass of the whole system. Increasing the force should lead to an increase in the acceleration of the trolley, so a is proportional to F.

This experiment has a lot of steps, so don't speed through it...
Make sure the string is the right length and there's enough space for the hanging masses to fall. There needs to be enough space so that the masses don't hit the floor before the trolley has passed through the light gate fully — if they hit the floor, the force won't be applied the whole way through the trolley's journey, so you won't get an accurate measurement for the speed.

Section 17 — Motion and Forces

Weight

*Now for something a bit more **attractive** — the force of **gravity**. Enjoy...*

Weight and Mass are Not the Same

1) Mass is just the amount of 'stuff' in an object. For any given object this will have the same value anywhere in the universe.
2) Mass is a scalar quantity. It's measured in kilograms with a mass balance (an old-fashioned pair of balancing scales).

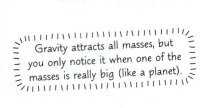
Gravity attracts all masses, but you only notice it when one of the masses is really big (like a planet).

3) Weight is the force acting on an object due to gravity (the pull of the gravitational force on the object). Close to Earth, this force is caused by the gravitational field around the Earth.
4) Weight is a force measured in newtons. You can think of the force as acting from a single point on the object, called its centre of mass (a point at which you assume the whole mass is concentrated).
5) Weight is measured using a calibrated spring balance (or newton meter).

Weight Depends on Mass and Gravitational Field Strength

1) You can calculate the weight of an object if you know its mass (m) and the strength of the gravitational field that it is in (g):

weight (N) = mass (kg) × gravitational field strength (N/kg)

2) Gravitational field strength varies with location. It's stronger the closer you are to the mass causing the field (and more massive objects create stronger fields).
3) This means that the weight of an object changes with its location.

EXAMPLE

What is the weight, in newtons, of a 2.0 kg object on Earth (g = 10 N/kg)?

1) Calculate the weight on Earth using the equation for weight given above.
   $W = m \times g = 2.0 \times 10 = 20$ N

The object has a weight of 16 N on a different planet. What is the gravitational field strength of this other planet?

1) Rearrange the weight equation for g.
2) Substitute the values in.
   $g = W \div m$
   $= 16 \div 2.0 = 8.0$ N/kg

Remember — the mass of the object is the same on every planet, it's the weight of the object that changes.

You might be experiencing déjà vu...

On p.269 you saw that 'g' was introduced as 'acceleration due to gravity' (m/s^2), and now it's being used for 'gravitational field strength' (N/kg). These two quantities have been given the same symbol because acceleration due to a gravitational field will always be equal to the strength of that field.

Q1 Calculate the weight in newtons of a 25 kg mass:
a) on Earth (g ≈ 10 N/kg)
b) on the Moon (g ≈ 1.6 N/kg)
[4 marks]

Q1 Video Solution

Warm-Up and Exam Questions

That's all you need to know about gravitational field strength... I bet that's a weight off your mind. Try out these questions and see how much really sunk in.

Warm-Up Questions

1) When carrying out the trolley-and-ramp practical (p.276), what is the purpose of adjusting the ramp so that the trolley is just about to move?
2) Give the definitions of mass and weight.
3) What are the units of weight?

Exam Questions

1 On Earth, the gravitational field strength is 10 N/kg.
   Calculate the weight of an 80 kg person on Earth.

   [2 marks]

PRACTICAL

2 A student investigates how the mass of a system affects its acceleration.
   Figure 1 is a graph of her results.

   (a) Name the independent variable in this experiment.
   [1 mark]

   (b) Name the dependent variable in this experiment.
   [1 mark]

   (c) Describe the relationship between mass and acceleration.
   [1 mark]

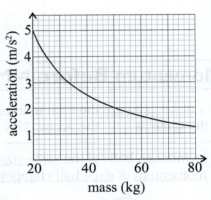

Figure 1

3 The weight of a space probe on the surface of Mars
   is 0.4 times its weight on the surface of Earth.

   (a) The gravitational field strength on Earth is 10 N/kg.
       Determine the gravitational field strength of Mars.
   [2 marks]

   (b) The weight of the probe on Mars is 3600 N. Calculate the mass of the probe.
   [3 marks]

PRACTICAL

4* A student is investigating how acceleration varies with force.
    He has a 1 kg trolley, attached by a pulley to a 0.5 kg hanging hook.
    He also has eight 100 g masses. When the trolley is released, it rolls down a ramp,
    and passes through two sets of light gates which each measure its velocity.

    Describe an experiment that the student can perform using this equipment
    to investigate the relationship between force and acceleration.
    [6 marks]

Section 17 — Motion and Forces

Momentum

*A **large rugby player** running very **fast** has much **more momentum** than a **skinny** bloke out for a Sunday afternoon **stroll**. Momentum's something that **all moving objects have**, so you better get your head around it.*

Momentum = Mass × Velocity

Momentum is mainly about how much 'oomph' an object has. It's a property that all moving objects have.
1) The greater the mass of an object, or the greater its velocity, the more momentum the object has.
2) Momentum is a vector quantity — it has size and direction.
3) You can work out the momentum of an object using:

$p = m \times v$ momentum (kg m/s) = mass (kg) × velocity (m/s)

EXAMPLE

A 50 kg cheetah is running at 60 m/s. Calculate its momentum.

$p = m \times v = 50 \times 60 = 3000$ kg m/s

EXAMPLE

A boy has a mass of 30 kg and a momentum of 75 kg m/s. Calculate his velocity.

$v = p \div m = 75 \div 30 = 2.5$ m/s

Momentum Before = Momentum After

In a closed system, the total momentum before an event (e.g. a collision) is the same as after the event. This is called conservation of momentum.

A closed system is just a fancy way of saying that no external forces act.

In snooker, balls of the same size and mass collide with each other. Each collision is an event where the momentum of each ball changes, but the overall momentum stays the same (momentum is conserved).

Before: The red ball is stationary, so it has zero momentum. The white ball is moving with a velocity *v*, so has momentum of $p = m \times v$.

After: The white ball hits the red ball, causing it to move. The red ball now has momentum. The white ball continues moving, but at a much smaller velocity (and so a much smaller momentum).
The combined momentum of the red and white ball is equal to the original momentum of the white ball, $m \times v$.

A moving car hits into the back of a parked car. The crash causes the two cars to lock together, and they continue moving in the direction that the original moving car was travelling, but at a lower velocity.

Before: The momentum was equal to mass of moving car × its velocity.
After: The mass of the moving object has increased, but its momentum is equal to the momentum before the collision. So an increase in mass causes a decrease in velocity.

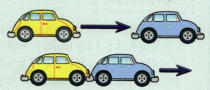

If the momentum before an event is zero, then the momentum after will also be zero. E.g. in an explosion, the momentum before is zero. After the explosion, the pieces fly off in different directions, so that the total momentum cancels out to zero.

Momentum

You can use the **equation** for **momentum**, along with the **conservation of momentum principle**, to **calculate** changes in **mass** and **velocity** in interactions. It's all about 'momentum before = momentum after'.

Calculations using Conservation of Momentum

You've already seen that momentum is conserved in a closed system (see last page).
You can use this to help you calculate things like the velocity or mass of objects in an event (e.g. a collision).

EXAMPLE

Misha fires a paintball gun. A 3.0 g paintball is fired at a velocity of 90 m/s. Calculate the velocity at which the paintball gun recoils if it has a mass of 1.5 kg. Momentum is conserved.

The word recoil means to move backwards.

1) Calculate the momentum of the pellet.
   $p = 0.003 \times 90 = 0.27$ kg m/s

2) The momentum before the gun is fired is zero. This is equal to the total momentum after the collision.
   Momentum before = momentum after
   $0 = 0.27 + (1.5 \times v)$

3) The momentum of the gun is $1.5 \times v$.

4) Rearrange the equation to find the velocity of the gun. The minus sign shows the gun is travelling in the opposite direction to the bullet.
   $v = -(0.27 \div 1.5)$
   $= -0.18$ m/s

EXAMPLE

Two skaters, Skater A and Skater B, approach each other, collide and move off together as shown in the image on the right. At what velocity do they move after the collision?

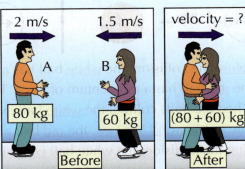

1) Choose which direction is positive. I'll say "positive" means "to the right".

2) Total momentum before collision = momentum of A + momentum of B.
   Momentum before = $(80 \times 2) + (60 \times (-1.5))$
   $= 70$ kg m/s

3) Total momentum after collision = momentum of A and B together.
   Momentum after = $140 \times v$

4) Set momentum before equal to momentum after, and rearrange for the answer.
   $140 \times v = 70$, so $v = 70 \div 140$
   $v = 0.5$ m/s to the right

Momentum questions may need you to analyse a scenario...

Make sure you read any momentum questions carefully. You need to identify what the objects and momentum were before the interaction, and what they are after the interaction. The question may not be a scenario you're familiar with, so you'll need to work out what's going on.

Q1 Video Solution

Q1 A 10 kg object is travelling at 6 m/s. It hits a stationary 20 kg object and the two objects join together and keep moving in the same direction. Calculate the velocity of the combined object, assuming that momentum is conserved. [3 marks]

Section 17 — Motion and Forces

Momentum

When a **resultant force** acts on an object, it causes the object to **change momentum**.

Forces Cause Changes in Momentum

1) When a resultant force acts on an object for a certain amount of time, it causes a change in momentum. Newton's 2nd Law can explain this:
   - A resultant force on an object causes it to accelerate: force = mass × acceleration (see p.25).
   - Acceleration is just change in velocity over time, so: force = $\frac{\text{mass} \times \text{change in velocity}}{\text{time}}$.

   This means a force applied to an object over any time interval will change the object's velocity.
   - Mass × change in velocity is equal to change in momentum, so you end up with the equation:

2) The faster a given change in momentum happens, the bigger the force causing the change must be (i.e. if *t* gets smaller in the equation above, *F* gets bigger).

3) So if someone's momentum changes very quickly, like in a car crash, the forces on the body will be very large, and more likely to cause injury. There's more about this on p.38.

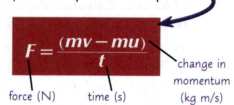

$$F = \frac{(mv - mu)}{t}$$

force (N)   time (s)   change in momentum (kg m/s)

Conservation of Momentum Shows Newton's Third Law

The equation above can help to show Newton's Third Law (reaction forces are equal and opposite). Take this example using snooker balls below:

Before

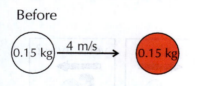

During

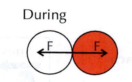

After

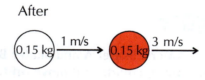

1) Before the collision, the white ball has a momentum of 0.15 × 4 = 0.6 kg m/s.
2) The red ball has a momentum of zero. The total momentum of the system is 0.6 kg m/s.
3) When the balls collide, the white ball exerts a force on the red ball.
4) Due to Newton's 3rd Law, the red ball also exerts an equal but opposite force on the white ball.
5) After the collision, the white ball continues moving at 1 m/s. The red ball begins moving at 3 m/s.
6) The total momentum is (0.15 × 1) + (0.15 × 3) = 0.6 kg m/s. Momentum is conserved.
7) The collision lasted 0.1 s. Given this information, you can calculate the size of the force that caused this change of velocity (and so change of momentum) for each ball:

Red Ball

$F = \frac{(mv - mu)}{t}$

$= \frac{(0.15 \times 3) - (0.15 \times 0)}{0.1}$

$= \frac{0.45}{0.1} = 4.5$ N

White Ball

$F = \frac{(mv - mu)}{t}$

$= \frac{(0.15 \times 1) - (0.15 \times 4)}{0.1}$

$= \frac{-0.45}{0.1} = -4.5$ N

8) The force exerted on the white ball (by the red ball) is equal and opposite to the force exerted on the red ball (by the white ball). This shows Newton's Third Law.

The larger the force, the larger the change in momentum...

Momentum is a fundamental bit of physics — learn it well. Then have a go at this question.

Q1 Calculate the force a tennis racket needs to apply to a 58 g tennis ball to accelerate it from rest to 34 m/s in 11.6 ms. [3 marks]

Section 17 — Motion and Forces

Warm-Up and Exam Questions

Don't lose momentum now. Throw yourself into these questions and you'll be done before you know it.

Warm-Up Questions

1) What are the units of momentum?
2) What is meant by the conservation of momentum?
3) What is the total momentum before and after an explosion?
4) How does increasing the time over which an object changes momentum change the force on it?

Exam Questions

1   A 60 kg gymnast lands on a crash mat. When they hit the crash mat, they are moving at 5.0 m/s and come to a stop in a period of 1.2 seconds (after which their momentum is zero).

(a) State the equation linking momentum, mass and velocity.
[1 mark]

(b) Calculate the momentum of the gymnast immediately before they hit the crash mat.
[2 marks]

(c) Calculate the size of the average force acting on the gymnast as they land on the crash mat. Use the correct equation from the Physics Equation Sheet on page 506.
[2 marks]

2   In a demolition derby, cars drive around an arena and crash into each other.

(a) One car has a mass of 650 kg and a velocity of 15.0 m/s. Calculate the momentum of the car.
[2 marks]

(b) The car collides head-on with another car with a mass of 750 kg. The two cars stick together. Calculate the combined velocity of the two cars immediately after the collision if the other car had a velocity of –10.0 m/s before the collision. Give your answer to 3 significant figures.
[4 marks]

3   A fast-moving neutron collides with a uranium-235 atom and bounces off. **Figure 1** shows the particles before and after the collision. The masses given in **Figure 1** are relative masses.

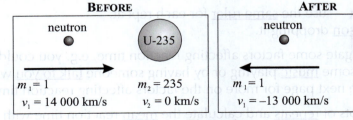

Figure 1

Calculate the velocity of the U-235 atom after the collision. Give your answer to 3 significant figures.
[4 marks]

Reaction Times

*Believe it or not, **reaction times** measure how quickly you react. They're also super easy to **test** for yourself. Read on for a simple **experiment** you can do in the lab.*

You can Measure Reaction Times with the Ruler Drop Test

Everyone's reaction time is different and many different factors can affect it.

You can do simple experiments to investigate your reaction time, but as reaction times are so short, you haven't got a chance of measuring one with a stopwatch. One way of measuring reaction times is to use a computer-based test (e.g. clicking a mouse when the screen changes colour). Another is the ruler drop test.

Here's how to carry it out:

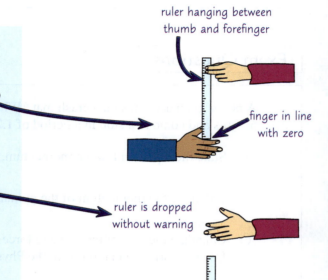

ruler hanging between thumb and forefinger

finger in line with zero

ruler is dropped without warning

ruler caught between thumb and finger

distance fallen

1) Sit with your arm resting on the edge of a table (this should stop you moving your arm up or down during the test). Get someone else to hold a ruler so it hangs between your thumb and forefinger, lined up with zero. You may need a third person to be at eye level with the ruler to check it's lined up.

2) Without giving any warning, the person holding the ruler should drop it. Close your thumb and finger to try to catch the ruler as quickly as possible.

3) The measurement on the ruler at the point where it is caught is how far the ruler dropped in the time it takes you to react.

4) The longer the distance, the longer the reaction time.

5) You can calculate how long the ruler falls for (the reaction time) because acceleration due to gravity is constant (roughly 10 m/s²).

> E.g. say you catch the ruler at 20 cm. From p.269 you know: $v^2 - u^2 = 2 \times a \times x$.
> $u = 0$, $a = 10$ m/s² and $x = 0.2$ m, so: $v = \sqrt{2 \times 10 \times 0.2 + 0}$ = 2 m/s
> v is equal to the change in velocity of the ruler.
> From page 268 you also know: $a = (v - u) \div t$ so $t = (v - u) \div a = 2 \div 10 = 0.2$ s
> This gives your reaction time.

6) It's pretty hard to do this experiment accurately, so you should do a lot of repeats and calculate a mean reaction time. The results will be better if the ruler falls straight down — you could add a blob of modelling clay to the bottom to stop it from waving about.

7) Make sure it's a fair test — use the same ruler for each repeat, and have the same person dropping it.

8) You could try to investigate some factors affecting reaction time, e.g. you could introduce distractions by having some music playing or by having someone talk to you while the test takes place (see the next page for more on the factors affecting reaction time).

9) Remember to still do lots of repeats and calculate the mean reaction time with distractions, which you can compare to the mean reaction time without distractions.

For an experiment like this, a typical reaction time is around 0.2-0.6 s.
A person's reaction time in a real situation (e.g. when driving) will be longer than that, though. Typically, an alert driver will have a reaction time of about 1 s.

Stopping Distances

*Knowing what affects **stopping distances** is especially useful for everyday life, as well as the exam.*

Stopping Distance = Thinking Distance + Braking Distance

In an emergency, a driver may perform an emergency stop. This is where the maximum force is applied by the brakes in order to stop the car in the shortest possible distance. The longer it takes a car to stop after seeing a hazard, the higher the risk of crashing.

The distance it takes to stop a car (stopping distance) is found by:

> **Stopping Distance = Thinking Distance + Braking Distance**

Thinking distance is the distance the car travels in the driver's reaction time (the time between noticing the hazard and applying the brakes).

Braking distance is the distance taken to stop once the brakes have been applied.

Many Factors Affect Your Total Stopping Distance

Thinking distance is affected by:
- Your speed — the faster you're going the further you'll travel during the time you take to react.
- Your reaction time — the longer your reaction time (see next page), the longer your thinking distance. This can be affected by tiredness, drugs or alcohol. Distractions can affect your ability to react.

Braking distance is affected by:
- Your speed — for a given braking force, the faster a vehicle travels, the longer it takes to stop.
- How much friction is between your tyres and the road — you're more likely to skid if the road is dirty, if it's icy or wet or if the tyres are bald (tyres must have a minimum tread depth of 1.6 mm).
- How good your brakes are — if brakes are worn or faulty, they won't be able to apply as much force as well-maintained brakes, which could be dangerous when you need to brake hard.
- The mass of the car — a car full of people and luggage won't stop as quickly as an empty car.

In the exam, you may need to spot the factors affecting thinking and braking distance in different situations.

> E.g. if a parent is driving her children to school early in the morning on an autumn day, her thinking distance could be affected by tiredness, or by her children distracting her. Her braking distance could be affected by ice, or by leaves on the road reducing the friction/grip.

 Stopping distance = thinking distance + braking distance...
The exam might ask you to give factors, other than speed, which affect thinking or braking distances, so make sure you know all the factors that affect each of these and what their effects are.

Section 17 — Motion and Forces

Stopping Safely

*Plotting a graph is always handy when there's a lot of info to take in. These **velocity/time graphs** illustrate really clearly how high speeds affect both **thinking and braking distances**.*

Thinking and Braking Distance can be Seen on v/t Graphs

The graph below shows the velocity of a vehicle as the driver performs an emergency stop.

See p.271 for more on v/t graphs.

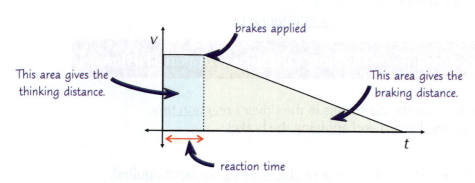

But if the driver is going faster, and he's a bit tired....

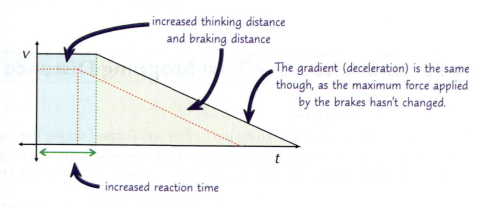

Large Decelerations can be Dangerous

1) Large decelerations of objects and people (e.g. in car crashes) can cause serious injuries. This is because a large deceleration requires a large force — $F = m \times a$.
2) The force can be lowered by slowing the object down over a longer time, i.e. decreasing its deceleration.
3) Safety features in vehicles are designed to increase collision times, which reduces the force, and so reduces the risk of injury. For example, seat belts stretch slightly and air bags slow you down gradually. Crumple zones are areas at the front and back of a vehicle which crumple up easily in a collision, increasing the time taken to stop.

EXAMPLE   **Estimate the resultant force acting on a car stopping quickly from 15 m/s.**

1) Estimate the deceleration of the car — you did that for this example on page 268.
2) Estimate the mass of the car.
3) Put these numbers into Newton's 2nd Law.

The car comes to a stop in ~1 s.
$a = (v - u) \div t = (0 - 15) \div 1 = -15$ m/s^2
Mass of a car is ~1000 kg.
$F = m \times a$
$= 1000 \times -15 = -15\,000$ N

The force here is negative as it acts in the opposite direction to the motion of the car.

4) The brakes of a vehicle do work on its wheels (see p.330). This transfers energy from the vehicle's kinetic energy store to the thermal energy store of the brakes. Very large decelerations may cause the brakes to overheat (so they don't work as well). They could also cause the vehicle to skid.

Section 17 — Motion and Forces

Warm-Up and Exam Questions

Time to apply the brakes for a second and put your brain through an MOT. Try out these questions. If you can handle these, your exam should be clear of hazards.

Warm-Up Questions

1) Describe an experiment you could carry out, using a ruler, to measure the reaction time of an individual.
2) What is meant by 'thinking distance'?
3) What must be added to the thinking distance to find the total stopping distance of a car?
4) Give an example of how poor weather can affect a driver's ability to stop a car before hitting a hazard.
5) Explain how crumple zones reduce the risk of harm in a car crash.

Exam Question

1   **Figure 1** shows how thinking distance and stopping distance vary with speed for a car travelling on a clear day on a dry road.

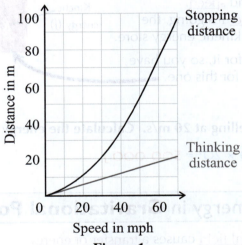

Figure 1

(a) Use **Figure 1** to determine the braking distance for a car travelling at 40 mph.

[3 marks]

(b) Using **Figure 1**, determine whether the thinking distance or braking distance is greater at 50 miles per hour.

[1 mark]

(c) Using **Figure 1**, determine whether stopping distance is directly proportional to speed. Explain your answer.

[1 mark]

(d) Describe how the shape of each of the graphs on **Figure 1** would change if the data was taken for the same driver travelling on an icy road.

[2 marks]

Section 18 — Conservation of Energy

Energy Stores

*Energy is **never used up**. Instead it's just **transferred** between different **energy stores** and different objects...*

Energy Exists in Stores

Energy can be transferred between and held in different energy stores. There are eight you need to know:

- Thermal — any object — the hotter it is, the more energy it has in this store.
- Kinetic — anything moving has energy in this store (see below).
- Gravitational potential — anything in a gravitational field (i.e. anything that can fall) (see below).
- Elastic potential — anything stretched, like springs, rubber bands, etc. (p.374).
- Chemical — anything that can release energy by a chemical reaction, e.g. food, fuels.
- Magnetic — e.g. two magnets that attract and repel each other.
- Electrostatic — e.g. two charges that attract and repel each other.
- Nuclear — atomic nuclei release energy from this store in nuclear reactions.

Movement Means Energy in an Object's Kinetic Energy Store

1) Anything that is moving has energy in its kinetic energy store. Energy is transferred to this store when an object speeds up and is transferred away from this store when an object slows down.
2) The energy in the kinetic energy store depends on the object's mass and speed. The greater its mass and the faster it's going, the more energy there will be in its kinetic energy store.
3) There's a slightly tricky formula for it, so you have to concentrate a little bit harder for this one.

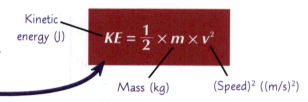

$$KE = \tfrac{1}{2} \times m \times v^2$$

Kinetic energy (J), Mass (kg), (Speed)² ((m/s)²)

EXAMPLE

A car of mass 2500 kg is travelling at 20 m/s. Calculate the energy in its kinetic energy store.

$KE = \tfrac{1}{2} \times m \times v^2 = \tfrac{1}{2} \times 2500 \times 20^2 =$ **500 000 J**

Raised Objects Store Energy in Gravitational Potential Energy Stores

1) Lifting an object in a gravitational field causes a transfer of energy to the gravitational potential energy (g.p.e.) store of the raised object. The higher the object is lifted, the more energy is transferred to this store.
2) The amount of energy in a gravitational potential energy store depends on the object's mass, its height and the strength of the gravitational field the object is in.
3) You can use this equation to find the change in energy in an object's gravitational potential energy store for a change in vertical height, Δh.

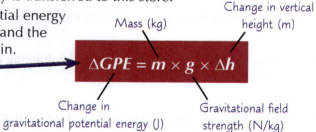

$$\Delta GPE = m \times g \times \Delta h$$

Mass (kg), Change in vertical height (m), Change in gravitational potential energy (J), Gravitational field strength (N/kg)

No speed means no kinetic energy...

Remember, the faster an object is travelling, the more energy it has in its kinetic energy store — just don't forget that squared sign when you're doing kinetic energy calculations.

Q1 A 2 kg object is dropped from a height of 10 m. Calculate the speed of the object after it has fallen 5 m, assuming there is no air resistance. g = 10 N/kg. [5 marks]

Energy Stores and Transfers

*Now you know about the different energy stores, it's time to find out how energy is **transferred** between them.*

Energy is Never Created or Destroyed

This is a really important principle in physics, it is called conservation of energy:

> Energy can be stored, transferred between stores, and dissipated, but it can never be created or destroyed.

See page 292 for more on dissipation.

The Total Energy of a Closed System Doesn't Change

1) A closed system is just a system (a collection of objects) that can be treated completely on its own. The total energy of a closed system has no net change.
2) If you get a question where the energy of a system increases or decreases, then it's not closed.
3) But you can make it into a closed system by increasing the number of things you treat as part of it.

> For example, a pan of water heating on a hob isn't a closed system, but the pan, the gas and the oxygen that burn to heat it, and their surroundings (e.g. if they're in a perfectly insulated room) are a closed system.

You Need to Identify Different Types of Energy Transfer

1) When a system changes, energy is transferred. Energy is transferred in four different ways:

- Mechanically — a force acting on an object (and doing work, p.330), e.g. pushing, stretching, squashing.
- Electrically — a charge doing work (p.339), e.g. charges moving round a circuit.
- By heating — energy transferred from a hotter object to a colder object, e.g. heating a pan on a hob.
- By radiation — energy transferred by waves, e.g. energy from the Sun reaching Earth by light.

2) You need to be able to describe how energy gets transferred from store to store. Here's one example (there's more on the next page):

> **A ball rolling up a slope**
> The ball does work against the gravitational force, so energy is transferred mechanically from the kinetic energy store of the ball to its gravitational potential energy store.

Before: the ball has energy in it's kinetic energy store.

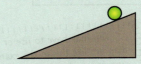
After: energy has been transferred to the ball's gravitational potential energy store.

EXAM TIP — No matter what store it's in, it's all energy...
In the exam, make sure you refer to energy in terms of the store it's in. For example, if you're describing energy in a hot object, say it 'has energy in its thermal energy store'.

Section 18 — Conservation of Energy

Energy Stores and Transfers

You can keep track of complicated **energy transfers** much more easily if you draw a **diagram**.

More Examples of Energy Transfers

Here come a few more examples of everyday energy transfers that you need to get to grips with...

A bat hitting a ball

The bat has energy in its kinetic energy store. Some of this is transferred mechanically to the ball's kinetic energy store. Some energy is also transferred mechanically to the thermal energy stores of the bat and the ball (and to the surroundings by heating). The rest is carried away by sound.

A rock dropped from a cliff

Assuming there's no air resistance, gravity does work on the rock, so the rock constantly accelerates towards the ground. Energy is transferred mechanically from the rock's gravitational potential energy store to its kinetic energy store.

A car slowing down (without braking)

Energy in the kinetic energy store of the car is transferred mechanically (due to friction between the tyres and road), and then by heating, to the thermal energy stores of the car and road.

A kettle boiling water

Energy is transferred electrically from the mains to the heating element of the kettle, and then by heating to the thermal energy store of the water.

You can Draw Diagrams to Show Energy Transfers

Diagrams can make it easier to see what's going on when energy is transferred. The diagram below shows the energy transferred when a ball is thrown upwards, taking air resistance into account. The boxes represent stores and the arrows show transfers:

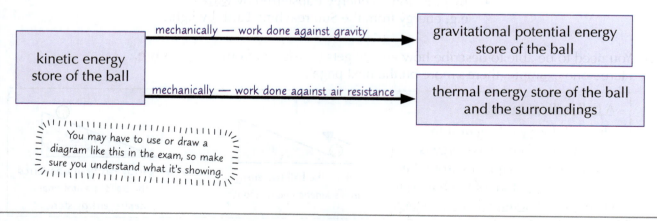

You may have to use or draw a diagram like this in the exam, so make sure you understand what it's showing.

Energy is transferred between the different stores of objects...

Energy stores pop up everywhere in physics. You need to be able to describe how energy is transferred, and which stores it gets transferred between, for any scenario. So, it's time to make sure you know all the energy stores and transfer methods like the back of your hand.

Q1 Describe the energy transfers that occur when the wind causes a windmill to spin. [3 marks]

Section 18 — Conservation of Energy

Warm-Up and Exam Questions

These questions give you chance to use your knowledge about energy stores and energy transfers.

Warm-Up Questions

1) State the equation that links energy in an object's kinetic energy store with mass and speed.
2) Which has more energy in its kinetic energy store: a person walking at 3 miles per hour, or a lorry travelling at 60 miles per hour?
3) Give two methods of energy transfer.
4) Describe the main energy transfer that takes place when the sun warms a glass of water.

Exam Questions

1 A motor lifts a load of mass 20 kg.
   The load gains 140 J of energy in its gravitational potential energy store.

   (a) State the equation that links change in gravitational potential energy, mass, gravitational field strength and change in vertical height.

   Use this equation to calculate the height through which the motor lifts the load.
   Assume the gravitational field strength = 10 N/kg.

   [4 marks]

   (b) The motor releases the load and the load falls.
   Ignoring air resistance, describe the changes in the way energy is stored that take place as the load falls.

   [2 marks]

   (c) Describe how your answer to (b) would differ if air resistance was not ignored.

   [1 mark]

2 A sling-shot is used to catapult a 60 g rock directly upwards.
   Figure 1 shows how the rock's height changes over time.

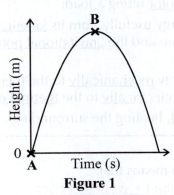

   Figure 1

   (a) From launch (**A**) to the peak of the rock's flight (**B**), describe how energy is transferred.

   [3 marks]

   (b) Initially, the speed of the rock is 18 m/s.
   Calculate the amount of energy in the rock's kinetic energy store at this time.

   [2 marks]

   (c) Use your answer to (b) to calculate the height of the rock at **B**.

   [3 marks]

Section 18 — Conservation of Energy

Unwanted Energy Transfers

So energy is **transferred** between different **stores**. But not all of the energy is transferred to **useful** stores.

Most Energy Transfers Involve Some Losses, Often by Heating

1) You've already met the principle of conservation of energy on page 289, but another important principle you need to know is:

> Energy is only useful when it is transferred from one store to a useful store.

2) Useful devices can transfer energy from one store to a useful store.
3) However, some of the input energy is always dissipated or wasted, often to thermal energy stores of the surroundings.
4) Whenever work is done mechanically (see p.289), frictional forces have to be overcome, including things like moving parts rubbing together, and air resistance. The energy needed to overcome these frictional forces is transferred to the thermal energy stores of whatever's doing the work and the surroundings.
5) This energy usually isn't useful, and is quickly dissipated.

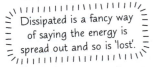
Dissipated is a fancy way of saying the energy is spread out and so is 'lost'.

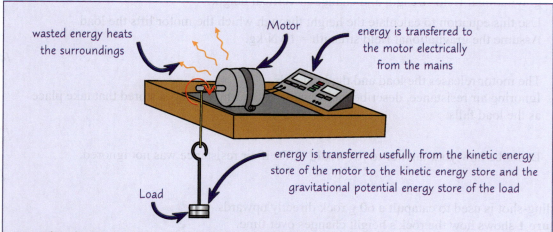

- The diagram shows a motor lifting a load.
- The motor transfers energy usefully from its kinetic energy store to the kinetic energy store and the gravitational potential energy store of the load.
- But it also transfers energy mechanically to the thermal energy stores of its moving parts, and electrically to the thermal energy stores of its circuits.
- This energy is dissipated, heating the surroundings.

6) The conservation of energy principle means that:
total energy input = useful energy output + wasted energy.
7) The less energy that's wasted, the more efficient the device is said to be. The amount of energy that's wasted can often be reduced — see page 294.

Before you know what's waste, you've got to know what's useful...

If you're trying to work out how a device is wasting energy, the first thing you should do is figure out which store is useful. For example, for a phone charger, only energy transferred to the chemical energy store of the phone's battery is useful. Then you know energy that ends up anywhere else is wasted.

Efficiency

Devices have **energy transferred** to them, but only transfer **some** of that energy to **useful energy stores**. Wouldn't it be great if we could tell **how much** the device **usefully transfers**? That's where **efficiency** comes in.

You can Calculate the Efficiency of an Energy Transfer

The efficiency of any device is defined as:

$$\text{efficiency} = \frac{\text{useful energy transferred by the device (J)}}{\text{total energy supplied to the device (J)}}$$

This will give the efficiency as a decimal. To give it as a percentage, you need to multiply the answer by 100.

EXAMPLE

A toaster transfers 216 000 J of energy electrically from the mains. 84 000 J of energy is transferred to the bread's thermal energy store. Calculate the efficiency of the toaster.

$$\text{efficiency} = \frac{\text{useful energy transferred by the device}}{\text{total energy supplied to the device}} = \frac{84\,000}{216\,000} = 0.388... = \mathbf{0.39 \text{ (to 2 s.f.)}}$$

This could also be written as 39% (to 2 s.f.).

All devices have an efficiency, but because some energy is <u>always wasted</u>, the efficiency <u>can never be</u> equal to or higher than <u>1 (or 100%)</u>.

You can Use Diagrams to Show Efficiency

<u>No device</u> is 100% efficient, but some are <u>more efficient</u> than others. You can use diagrams like the one below to show the different <u>energy transfers</u> made by a device, and so how <u>efficient</u> it is:

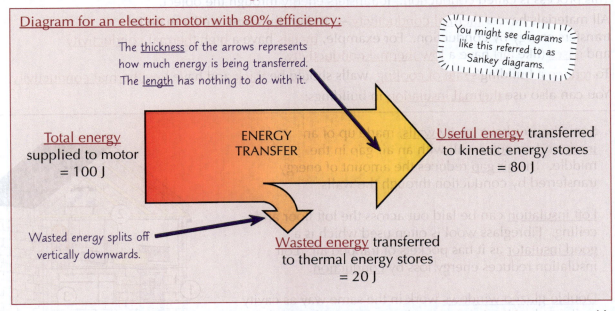

Diagram for an electric motor with 80% efficiency:

The <u>thickness</u> of the arrows represents how much energy is being transferred. The <u>length</u> has nothing to do with it.

Total energy supplied to motor = 100 J

ENERGY TRANSFER

Useful energy transferred to kinetic energy stores = 80 J

Wasted energy splits off vertically downwards.

Wasted energy transferred to thermal energy stores = 20 J

You might see diagrams like this referred to as Sankey diagrams.

You can <u>reduce</u> the amount of energy that's <u>wasted</u> in various ways — including by <u>lubrication</u> and by <u>thermal insulation</u>. <u>Decreasing</u> the amount of <u>wasted energy</u> means that a <u>higher proportion</u> of the <u>supplied</u> energy is transferred to <u>useful</u> stores, so the <u>efficiency</u> of the process is <u>increased</u>.

There's no such thing as perfect efficiency...

One really important thing to take from here — devices that <u>transfer energy</u> from one store to other stores will <u>always</u> transfer some energy to stores that aren't <u>useful</u>.

Q1 An electrical device wastes 420 J of energy when it has an input energy of 500 J. Calculate the efficiency of the device as a percentage. [3 marks]

Q1 Video Solution

Section 18 — Conservation of Energy

Reducing Unwanted Energy Transfers

*There are a few ways you can **reduce** the amount of energy scampering off to a **completely useless** store — **lubrication** and **thermal insulation** are the ones you need to know about. Read on to find out more...*

Lubrication Reduces Energy Transferred by Friction

1) Whenever something moves, there's usually at least one frictional force acting against it.
2) This transfers energy mechanically (work is done against friction) to the thermal energy store of the objects involved, which is then dissipated by heating to the surroundings.
3) For example, pushing a box along the ground causes energy to be transferred mechanically to the thermal energy stores of the box and the ground. This energy is then radiated away to the thermal energy store of the surroundings.

For objects that are touching each other, lubricants can be used to reduce the friction between the objects' surfaces when they move. Lubricants are usually liquids (like oil), so they can flow easily between objects and coat them.

Insulation Reduces the Rate of Energy Transfer by Heating

1) When one side of an object is heated, the particles in the hotter part vibrate more and collide with each other. This transfers energy from their kinetic energy stores to other particles, which then vibrate faster.
2) This process is called conduction. It transfers energy through the object.
3) All materials have a thermal conductivity — it describes how well a material transfers energy by conduction. For example, metals have a high thermal conductivity and gases (like air) have a low thermal conductivity.
4) To reduce a building's rate of cooling, walls should be thick and have low thermal conductivity.
5) You can also use thermal insulation in buildings:

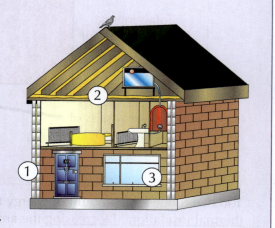

1) Some houses have cavity walls, made up of an inner and an outer wall with an air gap in the middle. The air gap reduces the amount of energy transferred by conduction through the walls.

2) Loft insulation can be laid out across the loft floor and ceiling. Fibreglass wool is often used which is a good insulator as it has pockets of trapped air. Loft insulation reduces energy loss by conduction.

3) Double-glazed windows work in the same way as cavity walls — they have an air gap between two sheets of glass to prevent energy transfer by conduction through the windows.

Having a well-insulated house can reduce your heating bills...

When people talk of energy loss, it's not that the energy has disappeared. It still exists (see conservation of energy on page 289), just not in the store we want. For example, in a car, you want the energy to transfer to the kinetic energy store of the wheels, and not to the thermal energy stores of the moving components.

Section 18 — Conservation of Energy

Warm-Up and Exam Questions

Don't let your energy dissipate. These questions will let you see how efficient your revision has been.

Warm-Up Questions

1) Which energy store does wasted energy typically end up in?
2) Why is the efficiency of an appliance always less than 100%?
3) Give one way you could reduce the frictional forces in the hinge of an automatic door.
4) For a given material, how does its thermal conductivity affect the rate of energy transfer through it?
5) How does the thickness of a building's walls affect the building's rate of cooling?

Exam Questions

1   Torch A transfers 1200 J of energy per minute.
480 J of this is transferred away usefully as light, 690 J is transferred
to useless thermal energy stores and 30 J is transferred away as sound.

(a) Write down the equation linking efficiency, useful energy transferred by the device and total energy supplied to the device.

[1 mark]

(b) Calculate the efficiency of torch A.

[2 marks]

Torch B transfers 10 J of energy away usefully as light each second.

(c) Torch B has an efficiency of 0.55. Calculate the total energy supplied to torch B each second.

[3 marks]

(d) Each torch is powered by an identical battery. A student claims that the battery in torch B will go 'flat' quicker than in torch A because it transfers more energy away as light each minute. Explain whether or not you agree with the student.

[1 mark]

2   A student investigates which type of window is the best at reducing unwanted energy transfers. The student places different samples of windows on a hot plate and measures how long it takes for the top surface of the window sample to reach 30 °C.

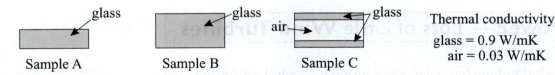

Figure 1

Figure 1 shows the cross-sections of each window sample. Rank them from best to worst for reducing unwanted energy transfers from a house and explain your choices.

[4 marks]

Energy Resources

There are lots of **energy resources** available on Earth. They are either **renewable** or **non-renewable** resources.

Non-Renewable Energy Resources Will Run Out One Day

Non-renewable energy resources are fossil fuels and nuclear fuel (e.g. uranium and plutonium). Fossil fuels are natural resources that form underground over millions of years. They are typically burnt to provide energy. The three main fossil fuels are:

1) Coal
2) Oil
3) (Natural) Gas

- These will all 'run out' one day.
- They all do damage to the environment.
- But they are reliable.

Renewable Energy Resources Will Never Run Out

Renewable energy resources include:

1) The Sun (Solar)
2) Wind
3) Hydro-electricity
4) Bio-fuel
5) Tides

- These will never run out — the energy can be 'renewed' as it is used.
- Most of them do damage the environment, but in less nasty ways than non-renewables.
- The trouble is they don't provide much energy and some of them are unreliable because they depend on the weather.

Solar Cells — Expensive but No Environmental Damage

1) Solar cells are made from materials that use energy transferred by light to create an electric current.
2) Solar power is often used in remote places where there's not much choice (e.g. the Australian outback) and to power electric road signs and satellites.
3) There's no pollution. (Although they do require quite a lot of energy to make.)
4) Initial costs are high, but there are basically no running costs.
5) They're mainly used to generate electricity on a relatively small scale.
6) Solar power is best in sunny countries, but it can be used in cloudy countries like Britain.
7) You can't make solar power at night or increase production when there's extra demand.

Wind Power — Lots of Little Wind Turbines

1) Each wind turbine has a generator inside it — wind rotates the blades, which turn the generator and produce electricity. So there's no pollution.
2) Initial costs are quite high, but running costs are minimal.
3) But lots of them are needed to produce as much power as, for example, a coal power plant. This means they can spoil the view. They can also be noisy, which can be annoying for people living nearby.
4) They only work when it's windy, so you can't always supply electricity, or respond to high demand.

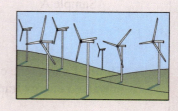

Section 18 — Conservation of Energy

More Renewable Energy Resources

Bio-fuels, *hydro-electricity* and *tidal barrages* — three more energy resources to get your head around.

Bio-fuels are Made from Plants and Waste

1) Bio-fuels are renewable energy resources created from either plant products or animal dung. They can be solid, liquid or gas and can be burnt to produce electricity or run cars.
2) They are supposedly carbon neutral, although there is some debate about this as it's only really true if you keep growing plants (or raising animals) at the rate that you're burning things.
3) Bio-fuels are fairly reliable, as crops take a relatively short time to grow and different crops can be grown all year round. However, they cannot respond to immediate energy demands. To combat this, bio-fuels are continuously produced and stored for when they are needed.
4) The cost to refine bio-fuels is very high. Also, some worry that growing crops specifically for bio-fuels will mean there isn't enough space or water for crops that are grown for food.
5) In some regions, large areas of forest have been cleared to make room to grow bio-fuels, resulting in lots of species losing their natural habitats. The decay or burning of this cleared vegetation also increases methane and CO_2 emissions.

Hydro-electricity — Building Dams and Flooding Valleys

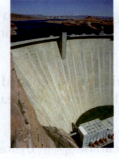

1) Producing hydro-electricity usually involves flooding a valley by building a big dam. Rainwater is caught and allowed out through turbines. There is no pollution (as such).
2) There is a big impact on the environment due to the flooding of the valley and possible loss of habitat for some species.
3) A big advantage is it can immediately respond to increased electricity demand — more water can be let out through the turbines to generate more electricity.
4) Initial costs are often high but there are minimal running costs and it's generally a reliable energy source.

Tidal Barrages — Using the Sun and Moon's Gravity

1) Tidal barrages are big dams built across river estuaries with turbines in them.
2) As the tide comes in it fills up the estuary. The water is then let out through turbines at a controlled speed to generate electricity.
3) There is no pollution but they affect boat access, can spoil the view and they alter the habitat for wildlife, e.g. wading birds.
4) Tides are pretty reliable (they're caused by the Sun and Moon's gravity and always happen twice a day). But the height of the tides is variable and barrages don't work when the water level is the same either side.
5) Initial costs are moderately high, but there are no fuel costs and minimal running costs.

Section 18 — Conservation of Energy

Non-Renewable Resources

*Renewable resources may sound like **great news** for the **environment**. But when it comes down to it, they **don't** currently meet all our needs so we still need those nasty, polluting **non-renewables**.*

Non-Renewables are Reliable and Cost Effective...

1) Fossil fuels and nuclear energy are reliable. There's enough fossil and nuclear fuels to meet current demand, and they are extracted from the Earth at a fast enough rate that power plants always have fuel in stock. This means that the power plants can respond quickly to changes in demand.

2) While the set-up costs of power plants can be quite high compared to some other energy resources, the running costs aren't that expensive. Combined with fairly low fuel extraction costs, using fossil fuels is a cost effective way to produce energy (which is why it's so popular).

...But Create Other Problems

1) Coal, oil and gas release carbon dioxide (CO_2) into the atmosphere when they're burned. All this CO_2 adds to the greenhouse effect, and contributes to global warming.

2) Burning coal and oil also releases sulfur dioxide, which causes acid rain — which can be harmful to trees and soils and can have far-reaching effects in ecosystems.

3) Acid rain can be reduced by taking the sulfur out before the fuel is burned, or cleaning up the emissions.

4) Views can be spoilt by fossil fuel power plants, and coal mining makes a mess of the landscape, especially "open-cast mining".

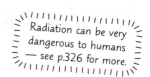

5) Oil spillages cause serious environmental problems, affecting mammals and birds that live in and around the sea. We try to avoid them, but they'll always happen.

6) Nuclear power is clean, since it does not directly release CO_2, but the nuclear waste is very dangerous and difficult to dispose of.

Radiation can be very dangerous to humans — see p.326 for more.

7) Nuclear fuel (e.g. uranium or plutonium) is relatively cheap but the overall cost of nuclear power is high due to the cost of the power plant and final decommissioning.

8) Nuclear power always carries the risk of a major catastrophe like the Fukushima disaster in Japan.

Trends in Energy Resource Use

*Over time, the types of **energy resources** we use **change**. There are lots of reasons for this — breakthroughs in **technology**, understanding more about how they affect the **environment** or changes in **cost** are just a few.*

Currently We Depend on Fossil Fuels

1) Over the 20th century, the electricity use of the UK hugely increased as the population grew and people began to use electricity for more and more things.
2) Since the beginning of the 21st century, electricity use in the UK has been decreasing (slowly), as we make appliances more efficient (p.293) and become more careful with energy use in our homes.
3) Some of our electricity is produced using fossil fuels and from nuclear power.
4) Generating electricity isn't the only reason we burn fossil fuels — oil (diesel and petrol) is used to fuel cars, and gas is used to heat homes and cook food.
5) However, renewable energy resources can be used for these purposes as well. Bio-fuels can be used to exclusively power vehicles, and solar water heaters can be used to heat buildings.

The Aim is to Increase Renewable Energy Use

1) Burning fossil fuels has a lot of negative effects on the environment (p.298). This has led to many people wanting to use more renewable energy resources that have less of an effect on the environment.
2) Pressure from other countries and the public has meant that governments have begun to introduce targets for using renewable resources. This in turn puts pressure on energy providers to build new power plants that use renewable resources to make sure they do not lose business and money.
3) Car companies have also been affected by this change in attitude towards the environment as the demand for electric cars is gradually increasing.

The Use of Renewables is Usually Limited by Reliability and Money

1) Building new renewable power plants costs money, so some smaller energy providers are reluctant to do this — especially when fossil fuels are such a cost effective way of meeting demand.
2) Even if new power plants are built, there are a lot of arguments over where they should be. E.g. many people don't want to live next to a wind farm, which can lead to protests.
3) Energy resources like wind power are not as reliable as traditional fossil fuels, whilst others cannot increase their power output on demand. This would mean either having to use a combination of different power plants (which would be expensive) or researching ways to improve reliability.
4) Research into improving the reliability and cost of renewable resources takes time and money. This means that, even with funding, it might be years before improvements are made. In the meantime, dependable, non-renewable power stations have to be used.
5) Making personal changes can be expensive or impractical. Things like solar panels for your home are still quite pricey and electric cars need to be charged which is harder in rural areas. The cost of these things is slowly going down and infrastructure is improving, but they are still not an option for many people.

Infrastructure is just the basic systems or services needed across the country for something to work, e.g. charging points for cars.

Going green is on-trend this season...

So with some people wanting to help the environment, others not wanting to be inconvenienced, and greener alternatives being expensive to set up, the energy resources we use are changing. Just not particularly quickly.

Section 18 — Conservation of Energy

Warm-Up and Exam Questions

This is the last set of warm-up and exam questions on Section 2. They're not too horrendous, I promise.

Warm-Up Questions

1) Name three non-renewable energy resources.
2) Give one advantage and one disadvantage associated with solar power.
3) Give two ways in which using coal as an energy resource causes environmental problems.
4) Suggest two reasons why we can't just stop using fossil fuels immediately.

Exam Questions

1   The government of a country needs to generate more electricity to support a growing population. They want to use renewable energy resources in order to achieve this.

   (a) The government has considered using wind, tides and hydro-electric power to generate electricity. Suggest **two** other renewable energy resources they could use.

   [2 marks]

   (b) In hydro-electric power stations, such as the one shown in **Figure 1**, water is held back behind a dam before being allowed to flow out through turbines.

   Give **one** environmental impact the government might be concerned about if they chose hydro-electric power to generate electricity.

   [1 mark]

   Figure 1

   (c) The government choose to generate electricity using tidal barrages.
   Give **one** environmental advantage of generating electricity using tidal barrages.

   [1 mark]

2   A family want to install solar panels on their roof. They have 8 m² of space on their roof for the solar panels. They use 32 500 000 J of energy per day. A 1 m² solar panel has an output of 200 J each second in good sunlight.

   (a) Calculate the minimum number of 1 m² solar panels required to cover the family's daily energy use, assuming there are 5 hours of good sunlight in a day.

   [4 marks]

   (b) Determine, using your answer from (a), whether the family can install enough solar panels to provide all of the energy they use, assuming there are 5 hours of good sunlight every day.

   [1 mark]

   (c) In reality, the number of hours of good sunlight in a day varies based on the weather and time of year. Discuss the reliability of energy from solar panels compared to from a local coal-fired power station.

   [3 marks]

Section 18 — Conservation of Energy

Section 19 — Waves and the Electromagnetic Spectrum

Wave Basics

*Waves **transfer energy** from one place to another **without** transferring any **matter** (stuff).*

Energy and Information are Transferred by Waves

1) Waves transfer energy and information in the direction they are travelling.
2) When waves travel through a medium, the particles of the medium vibrate and transfer energy and information between each other.
3) But overall, the particles stay in the same place — only energy and information are transferred.

> For example, if you drop a twig into a calm pool of water, ripples form on the water's surface. The ripples don't carry the water (or the twig) away with them though.
> Similarly, if you strum a guitar string and create sound waves, the sound waves don't carry the air away from the guitar and create a vacuum.

Waves have Amplitude, Wavelength and Frequency

1) The amplitude of a wave is the displacement from the rest position to a crest or trough.

2) The wavelength is the length of a full cycle of the wave, e.g. from crest to crest (see below) or from compression to compression (see the next page).

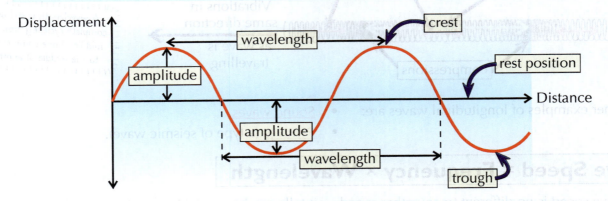

3) Frequency is the number of complete cycles of the wave passing a certain point per second. Frequency is measured in hertz (Hz). 1 Hz is 1 wave per second.

4) The period of a wave is the number of seconds it takes for a full cycle of the wave to pass a point. Period = 1 ÷ frequency.

Waves only transfer energy and information...

It's really important that you understand this stuff really well, or the rest of this topic will simply be a blur. Make sure you can sketch the wave diagram above and can label all the features from memory.

Transverse and Longitudinal Waves

*All waves are either **transverse** or **longitudinal**. Read on to find out more...*

Transverse Waves Have Sideways Vibrations

1) In transverse waves, the vibrations are perpendicular (at 90°) to the direction the wave travels.
2) A spring wiggled up and down gives a transverse wave:

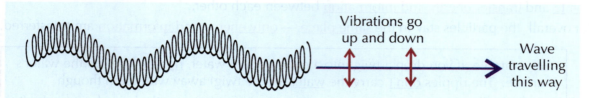

3) Most waves are transverse, including:
   - All electromagnetic waves, e.g. light (p.309).
   - S-waves (a type of seismic wave).
   - Ripples and waves in water (see p.303).

Longitudinal Waves Have Parallel Vibrations

1) In longitudinal waves, the vibrations are parallel to the direction the wave travels.
2) Longitudinal waves squash up and stretch out the arrangement of particles in the medium they pass through, making compressions (high pressure, lots of particles) and rarefactions (low pressure, fewer particles).
3) If you push the end of a spring, you get a longitudinal wave:

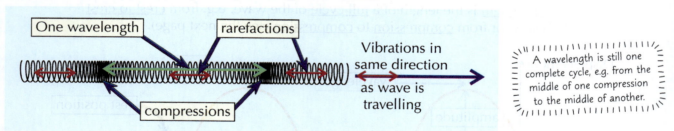

A wavelength is still one complete cycle, e.g. from the middle of one compression to the middle of another.

4) Other examples of longitudinal waves are:
   - Sound waves.
   - P-waves (a type of seismic wave).

Wave Speed = Frequency × Wavelength

1) Wave speed is no different to any other speed — it tells you how quickly a wave moves through space.
2) There are two ways to calculate wave speed:

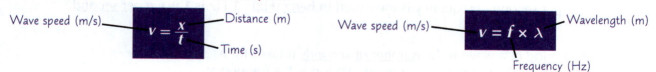

3) $v = f \times \lambda$ is sometimes referred to as 'the wave equation'.
4) Remember, velocity is speed in a given direction (p.266). So, if you know the direction of a wave, you can use these equations to work out wave velocity.

Learn both of those wave speed equations...

Whether a wave is transverse or longitudinal, you can find its speed using the wave equation.

Q1   A wave has a speed of 0.15 m/s and a wavelength of 7.5 cm. Calculate its frequency. [3 marks]

Investigating Waves

*The **speeds**, **frequencies** and **wavelengths** of waves can vary by huge amounts. So you have to use **suitable equipment** to measure waves in different materials, to make sure you get **accurate** and **precise** results.*

Use an Oscilloscope to Measure the Speed of Sound

By attaching a signal generator to a speaker you can generate sounds with a specific frequency. You can use two microphones and an oscilloscope to find the wavelength of the sound waves generated.

1) Set up the oscilloscope so the detected waves at each microphone are shown as separate waves.

2) Start with both microphones next to the speaker, then slowly move one away until the two waves are aligned on the display, but have moved exactly one wavelength apart.

3) Measure the distance between the microphones to find one wavelength (λ).

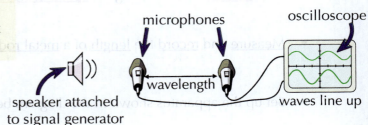

4) You can then use the formula $v = f \times \lambda$ (see previous page) to find the speed (v) of the sound waves passing through the air — the frequency (f) is whatever you set the signal generator to in the first place.

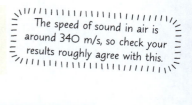

The speed of sound in air is around 340 m/s, so check your results roughly agree with this.

Measure the Speed of Water Ripples Using a Strobe Light

1) Using a signal generator attached to the dipper of a ripple tank you can create water waves at a set frequency.

2) Dim the lights and turn on the strobe light — you'll see a wave pattern made by the shadows of the wave crests on the screen below the tank.

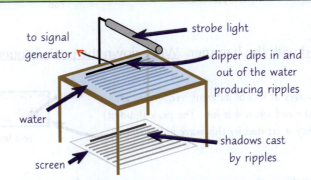

 PRACTICAL

3) Alter the frequency of the strobe light until the wave pattern on the screen appears to 'freeze' and stop moving. This happens when the frequency of the waves and the strobe light are equal — the waves appear not to move because they are being lit at the same point in their cycle each time.

4) The distance between each shadow line is equal to one wavelength. Measure the distance between lines that are 10 wavelengths apart, then find the average wavelength.

If you don't know the frequency of the strobe light, you can find the frequency by using a regular light, so you can see the waves moving. Count how many waves pass a mark on the screen in a given time, then divide this by the time in seconds to find the frequency.

5) Use $v = f \times \lambda$ to calculate the speed of the waves.

- Depending on the exact set-up of your apparatus, the waves seen on the screen may be magnified. In this case you'll need to work out the scale factor before you can find the wavelength.
- An easy way to do this it to stick a piece of tape of a known length, e.g. 10 cm, to the bottom of the ripple tank. Then measure the length of its shadow. If the shadow is longer than the tape, then what you're seeing on the screen is magnified.
- The length of the tape's shadow divided by the actual length of the tape will give the scale factor.

Section 19 — Waves and the Electromagnetic Spectrum

 ## Investigating Waves

There's one more **wave experiment** coming up. This time, it's to do with **waves in a solid**.

Use Peak Frequency to find the Speed of Waves in Solids

1) You can find the speed of waves in a solid by measuring the frequency of the sound waves produced when you hit the object, e.g. a rod, with a hammer.
2) Hitting the rod causes waves to be produced along the rod.
3) These waves make the rod vibrate and produce sound waves in the air around the rod (this is how a percussion triangle works).
4) These sound waves have the same frequencies as the waves in the rod.
5) Here is a method for measuring the speed of waves in a metal rod:

- Measure and record the length of a metal rod, e.g. a brass rod.

- Set up the apparatus shown in the diagram below, making sure to secure the rod at its centre.

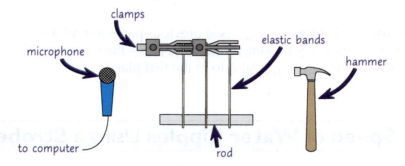

- Tap the rod with the hammer. Write down the peak frequency displayed by the computer.

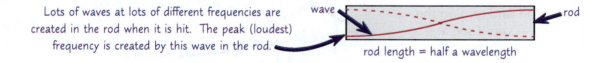

Lots of waves at lots of different frequencies are created in the rod when it is hit. The peak (loudest) frequency is created by this wave in the rod.

rod length = half a wavelength

- Repeat this three times to get an average peak frequency.

- Calculate the speed of the wave using $v = f \times \lambda$, where λ is equal to twice the length of the rod.

6) The peak frequency wave always has λ = rod length × 2, whatever the rod is made from. So this set-up is suitable for finding the wave speed in a rod of any type of solid material.

 ### Learn the methods for all these practicals...

These experiments might seem quite different, but the aim in all of them is to try and find values for f and λ. All the experiments then use the wave equation, $v = f \times \lambda$, to calculate wave speed.

Warm-Up and Exam Questions

Now to check what's actually stuck in your mind over the last four pages...

Warm-Up Questions

1) A twig is dropped on a pool of water and creates water ripples. Explain why the twig stays where it is, rather than being carried away by the ripples.
2) What are the units of frequency?
3) Give one example of a longitudinal wave.
4) State the equation that relates wave speed, frequency and wavelength.

Exam Questions

1 Figure 1 shows a graph of a water ripple.

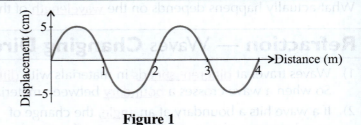

Figure 1

(a) State whether water ripples are transverse or longitudinal.

[1 mark]

(b) Give the amplitude of this wave.

[1 mark]

(c) Find the wavelength of this wave.

[1 mark]

(d) If the frequency of the wave doubles but its speed stays the same, state what will happen to its wavelength.

[1 mark]

PRACTICAL

2 Figure 2 shows how an oscilloscope can be used to display sound waves by connecting microphones to it. Trace 1 shows the sound waves detected by microphone 1 and trace 2 shows the sound waves detected by microphone 2.

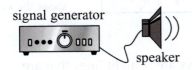
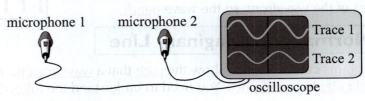

Figure 2

A student begins with both microphones at equal distances from the speaker and the signal generator set at a fixed frequency. He gradually moves microphone 2 away from the speaker, which causes trace 2 to move. He stops moving microphone 2 when both traces line up again as shown in Figure 2. He then measures the distance between the microphones.

(a) Explain how his measurement could be used to work out the speed of sound in air.

[2 marks]

(b) With the frequency set to 50 Hz, the distance between the microphones was measured as 6.8 m. Calculate the speed of sound in air.

[2 marks]

Section 19 — Waves and the Electromagnetic Spectrum

Wave Behaviour at Boundaries

How a wave behaves at a **boundary** depends on its **wavelength**, and the **materials** either side of the boundary.

Waves are Absorbed, Transmitted and Reflected at Boundaries

When a wave meets a boundary between two materials (a material interface), three things can happen:

1) The wave is absorbed by the second material — the wave transfers energy to the material's energy stores. Often, the energy is transferred to a thermal energy store, which leads to heating (this is how a microwave works, see page 311).
2) The wave is transmitted through the second material — the wave carries on travelling through the new material. This often leads to refraction (see below). Refraction is used in the lenses of glasses and cameras.
3) The wave is reflected — this is where the incoming ray is neither absorbed nor transmitted, but instead is 'sent back' away from the second material. This is how echoes are created.

What actually happens depends on the wavelength of the wave and the properties of the materials involved.

Refraction — Waves Changing Direction at a Boundary

1) Waves travel at different speeds in materials with different densities. So when a wave crosses a boundary between materials it changes speed.
2) If a wave hits a boundary at an angle, the change of speed causes a change in direction — refraction.
3) If the wave is travelling along the normal (see below) it will change speed, but it's not refracted.
4) The greater the change in speed, the more a wave bends (changes direction).
5) The wave bends towards the normal if it slows down, and away from the normal if it speeds up.
6) Electromagnetic (EM) waves (see p.309) like light usually travel more slowly in denser materials.
7) How much an EM wave refracts can be affected by its wavelength. Shorter wavelengths bend more. This can lead to the wavelengths spreading out (dispersion), e.g. white light becoming a spectrum.
8) The frequency of a wave stays the same when it crosses a boundary. As $v = f \times \lambda$, this means that the change in speed is caused by a change in wavelength — the wavelength decreases if the wave slows down, and increases if it speeds up.
9) You can show refraction using wavefront diagrams. When one part of the wavefront crosses a boundary into a denser material, that part travels slower than the rest of the wavefront, so the wave bends.

You might see refraction of light talked about in terms of 'optical density'.

less dense — This part of the wavefront travels slower than the rest.
The space between wavefronts shows the wavelength.

The Normal is an Imaginary Line

Ray diagrams can be used to show the path that a wave travels. Rays are straight lines that are perpendicular to wavefronts. You need to understand the following terms for ray diagrams:

1) The normal is an imaginary line that's perpendicular (at right angles) to the boundary, at the point where the incoming wave hits the boundary.
2) The angle of incidence is the angle between the incoming (incident) ray and the normal.
3) The angle of refraction is the angle between the refracted ray and the normal.

Hitting a boundary at an angle can lead to refraction.

Q1 Draw a ray diagram for light entering a less optically dense medium, 40° to the normal.

[3 marks]

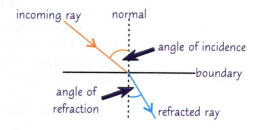

Investigating Refraction

*It's time to whip out your ray box and get some **refraction** going on.*

You Need to Do This Experiment in a Dim Room

1) This experiment uses a ray of light, so it's best to do it in a dim room so you can clearly see the ray.
2) The ray of light must be thin, so you can easily see the middle of the ray when tracing it and measuring angles from it.
3) To do this, you can use a ray box — an enclosed box that contains a light bulb. A thin slit is cut into one of the sides — allowing a thin ray of light out of the box that you can use for your experiment.

You Can Use a Glass Block to Investigate Refraction

Light is refracted at the boundary between air and glass. You can investigate this by looking at how much light is refracted when it passes through a glass block.

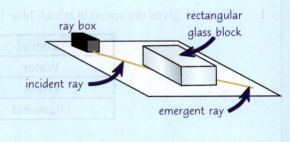

1) Place a rectangular glass block on a piece of paper and trace around it. Use a ray box to shine a ray of light at the middle of one side of the block.
2) Trace the incident ray and the emergent ray on the other side of the block. Remove the block and, with a straight line, join up the incident ray and the emergent ray to show the path of the refracted ray through the block.
3) Draw the normal at the point where the light ray entered the block. Use a protractor to measure the angle between the incident ray and the normal (the angle of incidence, *I*) and the angle between the refracted ray and the normal (the angle of refraction, *R*).
4) Do the same for the point where the ray emerges from the block.
5) You should end up with a diagram that looks like this.
6) Repeat this three times, keeping the angle of incidence as the ray enters the block the same. Calculate an average for each of the angles.

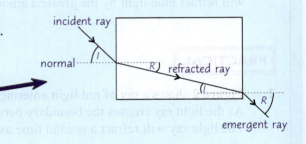

Here's what you should find:
- You should see that the ray of light bends towards the normal as it enters the block (so the angle of refraction is less than the angle of incidence). This is because air has a lower optical density than glass, so the light ray will always slow down when it enters the block.
- You should then see the ray of light bends away from the normal as it leaves the block. This is because the light ray speeds up as it leaves the block and travels through the air.
- It's important to remember that all electromagnetic waves can be refracted — this experiment uses visible light so that you can actually see the ray being refracted as it travels through the block.

Ray boxes produce a thin beam of light...

A thin, bright beam of light will be much easier to trace than a thicker, dimmer one. Not only will you be able to see the light more clearly, but your measurements will be more accurate too.

Section 19 — Waves and the Electromagnetic Spectrum

Warm-Up and Exam Questions

Well they were some refraction-heavy pages. Here are a few questions to check it all went in.

Warm-Up Questions

1) List the three things that can happen when a wave meets a boundary.
2) True or false? The shorter the wavelength of EM radiation, the less the wave is refracted at a boundary.
3) A wave's speed increases as it crosses the boundary between two materials. Assuming the wave hits the boundary at an angle to the normal, will the wave bend towards or away from the normal as it refracts?
4) Name a piece of equipment that can be used to produce a thin beam of light for use in refraction experiments.

Exam Questions

1   **Figure 1** gives the speed at which blue light travels through three different transparent materials.

Material	Speed of blue light (km/s)
Water	225 000
Glass	200 000
Diamond	125 000

Figure 1

The speed of blue light in air is 299 700 km/s. State and explain which of the materials in **Figure 1** will refract blue light by the greatest amount when blue light passes into it at an angle to the normal.

[2 marks]

PRACTICAL

2   **Figure 2** shows a ray of red light entering a glass prism.
As the light ray crosses the boundary between the air and the glass, it refracts.
The light ray will refract a second time as it leaves the glass prism on the other side.

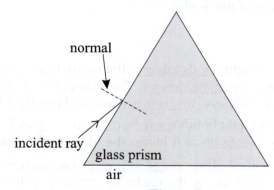

Figure 2

Describe an experiment that could be carried out to measure the angle of incidence, *I*, and the angle of refraction, *R*, at both boundaries.

[4 marks]

Section 19 — Waves and the Electromagnetic Spectrum

Electromagnetic Waves

*There are lots of different types of **electromagnetic wave**. Well, **seven** to be exact...*

There's a Continuous Spectrum of EM Waves

1) Electromagnetic (EM) waves are transverse waves (p.302).

2) They all travel at the same speed through a vacuum (space). But they travel at different speeds in different materials (which can lead to refraction and dispersion, p.306).

Electromagnetic waves aren't vibrations of particles, they're vibrations of electric and magnetic (p.356) fields. This means they can travel through a vacuum.

3) EM waves vary in wavelength from around 10^{-15} m to more than 10^4 m.

4) We group them based on their wavelength and frequency — there are seven basic types, but the different groups merge to form a continuous spectrum.

RADIO WAVES	MICRO WAVES	INFRA RED	VISIBLE LIGHT	ULTRA VIOLET	X-RAYS	GAMMA RAYS
1 m – 10^4 m	10^{-2} m	10^{-5} m	10^{-7} m	10^{-8} m	10^{-10} m	10^{-15} m

→ Wavelength

INCREASING FREQUENCY AND DECREASING WAVELENGTH

5) EM waves are generated by a variety of changes in atoms and their nuclei, giving a large range of frequencies. E.g. changes in the nucleus of an atom create gamma rays (p.321) and visible light is often produced by changes in an electron's energy level (p.318). This also explains why atoms can absorb a range of frequencies — each one causes a different change.

6) Our eyes can only detect a small part of this spectrum — visible light. Different colours of light have different wavelengths — from longest to shortest: red, orange, yellow, green, blue, indigo, violet.

7) All EM waves transfer energy from a source to an absorber. For example, when you warm yourself by an electric heater, infrared waves transfer energy from the thermal energy store of the heater (the source) to your thermal energy store (the absorber).

8) The higher the frequency of the EM wave, the more energy it transfers (and so the more dangerous it may be to humans — see p.314).

EM waves are sometimes called EM radiation.

You need to remember all seven types of EM waves...
You need to know the order of the EM waves too. A mnemonic can make this a whole lot easier. My favourite's 'Raging Martians Invaded Venus Using X-ray Guns'. You can make up your own.

Uses of EM Waves

*This page is all about how **radio waves** are **generated** and what they can be **used for**.*

Radio Waves are Made by Oscillating Charges

1) EM waves are made up of oscillating electric and magnetic fields.
2) Alternating currents (a.c.) (p.352) are made up of oscillating charges. As the charges oscillate, they produce oscillating electric and magnetic fields, i.e. electromagnetic waves.
3) The frequency of the waves produced will be equal to the frequency of the alternating current.
4) You can produce radio waves using an alternating current in an electrical circuit. The object in which charges (electrons) oscillate to create the radio waves is called a transmitter.
5) When transmitted radio waves reach a receiver, the radio waves are absorbed.
6) The energy transferred by the waves is transferred to the electrons in the material of the receiver.
7) This energy causes the electrons to oscillate and, if the receiver is part of a complete electrical circuit, it generates an alternating current.
8) This current has the same frequency as the radio waves that generated it.

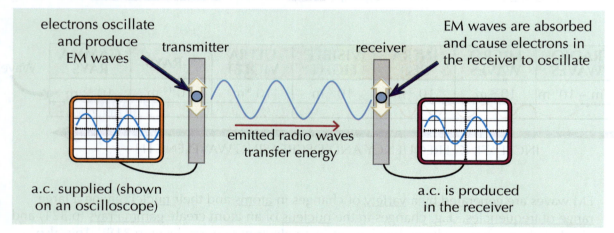

Radio Waves are Used for Communication and Broadcasting

1) Long-wave radio signals (wavelengths of 1 – 10 km) can be received halfway round the world from where they started, because long wavelengths bend around the curved surface of the Earth. This makes it possible for radio signals to be received even if the receiver isn't in the line of sight of the transmitter.

2) Short-wave radio signals (wavelengths of about 10 m – 100 m) can, like long-wave, be received at long distances from the transmitter. That's because they are reflected by the Earth's atmosphere.

3) Bluetooth® uses short-wave radio waves to send data over short distances between devices without wires (e.g. wireless headsets so you can use your phone while driving a car).

4) The radio waves used for TV and FM radio transmissions have very short wavelengths. To get reception, you must be in direct sight of the transmitter — the signal doesn't bend or travel far through buildings.

Section 19 — Waves and the Electromagnetic Spectrum

Uses of EM Waves

Believe it or not, microwaves are used in microwave ovens. For more uses of microwaves, read on.

Microwaves and Radio Waves are Used by Satellites

1) Communication to and from satellites (including satellite TV signals and satellite phones) uses EM waves which can pass easily through the Earth's watery atmosphere.

2) These waves are usually microwaves, but can sometimes be relatively high frequency radio waves.

3) For satellite TV, the signal from a transmitter is transmitted into space and picked up by the satellite receiver dish orbiting thousands of kilometres above the Earth.

4) The satellite transmits the signal back to Earth in a different direction, where it's received by a satellite dish on the ground.

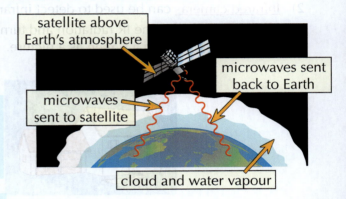

Microwave Ovens also Use Microwaves

1) In microwave ovens, the microwaves are absorbed by water molecules in food.

2) The microwaves penetrate up to a few centimetres into the food before being absorbed and transferring the energy they are carrying to the water molecules in the food, causing the water to heat up.

3) The water molecules then transfer this energy to the rest of the molecules in the food by heating — which quickly cooks the food.

Some microwaves pass through water, others are absorbed by water...

The wavelength of an EM wave affects whether it is absorbed, transmitted or reflected by a substance (p.306). The microwaves used in a microwave oven need the right wavelength to be absorbed by water. It's the water (and sometimes fat) in food absorbing the microwaves that causes the food to heat up.

Section 19 — Waves and the Electromagnetic Spectrum

Uses of EM Waves

Infrared radiation is another ridiculously useful EM wave. You can use it to **cook** your dinner, **catch criminals** in the dark, and change the **TV channel** without getting up from your favourite chair.

Infrared Radiation Can be Used to Monitor Temperature...

1) Infrared (IR) radiation is given out by all hot objects — the hotter the object, the more IR radiation it gives out.
2) Infrared cameras can be used to detect infrared radiation and monitor temperature.
3) The camera detects the IR radiation and turns it into an electrical signal, which is displayed on a screen as a picture. This is called thermal imaging.

Different colours represent different amounts of IR radiation being detected. Here, the redder the colour, the more infrared radiation is being detected.

4) Thermal imaging is used by police to see suspects that are trying to escape or hide in the dark.
5) Infrared sensors can be used in security systems. If a change in infrared radiation is detected, an alarm sounds or a security light turns on.

...Or Increase it

1) Absorbing IR radiation causes objects to get hotter. Food can be cooked using IR radiation — the temperature of the food increases when it absorbs IR radiation, e.g. from a toaster's heating element.
2) Electric heaters heat a room in the same way. Electric heaters contain a long piece of wire that heats up when a current flows through it. This wire then emits lots of infrared radiation (and a little visible light — the wire glows). The emitted IR radiation is absorbed by objects and the air in the room — energy is transferred by the IR waves to the thermal energy stores of the objects, causing their temperature to increase.

Infrared Can Also Transfer Information

Infrared radiation can also be used to transfer information.

1) For example, it can be used to send files between mobile phones or laptops. The distances must be fairly small and the receiver must be in the line of sight of the emitter.
2) This is also how TV remote controls work. In fact, some mobile phones now have built in software which means that you can use your phone as a TV remote.

3) Optical fibres are thin glass or plastic fibres that can carry data (e.g. from telephones or computers) over long distances as pulses of infrared radiation. They usually use a single wavelength to prevent dispersion (p.306), which can otherwise cause some information to be lost.

Uses of EM Waves

*And we're still not finished with **uses** of EM **waves** — there's just no end to their talents...*

Photography Uses Visible Light

1) Visible light is the light that we can see. We use it for illuminating things so that we can see them.
2) Photographic film reacts to light to form an image. This is how traditional cameras create photographs.
3) Digital cameras contain image sensors, which detect visible light and generate an electrical signal. This signal is then converted into an image that can be stored digitally or printed.

Ultraviolet is Used in Fluorescent Lamps

1) Fluorescence is a property of certain chemicals, where ultraviolet (UV) radiation is absorbed and then visible light is emitted. That's why fluorescent colours look so bright — they actually emit light.
2) Fluorescent lights use UV to emit visible light. They're energy-efficient (p.293) so they're good to use when light is needed for long periods (like in your classroom).
3) Security pens can be used to mark property (e.g. laptops). Under UV light the ink will glow, but it's invisible otherwise, helping to identify stolen property.
4) Bank notes and passports use a similar technique to detect forgeries — genuine notes and passports have special markings that only show up under UV light.
5) Ultraviolet radiation is sometimes used to sterilise water. It kills bacteria in the water, making it safe to drink. (Gamma rays are used in a similar way, see below.)

X-rays Let Us See Inside Things

1) X-rays can be used to view the internal structure of objects and materials, including our bodies.
2) They affect photographic film in the same way as light, meaning you can take X-ray photographs. But X-ray images are usually formed electronically these days.
3) Radiographers in hospitals take X-ray images to help doctors diagnose broken bones — X-rays are transmitted by flesh but are absorbed by denser material like bones or metal.
4) To produce an X-ray image, X-ray radiation is directed through the object or body onto a detector. The brighter bits of the image are where fewer X-rays get through, producing a negative image (the plate starts off all white).
5) X-rays are also used in airport security scanners to detect hidden objects that can't be detected with metal detectors.

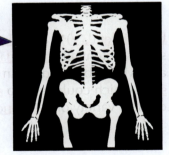

Gamma Rays are Used for Sterilising Things

1) Gamma rays are used to sterilise medical instruments — they kill microbes (e.g. bacteria).
2) Food can be sterilised in the same way — again by killing microbes. This keeps the food fresh for longer, without having to freeze it, cook it or preserve it some other way, and it's perfectly safe to eat.
3) Some medical imaging techniques use gamma rays to detect cancer.
4) Gamma radiation is used in cancer treatment, radiation is targeted at cancer cells to kill them. Doctors have to be careful to minimise the damage to healthy cells when treating cancer like this.

Section 19 — Waves and the Electromagnetic Spectrum

Dangers of EM Waves

*Okay, so you know how **useful** electromagnetic radiation can be — well, it can also be pretty **dangerous**.*

EM Radiation Can be Harmful to People

1) As you saw on p.306, when EM waves meet a boundary they can be absorbed, transmitted, refracted or reflected.
2) What happens depends on the materials at the boundary and the wavelength of the EM wave. E.g. some materials absorb some wavelengths of light but reflect others. This is what causes things to be a certain colour.
3) Differences in how EM waves are transmitted, reflected and absorbed have implications for human health.

> In general, the higher the frequency of the EM wave, the more energy it transfers and so the more potentially dangerous it is for humans.

Different EM Waves Have Different Effects on the Body

1) Radio waves are transmitted through the body without being absorbed.

2) Some wavelengths of microwaves can be absorbed, causing heating of cells, which may be dangerous.

3) Infrared (IR) and visible light are mostly reflected or absorbed by the skin, causing some heating too. IR can cause burns if the skin gets too hot.

4) Ultraviolet (UV) is also absorbed by the skin. But it has a higher frequency, so it is potentially more dangerous. It's a type of ionising radiation (p.321) and when absorbed it can cause damage to cells on the surface of your skin, which could lead to skin cancer. It can also damage your eyes and cause a variety of eye conditions or even blindness.

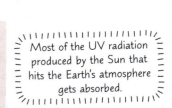
Most of the UV radiation produced by the Sun that hits the Earth's atmosphere gets absorbed.

5) X-rays and gamma rays are also ionising, so they can cause mutations and damage cells too (which can lead to cancer). But they have even higher frequencies, so transfer even more energy, causing even more damage. They can also pass through the skin and be absorbed by deeper tissues.

The risks and benefits must be weighed up...

Ionising radiation can be dangerous, but the risk can be worth taking. X-ray machines used to be installed in shoe shops for use in shoe fittings. They were removed when people realised X-rays were harmful and the risks far outweighed the benefits of using X-rays rather than tape measures...

Section 19 — Waves and the Electromagnetic Spectrum

Warm-Up and Exam Questions

EM radiation — so many uses, so many risks. Test your memory by answering these questions.

Warm-Up Questions

1) Are EM waves transverse or longitudinal?
2) True or false? The speed at which an EM wave travels in a vacuum depends on its wavelength.
3) Which type of EM wave has the highest frequency?
4) True or false? Changes in atoms can generate EM waves.
5) State one possible use of radio waves.
6) Explain how microwave ovens heat food.
7) What type of radiation is used in optical fibres?
8) Give one use of gamma radiation.
9) True or false? The higher the frequency of EM radiation, the more potentially dangerous it is for humans.

Exam Questions

1   **Figure 1** shows an image of the bones in a patient's foot.

(a) Name a type of EM radiation that could have been used to produce this photograph.

[1 mark]

(b) State **one** risk to the patient from being exposed to this type of radiation.

[1 mark]

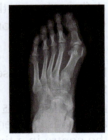

Figure 1

2   An alternating current is passed through a transmitter in order to produce radio waves with a wavelength of 8 km. The radio waves reach a receiver which is connected to a complete electrical circuit.

(a) Describe the effect of the incoming wave on the receiver and its circuit.

[3 marks]

The receiver is located in a built-up area. A resident is concerned that being exposed to radio waves may cause health problems.

(b) Explain whether the resident is right to be concerned.

[1 mark]

3   A patient is suffering with a skin condition called psoriasis. She is offered UVB phototherapy to treat the condition, where she will be exposed to ultraviolet radiation three times a week.

Describe the possible dangers involved with this treatment and any precautions that may be taken to minimise the risk of the patient being harmed by this treatment.

[4 marks]

Section 19 — Waves and the Electromagnetic Spectrum

Section 20 — Radioactivity

Developing the Model of the Atom

We used to think **atoms** were tiny solid spheres (like ball bearings), but they're **much more complex** than that.

The Theory of Atomic Structure Has Changed Over Time

1) In 1897 J. J. Thomson discovered that electrons could be removed from atoms, so atoms must be made up of smaller bits. He suggested the 'plum-pudding' model — that atoms were spheres of positive charge with tiny negative electrons stuck in them like fruit in a plum pudding.

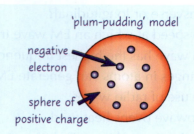

2) That "plum pudding" theory didn't last very long though. In 1909, Rutherford and Marsden tried firing a beam of alpha particles (see p.321) at thin gold foil. From the plum-pudding model, they expected the particles to pass straight through the gold sheet, or only be slightly deflected.

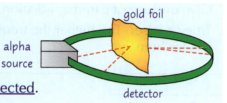

3) But although most of the particles did go straight through the sheet, some were deflected more than they had expected, and a few were deflected back the way they had come — something the plum-pudding model couldn't explain.

4) Rutherford realised this meant that most of the mass of the atom was concentrated at the centre in a tiny nucleus.

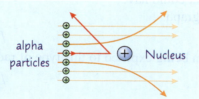

5) He also realised that most of an atom is just empty space, and that the nucleus must have a positive charge, since it repelled the positive alpha particles.

6) This led to the creation of the nuclear model of the atom (see next page).

7) Niels Bohr tweaked Rutherford's idea a few years later by proposing a model where the electrons were in fixed orbits at set distances from the nucleus. These fixed orbits were called energy levels (p.318).

8) He suggested that electrons can only exist in these fixed orbits (or shells), and not anywhere in between.

9) This is known as the Bohr model and is pretty close to our currently accepted model of the atom.

Rutherford's experiment helped adapt the model of the atom...

Rutherford and his lab of scientists made a hypothesis, did an investigation and then analysed the data they got from it. By doing this, they showed that the plum pudding model of the atom must be wrong, so it was changed. This is a great example of the scientific method (see page 2) in action.

Current Model of the Atom

*Due to lots of scientists doing lots of **experiments**, we now have a better idea of what the atom's really like. We now know about the particles in atoms — **protons**, **neutrons** and **electrons**.*

The **Current Model** of the Atom

Atoms are Made Up of Protons, Neutrons and Electrons...

1) The current model of the atom tells us that all atoms are made out of three different particles.
2) These particles are called protons, electrons and neutrons.
3) You need to know the relative mass and relative charge of each of these particles.

Particle	Relative Mass	Relative Charge
Proton	1	+1
Neutron	1	0
Electron	0.0005	−1

... and a lot of Empty Space

1) An atom is a positively charged nucleus surrounded by negatively charged electrons.
2) Virtually all the mass of the atom is in the nucleus. The nucleus is tiny — about 10 000 times smaller than the whole atom. It contains protons (which are positively charged) and neutrons (which are neutral). The rest of the atom is mostly empty space.
3) The negative electrons whizz round outside the nucleus in fixed orbits called energy levels or shells. They give the atom its overall size of around 1×10^{-10} m.
4) Atoms are neutral, so the number of protons = the number of electrons. This is because protons and electrons have an equal but opposite charge.
5) If an atom loses an electron it becomes a positive ion. If it gains an electron it becomes a negative ion (p.318).
6) Atoms can join together to form molecules — e.g. molecules of oxygen gas are made up of two oxygen atoms bonded together. Small molecules like this have a typical size of 1×10^{-10} m — the same sort of scale as an atom.

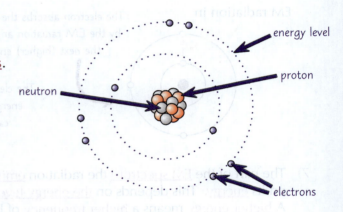

Lots of Atomic Quantities use **Standard Form**

The quantities to do with atoms are really tiny, so they're written in standard form:

A is a number between 1 and 10. — $A \times 10^n$ — n is the number of places the decimal point would move if you wrote the number out in decimal form.

If n is positive you know you're dealing with a large number. If n is negative you're dealing with a small number.

MATHS TIP — You'll find standard form all over the place...

Physics covers everything from tiny particles to giant stars. That means dealing with some really big numbers and some really small numbers. So, unless you want to spend all day writing zeros you've got to get used to standard form. 1×10^{-10} m is a lot easier than writing 0.0000000001 m.

Section 20 — Radioactivity

Electron Energy Levels

*There's some **quirky** stuff on this page — and the best part is that you can tell everyone you've been doing a little **quantum physics** today. Honestly. And if you study physics to a higher level, things get even **quirkier**.*

Electrons can be Excited to Higher Energy Levels

1) Electrons in an atom sit in different energy levels or shells.
2) Each energy level is a different distance from the nucleus.
3) An inner electron can move up to a higher energy level if it absorbs electromagnetic (EM) radiation with the right amount of energy.
4) When it does move up, it moves to an empty or partially filled shell and is said to be 'excited'.
5) The electron will then quickly fall back to its original energy level, and in doing so will emit (lose) the same amount of energy it absorbed.
6) The energy is carried away by EM radiation.

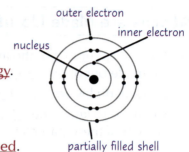

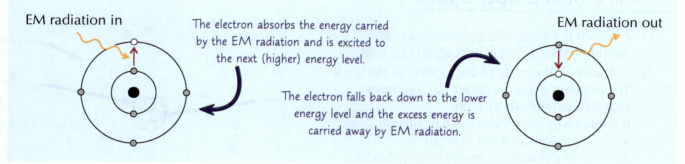

7) The part of the EM spectrum the radiation emitted from the atom is from depends on its energy. This depends on the energy levels the electron moves between. A higher energy means a higher frequency of EM radiation — p.309.

- As you move further out from the nucleus, the energy levels get closer together (so the difference in energy between two levels next to each other gets smaller).
- This means that an excited electron falling from the third energy level to the second would release less energy than an excited electron falling from the second energy level to the first. So the frequency of the generated radiation decreases as you get further from the nucleus.

8) Often, visible light is released when electrons move between energy levels.
9) Changes within the nucleus itself lead to the production of high energy, high frequency gamma rays (p.321).

An Atom is Ionised if it Loses an Electron

1) If an outer electron absorbs radiation with enough energy, it can move so far that it leaves the atom.

2) It is now a free electron and the atom is said to have been ionised.

3) The atom is now a positive ion. It's positive because there are now more protons than electrons.

4) An atom can lose more than one electron. The more electrons it loses, the greater its positive charge.

Section 20 — Radioactivity

Warm-Up and Exam Questions

Atoms may be tiny, but you could bag some big marks in your exams if you know them inside out. Here are some questions to check just how great your understanding of atoms really is...

Warm-Up Questions

1) Describe Thompson's 'plum pudding' model of the atom.
2) What are the relative masses of protons, neutrons and electrons?
3) True or false? Most of an atom's volume is made up of empty space.
4) In the current model of the atom, where are the protons located?
5) What is the overall charge of an atom?
6) What is the typical size of an atom?
7) True or false? An atom must gain an electron in order to become a positively charged ion.

Exam Questions

1   Figure 1 gives the number of protons, electrons and neutrons contained within an atom of Si-28.
    It also shows the relative charges of a proton, an electron and a neutron. The table is incomplete.

	Proton	Electron	Neutron
Relative Charge	+1	–1	
Number Present in Si-28	14		14

Figure 1

(a) Complete **Figure 1**.

[2 marks]

(b) Describe how electrons are arranged in the Bohr model of the atom.

[2 marks]

An electron in Si-28 absorbs 6.9×10^{-19} J of energy and as a result is excited to a higher energy level. After some time the electron returns to its original energy level by emitting electromagnetic radiation.

(c) State how much energy is emitted by the electron as it returns to its original energy level.

[1 mark]

Now the electron absorbs enough energy to be completely removed from the atom.

(d) State the relative charge of the silicon ion that is formed as a result.

[1 mark]

2   Rutherford investigated the structure of the atom by firing a beam of alpha particles at gold foil.
    Describe the results that Rutherford observed and the conclusions they led him to.

[4 marks]

Section 20 — Radioactivity

Isotopes

Isotopes of an element look pretty similar, but watch out — they have **different numbers of neutrons**.

Atoms of the Same Element have the Same Number of Protons

1) All atoms of each element have a set number of protons (so each nucleus has a given positive charge).

2) The number of protons in an atom is its atomic number or its proton number.

3) The mass (nucleon) number of an atom (the mass of the nucleus) is the number of protons + the number of neutrons in its nucleus.

> Example: An oxygen atom has the chemical symbol $^{16}_{8}O$.
>
> Mass number → 16
> Atomic number → 8 O ← Element symbol (oxygen)
>
> - Oxygen has an atomic number of 8. All oxygen atoms have 8 protons.
> - This atom of oxygen has a mass number of 16.
>   Since it has 8 protons, it must have 16 − 8 = 8 neutrons.

Isotopes are Different Forms of the Same Element

1) Isotopes of an element are atoms with the same number of protons (the same atomic number) but a different number of neutrons (a different mass number).

2) Isotopes can be written as, e.g., oxygen-18. This means that the mass number is 18.

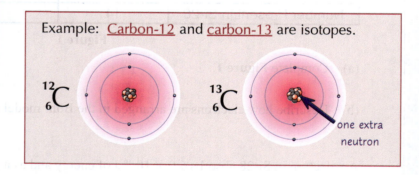

Example: Carbon-12 and carbon-13 are isotopes.

$^{12}_{6}C$ $^{13}_{6}C$ ← one extra neutron

3) All elements have different isotopes, but there are usually only one or two stable ones.

4) The other unstable isotopes tend to decay into other elements and give out radiation as they try to become more stable. This process is called radioactive decay.

5) Radioactive substances spit out one or more types of ionising radiation when they decay: alpha, beta or gamma (see next page). They can also emit neutrons (n).

Isotopes — Same-same, but different...

Isotopes of an element have lots in common — they have the same number of protons and electrons. What's different is their mass numbers — this is because they have different numbers of neutrons.

Ionising Radiation

Alpha, *beta* and *gamma radiation* — they all come from the nucleus, but they have some **key differences**...

Nuclear Radiation Ionises Atoms

1) Ionising radiation is any radiation that can knock electrons from atoms.
2) How likely it is that each type of radiation will ionise an atom varies.

Alpha Particles are Helium Nuclei

1) Alpha radiation is when an alpha particle (α) is emitted from the nucleus. An α-particle is two neutrons and two protons (like a helium nucleus).
2) They don't penetrate very far into materials and are stopped quickly — they can only travel a few cm in air and are absorbed by a thin sheet of paper.
3) Because of their size they are strongly ionising.

Beta Particles can be Electrons or Positrons

1) A beta-minus particle (β⁻) is simply a fast-moving electron released by the nucleus. Beta-minus particles have virtually no mass and a relative charge of −1.
2) A beta-plus particle (β⁺) is a fast-moving positron. The positron is the antiparticle of the electron. This just means it has exactly the same mass as the electron, but a positive (+1) charge.
3) They are both moderately ionising. Beta-minus particles have a range in air of a few metres and are absorbed by a sheet of aluminium (around 5 mm thick).
4) Positrons have a smaller range, because when they hit an electron the two destroy each other and produce gamma rays — this is called annihilation.

Gamma Rays are EM Waves with a Short Wavelength

1) After a nucleus has decayed, it often undergoes nuclear rearrangement and releases some energy. Gamma rays (γ) are waves of EM radiation (p.309) released by the nucleus that carry away this energy.
2) They penetrate far into materials without being stopped and will travel a long distance through air.
3) This means they are weakly ionising because they tend to pass through rather than collide with atoms. Eventually they hit something and do damage.
4) They can be absorbed by thick sheets of lead or metres of concrete.

Alpha particles are more ionising than beta particles...

... and beta particles are more ionising than gamma rays. Make sure you've got that clearly memorised, as well as what makes up each type of radiation, as this isn't the last you'll see of this stuff. No siree.

Section 20 — Radioactivity

Nuclear Equations

Nuclear equations show **radioactive decay** and once you get the hang of them they're **dead easy**. Get going.

Mass and Atomic Numbers Have to Balance

1) Nuclear equations are a way of showing radioactive decay by using element symbols (p.320).
2) They're written in the form: atom before decay → atom after decay + radiation emitted.
3) There is one golden rule to remember: the total mass and atomic numbers must be equal on both sides.

Alpha Decay Decreases the Charge and Mass of the Nucleus

When a nucleus emits an alpha particle, it loses two protons and two neutrons, so:
- the mass number decreases by 4.
- the atomic number decreases by 2.

$$^{238}_{92}U \rightarrow {}^{234}_{90}Th + {}^{4}_{2}\alpha$$

mass number: 238 → 234 + 4 (= 238)
atomic number: 92 → 90 + 2 (= 92)

Beta-minus Decay Increases the Charge of the Nucleus

In a beta-minus decay, a neutron changes into a proton and an electron, so:
- the mass number doesn't change — as it has lost a neutron but gained a proton.
- the atomic number increases by 1 — because it has one more proton.

$$^{14}_{6}C \rightarrow {}^{14}_{7}N + {}^{0}_{-1}\beta$$

mass number: 14 → 14 + 0 (= 14)
atomic number: 6 → 7 + (−1) (= 6)

Positron Emission Decreases the Charge of the Nucleus

In beta-plus decay, a proton changes into a neutron and a positron, so:
- the mass number doesn't change — as it has lost a proton but gained a neutron.
- the atomic number decreases by 1 — because it has one less proton.

$$^{18}_{9}F \rightarrow {}^{18}_{8}O + {}^{0}_{1}\beta$$

mass number: 18 → 18 + 0 (= 18)
atomic number: 9 → 8 + 1 (= 9)

Neutron Emission Decreases the Mass of the Nucleus

When a nucleus emits a neutron:
- the mass number decreases by 1 — as it has lost a neutron.
- the atomic number stays the same.

$$^{13}_{4}Be \rightarrow {}^{12}_{4}Be + {}^{1}_{0}n$$

mass number: 13 → 12 + 1 (= 13)
atomic number: 4 → 4 + 0 (= 4)

Gamma Rays Don't Change the Charge or Mass of the Nucleus

1) Gamma rays (γ) are a way of getting rid of excess energy from an atom. The nucleus goes from an excited state to a more stable state by emitting a gamma ray.
2) The mass and atomic numbers stay the same after a gamma ray has been emitted.

Make sure your equations are balanced on both sides...

Nuclear equations look intimidating, but they're quite straightforward once you get the hang of them.

Q1 Write the nuclear equation for $^{219}_{86}$Rn forming polonium (Po) by alpha decay. [3 marks]

Q1 Video Solution

Section 20 — Radioactivity

Warm-Up and Exam Questions

If you're confident you know your alpha particles from your gamma rays, try the questions below...

Warm-Up Questions

1) An atom of sodium has a mass number of 23 and an atomic number of 11. How many neutrons does it have?
2) True or false? Isotopes of an element have different atomic numbers.
3) What is meant by the term 'ionising radiation'?
4) Which type of ionising radiation has the greatest mass: alpha, beta or gamma?
5) True or false? A 5 mm sheet of aluminium will completely block gamma rays.
6) An atom undergoes a single beta-plus decay. What is the change in its atomic number?
7) An atom of Ar-40 undergoes gamma decay. What is the mass number of the resulting nucleus?

Exam Questions

1   Alpha, beta and gamma radiation sources were used to direct radiation at thin sheets of paper and aluminium. A detector was used to measure where radiation had passed through the sheets. The results are shown in **Figure 1**.

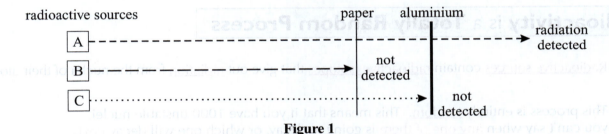

Figure 1

Name the type of radiation that source C emits. Explain your answer.

[2 marks]

2   **Figure 2** contains information about three atoms.

	Mass number	Atomic number
Atom A	32	17
Atom B	33	17
Atom C	32	16

Figure 2

(a) Define the term 'mass number' in the context of atoms.

[1 mark]

(b) State and explain which two atoms in **Figure 2** are isotopes of the same element.

[2 marks]

(c) Plutonium-219 decays by alpha emission to form an isotope of uranium. **Figure 3** shows an incomplete nuclear equation for this decay.
Determine the atomic number, X, of the uranium atom.

$$^{239}_{94}\text{Pu} \rightarrow\; ^{235}_{X}\text{U} + ^{4}_{2}\alpha$$

Figure 3

[1 mark]

Background Radiation and Activity

*Forget love — **radiation** is **all around**. Don't panic too much though — it's usually a pretty **small amount**.*

Background Radiation Comes from Many Sources

Background radiation is the low-level radiation that's around us all the time. It comes from:

1) Radioactivity of naturally occurring unstable isotopes which are all around us — in the air, in some foods, in building materials and in some of the rocks under our feet.

2) Radiation from space, which is known as cosmic rays. These come mostly from the Sun. Luckily, the Earth's atmosphere protects us from much of this radiation.

3) Radiation due to human activity, e.g. fallout from nuclear explosions or radiation from nuclear waste. But this represents a tiny proportion of the total background radiation.

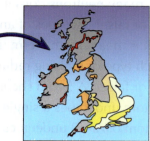

Coloured bits indicate more radiation from rocks.

Radioactivity is a Totally Random Process

1) Radioactive sources contain radioactive isotopes that give out radiation from the nuclei of their atoms.

2) This process is entirely random. This means that if you have 1000 unstable nuclei, you can't say when any one of them is going to decay, or which one will decay next.

3) If there are lots of nuclei though, you can predict how many will have decayed in a given time based on the half-life of the source (see next page). The rate at which a source decays is called its activity.

4) Activity is measured in becquerels, Bq. 1 Bq is 1 decay per second.

5) Activity can be measured with a Geiger-Müller tube, which clicks each time it detects radiation. The tube can be attached to a counter, which displays the number of clicks per second (the count-rate).

6) You can also detect radiation using photographic film. The more radiation the film's exposed to, the darker it becomes (just like when you expose it to light).

Your exposure to background radiation depends on where you live...

Background radiation comes from many sources, from food and drink to cosmic rays, but mostly it comes from the ground and is given out by certain rocks, like granite. That's why some parts of the UK have higher levels of background radiation than others. Areas like Cornwall and Devon, where there's lots of granite, have higher background radiation levels than is average for the UK. But they do have lovely beaches.

Section 20 — Radioactivity

Half-Life

*How quickly **unstable nuclei** decay is measured using **activity** and **half-life** — two very important terms.*

The Radioactivity of a Source Decreases Over Time

1) Each time a radioactive nucleus decays, that radioactive nucleus disappears. As the unstable nuclei all steadily disappear, the activity as a whole will decrease.
2) For some isotopes it takes just a few hours before nearly all the unstable nuclei have decayed, whilst others last for millions of years.
3) The problem with trying to measure this is that the activity never reaches zero, so we have to use the idea of half-life to measure how quickly the activity drops off.

> The half-life is the average time taken for the number of radioactive nuclei of an isotope to halve.

Half-life can also be described as the time taken for the activity to halve.

4) A short half-life means the activity falls quickly, because the nuclei are very unstable and rapidly decay.
5) Sources with a short half-life are dangerous because of the high amount of radiation they emit at the start, but they quickly become safe.
6) A long half-life means the activity falls more slowly because most of the nuclei don't decay for a long time — the source just sits there, releasing small amounts of radiation for a long time.
7) This can be dangerous because nearby areas are exposed to radiation for (millions of) years.

EXAMPLE
The activity of a radioactive sample is measured as 640 Bq. One hour later it has fallen to 160 Bq. Find its half-life.

1) Count how many half-lives it took to fall to 160 Bq.

   Initial activity: after 1 half-life: after 2 half-lives:
   640 ($\div 2$) $\rightarrow$ 320 ($\div 2$) $\rightarrow$ 160

2) Calculate the half-life of the sample.
   One hour is two half-lives — so the half-life is
   1 hour $\div$ 2 = **30 min**

Finding the Half-Life of a Sample using a Graph

1) If you plot a graph of activity against time (taking into account background radiation, see previous page), it will always be shaped like this one.
2) The half-life is found from the graph by finding the time interval on the bottom axis corresponding to a halving of the activity on the vertical axis.

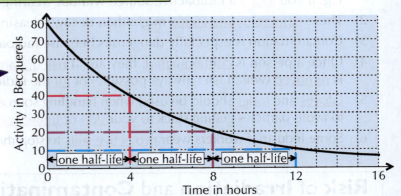

Isotopes with short half-lives decay quickly...
Half-life — the average time for the number of radioactive nuclei or the activity to halve. Simple.

Q1 The initial activity of a sample is 40 Bq. Show that the ratio of its final activity to its initial activity is 1:8 after three half-lives. [3 marks]

Ionisation, Irradiation and Contamination

Radioactive contamination comes about from *touching* and *handling* radioactive substances, whereas *irradiation* can result from just being near a source.

Radiation Damages Cells by Ionisation

1) Radiation can enter living cells and ionise atoms and molecules within them. This can lead to tissue damage.
2) Lower doses tend to cause minor damage without killing the cells. This can give rise to mutant cells which divide uncontrollably. This is cancer.
3) Higher doses tend to kill cells completely, causing radiation sickness (leading to vomiting, tiredness and hair loss) if a lot of cells all get affected at once.

Exposure to Radiation is called Irradiation

1) Objects near a radioactive source are irradiated by it. This simply means they're exposed to it (we're always being irradiated by background radiation sources).

2) Irradiating something does not make it radioactive.

3) Keeping sources in lead-lined boxes, standing behind barriers or being in a different room and using remote-controlled arms are all ways of reducing the effects of irradiation.

4) Radioactive materials can be used in some medical procedures. Patients are given the smallest possible dose of radiation necessary for their procedure to limit their exposure to it.

5) Medical staff who work with radiation wear photographic film badges to monitor their exposure.

Contamination is Radioactive Particles Getting onto Objects

1) If unwanted radioactive atoms get onto an object, the object is said to be contaminated. E.g. if you touch a radioactive source without wearing gloves, your hands would be contaminated.
2) These contaminating atoms might then decay, releasing radiation which could cause you harm.
3) Contamination is especially dangerous because radioactive particles could get inside your body.
4) Once a person is contaminated, they are at risk of harm until either the contamination is removed (which isn't always possible) or all the radioactive atoms have decayed.
5) Gloves and tongs should be used when handling sources, to avoid particles getting stuck to your skin or under your nails.
6) Some industrial workers wear protective suits to stop them breathing in particles.

Risk of Irradiation and Contamination Depends on the Radiation

1) Outside the body, beta and gamma radiation are the most dangerous, because they can penetrate the body and get to the delicate organs. Alpha is less dangerous, because it can't penetrate the skin.

2) Inside the body, alpha sources are the most dangerous. Alpha particles are strongly ionising, so they do all their damage in a very localised area. That means contamination, rather than irradiation, is the major concern when working with alpha sources.

Section 20 — Radioactivity

Warm-Up and Exam Questions

Get your Geiger-Müller counters out — it looks like there's some serious brain activity ahead. It's time to get stuck into some more radiation questions and start finishing this section off.

Warm-Up Questions

1) Give three sources of background radiation.
2) What does it mean if a radioactive source is said to have an activity of 1 becquerel?
3) Give an example of a detector that could be used to detect radiation.
4) A radioactive source has a half-life of three days. How long would it take for the source's activity to decrease by a factor of four?
5) What is the difference between radioactive contamination and irradiation?
6) Explain why you should wear gloves when handling radioactive materials.
7) Why is contamination by an alpha source more dangerous to humans than irradiation by an alpha source?

Exam Questions

1   Two different radioactive sources are being considered for use in a medical treatment. Their safety needs to be assessed.

    (a)   Give **two** possible effects of being exposed to a dose of ionising radiation.

[2 marks]

Source A emits beta-minus radiation. Source B emits alpha radiation.

    (b)   Explain which of the sources presents a greater danger to patients whilst outside the body.

[1 mark]

    (c)   Suggest **one** precaution the hospital should take when storing radioactive substances.

[1 mark]

2   A radioactive sample has a half-life of 40 seconds. The initial activity of the sample is 8000 Bq.

    (a)   Calculate the activity after 2 minutes. Give your answer in becquerels.

[2 marks]

    (b)   Determine the number of half-lives it would take for the activity to fall to 250 Bq.

[2 marks]

    (c)   The radioactive source is left until its activity falls to 100 Bq. Calculate the final activity as a percentage of the initial activity.

[2 marks]

Section 20 — Radioactivity

Revision Summary for Sections 17-20

That's the end of Section 20 — hopefully it wasn't too painful. Time to see how much you've absorbed.
- Try these questions and tick off each one when you get it right.
- When you're completely happy with a section, tick it off.

For even more practice, try the Retrieval Quizzes for Sections 17-20 — just scan these QR codes!

Section 17 — Motion and Forces (p.266-287) ☐

1) Give the equation relating distance travelled, speed and time.
2) Define acceleration in terms of velocity and time.
3) How would you find the distance travelled by an object from its velocity/time graph?
4) State Newton's First and Second Laws of Motion.
5) What is Newton's Third Law of Motion? Give an example of it in action.
6) State the formula used to calculate an object's momentum.
7) State four things that can affect the braking distance of a vehicle.

Section 18 — Conservation of Energy (p.288-300) ☑

8) Write down four energy stores.
9) Give the equation for finding the change in an object's gravitational potential energy.
10) What is a closed system?
11) Explain what is meant by the term 'dissipate'.
12) Give three ways to prevent unwanted energy transfers in a home.
13) What is the difference between renewable and non-renewable energy resources?
14) Explain why the UK plans to use more renewable energy resources in the future.

Section 19 — Waves and the Electromagnetic Spectrum (p.301-315) ☑

15) What is the amplitude, wavelength and frequency of a wave?
16) Describe an experiment you could do to measure the speed of ripples in water.
17) Explain, in terms of wave speed, what is meant by refraction.
18) Name two types of EM wave that have a higher frequency than ultraviolet radiation.
19) What kind of current is used to generate radio waves in an antenna?
20) Give a non-medical use of X-rays.
21) Which is potentially more dangerous, an EM wave with a high or a low frequency?

Section 20 — Radioactivity (p.316-327) ☐

22) Which has the lowest mass: a proton, an electron or a neutron?
23) What happens to an atom if it loses one or more of its outer electrons?
24) How do isotopes of the same element differ?
25) For alpha, beta and gamma radiation, give: a) their ionising power, b) their range in air.
26) What is background radiation?
27) What is the activity of a source? What are its units?
28) Define irradiation and contamination.

Section 20 — Radioactivity

Section 21 — Forces and Energy

Energy Transfers

Re-read pages 288-290. You'll need to remember everything on those pages for this section.

When a System Changes, Energy is Transferred

1) A system is just a fancy word for a single object (e.g. the air in a piston) or a group of objects (e.g. two colliding vehicles) that you're interested in. You can define your system to be anything you like.
2) When a system changes, energy is transferred. It can be transferred into or away from the system, between different objects in the system or between different types of energy stores (p.288).
3) Whenever a system changes, some energy is dissipated and stored in less useful ways (p.292).
4) The efficiency of a transfer is the proportion of the total energy supplied that ends up in useful energy stores (p.293).
5) You can use diagrams to show how efficient a transfer is, and which stores the energy is transferred to (see p.290 and 293).
6) How you define your system changes how you describe the energy transfers that take place (see below). A closed system is one that's defined so that the net change in energy is zero (p.289).

Energy can be Transferred by Heating...

1) A pan of water is heated on a gas camping stove.
2) When the system is the pan of water, energy is transferred into the system by heating to the thermal energy stores of the pan and the water, which increases their temperature.
3) When the system is the camping stove and the pan, energy is transferred within the system — from the chemical energy store of the gas to the thermal energy stores of the pan and the water, increasing their temperature.

...by Forces Doing Work...

1) A box is lifted up off of the floor. The box is the system.
2) As the box is lifted, work is done (see next page) against gravity.
3) This causes energy to be transferred to the box's kinetic and gravitational potential energy (GPE) stores.

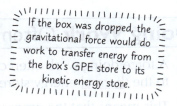

If the box was dropped, the gravitational force would do work to transfer energy from the box's GPE store to its kinetic energy store.

...or by Electrical Equipment

1) Electrical devices work by transferring energy between different energy stores.
2) For example, electric irons transfer energy electrically from the mains power supply to the thermal energy store of their metal plates.

An electric toothbrush is a system. It transfers energy electrically from the chemical energy store of its battery to the kinetic energy store of its bristles. Some of this energy is transferred out of the system to the surroundings by sound and by heating.

A hair dryer is a system. It transfers energy into the system electrically from the mains supply to the kinetic energy store of the fan inside of it. It also transfers energy electrically to the thermal energy store of the heating element and some energy is transferred away from the system by sound.

Work Done

*I'm sure you're no stranger to **doing work**, but in physics it's all to do with **forces** and **energy**.*

If A Force Moves An Object, Work is Done

When a force moves an object through a distance, work is done on the object and energy is transferred.

1) To make something move, some sort of force needs to act on it. The thing applying the force needs a source of energy (like fuel or food).
2) The force does 'work' to move the object and energy is transferred mechanically from one store to another.
3) Remember, you can calculate the amount of energy in the kinetic energy and gravitational potential energy stores using $KE = ½ \times m \times v^2$ and $\Delta GPE = m \times g \times \Delta h$ (p.42).
4) Whether energy is transferred 'usefully' (e.g. lifting a load) or is 'wasted' (p.46) you can still say that 'work is done'.
5) You can find out how much work has been done using:
6) One joule of work is done when a force of one newton causes an object to move a distance of one metre. You can also write this as 1 J = 1 Nm (newton metre).

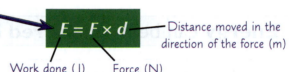

$E = F \times d$ — Distance moved in the direction of the force (m)
Work done (J)   Force (N)

EXAMPLE

A sled is pulled with a force of 10 N, for a distance of 4 m. Calculate the work done on the sled.
work done = force × distance = 10 × 4 = **40 J**

The sled started at rest. After travelling 4 m, its final velocity is 4 m/s. Calculate the sled's mass, assuming all the energy was transferred to the sled's kinetic energy store.

1) Rearrange the kinetic energy equation for m. $m = \dfrac{2 \times KE}{v^2}$
2) Substitute the values in. $= \dfrac{2 \times 40}{4^2} = $ **5 kg**

Doing Work Often Causes a Rise in Temperature

1) A force doing work often causes a rise in temperature as energy is dissipated to the thermal energy stores of a moving object and its surroundings.
2) This means that the process is often wasteful and so the efficiency of the process is reduced.
   Remember, efficiency = $\dfrac{\text{useful energy transferred by the device}}{\text{total energy supplied to the device}}$ (p.293).

> When you push something along a rough surface (like a carpet) you are doing work against frictional forces. Energy is being transferred to the kinetic energy store of the object because it starts moving, but some is also being transferred to thermal energy stores due to the friction. This causes the overall temperature of the object to increase. (Like rubbing your hands together to warm them up.)

3) Lubrication (p.294) reduces friction and unwanted energy transfers to thermal energy stores.

Get comfortable with work done calculations...

Make sure you're happy using the equations on this page before you move on.

Q1   A constant force of 20 N pushes an object 20 cm.
Calculate the work done on the object.   [2 marks]

Section 21 — Forces and Energy

Power

*The **more powerful** a device is, the **more energy** it will transfer in a certain amount of **time**.*

Power is How Much Work is Done per Second

1) Power is the rate of energy transfer.

2) The unit of power is the watt (W). 1 W = 1 J/s.

3) Remember, when work is done, energy is transferred (see previous page).

4) So, another way of describing power is how much work is being done every second.

5) This is the very easy formula for power:

$$\text{power (W)} = \frac{\text{work done (J)}}{\text{time taken (s)}} \quad \text{or} \quad P = \frac{E}{t}$$

The larger the power of an object, the more work it does per second. E.g. if an electric heater has a power of 600 W this means it transfers 600 J of energy every second. A 1200 W heater would transfer twice as much energy per second and so would heat a room quicker than the 600 W heater.

EXAMPLE

A microwave transfers 105 kJ of energy in 2 minutes. Find its power output.

1) Convert the values to the correct units first (p.12-13).   105 kJ = 105 000 J and 2 mins = 120 s
2) Substitute the values into the power equation. $P = E \div t = 105\,000 \div 120 = 875$ W

EXAMPLE

A 300 W motor lifts a 50 kg mass 5 m vertically upwards. Calculate the amount of energy transferred to the gravitational potential energy store of the mass.

Substitute values into the equation for ΔGPE (p.288).

$\Delta\text{GPE} = m \times g \times \Delta h$
$= 50 \times 10 \times 5 = 2500$ J

Calculate how long it takes the motor to lift the mass.

1) Rearrange the power equation for t. $t = E \div P$
2) Substitute the values in. $= 2500 \div 300 = 8.33...$ s
   $= 8$ s (to 1 s.f.)

A large power doesn't always mean a large force...

A powerful device is not necessarily one which can exert a strong force (although it usually ends up that way). A powerful device is one which transfers a lot of energy in a short space of time.

Section 21 — Forces and Energy

Warm-Up and Exam Questions

Do some work by answering these questions and transfer some knowledge to your brain store.

Warm-Up Questions

1) What is meant by the word 'system'?
2) True or false? Energy can be transferred into a system.
3) Describe the useful energy transfer that occurs in a battery powered fan.
4) State the equation linking work done, force and distance moved in the direction of the force.
5) True or false? Power measures how quickly energy is transferred.
6) Which unit for power is equivalent to joules per second?

Exam Questions

1   A ball rolls down a ramp, as shown in **Figure 1**.

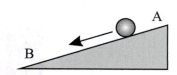

Figure 1

(a) The ball and ramp are assumed to be a closed system. Describe the energy transfer that takes place as the ball rolls from point A to point B.

[2 marks]

(b) State the change in total energy of the ball and ramp as this energy transfer occurs.

[1 mark]

2   The motor of an electric scooter moves the scooter 10 metres along a flat, horizontal course in 20 seconds. During this time the motor does a total of 1000 J of work.

(a) (i) Write down the equation that links power, work done and time taken.

[1 mark]

(ii) Calculate the power of the motor.

[1 mark]

(b) Whilst completing the course, 480 J of energy was transferred usefully to the kinetic energy stores of the scooter and its rider. Calculate the efficiency of the scooter.

[2 marks]

(c) The scooter's motor is replaced with a more powerful, but otherwise identical, motor. It moves along the same 10 m course. Describe how its performance will differ from before. Explain your answer.

[2 marks]

3   A train, initially at rest, moves 700 m in a straight line along a flat track. The force acting on the train is 42 000 N forwards along the track. You can assume there are no frictional forces acting on the train. The train has a mass of 150 000 kg.

(a) Calculate the work done by the force as the train moves 700 m. Give your answer in kJ.

[3 marks]

(b) Assuming that all of this energy was transferred to the train's kinetic energy store, calculate the final speed of the train.

[3 marks]

Section 21 — Forces and Energy

Forces

*Force is a **vector** — it has both a **size** and a **direction** (unlike **scalar** quantities which only have a **size** — p.266). This means you can use **arrows** to represent the forces acting on an object or a system.*

Interactions Between Objects Cause Forces

1) A force is a push or a pull on an object that is caused by it interacting with something.
2) Sometimes, objects need to be touching for a force to act.
   E.g. the normal contact force that acts between all touching objects, or friction between a car's tyre and the road. These are contact forces.
3) Other forces can act between objects that aren't touching (non-contact forces). They're usually caused by interacting fields. E.g. the gravitational attraction between objects (like the Earth and the Sun) is caused by their gravitational fields interacting.
4) Interacting magnetic fields (p.356) cause attraction or repulsion between magnetic objects, and the electrostatic force causing attraction and repulsion between electrical charges is due to interactions between their electric fields.
5) Whenever two objects interact, both objects feel an equal but opposite force (Newton's 3rd Law, p.274). This pair of forces is called an interaction pair. You can represent an interaction pair with a pair of vectors (arrows).

A chair exerts a force on the ground, whilst the ground pushes back at the chair with the same force (the normal contact force).
Equal but opposite forces are felt by both the chair and the ground.

This is NOT a free body force diagram (see below) — the forces are acting on different objects.

Chair pushes on ground
Ground pushes on chair

Free Body Force Diagrams Show All the Forces Acting on Objects

1) A free body force diagram shows an isolated body (an object or system on its own), and all the forces acting on it.
2) It should include every force acting on the body, but none of the forces it exerts on the rest of the world.
3) The sizes of the arrows show the relative magnitudes of the forces and the directions show the directions of the forces.

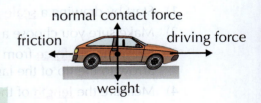

Drawing free body force diagrams can be relatively tricky...

Be careful — the arrows you draw need to have clearly different lengths for different sized forces.

Q1   A car has a driving force of 2000 N and a weight of 1600 N.
There is a total resistive force of 1200 N acting against the driving force.
Draw the free body force diagram for the car.   [2 marks]

Q1 Video Solution

Resultant Forces

*The **resultant force** acting on an object is found by **adding together** or **subtracting** all the forces acting on it.*

A Resultant Force is the Overall Force on a Point or Object

1) In most real situations there are at least two forces acting on an object along any direction.
2) If you have a number of forces acting at a single point, you can replace them with a single force (so long as the single force has the same effect as all the original forces together).
3) This single force is called the resultant force (or sometimes the net force on an object).
4) If the forces all act along the same line (they're all parallel), the overall effect is found by adding those going in the same direction and subtracting any going in the opposite direction.
5) Objects in equilibrium have a resultant force of zero — see the next page. Objects in equilibrium are either stationary, or moving at a steady speed (this is Newton's 1st Law — p.273).

- The normal contact force felt by the car is equal to its weight. These forces act in opposite directions, so there is no resultant force in the vertical direction (1500 N − 1500 N = 0 N).
- The frictional force acting on the car is smaller than the driving force pushing it forward, so there is a resultant force in the horizontal direction.
- 1200 N − 1000 N = 200 N. The resultant force is 200 N (to the left).

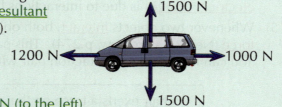

Use Scale Drawings to Find Resultant Forces

Scale drawings can help you resolve forces (see next page) or work out the resultant force.

1) Draw all the forces acting on an object, to scale, 'tip-to-tail'.
2) Then draw a straight line from the start of the first force to the end of the last force — this is the resultant (or net) force.
3) Measure the length of the resultant force on the diagram to find the magnitude of the force and the angle to find its direction.

Make sure the scale you use is sensible. You want large, clear diagrams that make your calculations easier to do.

EXAMPLE

A man is on an electric bicycle that has a driving force of 4 N north. However, the wind produces a force of 3 N east. Find the net force acting on the man.

1) Start by drawing a scale drawing of the forces acting.
2) Make sure you choose a sensible scale (e.g. 1 cm = 1 N).
3) Draw the net force from the tail of the first arrow to the tip of the last arrow.
4) Measure the length of the net force with a ruler and use the scale to find the force in N.
5) Use a protractor to measure the direction as a bearing.

A bearing is an angle measured clockwise from north, given as a 3-digit number, e.g. 10° = 010°.

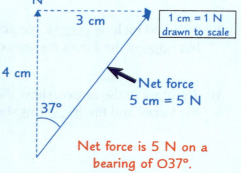

Net force is 5 N on a bearing of 037°.

When it comes to scale drawings, bigger is better...

EXAM TIP If you're asked to draw a scale drawing in an exam, try to use up as much of the space provided as possible. This will help you to measure angles and lengths more accurately.

Section 21 — Forces and Energy

Resolving Forces

*So, several forces can be **added tip-to-tail** to give a single **resultant force**. Sometimes it's helpful to reverse this process and **split up** a single force into components — this is known as **resolving a force**.*

An Object is in Equilibrium if the Forces on it are Balanced

1) If <u>all</u> of the forces acting on an object <u>combine</u> to give a resultant force of <u>zero</u>, the object is in <u>equilibrium</u>.

2) On a <u>scale diagram</u>, this means that the <u>tip</u> of the <u>last</u> force you draw should end where the <u>tail</u> of the first <u>force</u> you drew begins.

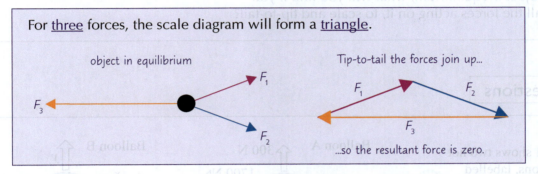

For <u>three</u> forces, the scale diagram will form a <u>triangle</u>.

3) You might be <u>given</u> forces acting on an <u>object</u> and told to <u>find</u> a <u>missing force</u>, given that the object is in <u>equilibrium</u>.

4) To do this, draw out the forces you <u>do</u> know (to <u>scale</u> and <u>tip-to-tail</u>), then <u>join</u> the <u>end</u> of the <u>last force</u> to the <u>start</u> of the <u>first force</u>. Make sure you draw this last force in the <u>right direction</u> — it's in the <u>opposite</u> direction to how you'd draw a <u>resultant</u> force.

5) This line is the <u>missing force</u>, you can measure its <u>size</u> and <u>direction</u>.

You Can Split a Force into Components

1) Not <u>all</u> forces act <u>horizontally</u> or <u>vertically</u> — some act at <u>awkward angles</u>.

2) To make these <u>easier</u> to deal with, they can be <u>split</u> into two <u>components</u> at <u>right angles</u> to each other (usually horizontal and vertical).

3) Acting <u>together</u>, these components have the <u>same effect</u> as the single force.

4) You can <u>resolve</u> a force (split it into components) by drawing it on a <u>scale grid</u>. Draw the force <u>to scale</u>, and then add the <u>horizontal</u> and <u>vertical</u> components along the <u>gridlines</u>. Then you can just <u>measure</u> them.

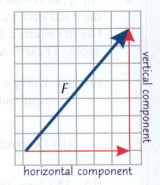

You might be given a scale to work with...

Scale drawings are really <u>useful</u>, so you need to make sure you're happy using <u>different scales</u>.

Q1 An object in equilibrium is being acted on by three forces. The first force is 0.50 N acting south and the second force is 0.30 N acting on a bearing of 045°. Find the magnitude and bearing of the third force. **[3 marks]**

Q1 Video Solution

Warm-Up and Exam Questions

Time to test your ability to force new information into your mind. That's right, there's more questions. Work through the warm-ups and when you're feeling happy with them, dive into the exam questions.

Warm-Up Questions

1) True or false? Objects can only exert a force on one another if they are touching.
2) What does the length of an arrow on a free body diagram represent?
3) What is meant by the resultant force acting on an object?
4) If an object is equilibrium, what will you find if you draw all the forces acting on it, to scale and tip-to-tail?

Exam Questions

1 **Figure 1** shows two hot air balloons, labelled with the forces acting on them. *Grade 4-6*

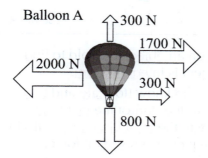 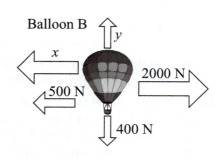

Figure 1

(a) Calculate the size of the resultant force acting on Balloon A and give its direction.

[3 marks]

(b) The resultant force acting on Balloon B is zero. Calculate the size of forces x and y.

[2 marks]

2 An apple is blown out of a tree on a windy day. As it falls, the wind exerts a force of 0.5 N horizontally on the apple. Gravity exerts a force of 1.2 N vertically downwards on the apple. These forces are shown in **Figure 2**. *Grade 6-7*

Figure 2

(a) (i) Using a scale drawing, determine the magnitude of the resultant force acting on the apple. Use a scale of 5 cm = 1 N.

[3 marks]

(ii) Determine the angle the resultant force makes with the vertical downwards direction.

[1 mark]

(b) The force the apple experiences due to gravity is an example of a non-contact interaction. Give **one** more example of a non-contact interaction.

[1 mark]

Section 21 — Forces and Energy

Section 22 — Electricity and Circuits

Circuit Basics

Current, *potential difference* and *resistance* are key to understanding circuits. But first up, **circuit symbols**.

Circuit Symbols You Should Know

You need to be able to use these symbols to interpret and draw circuit diagrams.

There's more about a.c. and d.c. on p.352.

cell	battery	open switch	closed switch	filament lamp	fuse	LED	power supply d.c. a.c.
resistor	variable resistor	ammeter (A)	voltmeter (V)	diode	LDR	thermistor	motor (M)

Current is the Flow of Electrical Charge

1) Current is the flow of electric charge (e.g. electrons, see below) around the circuit.
2) The unit of current is the ampere, A.
3) Potential difference (or voltage) is the driving force that pushes the charge round.
4) The unit of potential difference is the volt, V.
5) Resistance is anything that slows the flow down.
6) The unit of resistance is the ohm, Ω.
7) Current will only flow through an electrical component if there is a potential difference across that component, and if the circuit is closed (complete).
8) The current flowing through a component depends on the potential difference across it and the resistance of the component (p.339).
9) Generally speaking, the higher the potential difference across a component, the higher the current will be. And the greater the resistance of a component, the smaller the current that flows (for a given potential difference across the component). There's more on resistance on p.339.

potential difference of supply provides the 'push'
current flows
resistance — opposes the flow

Current in Metals is the Flow of Free Electrons

1) All atoms contain positive protons and neutral neutrons in the nucleus, with negatively charged electrons orbiting the nucleus (p.317).
2) The atoms in metals are bonded in such a way that metals are made up of a lattice (a grid) of positive ions (p.318) surrounded by free electrons.
3) These electrons are free to move through the whole metal. The current in metals is the flow of these free electrons.

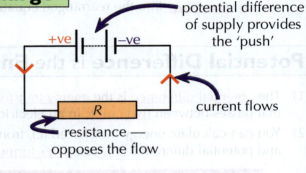

positive ion
free electron

Electrons flow the opposite way to the current...

Electrons in circuits actually move from −ve to +ve, but it's conventional to draw current as though it's flowing from +ve to −ve. It's what early physicists thought (before they discovered electrons), and it's stuck.

Circuit Basics

*Charges **transfer energy** round a circuit — you can work out **how much** with a couple of equations...*

Total Charge Through a Circuit Depends on Current and Time

1) Current is the rate of flow of charge.
2) If a current (*I*) flows past a point in a circuit for a length of time (*t*), then the charge (*Q*) that has passed this point is given by this formula:

$$\text{charge} = \text{current} \times \text{time}$$ or $$Q = I \times t$$

More charge passes around the circuit in a given time when a greater current flows.

3) To use this formula, you need current in amperes, A, charge in coulombs, C, and time in seconds, s.

EXAMPLE

A battery charger passes 18 000 C of charge to a battery over a period of 2.5 hours. Calculate the current flowing between the battery charger and the battery.

1) Convert the time into seconds. $2.5 \times 60 \times 60 = 9000$ s
2) Rearrange the equation for current. $I = Q \div t$
3) Substitute into the rearranged equation. $= 18\ 000 \div 9000 = 2$ A

Potential Difference is the Energy Transferred Per Unit Charge

1) The potential difference is the energy transferred per coulomb of charge that passes between two points in an electrical circuit.
2) You can calculate energy transferred (*E*), from charge moved (*Q*), and potential difference (*V*), using this formula:

$$\text{energy transferred} = \text{charge moved} \times \text{potential difference}$$ or $$E = Q \times V$$

3) To use this formula, you need energy transferred in joules, J, charge moved in coulombs, C, and potential difference in volts, V.
4) So, the potential difference (p.d.) across an electrical component is the amount of energy transferred by that electrical component (e.g. the amount of energy transferred by a motor to its kinetic energy store) per unit charge passed. One volt is one joule per coulomb.
5) Potential difference is sometimes called voltage. They're the same thing.

EXAMPLE

The motor in an electric toothbrush is attached to a 3 V battery. 140 C of charge passes through the circuit as it is used. Calculate the energy transferred.

$E = Q \times V = 140 \times 3 = 420$ J

Understanding potential difference is potentially difficult...

Potential difference can be harder to visualise than current or resistance. But if you know the definition for p.d. and are comfortable using the equations, you can't go far wrong.

Q1 A laptop charger passes a current of 8 A through a laptop battery. Calculate, in minutes, how long the charger needs to be connected to the battery for 28 800 C of charge to be transferred. **[4 marks]**

Section 22 — Electricity and Circuits

Potential Difference and Resistance

*Prepare yourself to meet one of the most **important equations** in electronics. It's all about **resistance**, **current** and **potential difference**... Now if that doesn't tempt you on to read this page, I don't know what will.*

Resistance, Potential Difference and Current: $V = I \times R$

1) Potential difference (V), current (I), and resistance (R) are all related through this formula:

   potential difference = current × resistance   or $V = I \times R$

2) To use this formula, you need potential difference in volts, V, current in amperes, A, and resistance in ohms, Ω.

3) If you rearrange this equation, you can use it to calculate the resistance of a component from measurements of potential difference and current (e.g. from the experiment on the next page).

EXAMPLE

A 4.0 Ω resistor in a circuit has a potential difference of 6.0 V across it. What is the current through the resistor?
1) Rearrange the equation for current. $I = V \div R$
2) Substitute into the rearranged equation. $= 6.0 \div 4.0 = 1.5$ A

Resistance Increases with Temperature (Usually)

1) When an electrical charge flows through a component, it has to do work against resistance.
2) This causes an electrical transfer of energy (work done = energy transferred, p.330).

3) Some of this energy is transferred usefully but some of it is dissipated to the thermal energy stores of the component and the surroundings.
4) So when a current flows through a resistor, the resistor heats up.

5) This happens because the electrons collide with the ions in the lattice that make up the resistor as they flow through it.
6) This gives the ions energy, which causes them to vibrate more (and the energy in the thermal energy store of the resistor to increase — see p.367).

7) The more the ions vibrate, the harder it is for electrons to get through the resistor (because there are more collisions).
8) So for a given p.d. the current decreases as the resistor heats up.
9) If the resistor gets too hot, no current will be able to flow.
10) There is one exception to this — the resistance of a thermistor decreases with an increase in temperature (p.341).

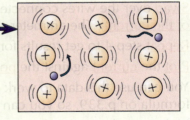

11) Low resistance wires (p.363) can be used to reduce the energy dissipated to thermal stores as the current flows between components.

The more ions vibrate, the lower the current passing through...

As a resistor heats up, current can't flow through it as easily — make sure you can explain why.

Q1   An appliance is connected to a 230 V source.
Calculate the resistance of the appliance if a current of 5.0 A is flowing through it.   [3 marks]

Q1 Video Solution

 # Investigating Components

*Time for a **practical** — the **set-up** described on this page can be used to **investigate any component**. Handy.*

You Can **Investigate** How **P.d.** Changes with **Current**

To investigate the relationship between current (*I*), p.d. (*V*) and resistance (*R*) for a range of components, such as a filament bulb or a fixed resistor:

1) Set up the test circuit as shown below.

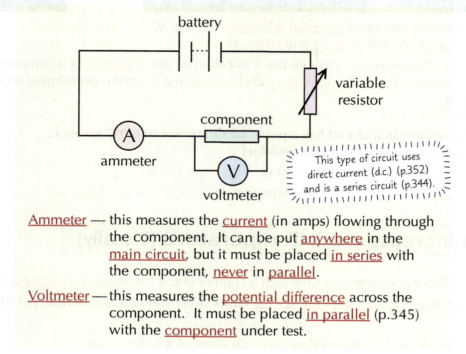

This type of circuit uses direct current (d.c.) (p.352) and is a series circuit (p.344).

- **Ammeter** — this measures the current (in amps) flowing through the component. It can be put anywhere in the main circuit, but it must be placed in series with the component, never in parallel.

- **Voltmeter** — this measures the potential difference across the component. It must be placed in parallel (p.345) with the component under test.

2) The variable resistor is used to change the current in the circuit.
3) As *I* = *V* ÷ *R* (p.339), increasing the resistance of the variable resistor lowers the current through the circuit at a fixed supply p.d.. This changes the potential difference across the component.
4) Now you need to get sets of current and potential difference readings:
   - Set the resistance of the variable resistor.
   - Measure the current through and potential difference across the component.
   - Take measurements at a number of different resistances.
5) Swap over the wires connected to the battery to reverse the direction of the current. The ammeter should now display negative readings.
6) Repeat step 4 to get results for negative values of current.
7) Plot the current against the potential difference to get *I-V* graphs like the ones on the next page.
8) You can use this data to work out the component's resistance for each measurement of *I* and *V*, using the formula on p.339, so you can see if the resistance of the component changes as *I* and *V* change.
9) Make sure the circuit doesn't get too hot over the course of your experiment, as this will mess up your results (see previous page). If the circuit starts to warm up, disconnect it for a while between readings so it can cool down. And, like any experiment, you should do repeats and calculate means.

Have a look at page 9 for more about calculating averages and interpreting your results.

 ### In this experiment, temperature is a control variable...

The temperature of the component needs to be kept constant, otherwise the investigation would not be a fair test. Variables that need to be kept the same are called control variables (page 6).

Section 22 — Electricity and Circuits

Circuit Devices

*With your current and your potential difference measured, you can now make some **sweet** graphs...*

Three Important Current-Potential Difference Graphs

I-V graphs show how the current varies as you change the potential difference (p.d.). Here are three examples, plotted from the experiment on the previous page:

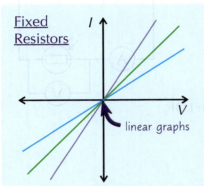
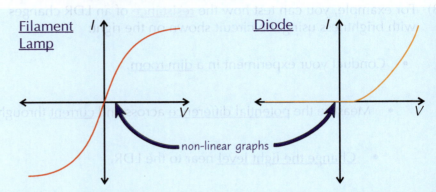

Current is directly proportional to p.d. (if the temperature stays the same). Different resistors have different resistances, so their I-V graphs have different slopes.

The increasing current increases the temperature of the filament, which makes the resistance increase (p.339) so their I-V graphs are curved.

Current will only flow through a diode in one direction, as shown. The diode has very high resistance in the opposite direction. Current flows this way through a diode:

1) **Linear** components have an I-V graph that's a straight line (e.g. a fixed resistor). **Non-linear** components have a curved I-V graph (e.g. a filament lamp or a diode).
2) For linear components, if the line goes through (0,0), the resistance of the component equals the inverse of the gradient of the line, or "1/gradient". The steeper the graph, the lower the resistance.
3) You can find the resistance for any point on any I-V graph by reading the p.d. and current at that point and sticking them into $V = I \times R$ (p.339).

LDR is Short for Light Dependent Resistor

1) An LDR is a resistor that is dependent on the intensity of light. Simple really.
2) In bright light, the resistance falls.
3) In darkness, the resistance is highest.
4) They have lots of applications including automatic night lights, outdoor lighting and burglar detectors.

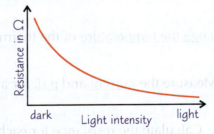

A Thermistor's Resistance Decreases as Temperature Increases

1) A thermistor is a temperature dependent resistor.
2) For negative temperature coefficient thermistors:
   - Their resistance drops in hotter conditions.
   - Their resistance goes up in cooler conditions.
3) Thermistors make useful temperature detectors, e.g. car engine temperature sensors and electronic thermostats.

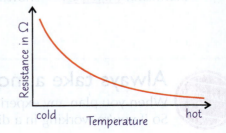

Section 22 — Electricity and Circuits

Investigating LDRs and Thermistors

*Whip out the ammeter, I feel another **experiment** coming on — this time it's **thermistors** and **LDRs**.*

You can Investigate How Resistance Changes for LDRs

1) You can create I-V graphs for LDRs using the method on p.340.
2) But the resistance of LDRs can depend on things other than current.
3) For example, you can test how the resistance of an LDR changes with brightness using the circuit shown on the right:

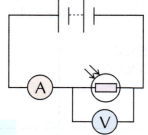

- Conduct your experiment in a dim room.
- Measure the potential difference across and current through the LDR.
- Change the light level near to the LDR.
- Measure the p.d. and current again. Repeat this for a range of light levels.
- Calculate the resistance for each measurement using $R = V \div I$.

4) You should find that as the light level gets brighter, the current through the LDR increases as the resistance decreases.

You can Investigate How Resistance Changes for Thermistors

1) As with LDRs, you can use the method on p.340 to create I-V graphs for thermistors.
2) Also, you can test how the resistance of a thermistor changes with temperature using the circuit on the right:

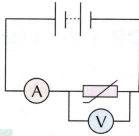

- Measure the p.d. across and current through the thermistor.
- Change the temperature of the thermistor by heating it.
- Measure the current and p.d. for a range of different temperatures.
- Calculate the resistance for each measurement using $R = V \div I$.

3) You should find that as the temperature increases, the current through the thermistor increases — showing that the resistance decreases.

Always take a moment to think about safety...

When you plan any experiment always assess the risks to try and reduce them as much as possible. So if you're working in a dim room, check there are no wires trailing across the floor.

Section 22 — Electricity and Circuits

Warm-Up and Exam Questions

Now you've had an intro to some circuit basics, check you've understood it all by trying these questions.

Warm-Up Questions

1) Draw the symbol for an LED.
2) What are the units of resistance?
3) True or false? Current in metals is the flow of positive ions.
4) State the equation linking energy transferred, charge moved and potential difference.
5) Explain, in terms of electrons and ions, why energy is transferred to a resistor's thermal energy store when a current flows through it.
6) How should a voltmeter be connected in a circuit to measure the p.d. across a component?
7) Sketch the current-potential difference graph for a filament lamp.
8) How does a thermistor's resistance change as the temperature of its surroundings increases?

Exam Questions

1 **Figure 1** shows a circuit diagram for a standard test circuit. When the switch is closed, the ammeter reads 0.30 A and the voltmeter reads 1.5 V.

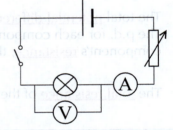

Figure 1

(a) (i) The switch is closed for 35 seconds. Calculate the total charge that flows through the filament lamp during this time.

[2 marks]

(ii) Calculate the energy transferred to the filament lamp during this time.

[2 marks]

(b) The variable resistor is used to increase the resistance in the test circuit. State how this will affect the current flowing through the circuit.

[1 mark]

PRACTICAL

2 A student carried out an experiment to measure what happened to the potential difference across a diode as the current through it was varied. **Figure 2** shows a graph of her results.

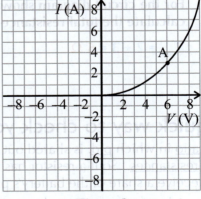

Figure 2

(a) State **one** variable that should be controlled in this experiment.

[1 mark]

(b) Calculate the resistance of the diode at the point marked A in **Figure 2**.

[4 marks]

Section 22 — Electricity and Circuits

Series Circuits

You'll need to make sure you know the **rules** for **current** and **p.d.** in series circuits. You also need to be able to explain what happens to a circuit's **total resistance** when you connect **resistors** in **series**.

Series Circuits — All or Nothing

1) In series circuits, the different components are connected in a line, end to end, between the +ve and −ve of the power supply (except for voltmeters, which are always connected in parallel, but they don't count as part of the circuit).
2) If you remove or disconnect one component, the circuit is broken and they all stop working. This is generally not very handy, and in practice very few things are connected in series.
3) You can use the following rules to design series circuits to measure quantities and test components. For a series circuit:

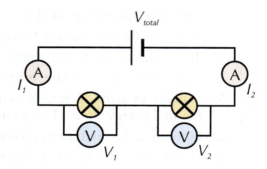

- There's a bigger supply p.d. when more cells are in series (if they're all connected the same way). E.g. when two cells with a p.d. of 1.5 V are connected in series they supply 3 V between them.

- The current is the same everywhere. $I_1 = I_2$ etc. The size of the current depends on the total p.d. and the total resistance of the circuit ($I = V \div R$).

- The total potential difference of the supply is shared between components. The p.d. for each component depends on its resistance. The bigger a component's resistance, the bigger its share of the total potential difference.

- The total resistance of the circuit increases as you add resistors (see below).

Adding Resistors in Series Increases Total Resistance

1) In series circuits the total resistance of two components is just the sum of their resistances.
2) This is because by adding a resistor in series, the two resistors have to share the total p.d..
3) The potential difference across each resistor is lower, so the current through each resistor is also lower. In a series circuit, the current is the same everywhere so the total current in the circuit is reduced when a resistor is added. This means the total resistance of the circuit increases.

EXAMPLE

For the circuit diagram shown, calculate the total resistance of the circuit.

$R_{total} = 2 + 3 = 5\ \Omega$

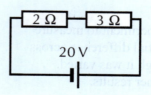

A quick way to check your p.d. calculations...

The ratio in which p.d. is shared out between components in series is the same as the ratio of their resistances. So if a resistor has a resistance three times greater than a light bulb, the resistor will receive a share of the battery's p.d. that is three times larger than that received by the bulb.

Q1 Video Solution

Q1 A battery is connected in series with a 4 Ω resistor, a 5 Ω resistor and a 6 Ω resistor. A current of 0.6 A flows through the circuit.
Calculate the potential difference of the battery.
[3 marks]

Parallel Circuits

Parallel circuits can be a little bit trickier to wrap your head around, but they're much more **useful** than series circuits. Most electronics use a combination of series and parallel circuitry.

Parallel Circuits — Everything is **Independent**

1) In parallel circuits, each component is separately connected to the +ve and −ve of the supply (except ammeters, which are always connected in series).
2) If you remove or disconnect one of them, it will hardly affect the others at all.
3) This is obviously how most things must be connected, for example in cars and in household electrics. You have to be able to switch everything on and off separately.
4) Everyday circuits often include a mixture of series and parallel parts — when looking at components on the same branch the rules for series circuits apply.

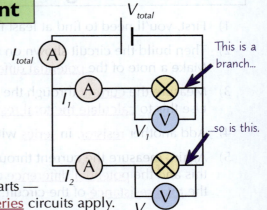

This is a branch...
...so is this.

Potential Difference in Parallel Circuits

1) In parallel circuits all components get the full source p.d., so the voltage is the same across all components: $V_1 = V_2 = V_3 = ...$
2) This means that identical bulbs connected in parallel will all be at the same brightness.

Current in Parallel Circuits

1) In parallel circuits the current is shared between branches.
2) The total current flowing around the circuit is equal to the total of all the currents through the separate components: $I_{total} = I_1 + I_2 + ...$
3) In a parallel circuit, there are junctions where the current either splits or rejoins. The total current going into a junction has to equal the total current leaving it.
4) If two identical components are connected in parallel then the same current will flow through each component.

Adding a Resistor in Parallel **Reduces** the **Total Resistance**

1) If you have two resistors in parallel, their total resistance is less than the resistance of the smallest of the two resistors.
2) This can be tough to get your head around, but think about it like this:

- In parallel, both resistors have the same potential difference across them as the source.
- This means the 'pushing force' making the current flow is the same as the source potential difference for each resistor that you add.
- But by adding another loop, the current has more than one direction to go in.
- This increases the total current that can flow around the circuit. Using $V = I \times R$, an increase in current means a decrease in the total resistance of the circuit.

Learn the difference between series and parallel circuits...

In series circuits, current is the same everywhere and p.d. is split between components.
In parallel circuits, p.d. is the same across each branch and current is split between branches.

Q1 A circuit contains three resistors, each connected in parallel with a cell. Explain what happens to the total current and resistance in the circuit when one resistor is removed. **[4 marks]**

Q1 Video Solution

Investigating Circuits

*Here's an **experiment** to see how placing **components** in series or parallel can affect a circuit's total resistance.*

You Can **Investigate** Adding **Resistors** in **Series**...

1) First, you'll need to find at least four identical resistors.
2) Then build the circuit shown on the right using one of the resistors. Make a note of the potential difference of the battery (V).
3) Measure the current through the circuit using the ammeter. Use this to calculate the total resistance of the circuit using $R = V \div I$.
4) Add another resistor, in series with the first.
5) Again, measure the current through the circuit and use this and the potential difference of the battery to calculate the total resistance of the circuit.
6) Repeat steps 4 and 5 until you've added all of your resistors.
7) Plot a graph of the number of resistors against the total resistance of the circuit (see below).

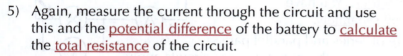

... or in **Parallel**

1) Using the same equipment as before (so the experiment is a fair test), build the same initial circuit.
2) Measure the total current through the circuit and calculate the total resistance of the circuit using $R = V \div I$ (again, V is the potential difference of the battery).
3) Next, add another resistor, in parallel with the first.
4) Measure the total current through the circuit and use this and the potential difference of the battery to calculate the total resistance of the circuit.
5) Repeat steps 3 and 4 until you've added all of your resistors.
6) Plot a graph of the number of resistors in the circuit against the total resistance.

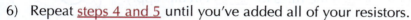
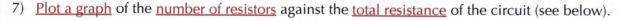

Your Results Should **Match** the **Resistance Rules**

You should find that adding resistors in series increases the total resistance of the circuit (adding a resistor decreases the total current through the circuit). The more resistors you add, the larger the resistance of the whole circuit.
If you measured the p.d. across one of the resistors, you would find the p.d. decreases as more resistors are added in series.

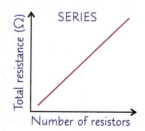

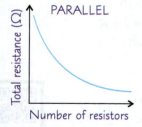

When you add resistors in parallel, the total current through the circuit increases — so the total resistance of the circuit has decreased.
The more resistors you add, the smaller the overall resistance becomes.
If you measured the p.d. across one of the resistors, you would find the p.d. remains the same regardless of how many resistors are added in parallel.

You can also do the experiments on this page with filament lamps instead of resistors:
- The lamps should get dimmer when a lamp is added in series (as the p.d. is being shared out).
- The lamps should be the same brightness in parallel (as they each have the same p.d.).

Warm-Up and Exam Questions

Time to see what you can remember about parallel and series circuits.

Warm-Up Questions

1) True or false? Current is the same everywhere in a series circuit.
2) How is the total resistance of a series circuit calculated from the resistance of each component in the circuit?
3) Two identical resistors are connected in parallel across a 3 V cell. What is the potential difference across each resistor?
4) Which circuit has the higher total resistance: two resistors connected in series, or the same two resistors connected in parallel?
5) Describe an experiment that could be used to investigate how increasing the number of resistors connected in series affects the total resistance of a circuit.

Exam Questions

1   **Figure 1** shows a series circuit.

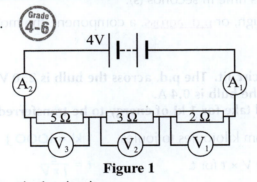

Figure 1

(a) Calculate the total resistance in the circuit.

[1 mark]

(b) The reading on A_1 is 0.4 A. Explain what the reading on A_2 is.

[2 marks]

(c) V_1 reads 0.8 V and V_2 reads 1.2 V. Calculate the reading on V_3.

[1 mark]

2   A parallel circuit is connected as shown in **Figure 2**.

(a) Find the reading on voltmeter V_1.

[1 mark]

(b) Calculate the reading on ammeter A_1.

[3 marks]

(c) Calculate the reading on ammeter A_2.

[1 mark]

(d) A third resistor is added to the circuit, connected in series with the 3 Ω resistor. Explain how this would affect the reading on A_2.

[3 marks]

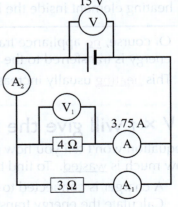

Figure 2

Energy in Circuits

You can think about **electrical circuits** in terms of **energy transfer** — the charge carriers take energy around the circuit. When they go through an electrical component energy is transferred to make the component work.

Energy Transferred Depends on Current, p.d. and Time

1) When an electrical charge goes through a change in potential difference, then energy is transferred (as work is done against resistance — p.339).
2) Energy is supplied to the charge at the power source to 'raise' it through a potential.
3) The charge gives up this energy when it 'falls' through any potential drop in components elsewhere in the circuit.
4) To find the energy transferred to an electrical component, you can use the equation:

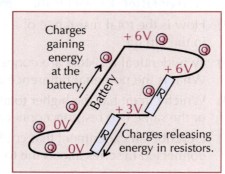

$$E = I \times V \times t$$

This equation comes from combining the two equations from p.338.

Where E is energy transferred in joules (J), I is current in amps (A), V is p.d. in volts (V) and t is time in seconds (s).

5) The larger the current through, or p.d. across, a component, the more energy is transferred to it.

EXAMPLE

A bulb is connected to a circuit. The p.d. across the bulb is 250 V and the current through the bulb is 0.4 A.
Calculate how long it will take for 1 kJ of energy to be transferred to the bulb.

1) Convert the energy from kilojoules to joules.   1 kJ = 1000 J
2) Then rearrange $E = I \times V \times t$ for t. $t = \dfrac{E}{I \times V}$
3) Substitute into the rearranged equation $t = \dfrac{1000}{0.4 \times 250} = 10$ s

Energy is Transferred from Cells and Other Sources

1) Electrical appliances are designed to transfer energy to components in the circuit when a current flows.

Kettles transfer energy electrically from the mains a.c. supply to the thermal energy store of the heating element inside the kettle.	Energy is transferred electrically from the battery of a handheld fan to the kinetic energy store of the fan's motor.

2) Of course, no appliance transfers all energy completely usefully. The higher the current, the more energy is transferred to the thermal energy stores of the components (and then the surroundings).
3) This heating usually increases the resistance of the components, like you saw on page 339.

$I \times V \times t$ will give the total energy transferred to a component...

The equation won't tell you how much of that energy is then transferred usefully by the component, or how much is wasted. To find that out, you need to know the component's efficiency (p.47).

Q1   A charger is connected to a 230 V source for an hour. A current of 4.0 A flows through it.
       Calculate the energy transferred by the charger.
       Give your answer to 2 significant figures.
       [3 marks]

Section 22 — Electricity and Circuits

Heating in Circuits and Power Ratings

Electrical devices are built to *transfer energy*. But nothing is perfect and some of this transferred energy ends up in *thermal* stores. This isn't always a bad thing though — devices like *toasters* and *heaters* make use of it.

Heating a Circuit isn't Always Bad

1) Heating up a component generally reduces its efficiency (p.293) — less energy is transferred to useful energy stores because more of it is being transferred to the thermal energy store of the component.
2) If the temperature gets too high, this can cause components in the circuit to melt — which means the circuit will stop working, or not work properly.
3) Fuses use this effect to protect circuits — they melt and break the circuit if the current gets too high (there's more on fuses on p.353).
4) The heating effect of an electric current can have other advantages. For example, it's ace if you want to heat something. Toasters contain a coil of wire with a really high resistance. When a current passes through the coil, its temperature increases so much that it glows and gives off infrared radiation. This radiation transfers energy to the bread and cooks it.
5) Filament bulbs and electric heaters work in a similar way.

Appliances Often Have a Power Rating

1) The total energy transferred by an appliance depends on how long the appliance is on for and its power.
2) The power of an appliance is the energy that it transfers per second. So the more energy it transfers in a given time, the higher its power. Power is measured in watts.
3) Appliances are often given a power rating — they're labelled with the maximum safe power that they can operate at. You can usually take this to be their maximum operating power.
4) The power rating tells you the maximum amount of energy transferred between stores per second when the appliance is in use.

> Microwaves have a range of power ratings. A microwave with a power rating of 500 W will take longer to cook food than one with a power rating of 750 W. This is because the 500 W microwave transfers less energy per second to the thermal energy store of the food, so it takes longer to cook.

5) This can help customers choose between models — the lower the power rating, the less electricity an appliance uses in a given time.
6) But, a higher power doesn't necessarily mean that it transfers more energy usefully. An appliance may be more powerful than another, but less efficient, meaning that it might still only transfer the same amount of energy (or even less) to useful stores (see p.292).

A higher power rating means more electricity is used per second...

The amount of electricity used by an appliance depends on its power rating and the amount of time it's switched on for. For example, the power rating of an electric lawn mower is typically about ten times higher than the power rating of a fridge (so the lawn mower will use more electricity per second), but a fridge probably uses more electricity in, for example, one year as it's always switched on.

Power in Circuits

*Here come three equations for **calculating** electrical **power**, just for you. An equation for every occasion.*

You can Calculate the Power of an Appliance

1) The power of an appliance can be found using:

   Power (W) = Energy transferred (J) ÷ Time (s)   or $P = \dfrac{E}{t}$

2) The power transferred by an appliance also depends on the potential difference (p.d.) across it, and the current flowing through it.
3) The p.d. tells you how much energy each unit of charge transfers (p.338), and the current tells you how much charge passes per unit time. So both will affect the rate that energy is transferred to an appliance, and the rate at which it transfers energy to other stores.
4) The power of an appliance can be found with:

   Electrical power (W) = Current (A) × Potential difference (V)   or $P = I \times V$

EXAMPLE

A blender is connected to the mains electricity supply. In one minute, 20 700 J of energy is transferred to the blender. Calculate the power of the blender.

P = E ÷ t = 20 700 ÷ 60 = **345 W**

The potential difference of the mains electricity supply is 230 V. Calculate the current through the blender during this one minute period.

1) Rearrange P = I × V for I.   I = P ÷ V
2) Substitute into the rearranged equation.   I = 345 ÷ 230 = **1.5 A**

You can also Calculate Power Using Current and Resistance

You can also find the power of an appliance if you don't know the potential difference. To do this, stick V = I × R from page 339 into P = I × V, which gives you:

$$P = I^2 \times R$$

Where P is the electrical power in watts (W), I is current in amperes (A) and R is the resistance in ohms (Ω).

EXAMPLE

A current of 5 A is passing through a motor, which has a resistance of 48 Ω. Calculate the power of the motor.

P = I² × R = 5² × 48 = **1200 W**

Make sure you use the right power equation...

If you're struggling to pick which power equation to use, it can be helpful to list the variables in the question, then decide which equation is suitable from the variables you've been given.

Q1 Calculate the difference in the amount of energy transferred by a 250 W TV and a 375 W TV when they are both used for two hours.   [3 marks]

Q1 Video Solution

Section 22 — Electricity and Circuits

Warm-Up and Exam Questions

Put the brakes on — it's time to see what you can remember about energy and power in circuits.

Warm-Up Questions

1) State the equation relating energy transferred, current, potential difference and time.
2) Describe the main energy transfer that occurs in an electric toaster when it's plugged into the mains and turned on.
3) Name one appliance that makes use of the heating effect of an electric current.
4) Give the unit used to measure power.
5) Will a 60 W light bulb or a 40 W light bulb transfer more energy in a given amount of time?
6) State the equation that relates electrical power, current and resistance.

Exam Questions

1   **Figure 1** shows the power ratings for two kettles and the potential difference across each kettle.

	Power (kW)	Potential Difference (V)
Kettle A	2.8	230
Kettle B	3.0	230

Figure 1

(a) State the equation linking electrical power, current and potential difference.

[1 mark]

(b) Calculate the current drawn from the mains supply by kettle A.

[3 marks]

(c) A student is deciding whether to buy kettle A or kettle B.
She wants to buy the kettle that boils water faster. Both kettles have the same efficiency.
State and explain which kettle she should choose.

[2 marks]

2   A torch uses a 3.0 V power supply. A current of 0.5 A passes through a torch bulb.

(a) The torch is on for half an hour.
Calculate the amount of energy transferred from the power supply in this time.
Use the correct equation from the Physics Equation Sheet on page 506.

[3 marks]

(b) The torch bulb is replaced. When the new torch bulb is connected to the 3.0 V power supply, 0.25 A of current passes through it.
State how the power of the torch will be affected by this change.

[1 mark]

3   A single 1.5 V battery contains 13 000 J of energy in its chemical energy store.
One of these batteries can be used to power a clock.
A current of 0.2 mA passes through the clock when the battery is connected.

Calculate how many batteries are needed to power the clock for 10 years.
Use the correct equation from the Physics Equation Sheet on page 506.

[3 marks]

Section 22 — Electricity and Circuits

Electricity in the Home

Now you've learnt the basics of **electrical circuits**, it's time to see how **electricity** is used in **everyday life**.

Mains Supply is a.c., Battery Supply is d.c.

1) There are two types of electricity supplies — alternating current (a.c.) and direct current (d.c.).
2) In a.c. supplies the movement of the charges is constantly changing direction. Alternating currents are produced by alternating voltages (the positive and negative ends of the p.d. keep alternating).
3) The UK mains supply (the electricity in your home) is an a.c. supply at around 230 V.
4) The frequency of the a.c. mains supply is 50 cycles per second or 50 Hz (hertz).
5) By contrast, cells and batteries supply direct current (d.c.).
6) In direct current the movement of the charges is only in one direction. It's created by a direct voltage (a p.d. that is only positive or negative, not both).

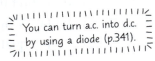
You can turn a.c. into d.c. by using a diode (p.341).

Most Cables Have Three Separate Wires

1) Most electrical appliances are connected to the mains supply by three-core cables. This means that they have three wires inside them, each with a core of copper and a coloured plastic coating.
2) The colour of the insulation on each cable shows its purpose.
3) The colours are always the same for every appliance. This is so that it is easy to tell the different wires apart.

NEUTRAL WIRE — blue.
The neutral wire completes the circuit — when the appliance is operating normally, current flows through the live and neutral wires. It is around 0 V.

LIVE WIRE — brown.
The live wire carries the voltage (potential difference, p.d.). It alternates between a high +ve and –ve voltage of about 230 V.

EARTH WIRE — green and yellow.
The earth wire is for safety and protecting the wiring. It carries the current away if something goes wrong and stops the appliance casing becoming live. It's also at 0 V.

- The p.d. between the live wire and the neutral wire equals the supply p.d. (230 V for the mains).
- The p.d. between the live wire and the earth wire is also 230 V for a mains-connected appliance.
- There is no p.d. between the neutral wire and the earth wire — they're both at 0 V.

4) Plug sockets have switches which are connected in the live wire of the circuit. This is so the circuit can be broken — the appliance becomes isolated and the risk of an electric shock is reduced.
5) Fuses and circuit breakers are also attached to the live wire in order to isolate the appliance if something goes wrong (p.353).

Mains electricity is always 230 V in the UK...

Make sure you can remember the potential differences between the three wires in mains wiring. Only the live wire has a potential difference that isn't zero, so there's a potential difference between the live wire and each of the other two wires (of 230 V). The potential difference between the earth and neutral wires is zero.

Electrical Safety

*The **live wire** is capable of giving a dangerous **electric shock**, so safety precautions such as **fuses** are needed.*

Touching the Live Wire Gives You an Electric Shock

1) Your body (just like the earth) is at 0 V.
2) This means that if you touch the live wire, a large potential difference is produced across your body and a current flows through you.
3) This causes a large electric shock which could injure or even kill you.
4) Even if a plug socket is turned off (i.e. the switch is open) there is still a danger of an electric shock. A current isn't flowing, but there is still a p.d. in the live wire. If you made contact with the live wire, your body would provide a link between the supply and the earth, so a current would flow through you.
5) Any connection between live and neutral can be dangerous. If the link creates a low resistance path to earth, a huge current will flow, which could result in a fire.

Earthing and Fuses Prevent Electrical Overloads

1) Surges (sudden increases) in current can occur because of changes in a circuit (e.g. an appliance suddenly switching off) or because of a fault in an electrical appliance.
2) Current surges can lead to the circuits and wiring in your appliances melting or causing a fire, and faulty appliances can cause deadly electric shocks.
3) The earth wire and a fuse are included in electrical appliances to prevent this from happening. The example below shows how they work:

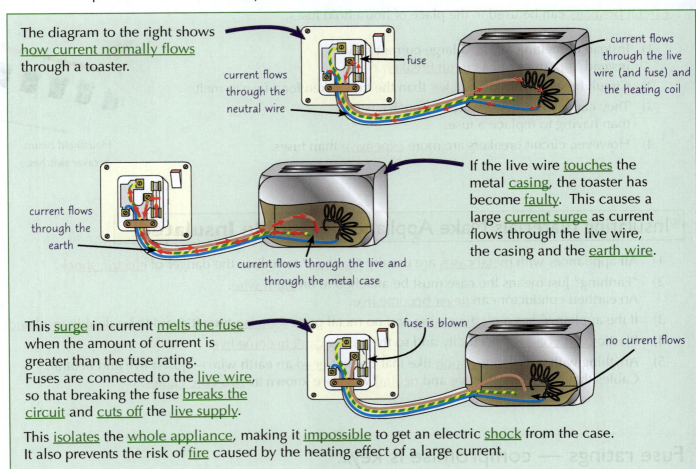

The diagram to the right shows how current normally flows through a toaster.
- current flows through the neutral wire
- fuse
- current flows through the live wire (and fuse) and the heating coil

If the live wire touches the metal casing, the toaster has become faulty. This causes a large current surge as current flows through the live wire, the casing and the earth wire.
- current flows through the earth
- current flows through the live and through the metal case

This surge in current melts the fuse when the amount of current is greater than the fuse rating. Fuses are connected to the live wire, so that breaking the fuse breaks the circuit and cuts off the live supply.
- fuse is blown
- no current flows

This isolates the whole appliance, making it impossible to get an electric shock from the case. It also prevents the risk of fire caused by the heating effect of a large current.

4) As well as the fuses in plugs, there are also household fuses (these are the ones that blow when a light bulb goes). These work in the same way, but protect the wiring in the house, not just in an appliance.

Section 22 — Electricity and Circuits

Electrical Safety

Fuses and *circuit breakers* are super important. And questions on them **cover a whole barrel of fun** — electrical current, resistance, potential difference... Read this page and make sure you've got it sussed.

A Fuse Rating is the Minimum Current needed to Break a Fuse

1) Fuses should be rated as near as possible but just higher than the normal operating current.
2) The larger the current, the thicker the cable you need to carry it (to stop the cable getting too hot and melting). That's why the fuse rating needed for cables usually increases with cable thickness.

> **EXAMPLE**
>
> A 1 kW hair dryer is connected to a 230 V supply.
> Suggest whether a 3 A, a 5 A or a 13 A fuse is needed.
>
> 1) Convert from kilowatts to watts.   1 kW = 1000 W
> 2) Then rearrange $P = I \times V$ (p.350) for I. $I = P \div V$
> 3) Substitute into the rearranged equation. $I = 1000 \div 230 = 4.3... A$
> 4) Choose the fuse with the rating just higher than the calculated current.   So a 5 A fuse is needed.

Circuit Breakers are Even Safer Than Fuses

Circuit breakers can be used in the place of household fuses.

1) Instead of melting a fuse, a large current may instead 'trip' (turn off) a circuit breaker.
2) Circuit breakers turn off quicker than the time taken for a fuse to melt.
3) They can also be reset, which is much easier than having to replace a fuse.
4) However, circuit breakers are more expensive than fuses.

Household circuit breaker switches.

Insulating Materials Make Appliances "Double Insulated"

1) All appliances with metal cases are usually "earthed" to reduce the danger of electric shock.
2) "Earthing" just means the case must be attached to an earth wire. An earthed conductor can never become live.
3) If the appliance has a plastic casing and no metal parts showing then it's said to be double insulated.
4) Plastic can't conduct electricity and so the casing can't become live.
5) Anything with double insulation like that doesn't need an earth wire — just a live and neutral. Cables that only carry the live and neutral wires are known as two-core cables.

Fuse ratings — compromise is key...

You want to be sure a fuse will melt if there's a surge in current, so the rating can't be too high. On the other hand you don't want it to be so low that it will blow whilst the appliance is functioning safely.

Warm-Up and Exam Questions

Time to see if you've been paying close attention to the last three pages — have a go at these delightful warm-up and exam questions. If you get any wrong, look back for a quick recap.

Warm-Up Questions

1) Is the electricity supplied by a battery alternating current or direct current?
2) Explain the function of the neutral wire in mains wiring.
3) What is the p.d. between the live wire and the neutral wire in mains wiring?
4) Which wire should a fuse be fitted to in mains wiring?
5) True or false? It is best to use a fuse with a rating that is much lower than the appliance's normal operating current.

Exam Questions

1   Appliances with a metal casing are usually connected to the mains using a three-core cable.

(a) Mains electricity provides alternating current.
State what is meant by alternating current.

[1 mark]

Figure 1

(b) **Figure 1** shows an electrical cable that has become frayed so that the metal part of the live wire is exposed. Explain why you would get an electric shock if you touched the exposed wire.

[3 marks]

2   A kettle is connected to the mains electricity supply.

The kettle develops a fault so that the live wire is in contact with the kettle's metal casing, causing it to become live.

(a) Explain how the earth wire and the fuse isolate the kettle in this situation.

[3 marks]

(b) Give an alternative to using a fuse to isolate a faulty appliance.

[1 mark]

(c) An appliance has a casing that is made entirely from plastic, and has no metal parts showing. Explain why the appliance does not need an earth wire.

[1 mark]

Section 22 — Electricity and Circuits

Section 23 — Magnetic Fields

Magnets and Magnetic Fields

Magnetic fields are *produced* by *magnets*, and can be shown with *field lines*. Well that was easy.

Magnets Produce **Magnetic Fields**

1) All magnets have two poles — north and south.
2) All magnets produce a magnetic field — a region where other magnets or magnetic materials (see next page) experience a force.
3) You can show a magnetic field by drawing magnetic field lines.
4) The lines always go from north to south and they show which way a force would act on a north pole at that point in the field.
5) The closer together the lines are, the stronger the magnetic field.
6) The further away from a magnet you get, the weaker the field is.
7) The magnetic field is strongest at the poles of a magnet. This means that magnetic forces are also strongest at the poles.

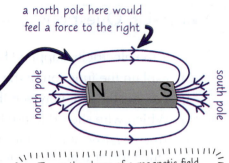

To see the shape of a magnetic field, place a piece of card over a magnet and sprinkle iron filings onto it. The filings line up with the field lines — but they won't show you the direction of the field.

Magnetic Fields Cause **Forces** between **Magnets**

1) Between two magnets there is a magnetic force that can be attractive or repulsive. Two poles that are the same (these are called like poles) will repel each other. Two unlike poles will attract each other.
2) Placing the north and south poles of two bar magnets near each other creates a uniform field between the two poles. The magnetic field is the same strength everywhere between the poles.
3) If you're asked to draw a uniform magnetic field, you need to draw at least three field lines, parallel to each other and all the same distance apart.

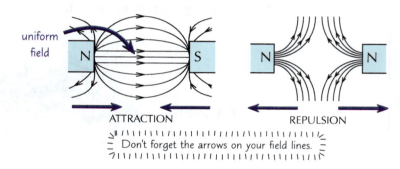

Don't forget the arrows on your field lines.

Plotting Compasses Show the **Directions** of Magnetic Fields

1) Inside a compass is a tiny bar magnet called a needle. A compass needle always lines up with the magnetic field it's in.
2) You can use a compass to build up a picture of what the field around a magnet looks like:
   - Put the magnet on a piece of paper and draw round it.
   - Place the compass on the paper near the magnet. The needle will point in the direction of the field line at this position.
   - Mark the direction of the compass needle by drawing two dots — one at each end of the needle.
   - Then move the compass so that the tail end of the needle is where the tip of the needle was in the previous position and put a dot by the tip of the needle. Repeat this and then join up the marks you've made — you'll end up with a drawing of one field line around the magnet.
   - Repeat this method at different points around the magnet to get several field lines. Make sure you draw arrows from north to south on your field lines.
3) When they're not near a magnet, compasses always point towards the Earth's North Pole. This is because the Earth generates its own magnetic field (and the North Pole is actually a magnetic south pole). This shows the inside (core) of the Earth must be magnetic.

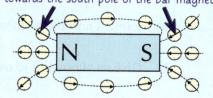

The compass follows the field lines and points towards the south pole of the bar magnet.

Permanent and Induced Magnets

*Magnetic fields don't just affect **magnets** — they affect a few special **magnetic materials** too.*

Very Few Materials are Magnetic

1) The main three magnetic elements are iron, nickel and cobalt.
2) Some alloys and compounds of these metals are also magnetic. For example, steel is magnetic because it contains iron.
3) If you put a magnetic material near a magnet, it is attracted to that magnet. The magnetic force between a magnet and a magnetic material is always attractive.

Magnets Can be Permanent or Induced

1) Permanent magnets (e.g. bar magnets) produce their own magnetic field all the time.
2) Induced (or temporary) magnets only produce a magnetic field while they're in another magnetic field.
3) If you put any magnetic material into a magnetic field, it becomes an induced magnet.
4) This magnetic induction explains why the force between a magnet and a magnetic material is always attractive — the south pole of the magnet induces a north pole in the material, and vice versa.
5) When you take away the magnetic field, induced magnets return to normal and stop producing a magnetic field. How quickly they lose their magnetism depends on the material they're made from.

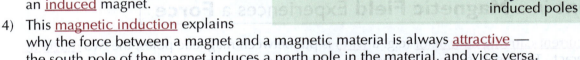

The magnetic material becomes magnetised when it is brought near the bar magnet. It has its own poles and magnetic field:

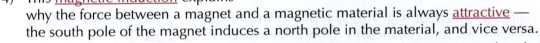

induced poles

- Magnetically 'soft' materials, e.g. pure iron and nickel-iron alloys, lose their magnetism very quickly.
- Magnetically 'hard' materials, e.g. steel, lose their magnetism more slowly. Permanent magnets are made from magnetically hard materials.

Magnetic Materials have Lots of Uses

There are many different uses of magnetic materials, the number of which has grown since the invention of electromagnets (p.360). For example:

1) Fridge doors — there is a permanent magnetic strip in your fridge door to keep it closed.
2) Cranes — these use induced electromagnets to attract and move magnetic materials — e.g. moving scrap metal in scrap yards.
3) Maglev trains — these use magnetic repulsion to make trains float slightly above the track (to reduce losses from friction) and to propel them along.
4) MRI machines — these use magnetic fields to create images of the inside of your body without having to use ionising radiation (like X-rays, p.313).
5) Speakers and microphones — these use magnets to create or detect vibrations.

Magnets attract magnetic materials due to magnetic induction...

However, once the permanent magnet is removed, the induced magnet becomes unmagnetised again.

Section 23 — Magnetic Fields

Electromagnetism and The Motor Effect

A **magnetic field** can be produced by a **current passing through a wire**. This can result in something called the **motor effect** if the current-carrying **wire** is placed in an **external magnetic field** (e.g. of a bar magnet).

A Moving Charge Creates a Magnetic Field

1) When a current flows through a long, straight conductor (e.g. a wire) a magnetic field is created around it.

2) The field is made up of concentric circles perpendicular to the wire, with the wire in the centre.

3) Changing the direction of the current changes the direction of the magnetic field — use the right-hand thumb rule to work out which way it goes.

4) In experiments, you can use a plotting compass to find its direction (see p.356).

5) The larger the current through the wire, or the closer to the wire you are, the stronger the field is.

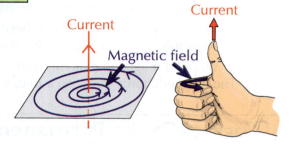

The Right-Hand Thumb Rule
Using your right hand, point your thumb in the direction of current and curl your fingers. The direction of your fingers is the direction of the field.

A Current in a Magnetic Field Experiences a Force

1) When a current-carrying conductor (e.g. a wire) is put between magnetic poles, the two magnetic fields interact. The result is a force on the wire. This is known as the motor effect.

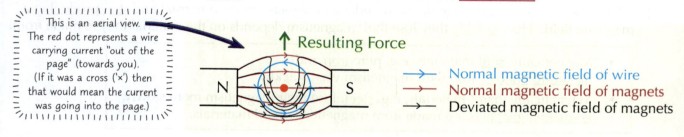

This is an aerial view. The red dot represents a wire carrying current "out of the page" (towards you). (If it was a cross ('x') then that would mean the current was going into the page.)

→ Normal magnetic field of wire
→ Normal magnetic field of magnets
→ Deviated magnetic field of magnets

2) To experience the full force, the wire has to be at 90° (right angles) to the magnetic field. If the wire runs along the magnetic field, it won't experience any force at all. At angles in between, it'll feel some force.

3) The force always acts in the same direction relative to the magnetic field and the direction of the current in the wire. So changing the direction of either the magnetic field or the current will change the direction of the force.

The wire also exerts an equal and opposite force on the magnet (from Newton's Third Law, see p.274) but we're just looking at the force on the wire.

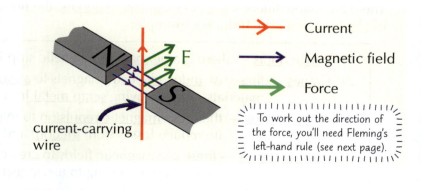

To work out the direction of the force, you'll need Fleming's left-hand rule (see next page).

Just point your thumb in the direction of the current...

... and your fingers show the direction of the field it produces. Remember, it's always your right thumb. Not your left. You'll use your left hand on the next page though, so it shouldn't feel left out...

Section 23 — Magnetic Fields

The Motor Effect

*So you know that a **current-carrying wire** experiences a **force** in a **magnetic field**. Time now to see how to find the **size** and the **direction** of this force.*

You Can Find the Size of the Force...

The size of the force acting on a conductor in a magnetic field depends on three things:

1) The magnetic flux density — how many field (flux) lines there are in a region. This shows the strength of the magnetic field (p.356).
2) The size of the current through the conductor.
3) The length of the conductor that's in the magnetic field.

When the current is at 90° to the magnetic field it is in, the force acting on it can be found using the equation:

$$F = B \times I \times l$$

Force (N)
Length (m)
Magnetic flux density (T, tesla or N/Am)
Current (A)

... and Which Way it's Acting

You can find the direction of the force on a current-carrying conductor with Fleming's left-hand rule.

1) Using your left hand, point your First finger in the direction of the magnetic Field.
2) Point your seCond finger in the direction of the Current.
3) Your thuMb will then point in the direction of the force (Motion).

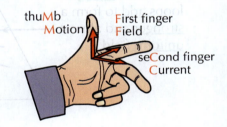

thuMb — Motion
First finger — Field
seCond finger — Current

EXAMPLE

In the diagram on the right, in which direction does the force act on the wire?

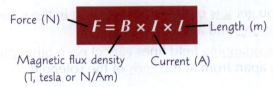

1) Draw in current arrows (positive to negative).

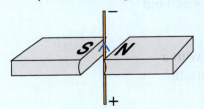

2) Use Fleming's LHR.

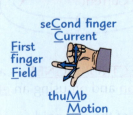

seCond finger — Current
First finger — Field
thuMb — Motion

3) Draw in direction of force (motion).

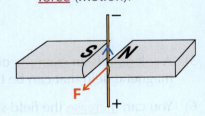

Fleming's left-hand rule can really come in handy...

Use the left-hand rule in the exam. You might look a bit silly, but as long as you remember which digit corresponds to motion, field and current, it makes getting those marks so much easier.

Q1 A section of a current-carrying wire is in a magnetic field, as shown in the diagram. The wire is at 90° to the magnetic field. Find the direction of the force acting on the wire. [1 mark]

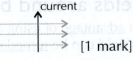

current

Section 23 — Magnetic Fields

Solenoids

A **solenoid** is a fancy way of saying **coils of wire** with a **current** flowing through them. The current means that solenoids produce a **magnetic field** which, as it turns out, is **similar** to the **field** around a **bar magnet**.

A Solenoid is a Long Coil of Wire

1) Around a single loop of current-carrying wire, the magnetic field looks like this:

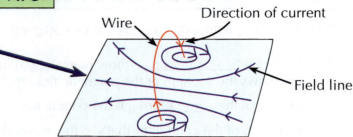

2) You can increase the strength of the magnetic field produced by a length of wire by wrapping it into a long coil with lots of loops, called a solenoid.

3) The field lines around each separate loop of wire line up.

- Inside the solenoid, you get lots of field lines pointing in the same direction. The magnetic field is strong and almost uniform.
- Outside the coil, the overlapping field lines cancel each other out — so the field is weak apart from at the ends of the solenoid.

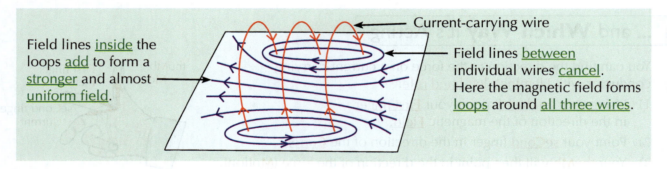

Field lines inside the loops add to form a stronger and almost uniform field.

Field lines between individual wires cancel. Here the magnetic field forms loops around all three wires.

4) You end up with a field that looks like the one around a bar magnet. The direction of the field depends on the direction of the current (p.358).

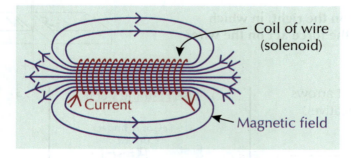

5) A solenoid is an example of an ELECTROMAGNET — a magnet with a magnetic field that can be turned on and off using an electric current.

6) You can increase the field strength of the solenoid even more by putting a block of iron in the centre of the coil. This iron core becomes an induced magnet (see p.357) whenever current is flowing.

The fields around bar magnets and solenoids are the same shape...

The main advantage of using an electromagnet (such as a solenoid) rather than a bar magnet is that the magnetic field can be turned on and off with the current. This makes an electromagnet pretty handy.

Warm-Up and Exam Questions

It's time for another page of questions to see how much you've absorbed. If you can do the warm-up questions without breaking into a sweat, then see how you get on with the exam questions below.

Warm-Up Questions

1) a) State whether there will be a force of attraction, repulsion, or no force between the two magnets on the right.
   b) Sketch the magnetic field lines occurring between the two bar magnets.
2) Describe how to plot the magnetic field lines of a bar magnet using a compass.
3) In which direction will a compass point if it is not near any magnets?
4) True or false? When a permanent magnet is placed next to a magnetic material, the magnetic material becomes an induced magnet that repels the permanent magnet.

Exam Questions

1 **Figure 1** shows an aerial view of a current-carrying wire in a magnetic field generated by two bar magnets. The circle represents the wire carrying current out of the page, towards you.

Figure 1

(a) Draw an arrow to show the direction of the force acting on the current-carrying wire.

[1 mark]

(b) Explain what causes the force to act on the current-carrying wire.

[1 mark]

(c) The magnetic field strength of the field generated by the bar magnets is 0.028 T.
7.0 cm of the current-carrying wire lies within the magnetic field of the bar magnets.
The current through the wire is 5.5 A.
Calculate the size of the force acting on the current-carrying wire.
Use the correct equation from the Physics Equation Sheet on page 506.

[2 marks]

(d) Describe what would happen to the force acting on the current-carrying wire if the direction of the current was reversed.

[1 mark]

2 A student makes an electromagnet by wrapping a current-carrying wire into a solenoid around a nail. When the nail is brought close to some paperclips, the paperclips are attracted to the nail.

(a) Explain why a strong uniform field is created within the coils of the solenoid.

[2 marks]

(b) Suggest an element that the nail might contain.

[1 mark]

(c) The student wants to increase the magnetic field strength of the electromagnet.
State **one** way in which he could do this.

[1 mark]

Electromagnetic Induction

Electromagnetic induction — sounds scary, but read this page **carefully** and it shouldn't be too complicated.

A **Changing** Magnetic Field Induces a **Potential Difference** in a **Wire**

Electromagnetic Induction: The induction of a potential difference (and current if there's a complete circuit) in a wire which is experiencing a change in magnetic field.

Induces is a fancy word for creates.

1) There are two different situations where you get electromagnetic induction. The first is if an electrical conductor (e.g. a coil of wire) and a magnetic field move relative to each other:

   - You can do this by moving/rotating either a magnet in a coil of wire OR a conductor (wire) in a magnetic field (the conductor "cuts through" the magnetic field lines).

   - If you move or rotate the magnet (or conductor) in the opposite direction, then the potential difference/current will be reversed. Likewise if the polarity of the magnet is reversed (by turning the magnet around), then the potential difference/current will be reversed too.

   - If you keep the magnet (or the coil) moving backwards and forwards, or keep it rotating in the same direction, you produce an alternating current (p.352).

2) You also get an induced p.d. when the magnetic field through an electrical conductor changes (gets bigger or smaller or reverses). This is what happens in a transformer (p.363).

3) You can increase the size of the induced p.d. by increasing the STRENGTH of the magnetic field, increasing the SPEED of movement/change of field or having MORE TURNS PER UNIT LENGTH on the coil of wire.

Induced Current **Opposes** the Change that Made It

1) So, a change in magnetic field can induce a current in a wire. But, as you saw on page 358, when a current flows through a wire, a magnetic field is created around the wire. (Yep, that's a second magnetic field — different to the one whose field lines were being cut in the first place.)

2) The magnetic field created by an induced current always acts against the change that made it (whether that's the movement of a wire or a change in the field it's in). Basically, it's trying to return things to the way they were.

3) This means that the induced current always opposes the change that made it.

Electromagnetic induction works whether the coil or the field moves

Electromagnetic induction may seem like a difficult concept to grasp, but there are really only a couple of key things to remember. It doesn't matter what's moving, electromagnetic induction occurs as long as field lines are being 'cut'. And the current that's induced will oppose the change that generated it.

Section 23 — Magnetic Fields

Transformers and The National Grid

Transformers are an *application* of *electromagnetic induction* for you to sink your teeth into.

Transformers Change the p.d. — but Only for Alternating Current

1) Transformers use induction to change the size of the potential difference of an alternating current.
2) They all have two coils of wire, the primary and the secondary coils, joined with an iron core.
3) When an alternating p.d. is applied across the primary coil, it produces an alternating magnetic field.
4) The iron in the core is a magnetic material (see p.357) that is easily magnetised and demagnetised. Because the coil is producing an alternating magnetic field, the magnetisation in the core also alternates.
5) This changing magnetic field induces a p.d. in the secondary coil.

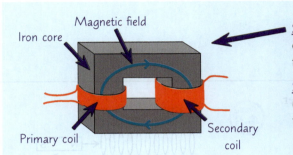

STEP-UP TRANSFORMERS step the potential difference up (i.e. increase it). They have more turns on the secondary coil than the primary coil.

STEP-DOWN TRANSFORMERS step the potential difference down (i.e. decrease it). They have more turns on the primary coil than the secondary.

6) Transformers are almost 100% efficient.
7) So you can assume that the input power is equal to the output power.
8) Using $P = I \times V$ (page 350), you can write this as:

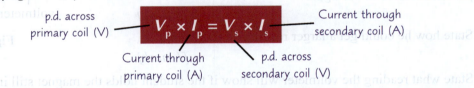

$$V_p \times I_p = V_s \times I_s$$

p.d. across primary coil (V)
Current through primary coil (A)
Current through secondary coil (A)
p.d. across secondary coil (V)

9) $V_p \times I_p$ is the power input at the primary coil. $V_s \times I_s$ is the power output at the secondary coil.

Transformers are Used in The National Grid

1) Once electricity has been generated in a power station, it goes into the national grid — a network of wires and transformers that connects UK power stations to consumers (anyone who uses electricity).
2) The national grid has to transfer loads of energy each second, which means it transmits electricity at a high power (as power = energy transferred ÷ time taken, $P = E \div t$, p.350).
3) Electrical power = current × potential difference ($P = I \times V$, p.350), so to transmit the huge amounts of power needed, you either need a high potential difference or a high current.
4) But a high current makes wires heat up, so loads of energy is wasted to thermal energy stores.
5) So to reduce these losses and make the national grid more efficient, high-potential difference, low-resistance cables, and transformers are used.
6) Step-up transformers at power stations boost the p.d. up really high (400 000 V) and keep the current low. Step-down transformers then bring it back down to safe, usable levels at the consumers' end.

Step-up transformers increase the potential difference...

To help remember the difference between step-up and step-down transformers, try to think about what's changing from the primary coil to the secondary coil. If the number of turns is increasing, the p.d. will also increase — both things have been "stepped up", so it's a step-up transformer.

Q1 A transformer has an input p.d. of 1.6 V. The output power is 320 W. Find the input current. [2 marks]

Warm-Up and Exam Questions

There were lots of new ideas in that section, not to mention that equation on page 363. Better have a go at these questions so you can really see what's gone in and what you might need to go over again.

Warm-Up Questions

1) What is meant by electromagnetic induction?
2) True or false? An induced current will always oppose the change that made it.
3) Do step-up transformers have more turns on their primary or secondary coil?
4) Why is a high current not used to transmit large amounts of power across the national grid?

Exam Questions

1   **Figure 1** shows a coil of wire connected to a voltmeter. A student moves a bar magnet into the coil as shown. The pointer on the voltmeter moves to the left.

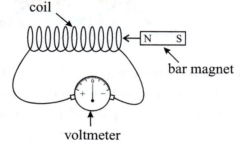

Figure 1

(a) Explain why the pointer moves.
   [1 mark]

(b) State how the student could get the voltmeter's pointer to move to the right.
   [1 mark]

(c) State how he could get a larger reading on the voltmeter.
   [1 mark]

(d) State what reading the voltmeter will show if the student holds the magnet still inside the coil.
   [1 mark]

2   The national grid supplies consumers across the UK with electricity from power stations.

(a) Describe what step-up and step-down transformers are used for in the national grid.
   [2 marks]

Figure 2 shows the structure of a transformer.

(b) Explain how an alternating current in the primary coil causes an alternating p.d. to occur in the secondary coil.
   [3 marks]

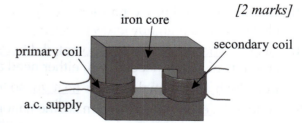

Figure 2

3   A student tests a transformer by connecting a power supply with an alternating current of 2.5 A and a potential difference of 12 V to the primary coil. The potential difference across the secondary coil is 4 V.

Calculate the current in the secondary coil, I_s.

[2 marks]

Section 24 — Matter

Density

Density tells you how much **mass** is packed into a given **volume** of space. You need to be able to work it out, as well as carry out **practicals** to work out the densities of liquids and solids. Lucky you.

Density is the Mass per Unit Volume of a Substance

Density is a measure of the 'compactness' of a substance. It relates the mass of a substance to how much space it takes up (i.e. it's a substance's mass per unit volume).

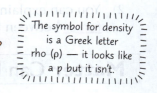

The symbol for density is a Greek letter rho (ρ) — it looks like a p but it isn't.

1) The units of density can be kg/m³ (where the mass is in kg and the volume is in m³) or g/cm³ (where the mass is in g and the volume is in cm³). 1 g/cm³ = 1000 kg/m³.

2) The density of an object depends on what it's made of. Density doesn't vary with size or shape.

3) The average density of an object determines whether it floats or sinks — a solid object will float on a fluid if it has a lower average density than the fluid.

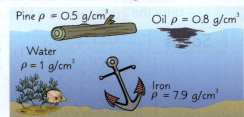

You Need to be Able to Measure Density in Different Ways

To Find the Density of a Liquid — PRACTICAL

1) Place a measuring cylinder on a balance and zero the balance (see p.380).
2) Pour 10 ml of the liquid into the measuring cylinder and record the liquid's mass.
3) Pour another 10 ml into the measuring cylinder and record the total volume and mass. Repeat this process until the measuring cylinder is full.
4) For each measurement, use the formula to find the density. (Remember that 1 ml = 1 cm³.)
5) Finally, take an average of your calculated densities to get an accurate value for the density of the liquid.

To Find the Density of a Solid Object — PRACTICAL

1) Use a balance to measure its mass (see p.380).
2) For some solid shapes, you can find the volume using a formula. E.g. the volume of a cube is just width × height × length.

Make sure you know the formulas for the volumes of basic shapes.

3) For a trickier shaped-solid, you can find its volume by submerging it in a eureka can filled with water. The water displaced by the object will be transferred to the measuring cylinder:
4) Record the volume of water in the measuring cylinder. This is the volume of the object.
5) Plug the object's mass and volume into the formula above to find its density.

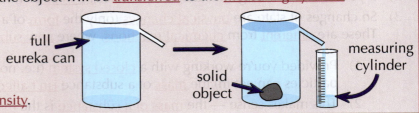

Light objects with large volumes aren't very dense...

Remember — density is all about how tightly packed the particles in a substance are.

Q1 A cube has edges of length 1.5 cm and an average density of 3500 kg/m³. What is its mass?   [3 marks]

Kinetic Theory and States of Matter

You've definitely met a lot of the terms on this page before, but that **doesn't** mean you can skip it...

Kinetic Theory is a Way of Explaining Matter

1) In kinetic theory, you can think of the particles that make up matter as tiny balls.
2) You can explain the ways that matter behaves in terms of how these balls move, and the forces between them. For example, kinetic theory is used to describe the states of matter.

Matter Can Be In Different States

1) Three states of matter are solid (e.g. ice), liquid (e.g. water) and gas (e.g. water vapour).
2) The particles of a substance in each state are the same — only the arrangement and energy of the particles are different.

Solids
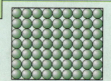
1) Strong forces of attraction hold the particles close together in a fixed, regular arrangement.
2) The particles don't have much energy in their kinetic energy stores so they can only vibrate about their fixed positions.

Liquids
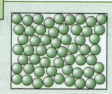
1) The forces of attraction between the particles are weaker.
2) The particles are close together, but can move past each other and form irregular arrangements.
3) They have more energy in their kinetic energy stores than the particles in a solid — they move in random directions at low speeds.

Gases
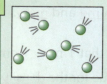
1) There are almost no forces of attraction between the particles.
2) For any given substance, in the gas state its particles will have more energy than in the solid state or the liquid state.
3) They are free to move, and travel in random directions and at high speeds.

You Need to Know the Changes of State

The energy transfers that take place during a change in state are covered on p.372.

1) You need to know the names of the different changes of state:
   - melting — solid to liquid
   - condensing — gas to liquid
   - sublimating — solid to gas
   - freezing — liquid to solid
   - evaporating/boiling — liquid to gas

2) If you reverse a change of state, the particles go back to how they were before.
3) So changes of state are physical changes (only the form of a substance changes). These are different from chemical reactions, where new substances are created by the reaction.

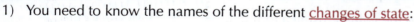

1) Provided you're working with a closed system (i.e. no particles can escape, and no new particles can get in) the mass of a substance isn't affected when it changes state.
2) This makes sense — the mass of a substance is the mass of its particles, and the particles aren't changing, they're just being rearranged.
3) However, when a substance changes state its volume does change. The particles in most substances are closer together when they're a solid than a liquid (ice and water are an exception), and are closer together when they're a liquid than a gas (see the diagrams above).
4) Since density = mass ÷ volume (p.365), then density must change too. Generally, substances are most dense when they're solids and least dense when they're gases.

Section 24 — Matter

Internal Energy and Absolute Zero

*According to kinetic theory, everything is made of **tiny little particles**.*
*The **energy** of a **system** is determined by the energy of the **particles** that make it up.*

Internal Energy is Stored by the Particles That Make Up a System

1) The particles in a system vibrate or move around — they have energy in their kinetic energy stores. The more energy they have in their kinetic energy stores, the faster the particles move.

2) They also have energy in their potential energy stores due to their positions. Usually, the further apart they are from each other, the more energy the particles have in this store.

3) The energy stored in a system is stored by its particles.

4) The internal energy of a system is the total energy that its particles have in their kinetic and potential energy stores.

5) The energy in the thermal energy store of a system is the energy in just the kinetic energy stores of its particles.

6) Heating a system transfers energy to its particles, so heating a system always increases its internal energy.

7) This leads to a change in temperature (when energy is transferred to the kinetic energy stores of the particles) or a change in state (when energy is transferred to the potential energy stores of the particles — see p.372).

Absolute Zero is as Cold as Stuff Can Get — 0 kelvin

1) If you increase the temperature of something, you give its particles more energy — they move about more quickly or vibrate more. In the same way, if you cool a substance down, you're reducing the energy of the particles.

2) In theory, the coldest that anything can ever get is -273 °C — this temperature is known as absolute zero.

3) At absolute zero, the particles have as little energy in their kinetic stores as it's possible to get — they're pretty much still.

4) Absolute zero is the start of the Kelvin scale of temperature.

5) A temperature change of 1 °C is also a change of 1 kelvin. The two scales are pretty similar — the only difference is where the zero occurs.

6) To convert from degrees Celsius to kelvins, just add 273.

7) And to convert from kelvins to degrees Celsius, just subtract 273.

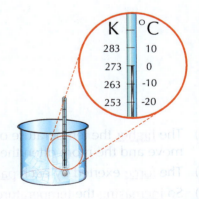

You can't get colder than absolute zero...

Always double check that your answer seems sensible in the exam. For example, nothing can get colder than 0 K or − 273 °C, so if your answer is below that, you've done something wrong in your calculations.

Section 24 — Matter

Gas Pressure

*Kinetic theory helps explain how **temperature**, **pressure** and the **energy in kinetic energy stores** are all related.*

The Average Speed of Particles Increases With Temperature

1) According to kinetic theory, the particles in a gas are constantly moving with random directions and speeds (see p.366).

2) If you increase the temperature of a gas, you transfer energy into the kinetic energy stores of its particles.

3) So as you increase the temperature of a gas, the average speed of its particles increases. This is because the energy in the particles' kinetic energy stores is $½ × m × v^2$ — p.288.

Colliding Gas Particles Create Pressure

1) Particles in a gas hardly take up any space. Most of the gas is empty space.
2) As gas particles move about at high speeds, they bang into each other and whatever else happens to get in the way. When they collide with something, they exert a force on it.
3) In a sealed container, the outward gas pressure is the total force exerted by all of the particles in the gas on a unit area of the container walls.

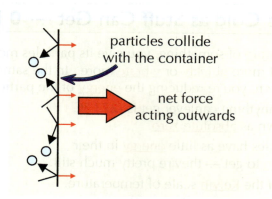
particles collide with the container
net force acting outwards

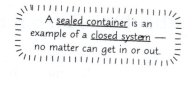
A sealed container is an example of a closed system — no matter can get in or out.

4) The higher the temperature of the gas, the faster the particles move and the more often they collide with the container.
5) The force exerted by each particle during a collision also increases as the temperature increases.
6) So increasing the temperature of a fixed volume of gas increases its pressure.

 The higher the temperature, the greater the pressure...
Imagine throwing a tennis ball at a wall. The faster you throw the tennis ball, the greater the force (and pressure) it exerts on the wall. It's the same idea with gases — when you increase the temperature of a gas, the particles move faster and create a greater pressure on the container walls.

Warm-Up and Exam Questions

Time to try your hand at some questions, before getting to grips with the rest of the section.

Warm-Up Questions

1) What is density a measure of?
2) In what state can the particles in a substance move in random directions at high speeds?
3) Name the change of state for a solid changing into a gas.
4) Are changes of state chemical or physical changes?
5) How does cooling a system affect its internal energy?
6) State the temperature of absolute zero in degrees Celsius.
7) If a gas is kept at a constant volume, explain why increasing the temperature of the gas causes the gas pressure to increase.

Exam Questions

1 A block of lead is solid at room temperature. *(Grade 4-6)*

   (a) Describe the arrangement and movement of the particles in a solid.
      [2 marks]

   (b) The lead block has a mass of 850.5 g and a volume of 75.0 cm^3.
      Calculate the density of the lead block. Give your answer in g/cm^3.
      [2 marks]

   (c) If the lead block is heated to 327.5 °C, it can change from a solid to a liquid.
      Give the name of this process.
      [1 mark]

PRACTICAL

2 A student has a collection of metal toy soldiers each made from the same metal. *(Grade 6-7)*
   Each toy soldier has a different volume.

   (a) Which of the following statements about the toy soldiers is true?

      ☐ **A** The masses and densities of each of the toy soldiers are the same.

      ☐ **B** The masses of each of the toy soldiers are the same, but their densities will vary.

      ☐ **C** The densities of each of the toy soldiers are the same, but their masses will vary.

      ☐ **D** The densities and masses of each toy soldier will vary.
      [1 mark]

   (b) The student wants to measure the density of one of the toy soldiers.
      He has a eureka can (a beaker with a spout in the side, as shown in
      Figure 1), a measuring cylinder, a mass balance and some water.
      State the **two** quantities the student must measure
      in order to calculate the density of the toy soldier.
      [2 marks]

   Figure 1

   *(c) Describe the steps the student could take to find the density
      of the toy soldier using the equipment he has.
      [6 marks]

Specific Heat Capacity

Specific heat capacity is really just a sciencey way of saying **how hard** it is to **heat** something up.

Specific Heat Capacity Relates Temperature and Energy

1) It takes more energy to increase the temperature of some materials than others.
2) For example, you need 4200 J to warm 1 kg of water by 1 °C, but only 139 J to warm 1 kg of mercury by 1 °C.
3) Materials that need to gain lots of energy to warm up also release loads of energy when they cool down again. They store a lot of energy for a given change in temperature.
4) The change in the energy stored in a substance when you heat it is related to the change in its temperature by its specific heat capacity.
5) The specific heat capacity of a substance is the change in energy in the substance's thermal energy store needed to raise the temperature of 1 kg of that substance by 1 °C.
6) You need to know how to use the equation relating energy, mass, specific heat capacity and temperature.

Change in thermal energy (J) — $\Delta Q = m \times c \times \Delta \theta$ — Temperature change (°C)
Mass (kg) — Specific heat capacity (J/kg°C)

7) The Δs in the equation just mean 'change in'.

You can Find the Specific Heat Capacity of Water   **PRACTICAL**

You can use the experiment below to find the specific heat capacity of water — or any liquid for that matter. In the experiment, an electric immersion heater is used to heat a container full of water. It is assumed that all of the energy transferred to the heater from its power supply is transferred usefully to the water — i.e. all of the energy transferred heats the water.

You can use this set up with solid blocks to find the SHC of solids.

1) First, place your container on a mass balance.
2) Zero the balance and fill the container with water. Record the mass of the water.
3) Set up the experiment as shown — make sure the joulemeter reads zero and place a lid on the container if you have one.
4) Measure the temperature of the water, then turn on the power.
5) Keep an eye on the thermometer. When the temperature has increased by e.g. ten degrees, stop the experiment and record the energy on the joulemeter, and the increase in temperature.
6) You can then calculate the specific heat capacity of the water by rearranging $\Delta Q = m \times c \times \Delta \theta$ to give you $c = \Delta Q \div (m \times \Delta \theta)$ and plugging in your measurements.
7) Repeat the whole experiment at least three times, then calculate an average of the specific heat capacity (p.9).

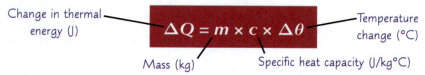

Alternatively, you could also use a voltmeter and ammeter instead of a joulemeter, time how long the heater was on for, then calculate the energy supplied (p.382).

Some substances can store more energy than others...

Learn the definition of specific heat capacity and make sure you know how to use the formula above.

Q1 Find the final temperature of 5 kg of water, at an initial temperature of 5 °C, after 50 kJ of energy has been transferred to it.
The specific heat capacity of water is 4200 J/kg°C.   [3 marks]

Q1 Video Solution

Specific Latent Heat

*The **energy needed** to change the state of a substance is called **specific latent heat**. But first, insulation...*

Use **Thermal Insulation** to get More **Accurate** Results

1) During <u>any</u> process, some energy is always <u>wasted</u>.
2) So in the experiment on the previous page, not <u>all</u> of the energy transferred from the power supply is used to heat the water (although we assume it's true to make calculations easier).
3) Some is <u>lost</u> heating up the wires of the immersion heater and some is transferred by heating to the container and the air around it.
4) To <u>reduce</u> these <u>unwanted energy transfers</u> and make your result more <u>accurate</u> (p.7), you should wrap the container in a <u>thermally insulating</u> material (e.g. cotton wool) and place it on an <u>insulating surface</u>, like a cork mat.
5) <u>Thermal insulators</u> reduce the <u>rate</u> at which energy is transferred by <u>heating</u>, which means that <u>less energy</u> is transferred to the thermal energy stores of the surroundings. There's more about thermal insulation on page 294.

Specific Latent Heat is the **Energy Needed** to **Change State**

1) The <u>specific latent heat</u> (SLH) of a <u>change of state</u> of a substance is the <u>amount of energy</u> needed to <u>change 1 kg</u> of it from <u>one state to another without changing its temperature</u>.
2) For <u>cooling</u>, specific latent heat is the energy <u>released</u> by a change in state.
3) Specific latent heat is <u>different</u> for <u>different materials</u>, and for changing between <u>different states</u>.

> The specific latent heat for changing between a <u>solid</u> and a <u>liquid</u> (<u>melting</u> or <u>freezing</u>) is called the <u>specific latent heat of fusion</u>. The specific latent heat for changing between a <u>liquid</u> and a <u>gas</u> (<u>evaporating</u>, <u>boiling</u> or <u>condensing</u>) is called the <u>specific latent heat of vaporisation</u>.

4) You can work out the <u>energy needed</u> (or <u>released</u>) when a substance of mass *m* changes state using this <u>formula</u>:

Thermal energy (J) = Mass (kg) × Specific Latent Heat (J/kg)

EXAMPLE The specific latent heat of vaporisation for water (boiling) is 2 260 000 J/kg. How much energy is needed to completely boil 1.50 kg of water at 100 °C?

1) Just plug the numbers into the <u>formula</u>. $Q = m \times L$
   $= 1.50 \times 2\,260\,000$
2) The units are <u>joules</u> because it's <u>energy</u>. $= 3\,390\,000$ J

Different changes of state mean different specific latent heats...

When it comes to the specific latent heat of <u>vaporisation</u> and <u>fusion</u>, the formula's the same, but the process is different. Make sure you understand which process you're actually looking at.

Q1 The SLH of fusion for a particular substance is 120 000 J/kg. How much energy is needed to melt 250 g of the substance when it is already at its melting temperature?   [2 marks]

Investigating Water

And now it's time to **investigate** what happens to the **temperature** of water during a **change of state**.

You Need to Put In Energy to Break Bonds between Particles

1) When a system is heated and its state changes (e.g. melting, boiling), energy is transferred to the potential energy stores of the particles instead of to their kinetic energy stores.
2) The particles in the system move apart from each other and the intermolecular forces between the particles get weaker (see p.366).
3) Because the amount of energy in the particles' kinetic energy stores stays the same, the average speed of the particles and the temperature of the system remain constant whilst the substance changes state.
4) During a change of state due to cooling, the particles lose energy from their potential energy stores. They move closer together and the intermolecular forces between them get stronger. Their average speed still doesn't change though (so the temperature still remains constant).
5) You can see this by doing this simple experiment:

PRACTICAL

1) Fill a beaker with crushed ice, and place a thermometer into the beaker to record the temperature of the ice.
2) Start a stopwatch and gradually heat the beaker full of ice using a Bunsen burner.
3) Every twenty seconds, record the temperature and the current state of the ice (e.g. partially melted, completely melted).
4) Continue this process until all of the ice has turned into water and the water begins to boil.
5) Stop the stopwatch and turn off the Bunsen burner.
6) Plot a graph of temperature against time for your experiment.

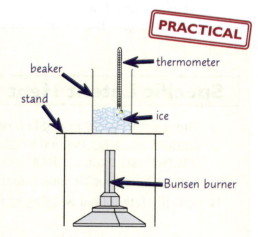

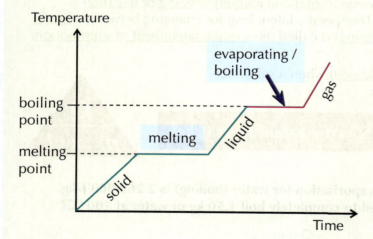

7) You should get a graph similar to the blue sections in the graph on the left.
8) The purple line shows what your graph would look like if you were able to trap and heat the water vapour produced.
9) Comparing the graph to your measurements, you should see that the flat spots occur when there is a change of state.
10) Energy is being transferred to the potential energy stores of the water particles at these points, so the temperature doesn't change.

11) If you carried out an experiment for cooling water instead of heating it, you would get a similar graph. However, the temperature-time graph for a substance cooled from a gas has a negative gradient and flat spots where the substance is condensing or freezing.

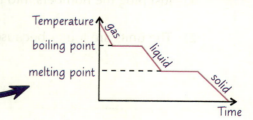

The temperature of a substance is constant as it changes state...

Energy isn't transferred to the particles' kinetic energy stores for a change of state, so the temperature of the substance stays the same and you get flat spots on a temperature-time graph. Learn that, and understand it.

Warm-Up and Exam Questions

Time to test yourself on specific heat capacity and specific latent heat. There's no escaping it, get going.

Warm-Up Questions

1) What is the specific heat capacity of a material?
2) In an experiment to find the specific heat capacity of water, a container of water is wrapped in a thermally insulating material and heated. Explain how this improves the results of the experiment.
3) What are the units of specific latent heat?
4) Sketch a temperature-time graph for water turning into ice.

Exam Questions

1. 47 100 J of energy is required to convert 40.8 g of liquid methanol to gaseous methanol without changing its temperature.

   Calculate the specific latent heat of vaporisation of methanol. Give your answer in J/kg.
   Use the correct equation from the Physics Equation Sheet on page 506.

   [2 marks]

2. 36 000 J of energy is transferred to a 0.5 kg concrete block. The block increases in temperature from 20 °C to 100 °C.

   (a) Calculate the specific heat capacity of the concrete block.
   Use the correct equation from the Physics Equation Sheet on page 506.

   [2 marks]

   (b) **Figure 1** shows a storage heater in a room. Energy is transferred to the thermal energy store of the electric storage heater at night, and then transferred away to the thermal energy stores of the surroundings during the day. Lead has a specific heat capacity of 126 J/kg°C.

   Using your answer to (a), explain why concrete blocks are used in storage heaters rather than lead blocks.

   [3 marks]

   Figure 1

PRACTICAL

3. A student uses an electrical immersion heater to transfer energy to a beaker containing 1.0 kg of water. She produces a graph of the energy supplied against the increase in temperature of the water, shown in **Figure 2**.

   (a) Use the gradient of the line of best fit in **Figure 2** to determine a value for the specific heat capacity of water in J/kg°C.

   [3 marks]

   (b) State and explain whether you would you expect the true value for the specific heat capacity of water to be higher or lower than the value found in this experiment.

   [2 marks]

   Figure 2

Elasticity

Forces don't just make objects *move*, they can also make them *change shape*. Whether they change shape *temporarily* or *permanently* depends on *the object* and the forces applied.

Stretching, Compressing or Bending Transfers Energy

1) When you apply a force to an object you may cause it to bend, compress or stretch.

2) To do this, you need more than one force acting on the object — otherwise the object would simply move in the direction of the applied force, instead of changing shape.

3) Work is done when a force stretches or compresses an object and causes energy to be transferred to the elastic potential energy store of the object.

4) If it is elastically distorted (see below), ALL this energy is transferred to the object's elastic potential energy store (see p.288).

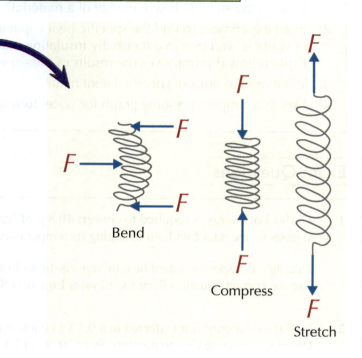
Bend
Compress
Stretch

Elastic Distortion

1) An object has been elastically distorted if it can go back to its original shape and length after the force has been removed.

2) Objects that can be elastically distorted are called elastic objects (e.g. a spring).

Inelastic Distortion

1) An object has been inelastically distorted if it doesn't return to its original shape and length after the force has been removed.

2) The elastic limit is the point where an object stops distorting elastically and begins to distort inelastically.

Elastic objects are only elastic up to a certain point...
Remember the difference between elastic distortion and inelastic distortion. If an object has been elastically distorted, it will return to its original shape when you remove the force. If it's been inelastically distorted, its shape will have been changed permanently — for example, an over-stretched spring will stay stretched even after you remove the force.

Elasticity

Springs obey a really handy little *equation* that relates the *force* on them to their *extension* — for a while at least. Thankfully, you can *plot a graph* to see where this equation is *valid*.

Extension is Directly Proportional to Force...

If a spring is supported at the top and a weight is attached to the bottom, it stretches.

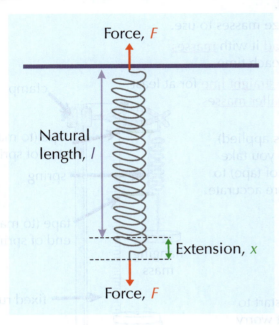

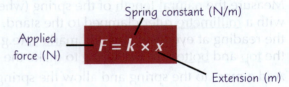

1) The extension of a stretched spring (or certain other elastic objects) is directly proportional to the load or force applied — so $F \propto x$.
2) This means that there is a linear relationship between force and extension. (If you plotted a force-extension graph for the spring, it would be a straight line.)
3) This is the equation:

$$F = k \times x$$

Spring constant (N/m), Applied force (N), Extension (m)

4) For a linear relationship, the gradient of an object's force-extension graph is equal to its spring constant.
5) The spring constant, depends on the material that you are stretching — a stiffer spring has a greater spring constant.
6) The equation also works for compression (where x is just the difference between the natural and compressed lengths — the compression).

...But this Stops Working when the Force is Great Enough

There's a limit to the amount of force you can apply to an object for the extension to keep on increasing proportionally.

1) The graph shows force against extension for an elastic object.
2) There is a maximum force above which the graph curves, showing that extension is no longer proportional to force.
3) The relationship is now non-linear — the object stretches more for each unit increase in force. This point is known as the limit of proportionality and is shown on the graph at the point marked P.
4) The elastic limit (see previous page) is marked as E. Past this point, the object is permanently stretched.

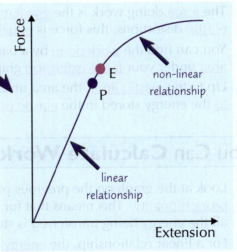

The spring constant is measured in N/m...

Be careful with units when doing calculations with springs. Some exam questions might have the extension in centimetres, but the spring constant is measured in newtons per metre. So convert the extension into metres before you do any calculations, or you'll get the wrong answer.

Q1 A spring is fixed at one end and a force of 1 N is applied to the other end, causing it to stretch. The spring extends by 2 cm. Calculate the spring constant of the spring.   [2 marks]

Section 24 — Matter

Investigating Elasticity

*You can do an easy **experiment** to see exactly how adding **masses** to a spring causes it to **stretch**.*

You Can Investigate the Link Between Extension and Work Done

Set up the apparatus as shown in the diagram. Make sure you have plenty of extra masses, then measure the mass of each (with a mass balance) and calculate its weight (the force applied) using $W = m \times g$ (p.30).

You could do a quick pilot experiment first to find out what size masses to use.

- Using an identical spring to the one you will be testing, load it with masses one at a time and record the force (weight) and extension each time.
- Plot a force-extension graph and check that you get a nice straight line for at least the first 6 points. If it curves too early, you need to use smaller masses.

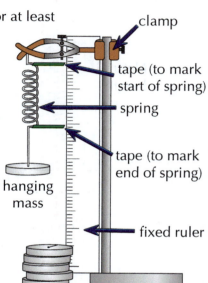

1) Measure the natural length of the spring (when no load is applied) with a millimetre ruler clamped to the stand. Make sure you take the reading at eye level and add markers (e.g. thin strips of tape) to the top and bottom of the spring to make the reading more accurate.
2) Add a mass to the spring and allow the spring to come to rest. Record the mass and measure the new length of the spring. The extension is the change in length.
3) Repeat this process until you have enough measurements (no fewer than 6).
4) Plot a force-extension graph of your results. It will only start to curve if you exceed the limit of proportionality, but don't worry if yours doesn't (as long as you've got the straight line bit).

1) You should find that a larger force causes a bigger extension.
2) You can also think of this as more work needing to be done to cause a larger extension.
3) The force doing work is the gravitational force and for linear elastic distortions, this force is equal to $F = k \times x$.
4) You can find the work done by a particular force by calculating the area under your force-extension graph up to that value of force.
5) Up to the elastic limit, the area under the graph (work done) is also equal to the energy stored in the elastic potential energy store (see below).

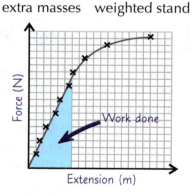

You Can Calculate Work Done for Linear Relationships

1) Look at the graph on the previous page. The elastic limit is always at or beyond the limit of proportionality. This means that for a linear relationship, the distortion is always elastic — all the energy being transferred is stored in the spring's elastic potential energy store.
2) For a linear relationship, the energy in the elastic potential energy store (and so the work done) can be found using:

$$E = \tfrac{1}{2} \times k \times x^2$$

- Extension² (m²)
- Spring constant (N/m)
- Energy transferred in stretching (J)

Take care when setting up to get more accurate measurements...

Make sure the ruler is vertical before you begin, otherwise you will have more error in your results.

Q1 A spring with a spring constant of 40 N/m extends elastically by 2.5 cm. Calculate the amount of energy stored in its elastic potential energy store. [2 marks]

Q1 Video Solution

Warm-Up and Exam Questions

Time to do some work and stretch yourself with these questions.

Warm-Up Questions

1) True or false? You can stretch a spring by only applying one force to it.
2) What is meant by elastic distortion?
3) State the formula linking force, spring constant and extension.

Exam Questions

PRACTICAL

1 A student investigates the relationship between the force applied to a spring and its extension.

   Figure 1 shows the force-extension graph of his results.

   Calculate the work done to stretch the spring by 4 cm.

   [2 marks]

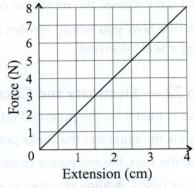

Figure 1

PRACTICAL

2 A teacher shows his students an experiment to show how a spring extends when masses are hung from it. He hangs a number of 90 g masses from a 50 g hook attached to the base of the spring. He records the extension of the spring and the total weight of the masses and hook each time he adds a mass to the bottom of the spring.

   (a) Give the independent variable in this experiment.

   [1 mark]

   (b) Give **one** control variable in this experiment.

   [1 mark]

   (c) When a force of 4 N is applied to the spring, the spring extends elastically by 2.5 cm. Calculate the spring constant of the spring.

   [3 marks]

   (d) The teacher applies a 15 N force to the spring. When he removes the force, the spring is 7 cm long. The original length of the spring was 5 cm. Describe what has happened to the spring.

   [1 mark]

3 A spring is compressed linearly and elastically. It takes 36 J of energy to compress the spring. The original length of the spring is 1.20 m. The spring has a spring constant of 400 N/m. Calculate the length of the spring after it has been compressed. Use the correct equation from the Physics Equation Sheet on page 506.

   [3 marks]

Revision Summary for Sections 21-24

Phew, that's the end of Section 24 — the last one in the book. Test yourself before you celebrate.
- Try these questions and tick off each one when you get it right.
- When you're completely happy with a section, tick it off.

For even more practice, try the Retrieval Quizzes for Sections 21-24 — just scan these QR codes!

Section 21 — Forces and Energy (p.329-336)

1) True or false? When a system changes, energy is transferred.
2) Give the equation that links kinetic energy, mass and speed.
3) True or false? A force doing work can cause a rise in temperature.
4) Give the equation that links power, work done and time taken.
5) Explain the difference between contact and non-contact forces.
6) What force causes the repulsion of two like electrical charges? What causes this force?
7) Describe how you would resolve a force into horizontal and vertical components using a scale drawing.

Section 22 — Electricity and Circuits (p.337-355)

8) What is meant by the potential difference in a circuit?
9) What is the equation that links potential difference, current and resistance?
10) Describe how the resistance of an LDR varies with light intensity.
11) True or false? Adding resistors in series increases the total resistance of the circuit.
12) State the equation that links power, energy transferred and time.
13) What is the frequency of the UK mains supply?
14) True or false? Circuit breakers must be replaced each time they 'trip'.

Section 23 — Magnetic Fields (p.356-364)

15) Sketch the magnetic field lines around a bar magnet.
16) Explain why a plotting compass points north when it is far away from a magnet.
17) Describe the magnetic field around a current-carrying wire.
18) What is Fleming's left-hand rule?
19) Describe how you can induce a current in a coil of wire.
20) A transformer has an input p.d. of 100 V and an output p.d. of 20 V. What kind of transformer is it?
21) Explain how transformers are used to improve efficiency when transmitting electricity across the national grid.

Section 24 — Matter (p.365-377)

22) What is the formula for density? What are the units of density?
23) True or false? Mass stays the same when a substance changes state.
24) What is absolute zero? What value does it have in kelvin?
25) Describe how a gas exerts a pressure on the walls of its container.
26) Define specific latent heat.
27) What is the difference between an elastic and an inelastic distortion?
28) Draw a typical force-extension graph for an elastic object being stretched past its elastic limit.

Practical Skills

Apparatus and Techniques

*Safety specs out, lab coats on — it's time to find out about the skills you'll need in **experiments**. Finally time to look like a real scientist. But you also need to know about this stuff in your exams...*

Three Ways to Measure Liquids

There are a few methods you might use to measure the volume of a liquid. Whichever method you use, always read the volume from the bottom of the meniscus (the curved upper surface of the liquid) when it's at eye level.

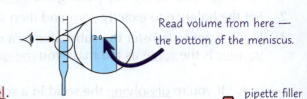

Read volume from here — the bottom of the meniscus.

Pipettes are long, narrow tubes that are used to suck up an accurate volume of liquid and transfer it to another container. A pipette filler attached to the end of the pipette is used so that you can safely control the amount of liquid you're drawing up. Pipettes are often calibrated to allow for the fact that the last drop of liquid stays in the pipette when the liquid is ejected. This reduces transfer errors.

Burettes measure from top to bottom (so when they're filled to the top of the scale, the scale reads zero). They have a tap at the bottom which you can use to release the liquid into another container (you can even release it drop by drop). To use a burette, take an initial reading, and once you've released as much liquid as you want, take a final reading. The difference between the readings tells you how much liquid you used.

Measuring cylinders are the most common way to measure out a liquid. They come in all different sizes. Make sure you choose one that's the right size for the measurement you want to make. It's no good using a huge 1000 cm³ cylinder to measure out 2 cm³ of a liquid — the graduations will be too big, and you'll end up with massive errors. It'd be much better to use one that measures up to 10 cm³.

If you only want a couple of drops of liquid, and don't need it to be accurately measured, you can use a dropping pipette to transfer it.

Gas Syringes Measure Gas Volumes

Gases can be measured with a gas syringe. They should be measured at room temperature and pressure as the volume of a gas changes with temperature and pressure. You should also use a gas syringe that's the right size for the measurement you're making. Before you use the syringe, you should make sure it's completely sealed (so that no gas can escape, making any results inaccurate) and that the plunger moves smoothly.

You could also count the bubbles of gas released. But the bubbles released could be different sizes and if they're produced quickly you might miss some. So this method is less accurate.

1) There are times when you might want to collect the gas produced by a reaction. For example, to investigate the rate of reaction.
2) The most accurate way to measure the volume of a gas that's been produced is to collect it in a gas syringe (see page 236).
3) You could also collect it by displacing water from a measuring cylinder.

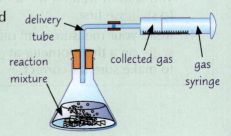

Apparatus and Techniques

Solids Should Be Measured Using a Balance

1) To weigh a solid, start by putting the container you're weighing your substance into on the balance.
2) Set the balance to exactly zero and then start weighing out your substance.
3) If you want to transfer the substance to a new container, you need to make sure that the mass you transfer is the same as the mass you measured. There are different ways you can do this. For example:

- If you're dissolving the solid in a solvent to make a solution, you could wash any remaining solid into the new container using the solvent. This way you know that all the solid you weighed has been transferred.
- You could set the balance to zero before you put your weighing container on the balance. Then reweigh the weighing container after you've transferred the solid. This lets you can work out exactly how much you added to your experiment.

You can also weigh the mass of liquids with balances.

Measure pH to Find Out How Acidic or Alkaline a Solution Is

1) Indicators are dyes that change colour depending on whether they're in an acid or an alkali. You use them by adding a couple of drops of the indicator to the solution you're interested in. Universal indicator is a mixture of indicators that changes colour gradually as pH changes. It's useful for estimating the pH of a solution based on its colour.
2) Indicator paper is useful if you don't want to colour the entire solution that you're testing. It changes colour depending on the pH of the solution it touches. You can also hold a piece of damp indicator paper in a gas sample to test its pH.
3) pH probes are attached to pH meters which have a digital display that gives a numerical value for the pH of a solution. They're used to give an accurate value of pH. (See p.193 for more on pH.)

Blue litmus paper turns red in acidic conditions and red litmus paper turns blue in alkaline conditions.

Measure Temperature and Time Accurately

TEMPERATURE
1) You can use a thermometer to measure the temperature of a substance.
2) Make sure the bulb of your thermometer is completely submerged in any substance you're measuring.
3) If you're taking an initial reading, you should wait for the temperature to stabilise first.
4) Read your measurement off the scale on a thermometer at eye level to make sure it's correct.

TIME
1) You should use a stopwatch to time most experiments — they're more accurate than regular watches.
2) Always make sure you start and stop the stopwatch at exactly the right time. Or alternatively, set an alarm on the stopwatch so you know exactly when to stop an experiment or take a reading.
3) In physics, you might be able to use a light gate (p.382). This will reduce errors in your experiment.

Practical Skills

Apparatus and Techniques

Measure **Most Lengths** with a **Ruler**

1) In most cases, a centimetre ruler can be used to measure length. It depends on what you're measuring though — metre rulers or long measuring tapes are good for large distances, and micrometers are used for measuring tiny things, like the diameter of a wire.

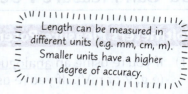
Length can be measured in different units (e.g. mm, cm, m). Smaller units have a higher degree of accuracy.

2) The ruler should always be parallel to what you want to measure.
3) If you're dealing with something where it's tricky to measure just one accurately (e.g. water ripples, p.303), you can measure the length of ten of them and then divide to find the length of one.
4) If you're taking multiple measurements of the same object (e.g. to measure changes in length) then make sure you always measure from the same point on the object.
It can help to put a marker or pointer onto the object to line up your ruler against.
5) Make sure the ruler and the object are always at eye level when you take a reading.
6) Sometimes you'll need to calculate the area of something. If you need to, here's how:

EXAMPLE Calculate the area of a rectangular field.

1) First, you'll need to take accurate measurements of its dimensions (see above for measuring lengths).
2) Then you can calculate its area.

Length = 30 m
Width = 55 m

Area of a rectangle = length × width.
= 30 × 55
= 1650 m²

Here are some examples of other area formulas that may come in useful:
Area of a triangle = ½ × base × height
Area of a circle = πr²

Use a **Protractor** to Find **Angles**

1) First align the vertex (point) of the angle with the mark in the centre of the protractor.

2) Line up the base line of the protractor with one line that forms the angle and then measure the angle of the other line using the scale on the protractor.

3) If the lines creating the angle are very thick, align the protractor and measure the angle from the centre of the lines. Using a sharp pencil to trace light rays or draw diagrams helps to reduce errors when measuring angles.

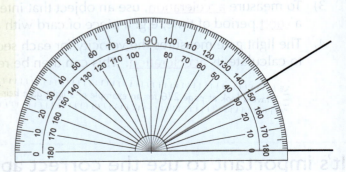

4) If the lines are too short to measure easily, you may have to extend them.

Practical Skills

Apparatus and Techniques

You Can Measure Potential Difference and Current

Voltmeters Measure Potential Difference

1) If you're using an analogue voltmeter, choose the voltmeter with the most appropriate unit (e.g. V or mV). If you're using a digital voltmeter, you'll most likely be able to switch between them.
2) Connect the voltmeter in parallel (p.345) across the component you want to test. The wires that come with a voltmeter are usually red (positive) and black (negative). These go into the red and black coloured ports on the voltmeter.
3) Then simply read the potential difference from the scale (or from the screen if it's digital).

Ammeters Measure Current

1) Just like with voltmeters, choose the ammeter with the most appropriate unit.
2) Connect the ammeter in series (p.344) with the component you want to test, making sure they're both on the same branch. Again, they usually have red and black ports to show you where to connect your wires.
3) Read off the current shown on the scale or by the screen.

Multimeters Measure Both

1) Instead of having a separate ammeter and voltmeter, many circuits use multimeters.
2) These are devices that measure a range of properties — usually potential difference, current and resistance.
3) If you want to find potential difference, make sure the red wire is plugged into the port that has a 'V' (for volts).
4) To find the current, use the port labelled 'A' or 'mA' (for amps).
5) The dial on the multimeter should then be turned to the relevant section, e.g. to 'A' to measure current in amps. The screen will display the value you're measuring.

Light Gates Measure Velocity and Acceleration

1) A light gate sends a beam of light from one side of the gate to a detector on the other side. When something passes through the gate, the beam of light is interrupted. The light gate then measures how long the beam was undetected.
2) To find the velocity of an object, connect the light gate to a computer. Measure the length of the object and input this using the software. It will then automatically calculate the velocity of the object as it passes through the beam.
3) To measure acceleration, use an object that interrupts the signal twice in a short period of time, e.g. a piece of card with a gap cut into the middle.
4) The light gate measures the velocity for each section of the object and uses this to calculate its acceleration. This can then be read from the computer screen.

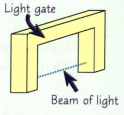
Light gate
Beam of light

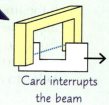
Card interrupts the beam

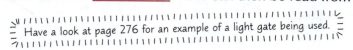
Have a look at page 276 for an example of a light gate being used.

It's important to use the correct apparatus when measuring

That's four pages filled with apparatus and techniques that you need to know for your exams and for your practicals too. In the exam, you might be asked to comment on how an experiment's been set up.

Practical Skills

Heating Substances

*Some more useful lab stuff for you now — a bit about **heating things up**.*

The Temperature of Water Baths & Electric Heaters Can Be Set

1) A water bath is a container filled with water that can be heated to a specific temperature.

2) A simple water bath can be made by heating a beaker of water over a Bunsen burner and monitoring the temperature with a thermometer. However, it can be hard to keep the temperature of the water constant.

3) An electric water bath will monitor and adjust the temperature for you. It's a much easier way of keeping the temperature of a reaction mixture constant. Here's how you use one:

- Set the temperature on the water bath, and allow the water to heat up.
- Place the vessel containing your substance in the water bath using test tube holders or tongs. The level of the water outside the vessel should be just above the level of the substance inside the vessel.
- The substance will then be warmed to the same temperature as the water.

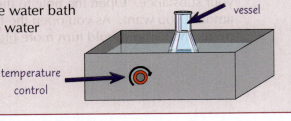

Handle any glassware you've heated with tongs until you're sure it's cooled down.

4) As the substance in the vessel is surrounded by water, the heating is very even. Water boils at 100 °C, so you can't use a water bath to heat something to a higher temperature than this — the water won't get hot enough.

5) Electric heaters are often made up of a metal plate that can be heated to a certain temperature. The vessel containing the substance you want to heat is placed on top of the hot plate. You can heat substances to higher temperatures than you can in a water bath but, as the vessel is only heated from below, you'll usually have to stir the substance inside to make sure it's heated evenly.

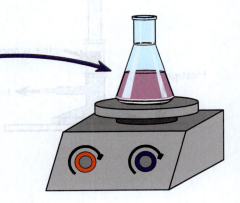

Water baths and electric heaters can be used to heat solutions

Electric water baths are great for keeping the temperature constant. Make sure you're clear on how to use both water baths and electric heaters, and more importantly, on how to use them safely.

Practical Skills

Heating Substances

Sometimes water baths and electric heaters aren't **appropriate** for what you want to do — e.g. if you want to heat a sample of a compound to see what **colour** flame it produces, you should use a **Bunsen burner** instead.

Bunsen Burners Have a Naked Flame

1) Bunsen burners are good for heating things quickly. You can easily adjust how strongly they're heating.

2) But you need to be careful not to use them if you're heating flammable compounds as the flame means the substance would be at risk of catching fire.

3) Here's how to use a Bunsen burner...

- Connect the Bunsen burner to a gas tap, and check that the hole is closed. Place it on a heat-proof mat.
- Light a splint and hold it over the Bunsen burner. Now, turn on the gas. The Bunsen burner should light with a yellow flame.
- The more open the hole is, the more strongly the Bunsen burner will heat your substance. Open the hole to the amount you want. As you open the hole more, the flame should turn more blue.

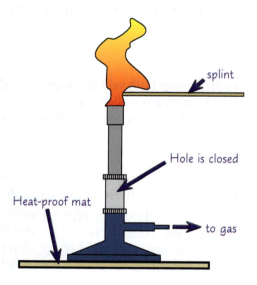

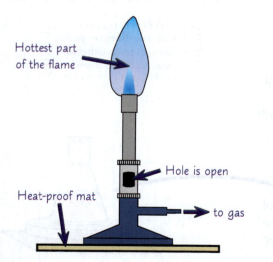

- The hottest part of the flame is just above the blue cone, so you should heat things here.
- If your Bunsen burner is alight but not heating anything, make sure you close the hole so that the flame becomes yellow and clearly visible.
- If you're heating something so that the container (e.g. a test tube) is in the flame, you should hold the vessel at the top, furthest away from the substance (and so the flame) using a pair of tongs.
- If you're heating something over the flame (e.g. an evaporating dish), you should put a tripod and gauze over the Bunsen burner before you light it, and place the vessel on this.

You might not expect the blue flame to be hotter, but it is

It's important to know your way around a Bunsen burner, particularly if you're going to be conducting an experiment that involves flammable chemicals. The flame should only be blue if you want to heat something. Otherwise, keep the hole closed so the flame is nice and visible.

Safety and Experiments

*Labs are **dangerous places**, so here's a page on things you can do to keep yourself and others **safe**.*

Be Careful When You Do Experiments

1) There are always hazards in any experiment, so <u>before</u> you start an experiment you should read and follow any <u>safety precautions</u> to do with your method or the apparatus you're using.

2) Stop masses and equipment falling by using <u>clamp stands</u>. Make sure masses are of a <u>sensible weight</u> so they don't break the equipment they're used with, and use <u>pulleys</u> of a sensible <u>length</u>.

3) When <u>heating</u> materials, make sure to let them <u>cool</u> before moving them, or wear <u>insulated gloves</u> while handling them. If you're using an <u>immersion heater</u> to heat liquids, you should always let it <u>dry out</u> in air, just in case any liquid has leaked inside the heater.

4) If you're using a <u>laser</u>, there are a few safety rules you must follow. Always wear <u>laser safety goggles</u> and never <u>look directly into</u> the laser or shine it <u>towards another person</u>. Make sure you turn the laser <u>off</u> if it's not needed to avoid any accidents.

5) When working with electronics, make sure you use a <u>low</u> enough <u>voltage</u> and <u>current</u> to prevent wires <u>overheating</u> (and potentially melting) and avoid <u>damage to components</u>, like blowing a filament bulb.

6) You also need to be aware of <u>general safety</u> in the lab — handle <u>glassware</u> carefully so it doesn't <u>break</u>, don't stick your fingers in sockets and avoid touching frayed wires.

7) Before starting an experiment, you should write out a <u>detailed risk assessment</u> (see page 142) and <u>method</u>. This way, you can make sure you carry out your experiment accurately and safely.

Make Sure You Can Draw Diagrams of Your Experiments

1) When you're writing out a <u>method</u> for your experiment, it's always a good idea to draw a <u>labelled diagram</u> showing how your apparatus will be <u>set up</u>.

2) The easiest way to do this is to use a scientific drawing, where each piece of apparatus is drawn as if you're looking at its <u>cross-section</u>. For example:

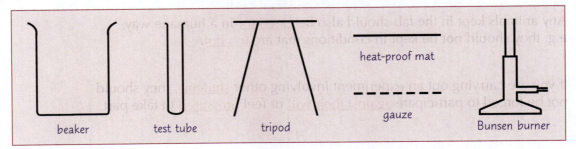

These simple diagrams are clear and easy to draw...

Have a go at <u>drawing diagrams</u> of the experimental set-ups for some of the practicals covered in this book. It'll give you practice at doing them, as well as reminding you how to set up the experiments.

Practical Skills

Safety and Ethics

*Science can be quite dangerous at times, so it's important that you keep yourself (and others) **safe** in the lab. Some experiments can also involve **ethical issues** that you must deal with respectfully and responsibly*

Make Sure you Work Safely Around Hazardous Chemicals

1) The substances used in chemical reactions are often hazardous. For example, they might catch fire easily (they're flammable), or they might irritate or burn your skin if you come into contact with them.

2) Whenever you're doing an experiment, you should wear a lab coat, safety goggles and gloves. Also, make sure that you're wearing sensible clothing when you're in the lab (e.g. open shoes won't protect your feet from spillages).

3) Always be careful that the chemicals you're using aren't flammable before you go lighting any Bunsen burners, and make sure you're working in an area that's well ventilated.

4) If you're doing an experiment that might produce nasty gases (such as chlorine), you should carry out the experiment in a fume hood so that the gas can't escape out into the room you're working in.

5) Never directly touch any chemicals (even if you're wearing gloves). Use a spatula to transfer solids between containers. Carefully pour liquids between different containers, using a funnel to avoid spillages.

6) Be careful when you're mixing chemicals, as a reaction might occur.

You Need to Think About Ethical Issues In Your Experiments

1) Any organisms involved in your investigations need to be treated safely and ethically.

2) Animals need to be treated humanely — they should be handled carefully and any wild animals captured for studying should be returned to their original habitat.

3) Any animals kept in the lab should also be cared for in a humane way, e.g. they should not be kept in conditions that are too hot.

4) If you are carrying out an experiment involving other students, they should not be forced to participate against their will or feel pressured to take part.

Proper lab attire includes a lab coat, safety goggles and gloves

The stuff on this page is all for your own good. It will help you in the exam, and make sure you stay safe in the lab. Make sure that you also pay attention to the specific hazards of the chemicals that you're using in your experiment. For a reminder, take a look at page 141.

Practical Skills

Practice Exams

Once you've been through all the questions in this book, you should feel pretty confident about the exams. As final preparation, here is a set of **practice exams** to really get you set for the real thing. The time allowed for each paper is 1 hour 10 minutes. These papers are designed to give you the best possible preparation for your exams.

GCSE Combined Science

Paper 1: Biology 1

Higher Tier

In addition to this paper you should have:
- A ruler.
- A calculator.

Centre name				
Centre number				
Candidate number				

Time allowed:
- 1 hour 10 minutes

Surname
Other names
Candidate signature

Instructions to candidates
- Write your name and other details in the spaces provided above.
- Answer **all** questions in the spaces provided.
- Do all rough work on the paper.
- Cross out any work you do not want to be marked.
- You are allowed to use a calculator.

Information for candidates
- The marks available are given in brackets at the end of each question.
- There are 60 marks available for this paper.
- You should use good English and present your answers in a clear and organised way.
- For questions marked with an asterisk (*) ensure that your answers have a logical structure, with points that link together clearly, and include detailed, relevant information.

Advice to candidates
- In calculations show clearly how you worked out your answers.
- Read each question carefully before answering it.
- Check your answers if you have time.

For examiner's use

Q	Attempt Nº			Q	Attempt Nº		
	1	2	3		1	2	3
1				4			
2				5			
3				6			
				Total			

1 **Figure 1** shows an animal cell.

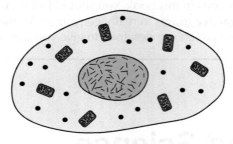

Figure 1

(a) Give **two** ways in which the cell in **Figure 1** is different from a bacterial cell.

....

....

....

[2 marks]

(b) Not all animal cells have the same structures as the cell in **Figure 1**. Explain why.

....

....

[1 mark]

Figure 2 shows a single-celled organism called *Euglena*, found in pond water.

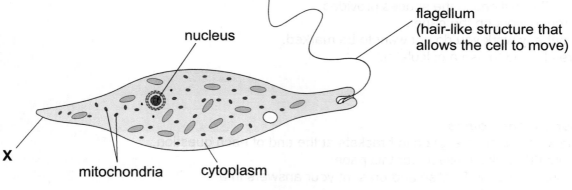

Figure 2

(c) What is the name of the subcellular structure labelled **X**?

☐ **A** ribosome

☐ **B** chloroplast

☐ **C** vacuole

☐ **D** cell membrane

[1 mark]

(d) A scientist viewed an individual *Euglena* under a microscope with × 150 magnification.
The real length of the *Euglena* was calculated to be 0.054 mm.
Calculate the length of the image of the *Euglena* in mm. Use the formula:

$$\text{magnification} = \frac{\text{image size}}{\text{real size}}$$

.... mm
[2 marks]

(e) When *Euglena* was first discovered, scientists disagreed over whether it was a plant or an animal. Give **two** similarities and **two** differences between plant and animal cells.

....

....

....

....

....

....

....

....

[4 marks]

[Total 10 marks]

Turn over for the next question

2 Communicable diseases can be spread between individuals.

(a) Zika virus disease is an example of a communicable disease.
The virus that causes the disease is spread by a mosquito vector.
Suggest **two** ways that the spread of the Zika virus disease could be reduced.

....

....

....

[2 marks]

(b) Which of the following communicable diseases is also spread by a vector?

☐ **A** influenza

☐ **B** malaria

☐ **C** HIV

☐ **D** athlete's foot

[1 mark]

(c) Tuberculosis (TB) is a communicable disease caused by *Mycobacterium tuberculosis* bacteria.
A strain of this bacteria was observed to have cells that divided every 18 hours on average.

Give the number of cells that would be produced from one bacterium of this strain in 3 days.

.... cells
[2 marks]

(d) The TB vaccine protects against tuberculosis.
Explain how immunisation helps to protect the body against a disease.

....

....

....

....

....

....

....

[4 marks]

[Total 9 marks]

3 Research from the Human Genome Project can be used to improve human health.

(a) What is meant by the term 'genome'?

☐ **A** A section of DNA that codes for a particular protein.

☐ **B** All of an organism's DNA.

☐ **C** A long coiled up molecule of DNA.

☐ **D** A unit containing a sugar, a phosphate group and a base.

[1 mark]

Cystic fibrosis is an inherited disorder caused by a recessive allele.

(b) Suggest how the Human Genome Project could have the potential to help people with cystic fibrosis.

....

....

[1 mark]

A couple have a baby boy. The doctor tells them that the baby has inherited cystic fibrosis. Neither parent shows signs of the disorder.

(c) In the space below, construct a diagram to show how the baby inherited cystic fibrosis.

Your diagram should show the genotypes of both parents, the genotypes of their gametes, and all the possible genotypes of their offspring.

Use **F** to represent the dominant allele and **f** to represent the recessive allele.

[3 marks]

Question 3 continues on the next page

Turn over ▶

The family pedigree in **Figure 3** shows a family with a history of cystic fibrosis.

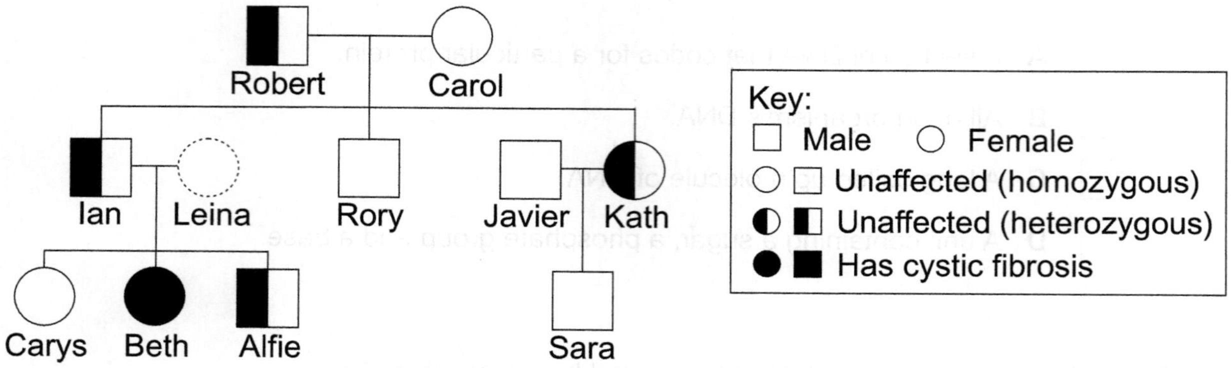

Figure 3

Key:
- ☐ Male ○ Female
- ○ ☐ Unaffected (homozygous)
- ◐ ◨ Unaffected (heterozygous)
- ● ■ Has cystic fibrosis

(d) Using the information in **Figure 3**, state what Leina's genotype must be. Explain your answer.

....
....
....
....
[2 marks]

(e) Carys and Beth are sisters. Carys has a scar on her hand. Beth does not.

Explain whether this is an example of genetic variation, environmental variation, or a combination of both.

....
....
....
[2 marks]
[Total 9 marks]

4   The peppered moth is an insect that lives on the trunks of trees in Britain.
    The moths are prey for birds such as thrushes.
    The peppered moth exists in two varieties, shown in **Figure 4**.

1. A light-coloured variety — they are better camouflaged on tree trunks in unpolluted areas.

2. A dark-coloured variety — they are better camouflaged on sooty tree trunks in badly polluted areas.

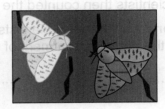

Figure 4

The bar charts in **Figure 5** show the percentages of dark- and light-coloured peppered moths in two different towns.

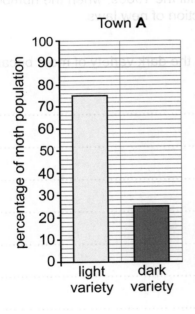
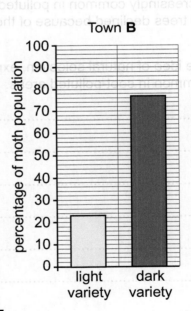

Figure 5

(a) State which town, **A** or **B**, is the most polluted. Give a reason for your answer.

....

....

[1 mark]

Question 4 continues on the next page

Turn over ▶

(b) Calculate the difference in percentage between the dark-coloured moth population in Town **A** and Town **B**. Show your working.

..............................%
[2 marks]

Collecting the data shown in **Figure 5** involved leaving traps overnight, with lights inside to attract moths. The scientists then counted the moths that had been captured, before releasing them.

(c) Suggest **one** way that the scientists carrying out this investigation could have helped to ensure the humane treatment of the moths.

....

....
[1 mark]

The dark variety of the moth was first recorded in the north of England in 1848.
It became increasingly common in polluted areas until the 1960s, when the number of soot-covered trees declined because of the introduction of new laws.

(d) Using the idea of natural selection, explain why the dark variety of moth became more common in soot-polluted areas.

....

....

....

....

....

....

....
[4 marks]

[Total 8 marks]

5 A student did an experiment to investigate the effect of pH on the action of the enzyme amylase. The method used is shown in **Figure 6**.

> 1. Add a set quantity of starch solution to a test tube and the same quantity of amylase solution to another.
> 2. Add a set quantity of a buffer solution with a pH of 5 to the tube containing starch solution.
> 3. Place all of the test tubes in a water bath at 35 °C.
> 4. Allow the starch and amylase solutions to reach the temperature of the water bath, then mix them together and return the mixture to the water bath.
> 5. Take a small sample of the mixture every minute and test for starch.
> 6. Stop the experiment when starch is no longer present in the sample, or after 30 minutes (whichever is sooner).
> 7. Repeat the experiment using buffer solutions of different pH values.

Figure 6

(a) What happens to the starch during the experiment?

☐ **A** It is converted into amino acids.

☐ **B** It is converted into sugars.

☐ **C** It is converted into glycerol.

☐ **D** It is converted into fatty acids.

[1 mark]

(b) Explain why a set quantity of starch solution was used for each repeat in the experiment.

....

....

[1 mark]

(c) Describe how the student could have tested for the presence of starch in **Step 5**.

....

....

....

....

....

[3 marks]

Question 5 continues on the next page

Turn over ▶

Figure 7 shows a graph of the student's results.

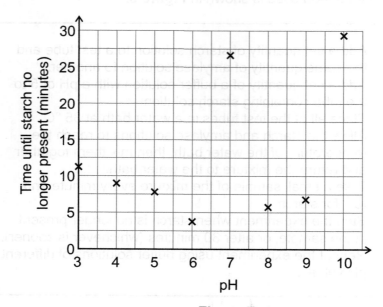

Figure 7

(d) Describe the trend shown in the graph in **Figure 7**, between **pH 3** and **pH 6**.

....

....
[1 mark]

(e) (i) The student thinks that one of the results shown on the graph is likely to be anomalous. Identify the anomalous result and give a reason for your answer.

....

....

....
[2 marks]

(ii) Suggest **one** factor that could have caused this anomalous result.

....

....

....
[1 mark]
[Total 9 marks]

6 A scientist was investigating the reflex actions of men and women.

The scientist made the following hypothesis:

'Men have faster reaction times than women.'

The reaction times of eight participants were tested in the investigation.
Each participant was tapped just below the knee with a small rubber hammer.
When the leg was tapped it automatically kicked outwards at the knee.

The scientist recorded how long it took each participant to respond to the stimulus of the tap on the leg. Each participant did the test 20 times, and a mean reaction time was calculated (to 2 decimal places).

The results are shown in **Figure 8**.

Sex	Participant	Mean reaction time (s)
Female	1	0.05
	2	0.06
	3	0.06
	4	0.04
Male	5	0.05
	6	0.04
	7	0.04
	8	0.05

Figure 8

(a) Using all the information above, give **two** reasons that support the idea that the participants' response was a reflex.

....

....

....

[2 marks]

(b) (i) What was the dependent variable in this experiment?

☐ A number of participants

☐ B stimulus

☐ C reaction time

☐ D sex

[1 mark]

Question 6 continues on the next page

Turn over ▶

(ii) What was the independent variable in this experiment?

☐ A number of participants
☐ B stimulus
☐ C reaction time
☐ D sex

[1 mark]

(c) **Figure 9** shows the mean reaction times for males and females in the investigation.

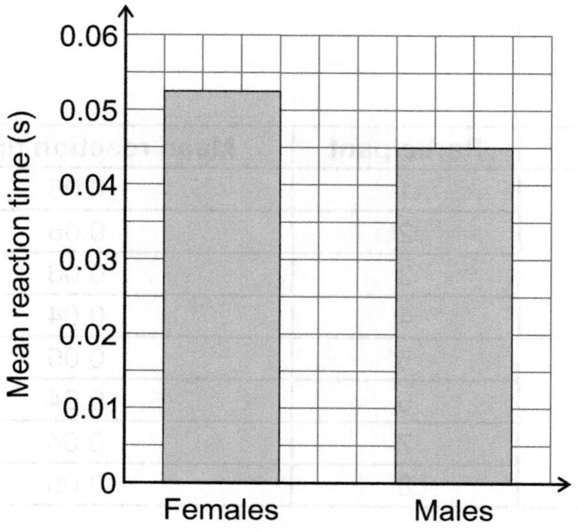

Figure 9

State whether or not the data shown in **Figure 9** supports the scientist's hypothesis. Explain your answer.

....
....

[2 marks]

(d) Suggest **two** variables that the scientist should have controlled in this experiment.

....
....

[2 marks]

Another example of a reflex is the response of moving your hand away from a painful stimulus. **Figure 10** shows the parts of the nervous system involved in this reflex.

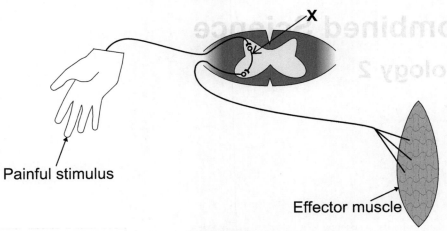

Figure 10

(e) (i) Name part **X** shown in **Figure 10**.

....

[1 mark]

*(ii) The pain stimulus is detected by receptors in the skin and causes a reflex response. Describe the path taken by a nervous impulse in this reflex, beginning at the receptors.

....

....

....

....

....

....

....

....

[6 marks]

[Total 15 marks]

END OF QUESTIONS

GCSE Combined Science
Paper 2: Biology 2
Higher Tier

In addition to this paper you should have:
- A ruler.
- A calculator.

Centre name				
Centre number				
Candidate number				

Time allowed:
- 1 hour 10 minutes

Surname	
Other names	
Candidate signature	

Instructions to candidates
- Write your name and other details in the spaces provided above.
- Answer **all** questions in the spaces provided.
- Do all rough work on the paper.
- Cross out any work you do not want to be marked.
- You are allowed to use a calculator.

Information for candidates
- The marks available are given in brackets at the end of each question.
- There are 60 marks available for this paper.
- You should use good English and present your answers in a clear and organised way.
- For questions marked with an asterisk (*) ensure that your answers have a logical structure, with points that link together clearly, and include detailed, relevant information.

Advice to candidates
- In calculations show clearly how you worked out your answers.
- Read each question carefully before answering it.
- Check your answers if you have time.

For examiner's use

Q	Attempt Nº			Q	Attempt Nº		
	1	2	3		1	2	3
1				4			
2				5			
3				6			
				Total			

1   A student was investigating the distribution of buttercups in an area around a school. The student counted the number of buttercups in 10 quadrats in five different fields. The quadrat measured 1 m². The results are shown in **Figure 1**.

Field	Mean number of buttercups per quadrat
A	10
B	35
C	21
D	37
E	21

Figure 1

(a) What is the median of the data in **Figure 1**?

Median = ...
[1 mark]

(b) The student used a random number generator to pick the coordinates to place the quadrats.
Suggest why the quadrats were placed randomly.

....
....
[1 mark]

(c) A week later, the student repeated the experiment in a sixth field, Field **F**.
The results for each quadrat are shown below:

6   15   9   14   20   5   3   11   10   7

Using this data, calculate the mean number of buttercups per m² in Field **F**.

Mean = ... buttercups per m²
[1 mark]

Question 1 continues on the next page

Turn over ▶

(d) Field **F** measures 90 m by 120 m.
Estimate the population of buttercups in Field **F**.

Estimated population = ... buttercups
[2 marks]

(e) The student observed that the distribution of buttercups changed across Field **A**.
Buttercups grow well in damp soil, so the student thinks that the change in the distribution of buttercups is due to variability in the moisture level of the soil across the field.

The student wants to investigate the hypothesis that more buttercups grow where there is a higher moisture level in the soil.
Describe how the student could investigate this hypothesis.

....

....

....

....

....

....

....

[4 marks]

[Total 9 marks]

2 Lactose is a reducing sugar commonly found in dairy products, such as milk and cheese. An enzyme called lactase breaks down lactose during digestion. The resulting products are the sugars glucose and galactose. These are absorbed into the blood from the small intestine.

(a) Suggest an explanation for why the breakdown of sugars like lactose into simpler sugars is necessary for organisms.

....

....

....
[2 marks]

(b) Glucose diffuses from the small intestine into the blood.
Describe how the concentration of glucose in the blood compares to that in the small intestine.

....

....
[1 mark]

(c) The optimum pH of lactase is pH 6.
State and explain what effect a pH of 12 would have on the break down of lactose by lactase.

....

....
[2 marks]

(d) Lactose intolerance is a digestive problem caused by insufficient production of lactase.
To test a person for lactose intolerance, they are given a drink of lactose solution.
A blood sample is then taken from them every 30 minutes for two hours.
The blood is tested to see how much glucose it contains.

Explain what will happen to the blood glucose level of a person who is lactose intolerant during the test.

....

....

....

....
[2 marks]

[Total 7 marks]

Turn over for the next question

Turn over ▶

3 The lung is a specialised gas exchange organ.
It contains millions of air sacs called alveoli.
Figure 2 shows an alveolus and a blood capillary.

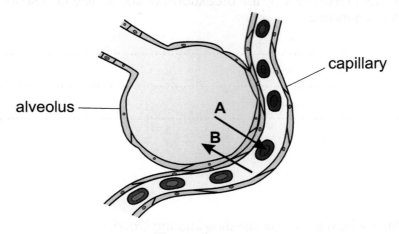

Figure 2

(a) The arrows in **Figure 2** show the net movement of two gases, **A** and **B**.
What are the names of gases **A** and **B**?

	Gas A	Gas B
☐ A	oxygen	nitrogen
☐ B	carbon dioxide	oxygen
☐ C	oxygen	carbon dioxide
☐ D	carbon dioxide	nitrogen

[1 mark]

(b) Explain why alveoli need a good blood supply.

....

....

....

[2 marks]

(c) **Figure 2** shows red blood cells travelling through a capillary.
Red blood cells are flexible, which allows them to fit through capillaries.

(i) State the function of red blood cells.

....
[1 mark]

(ii) Explain how red blood cells are adapted to their function.

....
....
....
....
[3 marks]

Sickle cell anaemia is a genetic disorder of the blood where the red blood cells become rigid and sickle-shaped. **Figure 3** shows a sickle-shaped red blood cell and some normal red blood cells.

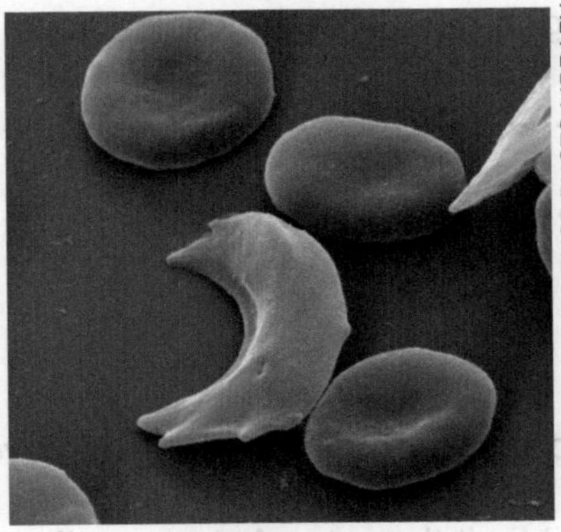

Figure 3

(d) A person with sickle cell anaemia may experience an increase in breathing rate.
Suggest why they may experience this symptom.

....
....
....
....
[2 marks]

[Total 9 marks]

Turn over for the next question

Turn over ▶

4 **Figure 4** shows the carbon cycle.

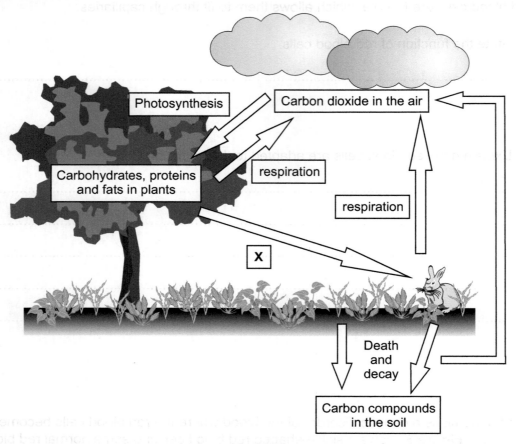

Figure 4

(a) Describe what is occurring at point **X** in the cycle shown in **Figure 4**.

....

....
[1 mark]

(b) Photosynthesis is an important process in the carbon cycle.

   (i) Give **three** factors that limit the rate of photosynthesis.

   1. ....

   2. ....

   3. ....
[3 marks]

   (ii) Photosynthesis is an endothermic reaction. Explain what this means.

   ....
[1 mark]

(c) What is the word equation for aerobic respiration?

☐ **A** glucose + oxygen → carbon dioxide + water

☐ **B** glucose → ethanol + carbon dioxide

☐ **C** glucose → carbon dioxide + water

☐ **D** glucose + oxygen → carbon dioxide

[1 mark]

(d) Explain how microorganisms are involved in the carbon cycle.

....

....

....
[2 marks]

(e) (i) Microorganisms also play a role in the nitrogen cycle.
Which type of microorganisms turn nitrates in the soil into nitrogen gas?

☐ **A** nitrifying bacteria

☐ **B** denitrifying bacteria

☐ **C** nitrogen fixing bacteria

☐ **D** decomposers

[1 mark]

(ii) Some microorganisms live in root nodules on legume plant and turn atmospheric nitrogen into ammonia. Farmers sometimes include these plants in a crop rotation cycle to help return nitrogen compounds to the soil which are lost when crops are harvested instead of being left to decompose.

Give **one** other way that farmers can increase the amount of nitrates in the soil.

....
[1 mark]
[Total 10 marks]

Turn over for the next question

Turn over ▶

5   A scientist measured the rate of transpiration in two plants over 48 hours. The results are shown in **Figure 5**.

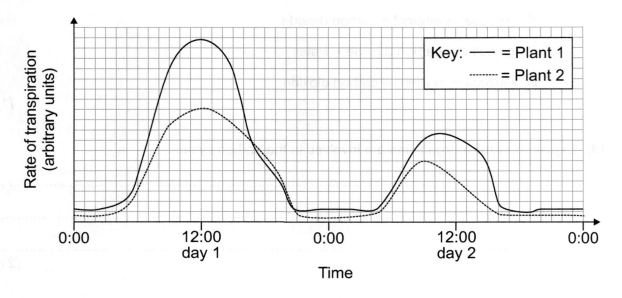

Figure 5

(a) Define the term 'transpiration'.

....

....
[1 mark]

(b) (i) At what time on **day 2** was the rate of transpiration highest for **plant 2**?

☐ A 06:00

☐ B 09:00

☐ C 11:00

☐ D 16:00

[1 mark]

(ii) The rate of transpiration for both plants was slower on **day 2** than on **day 1**. Suggest **one** reason for this and explain your suggestion.

....

....

....
[2 marks]

(c) Explain why the rate of transpiration is lower during the night.

....
....
....
....
[2 marks]

(d) Describe how a transpiration stream moves water through a plant.

....
....
....
....
....
[3 marks]

(e) (i) Plants absorb water from the soil through their roots.
What is the process by which mineral ions are absorbed into the root?

☐ A diffusion
☐ B active transport
☐ C osmosis
☐ D transpiration

[1 mark]

(ii) Describe how roots are adapted for absorbing water.

....
....
....
[2 marks]

[Total 12 marks]

Turn over for the next question

Turn over ▶

6 In humans, sexual reproduction involves the reproductive system.

(a) The male reproductive system includes the testes.
What hormone is produced by the testes?

☐ **A** testosterone

☐ **B** adrenaline

☐ **C** oestrogen

☐ **D** insulin

[1 mark]

Figure 6 shows the fluctuations in the levels of four different hormones during one 28 day menstrual cycle.

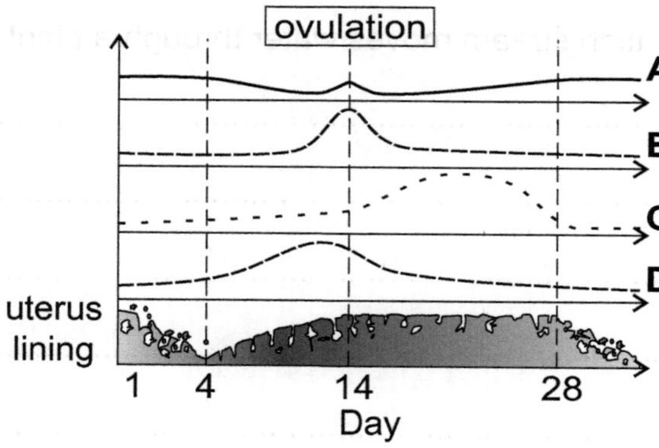

Figure 6

(b) State which line (**A-D**) in **Figure 6** represents progesterone and explain your answer.

....

....

[2 marks]

*(c) Describe how progesterone, LH, FSH and oestrogen interact to control the menstrual cycle.

....

....

....

....

....

....

....

....

....

[6 marks]

Some methods of contraception use reproductive hormones to control fertility.
One such method is the contraceptive implant, shown in **Figure 7**.

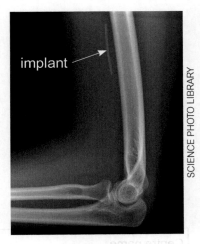

Figure 7

The contraceptive implant:

- is a small, plastic rod that is inserted by a doctor or nurse
- releases progesterone, which reduces fertility
- is effective for three years
- is over 99% effective at preventing pregnancy
- can cause side effects such as headaches and nausea
- can be made less effective by certain medications

Figure 8 shows a condom. The condom is a barrier method of contraception.

Figure 8

The condom:

- is worn over the penis during intercourse
- prevents sperm from entering the vagina
- can only be used once
- is 98% effective at preventing pregnancy when used correctly
- protects against sexually transmitted infections (STIs)

(d) Use the information to evaluate the implant and condom as methods of contraception.
Give a conclusion of which you think is the better method of contraception.
Justify your conclusion.

....

....

....

....

....

....

....

[4 marks]
[Total 13 marks]

END OF QUESTIONS

GCSE Combined Science
Paper 3: Chemistry 1
Higher Tier

In addition to this paper you should have:
- A ruler.
- A calculator.

Centre name				
Centre number				
Candidate number				

Time allowed:
- 1 hour 10 minutes

Surname	
Other names	
Candidate signature	

Instructions to candidates
- Write your name and other details in the spaces provided above.
- Answer **all** questions in the spaces provided.
- Do all rough work on the paper.
- Cross out any work you do not want to be marked.
- You are allowed to use a calculator.

Information for candidates
- The marks available are given in brackets at the end of each question.
- There are 60 marks available for this paper.
- You should use good English and present your answers in a clear and organised way.
- For questions marked with an asterisk (*) ensure that your answers have a logical structure with points that link together clearly, and include detailed, relevant information.

Advice to candidates
- In calculations show clearly how you worked out your answers.
- Read each question carefully before answering it.
- Check your answers if you have time.

For examiner's use

Q	Attempt Nº 1	2	3	Q	Attempt Nº 1	2	3
1				4			
2				5			
3				6			
				Total			

1   Atoms contain protons, neutrons and electrons.

(a) **Figure 1** shows the structure of an atom.
    Label a proton.

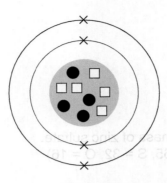

Figure 1

[1 mark]

(b) Where is most of the mass found in an atom?

☐ **A** in the neutrons

☐ **B** in the nucleus

☐ **C** in the electrons

☐ **D** in the electron shells

[1 mark]

Figure 2 shows the numbers of protons, neutrons and electrons in six different atoms.

Atom	Number of protons	Number of neutrons	Number of electrons
A	5	6	5
B	7	7	7
C	6	8	6
D	6	6	6
E	10	10	10
F	4	5	4

Figure 2

(c) Explain which **two** atoms in **Figure 2** are isotopes of the same element.

....

....

....

[2 marks]

Question 1 continues on the next page

Turn over ▶

(d) Zinc sulfate is an ionic compound with the formula $ZnSO_4$.

  (i) What is the charge on a sulfate ion?

  ☐ A +1

  ☐ B −1

  ☐ C +2

  ☐ D −2

  [1 mark]

  (ii) Calculate the relative formula mass of zinc sulfate.
  (relative atomic masses: Zn = 65, S = 32, O = 16)

  relative formula mass = ...
  [2 marks]

  (iii) Calculate the number of oxygen atoms in 1.4 moles of zinc sulfate.

  Give your answer to two significant figures.

  Number of oxygen atoms = ...
  [3 marks]
  [Total 10 marks]

2 Carbon dioxide is a simple molecular substance.

(a) Which one of the following is a typical size of a simple molecule such as carbon dioxide?

☐ A 10^{-10} m

☐ B 10^{-6} m

☐ C 10^{-12} m

☐ D 10^{-11} m

[1 mark]

(b) Explain why carbon dioxide does **not** conduct electricity.

Give your answer in terms of electrons.

....

....
[1 mark]

(c) Carbon dioxide is produced when a fuel reacts with oxygen in a combustion reaction.

Some data about the properties of oxygen is shown in **Figure 3**.

Melting point	Boiling point
−218 °C	−183 °C

Figure 3

(i) Predict the physical state of oxygen at −198 °C.

....
[1 mark]

(ii) Predict whether carbon dioxide would have a higher or lower boiling point than oxygen. Explain your answer.

....

....

....
[3 marks]

(d) Carbon dioxide can also be produced by heating zinc carbonate ($ZnCO_3$).

Zinc oxide (ZnO) is left behind.

The equation for the reaction is:

$$ZnCO_3 \rightarrow CO_2 + ZnO$$

1.32 kg of carbon dioxide is produced when a sample of zinc carbonate is heated.

Calculate the mass, in grams, of zinc carbonate that reacted.

(relative atomic masses: Zn = 65, C = 12, O = 16)

Mass of zinc carbonate = ... g
[4 marks]

[Total 10 marks]

Turn over ▶

3 A student reacts four different metals with dilute sulfuric acid.

The student controls all of the relevant variables to make sure that the test is fair.

The gas that is given off by each reaction is collected in a gas syringe.

Figure 4 shows all four reactions after 30 seconds.

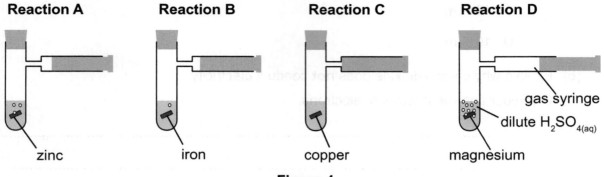

Figure 4

(a) State the dependent variable in this experiment.

....

[1 mark]

(b) Hydrogen gas is produced during the reaction.

Describe a method that could be used to test for hydrogen gas, and state the result you would expect to find.

....

....

....

[2 marks]

(c) Explain which reaction, **A**, **B**, **C**, or **D**, contains the **most reactive** metal.

....

....

....

[3 marks]

(d) In another experiment, the student placed pieces of different metals in metal salt solutions and leaves them for 10 minutes. The student then recorded whether any reaction had occurred. The results of this experiment are shown in **Figure 5**.

	Did any reaction occur with the following metal salt solutions?		
	Iron sulfate	**Magnesium sulfate**	**Copper sulfate**
Iron	No	No	....
Magnesium	....	No	Yes
Copper	No	No	No

Figure 5

Complete **Figure 5** by filling in the gaps.

[2 marks]

(e) The equation for the reaction between magnesium and copper sulfate solution is:

$$Mg_{(s)} + CuSO_{4(aq)} \rightarrow MgSO_{4(aq)} + Cu_{(s)}$$

In this reaction, magnesium loses electrons.

What is the name given to this process?

☐ A electrolysis

☐ B reduction

☐ C neutralisation

☐ D oxidation

[1 mark]

[Total 9 marks]

Turn over for the next question

Turn over ▶

4 A student is investigating how much calcium hydroxide is needed to neutralise 25 cm³ of 0.8 mol dm⁻³ hydrochloric acid.

The student used the following method:

1. Measure out the hydrochloric acid into a conical flask.
2. Measure out 0.1 g of solid calcium hydroxide using a mass balance.
3. Add the calcium hydroxide to the hydrochloric acid.
4. Wait for the calcium hydroxide to react completely.
5. Record the pH of the solution.
6. Repeat steps 2-5 until all of the hydrochloric acid has reacted.

(a) Suggest a piece of apparatus that the student could have used to measure out the hydrochloric acid.

....

[1 mark]

(b) Use the information above to calculate the mass of hydrochloric acid present in the 25 cm³ solution that the student used.
(relative formula mass of HCl = 36.5)

Mass of hydrochloric acid = ... g

[2 marks]

(c) (i) Describe what the student would have observed once all of the acid in the flask had reacted.

....

....

[1 mark]

(ii) Write the ionic equation for a neutralisation reaction.

Include state symbols in your answer.

....

[2 marks]

(d) (i) The student plotted a graph to show how the pH of the solution changed as the calcium hydroxide was added. The results are shown in **Figure 6**.

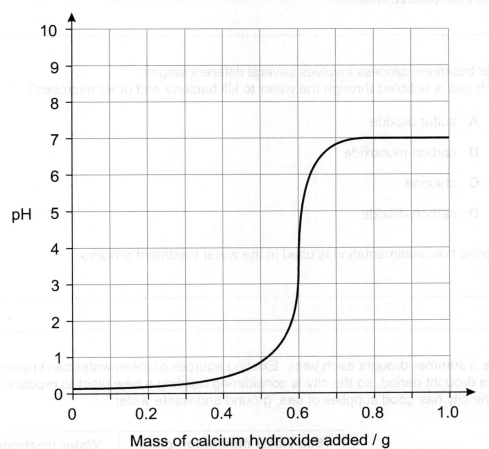

Figure 6

What mass of calcium hydroxide was required to completely neutralise the acid?

Mass of calcium hydroxide = ... g
[1 mark]

Another student is going to repeat the experiment using Universal indicator to measure how the pH of the solution changes during the experiment.

(ii) Explain why this student would not be able to produce a graph like **Figure 6** using the results they gather.

....

....
[1 mark]

(iii) Suggest a piece of equipment that could be used to accurately record the pH value of the solution over the course of the experiment.

....
[1 mark]

[Total 9 marks]

Turn over for the next question

Turn over ▶

5 Water is made potable using several methods.

(a) Define the term potable water.

....
[1 mark]

(b) The water treatment process involves several different stages.
   (i) Which gas is bubbled through the water to kill bacteria and other microbes?

   ☐ A sulfur dioxide

   ☐ B carbon monoxide

   ☐ C chlorine

   ☐ D carbon dioxide

[1 mark]

   (ii) Describe how sedimentation is used in the water treatment process.

....

....
[2 marks]

(c) A city has a summer drought each year. Existing sources of clean water can't meet demand during the drought period, so the city is considering building a new plant to produce clean water. The city has good supplies of sea, ground and waste water.

	Sea water distillation plant	Water treatment plant
Energy usage	very high	moderate
Suitable water source/s	sea water	ground and waste water

Figure 7

Using the information from **Figure 7** and your own knowledge, evaluate whether the city should build a sea water distillation plant or a water treatment plant.

....

....

....

....

....
[4 marks]

[Total 8 marks]

6 A student wanted to find out which of five dyes could be present in a particular black ink.

(a) The student was asked to suggest a method.

This is the method the student suggested:

- Take a piece of filter paper. Draw a pencil line near the bottom.
- Add spots of the dyes to the line at regular intervals.
- Put the paper into a beaker of water with the line just touching the water.
- Repeat these steps with a spot of the black ink on a second piece of filter paper, and put this paper into a beaker of ethanol.
- Place a lid on each beaker, and wait for the solvents to travel to the top of the paper.
- Compare the positions of the spots created by the black ink with those created by the dyes.

Identify **two** problems with this method. For each problem, suggest how you would alter the method to carry out the experiment correctly.

You can assume the student takes sensible safety precautions.

Problem 1 ....

....

Correction ....

....

....

Problem 2 ....

....

Correction ....

....

....

[4 marks]

Question 6 continues on the next page

Turn over ▶

(b) What property of the dyes makes them suitable for separation by chromatography?

☐ **A** They have different reactivities.

☐ **B** They have different melting points.

☐ **C** They have different solubilities.

☐ **D** They have different melting points.

[1 mark]

The student repeated the experiment using the correct method.
The results are shown in **Figure 8**.

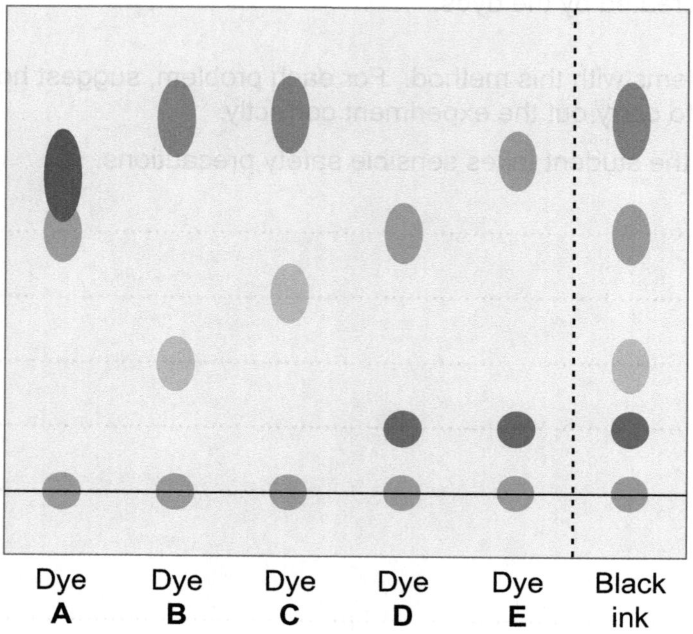

Diagram not to scale.

Dye A   Dye B   Dye C   Dye D   Dye E   Black ink

Figure 8

(c) Which dyes (**A-E**) could be present in the black ink? Explain your answer.

Dyes ....

Explanation ....

....

....

[2 marks]

(d) The student measured the distances moved by the solvent and one of the spots in the black ink. The student found that the solvent had moved 6.4 cm from the baseline, and that the spot had moved 4.8 cm.

Calculate the R_f value of the spot in the black ink.

R_f value = ...
[1 mark]

*(e) The ink is a mixture of dyes that are dissolved in a solvent.
The solvent has a much lower boiling point than all of the dyes in the ink.

Describe how simple distillation could be used to separate the solvent from the rest of the ink mixture.

....

[6 marks]

[Total 14 marks]

END OF QUESTIONS

424

GCSE Combined Science
Paper 4: Chemistry 2
Higher Tier

In addition to this paper you should have:
- A ruler.
- A calculator.

Centre name			
Centre number			
Candidate number			

Time allowed:
- 1 hour 10 minutes

Surname	
Other names	
Candidate signature	

Instructions to candidates
- Write your name and other details in the spaces provided above.
- Answer **all** questions in the spaces provided.
- Do all rough work on the paper.
- Cross out any work you do not want to be marked.
- You are allowed to use a calculator.

Information for candidates
- The marks available are given in brackets at the end of each question.
- There are 60 marks available for this paper.
- You should use good English and present your answers in a clear and organised way.
- For questions marked with an asterisk (*) ensure that your answers have a logical structure with points that link together clearly, and include detailed, relevant information.

Advice to candidates
- In calculations show clearly how you worked out your answers.
- Read each question carefully before answering it.
- Check your answers if you have time.

For examiner's use							
Q	Attempt Nº			Q	Attempt Nº		
	1	2	3		1	2	3
1				4			
2				5			
3				6			
				Total			

1 The halogens make up Group 7 of the periodic table.
Figure 1 shows some of the physical properties of the first four halogens.

Halogen	Atomic number	Melting Point / °C	Boiling Point / °C	Colour at room temperature
Fluorine	9	−220	−188	very pale yellow
Chlorine	17		−34	green
Bromine	35	−7	59	
Iodine	53	114	185	dark grey

Figure 1

(a) (i) Predict the melting point of chlorine, using the data in the table.

☐ **A** −231 °C

☐ **B** −216 °C

☐ **C** −101 °C

☐ **D** 107 °C

[1 mark]

(ii) Explain your answer to part **(i)**.

....

....
[1 mark]

(b) Which of the following options best describes the appearance of bromine at room temperature.

☐ **A** a red-brown gas

☐ **B** a green-brown gas

☐ **C** a dark green liquid

☐ **D** a red-brown liquid

[1 mark]

(c) Write down the balanced equation for the reaction between bromine (Br_2) and potassium iodide (KI).

....
[2 marks]

(d) Chlorine is bubbled through sodium iodide solution. Explain what will happen.
Give your answer in terms of the relative positions of chlorine and iodine in the periodic table.

....

....

....

....
[3 marks]

(e) The halogens can react with hydrogen (H_2) to form hydrogen halides.
Write the balanced equation for the reaction between hydrogen and fluorine (F_2).

....
[2 marks]

[Total 10 marks]

Turn over for the next question

Turn over ▶

2   A student is investigating how the rate of the reaction between marble chips (calcium carbonate) and hydrochloric acid is affected by the concentration of the acid.
The student compares different concentrations of acid by measuring how long it takes for the reaction to produce 20 cm³ of carbon dioxide gas.

The results of the experiment are shown in **Figure 2**.

Concentration of acid (mol dm⁻³)	Time (s)
0.2	58
0.4	29
0.6	18
0.8	15
1.0	12

Figure 2

(a) (i) Complete and balance the equation for the reaction between marble chips ($CaCO_3$) and hydrochloric acid (HCl).

.... + ... → $CaCl_2$ + ... + ...

[2 marks]

(ii) Plot the results shown in **Figure 2** on the axes below and draw a curve of best fit.

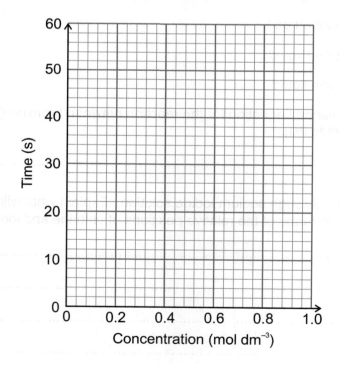

[2 marks]

(iii) Use your graph to predict the time that it would take for 20 cm³ of carbon dioxide gas to form with 0.5 mol dm⁻³ hydrochloric acid.

Time = ... s
[1 mark]

(b) Describe what the graph shows about the effect of concentration on the rate of reaction.

....

....
[1 mark]

(c) Explain, in terms of collision theory, why concentration affects the rate of a reaction.

....

....

....

....
[2 marks]

(d) The student carries out the experiment again using 0.6 mol dm⁻³ hydrochloric acid. This time powdered marble was used.

The student says "it will take longer than 18 seconds for 20 cm³ of carbon dioxide gas to form".

Is the student's prediction correct? Explain your answer.

....

....

....

....

....
[3 marks]
[Total 11 marks]

Turn over for the next question

Turn over ▶

3   Aqueous sodium thiosulfate and hydrochloric acid are clear, colourless solutions that react to form a yellow precipitate of sulfur.

An experiment is to be carried out to investigate the effect of temperature on the rate of this reaction.

25 cm³ of both reactants are used. Two different temperatures are investigated.

(a) Describe a method that could be used to carry out the experiment at each temperature being investigated.

....

....

....

....

....

....

....

....
[4 marks]

(b) Apart from the volumes of reactants, state **one** variable that needs to be kept constant throughout the experiment.

....
[1 mark]

(c) In terms of collision theory, explain how carrying out the experiment at a higher temperature will affect the rate of a reaction.

....

....

....

....
[2 marks]

[Total 7 marks]

4 Heptane and triacontane are two molecules that are present in two of the fractions produced by the fractional distillation of crude oil.

Figure 3 shows the boiling points of these two molecules.

Hydrocarbon	Chemical formula	Boiling point (°C)
Heptane	C_7H_{16}	98
Triacontane	$C_{30}H_{62}$	450

Figure 3

(a) Which of these two hydrocarbons would you expect to be collected further down the fractionating column?
Explain your answer, with reference to the boiling points of the hydrocarbons.

....

....

....

....
[2 marks]

(b) Cracking breaks down the products of fractional distillation into smaller molecules.

Figure 4 shows an example of cracking.

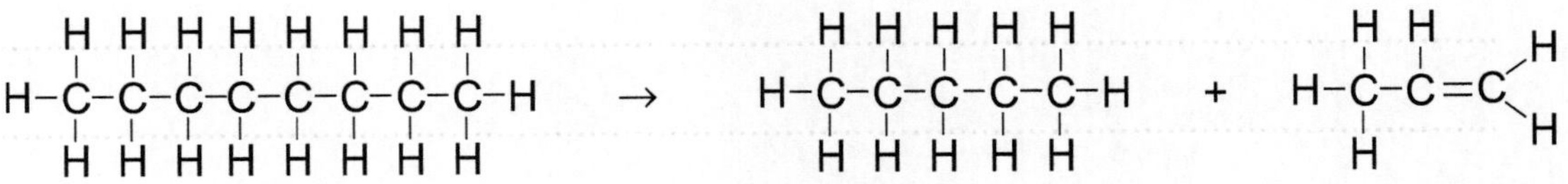

molecule X → pentane + propene

Figure 4

Which of the following is the chemical name given to molecule X?

☐ **A** ethanol

☐ **B** octane

☐ **C** decane

☐ **D** hept-1-ene

[1 mark]

Question 4 continues on the next page

Turn over ▶

(c) **Figure 5** shows the approximate supply and demand for some of the different fractions obtained from crude oil.

Fraction	Approximate % in crude oil	Approximate % demand
Gases	2	4
Petrol	16	27
Kerosene	13	
Diesel Oil	19	23
Fuel Oil and Bitumen	50	38

Figure 5

(i) Calculate the approximate percentage demand of kerosene.

.... %
[1 mark]

(ii) Using the data from **Figure 5**, suggest why fuel oil and bitumen, rather than diesel oil, are more likely to be cracked to provide petrol.

....

....

....

....

[2 marks]

[Total 6 marks]

5 Hydrogen can be burned in oxygen and used as a fuel.

$$2H_2 + O_2 \rightarrow 2H_2O$$

(a) Calculate the energy change for the reaction.
The bond energy values are given below.

Bond energy values (kJ mol⁻¹):

O=O 498

H–H 436

O–H 464

Energy change = ... kJ mol⁻¹

[4 marks]

(b) In another reaction, the energy change is exothermic.
Which of the following energy profiles shows the energy change of the reaction?

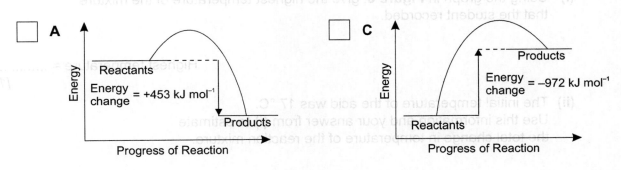

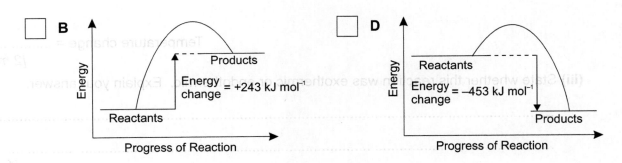

[1 mark]

Question 5 continues on the next page

(c) In another experiment, magnesium ribbon was reacted with dilute hydrochloric acid.

First, the initial temperature of the hydrochloric acid was recorded.

Magnesium was then added to the acid, and the temperature of the reaction mixture was measured at 10 second intervals.

The student's results are shown on the graph in **Figure 6**.

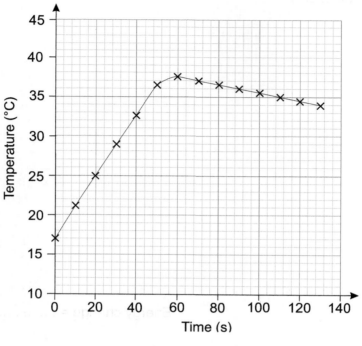

Figure 6

(i) Using the graph in **Figure 6**, give the highest temperature of the mixture that the student recorded.

Highest temperature = ... °C
[1 mark]

(ii) The initial temperature of the acid was 17 °C.
Use this information and your answer from **(i)** to estimate the total change in temperature of the reaction mixture.

Temperature change = ... °C
[2 marks]

(iii) State whether this reaction was exothermic or endothermic. Explain your answer.

....

....
[1 mark]
[Total 9 marks]

6   **Figure 7** shows the electronic structures of a sodium atom and a chlorine atom.

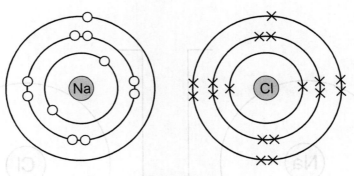

Figure 7

(a) Sodium is a group 1 metal.
Group 1 metals can react with non-metals to form ionic compounds.
Which of the following is the charge on a group 1 ion in an ionic compound?

☐ A   +2

☐ B   +3

☐ C   −1

☐ D   +1

[1 mark]

(b) Sodium and chlorine react to form the ionic compound sodium chloride.

(i) Which of the following is the correct balanced equation for the formation of sodium chloride?

☐ A   Na + Cl → NaCl

☐ B   2Na + Cl → Na$_2$Cl

☐ C   2Na + Cl$_2$ → 2NaCl

☐ D   4Na + Cl$_2$ → 2Na$_2$Cl

[1 mark]

Question 6 continues on the next page

Turn over ▶

(ii) Complete the dot and cross diagram of sodium chloride below.
Show only the outer electrons.

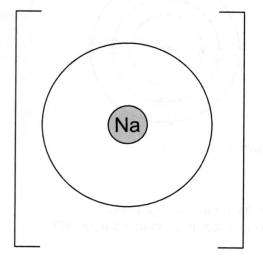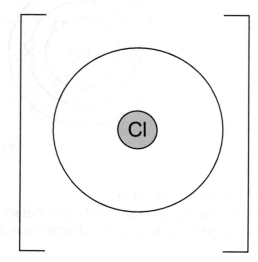

[4 marks]

(c) Chlorine has two major isotopes, ^{35}Cl and ^{37}Cl. ^{35}Cl has a relative abundance of 75%. Show that the relative atomic mass of chlorine is 35.5.

....

....

....
[2 marks]

(d) A teacher places small pieces of lithium, sodium and potassium into cold water. A student observes the reactions and decides that the order of reactivity of the three metals is:

- potassium (most reactive)
- sodium
- lithium (least reactive)

Explain the pattern of reactivity that the student has noticed in terms of the outer electrons of the atoms.

....

....

....

....
[3 marks]

*(e) The bonding between ions determines the properties of ionic structures. This is also true for the bonding between atoms in giant covalent structures such as diamond and graphite.

Figure 8 contains information about some of the properties of diamond and graphite.

	Hardness	Melting point	Conducts electricity?
Diamond	Hard	High	No
Graphite	Soft	High	Yes

Figure 8

Explain these properties of diamond and graphite in terms of their structure and bonding.

....

....

....

....

....

....

....

....

....

....

[6 marks]

[Total 17 marks]

END OF QUESTIONS

436

GCSE Combined Science
Paper 5: Physics 1
Higher Tier

In addition to this paper you should have:
- A ruler.
- A calculator.

Centre name	
Centre number	
Candidate number	

Time allowed:
- 1 hour 10 minutes

Surname	
Other names	
Candidate signature	

Instructions to candidates
- Write your name and other details in the spaces provided above.
- Answer **all** questions in the spaces provided.
- Do all rough work on the paper.
- Cross out any work you do not want to be marked.
- You are allowed to use a calculator.

Information for candidates
- The marks available are given in brackets at the end of each question.
- There are 60 marks available for this paper.
- You should use good English and present your answers in a clear and organised way.
- For questions marked with an asterisk (*) ensure that your answers have a logical structure with points that link together clearly, and include detailed, relevant information.

For examiner's use

Q	Attempt Nº			Q	Attempt Nº		
	1	2	3		1	2	3
1				4			
2				5			
3				6			
				Total			

Advice to candidates
- In calculations show clearly how you worked out your answers.
- Read each question carefully before answering it.
- Check your answers if you have time.

1   A group of students are investigating different types of energy transfer.

   (a) One student heats a metal spoon over a Bunsen burner.

   (i) Explain why the amount of energy transferred to the spoon and its surroundings cannot be greater than the amount of energy transferred from the Bunsen burner.

   ....

   ....
   [1 mark]

   (ii) Which energy store of the gas is energy being transferred from as the Bunsen is used?

   ☐ A Nuclear

   ☐ B Electrostatic

   ☐ C Chemical

   ☐ D Kinetic
   [1 mark]

   The student then uses tongs to place the hot spoon into an insulated flask full of cold water, like the one shown in **Figure 1**.
   The insulated flask is then sealed.

   Figure 1

   (iii) The sealed flask can be treated as a closed system.
   Which of the following statements is **true** for a closed system?

   ☐ A The net change in the energy of the system is always positive.

   ☐ B The net change in the energy of the system is always negative.

   ☐ C The net change in the energy of the system is always zero.

   ☐ D The net change in the energy of the system may be positive or negative.
   [1 mark]

Question 1 continues on the next page

Turn over ▶

(b) Another student is investigating how much a rubber ball heats up when it is bounced. During the experiment:

1. The ball is thrown horizontally at a wall.
2. The ball hits the wall, causing it to deform and heat up.
3. The ball bounces back to the student.
4. The student repeatedly throws the ball at the wall.
5. Every 20 seconds, the student uses a thermometer to measure the temperature of the ball's surface.

(i) Suggest **one** way to improve the student's experiment.

....
[1 mark]

(ii) Describe the energy transfers that occur as the ball collides with the wall and moves away from the wall.

....

....

....

....

....

....
[4 marks]

(c) The experiment is changed so that now the ball is released from a height of 1.75 metres and allowed to fall vertically. The ball has a mass of 30 grams. The gravitational field strength of Earth is 10 N/kg.

Calculate the energy transferred from the GPE store as the ball falls 1.75 m.
Use the equation:

change in GPE = mass × gravitational field strength × change in vertical height

Energy = ... J
[2 marks]
[Total 10 marks]

2 A home owner would like to make her home more energy efficient in order to reduce her impact on the environment.

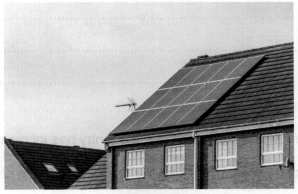

Figure 2

(a) **Figure 2** shows the solar panels the home owner has fitted to the roof to generate electricity. Solar panels are an example of a renewable energy resource.

(i) Give **one** other example of a renewable energy resource.

....
[1 mark]

Each hour the Sun's rays transfer 1.2 MJ of energy to the solar panels' surfaces. Of this energy, 0.2 MJ is transferred away usefully.

(ii) State the equation relating efficiency, total energy supplied to a device and useful energy transferred by the device.

....
[1 mark]

(iii) Calculate the efficiency of the home owner's solar panels.

Efficiency = ...
[2 marks]

(b) **Figure 3** shows a country's total energy use per year over 15 years.

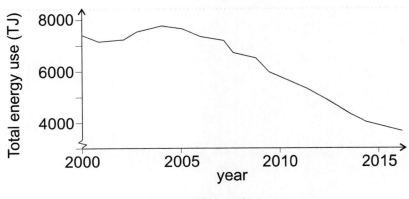

Figure 3

Question 2 continues on the next page

Turn over ▶

(i) Describe how the amount of energy used by the country has changed over time. Suggest **one** reason for this.

....

....

....

[2 marks]

The overall use of renewable resources in the country has increased over time.

(ii) Suggest **two** factors which might limit the use of renewable energy resources.

1. ....

2. ....

[2 marks]

(c) The home owner wants to build an extension.
The extension will be built with walls that are a single brick thick.
The home owner is trying to decide which type of brick to use to build the extension walls.
Figure 4 shows some types of brick that could be used.

Brick	Volume (cm^3)	Thickness (cm)	Thermal Conductivity (W/mK)
Brick X	150	8	0.84
Brick Y	150	12	0.62
Brick Z	150	10	0.84

Figure 4

Suggest which type of brick the home owner should use to minimise the rate of cooling of the extension. Justify your answer.

....

....

....

....

[3 marks]

[Total 11 marks]

3 **Figure 5** shows a couple doing a dance routine on an ice rink.

Figure 5

At the start of the routine, the first skater is at the entrance to the ice rink.

Figure 6 shows the first skater's distance-time graph for the first 35 seconds of the routine.

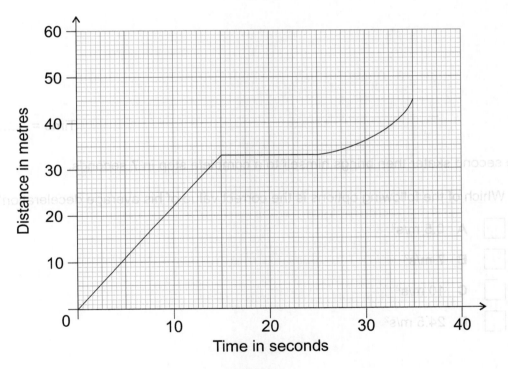

Figure 6

(a) Describe the motion of the first skater during the first 35 seconds of the routine.

....

....

....

....

[3 marks]

Question 3 continues on the next page

Turn over ▶

(b) After travelling 33 m the first skater arrives at the centre of the rink.
Use **Figure 6** to determine the speed of the first skater as she travels to the centre of the rink.

Speed = ... m/s
[2 marks]

The second skater is travelling at a constant speed of 3.5 metres per second.

(c) (i) State the equation relating speed, distance and time.

[1 mark]

(ii) Calculate the time it will take the second skater to travel a distance of 14 metres.

Time = ... s
[3 marks]

(d) The second skater then brings himself to a complete stop in 7 seconds.

(i) Which of the following options is the correct value of his average deceleration?

☐ **A** 0.5 m/s^2

☐ **B** 7 m/s^2

☐ **C** 10 m/s^2

☐ **D** 24.5 m/s^2

[1 mark]

(ii) Compare the magnitudes of the driving forces and the frictional forces acting on the second skater as he decelerates.

....

....
[1 mark]

[Total 11 marks]

4 A student wants to investigate how much different transparent materials will refract a beam of light. The student has three rectangular blocks made out of different transparent materials, similar to the one shown in **Figure 7**.

Figure 7

(a) Describe an experiment the student could carry out in order to investigate this.

....

....

....

....
[3 marks]

(b) (i) Name a piece of equipment that the student could use to create a thin beam of light.

....
[1 mark]

(ii) Explain **one** advantage of using a thin beam of light.

....

....
[1 mark]

Question 4 continues on the next page

Turn over ▶

(c) **Figure 8** shows the angles of refraction for three different materials, for a fixed angle of incidence.

Material	Angle of refraction (°)
Ice	37
Flint glass	24
Acrylic	31

Figure 8

(i) State the material in which light travels the slowest.

....

[1 mark]

(ii) Explain your answer to part (i).

....

....

[2 marks]

(d) When light of frequency 5.1×10^{14} Hz is travelling through flint glass, the wavelength of the light is 353 nm.

Calculate the speed of light in flint glass.

Speed of light in flint glass = ... m/s

[2 marks]

[Total 10 marks]

5 *(a) Models of the atom have developed over time.

Figure 9 shows an early model of the atom, Model X, and a currently used model of the atom, Model Y.

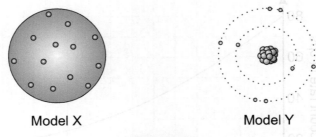

Model X   Model Y

Figure 9

Explain how experiments and scientific discoveries caused our understanding of the atom to develop from Model X to Model Y.
Your answer should include descriptions of the models shown in Figure 10.

....

....

....

....

....

....

....

....

....

[6 marks]

(b) (i) An unstable atom will emit radiation.

A student places a detector next to a radioactive sample of bismuth-212.
The student records the count-rate measured by the detector every 10 seconds.

Name a detector that the student could use to measure the count-rate.

....

[1 mark]

(ii) Bismuth-212 can decay by beta-minus emission to form an isotope of polonium (Po).
Figure 10 shows an incomplete nuclear equation showing this decay.

$$^{212}_{83}\text{Bi} \rightarrow\ ^{212}_{A}\text{Po} +\ ^{0}_{B}\beta$$

Figure 10

Determine the atomic number, A, of the polonium atom.

A = ...

[1 mark]

Question 5 continues on the next page

Turn over ▶

(iii) The student plots a graph of the count-rate of the bismuth-212 sample against time.

Figure 11 shows the student's graph.

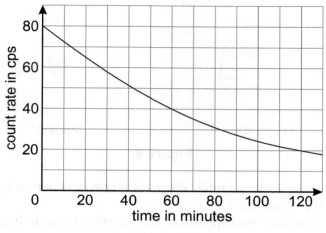

Figure 11

Use Figure 11 to calculate the half-life of bismuth-212.
Give your answer in minutes.

Half-life = ... minutes
[2 marks]

(c) Another radioactive isotope, iodine-131, emits gamma rays.
Iodine-131 is typically stored in a lead-lined box.

Figure 12 shows the radiation detected outside the box against the thickness of the box's lead lining.

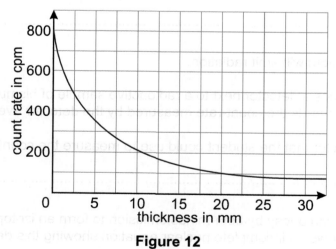

Figure 12

Using Figure 12, describe how the thickness of the box's lead lining affects the safety of people near to the box.

....

....

....

[2 marks]
[Total 12 marks]

6 A student is investigating sound waves. The experimental set-up is shown in **Figure 13**.

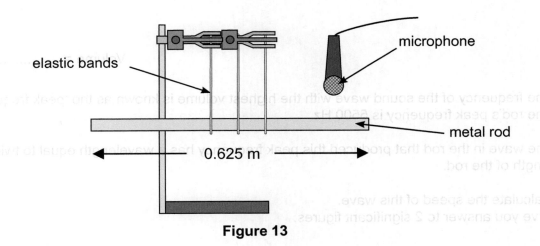

Figure 13

A 0.625 m metal rod is suspended by elastic bands.

The student strikes the metal rod with a hammer in order to produce a sound.
The sound that is produced is made up of sound waves of a range of frequencies.

A microphone connected to a computer records and measures the volume of all the sound waves produced by the metal rod.

The experiment is repeated three times and the measurements of volume are averaged.
Figure 14 shows the student's results.

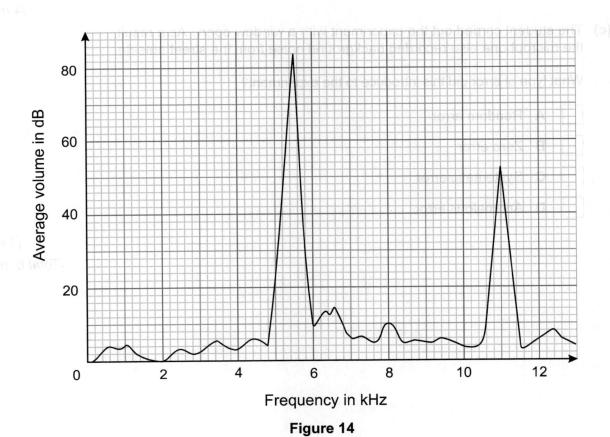

Figure 14

Question 6 continues on the next page

Turn over ▶

(a) What was the average volume of the 8 kHz sound wave produced by the rod?

Volume = ... dB
[1 mark]

(b) The frequency of the sound wave with the highest volume is known as the 'peak frequency'.
The rod's peak frequency is 5500 Hz.

The wave in the rod that produced this peak frequency has a wavelength equal to twice the length of the rod.

Calculate the speed of this wave.
Give you answer to 2 significant figures.

Wave speed = ... m/s
[4 marks]

(c) The student carried out the experiment with a window open. As a result, the microphone also recorded background noise from the street outside.

What type of error did this introduce to the experiment?

☐ A Random error

☐ B Zero error

☐ C Systematic error

☐ D Anomalous error

[1 mark]
[Total 6 marks]

END OF QUESTIONS

449

GCSE Combined Science
Paper 6: Physics 2
Higher Tier

In addition to this paper you should have:
- A ruler.
- A calculator.

Centre name
Centre number
Candidate number

Time allowed:
- 1 hour 10 minutes

Surname
Other names
Candidate signature

Instructions to candidates
- Write your name and other details in the spaces provided above.
- Answer **all** questions in the spaces provided.
- Do all rough work on the paper.
- Cross out any work you do not want to be marked.
- You are allowed to use a calculator.

Information for candidates
- The marks available are given in brackets at the end of each question.
- There are 60 marks available for this paper.
- You should use good English and present your answers in a clear and organised way.
- For questions marked with an asterisk (*) ensure that your answers have a logical structure with points that link together clearly, and include detailed, relevant information.

For examiner's use

Q	Attempt Nº			Q	Attempt Nº		
	1	2	3		1	2	3
1				4			
2				5			
3				6			
				Total			

Advice to candidates
- In calculations show clearly how you worked out your answers.
- Read each question carefully before answering it.
- Check your answers if you have time.

1 **Figure 1** shows a kettle that uses electricity to boil water.

Figure 1

(a) (i) Which of the following equations correctly relates charge, current and time?

☐ A charge = current × time

☐ B charge = ½ × current × time

☐ C charge = current ÷ time

☐ D charge = time ÷ current

[1 mark]

(ii) The current through the kettle is 12 A.
Calculate the time taken for 1440 C to pass through the kettle.

Time = ... s
[3 marks]

(b) The kettle has a power rating of 3000 W.
Explain what the term power rating means.

....

....

....

[1 mark]

(c) When the kettle is heating water, energy is transferred electrically from the mains to the heating element of the kettle.

Describe the energy transfer that occurs between the heating element and the water in the kettle.

....

....

....

....

[3 marks]

(d) To bring a full kettle of water to the boil, 740 kJ of energy is transferred to the kettle. 680 kJ of this energy is usefully transferred to the water.

Using this information, complete the energy transfer diagram in **Figure 2** for bringing a full kettle of water to the boil.

Label the diagram with the correct values for the energy transferred.

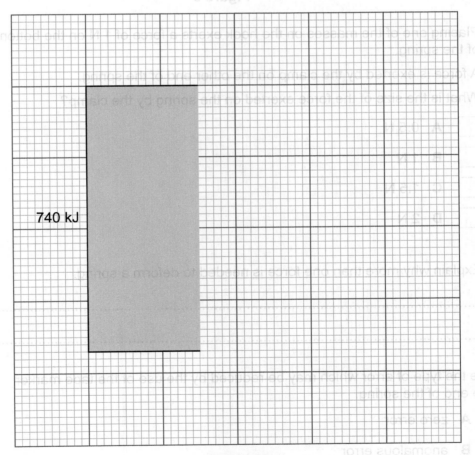

Figure 2

[2 marks]

[Total 10 marks]

Turn over for the next question

Turn over ▶

2   A student is given a set of apparatus, set up as shown in **Figure 3**.
    The hook is assumed to have zero mass.

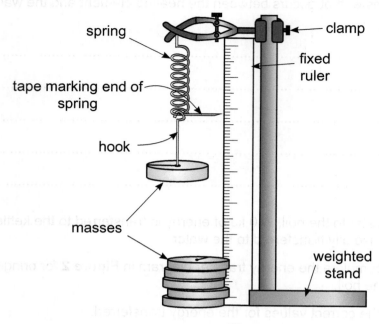

Figure 3

(a) (i) Placing one of the masses on the hook exerts a force of 1 N on the bottom of the spring.

A force is exerted by the clamp on the other end of the spring.

What is the size of the force exerted on the spring by the clamp?

☐ A 0.5 N

☐ B 1 N

☐ C 1.5 N

☐ D 2 N

[1 mark]

(ii) Explain why more than one force is needed to deform a spring.

....

....

[1 mark]

(b) Name the type of error which may be reduced by the use of the tape marker at the end of the spring.

☐ A zero error

☐ B anomalous error

☐ C systematic error

☐ D random error

[1 mark]

*(c) Describe how the student could use the experimental set-up in **Figure 3** to find the spring constant of the spring.

....
....
....
....
....
....
....
....
....
....
....
....

[6 marks]

The student used the apparatus in **Figure 3** to produce the graph shown in **Figure 4**.

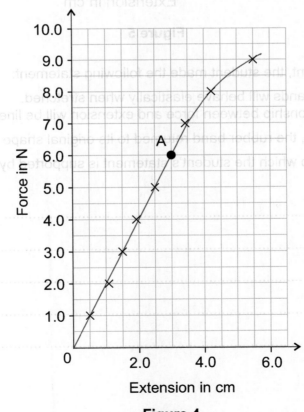

Figure 4

Question 2 continues on the next page

Turn over ▶

(d) Calculate the work done to stretch the spring to point A.

Work done = ... J

[3 marks]

(e) The student then decided to use the apparatus to create a force-extension graph for a rubber band. The student's graph is shown in **Figure 5**.

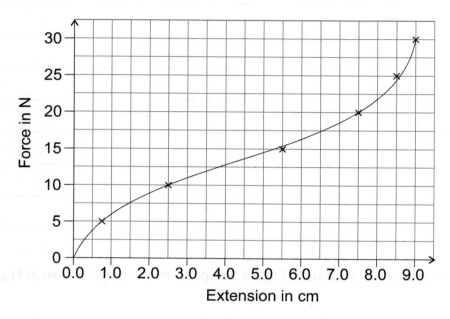

Figure 5

Before the experiment, the student made the following statement:

"I think that rubber bands will behave elastically when stretched.
I also think the relationship between force and extension will be linear."

After the experiment, the rubber band returned to its original shape and size.

Discuss the extent to which the student's statement is supported by the results of the experiment.

....

....

....

....

....

[2 marks]

[Total 14 marks]

3   A student has a length of wire.

(a) Which of the following shows the magnetic field around the wire when a current flows through the wire? The current is flowing into the paper.

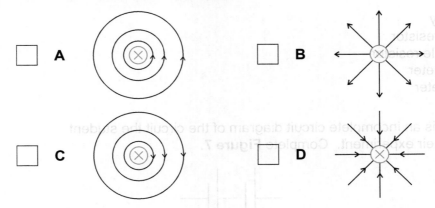

[1 mark]

(b) The current flowing through the wire is 2.4 A.
Calculate the amount of charge that will have flowed through the wire in 30 minutes.

Charge = ... C
[2 marks]

(c) The student passes the wire between the poles of two magnets, as shown in **Figure 6**.
The magnetic field between the poles has a magnetic flux density of 0.75 T.
The length of wire inside the magnetic field is 0.05 m.

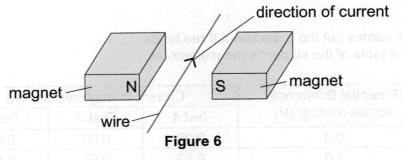

Figure 6

Calculate the size of the force on the wire.
Use the correct equation from the Physics Equation Sheet on page 506.

Force = ... N
[2 marks]

(d) Suggest **one** way the student could change their set-up to increase the size of the force on the wire.

....

....

[1 mark]
[Total 6 marks]

Turn over for the next question

Turn over ▶

4 A student wants to investigate the relationship between current and potential difference for a fixed resistor.

The student has:

- a battery
- a fixed resistor
- a variable resistor
- an ammeter
- a voltmeter

(a) **Figure 7** is an incomplete circuit diagram of the circuit the student uses in their experiment. Complete **Figure 7**.

Figure 7

[3 marks]

(b) The student carries out the experiment three times. **Figure 8** is a table of the student's measurements.

Potential Difference across resistor (V)	Current through resistor (A)		
	Test 1	Test 2	Test 3
0.0	0.00	0.00	0.00
1.0	0.52	0.51	0.50
2.0	0.99	0.99	1.00
3.0	1.52	1.50	1.50
4.0	1.98	1.99	1.99
5.0	2.53	2.52	2.51

Figure 8

Calculate the mean current flowing through the resistor when the potential difference across it was 5.0 V.

Current = ... A

[1 mark]

(c) The student notices that over time, the resistor being tested feels warm.
This is because energy is transferred when work is done against electrical resistance.

In terms of electrons and ions, explain the cause of this energy transfer in the resistor.

....
....
....
....
....
[2 marks]

(d) The student tests another fixed resistor, which has a resistance of 2 Ω.
Calculate the potential difference that needs to be applied across the resistor to cause a current of 5 A to flow through the resistor.

Potential difference = ... V
[2 marks]

(e) The student uses a similar experiment to investigate the relationship between current and potential difference in a filament lamp.

The student then plots the results on a graph of current against potential difference.

What should the graph look like?

☐ A

☐ B

☐ C

☐ D

[1 mark]
[Total 9 marks]

Turn over for the next question

Turn over ▶

5 A student is investigating the energy needed to boil different masses of water.
This is their method:

1. Place an empty beaker on a mass balance and zero the balance.
2. Add 0.25 kg of water to the beaker.
3. Use a clamp and stand to hold an electric immersion heater and a thermometer in the water.
4. Keeping the beaker on the mass balance, switch on the heater.
5. Record the current through and potential difference across the heater using an ammeter and a voltmeter.
6. Wait for the temperature of the water to reach 100 °C.
7. Start a stopwatch and record how long it takes the heater to boil off 0.025 kg of water.
8. Continue boiling the water, and record how long it takes to boil off the next 0.025 kg. Repeat the process until 0.05 kg of water remains in the beaker.
9. Calculate the energy transferred by the heater to boil the water using:
energy transferred = current × potential difference × time.

(a) (i) Suggest **one** safety precaution that should be taken during this experiment.

....
[1 mark]

(ii) Suggest **one** piece of equipment the student could use instead of the ammeter and voltmeter.

....
[1 mark]

Figure 9 shows a graph of the student's results.

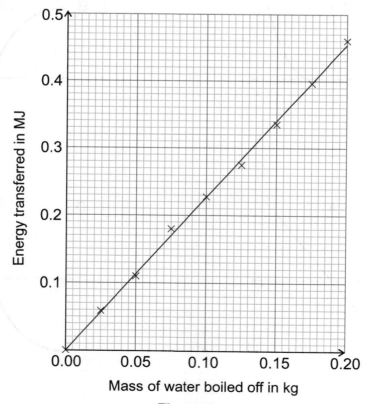

Figure 9

(b) Use **Figure 9** to determine the specific latent heat of vaporisation for water.

Specific latent heat = ... MJ/kg

[2 marks]

(c) The electric immersion heater had a potential difference of 12 V across it.
The current through the heater was 8 A.

Using **Figure 9**, how long had the water been boiling for when 0.185 kg of water had boiled off?

You can assume that no energy was transferred from the water to the surroundings, and that the immersion heater was 100% efficient.

Use the correct equation from the Physics Equation Sheet on page 506.

☐ A 4375 s

☐ B 4271 s

☐ C 40 s

☐ D 35 000 s

[1 mark]

(d) Describe **one** difference between particles in liquid water and particles in water vapour.

....

....

[1 mark]

[Total 6 marks]

Turn over for the next question

6 A student sets up the circuit shown in **Figure 10**.

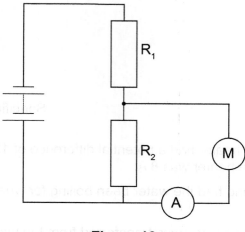

Figure 10

(a) (i) State the equation that links electrical power, current and potential difference.

....
[1 mark]

(ii) The battery used in the circuit is a 12 V battery.
The potential difference across R_1 is 4.0 V.
The current through R_1 is 5.0 A. The current through R_2 is 3.0 A.
Calculate the power of the motor.

Power = ... W
[3 marks]

(b) The motor is attached to fan blades.
The student decides to investigate how fast the fan blades will spin when different motors are used.

The student draws a graph of the speed of the blades over time for three different motors, as shown in **Figure 11**. All the motors have the same efficiency.

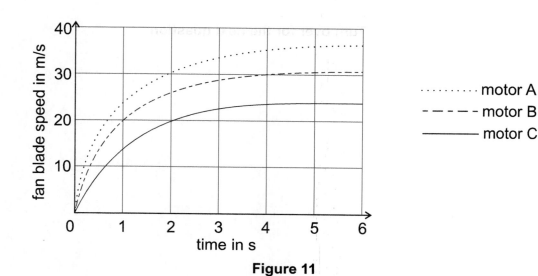

Figure 11

(i) Explain which motor has the highest power.

....
....
....
[3 marks]

(ii) Suggest one way to reduce energy losses from the motors.

....
[1 mark]

(c) The student creates a sensing circuit to control an electric heater, as shown in **Figure 12**.

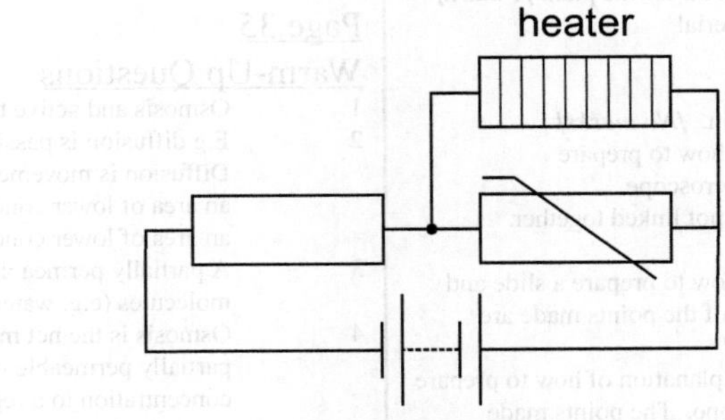

Figure 12

Explain what will happen to the potential difference across the heater as the room temperature increases.

....
....
....
[3 marks]

(d) The electric heater is used to heat 2.1 kg of water.
The water is heated from 16 °C to 65 °C.
The specific heat capacity of water is 4200 J/kg°C.

The heater is 85% efficient.
Calculate the energy transferred to the heater when it is used to heat the water.
Use the correct equation from the Physics Equation Sheet on page 506.

Energy transferred = ... J

[4 marks]

[Total 15 marks]

END OF QUESTIONS

Answers

Section 1 — Key Concepts in Biology

Page 23
More Microscopy
Q1   real size = image size ÷ magnification
      = 2.4 mm ÷ 40
      = 0.06 mm *[1 mark]*
      0.06 × 1000 = **60 µm** *[1 mark]*

Page 25
Warm-Up Questions
1. mitochondria
2. Any two from: e.g. it has a long tail to help it swim. / It has lots of mitochondria to provide energy for swimming. / It has an acrosome to store the enzymes for digesting the egg cell membrane.
3. electron microscope.
4. 4.5×10^{-4} µm

Exam Questions
1. B *[1 mark]*
Remember, DNA in prokaryotic cells floats freely in the cytoplasm — it's not stored in a nucleus.
2. a) C *[1 mark]*
    b) It is the site of photosynthesis, which makes food for the plant *[1 mark]*
    c) They're involved in translation of genetic material in the synthesis of proteins *[1 mark]*
3. a) How to grade your answer:
      Level 0: There is no relevant information. *[No marks]*
      Level 1: There is a brief explanation of how to prepare a slide or how to use a light microscope. The points made are basic and not linked together. *[1 to 2 marks]*
      Level 2: There is some explanation of how to prepare a slide and use a light microscope. Some of the points made are linked together. *[3 to 4 marks]*
      Level 3: There is a clear and detailed explanation of how to prepare a slide and use a light microscope. The points made are well linked and the answer has a clear and logical structure. *[5 to 6 marks]*

Here are some points your answer may include:
To prepare a slide:
Add a drop of water to the middle of a clean slide.
Cut up an onion and separate it out into layers.
Use tweezers to peel off some tissue from the bottom of one of the layers.
Use tweezers to place the tissue into the water on the slide.
Add a drop of stain.
Place a cover slip on top by standing it upright on the slide, next to the water droplet, then carefully tilting and lowering it so it covers the onion tissue without trapping any air bubbles.
To use a light microscope:
Clip the slide onto the stage.
Select the lowest-powered objective lens.
Use the coarse adjustment knob to move the stage up to just below the objective lens (without looking down the eyepiece).
Look down the eyepiece and use the coarse adjustment knob to move the stage downwards until the image is roughly in focus.
Adjust the focus with the fine adjustment knob, until a clear image of the cells is visible.
To see the cells with greater magnification, swap to a higher-powered objective lens and refocus.

    b) real size = image size ÷ magnification
      = 7.5 mm ÷ 100
      = 0.075 mm
      0.075 × 1000 = **75 µm** *[3 marks for correct answer, otherwise 1 mark for correctly rearranging the equation and 1 mark for 0.075 mm.]*

Page 29
Investigating Enzyme Activity
Q1   2 minutes = 2 × 60 = 120 seconds
      36 ÷ 120 = **0.3 cm³ s⁻¹** *[1 mark]*

Page 31
Warm-Up Questions
1. The part of an enzyme which joins to a substrate.
2. The pH at which the enzyme works best.
3. temperature and substrate concentration
4. a) carbohydrase/amylase
    b) protease
    c) lipase
Carbohydrases (e.g. amylase) break down carbohydrates, such as starch. Proteases break down proteins, and lipases break down lipids (fats).

5. a) (simple) sugars
    b) amino acids
6. amino acids

Exam Questions
1. a) Accept answers between 38 °C and 40 °C *[1 mark]*.
    b) Enzyme B, e.g. because it has an unusually high optimum temperature which it would need to work in the hot vent *[1 mark]*.
2. a) To prevent the starch coming into contact with amylase in the syringe, which would have started the reaction before he had started the stop clock *[1 mark]*
    b) Rate = 1000 ÷ 60 = **17 s⁻¹** (2 s.f.) *[1 mark]*
    c) Repeat the experiment using buffers with a range of different pH values and compare the results *[1 mark]*

Page 32
Diffusion and Active Transport
Q1   active transport *[1 mark]*

Page 34
Osmosis
Q1   Water will move out of the piece of potato by osmosis *[1 mark]*, so its mass will decrease *[1 mark]*.

Page 35
Warm-Up Questions
1. Osmosis and active transport.
2. E.g. diffusion is passive whereas active transport requires energy. Diffusion is movement from an area of higher concentration to an area of lower concentration, whereas active transport is from an area of lower concentration to higher concentration.
3. A partially permeable membrane only allows small molecules (e.g. water) to diffuse through it.
4. Osmosis is the net movement of water molecules across a partially permeable membrane from a region of higher water concentration to a region of lower water concentration.

Exam Questions
1. The ink will diffuse / spread out through the water *[1 mark]*. This is because the ink particles will move from where there is a higher concentration of them (the drop of ink) to where there is a lower concentration of them (the surrounding water) *[1 mark]*.
2. a) The potato cylinder in tube D *[1 mark]*, because this tube contains the most concentrated sugar solution so this cylinder will have lost the most water *[1 mark]* by osmosis *[1 mark]*.
    b) Tube A contained distilled water, so some of the water moved by osmosis into the potato cylinder *[1 mark]* from an area of high water concentration to an area of low water concentration *[1 mark]*.

Section 2 — Cells and Control

Page 38
Mitosis
Q1 a) 11 ÷ (62 + 11) = 0.150...
      0.150... × 100 = **15%** *[1 mark]*
    b) E.g. she could see the X-shaped chromosomes in the middle of the cells *[1 mark]*.

Page 43
Warm-Up Questions
1. It's the process by which a cell changes to become specialised for its job.
2. True
3. 25% of two-month-olds are lighter than the baby.
4. in the nucleus

Exam Questions
1. a) The amount of DNA is doubling *[1 mark]* so that there is one copy for each new cell *[1 mark]*.
    b) The two new cells separate *[1 mark]*.
    c) two *[1 mark]*
    d) A change in one of the genes controlling cell division can cause cells to divide uncontrollably *[1 mark]*. This can lead to a mass of cells called a tumour, which can invade and destroy surrounding cells *[1 mark]*.
2. a) E.g. they could be grown into a particular type of cell, which can then be used to replace faulty cells *[1 mark]*
    b) Embryonic stem cells have the potential to develop into any kind of cell, whereas adult stem cells can only develop into certain types of cell *[1 mark]*.
3. 3 hours = 60 × 3 = 180 minutes
    180 ÷ 30 = 6 divisions
    $2^6 = 2 \times 2 \times 2 \times 2 \times 2 \times 2$ = **64 cells** *[2 marks for correct answer, otherwise 1 mark for correct working.]*

Page 46
Reflexes
Q1   A rapid, automatic response to a stimulus *[1 mark]*.
Q2a)   muscle *[1 mark]*
    b)   The heat stimulus is detected by receptors in the hand *[1 mark]*, which send impulses along a sensory neurone to the CNS *[1 mark]*. The impulses are transferred to a relay neurone *[1 mark]*. They are then transferred to a motor neurone and travel along it to the effector/muscle *[1 mark]*.

Page 47
Warm-Up Questions
1. A stimulus is a change in the environment.
2. An axon carries nerve impulses away from the cell body.
3. A myelin sheath surrounds an axon, acting as an electrical insulator.
4. sensory neurone, relay neurone, motor neurone
5. synapse

Exam Questions
1 a)   Stimulus: appearance of red triangle *[1 mark]*
        Receptors: cells in the eye / light receptor cells *[1 mark]*
        Effectors: muscles (in hand controlling mouse) *[1 mark]*
  b) $343 \times 3 = 1029$
        $1029 - 328 - 346 = $ **355 ms** *[2 marks for the correct answer, otherwise 1 mark for correct working.]*
2 a)   motor neurone *[1 mark]*
  b)   Muscle *[1 mark]*, which contracts to move the baby's fingers *[1 mark]*.
  c)   When the electrical impulse reaches the end of the neurone, it stimulates the release of a neurotransmitter *[1 mark]*. The neurotransmitter diffuses across the synapse to activate an electrical impulse in the next neurone *[1 mark]*.
  d)   E.g. in a baby older than 6 months, the pathway will involve conscious parts of the brain, whereas in a newborn baby it won't. / In a baby older than 6 months, the response will not be produced as rapidly as in the newborn baby *[1 mark]*.

The response in the baby older than 6 months is not a reflex — it chooses whether it wants to grasp an object. Remember, reflexes are automatic — they don't involve conscious parts of the brain, which makes the response much faster.

Section 3 — Genetics
Page 49
Meiosis
Q1   32 *[1 mark]*

Page 51
Warm-Up Questions
1. two
2. A and T. C and G.
3. A section of DNA on a chromosome that codes for a particular protein.

Exam Questions
1 a)   (ice cold) alcohol *[1 mark]*
  b)   DNA *[1 mark]*
2 a)   C *[1 mark]*
  b)   hydrogen bonds *[1 mark]*
  c)   DNA contains genes *[1 mark]*. Each gene codes for a particular sequence of amino acids *[1 mark]*, which are put together to make a specific protein *[1 mark]*.
3 a)   three *[1 mark]*
When a cell undergoes meiosis, each new cell ends up with half the number of chromosomes as in the original cell.
  b)   four *[1 mark]*
Remember, when a cell undergoes meiosis, four gametes are produced — it doesn't matter whether you're talking about human cells or mosquito cells.

Page 54
Genetic Diagrams
Q1

	R	r
r	Rr	rr
r	Rr	rr

round peas : wrinkly peas, **1 : 1**
[1 mark for correct gametes, 1 mark for correct offspring genotypes and 1 mark for correct ratio.]

Page 55
Genetic Diagrams
Q1   Ff *[1 mark]*

Page 56
Warm-Up Questions
1. Different versions of the same gene.
2. What characteristics you have.
3. White fur, because you need two copies of the recessive allele (b) for this characteristic to be shown / if you have one recessive allele and one dominant allele (Bb) you get brown fur, so brown fur must be the dominant characteristic.
4. XX

Exam Questions
1 a)

	F	f
F	FF	Ff
f	Ff	ff

[1 mark for correct genotype of offspring, 1 mark for correct genotypes of gametes]
  b)   1 in 2 / 50% *[1 mark]*
  c)   Has cystic fibrosis *[1 mark]*.
2 a)   AA, Aa *[1 mark]*
  b)   E.g.
Genotypes of parents: aa, Aa
Genotypes of gametes: a, a, A, a
Genotypes of offspring: Aa, Aa, aa, aa
[1 mark for parent with genotype aa, 1 mark for parent with genotype Aa, 1 mark for correct genotypes of offspring]
  c)   50% *[1 mark]*
Offspring with the genotype aa will have albinism.
  d)   Fertilisation is random/the genetic diagram only shows the probability of the outcome, so the numbers of offspring produced will not always be exactly in those proportions *[1 mark]*.

Page 60
Warm-Up Questions
1. Differences between members of the same species that have been caused by the environment/conditions an organism lives in.
2 a)   E.g. Amy and Beth could have inherited different alleles/genes for hair type (curly or straight) from their parents.
  b)   E.g. one of the sisters might use curling tongs or hair straighteners to alter their natural hair type. / Amy might use curling tongs to make her hair curly. / Beth might use hair straighteners to make her hair straight.
3. False

Exam Questions
1 a)   D
  b)   The difference in weight must be caused by the environment *[1 mark]*, because the twins have exactly the same genes *[1 mark]*.
In this case, the environment can mean the amount of food each twin eats or the amount of exercise they each do.
  c)   No, because if it was caused by genes, both twins should have the birthmark *[1 mark]*.
2 a)   E.g. if Eshan has the allele he could get tailored advice on lifestyle factors to reduce the likelihood of developing colorectal cancer. / He can have regular checks to ensure early treatment if he develops colorectal cancer *[1 mark]*.
  b)   E.g. if Eshan has the allele he could be discriminated against by life insurers / he could be discriminated against by employers / he could be put under pressure not to have children so that the gene is not passed on / he could have increased stress levels from worrying about potentially developing colorectal cancer *[1 mark]*.
3 a)   Mutations change the base sequence of DNA *[1 mark]*, which can result in a new allele *[1 mark]*. New alleles can lead to differences in phenotype, increasing variation *[1 mark]*.
  b)   E.g the mutation could result in the production of a protein that is very different *[1 mark]*, so the activity of the protein would be affected, which would affect phenotype *[1 mark]*.

Section 4 — Natural Selection and Genetic Modification

Page 61
Natural Selection and Evidence for Evolution
Q1   There was a variety of tongue lengths in the moth population *[1 mark]*. Moths with longer tongues got more food/nectar and were more likely to survive *[1 mark]*. These moths were more likely to reproduce and pass on the genes responsible for their long tongues *[1 mark]*. So, over time, longer tongues became more common in the moth population *[1 mark]*.

Page 66
Selective Breeding
Q1   Select rabbits with floppy ears *[1 mark]* and breed them together to produce offspring *[1 mark]*. Select offspring with floppy ears and breed them together *[1 mark]*. Repeat this over many generations until all of the offspring have floppy ears *[1 mark]*.

Page 68
Genetic Engineering
Q1   A plasmid could be removed from the bacterial cell and cut open with a restriction enzyme *[1 mark]*. The rennin gene could be cut out of a cow chromosome using the same restriction enzyme *[1 mark]*. The plasmid and rennin gene could then be joined together using ligase enzymes *[1 mark]*. The plasmid could then be re-inserted into the bacterial cell *[1 mark]*.

Pages 69-70
Warm-Up Questions
1. Organisms with the beneficial characteristic are better adapted to their environment, so they have a better chance of survival. This makes them more likely to breed successfully and pass on the alleles for the beneficial characteristic to their offspring.
2. Any trace of an animal or plant that lived a long time ago.
3. E.g. genetic analysis showed that Archaea and Bacteria were less closely related than first thought.
4. Restriction enzymes and ligase enzymes.

Exam Questions
1. a) New alleles arise though mutations *[1 mark]*.
   b) i) Any two from: e.g. predation / competition for resources/food/water/mates / disease *[1 mark for each correct answer]*.
     ii) They may lack the characteristics needed to adapt to the new selection pressure *[1 mark]* and so are less able to survive and reproduce *[1 mark]*.
2. a) The tall and dwarf wheat plants could be bred together *[1 mark]*. The best of the offspring/the offspring with the highest grain yield and highest bad weather resistance could then be bred together *[1 mark]*, and this process repeated over several generations *[1 mark]*.
   b) There will be less genetic variation within the population of selectively bred wheat plants *[1 mark]*, so there is a smaller chance of disease resistance alleles being present *[1 mark]*. This means that there is a greater chance that all of the plants will be affected/killed by the disease *[1 mark]*.
3. a) Organism C *[1 mark]* because its DNA sequence has the highest percentage similarity to humans *[1 mark]*.
   b) Archaea *[1 mark]*, Bacteria *[1 mark]*, and Eukarya *[1 mark]*.
4. Variation in the population meant that some Clostridium difficile bacteria had alleles which gave resistance to the antibiotic *[1 mark]*. When exposed to this antibiotic, resistant bacteria were more likely to survive *[1 mark]* and pass on the resistance allele to offspring *[1 mark]*. The resistance allele became more common in the population and soon all bacteria in the population were resistant *[1 mark]*.
5. How to grade your answer:
   Level 0:   There is no relevant information. *[No marks]*
   Level 1:   There is some information about evolution by natural selection. The points are basic and not linked together. *[1 to 2 marks]*
   Level 2:   There is some explanation about how evolution by natural selection may have led to a change in appearance of the stingray. Some of the points made are linked together. *[3 to 4 marks]*
   Level 3:   There is a clear and detailed explanation of how evolution by natural selection may have led to a change in the appearance of the stingray. The points made are well-linked and the answer has a clear and logical structure. *[5 to 6 marks]*

Here are some points your answer may include:
Ancestors of this stingray showed variation in their appearance.
The stingrays that looked more like flat rocks were better camouflaged and so less likely to be seen by prey, meaning they could obtain more food / they were less likely to be seen and eaten by predators.
This means they were more likely to survive and reproduce.
As a result, the alleles that caused the stingrays to look like flat rocks were more likely to be passed on to the next generation.
Over time, the flat rock appearance became more common in the population, until all of the stingrays in the population had this appearance.

Section 5 — Health, Disease and the Development of Medicines

Page 74
Warm-Up Questions
1. A state of complete physical, mental and social well-being and not merely the absence of disease of infirmity.
2. It can be spread between individuals.
3. Any two from: e.g. cholera / tuberculosis / some stomach ulcers / Chlamydia.
4. Sexual contact allows the exchange of infected bodily fluids such as semen and vaginal fluids. The exchange of such fluids transmits the virus between individuals.
5. E.g. wearing a condom when having sex. / Screening individuals so they can be treated. / Avoiding sexual contact.

Exam Questions
1. a) An organism that can cause disease *[1 mark]*.
   b) D *[1 mark]*
   c) The fungus is carried through the air by the wind. / Diseased ash trees are moved between areas *[1 mark]*.
2. a) Malaria is spread by vectors *[1 mark]* and not through contaminated food/surfaces / skin to skin contact *[1 mark]*.
   b) E.g. mosquitoes are the vectors of malaria, so destroying mosquitoes will prevent malaria being spread between people *[1 mark]*.
   c) E.g. by having clean water supplies / hygienic living conditions *[1 mark]*.

Page 77
Immunisation
Q1   Basia has memory lymphocytes that recognise the antigens on the flu virus and rapidly produce antibodies, which kill the pathogen *[1 mark]*. Cassian doesn't have memory lymphocytes so it takes his immune system longer to produce antibodies and he becomes ill in the meantime *[1 mark]*.

Page 79
Warm-Up Questions
1. The skin acts as a barrier to pathogens, and, if it gets damaged, blood clots quickly seal cuts and keep microorganisms out.
2. To destroy specific pathogens that enter the body.
3. a (B-)lymphocyte
4. False
5. A placebo is a substance that looks like the real drug but doesn't do anything.

Exam Questions
1. a) Mucus traps particles that could contain pathogens *[1 mark]*.
   b) They waft the mucus up to the back of the throat where it can be swallowed *[1 mark]*.
   c) hydrochloric acid *[1 mark]*
   d) lysozyme *[1 mark]*
2. a) B *[1 mark]*
Drugs are tested on human cells, live animals and human tissue in preclinical trials. If a drug makes it through the preclinical trials, it's then tested on human volunteers in a clinical trial.
   b) In a double blind trial neither the patient nor the doctor *[1 mark]* knows who is receiving the drug and who is receiving the placebo until all the results have been gathered *[1 mark]*.
   c) E.g. dosage *[1 mark]*, efficacy/how well the drug works *[1 mark]*

Page 82
Measures of Obesity
Q1 a) $76.0 \text{ kg} \div (1.62 \text{ m})^2 =$ **29.0 kg m^{-2}** *[1 mark]*
   b) obese *[1 mark]*

Page 85
Warm-Up Questions
1. E.g. nicotine increases heart rate, which increases blood pressure. High blood pressure damages artery walls, contributing to the build up of fatty deposits, which can restrict blood flow in the arteries. / Smoking increases the risk of blood clots forming in arteries, which can restrict or block blood flow.
2. Alcohol is broken down by enzymes in the liver and some of the products are toxic. Drinking too much over a long period of time can cause permanent liver damage.
3. E.g. the National Health Service has to provide resources for the treatment of patients with non-communicable diseases all over the country. / People with non-communicable diseases may be unable to work, which may negatively affect the country's economy.

4   E.g. muscle weighs more than fat, so muscular people can have a high BMI even though they're not overweight.
5   E.g. they don't usually have any downsides/side effects.

Exam Questions
1. a) E.g drinking too much alcohol *[1 mark]*.
   b) E.g the cost of treating patients with liver disease in local hospitals *[1 mark]*.
2. a) 31 cm ÷ 33 cm = **0.94 (2 s.f.)** *[1 mark]*
   b) Person A's sex / whether person A is male or female *[1 mark]*.
   c) Height and mass *[1 mark]*.
3. a) A disease that cannot be spread between individuals *[1 mark]*.
   b) E.g. nicotine in cigarette smoke increases heart rate which increases blood pressure *[1 mark]*. High blood pressure damages artery walls, which contributes to the build up of fatty deposits in the arteries *[1 mark]*. Smoking also increases the risk of blood clots forming in arteries *[1 mark]*. Fatty deposits and blood clots can both restrict blood flow, increasing the risk of heart attack or a stroke *[1 mark]*.

Section 6 — Plant Structures and Their Functions
Page 89
Investigating Photosynthesis
Q1   E.g. light intensity *[1 mark]*, CO_2 *[1 mark]*.
Q2   light intensity $\propto \dfrac{1}{\text{distance}^2}$

$1 \div 15^2 = $ **0.00444... a.u.** *[1 mark]*
$1 \div 5^2 = $ **0.04 a.u.** *[1 mark]*
$0.04 \div 0.00444... = $ **9** *[1 mark]*

Page 90
Warm-Up Questions
1. False
2. A limiting factor is something that stops photosynthesis from happening any faster.
3. If the temperature's too high, the plant's enzymes will be denatured, so the rate of photosynthesis rapidly decreases.

Remember, if the temperature is too high for an enzyme, the bonds holding it together may break. This causes the shape of the enzyme's active site to change, denaturing the enzyme.

4. light intensity $\propto \dfrac{1}{\text{distance}^2}$

Exam Questions
1. a) By counting the number of bubbles produced / by measuring the volume of gas produced, in a given time/at regular intervals *[1 mark]*.
   b) Dependent variable — rate of photosynthesis/number of bubbles in a given time/volume of gas in a given time *[1 mark]*. Independent variable — light intensity *[1 mark]*.
2. a) Light intensity *[1 mark]*, because between these two points increasing the light intensity increases the rate of photosynthesis *[1 mark]*.
   b) After point B, increasing light intensity did not increase the rate of photosynthesis *[1 mark]*, so light intensity was no longer the limiting factor / a factor other than light intensity (e.g CO_2 concentration or temperature) was limiting the rate of photosynthesis *[1 mark]*.
3. light intensity $= \dfrac{1}{d^2} = \dfrac{1}{7.5^2} = $ **0.018 a.u. (2 s.f.)**

[2 marks for correct answer, otherwise 1 mark for correct working.]

Page 95
Warm-Up Questions
1. The lower surface of leaves.
2. False
3. light intensity, temperature, air flow

Exam Questions
1. a) xylem vessels *[1 mark]*
   b) They are made of dead cells joined end to end *[1 mark]* with no end walls between them and a hole down the middle *[1 mark]*. They're strengthened with a material called lignin *[1 mark]*.
   c) transpiration *[1 mark]*
2. a) phloem *[1 mark]*
   b) Phloem vessels are made of columns of living cells *[1 mark]*, which provide the energy needed to move substances through the vessel *[1 mark]*. The cells have small pores in the end walls *[1 mark]* to allow substances to flow through *[1 mark]*.
3. a) $(10 + 11 + 9) \div 3 = $ **10%** *[2 marks for correct answer, otherwise 1 mark for correct working]*
   b) How to grade your answer:
   Level 0: There is no relevant information. *[No marks]*
   Level 1: There is a brief explanation of how the increased air flow from the fan and the higher temperature increases the rate of transpiration. The points made are basic and not linked together. *[1 to 2 marks]*
   Level 2: There is some explanation of how the increased air flow from the fan and the higher temperature increases the rate of transpiration. Some of the points made are basic and not linked together. *[3 to 4 marks]*
   Level 3: There is a clear and detailed explanation of how the increased air flow from the fan and the higher temperature increases the rate of transpiration. The points made are well-linked and the answer has a clear and logical structure. *[5 to 6 marks]*

Here are some points your answer may include:
The movement of air from the fan moves water vapour away from plants in group D, maintaining a low concentration of water outside the leaf.
The low concentration of water outside the leaf increases the rate at which water diffuses out of the leaf.
Therefore, the plants in group D would lose more water, and so more mass, than the plants in group A.
At warmer temperatures, water particles have more energy to evaporate and diffuse out of the stomata.
The rate of transpiration will be higher in the plants at 25 °C than at 20 °C. So the plants in Group D will lose more water, and so more mass than the plants in Group A.

Section 7 — Animal Coordination, Control and Homeostasis
Page 98
Adrenaline and Thyroxine
Q1   TSH stimulates the release of thyroxine into the blood *[1 mark]*, but the amount of TSH falls when the level of thyroxine gets above the normal level *[1 mark]*. This negative feedback won't affect the antibody, so it will keep stimulating the release of thyroxine above the normal level *[1 mark]*.

Page 99
Warm-Up Questions
1. target organ
2. a) E.g. pituitary gland, thyroid gland, adrenal gland, pancreas, testes.
   b) ovaries
3. adrenal glands
4. thyroid

Exam Questions
1. a) a negative feedback system *[1 mark]*
   b) C *[1 mark]*
2. The pituitary gland releases a hormone/TSH which acts on the thyroid gland to make it release another hormone/thyroxine *[1 mark]*. If this hormone/TSH is not released, then the thyroid gland will stop releasing its hormone/thyroxine *[1 mark]*, so the person will experience symptoms linked to low thyroid hormone levels *[1 mark]*.
3. How to grade your answer:
   Level 0: There is no relevant information. *[No marks]*
   Level 1: There is a brief explanation of how the release of a hormone (adrenaline) in response to seeing the dog will affect the cat's heart rate and blood glucose level. The answer shows basic understanding, but lacks coherency. *[1 to 2 marks]*
   Level 2: There is some explanation of how the release of a hormone (adrenaline) in response to seeing the dog will affect the cat's heart rate and blood glucose level. There is some attempt to explain why such a response is beneficial to the cat. The answer shows mostly accurate understanding and has some structure. *[3 to 4 marks]*
   Level 3: There is a clear and detailed explanation of how the release of a hormone (adrenaline) in response to seeing the dog will affect the cat's heart rate and blood glucose level. There is a good explanation of why such a response is beneficial to the cat. The answer shows an accurate understanding of the relevant biology and is well structured. *[5 to 6 marks]*

Here are some points your answer may include:
When the cat sees the dog a nervous impulse is sent to the adrenal glands.
The adrenal glands release adrenaline.
Adrenaline travels to the heart, where it binds to specific receptor cells.
This causes the cat's heart muscle to contract more frequently, increasing the cat's heart rate.
Adrenaline also binds to receptors in the liver.
This causes the liver to break down its glycogen stores, releasing glucose. This increases the blood glucose level.
The increased heart rate increases the rate of delivery of oxygen and glucose to muscle cells..
The increased blood glucose increases the rate of delivery of glucose to muscle cells.
Both these processes will help to increase respiration rate, to produce extra energy for a 'fight or flight' response / in case the cat needs to fight or run away.

Page 104
Warm-Up Questions
1. FSH/follicle-stimulating hormone
2. condoms

3   A fertility treatment that involves eggs being handled outside of the body.
4   Clomifene increases the release of FSH and LH.

Exam Questions
1 a)   It inhibits it *[1 mark]*.
  b)   LH/luteinising hormone *[1 mark]*
  c)   day 14 *[1 mark]*
  d)   It breaks down *[1 mark]*.
  e)   It will maintain the lining of the uterus *[1 mark]*.
2 a)   Keeping oestrogen levels permanently high inhibits production of FSH *[1 mark]*, so no eggs will mature / so egg development and production will stop *[1 mark]*.
  b)   E.g. progesterone stimulates the production of thick cervical mucus *[1 mark]*, which will prevent any sperm getting through and reaching the woman's egg *[1 mark]*. / Progesterone inhibits the release of FSH *[1 mark]*, which will stop a follicle/an egg maturing in the ovaries *[1 mark]*. / Progesterone inhibits the release of LH *[1 mark]*, which will prevent ovulation from occurring *[1 mark]*.
  c)   By preventing sperm from reaching the egg *[1 mark]*.
  d)   Advantage: e.g. they have no unpleasant side effects. / They protect against sexually transmitted infections *[1 mark]*. Disadvantage: e.g. barrier methods are less effective at preventing pregnancy. / They need to be available at the time of intercourse *[1 mark]*.

Page 106
Blood Glucose Regulation
Q1   Curve 1, because the secretion rate is high when the blood glucose level is low / the secretion rate decreases as the blood glucose level rises *[1 mark]*. Glucagon increases the blood glucose level, so it is secreted when the blood glucose level becomes too low *[1 mark]*.

Page 108
Warm-Up Questions
1   The maintenance of a constant internal environment in response to internal and external changes.
2   Removes glucose from the blood and makes the liver turn glucose into glycogen for storage.
3   A condition in which the pancreas doesn't produce enough insulin, or the body becomes resistant to insulin.
4   E.g. having a high body mass index/obesity.

Exam Questions
1 a)   D
  b)   Eating carbohydrates *[1 mark]*.
  c)   The pancreas/organ A produces very little or no insulin *[1 mark]*. This means that the liver/organ B is unable to remove glucose from the blood for storage *[1 mark]*. So the blood glucose level is able to rise to a dangerously high level *[1 mark]*.
  d)   It makes the liver/organ B turn glycogen into glucose increasing blood sugar levels *[1 mark]*.

Section 8 — Exchange and Transport in Animals
Page 109
Exchange of Materials
Q1   Surface area:
$(2 \times 2) \times 2 = 8$
$(2 \times 1) \times 4 = 8$
$8 + 8 = 16 \, \mu m^2$ *[1 mark]*
Volume:
$2 \times 2 \times 1 = 4 \, \mu m^3$ *[1 mark]*
So the surface area to volume ratio is **16 : 4, or 4 : 1** *[1 mark]*.

Page 112
Respiration
Q1   Running is a more intense type of exercise than walking *[1 mark]*, so more anaerobic respiration will be taking place in the muscles *[1 mark]*. Anaerobic respiration produces lactic acid, so running will lead to more lactic acid being in the blood *[1 mark]*.

Page 114
Warm-Up Questions
1   For efficient diffusion, as they have a small surface area compared to their volume, it's difficult to exchange enough substances across their outside surface alone.
2   Any two from: e.g. metabolic processes/to build up larger molecules from smaller ones. / To contract muscles. / To keep body temperature steady.
3   E.g. carbon dioxide and urea.
4   Glucose and oxygen.
5   respirometer

Exam Questions
1 a)   C *[1 mark]*
  b)   The alveoli walls are thin *[1 mark]* which minimises the distance that gases have to move *[1 mark]*.

2 a)   To release energy from the breakdown of organic compounds *[1 mark]*
  b)   Any two from: e.g. aerobic respiration uses oxygen, anaerobic respiration does not. / Glucose is broken down fully during aerobic respiration but is only partially broken down during anaerobic respiration. / Aerobic respiration doesn't produce lactic acid/ethanol, anaerobic respiration does. / Aerobic respiration releases more energy than anaerobic respiration. *[2 marks]*
  c)   glucose *[1 mark]* → lactic acid *[1 mark]*

Page 119
Circulatory System — The Heart
Q1   stroke volume = cardiac output ÷ heart rate
= 4221 cm^3 min^{-1} ÷ 67 bpm
= **63 cm^3** *[2 marks for the correct answer, or 1 mark for the correct calculation]*

Page 120
Warm-Up Questions
1   They carry blood back to the heart.
2   They help the blood to clot at a wound.
3   Any three from: e.g. red blood cells / white blood cells / platelets / glucose / amino acids / carbon dioxide / urea / hormones / proteins / antibodies / antitoxins.
4   cardiac output = heart rate × stroke volume

Exam Questions
1 a)   White blood cells *[1 mark]*. They defend the body against infection *[1 mark]*.
  b)   Any two from: e.g. they have permeable walls *[1 mark]*, so substances can diffuse in and out *[1 mark]*. / Their walls are usually only one cell thick *[1 mark]*, which increases the rate of diffusion by decreasing the distance over which it occurs *[1 mark]*. / They are very narrow *[1 mark]*, so they can squeeze into the gaps between cells *[1 mark]*.
2 a)   A — aorta, B — vena cava, C — left atrium *[1 mark]*
  b)   It pumps blood around the body *[1 mark]*.
  c)   To prevent the backflow of blood *[1 mark]*.
  d)   Deoxygenated blood enters the right atrium *[1 mark]* through the vena cava *[1 mark]*. The blood moves through to the right ventricle *[1 mark]* which pumps it through the pulmonary artery to the lungs *[1 mark]*.

Section 9 — Ecosystems and Material Cycles
Page 123
Investigating Ecosystems
Q1   0.75 × 4 = 3 buttercups per m^2 *[1 mark]*.
3 × 1200 = **3600 buttercups in total** *[1 mark]*.

Page 125
Warm-Up Questions
1   a community
2   A community of living organisms (biotic) with the non-living (abiotic) conditions.
3   E.g. amount of water, light intensity, temperature, levels of pollutants.

Exam Questions
1 a)   E.g. they could have marked out a transect/straight line from the wood to the opposite side of the field *[1 mark]* and placed quadrats along it at regular intervals *[1 mark]*. They then could have counted the number of poppies in each quadrat *[1 mark]*.
  b)   E.g. the number of poppies increases with increasing distance from the wood *[1 mark]*.
2 a)   At first, the population size of the cutthroat trout would decrease as the lake trout eat the cutthroat trout *[1 mark]*. This would lead to a decline in the population of the lake trout (as they'd have less to eat) *[1 mark]*. That would allow the population of cutthroat trout to increase again *[1 mark]*. The population of lake trout would then increase as they have more to eat (and the cycle would start again) *[1 mark]*.
  b)   E.g. competition with other fish species *[1 mark]*.

Page 130
Warm-Up Questions
1   Biodiversity is the variety of living organisms in an ecosystem.
2   Excess nitrates cause algae in the water to grow more quickly, which stops light reaching plants growing in the water. This means that the plants cannot photosynthesise, so they die and then decompose. This provides more food for microorganisms that feed on the decomposing plants. They increase in number, using up the oxygen in the water. This leads to the death of organisms in the water that need oxygen for aerobic respiration, like fish.
3   Conservation schemes maintain biodiversity by preventing species from dying out.

4. Any two from: e.g. food is added to the nets to feed the fish, which also produce lots of waste. The food and waste can leak into the water system, causing eutrophication and the death of wild species. / Open water fish farms can be a breeding ground for parasites, which can then escape and infect wild animals, killing them. / Predators can be attracted to the nets, become trapped in them and die. / Farmed fish can escape into the wild and can out-compete indigenous species.

Exam Questions

1. E.g. black rats could compete with the island's indigenous species for resources *[1 mark]*. If the rats out-compete other species this could cause them to die out, reducing biodiversity *[1 mark]*. The black rats might bring new diseases to the island habitat *[1 mark]*. These new diseases might infect and kill lots of indigenous species, reducing the habitat's biodiversity *[1 mark]*.

You don't have to have given these exact answers here. You get one mark each for giving any two sensible ways that introducing the rats could reduce biodiversity, and one mark each for explaining how each one could reduce biodiversity.

2. a) Planting only white spruce will result in low biodiversity because of the low number of tree species *[1 mark]*. A lower number of tree species will also mean that the number of different animal species using the trees for food and shelter will be lower *[1 mark]*.
   b) E.g. protect the forest so that the natural habitat of the species is preserved. / Protect the species in a safe area outside of the forest. / Use a captive breeding programme to increase their numbers *[1 mark]*.

3. How to grade your answer:
   Level 0: There is no relevant information. *[0 marks]*
   Level 1: There is some information about the possible benefits of conservation schemes for species within the ecosystem, the people of Ecuador or people from other countries. The points made are basic and not linked together. *[1 to 2 marks]*
   Level 2: There is some discussion of the possible benefits of conservation schemes for at least two of species within the ecosystem, the people of Ecuador or people from other countries. Some of the points made are linked together. *[3 to 4 marks]*
   Level 3: There is a clear and detailed discussion of the possible benefits of conservation schemes for species within the ecosystem, the people of Ecuador and people from other countries. The points made are well-linked and the answer has a clear and logical structure. *[5 to 6 marks]*

Here are some points your answer may include:
If at-risk species go extinct it will affect all the organisms that feed on and are eaten by that species, so the whole food chain is affected.
This means that protecting at-risk species from extinction is likely to help maintain the biodiversity of the area,
by ensuring minimal damage to food chains.
Protecting at-risk plant species may also protect the habitat of other animal and plant species in the ecosystem.
High biodiversity may bring more money to Ecuador through ecotourism, which will help to benefit the people of Ecuador. Ecotourism and the conservation schemes themselves will create new employment opportunities for local people.
Ecotourism also provides opportunities for people from outside Ecuador to see the rare species that live there.
Conservation schemes may help to protect species that are important to Ecuador's cultural heritage. Conserving rainforest areas may protect plants that will, in future, turn out to be medically useful. If these species were lost, people all over the world could miss out on valuable medicines.

Page 132
The Water Cycle
Q1 Energy from the Sun makes water from the sea evaporate, turning it into water vapour *[1 mark]*. The water vapour is carried upwards, as warm air rises *[1 mark]*. When it gets higher up, it cools and condenses to form clouds *[1 mark]*. Water then falls from the clouds as precipitation, usually as rain *[1 mark]*.

Page 135
The Nitrogen Cycle
Q1 Decomposers break down dead leaves and release ammonia *[1 mark]*. Then nitrifying bacteria turn the ammonia into nitrites *[1 mark]* and then into nitrates *[1 mark]*.

Page 136
Warm-Up Questions
1. Fossil fuels release carbon dioxide as they are burned (to produce energy).
2. Water vapour rises, then cools and condenses to form clouds.
3. Nitrifying bacteria turn ammonia in decaying matter into nitrites and then into nitrates.
4. Using fertilisers increases the amount of nitrates in the soil. This increases the growth of the crops and so the crop yield.

Exam Questions
1. a) Animals are eating plants (and gaining nitrogen compounds from the plant proteins) *[1 mark]*.
   b) denitrifying bacteria *[1 mark]*
   c) nitrogen-fixing bacteria *[1 mark]*

2. E.g. salt water is treated to remove solids *[1 mark]*, then fed at high pressure into a vessel containing a partially permeable membrane *[1 mark]*. The pressure causes water molecules to move from a higher salt concentration to a lower salt concentration *[1 mark]*. As water moves through the membrane, the salts are left behind, removing them from the water *[1 mark]*.

3. How to grade your answer:
   Level 0: There is no relevant information. *[No marks]*
   Level 1: There is a brief description of one or two ways in which carbon stored in the vegetation could be returned to the atmosphere. The answer shows some basic understanding, but lacks coherency. The points made do not link together. *[1 to 2 marks]*
   Level 2: There is some description of more than two of the ways that carbon stored in the vegetation could be returned to the atmosphere. The answer shows mostly accurate understanding and has some structure. *[3 to 4 marks]*
   Level 3: There is a clear and detailed description of more than three of the ways that carbon stored in the vegetation could be returned to the atmosphere. The answer shows an accurate understanding of the relevant biology and is well structured. *[5 to 6 marks]*

Here are some points your answer may include:
Carbon stored in the small branches will be returned to the atmosphere as carbon dioxide when the branches are burnt.
The green plants could be broken down by microorganisms/decomposers, which will release carbon as carbon dioxide as they respire.
Some of the green plants may be eaten by other organisms. Some of the carbon from these plants will be released as carbon dioxide when the animals respire.
Some of the carbon from these plants will be lost as carbon compounds in the animals' waste.
Microorganisms/decomposers will break this material down and release carbon dioxide as they respire.
Some of the carbon from these plants will be stored as carbon compounds in the animals' biomass.
This carbon will not be released until the animals are dead.
It will be released as carbon dioxide by the microorganisms/decomposers that break down the dead material as they respire.
The wood that is taken away to be made into furniture will eventually return the carbon to the atmosphere through decay/ burning when the lifespan of the furniture is over.

Section 10 — Key Concepts in Chemistry
Page 139
Chemical Equations
Q1 $2Fe + 3Cl_2 \rightarrow 2FeCl_3$ *[1 mark]*
Q2 a) water $\rightarrow$ hydrogen + oxygen *[1 mark]*
   b) $2H_2O \rightarrow 2H_2 + O_2$
   [1 mark for correct reactants and products, 1 mark for a correctly balanced equation]

Page 143
Warm-Up Questions
1. $2Al + 3Cl_2 \rightarrow 2AlCl_3$
2. $H^+_{(aq)} + OH^-_{(aq)} \rightarrow H_2O_{(l)}$
3. The student should wear gloves, a lab coat and goggles when handling chemical A / should only use low concentrations of chemical A. When handling chemical B, the student should take care to keep it away from naked flames.

Exam Questions
1. a) Sodium hydroxide + hydrochloric acid $\rightarrow$ sodium chloride + water *[1 mark]*
   b) (aq) *[1 mark]*
2. a) methane and oxygen *[1 mark]*
   b) carbon dioxide and water *[1 mark]*
   c) $CH_4 + 2O_2 \rightarrow CO_2 + 2H_2O$
   [1 mark for correct missing reactant, 1 mark for correctly balancing the equation]
3. a) $H_2SO_4 + 2NH_3 \rightarrow (NH_4)_2SO_4$ *[1 mark for correct missing reactant, 1 mark for correctly balancing the equation]*
   b) 15 *[1 mark]*
   There are eight atoms of hydrogen, one atom of sulfur, four atoms of oxygen, and two atoms of nitrogen.
   c) 8 *[1 mark]*
   There are 4 hydrogen atoms in NH_4 and there are two of these.

Page 146
The Atom
Q1 protons = atomic number = 31 *[1 mark]*
electrons = protons = 31 *[1 mark]*
neutrons = mass number − atomic number
= 70 − 31 = **39** *[1 mark]*

Page 147
Warm-Up Questions
1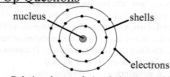

2 Relative charge of −1, relative mass of 0.0005.
3 The total number of protons and neutrons in the atom.
4 electrons = 19, protons = 19, neutrons = 39 − 19 = **20**

Exam Questions
1 a) proton: +1, neutron: 0
[2 marks — 1 mark for each correct charge]
b) In the nucleus *[1 mark]*.
c) 8 *[1 mark]*
d) 1 *[1 mark]*
2 a) 7 *[1 mark]*
b) The number of protons is the same as the atomic number *[1 mark]*
3 How to grade your answer:
Level 0: No description is given. *[No marks]*
Level 1: Brief description of how the theory of atomic structure has changed. The points made do not link together.
[1 to 2 marks]
Level 2: Some detail given of how the theory of atomic structure has changed. The answer has some structure.
[3 to 4 marks]
Level 3: A clear and detailed description of how the theory of atomic structure has changed. The answer is well structured. *[5 to 6 marks]*

Here are some points your answer may include:
John Dalton described atoms as solid spheres that make up the different elements.
J J Thomson concluded that atoms weren't solid spheres and that an atom must contain smaller, negatively charged particles (electrons). He called this the 'plum pudding model'.
Ernest Rutherford conducted a gold foil experiment, firing positively charged particles at an extremely thin sheet of gold. Most of the particles went straight through, but a few were deflected more than expected and a small number were deflected backwards. This made him think that the plum pudding model of the atom couldn't be correct. He concluded that there was a positively charged nucleus at the centre, surrounded by a 'cloud' of negative electrons.
Niels Bohr proposed a new model of the atom where all the electrons were contained in shells. He suggested that electrons can only exist in fixed orbits, or shells. This theory was supported by lots of evidence.
The currently accepted model of the atom is a nucleus containing protons and neutrons, orbited by electrons in shells. The nucleus contains most of the mass of the atom, but is very small compared to the size of the atom.

Page 149
Isotopes and Relative Atomic Masses
Q1 Relative atomic mass = $\frac{(92.2 \times 28) + (4.7 \times 29) + (3.1 \times 30)}{92.2 + 4.7 + 3.1}$ *[1 mark]*
= $\frac{2581.6 + 136.3 + 93}{100}$ = $\frac{2810.9}{100}$
= 28.109 = **28.1** *[1 mark]*

Page 152
Electronic Configurations
Q1 2.8.3 or *[1 mark]*

Page 153
Warm-Up Questions
1 The average mass of one atom of an element, compared to 1/12 the mass of one atom of carbon-12.
2 a) by atomic mass and chemical properties
  b) by atomic number
3 a) 2
  b) 8
  c) 8
4 2.8.7

Exam Questions
1 a) 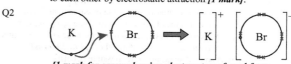 *[1 mark]*
b) Any one of: lithium / potassium / rubidium / caesium / francium *[1 mark]*
c) 1 *[1 mark]*
2 a) An isotope is a different atomic form of the same element *[1 mark]*, which has the same number of protons *[1 mark]* but a different number of neutrons *[1 mark]*.
b) Protons = 6 *[1 mark]*, neutrons = 7 *[1 mark]*, electrons = 6 *[1 mark]*
c) It has a different atomic number from carbon *[1 mark]*.
d) (13 × 79) + (14 × 21) = 1321
Relative atomic mass = $\frac{1321}{100}$ = 13.21 = **13.2** (to 1 d.p.)
[3 marks for correct answer to one decimal place, otherwise 1 mark for multiplying each relative isotopic mass by its percentage abundance and adding them together and 1 mark for dividing by 100.]

Page 156
Ionic Bonding
Q1 Each sodium atom loses an electron to form an Na+ ion *[1 mark]*. Each chlorine atom gains an electron to form a Cl− ion *[1 mark]*. The oppositely charged ions are attracted to each other by electrostatic attraction *[1 mark]*.

Q2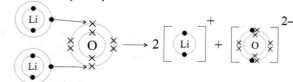

[1 mark for arrow showing electron transferred from potassium to bromine 1 mark for both ions having correct electron configurations — you only need to show the outer shells, 1 mark for correct charges on ions]

Page 158
Ionic Compounds
Q1 Li$_2$O *[1 mark]*

Page 159
Warm-Up Questions
1 A charged atom or group of atoms.
2 +2
3 Because the lattice is held together by a lot of strong ionic bonds, it takes a lot of energy to overcome these attractions and melt/boil the sodium chloride.
4 When ionic compounds are dissolved, the ions separate and are free to move in the solution. These free-moving charged particles allow the solution to carry electric charge.
5 Al(OH)$_3$

Exam Questions
1 a) Sodium will lose the electron from its outer shell to form a positive ion *[1 mark]*. Fluorine will gain an electron to form a negative ion *[1 mark]*.
b) Ionic compounds have a giant ionic lattice structure *[1 mark]*. The ions form a closely packed regular lattice arrangement *[1 mark]*, held together by strong electrostatic forces of attraction between oppositely charged ions *[1 mark]*.
2 a) lithium oxide *[1 mark]*
b)

[1 mark for arrows shown correctly, 1 mark for correct electron arrangement and charge on lithium ion, 1 mark for correct electron arrangement and charge on oxygen ion]
c) When molten, the Li+ and O^{2-} ions are able to move *[1 mark]*. These ions are able to carry electric charge *[1 mark]*.
d) The formula of the compound is **LiCl** *[1 mark]*. Lithium is in Group 1, so forms +1 ions. Chlorine is in Group 7, so forms −1 ions. Therefore there needs to be one lithium ion for every chloride ion for the compound to be neutral *[1 mark]*.

Page 162
Warm-Up Questions
1 A strong bond made by the sharing of a pair of electrons between two atoms.
2 2

3	10^{-10} m
4	gas or liquid
5	covalent bonds
6	intermolecular forces

Exam Questions

1. 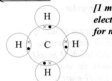 *[1 mark for showing pairs of shared electrons between C and H. 1 mark for no other electrons shown.]*

2. a) *[1 mark for showing a pair of shared electrons between H and Cl atoms. 1 mark for showing three non-bonding pairs of electrons on the chlorine atom]*

   b) 2 *[1 mark]*

   It makes two single bonds (one double bond).

3. a) Hydrogen chloride doesn't contain any ions or free electrons to carry a charge *[1 mark]*.

   b) Chlorine is a larger molecule than hydrogen chloride *[1 mark]* and therefore there are greater intermolecular forces between molecules *[1 mark]*. As the intermolecular forces are greater between chlorine molecules, its boiling point is higher than hydrogen chloride's *[1 mark]*.

   Chlorine has three shells of electrons, whereas hydrogen only has one. So Cl_2 is a bigger molecule than HCl.

Page 163
Giant Covalent Structures

Q1 Graphite is made up of carbon atoms. Each carbon atom forms three covalent bonds *[1 mark]* to form layers of carbon atoms *[1 mark]* arranged in hexagons *[1 mark]*. There are no covalent bonds between the sheets (only weak forces of attraction) *[1 mark]*.

Page 166
Warm-Up Questions

1. E.g. diamond is much harder than graphite. Diamond doesn't conduct electricity whereas graphite does.
2. Molecules of carbon, shaped like closed tubes or hollow balls.
3. A molecule made up of long chains of covalently bonded carbon atoms.
4. The electrostatic forces between the metal ions and the delocalised sea of electrons are very strong. To melt a metal, these forces need to be broken, and this requires lots of energy.

Exam Questions

1. a) In a giant covalent structure, all of the atoms are bonded to each other with strong covalent bonds *[1 mark]*. It takes lots of energy to break these bonds and melt the solid *[1 mark]*.
   b) E.g. diamond / graphite / graphene *[1 mark]*

2. a) E.g. copper is a good electrical conductor as it contains delocalised electrons *[1 mark]* which are able to carry an electrical charge *[1 mark]*.
   b) The layers of atoms in copper are able to slide over each other *[1 mark]*.

3. a) The layers of carbon atoms that make up graphite are held together weakly *[1 mark]*. The layers can easily slide over each other, making graphite soft and slippery *[1 mark]*.
   b) E.g. each carbon atom has a delocalised electron/ an electron that is able to move *[1 mark]*.
   The delocalised electrons can carry an electrical charge through the material.
   c) In diamond, each carbon atom forms four covalent bonds in a rigid lattice structure *[1 mark]*. This makes diamond very hard, so it would be good at cutting other substances *[1 mark]*.
   d) i) graphene *[1 mark]*
      ii) E.g. they have a very large surface area which catalyst molecules could be attached to *[1 mark]*.

Page 167
Conservation of Mass

Q1 The mass of the reaction container will increase *[1 mark]*. One of the reactants is a gas and the product is a solid *[1 mark]*, so as the gas reacts to form the product it will become contained in the reaction container *[1 mark]*.

Page 170
Moles and Calculations

Q1 moles = mass ÷ M_r
= 90 ÷ 18 = **5.0 moles** *[1 mark]*

Q2 $3.5 \times 6.02 \times 10^{23} = \mathbf{2.107 \times 10^{24}}$ *[1 mark]*

Q3 moles = mass ÷ M_r
= 81.4 ÷ 74 = 1.1 moles *[1 mark]*
$1.1 \times 6.02 \times 10^{23} = 6.622 \times 10^{23}$ *[1 mark]*
In one particle of $Ca(OH)_2$, there are 5 atoms, so in 1.1 moles, there are: $6.622 \times 10^{23} \times 5 = \mathbf{3.311 \times 10^{24}}$ **atoms** *[1 mark]*

Page 171
Moles and Calculations

Q1 Volume = 15 ÷ 1000 = 0.015 dm³ *[1 mark]*
concentration = mass ÷ volume = 0.60 ÷ 0.015
= **40 g dm⁻³** *[1 mark]*

Page 172
Warm-Up Questions

1. The sum of the relative atomic masses of all the atoms in a compound.
2. C_2H_4Cl
3. E.g. an amount of particles in a substance equal to Avogadro's constant (6.02×10^{23}).
4. moles = mass ÷ M_r = 184 ÷ 46 = **4.0 moles**
5. M_r = mass ÷ moles = 87.0 ÷ 0.500 = **174**
6. 200 cm³ = (200 ÷ 1000) dm³ = 0.2 dm³
mass = concentration × volume = 55 × 0.2 = **11 g**

Exam Questions

1. C *[1 mark]*
   Mr of $CaCl_2$ = 40 + (2 × 35.5) = 111

2. a) $M_r(MgCO_3)$ = 24 + 12 + (3 × 16) = **84** *[1 mark]*
   b) The mass of the reaction vessel and its contents is likely to decrease over the course of the reaction *[1 mark]* as one of the products is a gas *[1 mark]*. Since the reaction vessel isn't sealed, the gas will escape from the reaction vessel and so its mass won't be measured *[1 mark]*.

3. a) M_r of KOH = (39 + 16 + 1) = 56
   Mass of 4 moles of KOH = 4 × 56 = 224 g
   Extra mass needed = 224 − 140 = **84 g**
   [3 marks for correct answer, otherwise 1 mark for M_r of KOH and 1 mark for mass of 4 moles of KOH]
   b) M_r of K_2SO_4 = (2 × 39) + 32 + (4 × 16) = 174
   mass of K_2SO_4 = moles × M_r = 1.25 × 174 = 217.5 = **218 g**
   [2 marks for correct answer, otherwise 1 mark for M_r of K_2SO_4]
   c) volume = 1500 ml = 1.5 dm³
   mass of copper ions = concentration × volume = 12 × 1.5 = 18 g
   moles of copper ions = mass ÷ M_r = 18 ÷ 63.5 = 0.28346... moles
   no. of copper ions = moles × Avogadro's constant
   = 0.28346... × 6.02 × 10^{23}
   = 1.70645... × 10^{23} = $\mathbf{1.7 \times 10^{23}}$ **(2 s.f.)**
   [4 marks for correct answer, otherwise 1 mark for mass of copper ions, 1 mark for number of moles of copper ions and 1 mark for correct working used to calculate the number of copper ions]

Page 173
Calculating Empirical Formulas

Q1 mass of oxygen = 45.6 − 13.9 = 31.7 g *[1 mark]*
moles = mass ÷ A_r
moles of oxygen = 31.7 ÷ 16 = 1.98125
moles of nitrogen = 13.9 ÷ 14 = 0.99... *[1 mark]*
Divide by the smallest number (0.99...).
oxygen = 1.98125 ÷ 0.99... = 2
nitrogen = 0.99... ÷ 0.99... = 1
Ratio of O : N = 2 : 1.
So empirical formula = NO_2 *[1 mark]*

Page 175
Limiting Reactants

Q1 $M_r(KBr)$ = 119, $M_r(KCl)$ = 74.5 *[1 mark]*
No. of moles of KBr = 23.8 ÷ 119 = 0.200 mol *[1 mark]*
From the equation, 2 moles of KBr react to form 2 moles of KCl.
So 0.200 moles of KBr will form 0.200 mol of KCl *[1 mark]*.
So mass of KCl = 74.5 × 0.200
= **14.9 g** *[1 mark]*

Page 176
Balancing Equations Using Masses

Q1 a) N_2: $\frac{84}{28} = 3$ mol *[1 mark]*

H_2: $\frac{18}{2} = 9$ mol *[1 mark]*

NH_3: $\frac{102}{17} = 6$ mol *[1 mark]*

b) Divide by the smallest number of moles (3):
N_2: $\frac{3}{3} = 1$ H_2: $\frac{9}{3} = 3$ NH_3: $\frac{6}{3} = 2$ *[1 mark]*
The balanced symbol equation is:
$N_2 + 3H_2 \rightarrow 2NH_3$ *[1 mark]*

Page 177
Warm-Up Questions
1. moles = mass ÷ A_r
   moles of boron = 5.5 ÷ 11 = 0.5
   moles of fluorine = 28.5 ÷ 19 = 1.5
   Divide by the smallest number (0.5).
   boron = 0.5 ÷ 0.5 = 1
   nitrogen = 1.5 ÷ 0.5 = 3
   Ratio of B : F = 1 : 3.
   So empirical formula = BF_3
2. The reactant that gets used up in a reaction and therefore limits the amount of product formed.
3. It halves.

Exam Questions
1. a) moles of metal X = mass ÷ A_r = 3.5 ÷ 7 = **0.5 mol**
   moles of oxygen = mass ÷ M_r = 4.0 ÷ 32 = **0.125 mol**
   moles of metal oxide = mass ÷ M_r = 7.5 ÷ 30 = **0.25 mol**
   [2 marks for all three correct answers, otherwise 1 mark for two correct answers]
   b) Divide by the smallest number of moles (0.125):
   X: $\frac{0.5}{0.125} = 4$ O_2: $\frac{0.125}{0.125} = 1$ Oxide: $\frac{0.25}{0.125} = 2$ *[1 mark]*
   The balanced symbol equation is:
   $4X + O_2 \rightarrow 2X_2O$ *[1 mark]*
   Even if your answer to (a) was wrong, you'd still gets the marks for part (b) if you used the correct method.
2. a) i) M_r of $NaHCO_3$ = 23 + 1 + 12 + (3 × 16) = 84
   Moles of $NaHCO_3$ = 6.0 ÷ 84 = 0.0714... mol
   1 mole of Na_2SO_4 is made for every 2 moles of $NaHCO_3$ that reacts, so moles of Na_2SO_4 = 0.0714... ÷ 2
   = 0.0357... = **0.036 mol**
   [3 marks for correct answer, otherwise 1 mark for M_r of $NaHCO_3$ and 1 mark for moles of $NaHCO_3$]
   ii) M_r of Na_2SO_4 = (2 × 23) + 32 + (4 × 16) = 142
   Mass of Na_2SO_4 = 142 × 0.036 = 5.112 = **5.1 g (2 s.f.)**
   [2 marks for correct answer, otherwise 1 mark for M_r of Na_2SO_4]
   Even if your answer to (i) was wrong, you'd still gets the marks for part (ii) if you used the correct method.
   b) H_2SO_4 is in excess/$NaHCO_3$ is the limiting reactant *[1 mark]*
3. a) M_r (Fe_2O_3) = (2 × 56) + (3 × 16) = 160
   A_r (C) = 12 *[1 mark]*
   Moles = mass ÷ M_r (or A_r)
   Moles of Fe_2O_3 = 2.4 ÷ 160 = 0.015 mol
   Moles of C = 0.36 ÷ 12 = 0.03 mol *[1 mark]*
   Dividing by the smallest number of moles (0.015): Fe_2O_3 = 1, C = 2
   In the balanced equation, Fe_2O_3 and C react in a ratio of 2 : 3.
   Using the masses, there is a 1 : 2 ratio of Fe_2O_3 to C (which is the same as 2 : 4) *[1 mark]*, so Fe_2O_3 is the reactant that is not in excess *[1 mark]*.
   [4 marks for correct answer, otherwise 1 mark for each stage of the working as shown in the answer above]
   b) mass of element Y present = 52.00 − 17.92 = 34.08 g *[1 mark]*
   moles = mass ÷ M_r (or A_r)
   moles of Fe = 17.92 ÷ 56 = 0.32 moles
   moles of product = 52.00 ÷ 162.5 = 0.32 moles
   moles of Y_2 = 34.08 ÷ 71 = 0.48 *[1 mark]*
   So ratio of Fe : Y_2 : product = 0.32 : 0.48 : 0.32.
   Divide them all by the smallest number of moles, which is 0.32:
   Ratio of Fe : Y_2 : product = 1 : 1.5 : 1.
   Multiply by 2 to make everything a whole number:
   Ratio of Fe : Y_2 : product = 2 : 3 : 2 *[1 mark]*
   So balanced equation: $2Fe + 3Y_2 \rightarrow$ 2(product). To make the equation balance, the product must contain 1 atom of Fe and 3 atoms of Y.
   So the balanced equation is:
   $2Fe + 3Y_2 \rightarrow 2FeY_3$ *[1 mark]*
   [4 marks for the correct balanced equation, otherwise 1 mark for each stage of the working as shown in the answer above]

Section 11 — States of Matter and Mixtures
Page 181
States of Matter
Q1 a) solid *[1 mark]*
   b) liquid *[1 mark]*
   c) liquid *[1 mark]*
   d) gas *[1 mark]*

Page 182
Warm-Up Questions
1. gas, liquid, solid
2. The particles move faster.
3. a) freezing
   b) condensing
   c) melting
   d) subliming

Exam Questions
1. a) Particles are held in fixed positions in a regular lattice arrangement *[1 mark]*.
   b) The particles gain energy, so they move faster *[1 mark]*. The intermolecular bonds are weakened and, when the particles have enough energy, the bonds break *[1 mark]*. This means the particles are free to move far apart from each other and the liquid becomes a gas *[1 mark]*.
2. a) liquid *[1 mark]*
   b) gas *[1 mark]*
3. a) The particles are free to move about / have virtually no forces of attraction between them *[1 mark]*, so they move randomly, spreading out to fill the container *[1 mark]*.
   b) Liquids can flow because the particles in a liquid are free to move past each other but tend to stick together *[1 mark]*. Solids cannot flow because the particles in a solid are held in fixed positions *[1 mark]*.

Page 185
Distillation
Q1 Ethanol *[1 mark]*. Ethanol has the second lowest boiling point and will be collected once all the methanol has been distilled off and the temperature increased *[1 mark]*.

Page 187
Warm-Up Questions
1. A pure substance is a substance that only contains one compound or one element.
2. Impurities in a substance will result in it boiling over a wider temperature range.
3. fractional distillation
4. crystallisation

Exam Questions
1. The compound is likely to be pure *[1 mark]*, because it has a single, sharp melting point *[1 mark]*.
2. a) E.g. mix the lawn sand with water to dissolve the ammonium sulfate *[1 mark]*. Filter the mixture using filter paper to remove the sharp sand and leave it to dry in a warm place/desiccator/drying oven *[1 mark]*. Pour the remaining solution into an evaporating dish and slowly heat it to evaporate the water and crystallise the ammonium sulfate until you have a dry product *[1 mark]*.
   b) E.g. the products were not completely dry *[1 mark]*.
3. a) The boiling points of water and methanoic acid are too close together to allow them to be separated by simple distillation *[1 mark]*.
   b)

Temperature on thermometer	Contents of the flask	Contents of the beaker
30 °C	both liquids	no liquid
65 °C	water	propanone
110 °C	no liquid	both liquids

[3 marks for whole table correct otherwise 1 mark for each correct row]

Page 189
Interpreting Chromatograms
Q1 $R_f = \frac{6.3}{8.4} = 0.75$ *[1 mark]*.

Page 191
Water Treatment
Q1 The water is first filtered through a wire mesh to filter out large objects and through gravel and sand to filter out smaller solid objects *[1 mark]*. Then a sedimentation process is used in which chemicals are added to the water to make fine particles clump together and settle at the bottom *[1 mark]*. Finally, chlorine gas is bubbled through the water to kill harmful bacteria *[1 mark]*.

Page 192
Warm-Up Questions
1. a piece of filter paper
2. Pencil marks are insoluble, so the baseline won't dissolve into the solvent and separate along with the substance being analysed.
3. Chemical A will end up closer to the solvent front than B.
4. distillation

Exam Questions
1. Tap water could contain other ions that might interfere with the reaction *[1 mark]*. He should use deionised water instead *[1 mark]*
2. a) All of the inks in Figure 1 have separated into at least two different substances, so none of them can be pure *[1 mark]*.
   b) A *[1 mark]*
   c) C *[1 mark]* because the spots in the chromatogram for C match those in sunrise yellow *[1 mark]*.

d) R_f = distance travelled by substance in sunrise yellow ÷ distance travelled by solvent
$R_f = 9.0 ÷ 12.0 = $ **0.75**
[2 marks for correct answer, otherwise 1 mark for using the correct formula to calculate R_f]
e) distillation *[1 mark]*

Section 12 — Chemical Changes
Page 193
Acids and Bases
Q1 The H$^+$ ions from the acid *[1 mark]* react with the OH$^-$ ions from the alkali to form water *[1 mark]*.

Page 197
Warm-Up Questions
1 A substance that reacts with an acid to produce a salt and water.
2 0 to 14
3 neutral
4 a) Strong acids ionise almost completely in water, so a large proportion of the acid molecules dissociate to release H$^+$ ions. Weak acids do not fully ionise, so only a small proportion of the acid molecules dissociate to release H$^+$ ions.
b) A concentrated acid has a much larger number of acid molecules per litre of water than a dilute acid.
5 sodium chloride and hydrogen
6 $H_2SO_4 + CaCO_3 \rightarrow CaSO_4 + H_2O + CO_2$
7 Carbon dioxide turns limewater cloudy.

Exam Questions
1 a) H$^+$ ions/hydrogen ions *[1 mark]*
b) neutralisation *[1 mark]*
2 a) $2HCl + Ca(OH)_2 \rightarrow CaCl_2 + 2H_2O$
[1 mark for formulas of both products correct, 1 mark for putting a 2 in front of H_2O to balance the equation]
b) From red *[1 mark]* through orange/yellow to green *[1 mark]*.
c) Difference in pH = 5 − 2 = 3
So the H$^+$ concentration decreased by a factor of 10^3 / 1000 *[1 mark]*
d) Because a lot of the H$^+$ ions will react with OH$^-$ ions to form water during the reaction *[1 mark]*.
e) alkali *[1 mark]*

Page 198
Making Insoluble Salts
Q1 E.g. barium nitrate/barium chloride and copper sulfate *[1 mark for any soluble barium salt and 1 mark for any soluble sulfate]*

Page 201
Warm-Up Questions
1 a) soluble
b) insoluble
c) insoluble
d) soluble
2 Because if you don't use a titration, you can't tell when the reaction is complete. Also you can't add an excess of alkali/acid, because alkalis/acids are soluble and would contaminate the soluble salt produced.

Exam Questions
1 lead chloride — insoluble *[1 mark]*
potassium nitrate — soluble *[1 mark]*
2 Filter the product mixture through some filter paper *[1 mark]*. Rinse the solid/calcium sulfate left behind on the filter paper with deionised water *[1 mark]*. Scrape the solid/calcium sulfate onto fresh filter paper and leave it to dry in an oven/desiccator *[1 mark]*.
3 a) The excess copper oxide will sink to the bottom of the flask and stay there *[1 mark]*.
b) filtration *[1 mark]*
c) Heat the copper sulfate solution gently using a Bunsen burner to evaporate some of the water *[1 mark]*. Leave the solution to cool until crystals form *[1 mark]*. Filter out the crystals and dry them *[1 mark]*.
4 How to grade your answer:
Level 0: There is no relevant information. *[No marks]*
Level 1: There is a brief explanation of how to prepare the salt, but it has limited detail and little technical equipment is mentioned. The points made are basic and not linked together. *[1 to 2 marks]*
Level 2: There is an explanation of how to prepare a pure sample of the salt and some of the equipment required is named, but there are limited details. Some of the points made are linked together. *[3 to 4 marks]*
Level 3: There is a clear and detailed explanation of how to prepare a pure, dry sample of the salt and all the equipment needed is clearly named. The points made are well-linked and the answer has a clear and logical structure. *[5 to 6 marks]*

Here are some points your answer may include:
Measure out a set amount of hydrochloric acid into a conical flask using a pipette.
Add a few drops of indicator, e.g. methyl orange or phenolphthalein.
Slowly add the sodium hydroxide solution to the acid in the flask using a burette, until the acid has been exactly neutralised and the indicator changes colour.
This is the volume of sodium hydroxide solution needed to neutralise this volume of acid.
Carry out the reaction again using exactly the same volumes of hydrochloric acid and sodium hydroxide solution but with no indicator.
Slowly evaporate off some of the water from the solution in the flask, then leave the solution to cool and crystallise.
Filter off the solid and dry it.
You'll be left with a pure, dry sample of sodium chloride.

Page 204
Electrolysis of Molten Substances
Q1 a) chlorine gas/Cl_2 *[1 mark]*
b) calcium atoms/Ca *[1 mark]*

Page 207
Warm-Up Questions
1 a) Oxidation is a loss of electrons.
b) the anode
2 E.g. clean the surfaces of two inert electrodes with emery paper/sandpaper. Place both electrodes into a beaker filled with the electrolyte solution. Connect the electrodes to a power supply using crocodile clips and wires. Turn the power supply on.
3 zinc and chlorine
4 oxygen
5 copper

Exam Questions
1 a) $Al^{3+} + 3e^- \rightarrow Al$ *[1 mark]*
b) $2O^{2-} \rightarrow O_2 + 4e^-$ *[1 mark]*
c) The oxygen made at the positive electrode reacts with the carbon (to make carbon dioxide) *[1 mark]*, wearing the electrode away *[1 mark]*.
2 a) hydrogen *[1 mark]*
b) $2H^+ + 2e^- \rightarrow H_2$ *[1 mark]*
c) chlorine *[1 mark]*
d) $2Cl^- \rightarrow Cl_2 + 2e^-$ / $2Cl^- - 2e^- \rightarrow Cl_2$ *[1 mark]*
e) Sodium is more reactive than hydrogen, so the sodium ions from the sodium chloride stay in solution *[1 mark]*. Hydroxide ions are also left in solution when hydrogen is produced from water *[1 mark]*.
f) Copper is less reactive than hydrogen *[1 mark]*.

Section 13 — Extracting Metals and Equilibria
Page 213
Warm-Up Questions
1 How easily it loses electrons to form positive ions/cations.
2 Gold is less easily oxidised.
3 metal + water → metal hydroxide + hydrogen
4 A gain of electrons.
5 zinc/Zn

Exam Questions
1 a) any one from: potassium/sodium/calcium *[1 mark]*
b) copper *[1 mark]*
c) i) hydrogen *[1 mark]*
ii) Bubbles of hydrogen gas would be produced *[1 mark]* more slowly than zinc and dilute acid / very slowly *[1 mark]*.
You don't need to use these exact words — the two points you need to cover are that it would still produce hydrogen gas, but at a slower rate than the zinc.
2 In tube A there will be no change *[1 mark]*. In tube B the solution will have changed from blue to green *[1 mark]*. Iron is more reactive than copper, so in tube A the copper cannot displace the iron from iron sulfate *[1 mark]*, but in tube B the iron does displace the copper from copper sulfate, forming green iron sulfate *[1 mark]*.

Page 214
Extracting Metals Using Carbon
Q1 $2PbO + C \rightarrow 2Pb + CO_2$
[1 mark for the correct products, 1 mark for the correctly balanced equation]
Q2 Tin is less reactive than carbon *[1 mark]* so you could extract tin from its ore by reducing it with carbon *[1 mark]*.

Page 215
Extracting Metals Using Electrolysis
Q1   Aluminium would be more expensive to extract than iron *[1 mark]* as aluminium is more reactive than carbon, so has to be extracted using electrolysis, whereas iron can be extracted by reduction with carbon *[1 mark]*. Extracting metals using electrolysis is much more expensive than using reduction with carbon as it requires high temperatures to melt the metal ore which is expensive/there are costs associated with using electricity, whereas reduction using carbon is much cheaper *[1 mark]*.

Page 220
Warm-Up Questions
1   Carbon can only take away the oxygen from metals which are less reactive than carbon itself.
2   Plants are grown in soil that contains metal compounds. The plants are harvested, dried and burned in a furnace. The ash contains metal compounds from which the metal can be extracted by electrolysis or displacement reactions.
3   E.g. it saves money (compared to extracting new metals) and creates jobs.
4   Choice of material used to make the product / obtaining the raw materials, how the product is manufactured, product use and product disposal.

Exam Questions
1 a) $2Fe_2O_3 + 3C \rightarrow 4Fe + 3CO_2$ *[1 mark for all reactants and products correct, 1 mark for correctly balancing the equation]*
   b)   Oxygen is being lost from iron oxide *[1 mark]*.
2 a)   To lower the melting point of the aluminium oxide *[1 mark]*
   b) $Al^{3+} + 3e^- \rightarrow Al$ *[1 mark]*
3 a)   Bacteria get energy from the bonds between atoms in the ore and separate copper from its ore in the process *[1 mark]*. A solution called a leachate is produced which contains copper ions *[1 mark]*. Copper ions are extracted from the leachate using electrolysis/displacement with a more reactive metal *[1 mark]*.
   b)   Advantage: e.g. they have a smaller impact on the environment *[1 mark]*. Disadvantage: e.g. they are slower *[1 mark]*.
4   How to grade your answer:
     Level 0: There is no relevant information. *[No marks]*
     Level 1: There is a brief discussion of some environmental impacts of each type of bag. The points made are basic, don't link together and don't cover all of the information given in Figure 1. If a conclusion is present it may not link to points made. *[1 to 2 marks]*
     Level 2: There is a logical discussion of possible environmental impacts of each type of bag, but there is limited detail. There is a good coverage of the information given in Figure 1 and the answer has some structure. A clear conclusion is given. *[3 to 4 marks]*
     Level 3: There is a clear and detailed discussion of the possible environmental impacts of each type of bag. The answer has a logical structure and makes good use of the information given in Figure 1. A conclusion is present that fits with the points given in the answer. *[5 to 6 marks]*

Here are some points your answer may include:
The raw materials used to make plastic bags come from crude oil, which is a non-renewable resource.
Obtaining crude oil from the ground and refining it requires a lot of energy and generates air pollution due to the release of greenhouse gases.
The raw materials used to make paper bags come from trees.
Trees are a renewable resource, although they take up land that could be used for other uses e.g. growing crops.
Cutting down trees and processing the raw timber requires power.
This power is often generated by burning fossil fuels, which releases harmful greenhouse gases into the atmosphere.
Cutting down trees to make paper also reduces the amount of carbon dioxide that can be absorbed by trees, which contributes to climate change.
The manufacture of plastic bags involves fractional distillation, cracking and polymerisation, which all require large amounts of energy.
As this energy often comes from burning fossil fuels, the manufacture causes the release of pollution (e.g. greenhouse gases) into the atmosphere.
Manufacturing paper bags also requires lots of energy. This could come from burning fossil fuels and so would generate pollution, such as greenhouses gases, which have a negative impact on the environment.
In addition, the manufacture of paper bags also creates lots of waste, which has to be disposed of and may cause pollution (e.g. if sent to landfill).
Plastic bags are reusable, which could reduce the amount of waste sent to landfill.
Paper bags are usually single-use, which could increase the amount of waste sent to landfill.
Plastic bags are not biodegradable so will stay in the environment for a long time if disposed of in landfill sites.
Plastic bags can be recycled, which would reduce the need to extract raw materials to make new bags.
Paper bags are biodegradable so will break down more easily than plastic bags if sent to landfill sites, reducing the impact on the environment.
Paper bags are also non-toxic, so won't releases poisonous/toxic substances into the environment after being disposed of.
Paper bags can be recycled, which would reduce the need to gather raw materials to make new bags.

Page 223
Le Chatelier's Principle
Q1 a)   More $H_2CO_{3(aq)}$ would be produced *[1 mark]*.
   b)   Less $NH_{3(g)}$ and $HCl_{(g)}$ would be produced *[1 mark]*.
   c)   More $CO_{2(g)}$ would be produced *[1 mark]*.

Page 224
Warm-Up Questions
1   They are the same.
2   A system in which none of the reactants or products can escape.
3   It would have no effect (because there are equal numbers of gas molecules on both sides).
4   The equilibrium will move to the left/towards reactants and the amount of reactants will increase.

Exam Questions
1 a)   The reaction is reversible *[1 mark]*.
   b)   Both (the forward and reverse) reactions are taking place at exactly the same time and rate *[1 mark]*.
2 a)   Less $NO_{2(g)}$ will be produced *[1 mark]*, because there are more moles of gas on the right hand side of the equation *[1 mark]*.
   b)   It will have no effect *[1 mark]*, because there are the same number of moles of gas on both sides of the equation *[1 mark]*.
3 a)   It gives out energy *[1 mark]*, because it's exothermic *[1 mark]*.
As the forward reaction is endothermic, you know that the reverse reaction is exothermic and therefore gives out energy.
   b)   A reversible reaction is always exothermic in one direction and endothermic in the other direction *[1 mark]*, so a change in temperature will always favour one reaction more than the other *[1 mark]*.
   c)   It would move to the right *[1 mark]*.

Section 14 — Groups in the Periodic Table
Page 227
Group 1 — Alkali Metals
Q1   lithium + water → lithium hydroxide + hydrogen *[1 mark]*

Pages 233-234
Warm-Up Questions
1   1
2   more reactive
3   It increases.
4   sodium chloride/NaCl
5   A reaction where a more reactive element displaces a less reactive element from a compound.
6   negative
7   Group 0

Exam Questions
1 a)   Highest (X): fluorine *[1 mark]*
      Lowest (Y): iodine *[1 mark]*
Halogens at the top of Group 7 are more reactive than those at the bottom of the group.
   b)   iodine *[1 mark]*
2 a)   Group 1 *[1 mark]*
   b)   *[2 marks — 1 mark for correct number of electrons in correct shells, 1 mark for square brackets and charge]*
3 a)   Hold a piece of damp blue litmus paper in the gas *[1 mark]*. If the litmus paper turns from blue to white, chlorine is present *[1 mark]*.
   b)   E.g. displacement reaction *[1 mark]*
   c)   Iodine/I_2 *[1 mark]* as it is displaced from potassium iodide *[1 mark]*.
A more reactive halogen will displace a less reactive halogen from a compound.
   d)   The products of the reaction will be aqueous potassium chloride/$KCl_{(aq)}$ *[1 mark]* and bromine gas/$Br_{2(g)}$ *[1 mark]*. Chlorine is more reactive than bromine as its outer shell is closer to the nucleus *[1 mark]*. This results in chlorine displacing bromine from potassium bromide *[1 mark]*.
   e)   Group 0 elements are generally inert *[1 mark]*. This is because they don't need to lose or gain electrons to have a full outer shell *[1 mark]*.
4 a)   They have a single outer electron which is easily lost, so they are very reactive *[1 mark]*.
   b)   As you go down Group 1, the outer electron is further from the nucleus *[1 mark]*. So the attraction between the nucleus and the electron decreases *[1 mark]*. This means the outer electron is more easily lost and the metal is more reactive *[1 mark]*.

c) i) hydrogen *[1 mark]* and potassium hydroxide *[1 mark]*
ii) $2K + 2H_2O \rightarrow 2KOH + H_2$ *[1 mark for correct products and reactants, 1 mark for correct balancing]*

Section 15 — Rates of Reaction and Energy Changes

Page 235

Rates of Reaction

Q1 Average rate = amount of reactant used ÷ time
= 6.0 g ÷ 200 s *[1 mark]*
= **0.03 g s^{-1}** *[1 mark]*

Pages 241-242

Warm-Up Questions

1 E.g. how quickly a reaction happens.
2 Reaction A
3 It increases the rate of the reaction.
4 gradient = change in y ÷ change in x

Exam Questions

1 a) stopwatch/stopclock/timer *[1 mark]*
b) gas syringe *[1 mark]*
c) E.g. place a conical flask on a mass balance *[1 mark]* and record the change in mass at regular intervals as the gas leaves the flask *[1 mark]*.
2 a) Any two from: e.g. the concentration of sodium thiosulfate/ hydrochloric acid / the depth of liquid / the person judging when the black cross is obscured / the black cross used (size, darkness etc.) *[2 marks — 1 mark for each correct answer]*
Judging when a cross is completely obscured is quite subjective — two people might not agree on exactly when it happens. You can try to limit this problem by using the same person each time, but you can't remove the problem completely. The person might have changed their mind slightly by the time they do the next experiment — or be looking at it from a different angle, be a bit more bored, etc.

b)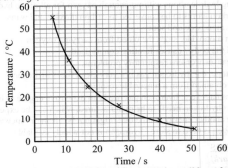
[1 mark for correctly drawn axes with a sensible scale, 2 marks for all points plotted correctly, otherwise 1 mark if 5 of 6 points plotted correctly, 1 mark for a suitable line of best fit]
c) As the temperature decreases, the time taken for the mark to disappear decreases *[1 mark]*.
d) At each temperature it would take longer for the reaction to complete *[1 mark]*.
e) E.g. by repeating the experiment *[1 mark]*. If the results gained are similar then the experiment is repeatable *[1 mark]*.
3 a) A *[1 mark]*
b) The temperature needed to be controlled so that the teacher could tell if the variable she changed/the independent variable/the change in HCl concentration caused the change in rate *[1 mark]*.
c) 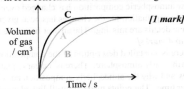 *[1 mark]*
Curve C should be to the left of the curves A and B — this shows that curve C has a steeper gradient than curves A and B. It should also finish with the same volume of gas produced as curves A and B.
4 a) Rate = amount of product formed ÷ time
= 40 ÷ 60 = **0.67 cm^3 s^{-1}** *[1 mark]*

b)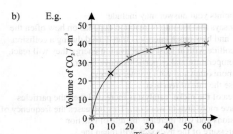
[1 mark for correctly plotting the two missing points, 1 mark for a suitable line of best fit.]

c) E.g.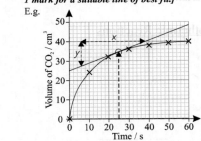
change in y = 40 − 27 = 13, change in x = 38 − 6 = 32,
rate = change in y ÷ change in x = 13 ÷ 32 = **0.4 cm^3 s^{-1}**
[1 mark for drawing a tangent at 25 s, 1 mark for correctly calculating a change in y from the tangent, 1 mark for correctly calculating a change in x from the tangent and 1 mark for a rate between 0.3 cm^3 s^{-1} and 0.5 cm^3 s^{-1}]

Page 244

Collision Theory

Q1 Increasing the temperature of a reaction mixture causes the particles to move faster *[1 mark]*, therefore they will collide more often *[1 mark]*.
Q2 Breaking a solid into smaller pieces will increase the surface area to volume ratio *[1 mark]*. This means that particles of the other reactant will have more area to work on *[1 mark]*. This increases the frequency of collisions and speeds up the rate of reaction *[1 mark]*.

Page 246

Warm-Up Questions

1 They must collide with at least the activation energy.
2 Increasing the temperature causes the particles to move faster. This increases the frequency and energy of their collisions. This means there are more successful collisions, increasing the rate of their reaction.
3 True
4 Enzymes help to speed up chemical reactions in living cells.

Exam Questions

1 a) Any two from: e.g. volume of acid / mass of calcium carbonate / size of solid particles / temperature *[2 marks — 1 mark for each correct answer]*
b) 140 − 87.5 = **52.5 cm^3** *[1 mark]*
c) The gradient of the graph at the start of the reaction is steeper for 0.4 mol dm^{-3} / the curve for the 0.4 mol dm^{-3} reaction finishes/flattens out first, so the rate of reaction is faster than when 0.2 mol dm^{-3} HCl was used *[1 mark]*.
This is because increasing the concentration of a reactant increases the number of particles of that substance in the reaction mixture *[1 mark]*. This increases the frequency of collisions between particles of the reactants, increasing the rate of the reaction *[1 mark]*.
2 How to grade your answer:
Level 0: There is no relevant information. *[No marks]*
Level 1: One or two ways of increasing the rate are described and there's reference to collision theory. The points made do not link together. *[1 to 2 marks]*
Level 2: At least two ways of increasing the rate are given with appropriate reference to collision theory. The answer has some structure. *[3 to 4 marks]*
Level 3: There is a clear and detailed discussion of three ways by which the rate can be increased, which includes relevant references to collision theory. The answer is well structured. *[5 to 6 marks]*

Page 247
Endothermic and Exothermic Reactions
Q1
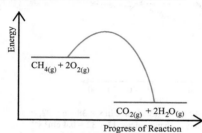

[1 mark for correct axes, 1 mark for correct energy levels of reactants and products, 1 mark for correct shape of curve linking the reactants to the products]

Page 250
Bond Energies
Q1 Energy required to break original bonds:
$(1 \times N \equiv N) + (3 \times H-H)$
$= 941 + (3 \times 436) = 941 + 1308$
$= 2249$ kJ mol^{-1} *[1 mark]*
Energy released by forming new bonds:
$(6 \times N-H)$
$= 6 \times 391 = 2346$ kJ mol^{-1} *[1 mark]*
Overall energy change:
$= 2249 - 2346 = -97$ **kJ mol^{-1}** *[1 mark]*

Page 251
Warm-Up Questions
1. An exothermic reaction is one which gives out energy to the surroundings.
2. An endothermic reaction is one which takes in energy from the surroundings.
3. The activation energy is the minimum amount of energy the reactants need to collide in order to react.
4. An increase in the temperature of the surroundings.
5. When bonds are formed.

Exam Questions
1. B *[1 mark]*
2. a) Exothermic, because the temperature of the mixture has increased *[1 mark]*, therefore the particles have transferred energy to the reaction mixture *[1 mark]*.
   b) A lid was placed on the cup to reduce energy lost to the surroundings (by evaporation) *[1 mark]*.
3. a) C – H and O = O *[1 mark]*
   b) $(4 \times 414) + (2 \times 494) = 2644$ kJ mol^{-1}
   This is the amount of energy required to break the bonds in CH_4 and $2O_2$.
   $(2 \times 800) + (4 \times 459) = 3436$ kJ mol^{-1}
   This is the amount of energy released by forming the bonds in CO_2 and $2H_2O$.
   $2644 - 3436 = -792$ **kJ mol^{-1}**
   [4 marks for correct answer, otherwise 1 mark for finding the energy needed to break the bonds in the reactants, 1 mark for finding the energy released by forming bonds in the products, 1 mark for subtracting the energy released by forming bonds from the energy required to break bonds.]

Section 16 — Fuels and Earth Science
Page 252
Fractional Distillation
Q1 The diagram shows that the hydrocarbons in petrol have a shorter chain length than the hydrocarbons in diesel, so petrol has a lower boiling point than diesel *[1 mark]*.

Page 253
Hydrocarbons
Q1 $C_2H_6 + 3½O_2 \rightarrow 2CO_2 + 3H_2O$ or
$2C_2H_6 + 7O_2 \rightarrow 4CO_2 + 6H_2O$
[1 mark for correct reactants and products, 1 mark for correctly balancing]

Page 256
Warm-Up Questions
1. a) e.g. aircraft fuel
   b) e.g. as fuel in some cars / trains
   c) e.g. surfacing roads and roofs
2. water and carbon dioxide
3. e.g. alkanes / alkenes
4. E.g. the longer the hydrocarbon molecules, the less easily it ignites. / The shorter the hydrocarbon molecules, the more easily it ignites.

Exam Question
1. a) A *[1 mark]*
   b) F *[1 mark]*
   c) Inside the fractionating column there is a temperature gradient with the hottest part at the bottom and coolest at the top *[1 mark]*. Crude oil that is gaseous moves up the column and when hydrocarbons in the gas reach a part of the column where the temperature is lower than their boiling point they condense and drain out of the column *[1 mark]*. Hydrocarbons with longer chain lengths have higher boiling points so condense lower down the column whereas hydrocarbons with shorter chain lengths have lower boiling points so condense higher up the column *[1 mark]*
   d) Because shorter-chain hydrocarbons generated by cracking tend to be more useful than longer ones *[1 mark]*.
   e) $C_8H_{18} \rightarrow \mathbf{C_2H_6} + 2C_3H_6$ *[1 mark]*

Page 260
Warm-Up Questions
1. Burning hydrocarbons without enough oxygen for all of the hydrogen and carbon atoms to be converted to carbon dioxide and water.
2. a) carbon monoxide and soot
   b) Carbon monoxide: stops the blood from carrying oxygen around the body / causes fainting/comas/death.
   Soot: causes/worsens respiratory problems.
3. Advantage: e.g. hydrogen gas is a very clean fuel / hydrogen can be obtained from a renewable resource.
   Disadvantage: e.g. hydrogen gas needs an expensive engine to be used as fuel / hydrogen needs to be manufactured, which can be expensive/ require another energy source that might not be clean or renewable / hydrogen is hard to store / hydrogen is not widely available.

Exam Questions
1. B *[1 mark]*
2. a) Fossil fuels contain sulfur impurities *[1 mark]*.
   b) When sulfur dioxide mixes with water in clouds *[1 mark]* it forms dilute sulfuric acid, which falls as acid rain *[1 mark]*.
   c) E.g. it kills plants/animals / damages buildings and statues / makes metals corrode *[1 mark]*.
3. How to grade your answer:
   Level 0: There is no relevant information. *[No marks]*
   Level 1: There is a brief description of the Earth's early atmosphere and how the atmospheric composition has changed over time, but no explanation for the changes has been given. The points made are basic and not linked together. *[1 to 2 marks]*
   Level 2: There is a description of the Earth's early atmosphere and how atmospheric composition has changed over time. Some explanation for the changes has been given, but some details are missing. The answer has some structure. *[3 to 4 marks]*
   Level 3: There is a detailed description of the composition of Earth's early atmosphere. There is a clear explanation of how and why the atmospheric composition has changed over time. The points made are well-linked and the answer has a clear and logical structure. *[5 to 6 marks]*
   Here are some points your answer may include:
   The early atmosphere was mostly made up of carbon dioxide and water vapour, with very little oxygen.
   Most of the early water vapour condensed to form the oceans, so the amount of water vapour in the atmosphere has decreased over time to just 0.25%.
   A lot of the early carbon dioxide dissolved in the oceans.
   Green plants then evolved. These removed more carbon dioxide from the atmosphere during photosynthesis.
   Much of this carbon dioxide became locked up in fossil fuels and sedimentary rocks.

So the amount of atmospheric carbon dioxide has decreased significantly over time, to just 0.04%. Photosynthesis also produced oxygen. This increased the level of oxygen to the present day concentration of 21%.

Page 261
The Greenhouse Effect
Q1 The sun gives out short wavelength radiation *[1 mark]* which is reflected back by the Earth as long wavelength/thermal radiation *[1 mark]*. The thermal radiation is absorbed by greenhouse gases in the atmosphere *[1 mark]*. Greenhouse gases give out the thermal radiation in all directions including back towards the Earth, causing the temperature to rise *[1 mark]*.

Page 264
Warm-Up Questions
1 e.g. water vapour, methane
2 a) E.g. plants take carbon dioxide out of the atmosphere, so removing trees causes carbon dioxide levels to rise.
  b) E.g. an increase in energy consumption means more fossil fuels are burnt. Burning fossil fuels releases carbon dioxide into the atmosphere, so it would increase atmospheric CO_2.
  c) E.g. methane is a greenhouse gas that is produced from the digestive processes of certain livestock. An increase in livestock farming will cause an increase in methane emissions to the atmosphere.
3 The increase in the average temperature of the Earth's surface.

Exam Questions
1 a) Any one from: e.g. less data was collected / data was collected at fewer locations / the methods used to collect the data were less accurate *[1 mark]*
  b) E.g. 317 + ((317 × 22.7) ÷ 100) = 388.959 = **389 ppm** (to 3 s.f.)
    [2 marks for correct answer to three significant figures, otherwise 1 mark for 388.959 ppm.]
  c) E.g. the temperature at the Earth's surface is correlated to the concentration of carbon dioxide in the atmosphere *[1 mark]*.
2 a) Carbon dioxide absorbs long wavelength radiation emitted from the Earth *[1 mark]*. It is then re-radiated back towards the Earth, warming the Earth's surface *[1 mark]*.
  b) Any two from: e.g. flooding / melting of the polar ice caps / changes in rainfall patterns *[2 marks]*.
  c) i) E.g. walking/cycling instead of driving / turning down their central heating *[1 mark]*.
    ii) E.g. they could create financial incentives that encourage people to cut their own personal carbon dioxide emissions / they could encourage an increase in research into new/renewable energy sources *[1 mark]*.

Section 17 — Motion and Forces
Page 267
Speed
Q1 $s = d \div t = 200 \div 25$ *[1 mark]*
    = **8 m/s** *[1 mark]*

Page 269
Acceleration
Q1 $u = 0$ m/s, $v = 5$ m/s, $a = g = 10$ m/s^2,
    $x = (v^2 - u^2) \div 2a$
    $= (25 - 0) \div (2 \times 10)$ *[1 mark]*
    = **1.25 m** *[1 mark]*

Page 270
Distance/Time Graphs
Q1 E.g.

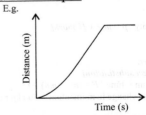

[1 mark for a curved line with an increasing positive gradient, 1 mark for the line becoming a straight line with a positive gradient, 1 mark for the line then becoming horizontal]

Page 271
Velocity/Time Graphs
Q1

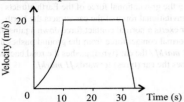

[1 mark for an upwards curved acceleration line to 20 m/s, 1 mark for a straight line representing steady speed, 1 mark for a straight line representing deceleration]

Page 272
Warm-Up Questions
1 Speed is scalar, velocity is a vector / velocity has a direction, speed does not.
2 a) E.g. 3 m/s
  b) E.g. 250 m/s
  c) E.g. 340 m/s
Your answers may be slightly different to these, but as long as they're about the same size, you should be fine to use them in the exam.
3 Velocity is calculated from the gradient.
4 A straight, horizontal line.

Exam Questions
1 a) The cyclist travels at a constant speed (of 3 m/s) between 5 s and 8 s *[1 mark]*, then decelerates between 8 s and 10 s *[1 mark]*.
  b) Area of triangle = 0.5 × width × height
    Width = 5 − 2 = 3 s
    Height = 3 m/s
    Distance = 0.5 × 3 × 3 = **4.5 m**
    [2 marks for correct answer, otherwise 1 mark for a correct method to calculate the area under the graph between 2 and 5 seconds]
You can also answer this question by counting the number of squares under the graph between 2 and 5 s — there are 4.5 squares, and the area of one square is equivalent to 1 m (height of one square × width of one square = 1 m/s × 1 s), so the cyclist has travelled 4.5 m.
  c) Acceleration is given by the gradient of a velocity-time graph.
    change in $y = 3 - 0 = 3$ m/s
    change in $x = 5 - 2 = 3$ s
    acceleration = 3 ÷ 3 = **1 m/s^2**
    [2 marks for correct answer, otherwise 1 mark for a correct method to calculate the gradient of the line between 2 and 5 seconds]
You could also have used $a = (v - u) \div t$ here.
  d) average acceleration = change in velocity ÷ change in time /
    $a = (v - u) \div t$
    velocity at 8 s = 3 m/s; velocity at 10 s = 2 m/s
    so $v - u = 2 - 3 = -1$ m/s
    So, $a = -1 \div 2$
    = −0.5 m/s^2
    So, deceleration = **0.5 m/s^2**
    [3 marks for correct answer, otherwise 1 mark for correct calculation of change in velocity and 1 mark for correct substitution]
Your answer should be positive since the question asks for deceleration, rather than acceleration.
2 a) E.g. 31 m/s *[1 mark]*
  b) i) acceleration = change in velocity ÷ change in time
    $a = (v - u) \div t$
    $v - u = 31 - 0 = 31$ m/s
    $a = 31 \div 5$
    = **6.2 m/s^2**
    [2 marks for correct answer, otherwise 1 mark for correct substitution]
    ii) $v^2 - u^2 = 2 \times a \times x$
    rearrange for x
    $x = (v^2 - u^2) \div (2 \times a)$
    = $(31^2 - 0^2) \div (2 \times 6.2)$
    = **77.5 m**
    = **78 m (to 2 s.f.)**
    [3 marks for correct answer, otherwise 1 mark for correct rearrangement and 1 mark for correct substitution]
Even if you got the answer to (a) wrong, award yourself the marks for (b) if you did the sums above correctly.

Page 273
Newton's First and Second Laws
Q1 $F = ma = (80 + 10) \times 0.25$ *[1 mark]*
    = **22.5 N** *[1 mark]*

Page 274
Inertia and Newton's Third Law
Q1 Any one from: e.g the gravitational force of the Earth attracts the car and the gravitational force of the car attracts the Earth *[1 mark]* / the car exerts a normal contact force down against the ground and the normal contact force from the ground pushes up against the car *[1 mark]* / the car (tyres) pushes the road backwards and the road pushes the car (tyres) forwards *[1 mark]*.

Page 275
Warm-Up Questions
1   0 N
2   force = mass × acceleration
This is Newton's Second Law.
3   false
4   Boulder B
Boulder B needs a greater force to accelerate it by the same amount as boulder A.
5   true
This is Newton's Third Law.

Exam Questions
1 a) The ball exerts a force of −500 N on the bat *[1 mark]*, because, from Newton's Third Law, if the bat exerts a force on the ball, the ball exerts an equal force on the bat in the opposite direction *[1 mark]*.
   b) The acceleration of the ball is greater *[1 mark]* because it has a smaller mass, but is acted on by the same size force (and $F = m \times a$) *[1 mark]*.
2 a) Force = mass × acceleration / $F = m \times a$
So, $a = F \div m$
Set direction of van's motion to be positive, so $F = -200$ N
$a = -200 \div 2500$
$= -0.08$ m/s^2
So, deceleration = **0.08 m/s^2**
[3 marks for correct answer, otherwise 1 mark for correct rearrangement and 1 mark for correct substitution]
   b) Force = mass × acceleration / $F = m \times a$
$F = 4.50 \times 28.0$
$= \mathbf{126}$ **N**
[2 marks for correct answer, otherwise 1 mark for correct substitution]
   c) By Newton's Third Law, force on van due to the cone in the collision is −126 N.
force = mass × acceleration / $F = m \times a$
So, $a = F \div m$
$a = -126 \div 2500$
$= -0.0504$ m/s^2
So deceleration = **0.0504 m/s^2**
[3 marks for correct answer, otherwise 1 mark for correct rearrangement and 1 mark for correct substitution]
You'd still get the marks here, even if you got (b) wrong, as long as your method's correct.

Page 278
Weight
Q1 a) $W = mg = 25 \times 10$ *[1 mark]*
$= \mathbf{250}$ **N** *[1 mark]*
   b) $W = 25 \times 1.6$ *[1 mark]*
$= \mathbf{40}$ **N** *[1 mark]*

Page 279
Warm-Up Questions
1 It means that the force due to gravity caused by the hanging mass will be the main cause of the trolley accelerating.
2 Mass is the amount of 'stuff' in an object. Weight is the force acting on an object due to gravity.
3 Newtons

Exam Questions
1 Weight = mass × gravitational field strength / $W = m \times g$
$W = 80 \times 10$
$= \mathbf{800}$ **N**
[2 marks for correct answer, otherwise 1 mark for correct substitution]
2 a) mass *[1 mark]*
   b) acceleration *[1 mark]*
   c) As the mass increases, the acceleration decreases at a decreasing rate / mass and acceleration are inversely proportional *[1 mark]*.
3 a) $W = m \times g$, so if the weight of an object on Mars is 0.4 times its weight on Earth, then Mars's gravitational field strength must be 0.4 times Earth's gravitational field strength (since mass is constant).
$0.4 \times 10 = \mathbf{4}$ **N/kg**
[2 marks for correct answer, otherwise 1 mark for correct reasoning of gravitational field strength being 0.4 times the gravitational field strength on Earth]

   b) $W = m \times g$
$m = W \div g$
$= 3600 \div 4$
$= \mathbf{900}$ **kg**
[3 marks for correct answer, otherwise 1 mark for correct rearrangement and 1 mark for correct substitution]
Even if you got the answer to (a) wrong, you get full marks for (b) if you did the calculations correctly with your answer for (a).

4 How to grade your answer:
Level 0: There is no relevant information. *[No marks]*
Level 1: A simple experiment to investigate force and acceleration which can be performed with the given equipment is partly outlined. The answer lacks structure. *[1 to 2 marks]*
Level 2: An experiment to investigate force and acceleration which can be performed with the given equipment is outlined in some detail. The answer has some structure. *[3 to 4 marks]*
Level 3: An experiment to investigate force and acceleration which can be performed with the given equipment is fully described in detail. The answer is well structured. *[5 to 6 marks]*

Here are some points your answer may include:
Place all of the masses on the trolley.
Calculate the weight of the hanging hook using $W = m \times g$ — this is the accelerating force.
Place the trolley on the ramp and adjust the height of the ramp until the trolley just starts to move.
Mark a line on the ramp just before the first light gate.
Hold the trolley at the start line and release the trolley, so that it moves through the light gates.
Record the time and velocity as the trolley passes through each light gate.
Calculate and record the trolley's acceleration using
$a = (v − u) \div t$.
Take one of the masses from the trolley, and add it to the hook.
Repeat the steps above (starting with calculating the new total weight of the hanging hook) until all the masses from the trolley have been moved to the hook.
Plot the results on a graph of acceleration against accelerating force (the total weight of the hook), and draw a line of best fit.

Page 281
Momentum
Q1 $p_{before} = (10 \times 6) + (20 \times 0)$
$= 60$ kg m/s *[1 mark]*
$p_{after} = (10 + 20) \times v = 30v$ *[1 mark]*
$p_{before} = p_{after}$
$60 = 30v$
so $v = 60 \div 30 = \mathbf{2}$ **m/s** *[1 mark]*

Page 282
Momentum
Q1 First, convert quantities to the correct units: 58 g = 0.058 kg
11.6 ms = 0.0116 s *[1 mark]*
$F = ((m \times v) − (m \times u)) \div t$
$= ((0.058 \times 34) − (0.058 \times 0)) \div 0.0116$ *[1 mark]*
$F = \mathbf{170}$ **N** *[1 mark]*

Page 283
Warm-Up Questions
1 kg m/s
2 In a closed system, the total momentum before an interaction must equal the total momentum after the interaction.
3 The total momentum is zero.
4 It decreases the force.

Exam Questions
1 a) momentum = mass × velocity / $p = m \times v$ *[1 mark]*
   b) $p = 60 \times 5.0$
$= \mathbf{300}$ **kg m/s**
[2 marks for correct answer, otherwise 1 mark for correct substitution]
   c) force = change in momentum ÷ time / $F = (mv − mu) \div t$
Gymnast comes to a stop, so change in momentum = 300 kg m/s
$F = 300 \div 1.2$
$= \mathbf{250}$ **N**
[2 marks for correct answer, otherwise 1 mark for correct substitution]
2 a) momentum = mass × velocity / $p = m \times v$
$p = 650 \times 15.0$
$= \mathbf{9750}$ **kg m/s**
[2 marks for correct answer, otherwise 1 mark for correct substitution]

b) momentum before = momentum after
momentum of first car = 9750 kg m/s
momentum of second car = 750 × (−10.0)
= −7500 kg m/s
Total momentum before = 9750 + (−7500)
= 2250 kg m/s
Total momentum after = (mass of car 1 + mass of car 2) × v
2250 = (650 + 750) × v
so, v = 2250 ÷ (650 + 750)
= 2250 ÷ 1400
= 1.607142...
= **1.61 m/s (to 3 s.f.)**
[4 marks for correct answer, otherwise 1 mark for correct calculation of total momentum before the collision, 1 mark for correctly equating momentum before and after the collision and 1 mark for correct unrounded answer]

3   momentum before = momentum after
momentum of neutron before = 1 × 14 000
= 14 000
momentum of uranium before = 235 × 0
= 0
momentum of neutron after = 1 × −13 000
= −13 000
momentum of uranium after = 235 × v
So, 14 000 = −13 000 + 235 × v
so, v = (14 000 + 13 000) ÷ 235
= 114.8936...
= **115 km/s (to 3 s.f.)**
[4 marks for correct answer, otherwise 1 mark for correct calculations of momentum, 1 mark for correctly equating momentum before and after the collision and 1 mark for correct unrounded answer]

Don't worry too much about the units in this question. The masses given are relative masses, with no units, so we couldn't use the standard units for momentum. As you're only looking for the velocity though, you can just do the calculation as normal, and make sure that the units on your final answer match the units for velocity given in the question.

Page 287
Warm-Up Questions
1   Get the individual to sit with their arm resting on the edge of a table. Hold a ruler end-down so that the 0 cm mark hangs between their thumb and forefinger. Drop the ruler without warning. The individual must grab the ruler between their thumb and forefinger as quickly as possible. Measure the distance at which they have caught the ruler. Use $v^2 - u^2 = 2 \times a \times x$ and $a = 10$ m/s² to calculate v, and $a = (v - u) \div t$ to calculate the time taken for the ruler to fall that distance. This is their reaction time.
2   The thinking distance is the distance travelled during a person's reaction time (the time between seeing a hazard, and applying the brakes).
3   The braking distance.
4   Any one from: e.g. poor grip on the roads increases braking distance / poor visibility delays when you see the hazard / distraction by the weather delays when you see the hazard.
5   Crumple zones increase collision time, which reduces the force on the vehicle and passengers (since $F = (mv - mu) \div t$). This reduces the risk of harm in a crash.

Exam Question
1 a) stopping distance = braking distance + thinking distance,
So, braking distance = stopping distance − thinking distance
At 40 mph,
stopping distance = 35 m (accept between 34 m and 36 m)
thinking distance = 12 m (accept between 11 m and 13 m)
braking distance = 35 − 12 = **23 m**
(Accept correct for above readings)
[3 marks for correct answer, otherwise 1 mark for correctly reading stopping and thinking distances from the graph and 1 mark for correct substitution]
b) braking distance *[1 mark]*
The stopping distance is over twice as high as the thinking distance at 50 mph, so the braking distance must be bigger than the thinking distance.
c) Stopping distance is not directly proportional to speed. If stopping distance and speed were directly proportional, the relationship between them would be shown by a straight line / would be linear *[1 mark]*.
d) If the road were icy, the thinking distance graph would not change *[1 mark]* but the stopping distance graph would get steeper (as the braking distance would increase) *[1 mark]*.
The thinking distance graph doesn't change, because the icy road won't change your reaction time. But it will decrease the friction between the car and the road, so the braking distance increases.

Section 18 — Conservation of Energy
Page 288
Energy Stores
Q1 The change in height is 5 m.
So the energy transferred from the gravitational potential energy store is:
$\Delta GPE = m \times g \times \Delta h = 2 \times 10 \times 5$ *[1 mark]*
= 100 J *[1 mark]*
This is transferred to the kinetic energy store of the object,
so KE = 100 J *[1 mark]*
$KE = ½ \times m \times v^2$
so $v^2 = (2 \times KE) \div m$
= $(2 \times 100) \div 2$ *[1 mark]*
= 100 m²/s²
$v = \sqrt{100}$ = **10 m/s** *[1 mark]*

Page 290
Energy Stores and Transfers
Q1 Energy is transferred mechanically *[1 mark]* from the kinetic energy store of the wind *[1 mark]* to the kinetic energy store of the windmill *[1 mark]*.

Page 291
Warm-Up Questions
1   kinetic energy = ½ × mass × (speed)² / $KE = ½ \times m \times v^2$
2   A lorry travelling at 60 miles per hour.
3   Any two from: e.g. mechanically (by a force doing work) / electrically (work done by a charge) / by heating / by radiation.
4   Energy is transferred by radiation to the thermal energy store of the water.

Exam Questions
1 a) Change in gravitational potential energy = mass × gravitational field strength × change in height /
$\Delta GPE = m \times g \times \Delta h$ *[1 mark]*
So, $\Delta h = \Delta GPE \div (m \times g)$
= 140 ÷ (20 × 10)
= **0.7 m**
[3 marks for the correct answer, otherwise 1 mark for correct rearrangement and 1 mark for correct substitution]
b) Energy is transferred from the gravitational potential energy store *[1 mark]* to the kinetic energy store of the load *[1 mark]*.
c) Some of the energy would also be transferred to the thermal energy store of the air (and the thermal energy store of the load) *[1 mark]*.
2 a) Energy is transferred mechanically from the elastic potential energy store of the sling-shot *[1 mark]* to the kinetic energy store of the rock *[1 mark]*. This energy is then transferred mechanically to the gravitational potential energy store of the rock as it rises *[1 mark]*.
b) Kinetic energy = ½ × mass × (speed)² / $KE = ½ \times m \times v^2$
$KE = ½ \times 0.06 \times (18)^2$
= 9.72 J
= **9.7 J (to 2 s.f.)**
[2 marks for correct answer, otherwise 1 mark for correct substitution]
c) At B all energy from the kinetic store has been transferred to the gravitational potential energy store.
So, ΔGPE = 9.72 J
$\Delta GPE = m \times g \times \Delta h$
$\Delta h = \Delta GPE \div (m \times g)$
= 9.72 ÷ (0.06 × 10)
= **16.2 m**
[3 marks for the correct answer, otherwise 1 mark for correct rearrangement and 1 mark for correct substitution]

Page 293
Efficiency
Q1 Useful energy transferred by device
= 500 − 420 = 80 J *[1 mark]*
Efficiency = $\frac{\text{useful energy transferred by device}}{\text{total energy supplied to device}}$
= 80 ÷ 500 = 0.16 *[1 mark]*
0.16 × 100 = **16%** *[1 mark]*

Page 295
Warm-Up Questions
1   Thermal energy stores.
2   Some energy is always dissipated, so less than 100% of the energy supplied to a device is transferred usefully.
3   E.g. lubrication
4   The higher the thermal conductivity, the greater the rate of the energy transfer (i.e. the faster energy is transferred) through it.
5   The thicker the walls, the slower the rate of cooling.

Exam Questions
1 a) efficiency = useful energy transferred by the device ÷ total energy supplied to the device *[1 mark]*
b) efficiency = 480 ÷ 1200
= **0.4 (or 40%)**
[2 marks for correct answer, otherwise 1 mark for correct substitution]

c) efficiency = useful energy transferred by the device ÷ total energy supplied to the device
total energy supplied to the device = useful energy transferred by the device ÷ efficiency
= 10 ÷ 0.55
= 18.181... = **18 J** (to 2 s.f)
[3 marks for the correct answer, otherwise 1 mark for correct rearrangement and 1 mark for correct substitution]
d) Disagree. Torch B has a lower input energy transfer than torch A, i.e. it transfers less energy per minute than torch A (as 18.181... × 60 = 1090.9..., and 1090.9... < 1200) *[1 mark]*.
Even if you got the answer to (c) wrong, if your conclusion is correct for your answer to (d), you'd get the marks for this question.
2 Best: C Second best: B Worst: A *[1 mark]*
The thicker a sample is, the slower the rate of energy transfer through it so sample B will be a better insulator than sample A *[1 mark]*. Air has a lower thermal conductivity than glass (so it transfers energy at a slower rate than glass does) *[1 mark]* so even though samples B and C are the same thickness, sample C is a better insulator than sample B *[1 mark]*.

Page 300
Warm-Up Questions
1 Any three from: coal / oil / natural gas / nuclear fuel (plutonium or uranium).
2 Advantage: e.g. low running costs / won't run out / doesn't create pollution
Disadvantage: e.g. cannot produce energy at night.
3 Any two from: e.g. it releases greenhouse gases and contributes to global warming / it causes acid rain / coal mining damages the landscape.
4 Any two from: e.g. renewable resources don't currently provide enough energy / energy from renewables cannot be relied upon currently / it's expensive to build new renewable power plants / it's expensive to switch to cars running on renewable energy. / it's impractical to switch to cars running on renewable energy.

Exam Questions
1 a) Solar *[1 mark]*, bio-fuels *[1 mark]*
b) E.g. flooding a valley for a dam can destroy habitats for some species *[1 mark]*.
c) E.g. they cause no pollution *[1 mark]*
2 a) Seconds in 5 hours = 5 × 60 × 60 = 18 000 s
Energy provided by 1 m² solar panel in 5 hours = 200 × 18 000
= 3 600 000 J
Number of panels needed = energy needed ÷ energy provided
= 32 500 000 ÷ 3 600 000
= 9.027... = **10 panels** (to next whole number)
[4 marks for correct answer, otherwise 1 mark for correct method of calculation of energy provided by one panel, 1 mark for correct value of energy provided by one panel and 1 mark for correct method of calculation of number of panels needed]
Remember, because you have to have a set number of whole panels, if you get a decimal answer, you need to round up to the next whole number to be able to provide the right amount of energy.
b) Ten 1 m² solar panels are needed, so they will need at least 10 × 1 m² = 10 m² of space. However, they only have 8 m² of space on their roof, so the family cannot install sufficient solar panels *[1 mark]*.
c) E.g. solar panels are less reliable than coal-fired power stations *[1 mark]*. The energy output of the solar panels will vary based on the number of hours of good sunlight, and may not be able to provide enough energy on a given day *[1 mark]*. The energy output of coal-fired power stations is not influenced by environmental factors like weather, and energy output can be increased to meet demand *[1 mark]*.

Section 19 — Waves and the Electromagnetic Spectrum
Page 302
Transverse and Longitudinal Waves
Q1 7.5 ÷ 100 = 0.075 m
wave speed = frequency × wavelength, so
frequency = wave speed ÷ wavelength *[1 mark]*
= 0.15 ÷ 0.075 *[1 mark]*
= **2 Hz** *[1 mark]*

Page 305
Warm-Up Questions
1 Waves only transfer energy and information, they do not transfer matter (in this case, the twig and the water particles around the twig).
2 hertz (Hz)
3 e.g. sound / P-waves
4 wave speed = frequency × wavelength / $v = f \times \lambda$

Exam Questions
1 a) transverse *[1 mark]*
b) 5 cm *[1 mark]*
c) 2 m *[1 mark]*
d) It will halve *[1 mark]*.
$v = f \times \lambda$, so if f doubles, then λ must halve, so that v stays the same.
2 a) The distance he measures is 1 wavelength *[1 mark]*. This can be used, together with the frequency set by the signal generator, in the formula for wave speed, wave speed = frequency × wavelength / $v = f \times \lambda$ *[1 mark]*
b) wave speed = frequency × wavelength / $v = f \times \lambda$
So $v = 50 \times 6.8$
= **340 m/s**
[2 marks for correct answer, otherwise 1 mark for correct substitution]

Page 306
Wave Behaviour at Boundaries
Q1

[1 mark for a correct diagram showing rays and the normal, 1 mark for an angle of incidence of 40°, 1 mark for an angle of refraction greater than 40°]

Page 308
Warm-Up Questions
1 reflection, transmission and absorption
2 false
The shorter the wavelength, the more an EM wave will be refracted as it hits a boundary at an angle to the normal.
3 Away from the normal.
4 e.g. a ray box

Exam Questions
1 Diamond *[1 mark]* slows down the blue light by the greatest amount, causing it to refract the most. *[1 mark]*
2 E.g. place the prism on a piece of paper and shine a ray of light at the prism. Trace the incident and emergent rays and the boundaries of the prism on the piece of paper *[1 mark]*. Remove the prism and draw in the refracted ray through the prism by joining the ends of the other two rays with a straight line *[1 mark]*. Draw in the normals using a protractor and ruler *[1 mark]* and use the protractor to measure I and R at both boundaries *[1 mark]*.

Page 315
Warm-Up Questions
1 transverse
2 false
All EM waves travel at the same speed in a vacuum.
3 gamma rays
4 true
5 e.g. communication / broadcasting / satellite transmissions
6 The microwaves penetrate a few centimetres into the food before being absorbed by water molecules in the food. The microwaves transfer their energy to the water molecules, causing the water to heat up. Energy is then transferred from the water to the rest of the food by heating, causing the food to cook.
7 infrared radiation
8 E.g. to sterilise medical equipment / to sterilise food / medical imaging / cancer treatment.
9 true

Exam Questions
1 a) X-rays *[1 mark]*
b) E.g. could cause cancer / cell mutations / damage cells *[1 mark]*.
2 a) The incoming wave transfers energy to electrons in the receiver *[1 mark]*. This causes the electrons to oscillate *[1 mark]*, generating an alternating current in the circuit *[1 mark]*.
b) The resident shouldn't be concerned as radio waves have a very low frequency so are not dangerous / are not absorbed by the body *[1 mark]*.
3 E.g. ultraviolet radiation is a type of ionising radiation, exposure to this type of radiation can damage skin cells / could lead to skin cancer *[1 mark]*. The damage to cells and risk of developing cancer could be minimised by limiting the patient's exposure to the ultraviolet radiation while still exposing her to enough so that it is an effective treatment for her psoriasis *[1 mark]*. Exposure to ultraviolet radiation could also damage the patient's eyes and cause a variety of eye conditions including blindness *[1 mark]*. The risk of eye damage could be reduced by the patient wearing protective goggles during treatments *[1 mark]*.

Section 20 — Radioactivity
Page 319
Warm-Up Questions
1 The atom consists of a sphere of positive charge throughout which electrons are embedded like fruit in a plum pudding.

2. proton: 1, neutron: 1, electron: 0.0005
3. true
4. In the nucleus.
5. 0; an atom has no overall charge.
6. 1×10^{-10} m
7. false

An atom must lose an electron to become a positive ion.

Exam Questions
1. a)

	Proton	Electron	Neutron
Relative Charge	+1	-1	0
Number Present in Si-28	14	14	14

[2 marks — 1 mark for each correct answer]

b) Electrons may only occupy fixed energy levels *[1 mark]* at set distances from the nucleus *[1 mark]*.

c) 6.9×10^{-19} J *[1 mark]*

d) +1 *[1 mark]*

2. Most of the alpha particles passed straight through the gold foil *[1 mark]*. However, some were deflected back in the direction they came from *[1 mark]*. He concluded most of the atom is empty space *[1 mark]* whilst positive charge and mass is concentrated in a small nucleus *[1 mark]*.

Page 322
Nuclear Equations
Q1 $^{219}_{86}\text{Rn} \rightarrow \,^{215}_{84}\text{Po} + \,^{4}_{2}\alpha$

[1 mark for correct layout, 1 mark for correct symbol for an alpha particle, 1 mark for total atomic and mass numbers being equal on both sides]

Page 323
Warm-Up Questions
1. $23 - 11 = 12$ neutrons
2. false

Isotopes of an element will have identical atomic numbers and different mass numbers.

3. Any radiation that can knock electrons from atoms.
4. alpha
5. false

Gamma rays are stopped by thick sheets of lead or metres of concrete.

6. The atomic number will decrease by 1.
7. 40

Mass number is unchanged by the emission of gamma radiation.

Exam Questions
1. Beta (particles) *[1 mark]*, because the radiation passes through the paper, but not the aluminium, so it is moderately penetrating in comparison to the other two *[1 mark]*.

2. a) The total number of protons and neutrons in the nucleus/atom. *[1 mark]*
   b) Atom A and atom B *[1 mark]* because isotopes of the same element have the same atomic number, but different mass numbers *[1 mark]*.
   c) $X = 86 - 2$
      $= 84$ *[1 mark]*

Page 325
Half-Life
Q1 After one half-life the activity will be
$40 \div 2 = 20$ Bq *[1 mark]*
After a second: $20 \div 2 = 10$ Bq
After a third: $10 \div 2 = 5$ Bq *[1 mark]*
So the ratio is 5:40 = **1:8** *[1 mark]*

Page 327
Warm-Up Questions
1. Any three from: e.g. the air / some foods / building materials / rocks / space / fallout from nuclear explosions / nuclear waste.
2. One decay occurs each second.
3. E.g. a Geiger-Müller tube
4. 6 days.

To decrease by a factor of four, two half-lives must pass. $2 \times 3 = 6$.

5. Irradiation occurs when an object is exposed to radiation. Contamination occurs when a radioactive source gets onto or into an object.
6. To prevent your hands from becoming contaminated with radioactive materials / to prevent radioactive particles getting stuck to your skin or under your nails.
7. If you are exposed to alpha radiation from an external source (i.e. if you are irradiated), the alpha particles will be blocked by your skin. However, if an alpha source gets inside your body it can do a lot of damage to nearby cells, as it's strongly ionising.

Exam Questions
1. a) E.g. radiation sickness / cancer.
   [2 marks — 1 mark for each correct answer]
   b) Source A, because beta radiation is able to penetrate the skin and get to delicate organs *[1 mark]*.
   c) E.g. store them in a lead-lined box *[1 mark]*.

2. a) $2 \times 60 = 120$ seconds
   $120 \div 40 = 3$ half-lives
   Activity after 1 half life: $8000 \div 2 = 4000$,
   Activity after 2 half lives: $4000 \div 2 = 2000$,
   Activity after 3 half lives: $2000 \div 2 = \mathbf{1000\ Bq}$
   [2 marks for correct answer, otherwise 1 mark for correctly calculating the number of half-lives]

   b) Activity after 1 half life: $8000 \div 2 = 4000$,
   Activity after 2 half lives: $4000 \div 2 = 2000$,
   Activity after 3 half lives: $2000 \div 2 = 1000$,
   Activity after 4 half lives: $1000 \div 2 = 500$,
   Activity after 5 half lives: $500 \div 2 = 250$.
   So it takes **5 half-lives** to drop to 250 Bq
   [2 marks for correct answer, otherwise 1 mark for attempting to halve values to find number of half-lives]

   c) $(100 \div 8000) \times 100$ *[1 mark]* = **1.25%** *[1 mark]*

Section 21 — Forces and Energy
Page 330
Work Done
Q1 First change the distance to metres:
$20 \div 100 = 0.2$ m
Then substitute into the equation:
$E = F \times d = 20 \times 0.2$ *[1 mark]*
$= 4$ J *[1 mark]*

Page 332
Warm-Up Questions
1. A system is the object or group of objects that you are interested in.
2. true
3. Energy is transferred electrically from the chemical energy store of the battery to the kinetic energy store of the fan's blades.
4. work done = force × distance moved in the direction of the force / $E = F \times d$
5. true
6. watts

Exam Questions
1. a) Energy is transferred from the ball's gravitational potential energy store *[1 mark]* to its kinetic energy store *[1 mark]*.
   b) There will be no change in total energy *[1 mark]*.

In a closed system, the net change in energy is always zero.

2. a) i) power = work done ÷ time taken / $P = E \div t$ *[1 mark]*
      ii) $P = 1000 \div 20$
         $= 50$ W *[1 mark]*
   b) efficiency = useful energy transferred by the device ÷ total energy supplied to the device
      efficiency = $480 \div 1000$
      $= 0.48\ (= 48\%)$
      [2 marks for correct answer, otherwise 1 mark for correct substitution]
   c) It will be faster / complete the course in less time *[1 mark]* because the motor transfers the same amount of energy, but over a shorter time *[1 mark]*.

3. a) work done = force × distance moved in the direction of the force / $E = F \times d$
   $E = 42\ 000 \times 700$
   $= 29\ 400\ 000$ J
   $= \mathbf{29\ 400\ kJ}$
   [3 marks for correct answer, otherwise 1 mark for correct substitution and 1 mark for correct answer in J]

   b) $KE = \tfrac{1}{2} \times m \times v^2$
   $v = \sqrt{\dfrac{2 \times KE}{m}}$
   $= \sqrt{\dfrac{2 \times 29\ 400\ 000}{150\ 000}} = 19.79...$ m/s = **20 m/s (to 1 s.f.)**
   [3 marks for correct answer, otherwise 1 mark for correct rearrangement and 1 mark for correct substitution]

Even if you got the answer to (a) wrong, you get full marks for (b) if you did the calculations correctly with your answer for (a).

Page 333
Forces
Q1 E.g.

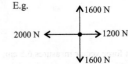

[2 marks for all forces correctly drawn, 1 mark for three forces correctly drawn — weight and normal contact force arrows should be the same length, the arrow for the driving force should be longer than the weight arrow and the arrow for the resistive force should be shorter]

Page 335
Resolving Forces
Q1 Draw the given forces to scale and tip-to-tail. The third force is found by joining the end of the second force to the start of the first force. E.g.

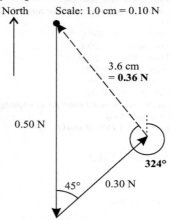

Third force = **0.36 N on a bearing of 324°**.
[1 mark for a correct scale drawing with a sensible scale, 1 mark for a magnitude between 0.35 and 0.37 N, 1 mark for a bearing between 323 and 325°]

Page 336
Warm-Up Questions
1. false
Non-contact forces occur between objects that aren't touching.
2. The relative magnitude of the forces.
3. A resultant force is the single force obtained by combining all the forces acting on an object. The resultant force has the same effect on the object as all the original forces together.
4. The tip of the last force you draw should end where the tail of the first force you drew began. E.g. for three forces the scale diagram will form a triangle.

Exam Questions
1. a) Total force to the right = 1700 + 300 = 2000 N
Total force to the left = 2000 N
Total horizontal force = 2000 − 2000 = 0 N
Resultant force = downwards force − upwards force
= 800 − 300
= **500 N downwards**
[3 marks for correct answer, otherwise 1 mark for correctly calculating that the total horizontal force is zero and 1 mark for giving the correct direction of the resultant force]
b) Total vertical force = 0 N
so, y = **400 N**
Total horizontal force = 0 N
so, x + 500 N = 2000 N
x = 2000 − 500 = **1500 N**
[2 marks — 1 mark for each correct answer]

2. a) i)

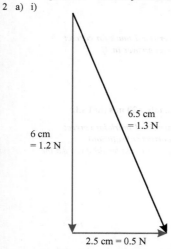

On the scale diagram the resultant force vector measures 6.5 cm.
6.5 ÷ 5 = 1.3 N
1.3 N (±0.02 N)
[3 marks for correct answer, otherwise 1 mark for drawing forces tip-to-tail and 1 mark for drawing the vertical force 6 cm long and the horizontal force 2.5 cm long]
When creating a scale drawing, use a protractor to help you draw forces that are at right angles.

ii) Using the scale drawing from a) i):

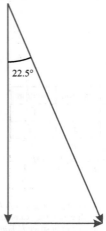

22.5° (±1°) *[1 mark]*
b) E.g. electrostatic / magnetic *[1 mark]*.

Section 22 — Electricity and Circuits
Page 338
Circuit Basics
Q1 $Q = It$ so $t = Q \div I$ *[1 mark]*
= 28 800 ÷ 8 *[1 mark]*
= 3600 s *[1 mark]*
$t = 3600 \div 60 = $ **60 minutes** *[1 mark]*

Page 339
Potential Difference and Resistance
Q1 $V = IR$ so $R = V \div I$ *[1 mark]*
= 230 ÷ 5.0 *[1 mark]*
= **46 Ω** *[1 mark]*

Page 343
Warm-Up Questions
1.
2. ohms
3. false
Current in metals is the flow of free electrons.
4. energy transferred = charge moved × potential difference / $E = Q \times V$
5. Electrons collide with the ions in the lattice that make up the resistor as they flow through it. These collisions transfer energy to the kinetic energy store of the ions, causing them to vibrate more (so the energy in the thermal energy store of the resistor will increase).
6. In parallel with the component.
7.
8. It decreases.

Exam Questions
1. a) i) $Q = I \times t$
= 0.30 × 35
= **10.5 C**
[2 marks for correct answer, otherwise 1 mark for correct substitution]
ii) $E = Q \times V$
= 10.5 × 1.5
= **15.75 J**
= **16 J (to 2 s.f.)**
[2 marks for correct answer, otherwise 1 mark for correct substitution]
If you got the answer to (i) wrong, you still get full marks for (ii) if you did the calculations correctly using your answer to (i).
b) It will decrease *[1 mark]*.
2. a) The temperature of the circuit/diode *[1 mark]*.
b) At point A, $V = 6$ V, $I = 3$ A
potential difference = current × resistance / $V = I \times R$
$R = V \div I$
= 6 ÷ 3
= **2 Ω**
[4 marks for correct answer, otherwise 1 mark for obtaining correct values from the graph, 1 mark for correct rearrangement and 1 mark for correct substitution]

Page 344
Series Circuits
Q1 R_{total} = 4 + 5 + 6 = 15 Ω *[1 mark]*
    $V = I \times R$ = 0.6 × 15 *[1 mark]*
    = **9 V** *[1 mark]*

Page 345
Parallel Circuits
Q1 The total current through the circuit decreases *[1 mark]* as there are fewer paths for the current to take *[1 mark]*. The total resistance of the circuit increases *[1 mark]* as, using $V = IR$, a decrease in the total current means an increase in the total resistance *[1 mark]*.

Page 347
Warm-Up Questions
1 true
2 The resistances of all the components are added together.
3 3 V
   In a parallel circuit all of the components get the full source potential difference.
4 Two resistors connected in series.
5 One by one, connect identical resistors in series. Each time a new resistor is added, measure the current passing through the circuit using an ammeter, and then calculate the total resistance using $R = V \div I$, where V is the potential difference of the power supply. Plot a graph of total resistance against number of resistors.

Exam Questions
1 a) total resistance = $R_1 + R_2 + R_3$
      = 2 + 3 + 5
      = **10 Ω** *[1 mark]*
   b) The reading on A_2 will be **0.4 A** *[1 mark]* because in a series circuit, the same current flows through all parts of the circuit *[1 mark]*.
   c) $V_3 = V_{supply} - V_1 - V_2$
      = 4 – 0.8 – 1.2
      = **2 V** *[1 mark]*
2 a) **15 V** *[1 mark]*
   Potential difference is the same across each branch in a parallel circuit.
   b) $V = I \times R$
      $I = V \div R$
      = 15 ÷ 3
      = **5 A**
      [3 marks for correct answer, otherwise 1 mark for correct rearrangement and 1 mark for correct substitution]
   c) I_2 = 5 + 3.75
      = **8.75 A** *[1 mark]*
   Even if you got the answer to (b) wrong, you still get full marks for (c) if you did the calculations correctly with your answer to (b).
   d) The reading on A_2 will decrease *[1 mark]* since current through the branch with two resistors will decrease *[1 mark]*, decreasing the total current in the circuit *[1 mark]*.

Page 348
Energy in Circuits
Q1 t = 60 × 60 *[1 mark]*
    $E = I \times V \times t$
    = 4.0 × 230 × (60 × 60) *[1 mark]*
    = 3 312 000 J
    = **3 300 000 J** (to 2 s.f.) *[1 mark]*

Page 350
Power in Circuits
Q1 $E = P \times t$ = 250 × (2 × 60 × 60)
    = 1 800 000 J *[1 mark]*
    E = 375 × (2 × 60 × 60)
    = 2 700 000 J *[1 mark]*
    So difference in the energy transferred is
    2 700 000 – 1 800 000
    = **900 000 J** *[1 mark]*

Page 351
Warm-Up Questions
1 energy transferred = current × potential difference × time / $E = I \times V \times t$
2 Energy is transferred electrically from the mains supply to the thermal energy store of the toaster's heating element.
3 E.g. electric heaters/toasters
4 watts
5 The 60 W light bulb.
6 $P = I^2 \times R$

Exam Questions
1 a) electrical power = current × potential difference / $P = I \times V$ *[1 mark]*
   b) $I = P \div V$
      = (2.8 × 1000) ÷ 230
      = **12.17... A**
      = **12 A** (to 2 s.f.)
      [3 marks for correct answer, otherwise 1 mark for correct rearrangement and 1 mark for correct substitution]
   c) She should choose kettle B because it has the higher power rating *[1 mark]*. This means that it transfers more energy to heat the water per unit time, so it will boil the water faster *[1 mark]*.
2 a) $E = I \times V \times t$
      t = 0.5 hours = 30 minutes
      Convert minutes into seconds: 30 × 60 = 1800 s
      E = 0.5 × 3.0 × 1800
      = **2700 J**
      [3 marks for correct answer, otherwise 1 mark for correctly converting time into seconds and 1 mark for correct substitution]
   b) The power of the torch will be halved *[1 mark]*.
   The current has been halved, and as $P = I \times V$, halving the current and keeping the potential difference the same means the power will also be halved.
3 Calculate the lifetime of a single battery:
   $E = I \times V \times t$
   $t = \dfrac{E}{I \times V}$
   $= \dfrac{13\,000}{(0.2 \times 10^{-3}) \times 1.5}$ = 4.333... × 10⁷ s

   Then calculate the number of batteries required for ten years:
   $= \dfrac{\text{ten years (seconds)}}{\text{lifetime of one battery (seconds)}}$
   $= \dfrac{10 \times 365 \times 24 \times 60 \times 60}{4.333... \times 10^7}$ = 7.2775... batteries
   So **8 batteries** are needed to power the clock for ten years.
   [3 marks for correct answer, otherwise 1 mark for correctly calculating the lifetime of a single battery and 1 mark for dividing the number of seconds in ten years by the lifetime of a single battery]
   Alternative method:
   Number of seconds in ten years = 10 × 365 × 24 × 60 × 60
   = 315 360 000 s
   Calculate the energy required by the clock in ten years:
   $E = I \times V \times t$
   = (0.2 × 10⁻³) × 1.5 × 315 360 000
   = 94 608 J
   Then calculate the total number of batteries needed to supply this amount of energy:
   Number of batteries = 94 608 ÷ 13 000
   = 7.2775...
   So **8 batteries** are needed to power the clock for ten years.
   [3 marks for correct answer, otherwise 1 mark for correctly calculating the total energy required for ten years and 1 mark for dividing this by the energy of a single battery]

Page 355
Warm-Up Questions
1 direct current
2 The neutral wire completes the circuit, allowing current to flow out of the appliance.
3 230 V
4 the live wire
5 false
Fuses should be rated as near as possible but just higher than the normal operating current.

Exam Questions
1 a) In alternating current the movement of charges constantly changes direction *[1 mark]*.
   b) Your body is at 0 V, so there's a potential difference of around 230 V between the live wire and you *[1 mark]*. Touching the wire forms a link from the supply to the earth through your body *[1 mark]*, causing a large current to flow through you, which is an electric shock *[1 mark]*.
2 a) The earth wire is connected to the kettle's metal casing *[1 mark]*. When the casing becomes live, a large current is able to surge from the live wire, through the casing and out through the earth wire *[1 mark]*. The surge in current causes the fuse attached to the live wire to melt, isolating the kettle from the live supply *[1 mark]*.
   b) a circuit breaker *[1 mark]*
   c) Because plastic is a good electrical insulator, the casing cannot become live, so an earth wire is not needed *[1 mark]*.

Section 23 — Magnetic Fields
Page 359
The Motor Effect
Q1 Into the page *[1 mark]*.

Page 361

Warm-Up Questions

1 a) attraction
   Opposite poles are facing each other and opposite poles attract.
   b)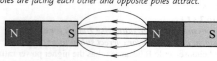
   The magnetic field is uniform between the two bar magnets, so you need to draw at least 3 parallel field lines that are equally spaced.
2 Put the magnet on a piece of paper and put a compass next to it. Make a mark on the paper at each end of the compass needle. Then move the compass so that the tail of the compass needle is where the tip of the needle was previously, and mark again where the needle is pointing. Repeat this several times and then join up the markings for a complete sketch of a field line around the magnet. Do this several times for different points around the magnet to get several field lines. Add arrows to each field line, pointing from north to south.
3 north/towards the Earth's North Pole
4 false
   A permanent magnet will always attract an induced magnet/magnetic material.

Exam Questions

1 a)   *[1 mark]*
   b) The interaction between the magnetic field generated by the wire and the magnetic field between the north and south poles of the bar magnets *[1 mark]*.
   c) $l = 7.0$ cm $= 0.070$ m
      $F = B \times I \times l$
      $= 0.028 \times 5.5 \times 0.070$
      $= 0.01078$ N $= 0.011$ N (to 2 s.f.)
      [2 marks for correct answer, otherwise 1 mark for correct substitution]
   d) The direction of the force would be reversed *[1 mark]*.
2 a) The field lines inside each loop of the solenoid all point in the same direction, so they add together to create a strong uniform field *[1 mark]*.
   b) e.g. iron / nickel / cobalt *[1 mark]*
   c) E.g. increase the current flowing through the solenoid *[1 mark]*.

Page 363

Transformers and The National Grid

Q1 Power output $= V_s \times I_s = 320$ W
    $V_p \times I_p = V_s \times I_s$, so
    $I_p = (V_s \times I_s) \div V_p$
    $= 320 \div 1.6$ *[1 mark]*
    $= 200$ A *[1 mark]*

Page 364

Warm-Up Questions

1 The induction of a potential difference in a conductor which is experiencing a changing magnetic field.
2 true
3 More turns on the secondary coil.
4 Because the high current would result in inefficient transmission of power/a large loss of energy to thermal energy stores.

Exam Questions

1 a) The coil experiences a change in magnetic field, so a potential difference is induced *[1 mark]*.
   b) Any one from: e.g. move the magnet out of the coil / move the coil away from the magnet / insert the south pole of the magnet into the same end of the coil / insert the north pole of the magnet into the other end of the coil *[1 mark]*.
   c) Any one from: e.g. push the magnet into the coil more quickly / use a stronger magnet / add more turns per unit length of wire *[1 mark]*.
   d) Zero / no reading *[1 mark]*.
   A moving/changing magnetic field is needed to generate a potential difference.
2 a) Step-up transformers are used at power stations to increase the potential difference (and so decrease the current) of the electricity produced for efficient transmission *[1 mark]*. Step-down transformers at the consumers' end reduce the potential difference to safe levels that can be used by consumers *[1 mark]*.
   b) An alternating current in the primary coil produces an alternating magnetic field *[1 mark]*. This causes an alternating magnetic field in the iron core and through the secondary coil *[1 mark]*. The changing magnetic field through the secondary coil induces a potential difference in the secondary coil *[1 mark]*.
3 $V_p \times I_p = V_s \times I_s$
   $I_s = \dfrac{V_p \times I_p}{V_s} = \dfrac{12 \times 2.5}{4}$
   $I_s = 7.5$ A
   [2 marks for correct answer, otherwise 1 mark for correct substitution]

Section 24 — Matter

Page 365

Density

Q1 First find the cube's volume:
    $0.015 \times 0.015 \times 0.015 = 3.375 \times 10^{-6}$ m³ *[1 mark]*
    The cube's density is 3500 kg/m³.
    $m = \rho \times V$
    $= 3500 \times (3.375 \times 10^{-6})$ *[1 mark]*
    $= 0.01181...$ kg
    $= \mathbf{12\ g}$ (to 2 s.f.) *[1 mark]*

Page 369

Warm-Up Questions

1 Density is a measure of the amount of mass in a given volume / compactness of a substance.
2 gas
3 sublimation
4 physical changes
5 Cooling a system decreases its internal energy.
6 -273 °C
7 The higher the temperature of the gas, the faster the gas particles move. This means the gas particles collide with the walls of the container more often and with a greater force. This causes the gas pressure to increase.

Exam Questions

1 a) Particles are held close together in a fixed, regular pattern *[1 mark]*. They vibrate about fixed positions *[1 mark]*.
   b) density = mass ÷ volume
      $= 850.5 \div 75.0$
      $= \mathbf{11.34\ g/cm^3}$
      [2 marks for correct answer, otherwise 1 mark for correct substitution]
   c) melting *[1 mark]*
2 a) C *[1 mark]*.
   b) The volume of the toy soldier / the volume of water displaced by the toy soldier *[1 mark]*. The mass of the toy soldier *[1 mark]*.
   c) How to grade your answer:
      Level 0: There is no relevant information. *[No marks]*
      Level 1: There is a brief description of an experiment to measure the density of the toy soldier, but the answer isn't very clear. The points made do not link together.
                [1 to 2 marks]
      Level 2: There is a description of an experiment to measure the mass and volume of the toy soldier, with reference to the equipment needed. The answer has some structure.
                [3 to 4 marks]
      Level 3: There is a clear and detailed description of an experiment to measure the density of the toy soldier. The method includes details of how to use the equipment and how to process the results to work out the density of the toy soldier. The answer is well structured. *[5 to 6 marks]*
      Here are some points your answer may include:
      Measure and record the mass of the toy soldier using the mass balance.
      Fill a eureka can with water.
      Place an empty measuring cylinder beneath the spout of the eureka can.
      Submerge the toy soldier in the eureka can.
      Measure the volume of water displaced from the eureka can using the measuring cylinder.
      The volume of water displaced is equal to the volume of the soldier.
      Use the equation density = mass ÷ volume / $\rho = m \div V$ to calculate the density of the toy soldier.
   With questions where you have to describe a method, make sure your description is clear and detailed.

Page 370

Specific Heat Capacity

Q1 $\Delta Q = mc\Delta\theta$ so
    $\Delta\theta = \Delta Q \div (m \times c)$ *[1 mark]*
    $= 50\ 000 \div (5 \times 4200)$
    $= 2.380...$ °C *[1 mark]*
    So the new temperature
    $= 5 + 2.380... = 7.380...$
    $= \mathbf{7}$ °C (to 1 s.f.) *[1 mark]*

Page 371

Specific Latent Heat

Q1 $Q = m \times L = 0.25 \times 120\ 000$ *[1 mark]*
    $= \mathbf{30\ 000\ J}$ *[1 mark]*

Page 373

Warm-Up Questions

1 The change in energy in the substance's thermal energy store needed to raise the temperature of 1 kg of that substance by 1 °C.

2. The thermally insulating material reduces unwanted energy transfers to the surroundings. More of the energy supplied is transferred to the thermal energy stores of the water, so the ΔE value used to calculate the specific heat capacity is a more accurate value. This improves the accuracy of the value of specific heat capacity.

3. J/kg

4.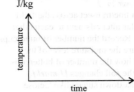

Exam Questions

1. $Q = m \times L$
   So, $L = Q \div m$
   $m = 40.8$ g $= (40.8 \div 1000)$ kg $= 0.0408$ kg
   $L = 47\,100 \div 0.0408 = $ **1.1544... × 10⁶ J/kg**
   $= $ **1.15 × 10⁶ J/kg (to 3 s.f.)**
   [2 marks for correct answer, otherwise 1 mark for correct substitution]

2. a) $\Delta Q = m \times c \times \Delta\theta$
   So, $c = \Delta Q \div (m \times \Delta\theta)$
   $\Delta\theta = 100 - 20 = 80$ °C
   $c = 36\,000 \div (0.5 \times 80)$
   $= $ **900 J/kg°C**
   [2 marks for correct answer, otherwise 1 mark for correct substitution]
   b) Concrete has a higher specific heat capacity *[1 mark]* and so will be able to store a lot more energy in its thermal energy store for the same temperature change, and therefore emit a lot more energy during the day *[1 mark]*. This means it will be able to heat the room to a higher temperature / for longer *[1 mark]*.

3. a) In the graph, $y = \Delta\theta$ and $x = \Delta Q$.
   $\Delta Q = m \times c \times \Delta\theta$
   Rearrange this equation to make it look like $y = mx + c$:
   $\Delta\theta = \frac{1}{m \times c} \times \Delta Q$
   Comparing this to $y = mx + c$,
   the gradient of the graph must equal $\frac{1}{m \times c}$ *[1 mark]*
   Coordinates of two points on the line of best fit are (0,0) and (3000, 0.70), where x has been converted from kJ to J.
   Gradient $= \Delta y \div \Delta x = (0.70 - 0) \div (3000 - 0)$
   $= 0.0002333...$ *[1 mark]*
   $c = \frac{1}{m \times \text{gradient}}$
   $m = 1.0$ kg, so $c = \frac{1}{1 \times 0.0002333...} = 4285.71...$ J/kg °C
   $= $ **4300 J/kg °C (to 2 s.f.)** *[1 mark]*
   b) Lower — in the investigation, some of the energy transferred by the heater would have been transferred to the thermal energy stores of the surroundings rather than the water *[1 mark]*. For the same temperature change to have occurred for a smaller amount of energy transferred, the specific heat capacity must be smaller *[1 mark]*.

Page 375
Elasticity
Q1 $k = F \div x = 1 \div 0.02$ *[1 mark]*
$= $ **50 N/m** *[1 mark]*

Page 376
Investigating Elasticity
Q1 $E = \frac{1}{2}kx^2$
$= \frac{1}{2} \times 40 \times (0.025)^2$ *[1 mark]*
$= $ **0.0125 J** *[1 mark]*

Page 377
Warm-Up Questions
1. false
In order to distort a spring, at least two forces must be applied to the spring.
2. An object undergoing elastic distortion will go back to its original shape and length after the distorting forces have been removed.
3. force = spring constant × extension / $F = k \times x$

Exam Questions
1. extension = 4 cm = 0.04 m
   work done = area under graph
   $= \frac{1}{2} \times 8 \times 0.04$
   $= $ **0.16 J**
   [2 marks for correct answer, otherwise 1 mark for attempting to find the area under the graph]
2. a) The mass on the bottom of the spring / the force applied to the bottom of the spring *[1 mark]*.
   b) Any one from: e.g. the spring used throughout the experiment / the temperature the experiment is carried out at *[1 mark]*.

c) extension = 2.5 cm = 0.025 m
$F = k \times x$
so $k = F \div x$
$= 4 \div 0.025$
$= $ **160 N/m**
[3 marks for correct answer, otherwise 1 mark for correct rearrangement and 1 mark for correct substitution]
Remember to convert the measurement of extension from cm into m before you do your calculation.
d) The spring has been inelastically distorted *[1 mark]*.

3. $E = \frac{1}{2} \times k \times x^2$
Rearrange for x:
$x = \sqrt{\frac{2 \times E}{k}} = \sqrt{\frac{2 \times 36}{400}} = 0.42426...$ m
So length of spring after compression $= 1.20 - 0.42426...$
$= $ **0.77573... m**
$= $ **0.78 m (to 2 s.f.)**
[3 marks for correct answer, otherwise 1 mark for correct substitution and 1 mark for calculating compression = 0.42426... m]

Paper 1: Biology 1
Pages 387-399

1. a) Any two from: e.g. it has a nucleus / it contains mitochondria / it doesn't contain plasmids *[2 marks]*.
   b) E.g. most cells have a structure that is specialised for their function, so they will contain different subcellular structures *[1 mark]*.
   c) D *[1 mark]*
   d) image size = real size × magnification
   image size = 0.054 × 150
   image size = **8.1 mm** *[2 marks for correct answer, otherwise 1 mark for correct working]*.
   e) Similarities
   Any two from: e.g. both plant and animal cells have a nucleus. / Both plant and animal cells contain cytoplasm. / Plant cells and animal cells both have a cell membrane. / Mitochondria are found in both plant cells and animal cells. / Both plant cells and animal cells have ribosomes *[2 marks]*.
   Differences
   Any two from: e.g. chloroplasts are present in plant cells, but not in animal cells. / Plant cells have a cell wall, but animal cells do not. / Plant cells contain a permanent vacuole, but animal cells do not *[2 marks]*.

2. a) Any two from: e.g. stop the mosquitoes from breeding / protect people from mosquito bites using mosquito nets / protect people from mosquito bites by using insect repellent *[2 marks]*.
   b) B *[1 mark]*
   c) 3 days = 3 × 24 = 72 hours
   72 ÷ 18 = 4 divisions
   1 bacterial cell × 2⁴ = 1 × 2 × 2 × 2 × 2 = **16 cells** *[2 marks for correct answer, otherwise 1 mark for correct working.]*
   d) The body is injected with small amounts of dead or inactive pathogens (which are harmless) *[1 mark]*. The pathogens carry antigens, which cause the B-lymphocytes in the body to produce antibodies *[1 mark]* and cause memory lymphocytes to be made *[1 mark]*. If live pathogens of the same type are detected again, the memory lymphocytes can cause a much faster secondary immune response, so the person is less likely to get ill *[1 mark]*.

3. a) B *[1 mark]*
   b) E.g. research from the project about the cystic fibrosis gene could be used to develop more effective treatments for the disorder *[1 mark]*.
   c) E.g.

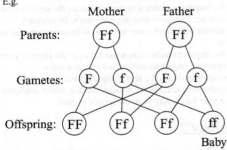

[1 mark for showing that the parents both have the Ff genotype, 1 mark for showing the gametes' genotypes as F or f, 1 mark for correctly showing all possible genotypes of the couple's offspring and identifying the baby's genotype as ff.]
   d) Ff *[1 mark]*. E.g. Ian has the genotype Ff, so Leina must also have the genotype Ff in order for her children to inherit the genotypes: FF (Carys), ff (Beth) and Ff (Alfie) *[1 mark]*.
   e) Environmental variation *[1 mark]*. The scar would have been caused by an environmental factor rather than being determined by genes *[1 mark]*.

4 a) Town B is the most polluted because it contains a higher percentage of dark moths *[1 mark]*.
   b) 77% − 25% = **52%**
      [2 marks for correct answer, otherwise 1 mark for correctly reading 77% and 25% off the graph]
   c) Any one from: e.g. avoid leaving the moths inside the trap for too long. / Avoid touching the moths. / Release the moths in their original habitat *[1 mark]*.
   d) The dark variety is better camouflaged in soot-polluted areas, so it is less likely to be eaten by predators *[1 mark]*. This means more dark moths survive to breed *[1 mark]* and pass the gene(s)/allele for this characteristic on to the next generation *[1 mark]*. As this process continues over time, the dark variety of moth becomes more common *[1 mark]*.

It makes sense that if an organism blends in with its background it'll be harder for predators to spot it.

5 a) B *[1 mark]*
   b) To make the experiment a fair test. / To ensure the same amount of substrate was available in each experiment. / To make the results valid/repeatable *[1 mark]*.
   c) They could have added the sample to a drop of iodine solution *[1 mark]*. If starch was present the iodine solution would have changed to blue-black *[1 mark]*. If starch was no longer present, the iodine solution would have remained browny-orange *[1 mark]*.
   d) As the pH increases from pH 3 to pH 6, the time until the starch is no longer present decreases / the rate of reaction increases *[1 mark]*.
   e) i) The result for pH 7 is anomalous *[1 mark]* because the time taken until starch is no longer present is much slower than expected *[1 mark]*.
      ii) E.g. the student may not have used the correct volume/concentration of starch solution. / The student may have used the incorrect volume/concentration of amylase solution. / The student may have used a buffer solution with the wrong pH. / The student may have carried out the experiment at a different temperature. / The student may have started timing the experiment too early *[1 mark]*.

6 a) Any two from: e.g. there is very little variation in the mean reaction time among all participants. / Their reaction time was very fast. / Their response was automatic *[2 marks]*.

If you have to think about what physical response to give then it's not a reflex action.

   b) i) C *[1 mark]*
      ii) D *[1 mark]*
   c) The men in this experiment had a faster mean reaction time than the women *[1 mark]*, so the data supports the scientist's hypothesis *[1 mark]*.
   d) Any two from: e.g. the age of the participants. / The strength of the tap on the knee. / Caffeine consumption of the participants prior to the investigation / Using the same timing method/equipment *[2 marks]*.
   e) i) relay neurone *[1 mark]*
      ii) How to grade your answer:
         Level 0: There is no relevant information. *[No marks]*
         Level 1: There is a brief description of some parts of the path taken by a nervous impulse in the reflex. The answer shows basic understanding, but lacks coherency. *[1 to 2 marks]*
         Level 2: There is some description of the path taken by a nervous impulse in the reflex, but some detail is missing. The answer shows mostly accurate understanding and has some structure. *[3 to 4 marks]*
         Level 3: There is a clear and detailed description of the path taken by a nervous impulse in the reflex. The answer shows an accurate understanding of the relevant biology and is well structured. *[5 to 6 marks]*

      Here are some points your answer may include:
      The impulse travels from the receptors, along a sensory neurone, to the central nervous system/spinal cord.
      When the impulse reaches a synapse between the sensory neurone and a relay neurone, it triggers neurotransmitters to be released.
      These neurotransmitters cause impulses to be sent along the relay neurone.
      When the impulse reaches a synapse between the relay neurone and a motor neurone, neurotransmitters are released again.
      This causes impulses to be sent along the motor neurone.
      The impulse then reaches the muscle/effector, which contracts to move your hand away from the source of pain.

Paper 2: Biology 2
Pages 400-411

1 a) Put data in order: 10, 21, 21, 35, 37
      Median = 21 *[1 mark]*
   b) To avoid bias. / To make sure the results were representative of the whole sample area *[1 mark]*.
   c) (6 + 15 + 9 + 14 + 20 + 5 + 3 + 11 + 10 + 7) ÷ 10
      = 100 ÷ 10
      = **10 buttercups per m²** *[1 mark]*
   d) 90 × 120 = 10 800 m²
      10 × 10 800 = **108 000 buttercups**
      [2 marks for correct answer, otherwise 1 mark for finding the area of the field.]

Even if you got your answer to c) wrong, you still get full marks for d) if you did the calculation correctly with your answer to c).

   e) Use a tape measure to mark out a line/transect across the field *[1 mark]*. Place quadrats at regular intervals/next to each other along the line/transect *[1 mark]*. Record the number of buttercups in each quadrat *[1 mark]*. Measure the moisture level of the soil at each sample point and see how the number of buttercups changes as the moisture level of the soil changes *[1 mark]*.

2 a) Organisms need to be able to break down sugars like lactose into smaller components so that they can be absorbed into the bloodstream and into cells *[1 mark]* to be used for other life processes, such as respiration *[1 mark]*.
   b) The concentration of glucose is higher in the small intestine than in the blood *[1 mark]*.
   c) Lactose would no longer be broken down *[1 mark]* because lactase would be denatured *[1 mark]*.
   d) Their blood glucose level will not rise very much at all *[1 mark]*. This is because a person with lactose intolerance has little or no lactase to break down the lactose, so there will be little or no glucose to be absorbed from the small intestine *[1 mark]*.

3 a) C *[1 mark]*
   b) To maintain the concentration gradients of oxygen and carbon dioxide *[1 mark]* to maximise the rate of diffusion of the gases into and out of the alveoli *[1 mark]*.
   c) i) To carry oxygen from lungs to the cells *[1 mark]*.
      ii) Their biconcave disc shape gives them a large surface area for absorbing oxygen *[1 mark]*. They don't have a nucleus, so they have more room to carry oxygen *[1 mark]*. They contain lots of haemoglobin, which combines with oxygen in the lungs to become oxyhaemoglobin *[1 mark]*.
   d) E.g. the sickle-shaped cells are more rigid than normal red blood cells so they may not be able to carry as much oxygen / the sickle-shaped cells are a different shape from normal red blood cells, so they may not be able to fit through the capillaries *[1 mark]*. This could reduce the amount of oxygen transported to cells, causing an increase in breathing rate *[1 mark]*.

If you don't have enough oxygen for respiration, your breathing rate increases to get more oxygen into your blood. In a person with sickle cell anaemia, the lack of oxygen may cause their breathing rate to increase so much that they feel breathless.

4 a) Carbon compounds in the plants are being transferred to animals as they eat the plants *[1 mark]*.
   b) i) light intensity *[1 mark]*, carbon dioxide concentration *[1 mark]*, temperature *[1 mark]*.
      ii) Energy is taken in during photosynthesis / the reaction *[1 mark]*.
   c) A *[1 mark]*
   d) Microorganisms break down waste products and dead organisms *[1 mark]* and release carbon dioxide into the atmosphere as they respire *[1 mark]*.
   e) i) B *[1 mark]*
      ii) E.g. using fertilisers *[1 mark]*.

5 a) The loss of water from a plant's surface by evaporation or diffusion *[1 mark]*.
   b) i) B *[1 mark]*
      ii) E.g. day 2 was less bright, so the stomata weren't fully open and less water could move out of the leaves. / Day 2 was colder, so the water evaporated/diffused more slowly. / Day 2 was less windy, so the water vapour was carried away more slowly, meaning that diffusion couldn't happen as quickly.
      [1 mark for reason, 1 mark for explanation].

The rate of transpiration varies throughout the day due to the changing light intensity, but it can also be affected by the temperature, and the air flow around the leaves.

   c) At night, the light intensity is low *[1 mark]* so the stomata close, allowing less water vapour to escape *[1 mark]*.
   d) Transpiration creates a slight shortage of water in the leaf *[1 mark]*. More water is drawn up from the rest of the plant through the xylem vessels to replace it *[1 mark]*. This in turn means that more water is drawn up from the roots *[1 mark]*.
   e) i) B *[1 mark]*
      ii) Each branch of a root is covered in microscopic root hair cells *[1 mark]* giving them a large surface area for absorbing water *[1 mark]*.

6 a) A *[1 mark]*
   b) C *[1 mark]* — e.g. because the level corresponds to the thickness of the uterus lining, which is maintained by progesterone *[1 mark]*.

There are a few different ways that you can tell that this line represents progesterone. As long as you're able to justify your answer, you'll get the marks.

c) How to grade your answer:
Level 0: There is no relevant information. *[No marks]*
Level 1: There is a basic description of how at least two of the hormones help to control the menstrual cycle, but little description of how they interact with each other. The points made are not linked together. *[1 to 2 marks]*
Level 2: There is a clear description of how at least three of the hormones help to control the menstrual cycle and some description of how they interact with each other. Some of the points are linked together. *[3 to 4 marks]*
Level 3: There is a detailed description of how each of the four hormones helps to control the menstrual cycle and how they interact with each other. The points made are well linked and the answer has a clear and logical structure. *[5 to 6 marks]*

Here are some points your answer may include:
FSH is released by the pituitary gland at the start of the menstrual cycle.
It causes a follicle in one of the ovaries to mature.
It also stimulates the production of oestrogen.
Oestrogen is released by the ovaries and causes the lining of the uterus to thicken and grow.
At a high level it stimulates a surge/rapid increase in levels of LH.
LH is released by the pituitary gland.
It stimulates ovulation and also stimulates the remains of the follicle to develop into a corpus luteum.
The corpus luteum secretes progesterone.
Progesterone maintains the lining of the uterus and inhibits the release of FSH and LH.
When the level of progesterone falls and there's a low oestrogen level, the uterus lining breaks down.
A low progesterone level allows FSH to increase so that the menstrual cycle can begin again.

d) Advantages of the implant: e.g. it works for three years / protection is always available / you do not have to remember to take a pill every day / it is highly effective.
Disadvantages of the implant: e.g. it has to be inserted by a doctor or nurse which may be painful/inconvenient / if certain medications are taken, a different contraceptive method would have to be used / you could suffer from side effects / it does not protect against STIs.
Advantages of the condom: e.g. it protects against STIs / there are no side effects / it is not affected by medication.
Disadvantages of the condom: e.g. it needs to be available at the time of intercourse / if it isn't used correctly it may not be effective / it can only be used once.
Conclusion: e.g. The condom is the better method of contraception because it prevents the spread of STIs.
[3 marks for at least one advantage and one disadvantage of each method, otherwise 2 marks for at least two advantages or disadvantages of either method or 1 mark for one advantage or disadvantage of either method. 1 mark for giving a justified conclusion.]

Paper 3: Chemistry 1
Pages 412-423

1 a) E.g.

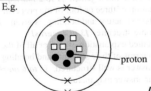

[1 mark]
Remember that atoms have the same number of electrons and protons.
b) B *[1 mark]*
c) C and D *[1 mark]* — they are the only pair with the same number of protons *[1 mark]*
d) i) D *[1 mark]*
ii) $M_r = 65 + 32 + (4 \times 16) = \mathbf{161}$
[2 marks for the correct answer, otherwise 1 mark for correct working]
iii) moles of oxygen atoms = $1.4 \times 4 = 5.6$ moles *[1 mark]*
This is because there are 4 moles of oxygen atoms for every 1 mole of $ZnSO_4$.
atoms of oxygen = moles of oxygen × Avogadro's constant
$= 5.6 \times 6.02 \times 10^{23}$ *[1 mark]*
$= 3.3712 \times 10^{24} = \mathbf{3.4 \times 10^{24}}$ atoms *[1 mark]*
[3 marks for correct answer given to 2 significant figures without working, otherwise 1 mark for correct number of moles of oxygen atoms, 1 mark for multiplying number of moles of oxygen atoms by Avogadro's constant]
Make sure you give your final answer to the number of significant figures stated in the question. If you don't do this you won't get full marks.

2 a) A *[1 mark]*
b) It has no free electrons *[1 mark]*

c) i) liquid *[1 mark]*
ii) Carbon dioxide would have a higher boiling point than oxygen. Because carbon dioxide is a larger molecule *[1 mark]*, the intermolecular forces would be stronger *[1 mark]* so would require more energy to break *[1 mark]*

d) mass of CO_2 = 1.32 kg = 1320 g
M_r of CO_2 = 12 + (2 × 16) = 44 *[1 mark]*
moles of CO_2 = mass ÷ M_r = 1320 ÷ 44 = 30 moles *[1 mark]*
moles of $ZnCO_3$ = 30 moles
This is because one mole of $ZnCO_3$ reacts to produce one mole of CO_2.
M_r of $ZnCO_3$ = 65 + 12 + (16 × 3) = 125 *[1 mark]*
mass of $ZnCO_3$ = moles × M_r = 30 × 125 = **3750 g** *[1 mark]*
[4 marks for correct answer without working]

3 a) The volume of gas produced *[1 mark]*.
b) Place a lighted splint in the gas *[1 mark]* and it will make a squeaky pop sound *[1 mark]*.
c) Reaction D *[1 mark]*. The most reactive metal will react fastest with the acid *[1 mark]*. In reaction D the largest volume of gas has been collected in the syringe / the most bubbles are being given off *[1 mark]*.
d) Reaction of copper sulfate with iron: yes *[1 mark]*
Reaction of iron sulfate with magnesium: yes *[1 mark]*
e) D *[1 mark]*
A more reactive metal will displace a less reactive metal in a salt.

4 a) E.g. a pipette / measuring cylinder *[1 mark]*
b) volume of HCl = 25 cm³ = 0.025 dm³
moles of HCl = concentration × volume
= 0.8 × 0.025 = 0.02 moles
mass of HCl = moles × M_r
= 0.02 × 36.5 = **0.73 g**
[2 marks for correct answer, otherwise 1 mark for correct number of moles of HCl]
c) i) There would be unreacted calcium hydroxide/solid at the bottom of the flask *[1 mark]*
ii) $H^+_{(aq)} + OH^-_{(aq)} \rightarrow H_2O_{(l)}$
[1 mark for correct ionic equation, 1 mark for correct state symbols]
d) i) 0.75 g *[1 mark — accept any answer between 0.72 g and 0.78 g]*
ii) E.g. monitoring pH using Universal indicator doesn't provide accurate data for the value of pH as the reaction progresses *[1 mark]*.
iii) a pH meter/probe *[1 mark]*

5 a) Potable water is water that is fit to drink *[1 mark]*.
b) i) C *[1 mark]*
ii) Iron sulfate/aluminium sulfate is added to the water *[1 mark]*, which makes fine particles clump together and settle at the bottom *[1 mark]*.
c) E.g. the sources of water available to the city mean that either plant is possible to use *[1 mark]*. The sea water distillation plant would be more costly to run since it uses more energy than a water treatment plant *[1 mark]*. The higher energy usage of sea water distillation means that this type of plant is likely to have a larger environmental impact due to greenhouse gas emissions linked to power generation *[1 mark]*. In conclusion, a water treatment plant is likely to have lower costs and less environmental impact, which suggests that this may be a better option that sea water distillation *[1 mark]*.
In questions that ask you to evaluate you need to include a conclusion that supports what you've talked about in the rest of your answer — that's what the last mark is for in the example answer shown above.

6 a) Any two from: Problem — the spots of dye/ink are touching the solvent *[1 mark]*. Correction — the student should put the filter paper in a beaker of solvent with the pencil line above the level of the solvent *[1 mark]*. / Problem — the ink and dyes are compared using different solvents *[1 mark]*. Correction — the student should use the same solvent for the black ink and the dyes so that it's a fair test *[1 mark]*. / Problem — the ink and dyes are compared on different pieces of filter paper which could make it difficult to directly compare them *[1 mark]*. Correction — the student should put the spots of the dyes and the ink on the same piece of filter paper *[1 mark]*.
b) C *[1 mark]*
c) Dyes B and D *[1 mark]*
Explanation — all of the spots from these two dyes are in the same positions as the spots from the black ink *[1 mark]*.
d) R_f = distance travelled by solute ÷ distance travelled by solvent = 4.8 ÷ 6.4 = **0.75** *[1 mark]*
e) How to grade your answer:
Level 0: There is no relevant information. *[No marks]*
Level 1: There is a brief explanation of how to carry out simple distillation but it has limited detail and is incomplete. Several errors are present. There is no clear explanation of how the solvent is separated from the ink mixture. The points made do not link together. *[1 to 2 marks]*
Level 2: There is an explanation of how to carry out simple distillation that contains correctly named pieces of equipment. The explanation may miss small details and contain a few small errors. An attempt is made to explain how the solvent is separated from the ink mixture, but it may contain small errors. The answer has some structure. *[3 to 4 marks]*

Level 3: There is a clear and detailed explanation of how to carry out simple distillation with all equipment correctly named. The answer explains accurately how distillation could separate the solvent from the ink mixture. The answer is well structured. *[5 to 6 marks]*
Here are some points your answer may include: e.g.
Attach a distillation flask to a condenser.
Place the end of the condenser over a beaker/conical flask.
Connect the bottom end of the condenser to a cold tap using rubber tubing.
Run cold water through the condenser to keep it cool.
Pour the ink into a distillation flask.
Place a thermometer and a bung in the top of the distillation flask.
Gradually heat the distillation flask using a Bunsen burner.
The solvent will evaporate, as it has the lowest boiling point, whilst the rest of the ink mixture will stay in liquid form.
The gaseous solvent will then pass into the condenser.
In the condenser, the gaseous solvent will cool and condense.
It will then flow into the beaker/conical flask, where it is collected separately from the rest of the ink mixture.

Paper 4: Chemistry 2
Pages 424-435
1 a) i) C *[1 mark]*
Melting point increases down the group, so chlorine will have a melting point about halfway between the melting points of fluorine and bromine.
   ii) It is around halfway between the melting points of bromine and fluorine *[1 mark]*.
  b) D *[1 mark]*
  c) $Br_2 + 2KI \rightarrow I_2 + 2KBr$
     [1 mark for correct products, 1 mark for correct balancing]
  d) Chlorine is higher up group 7 than iodine, which means that chlorine is more reactive than iodine *[1 mark]*. This is because chlorine can attract an electron to its outer shell more easily than iodine, because the nucleus is closer to the outermost shell *[1 mark]*. This means that chlorine will displace iodine in the solution *[1 mark]*.
  e) $H_2 + F_2 \rightarrow 2HF$
     [1 mark for correct reactants and products, 1 mark for correct balancing]
2 a) i) $CaCO_3 + 2HCl \rightarrow CaCl_2 + CO_2 + H_2O$
       [1 mark for correct reactants and products, 1 mark for correct balancing]
   ii)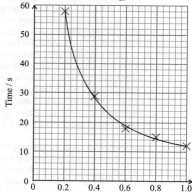
       [1 mark for plotting points correctly, 1 mark for sensible curve of best fit]
  iii) E.g. 23 s (accept 22-24 s) *[1 mark]*
  b) The rate increases as the concentration increases *[1 mark]*.
  c) At higher concentration there are more particles of reactant in a certain volume *[1 mark]*. This means that collisions between particles are more likely, so the reaction rate increases *[1 mark]*.
  d) No. The powdered marble has a larger surface area *[1 mark]*. This will increase the rate of the reaction *[1 mark]*, so it will take less than 18 seconds for 20 cm³ of carbon dioxide to form *[1 mark]*.
3 a) E.g. measure out 25 cm³ of sodium thiosulfate solution and 25 cm³ of hydrochloric acid using measuring cylinders *[1 mark]*. Use a water bath to gently heat the separate solutions to the required temperature *[1 mark]*. Place a flask over a black mark on a piece of paper, and add both solutions to the flask *[1 mark]*. Use a stopwatch to time how long it takes for the black mark to disappear due to the formation of the yellow sulfur precipitate *[1 mark]*.
  b) E.g. the concentrations of reactants / the depth of liquid in the flask *[1 mark]*. *[Accept any other valid answer]*
  c) E.g. at higher temperatures, particles move faster, so they collide more often and with more energy *[1 mark]*. This means more particles collide with enough energy to react, so the reaction rate is faster at a higher temperature *[1 mark]*.

4 a) Triacontane has a higher boiling point than heptane because it is a larger hydrocarbon *[1 mark]*. This means that triacontane will turn to liquid and drain out / be collected lower down the column where the temperature is higher *[1 mark]*.
  b) B *[1 mark]*
  c) i) 8% *[1 mark]*
    ii) E.g. the supply of fuel oil and bitumen (50%) is larger than the demand (38%), so there is plenty of unused fuel oil and bitumen that can be cracked to provide petrol *[1 mark]*. However, the demand for diesel oil (23%) is already greater than the amount in crude oil (19%), so there isn't any spare for cracking *[1 mark]*.
5 a) Bonds broken (2 × 436) + 498 = 1370
     Bonds formed (4 × 464) = 1856
     Energy change = 1370 − 1856 = **−486 kJ mol⁻¹**
     [4 marks for the correct answer, otherwise 3 marks for the correct answer with the wrong sign, 1 mark for calculating the correct amount of energy needed to break the bonds and 1 mark for calculating the correct amount of energy released in bond formation]
  b) D *[1 mark]*
  c) i) 37.5 °C *[1 mark]*
    ii) Temperature change = final temperature − initial temperature
        = 37.5 − 17 = **20.5 °C**
       [2 marks for correct answer, otherwise 1 mark for writing a correct expression for calculating the temperature change]
If your answer to i) was wrong, you can still have both marks for correctly subtracting 17 from it to find the temperature change.
   iii) The reaction was exothermic as the temperature of the surroundings increased during the reaction *[1 mark]*.
6 a) D *[1 mark]*
  b) i) C *[1 mark]*
    ii) E.g.
        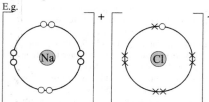
       [1 mark for 8 electrons in sodium, 1 mark for 8 electrons in chlorine, 1 mark for each correct charge]
  c) Cl is 25% ³⁷Cl and 75% ³⁵Cl *[1 mark]*
     To find the relative atomic mass of chlorine these abundances need to be taken into account using the calculation:
     $A_r = ((37 \times 25) + (35 \times 75)) \div 100 = 35.5$ *[1 mark]*
  d) E.g. as you go down group 1 the outer electron gets further from the nucleus *[1 mark]*. This means that the outer electron is more easily lost because it feels less attraction from the nucleus *[1 mark]*. The more readily a metal loses its outer electrons, the more reactive it is, so reactivity increases as you go down group 1/from lithium to sodium to potassium *[1 mark]*.
  e) How to grade your answer:
     Level 0: There is no relevant information. *[No marks]*
     Level 1: A brief attempt is made to explain one or two of these properties in terms of structure and bonding. The points made do not link together. *[1 to 2 marks]*
     Level 2: Some explanation of three or four of the properties, in terms of their structure and bonding, is given. The answer has some structure. *[3 to 4 marks]*
     Level 3: Clear and detailed explanation of five or all of the properties, in terms of their structure and bonding, is given. The answer is well structured. *[5 to 6 marks]*
Here are some points your answer may include:
<u>Diamond</u>
Each carbon atom in diamond forms four covalent bonds in a rigid giant covalent/lattice structure, making it very hard.
Because it is made up of lots of covalent bonds, which take a lot of energy to break, diamond has a very high melting point.
There are no free electrons or ions in the structure of diamond, so it can't conduct electricity.
<u>Graphite</u>
Each carbon atom in graphite forms three covalent bonds, creating sheets of carbon atoms that can slide over each other. The carbon layers are only held together weakly, which is what makes graphite soft and slippery.
The covalent bonds between the carbon atoms take a lot of energy to break, giving graphite a very high melting point.
Only three out of each carbon's four outer electrons are used in bonds, so graphite has lots of free/delocalised electrons and can conduct electricity.

Paper 5: Physics 1
Pages 436–448

1. a) i) E.g. total energy must be conserved / energy cannot be created or destroyed, only transferred. *[1 mark]*
   ii) C *[1 mark]*
   iii) C *[1 mark]*
   b) i) E.g. measure the temperature after a set number of bounces instead of after a set time *[1 mark]*
   This is a sensible idea as the number of bounces in a given time may vary.
   ii) E.g. energy is transferred mechanically from the ball's kinetic energy store *[1 mark]* to its elastic potential energy store as it hits the wall and deforms *[1 mark]*. Some energy is transferred by heating to the thermal energy store of the ball *[1 mark]*. Energy is transferred mechanically from the elastic potential energy store of the ball to the kinetic energy store of the ball as the ball rebounds from the wall *[1 mark]*.
   c) change in GPE = $0.03 \times 10 \times 1.75$
   = **0.525 J**
   [2 marks for correct answer, otherwise 1 mark for correct substitution]

2. a) i) E.g. bio-fuel / wind power / hydroelectricity / the tides *[1 mark]*
   ii) Efficiency = useful energy transferred by the device ÷ total energy transferred to the device. *[1 mark]*
   iii) Efficiency = useful energy transferred by the device ÷ total energy transferred to the device
   = $0.2 \div 1.2$
   = $0.1666...$
   = **0.17 (= 17%) (to 2 s.f.)**
   [2 marks for correct answer, otherwise 1 mark for correct substitution]
   b) i) The amount of energy used has decreased over time *[1 mark]*. E.g. this could be because electrical devices have become more efficient over time *[1 mark]*.
   ii) Any two from: e.g. building renewable power plants is expensive / using fossil fuels is fairly cheap / some people don't want to live near renewable power plants / renewable energy resources are not as reliable as fossil fuels / research into improving the reliability and reducing the cost of renewable resources is expensive and time consuming / making personal changes (such as installing solar panels) can be expensive for an individual *[2 marks — 1 mark for each correct point]*.
   c) The home owner should use brick Y *[1 mark]*, because brick Y has the lowest thermal conductivity of all the options. This means the rate of energy transfer by heating will be slowest through this type of brick *[1 mark]*. Also brick Y is the thickest brick and the thicker the walls of a building, the lower the rate of cooling of the building will be *[1 mark]*.

3. a) The first skater travels at a constant speed for the first 15 s (travelling 33 m) *[1 mark]*. The skater then remains stationary (at 33 m) for 10 s *[1 mark]* before accelerating away for the next 10 s (and travelling another 12 m) *[1 mark]*.
   b) The gradient of the line between 0 s and 15 s will give speed.
   speed = gradient = $\frac{\text{change in } y}{\text{change in } x}$
   = $\frac{33 - 0}{15 - 0}$
   = **2.2 m/s**
   [2 marks for correct answer, otherwise 1 mark for correct method of calculating speed from the graph]
   c) i) Speed = distance ÷ time *[1 mark]*
   ii) Time = distance ÷ speed
   = $14 \div 3.5$
   = **4 s**
   [3 marks for the correct answer, otherwise 1 mark for correct rearrangement and 1 mark for correct substitution]
   d) i) A *[1 mark]*
   ii) The total frictional force must be larger than the total driving forces *[1 mark]*.

4. a) E.g. place a block on a sheet of paper and draw around it. Shine a light beam through the block *[1 mark]*. Trace the path of the ray using a pencil and a ruler. Measure and record the angles of incidence and refraction *[1 mark]*. Repeat this for different materials, keeping the angle of incidence the same *[1 mark]*.
   b) i) e.g. ray box *[1 mark]*
   ii) E.g. it allows the centre of the beam to be traced more accurately, meaning better angle measurements *[1 mark]*.
   c) i) Flint glass *[1 mark]*
   ii) Flint glass refracts the light beam by the greatest amount *[1 mark]* and refraction is caused by light being slowed down by a material *[1 mark]*.
   d) $v = f \times \lambda$
   = $(5.1 \times 10^{14}) \times (353 \times 10^{-9})$
   = $1.800... \times 10^8$
   = **1.8×10^8 m/s (to 2 s.f.)**
   [2 marks for correct answer, otherwise 1 mark for correct substitution]

5. a) How to grade your answer:
   Level 0: There is no relevant information. *[No marks]*
   Level 1: There is a brief description of both models of the atom. The points made do not link together. *[1 to 2 marks]*
   Level 2: There is a description of both models of the atom, and some description of the scientific discoveries that led to the development of the nuclear model. The answer has some structure. *[3 to 4 marks]*
   Level 3: There is a clear and detailed description of both models of the atom, and of the scientific discoveries and experiments which led to the development of the nuclear model. The answer is well structured. *[5 to 6 marks]*
   Here are some points your answer may include:
   Model X is the plum pudding model of the atom.
   The plum pudding model describes the atom as a sphere of positive charge, with negatively charged electrons within it.
   Model Y is the nuclear/Bohr model of the atom.
   The nuclear/Bohr model of the atom describes the atom as a nucleus, made up of positively charged protons and uncharged neutrons, orbited by electrons.
   In the early 20th century (1909), Rutherford and Marsden performed the alpha scattering experiment.
   They fired a beam of positively charged alpha particles at a thin gold foil.
   Based on the plum pudding model, they expected all the alpha particles to pass through the foil, with some deflection.
   However, they found that most alpha particles passed through the foil without deflecting, while a small few were deflected back towards the emitter.
   This suggested that most of the atom is empty space, since so many of the alpha particles passed through without deflecting.
   It also suggested there was a small, positively charged 'nucleus' in the centre of the atom, which caused the backwards deflection of the alpha particles.
   Later, Bohr proposed that the electrons in an atom could only be found in fixed orbits named energy levels.
   b) i) E.g. a Geiger-Müller tube *[1 mark]*
   ii) The charge on a beta particle, B = –1
   83 = A – 1
   A = **84** *[1 mark]*
   iii) The initial count-rate was 80 cps.
   $80 \div 2 = 40$
   So after one half-life, the count-rate will be 40 cps.
   From the graph, 40 cps is reached after 60 minutes.
   So half-life = **60 minutes**.
   [2 marks for correct answer, otherwise 1 mark for correct method of calculating half-life graphically]
   c) A thicker lead lining blocks more gamma radiation *[1 mark]*, which improves the safety of people nearby since gamma radiation can damage or kill cells *[1 mark]*.

6. a) 10 dB *[1 mark]*
   b) wavelength = $2 \times 0.625 = 1.25$ m
   wave speed = frequency × wavelength
   = 5500×1.25
   = 6875 m/s
   = **6900 m/s (to 2 s.f.)**
   [4 marks for correct answer, otherwise 1 mark for correctly calculating wavelength, 1 mark for correct substitution and 1 mark for correct unrounded answer]
   c) A *[1 mark]*

Paper 6: Physics 2
Pages 449–461

1. a) i) A *[1 mark]*
   ii) time = charge ÷ current = $1440 \div 12$ = **120 s**
   [3 marks for correct answer, otherwise 1 mark for correct rearrangement and 1 mark for correct substitution]
   b) E.g. the maximum safe power that an appliance can operate at / the maximum amount of energy an appliance can transfer between stores per second *[1 mark]*.
   c) Energy is transferred from the thermal energy store of the heating element *[1 mark]* to the thermal energy store of the water *[1 mark]* by heating *[1 mark]*.

d) E.g.

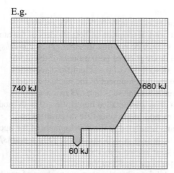

[2 marks for a correctly drawn diagram, otherwise 1 mark for correct width of one arrow or correct calculation of waste energy]

2 a) i) B *[1 mark]*
The clamp must apply 1 N of force to balance the weight of the mass. Otherwise, there will be a resultant force on the spring causing it to move.
  ii) If only one force was applied, this would simply cause the spring to move in the direction of the force *[1 mark]*.
  b) D *[1 mark]*
  c) How to grade your answer:
  Level 0:   There is no relevant information. *[No marks]*
  Level 1:   There is a brief description of an experiment using the equipment shown. The points made are not linked together. *[1 to 2 marks]*
  Level 2:   There is a description of an experiment that can be performed with the equipment shown, and a valid statement of how to calculate the spring constant. The answer has some structure. *[3 to 4 marks]*
  Level 3:   There is a clear and detailed description of an experiment that can be performed using the equipment shown, and of how to calculate the spring constant from the resulting force-extension graph. The answer is well structured. *[5 to 6 marks]*
  Here are some points your answer may include:
  Measure the mass of the masses that are to be hung from the spring using a mass balance.
  Calculate the weight of each of the masses using $W = m \times g$.
  Using the ruler, measure the length of the spring when it has no masses hanging from it (the unstretched length).
  Hang a mass from the spring, and record the new length of the spring.
  Calculate the extension of the spring by subtracting the unstretched length from the new length.
  Increase the number of masses hanging from the spring in steps, recording the new weight and calculating the extension each time.
  Once there are a suitable number of points, plot the results on a force-extension graph, with force on the y-axis, and extension on the x-axis.
  Draw a line of best fit through the results.
  Spring constant = force ÷ extension ($k = F \div e$).
  So the spring constant can be calculated by finding the gradient of the linear part of the graph.
  d) Work done is equal to area under the graph up to point A.
  Extension = 3.0 cm = 0.030 m
  Area = area of a triangle = ½ × base × height
       = ½ × 0.030 × 6.0
       = **0.09 J**
  [3 marks for correct answer, otherwise 1 mark for correctly converting cm to m and 1 mark for a correct method of calculating the area under the graph]
  You could have used the counting the squares method here instead if you had wanted to. Either method used correctly will get you full marks.
  e) The rubber band did behave elastically, as it returned to its original shape and size once the forces acting on it were removed *[1 mark]*. However, the force-extension graph for the rubber band was a curve, so the relationship between force and extension was not linear *[1 mark]*.

3 a) C *[1 mark]*
  b) 30 minutes = 30 × 60 = 1800 s
     $Q = I \times t = 2.4 \times 1800 = 4320 =$ **4300 C (to 2 s.f.)**
     [2 marks for correct answer, otherwise 1 mark for correct substitution.]
  c) $F = B \times I \times l$
     $= 0.75 \times 2.4 \times 0.05 =$ **0.09 N**
     [2 marks for correct answer, otherwise 1 mark for correct substitution.]
  d) Any one from: e.g. increase the current through the wire / increase the magnetic flux density/strength of the magnetic field / increase the length of the wire inside the magnetic field *[1 mark]*.

4 a) E.g.

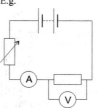

[1 mark for variable resistor, fixed resistor and ammeter drawn in series with the battery, 1 mark for voltmeter drawn in parallel to the fixed resistor, 1 mark for all circuit symbols drawn correctly]
  b) mean = $\frac{2.53 + 2.52 + 2.51}{3}$ = **2.52 A** *[1 mark]*
  c) E.g. when a current flows through the resistor, electrons collide with the ions in the lattice that make up the resistor *[1 mark]*. This gives energy to the ions, which makes them vibrate more (causing the resistor to heat up) *[1 mark]*.
  d) $V = I \times R = 5 \times 2 =$ **10 V**
     [2 marks for correct answer, otherwise 1 mark for correct substitution]
  e) D *[1 mark]*

5 a) i) E.g. wear insulated gloves to move the container / don't move the container until it is cool / keep all electronics (apart from the immersion heater) away from the water *[1 mark]*
  ii) E.g. joulemeter *[1 mark]*
  b) Comparing $y = mx + c$ and $Q = m \times L$, with Q on the y-axis and m on the x-axis, you can see that the gradient of the graph is equal to L.
     Gradient = change in y ÷ change in x
              = 0.34 ÷ 0.15 = 2.266... = **2.3 MJ/kg (to 2 s.f.)**
     (accept between 2.2 and 2.3 MJ/kg)
     [2 marks for correct answer, otherwise 1 mark for correct method for calculating the gradient of the graph]
  c) A *[1 mark]*
  Reading from the graph, 0.42 MJ of energy was required to boil off 0.185 kg of water.
  $E = IVt$, so $t = \frac{E}{IV} = \frac{0.42 \times 10^6}{8 \times 12} =$ **4375 s**.
  d) E.g. particles of liquid water are closer together than particles of water vapour. / Particles of liquid water have less energy in their kinetic stores/move slower than particles of water vapour *[1 mark]*.

6 a) i) electrical power = current × potential difference / $P = I \times V$ *[1 mark]*
  ii) Potential difference across the motor = 12.0 – 4.0 = 8.0 V
     Current through the motor = 5.0 – 3.0 = 2.0 A
     $P = I \times V = 2.0 \times 8.0 =$ **16 W**
     [3 marks for correct answer, otherwise 1 mark for correct calculation of potential difference across the motor or current through the motor and 1 mark for correct substitution into the power equation.]
  b) i) The motors transfer energy to the kinetic energy store of the fan blades *[1 mark]*. Power is the rate of energy transfer, so using a more powerful motor will cause the fan blades to increase their speed at a higher rate / reach a higher maximum speed *[1 mark]*. So motor A has the highest power *[1 mark]*.
  ii) E.g. lubricate the motors *[1 mark]*.
  c) As the temperature increases, the resistance of the thermistor will decrease *[1 mark]*, so the potential difference across the thermistor will decrease *[1 mark]*. As the thermistor is in parallel with the heater, the potential difference across the heater will decrease *[1 mark]*.
  d) Energy usefully transferred = $\Delta Q = m \times c \times \Delta \theta$
     $\Delta \theta = 65 - 16 = 49$ °C
     $\Delta Q = 2.1 \times 4200 \times 49 = 432\,180$ J
     Total useful energy transferred by device = 432 180 J
     efficiency = $\frac{\text{useful energy transferred by device}}{\text{total energy supplied to device}}$
     total energy supplied to device
     = useful energy transferred by device ÷ efficiency
     = 432 180 ÷ 0.85
     = **508 447.058... J = 510 000 J (to 2 s.f.)**
     [4 marks for correct answer, otherwise 1 mark for correct substitution to find energy usefully transferred, 1 mark for correct rearrangement of efficiency equation and 1 mark for correct substitution into rearranged efficiency equation]

Glossary

Abiotic factor	A non-living factor of the environment.
Absolute zero	Theoretically the coldest temperature an object could reach. At absolute zero, particles have the minimum amount of energy in their kinetic energy stores. Absolute zero is at 0 K, or −273 °C.
Absorption (of waves)	When a wave transfers energy to the energy stores of a material.
Acceleration	A change in velocity in a certain amount of time.
Accurate result	A result that is very close to the true answer.
Acid	A substance with a pH of less than 7 that forms H^+ ions in water.
Acrosome	The part of the sperm that contains the enzymes needed to digest through the membrane of the egg cell.
Activation energy	The minimum amount of energy that reactant particles must have when they collide in order to react.
Active transport	The movement of particles across a membrane against a concentration gradient (i.e. from an area of lower concentration to an area of higher concentration) using energy transferred during respiration.
Activity (radioactive)	The number of nuclei of a sample that decay per second, measured in Bq.
Adaptation	A feature that helps an organism to survive in its natural environment.
Aerobic respiration	Respiration taking place in the presence of oxygen.
Air resistance	The frictional force caused by air on a moving object.
Alkali	A substance with a pH of more than 7 that forms OH^- ions in solution.
Alkali metal	An element in Group 1 of the periodic table. E.g. sodium, potassium etc.
Alkane	A saturated hydrocarbon with the general formula C_nH_{2n+2}. E.g. methane, ethane etc.
Alkene	An unsaturated hydrocarbon that contains a carbon-carbon double bond.
Allele	A version of a gene.
Alpha decay	A type of radioactive decay in which an alpha particle is given out from a decaying nucleus.
Alpha particle	A positively-charged particle made up of two protons and two neutrons (a helium nucleus).
Alpha particle scattering experiment	An experiment in which alpha particles were fired at gold foil to see if they were deflected. It led to the plum pudding model being abandoned in favour of the nuclear model of the atom.
Alternating current (a.c.)	Current that is constantly changing direction.
Alveolus	A tiny air sac in the lungs, where gas exchange occurs.
Amino acid	A small molecule that is a building block of proteins.
Ammeter	A component used to measure the current through a component. It is always connected in series with the component.
Amplitude	The maximum displacement of a point on a wave from its rest position.
Anaerobic respiration	Respiration taking place in the absence of oxygen.
Angle of incidence	The angle the incoming ray makes with the normal at a boundary.
Angle of refraction	The angle a refracted ray makes with the normal when a wave refracts at a boundary.
Anion	A particle with a negative charge, formed when one or more electrons are gained.
Anode	An electrode where oxidation happens. The positive electrode in electrolysis.
Anomalous result	A result that doesn't fit with the rest of the data.
Antibiotic	A drug used to kill or prevent the growth of bacteria.
Antibiotic resistance	When bacteria aren't killed by an antibiotic.
Antibody	A protein produced by B-lymphocytes in response to the presence of an antigen.
Antigen	A molecule on the surface of a cell or a pathogen that can trigger an immune response. Foreign antigens trigger B-lymphocytes to produce antibodies.
Aqueous solution	A solution made up of a solute dissolved in water.
Artery	A blood vessel that carries blood away from the heart.
Asexual reproduction	Where organisms reproduce by mitosis to produce genetically identical offspring.
Atmosphere	The layer of gases that surrounds a planet.

Glossary

Atom	A small particle that makes up matter. It is made up of a small, central, positively-charged nucleus, consisting of protons and neutrons, surrounded by negatively-charged electrons.
Atomic number	The number of protons in the nucleus of an atom. It's also known as proton number.
Avogadro constant	The number of particles in one mole of a substance, which is 6.02×10^{23}.
Axon	The part of a neurone that carries nerve impulses away from the cell body.
B-lymphocyte	A type of white blood cell involved in the specific immune response that produces antibodies.
Background radiation	The low-level radiation which surrounds us at all times, arising from both natural and man-made sources.
Base	A substance that reacts with acids in neutralisation reactions.
Beta-minus particle	A high-speed electron emitted by the nucleus.
Beta-plus particle	A high-speed positron emitted by the nucleus.
Beta decay	A type of radioactive decay in which either a beta-minus particle or a beta-plus particle is given out from a decaying nucleus.
Bias	Unfairness in the way data is presented, possibly because the presenter is trying to make a particular point (sometimes without knowing they're doing it).
Bio-fuel	A renewable energy resource made from plant products or animal dung.
Biodiversity	The variety of living organisms in an ecosystem.
Bioleaching	The process by which a metal is separated from its ore using bacteria.
Biomass	The mass of living material in an organism or a group of organisms.
Biotic factor	A living factor of the environment.
BMI	Body Mass Index. Used as a guide to help decide whether someone is underweight, of healthy weight, overweight or obese.
Bond energy	The amount of energy required to break a bond (or the amount of energy released when a bond is made).
Braking distance	The braking distance is the distance a vehicle travels after the brakes are applied until it comes to a complete stop, as a result of the braking force.
Calibrate	Check the accuracy of an instrument by using it to measure a known value.
Capillary	A type of blood vessel involved in the exchange of materials at tissues.
Carbohydrase	A type of digestive enzyme that catalyses the breakdown of a carbohydrate into sugars.
Cardiovascular disease	Disease of the heart or blood vessels.
Catalyst	A substance that increases the speed of a reaction, without being changed or used up.
Categoric data	Data that comes in distinct categories (e.g. flower colour or blood group).
Cathode	An electrode where reduction happens. The negative electrode in electrolysis.
Cation	A particle with a positive charge, formed when one or more electrons are lost.
Cell membrane	A membrane surrounding a cell, which holds it together and controls what goes in and out.
Cellulose	A molecule which strengthens cell walls in plants and algae.
Cell wall	A structure surrounding some cell types, which gives strength and support.
Central Nervous System (CNS)	The brain and spinal cord. It's where reflexes and actions are coordinated.
Centripetal force	The resultant force that acts on any object moving in a circle. It acts towards the centre of the circle.
Chemical bond	The attraction of two atoms for each other, caused by the sharing or transfer of electrons.
Chlorophyll	A green substance found in chloroplasts which absorbs light for photosynthesis.
Chloroplast	A structure found in plant cells and algae. It is the site of photosynthesis.
Chromatogram	The pattern of spots formed as a result of separating a mixture using chromatography.
Chromatography	A method used to separate the substances in a mixture based on how the components interact with a mobile phase and a stationary phase.
Chromosome	A long molecule of DNA found in the nucleus. Each chromosome carries many genes.

Glossary

Cilia	Hair-like structures on the surface of a cell, used to move substances in one direction.
Circuit breaker	A circuit component that 'trips' and breaks the circuit when the current through it goes above a certain point. They are used to protect circuits and to prevent electrical fires and electric shocks.
Climate change	A change in the Earth's climate. E.g. global warming, changing rainfall patterns etc.
Clinical trial	A set of drug tests on human volunteers.
Closed system (chemistry)	A reaction system where no substances can get in or out.
Closed system (physics)	A system where the net change in energy is zero.
Collision theory	The theory that in order for a reaction to occur, particles must collide with sufficient energy.
Combustion	An exothermic reaction between a fuel and oxygen.
Communicable disease	A disease that can spread between individuals.
Community	All the organisms of different species living in a habitat.
Complete combustion	Combustion in plenty of oxygen, where the only products are carbon dioxide and water.
Compound	A substance made up of atoms of at least two different elements, chemically joined together.
Concentration	The amount of a substance in a certain volume of solution.
Conclusion	A summary of the findings of a scientific investigation.
Conduction	A method of energy transfer by heating where vibrating particles transfer energy through a material by colliding with neighbouring particles and transferring energy between their kinetic energy stores.
Conductor (electrical)	A material through which electrical charges can easily move.
Conductor (heat)	A material that heat or can pass through easily.
Conservation of energy	Energy can be stored, transferred between energy stores and dissipated — but it can never be created or destroyed. The total energy of a closed system has no net change.
Conservation of momentum	In a closed system, the total momentum before an event is the same as the total momentum after the event.
Contact force	A force that only acts between touching objects.
Contamination (radioactive)	The presence of unwanted radioactive atoms on or inside an object.
Continuous data	Numerical data that can have any value within a range (e.g. length, volume or temperature).
Contraceptive	A method of preventing pregnancy.
Control experiment	An experiment that's kept under the same conditions as the rest of the investigation, but where the independent variable isn't altered.
Control variable	A variable in an experiment that is kept the same.
Conversion factor	A number which you must multiply or divide a unit by to convert it to a different unit.
Correlation	A relationship between two variables.
Cosmic ray	Radiation from space.
Covalent bond	A chemical bond formed when atoms share a pair of electrons.
Cracking	The process that is used to break long-chain hydrocarbons down into shorter, more useful hydrocarbons.
Crystallisation	The formation of solid crystals as water evaporates from a solution. For example, salt solutions undergo crystallisation to form solid salt crystals.
Current	The flow of electric charge. The size of the current is the rate of flow of charge. Measured in amperes (A).
Cytokinesis	The stage of the cell cycle when the cytoplasm and cell membrane divide to form two separate cells.
Cytoplasm	A gel-like substance in a cell where most of the chemical reactions take place.
Decomposer	An organism (usually a microorganism) that breaks down waste products and dead organisms.
Delocalised electron	An electron that isn't associated with a particular atom or bond and is free to move within a structure.
Dendron	The part of a neurone that carries nervous impulses towards the cell body.
Density	A substance's mass per unit volume.
Dependent variable	The variable in an experiment that is measured.
Desalination	The removal of salts from salt water to produce potable (drinking) water.

Glossary

Diabetes	A condition that affects the body's ability to control its blood glucose level.
Differentiation	The process by which a cell becomes specialised for its job.
Diffusion	The spreading out of particles from an area of higher concentration to an area of lower concentration.
Diode	A circuit component that only allows current to flow through it in one direction. It has a very high resistance in the other direction.
Diploid cell	A cell with two copies of each chromosome.
Direct current (d.c.)	A current where the charges only move in one direction.
Discrete data	Numerical data that can only take a certain value, with no in-between value, e.g. number of people.
Displacement	The straight-line distance and direction from an object's starting position to its finishing position.
Displacement reaction	A reaction where a more reactive element replaces a less reactive element in a compound.
Displayed formula	A chemical formula that shows the atoms in a covalent compound and all the bonds between them.
Dissipation	The transfer of energy to thermal energy stores of an object and its surroundings. Also called wasted energy.
Distance/time graph	A graph showing how the distance travelled by an object changes over a period of time.
Distillation	A way of separating out a liquid from a mixture. You heat the mixture until the bit you want evaporates, then cool the vapour to turn it back into a liquid.
Distribution	Where organisms are found in a particular area.
DNA	Deoxyribonucleic acid. The molecule in cells that stores genetic information.
Dominant allele	The allele for the characteristic that's shown by an organism if two different alleles are present for that characteristic.
Double-blind trial	A clinical trial where neither the doctors nor the patients know who has received the drug and who has received the placebo until all the results have been gathered.
Dynamic equilibrium	The point at which the rates of the forward and backward reactions in a reversible reaction are the same, and so the amounts of reactants and products in the reaction container don't change.
Earth wire	The green and yellow wire in an electrical cable that only carries current when there's a fault. It stops exposed metal parts of an appliance from becoming live. It is at 0 V.
Ecosystem	A community of living organisms along with the abiotic parts of their environment.
Effector	Either a muscle or gland which responds to nervous impulses.
Efficiency	The proportion of energy supplied to a device which is usefully transferred.
Elastic distortion	An object undergoing elastic distortion will return to its original shape and length once any forces being applied to it are removed.
Elastic object	An object which can be elastically distorted.
Elastic potential energy store	Anything that has been stretched or compressed, e.g. a spring, has energy in its elastic potential energy store.
Electrode	An electrical conductor which is submerged in the electrolyte during electrolysis.
Electrolysis	The process of breaking down a substance using electricity.
Electrolyte	A molten or dissolved ionic compound used in electrolysis that can conduct electricity between the two electrodes.
Electromagnet	A magnet whose magnetic field can be turned on and off by an electric current.
Electromagnetic induction	The induction of a potential difference across a conductor which is experiencing a change in external magnetic field. If the conductor is part of a complete circuit, this will cause a current to flow.
Electromagnetic (EM) spectrum	A continuous spectrum of all the possible wavelengths of electromagnetic waves.
Electron	A negatively charged subatomic particle with hardly any mass.
Electronic configuration	The number of electrons in an atom (or ion) and how they are arranged.
Electron shell	A region of an atom that contains electrons. It's also known as an energy level.
Electrostatic force	A force of attraction between opposite charges.
Element	A substance that is made up only of atoms with the same number of protons.
Empirical formula	A chemical formula showing the simplest possible whole number ratio of atoms in a compound.

Glossary

Endocrine gland	An organ that hormones are produced and secreted from.
Endothermic reaction	A reaction which takes in energy from the surroundings.
End point	The point at which an acid or alkali is completely neutralised during a titration.
Energy store	A means by which an object stores energy. Common energy stores are: thermal, kinetic, gravitational potential, elastic potential, chemical, magnetic, electrostatic and nuclear.
Enzyme	A protein that acts as a biological catalyst.
Equilibrium (physics)	A state in which all the forces acting on an object are balanced, so the resultant force is zero.
Erythrocyte	A red blood cell.
Eukaryotic cell	A complex cell, such as a plant or animal cell.
Eutrophication	An excess of nutrients in water, leading to increased algal growth, oxygen depletion and the eventual death of other organisms in the water.
Evaluation	A critical analysis of a scientific investigation.
Evolution	The changing of the inherited characteristics of a population over time.
Exothermic reaction	A reaction which transfers energy to the surroundings.
Extinct	When no living individuals of a species remain.
Fair test	A controlled experiment where the only thing that changes is the independent variable.
Family pedigree	A diagram that shows how a characteristic (or disorder) is inherited in a group of related people.
Feedstock	A raw material used to produce other substances through industrial processes.
Fertilisation	The fusion of male and female gametes during sexual reproduction.
Fertiliser	A substance added to soil to provide nutrients for plant growth. E.g. animal manure, compost and artificial fertilisers.
Fertility	The ability to conceive a child.
Filtration	A physical method used to separate an insoluble solid from a liquid.
Finite resource	A resource that isn't produced at a quick enough rate to be considered replaceable. Also known as a non-renewable resource.
Flagellum	A long, hair-like structure that rotates to make a bacterium move.
Fleming's left-hand rule	The rule used to work out the direction of the force produced by the motor effect. Your first finger points in the direction of the magnetic field, your second finger points in the direction of the current and your thumb points in the direction of the force (or motion).
Force	A push or a pull on an object caused by it interacting with something.
Fossil	The remains of an organism from many years ago, which is found in rock.
Fossil fuel	A group of natural, non-renewable resources used as fuels. E.g. oil, coal, natural gas.
Fraction	A group of hydrocarbons that condense together when crude oil is separated using fractional distillation. E.g. petrol, diesel oil, kerosene etc.
Fractional distillation	A process that can be used to separate substances in a mixture according to their boiling points.
Free body force diagram	A diagram that shows all the forces acting on an isolated object, the direction in which the forces are acting and their (relative) magnitudes.
Frequency	The number of complete wave cycles passing a certain point per second. Measured in hertz, Hz.
Friction	A force that opposes an object's motion. It acts in the opposite direction to motion.
Fullerene	A molecule made up of carbon atoms arranged into rings and shaped like a closed tube or hollow ball.
Fuse	A circuit component that contains a thin piece of wire which melts when the current through the fuse goes above a certain point. Fuses are used to protect circuits and to prevent electrical fires and electric shocks.
Gamete	A sex cell, e.g. an egg cell or a sperm cell in animals.
Gamma decay	A type of radioactive decay in which a gamma ray is given out from a decaying nucleus.
Gamma ray	A high-frequency, short-wavelength electromagnetic wave.
Geiger-Müller tube	A radiation detector that is used with a counter to measure count-rate.
Gene	A short section of DNA, found on a chromosome, which contains the instructions needed to make a protein (and so controls the development of a characteristic).

Glossary

General formula	A formula that can be used to find the molecular formula of any member of a homologous series.
Genetically modified organism	An organism, e.g. a type of crop, which has had its genes modified through genetic engineering.
Genetic disorder	A health condition caused by a fault in an individual's genetic material, which can be passed on to offspring.
Genetic engineering	The process of cutting out a useful gene from one organism's genome and inserting it into another organism's cell(s).
Genome	All of the genetic material in an organism.
Genotype	What alleles an individual has, e.g. Tt.
Giant covalent structure	A large molecule made up of a very large number of atoms held together by covalent bonds.
Global warming	The rise in the average global temperature.
Glucagon	A hormone produced and secreted by the pancreas when blood glucose level is too low.
Glycogen	A molecule that acts as a store of glucose in liver and muscle cells.
Gradient	The slope of a line graph. It shows how quickly the variable on the y-axis changes with the variable on the x-axis.
Gravitational potential energy (GPE) store	Anything that has mass and is in a gravitational field has energy in its gravitational potential energy store.
Gravity	The force of attraction between all objects with mass.
Greenhouse effect	When greenhouse gases in the atmosphere absorb long wavelength radiation and re-radiate it in all directions, including back towards Earth, helping to keep the Earth warm.
Greenhouse gas	A gas in the atmosphere that can absorb and reflect heat radiation.
Group	A column in the periodic table.
Guard cell	A type of cell found on either side of a stoma. A pair of these cells control the stoma's size.
Haber process	A process used to make ammonia by reacting nitrogen with hydrogen.
Habitat	The place where an organism lives.
Haemoglobin	A red pigment found in red blood cells that carries oxygen.
Half equation	An equation which shows how electrons are transferred when a substance is reduced or oxidised. E.g. at an electrode during electrolysis.
Half-life	The average time taken for the number of radioactive nuclei in an isotope to halve.
Halogen	An element in Group 7 of the periodic table. E.g. bromine, chlorine etc.
Haploid cell	A cell containing half the number of chromosomes of a normal body cell.
Hazard	Something that has the potential to cause harm (e.g. fire, electricity, etc.).
Heterozygous	Where an organism has two alleles for a particular gene that are different.
Homeostasis	The regulation of conditions inside your body (and cells) to maintain a stable internal environment, in response to changes in both internal and external conditions.
Homologous series	A family of molecules which have the same general formula and similar chemical properties. E.g. alkanes.
Homozygous	Where an organism has two alleles for a particular gene that are the same.
Hormone	A chemical messenger which travels in the blood to activate target cells.
Hydrocarbon	A compound that is made from only hydrogen and carbon.
Hydroelectric dam	A power station in which a dam is built across a valley or river. This holds back water, forming a reservoir. Water is allowed to flow out of the reservoir through turbines at a controlled rate. This turns the turbines, which are attached to generators and can generate electricity.
Hypothalamus	A structure in the brain. It releases TRH to regulate thyroxine levels when blood thyroxine is low.
Hypothesis	A possible explanation for a scientific observation.
Immunisation	The injection of dead or inactive pathogens, in order to trigger an immune response that will help to protect you against a particular pathogen in the future.
Inbreeding	When closely related animals or plants are bred together.

Glossary

Incomplete combustion	When a fuel burns but there isn't enough oxygen for it to burn completely. Products can include carbon monoxide and carbon particulates.
Independent variable	The variable in an experiment that is changed.
Indicator	A substance that changes colour above or below a certain pH.
Induced (temporary) magnet	A magnetic material that only has its own magnetic field while it is inside another magnetic field.
Inelastic distortion	An object undergoing inelastic distortion will not return to its original shape and length once the forces being applied to it are removed.
Inert	Unreactive (unlikely to take part in chemical reactions).
Inertia	The tendency of an object to remain stationary or continue travelling at a constant velocity.
Inertial mass	The ratio of the force on an object over its acceleration.
In excess	A reactant that is not used up during a reaction.
Insoluble	A substance is insoluble if it does not dissolve in a particular solvent.
Insulator	A material that heat or electricity cannot pass through easily.
Insulin	A hormone produced and secreted by the pancreas when blood glucose level is too high.
Interdependence	Where, in a community, species depend on other species for things such as food and shelter in order to survive and reproduce.
Intermolecular force	A force of attraction that exists between molecules.
Internal energy	The total energy that a system's particles have in their kinetic and potential energy stores.
Interphase	The stage of the cell cycle when the cell is not dividing. During this stage, the cell grows, increases its amount of subcellular structures and copies its DNA.
Ion	A charged particle formed when one or more electrons are lost or gained from an atom or molecule.
Ionic bond	A strong attraction between oppositely charged ions.
Ionic compound	A compound that contains positive and negative ions held together in a regular arrangement (a lattice) by electrostatic forces of attraction.
Ionic equation	An equation that shows only the particles that react and the products they form.
Ionising radiation	Radiation that has enough energy to knock electrons off atoms.
Iris	The coloured part of the eye, which controls how much light enters the pupil.
Irradiation	Exposure to radiation.
Isotope	A different form of the same element, which has atoms with the same number of protons (atomic number), but a different number of neutrons (and so different mass number).
IVF	*In vitro* fertilisation. The artificial fertilisation of eggs in the lab.
Kinetic energy store	Anything that's moving has energy in its kinetic energy store.
Kinetic theory of matter	A theory explaining how particles in matter behave by modelling these particles as tiny balls.
Lattice	A closely-packed regular arrangement of particles.
Le Chatelier's principle	The idea that if the reaction conditions are changed when a reversible reaction is at equilibrium, the system will try to counteract the change.
Life cycle assessment	An assessment of the environmental impact of a product over the course of its life.
Light-dependent resistor (LDR)	A resistor whose resistance is dependent on light intensity. The resistance decreases as light intensity increases.
Limiting factor	A factor which prevents a reaction from going any faster.
Limiting reactant	A reactant that gets completely used up in a reaction, so limits the amount of product that's formed.
Limit of proportionality	The point beyond which the force applied to an object is no longer directly proportional to the extension of the object.
Linear graph	A straight line graph.
Lipase	A type of digestive enzyme that catalyses the breakdown of lipids into fatty acids and glycerol.
Litmus	An indicator that's blue in alkalis and red in acids.
Live wire	The brown wire in an electrical cable that carries an alternating potential difference from the mains. It is at 230 V.

Glossary

Longitudinal wave	A wave in which the vibrations are parallel to the direction the wave travels.
Lubricant	A substance (usually a liquid) that can flow easily between two objects. Used to reduce friction between surfaces.
Magnetic field	A region where magnets, magnetic materials (like iron and steel) and current-carrying wires experience a force.
Magnetic flux density	The number of magnetic field lines per unit area. Its symbol is B and it is measured in tesla, T.
Magnetic material	A material (such as iron, steel, cobalt or nickel) which can become an induced magnet while it's inside another magnetic field.
Malleable	Can be easily hammered or rolled into different shapes.
Mass number	The total number of protons and neutrons in an atom.
Mean (average)	A type of average found by adding up all the data and dividing by the number of values.
Median (average)	The middle value in a set of data when the values are put in order of size.
Meiosis	A type of cell division where a cell divides twice to produce four genetically different gametes. It occurs in the reproductive organs.
Memory lymphocyte	A type of white blood cell produced in response to a foreign antigen. They remain in the body for a long time, and respond quickly to a second infection.
Menstrual cycle	A monthly sequence of events during which the body prepares the lining of the uterus (womb) in case it receives a fertilised egg, and releases an egg from an ovary. The uterus lining then breaks down if the egg has not been fertilised.
Meristem tissue	Tissue found at the growing tips of plant shoots and roots that is able to differentiate.
Metabolism	All the chemical reactions that happen in a cell or the body.
Metallic bond	The attraction between metal ions and delocalised electrons in a metal.
Metal ore	Rocks that are found naturally in the Earth's crust containing enough metal to make the metal profitable to extract.
Methyl orange	An indicator that's yellow in alkalis and red in acids.
Mitochondria	Structures in a cell which are the site of most of the reactions for aerobic respiration.
Mitosis	A type of cell division where a cell reproduces itself by splitting to form two identical offspring.
Mixture	A substance made from two or more elements or compounds that aren't chemically bonded to each other.
Mobile phase	In chromatography, the mobile phase is a gas or liquid where the molecules are able to move.
Mode (average)	A measure of average found by selecting the most frequent value from a data set.
Model	Something used to describe or display how an object or system behaves in reality.
Mole	A unit of amount of substance. One mole of a substance contains 6.02×10^{23} particles and its mass is equal to the relative formula mass of that substance in grams.
Molecular formula	A chemical formula showing the actual number of atoms of each element in a compound.
Molecule	A particle made up of at least two atoms held together by covalent bonds.
Momentum	A property of a moving object that is the product of its mass and velocity.
Monohybrid inheritance	The inheritance of a single characteristic.
Monomer	A small molecule that can be joined together with other small molecules to form a polymer.
Motor effect	When a current-carrying conductor is placed in a magnetic field, the conductor and the magnet producing the magnetic field exert a force on each other.
Motor neurone	A nerve cell that carries electrical impulses from the CNS to effectors.
Mutation	A random change in an organism's DNA.
Mutualism	A relationship between two organisms, from which both organisms benefit.
Myelin sheath	A layer surrounding the axon of some neurones, acting as an electrical insulator to speed up electrical impulses.
National grid	The network of transformers and cables that distributes electrical power from power stations to consumers.
Natural selection	The process by which species evolve.
Negative feedback	A mechanism that restores a level back to optimum in a system.

Glossary

Nervous system	The organ system in animals that allows them to respond to changes in their environment.
Neurone	A nerve cell. Neurones transmit information around the body, including to and from the CNS.
Neurotransmitter	A chemical that diffuses across a synapse in order to transfer a nerve signal from one neurone to the next.
Neutralisation reaction	The reaction between acids and bases that leads to the formation of neutral products — usually a salt and water.
Neutral substance	A substance with a pH of 7.
Neutral wire	The blue wire in an electrical cable that current in an appliance normally flows through. It is around 0 V.
Neutron	A subatomic particle that has no charge (is neutral). Found in the nucleus of an atom.
Newton's First Law	An object will remain at rest or travelling at a constant velocity unless it is acted on by a resultant force.
Newton's Second Law	The acceleration of an object is directly proportional to the resultant force acting on it, and inversely proportional to its mass. Often given as $F = m \times a$.
Newton's Third Law	When two objects interact, they exert equal and opposite forces on each other.
Noble gas	An element in Group 0 of the periodic table. E.g. helium, neon etc.
Non-communicable disease	A disease that cannot spread between individuals.
Non-contact force	A force that can act between objects that are not touching, usually as a result of interacting fields.
Non-renewable resource	A resource that isn't produced at a quick enough rate to be considered replaceable. Also known as a finite resource.
Normal (at a boundary)	A line that's perpendicular (at 90°) to a boundary at the point of incidence (where a wave hits the boundary).
Normal contact force	A force that acts between all touching objects.
Nuclear model	A model of the atom that says that the atom has a small, central positively-charged nucleus with negatively-charged electrons moving around the nucleus, and that most of the atom is empty space.
Nucleotide	A repeating unit in DNA that consists of a sugar, a phosphate group and a base.
Nucleus (of an atom)	The centre of an atom, containing protons and neutrons.
Nucleus (of a cell)	A structure found in animal and plant cells which contains the genetic material.
Obesity	A condition where a person has an excessive amount of body fat, to the point where it poses a risk to their health.
Orbit	The path on which one object moves around another.
Organelle	A subcellular structure, e.g. nucleus, ribosome.
Osmosis	The movement of water molecules across a partially permeable membrane from a region of higher water concentration to a region of lower water concentration.
Oxidation	A reaction where electrons are lost or oxygen is gained by a species.
Paper chromatography	A technique that can be used to separate and analyse soluble substances.
Parallel circuit	A circuit in which every component is connected separately to the positive and negative ends of the supply.
Parasitism	The relationship between a parasite and its host. The parasite takes what it needs to survive and the host doesn't benefit.
Partially permeable membrane	A membrane with tiny holes in it, which lets some molecules through it but not others.
Pathogen	A microorganism that causes disease, e.g. a bacterium, virus, protist or fungus.
Peer-review	The process in which other scientists check the results and explanations of an investigation before they are published.
Period (chemistry)	A row in the periodic table.
Period (of a wave)	The time taken for one full cycle of a wave to be completed.
Periodic table	A table of all the known elements, arranged in order of atomic number so that elements with similar chemical properties are in groups.
Permanent magnet	A magnetic material that always has its own magnetic field around it.
Phagocyte	A white blood cell that engulfs foreign cells and digests them.

Glossary

Phenolphthalein	An indicator that's pink in alkalis and colourless in acids.
Phenotype	The characteristics an individual has, e.g. brown eyes.
Phloem	A type of plant tissue which transports food substances (mainly sucrose) around the plant.
Photosynthesis	The process by which plants use energy to convert carbon dioxide and water into glucose and oxygen.
pH scale	A scale from 0 to 14 that is used to measure how acidic or alkaline a solution is.
Physical change	A change where you don't end up with a new substance — it's the same substance as before, just in a different form. (A change of state is a physical change.)
Phytoextraction	The process by which a metal is extracted from soil using plants.
Placebo	A substance that is like a drug being tested, but which doesn't do anything.
Plasma	The liquid component of blood, which carries blood cells and other substances around the body.
Plasmid	A small loop of extra DNA that isn't part of the chromosome, found in bacterial cells.
Platelet	A small fragment of a cell found in the blood, which helps blood to clot at a wound.
Polymer	A long chain molecule that is formed by joining lots of smaller molecules (monomers) together.
Positron	A subatomic particle with a relative charge of +1 and a relative mass of 0.0005. It is the antiparticle of an electron.
Potable water	Water that is safe for drinking.
Potential difference	The driving force that pushes electric charge around a circuit, measured in volts (V). Also known as p.d. or voltage.
Power	The rate of transferring energy (or doing work). Normally measured in watts (W).
Power rating	The maximum safe power an appliance can operate at.
Precipitate	A solid that is formed in a solution during a chemical reaction.
Precise result	When all the data is close to the mean.
Predation	When an organism hunts and kills other organisms for food.
Prediction	A statement based on a hypothesis that can be tested.
Pressure	The force per unit area exerted on a surface.
Prey	An animal that is hunted and killed by another animal for food.
Producer	An organism at the start of a food chain that makes its own food using energy from the Sun.
Product	A substance that is formed in a chemical reaction.
Prokaryotic cell	A small, simple cell, e.g. a bacterium.
Protease	A type of digestive enzyme that catalyses the breakdown of proteins into amino acids.
Protein	A large biological molecule made up of long chains of amino acids.
Protist	A eukaryotic single-celled organism, e.g. algae.
Proton	A subatomic particle with a positive charge. Found in the nucleus of an atom.
Punnett square	A type of genetic diagram.
Pure substance	A substance that is completely made up of only one compound or element.
Quadrat	A square frame enclosing a known area. It is used to study the distribution of organisms.
Radioactive decay	The random process of a radioactive substance giving out radiation from the nuclei of its atoms.
Radioactive substance	A substance that spontaneously gives out radiation from the nuclei of its atoms.
Random error	A difference in the results of an experiment caused by unpredictable events, e.g. human error in measuring.
Range	The difference between the smallest and largest values in a set of data.
Rate of reaction	How fast the reactants in a reaction are changed into products.
Ray	A straight line showing the path along which a wave moves.
Reactant	A substance that reacts in a chemical reaction.
Reaction profile	A graph that shows how the energy in a reaction changes as the reaction progresses.
Reaction time	The time taken for a person to react after an event (e.g. seeing a hazard).

Glossary

Reactivity series	A list of elements arranged in order of their reactivity. The most reactive elements are at the top and the least reactive at the bottom.
Receptor	A group of cells that are sensitive to a stimulus (e.g. receptor cells in the eye detect light).
Recessive allele	An allele whose characteristic only appears in an organism if there are two copies present.
Redox reaction	A reaction where one substance is reduced and another is oxidised.
Reduction	A reaction where electrons are gained or oxygen is lost.
Reflection	When a wave bounces back as it meets a boundary between two materials.
Reflex	A fast, automatic response to a stimulus.
Reforestation	When land where a forest previously stood is replanted to form a new forest.
Refraction	When a wave changes direction as it passes across the boundary between two materials at an angle to the normal.
Relative atomic mass (A_r)	The average mass of one atom of an element compared to $1/12$ of the mass of one atom of carbon-12.
Relative formula mass (M_r)	All the relative atomic masses (A_r) of the atoms in a compound added together.
Relay neurone	A nerve cell that carries electrical impulses from sensory neurones to motor neurones.
Reliable result	A result that is repeatable and reproducible.
Renewable resource	A resource that can be made at the same or similar rate as it's being used.
Repeatable result	A result that will come out the same if the experiment is repeated by the same person using the same method and equipment.
Reproducible result	A result that will come out the same if someone different does the experiment, or a slightly different method or piece of equipment is used.
Resistance	Anything in a circuit that reduces the flow of current. Measured in ohms, Ω.
Resolution	The smallest change a measuring instrument can detect.
Respiration	The process of breaking down glucose to transfer energy, which occurs in every cell.
Resultant force	A single force that can replace all the forces acting on an object to give the same effect as the original forces acting altogether.
Reversible reaction	A reaction where the products of the reaction can themselves react to produce the original reactants.
R_f value	In chromatography, the ratio between the distance travelled by a dissolved substance and the distance travelled by the solvent.
Ribosome	A structure in a cell, where proteins are made.
Right-hand thumb rule	The rule to work out the direction of the magnetic field around a current-carrying wire. Your thumb on your right hand points in the direction of the current, and your fingers curl in the direction of the magnetic field.
Risk	The chance that a hazard will cause harm.
Risk factor	Something that is linked to an increased likelihood that a person will develop a certain disease.
S.I. unit	A standard unit of measurement, recognised by scientists all over the world.
Scalar	A quantity that has magnitude but no direction.
Scaling prefix	A word or symbol which goes before a unit to indicate a multiplying factor (e.g. 1 km = 1000 m).
Selective breeding (artificial selection)	When humans artificially select the plants or animals that are going to breed, so that the genes for particular characteristics remain in the population.
Sensory neurone	A nerve cell that carries electrical impulses from a receptor in a sense organ to the CNS.
Series circuit	A circuit in which every component is connected in a line, end to end.
Sex chromosome (humans)	One of the 23rd pair of chromosomes, X or Y. Together they determine whether an individual is male or female.
Sexual reproduction	Where two gametes combine at fertilisation to produce a genetically different new individual.
Significant figure	The first significant figure of a number is the first non-zero digit. The second, third and fourth significant figures follow on immediately after it.
Simple distillation	A way of separating a liquid out from a mixture if there are large differences in the boiling points of the substances.
Simple molecule	A molecule made up of only a few atoms held together by covalent bonds.
Solar cell	A device that generates electricity directly from the Sun's radiation.

Glossary

Solenoid	A coil of wire often used in the construction of electromagnets.
Soluble	A substance is soluble if it dissolves in a particular solvent.
Solute	A substance dissolved in a solvent to make a solution.
Solution	A mixture made up of one substance (the solute) dissolved in another (the solvent).
Solvent	A liquid in which another substance (a solute) can be dissolved.
Solvent front	The point the solvent has reached up the filter paper during paper chromatography.
Specific heat capacity (SHC)	The amount of energy (in joules) needed to raise the temperature of 1 kg of a material by 1°C.
Specific latent heat (SLH)	The amount of energy needed to change 1 kg of a substance from one state to another without changing its temperature. (For cooling, it is the energy released by a change in state.)
Specific latent heat of fusion	The specific latent heat for changing between a solid and a liquid (melting or freezing).
Specific latent heat of vaporisation	The specific latent heat for changing between a liquid and a gas (evaporating, boiling or condensing).
Standard form	A number written in the form $A \times 10^n$, where A is a number between 1 and 10.
State of matter	The form which a substance can take — e.g. solid, liquid or gas.
State symbol	The letter, or letters, in brackets that are placed after a substance in an equation to show what physical state it's in. E.g. gaseous carbon dioxide is shown as $CO_{2(g)}$.
Statins	A group of medicinal drugs that are used to decrease the risk of cardiovascular disease by reducing the amount of cholesterol in the bloodstream.
Stationary phase	In chromatography, the stationary phase is a solid or really thick liquid where molecules are unable to move.
Stem cell	An undifferentiated cell which has the ability to become one of many different types of cell, or to produce more stem cells.
Stent	A tube that's inserted inside an artery to help keep it open.
STI	An infection spread through sexual contact.
Stimulus	A change in the environment.
Stoma	A tiny hole in the surface of a leaf.
Stopping distance	The distance covered by a vehicle in the time between the driver spotting a hazard and the vehicle coming to a complete stop. It's the sum of the thinking distance and the braking distance.
Strong acid	An acid which fully ionises in an aqueous solution.
Surface area to volume ratio	The amount of surface area per unit volume.
Synapse	The connection between two neurones.
System	The object, or group of objects, that you're considering.
Systematic error	An error that is consistently made throughout an experiment.
Tangent	A straight line that touches a curve at a particular point without crossing it.
Theory	A hypothesis which has been accepted by the scientific community because there is good evidence to back it up.
Thermal conductivity	A measure of how quickly an object transfers energy by heating through conduction.
Thermal insulator	A material with a low thermal conductivity.
Thermistor	A resistor whose resistance is dependent on the temperature. The resistance decreases as temperature increases.
Thinking distance	The distance a vehicle travels during the driver's reaction time (the time between seeing a hazard and applying the brakes).
Three-core cable	An electrical cable containing a live wire, a neutral wire and an earth wire.
Tidal barrage	A dam built across a river estuary, containing turbines connected to generators. When there's a difference in water height on either side, water flows through the dam, turning the turbines and generating electricity.

Glossary

Tissue	A group of similar cells that work together to carry out a particular function.
Toxin	A poison. Toxins are often produced by bacteria.
Transect	A line which can be used to study the distribution of organisms across an area.
Transformer	A device which can change the size of an alternating potential difference.
Translocation	The movement of food substances around a plant.
Transmission (of waves)	When a wave passes across a boundary from one material into another and continues travelling.
Transpiration stream	The movement of water from a plant's roots, through the xylem and out of the leaves.
Transverse wave	A wave in which the vibrations are perpendicular (at 90°) to the direction the wave travels.
Tumour	A mass of abnormal cells.
Uncertainty	The amount by which a given result may differ from the true value.
Uniform field	A field that has the same strength everywhere.
Universal indicator	A mixed indicator that gradually changes colour depending on the pH of the solution that it's in.
Urea	A waste product produced from the breakdown of amino acids in the liver.
Vacuole	A structure in plant cells that contains cell sap that maintains the internal pressure to support the cell.
Valid result	A result that is repeatable, reproducible and answers the original question.
Valve	A structure within the heart or a vein which prevents blood flowing in the wrong direction.
Variable	A factor in an investigation that can change or be changed (e.g. temperature or concentration).
Variation	The differences that exist between individuals.
Vector (in disease)	An organism that transfers a disease from one animal or plant to another, which doesn't get the disease itself.
Vector (in genetic engineering)	Something used to transfer DNA into a cell, e.g. a virus or a bacterial plasmid.
Vector (physics)	A quantity which has both magnitude (size) and a direction.
Vein	A blood vessel that carries blood to the heart.
Velocity	The speed and direction of an object.
Velocity/time graph	A graph showing how the velocity of an object changes over a period of time.
Virus	A tiny pathogen that can only replicate within host body cells.
Viscosity	How runny or gloopy a substance is.
Voltmeter	A component used to measure the potential difference across a component. It is always connected in parallel with the component.
Wave	An oscillation that transfers energy and information without transferring any matter.
Wavefront diagram	A representation of a wave made up of a series of 'wavefronts'. These are lines drawn through identical points on a wave, e.g. through each crest, perpendicular to the wave's direction of travel.
Wavelength	The length of a full cycle of a wave, e.g. from a crest to the next crest.
Weak acid	An acid which doesn't fully ionise in an aqueous solution.
Weight	The force acting on an object due to gravity.
White blood cell	A blood cell that is part of the immune system, defending the body against disease.
Work done	Energy transferred, e.g. when a force moves an object through a distance, or by an appliance.
Xylem	A type of plant tissue which transports water and mineral ions around the plant.
Yield	The amount of product made in a reaction.
Zero error	A type of systematic error caused by using a piece of equipment that isn't zeroed properly.
Zygote	A fertilised egg cell.

Index

A
abiotic factors 122
absolute zero 367
absorption of EM waves 306, 314
acceleration 268, 269, 273, 382
  due to gravity 269, 284
accuracy (of data) 7
acid rain 257
acids 193-196, 199, 200
  concentration 194, 195
acquired characteristics 57
activation energy 243, 245, 248
active sites 26, 27
active transport 32
activity 324, 325
adrenal glands 96, 98
adrenaline 98
adult stem cells 42
aerobic respiration 111
AIDS 73
alcohol 80, 81
alkali metals 226, 227
alkalis 193, 200
alkanes 252, 253, 255
alkenes 255
alleles 52-55, 57, 58
alpha particles 321, 322
alternating currents 352, 362, 363
alveoli 110
amino acids 30
ammeters 337, 340, 382
amplitude 301
amylase 28, 29
anaerobic respiration 112
angle of incidence 307
angle of refraction 307
animal cells 17
anions 154, 202
anomalous results 8, 9
antibiotic resistance 62
antibiotics 78
antibodies 75-77, 115, 116
antigens 75-77
apparatus in experiments 379-382
Archaea (domain) 65
Ardi (fossil) 63
arteries 117
asexual reproduction 37, 38
Assisted Reproductive Technology (ART) 102
atmosphere (of the Earth) 261-263
  evolution of 259
atomic models 316, 317

atomic numbers 146
atomic (proton) number 320
atomic structure 146
  history of 144, 145
atoms 316-318, 320
averages 9
Avogadro's constant 169, 170
axons 44, 45

B
background radiation 324
bacteria 18, 72
Bacteria (domain) 65
balancing equations 138, 139, 176
ball and stick models 157, 158
barrier contraceptives 103
bases 193, 196, 199, 200
bases (DNA) 50
batteries 337, 352
belt transects 124
beta particles 321, 322
bias 3
biodiversity 126-129
bio-fuels 297
biological catalysts 26
biological molecules 30
biomass 87
biotic factors 122
blood 115, 116
  glucose 106, 107
  vessels 117
B-lymphocytes 75-77
BMI (body mass index) 82, 107
Bohr model 316
boiling 180
bond energies 250
bonding
  covalent 160, 161, 163, 164
  ionic 155-158
  metallic 165
braking distances 285, 286
Bunsen burners 384
burettes 379

C
cancer 39, 326
capillaries 117
carbohydrases 30
carbohydrates 30
carbon-14 dating 64
carbon cycle 131
carbon dioxide
  as a greenhouse gas 261-263
carbon monoxide 257
cardiac output 119
cardiovascular disease 80, 81, 83, 84

catalysts 26, 245
categoric data 10
cations 154, 202
cell
  cycle 37
  differentiation 39
  division 37-39
  elongation 39
  membranes 17, 18, 32
  structure 17, 18
  walls 18
central nervous system (CNS) 44, 45
Chalara ash dieback 71
changes of state 366, 371, 372
charge 338
Chlamydia 73
chloroplasts 18, 87
cholera 72
chromatography 188-190
chromosomes 37, 38, 50
ciliated epithelial cells 20
circuit breakers 354
circuits 337-354
circuit symbols 337
circular motion 273
circulatory system 115-119
classification 65
climate change 262, 263
clinical testing 78
clomifene therapy 102
closed systems 289
collision theory 243, 244
colours 309
combustion 208, 253
communicable diseases 71-73
communities 121, 122
compasses (plotting) 356
competition 122
complementary base pairing 50
concentration 171
conclusions 14
condensation 132, 180
conservation 128, 129
conservation of energy 289
conservation of mass 167
conservation of momentum 280-282
contact forces 333
contamination 326
continuous data 10
continuous sampling 28
contraceptives 103
control variables 6
converting units 24
correlation 11, 14
count-rate 324
covalent bonding 160, 161, 163, 164
cracking 255

crop rotation 135
crude oil 252, 253
crystallisation 186
current 337-340, 350
  in parallel 345
  in series 344
cytoplasm 17

D
dangers
  of EM waves 314
  of large accelerations 286
  of radiation 326
Darwin, Charles 61
decomposition 131, 134, 135
defences against disease 75
delocalised electrons 163, 165
denaturation (enzymes) 27
dendrites 44, 45
dendrons 44, 45
denitrifying bacteria 135
density 365, 366
desalination 133
diabetes 107
diamond 163
differentiation 39, 41, 42
diffusion 32
diodes 337, 341
diploid cells 38, 48
direct current 352
discrete data 10
diseases 71-73, 80, 81, 83, 84
displacement 266
displacement reactions 211, 212, 230, 231, 249
dissociation of acids 194
distance 266, 267
distance-time graphs 270
distillation 252
  fractional 185, 252
  of seawater 191
  simple 184, 190
distortion 374-376
distribution of organisms 123, 124
DNA 50
  extraction from fruit 50
  structure of 50
dominant alleles 52, 53
dot and cross diagrams 155, 156, 160, 161
drought 133
drug development 78

Index

E

earthing 352, 353
earth wires 352, 353
ecosystems 121, 122
   investigating 123, 124
   levels of organisation 121
effectors 44-46
efficiency 292, 293, 330
egg cells 19, 48
elasticity 374-376
elastic potential energy stores 376
electric heaters 383
electric shocks 353
electrolysis 202-206, 215
electrolytes 202, 203
electromagnetic induction 362, 363
electromagnetic spectrum 309
electromagnetic waves 309-314
electromagnets 360
electron configurations 152
electron microscopes 21
electrons 317, 318
electron shells 146, 152
elements 320
embryonic stem cells 41, 42
empirical formulas 168, 173
endocrine glands 96
endothermic reactions 247-250
energy in circuits 348-350
energy levels 317, 318
energy of particles 366-368, 372
energy resources 296-299
energy stores 288, 329
   elastic potential 376
   gravitational potential 288
   kinetic 288
energy transfer diagrams 290, 293
energy transfers 289, 290, 292, 293, 329
environmental variation 57
enzymes 26-30, 245
   investigating activity 28, 29
equations (chemical) 138-140
equilibria 221-223
equilibrium 274, 335
errors 8, 15
erythrocytes 115, 116
estimating
   acceleration 268
   forces 286
ethical issues 386
Eukarya (domain) 65
eukaryotic cells 17
eutrophication 126
evaluations 16
evaporation 132, 180
evolution 61-64
   of humans 63, 64
exchange surfaces 110
exothermic reactions 247-250
experimental safety 385
extraction of metals 214-216

F

fair tests 6
family pedigrees 55
fatty acids 30
fermentation 245
fertilisation (reproduction) 48
fertilisers 126, 135
fields (magnetic) 356, 358, 360
fight or flight response 98
filament lamps 337, 341
filtration 186, 191
fish farms 127
five kingdom classification 65
flagella 18
Fleming's left-hand rule 359
force-extension graphs 375, 376
forces 273, 274, 282, 333-335
   equilibrium 335
   free body force diagrams 333
   magnetic 356
   resolving 335
   resultant 334
   scale drawings 334, 335
fossil fuels 298
fossils 61, 63, 64
fractional distillation 185, 252
fractions 252, 254, 255
free body force diagrams 333
freezing 180
frequency 301
FSH (follicle-stimulating hormone) 101-103
fullerenes 164
fungi 71, 131
fuses 337, 349, 353, 354

G

gametes 48, 49
gamma rays 309, 313, 314, 321, 322
gases 179, 180
gas exchange
   mammals 110
   plants 92
gas pressure 368
gas syringes 236, 237, 379
Geiger-Müller tubes 324
genes 50, 52, 58, 59
genetic
   diagrams 53-55
   engineering 67, 68
   variation 57, 58
genetically modified organisms (GMOs) 67, 68
genomes 50, 58, 59
genotypes 52
giant covalent structures 163
giant ionic lattices 157
global warming 298
glucagon 106
glucose 87, 106, 107, 111, 112
glycerol 30
gradients 11
graphene 163, 164
graphite 163
graphs 10, 11
gravitational field strength 278
gravitational potential energy stores 288
greenhouse effect 261
greenhouse gases 261-263
Group 0 elements 232
Group 1 elements 226, 227
Group 7 elements 228-231
growth 39
guard cells 92

H

Haber process 221
half equations 202, 204-206
half-life 324, 325
halogens 228-231
haploid cells 19, 20, 48, 49
hazards 5, 8, 141, 142, 385
health 71
heart (structure of) 118
heating 289, 382
heating in circuits 339, 349
heterozygous organisms 52, 53
HIV 73
homeostasis 105
hominids 63
homologous series 253
homozygous organisms 52, 53
hormonal contraceptives 103
hormones 96-98, 101-103, 106
human evolution 63, 64
Human Genome Project 58, 59
hydrocarbons 252-255
hydro-electricity 296, 297
hydrogen (as a fuel) 258
hypothalamus 98
hypotheses 2, 6

I

immune system 75-77
incomplete combustion 257
indicators 193, 196, 380
induced magnets 357
inertia 274
infrared radiation 309, 312, 314
insoluble salts 198
insulin 106, 107
interdependence 121
intermolecular forces 161, 254
internal energy 367
interphase 37
inverse square law 88
investigating
   circuits 340, 346
   density 365
   elasticity 376
   Newton's Second Law 276, 277
   properties of water 370-372
   reaction times 284
   refraction 307
   wave speed 303, 304
iodine test (for starch) 28
ionic compounds 155-158
ionic equations 140
ionising radiation 314, 321, 322
   dangers of 326
ions 154, 317, 318
irradiation 326
isotopes 148, 149, 320
IVF 102
I-V graphs 341

K

Kelvin scale 367
kinetic energy stores 288
kinetic theory 366, 367

L

LDRs 337, 341, 342
Leakey's fossils 64
Le Chatelier's principle 222, 223
LH (luteinising hormone) 101
life cycle assessments 218, 219
ligases 68
light gates 382
light microscopes 21, 22
limewater 195
limiting factors (photosynthesis) 87, 88
limiting reactants 174, 175
limit of proportionality 375, 376
lipases 30
lipids 30
liquids 179, 180
litmus paper 380
liver disease 80, 81
live wires 352, 353
lock and key model 26
longitudinal waves 302
lubrication 293, 294
Lucy (fossil) 63
lymphocytes 75-77, 115
lysozymes 75

Index

M

magnetic fields 356, 358, 360
magnetic flux density 359
magnets 356, 357
magnification 23, 24
mains electricity 352
malaria 72
malnutrition 80
mass 278
mass balances 380
mass (nucleon) number 146, 320
mass transport systems 110
meiosis 49
melting 180
memory lymphocytes 76, 77
Mendeleev, Dmitri 150, 151
menstrual cycle 100, 101
meristems 41
metallic bonding 165
metals 165, 226, 227
  reactions of 195, 209-212
microscopes 21-24
microwaves 309, 311, 314
mitochondria 17, 18
mitosis 37-39
moles 169-171
momentum 280-282
monohybrid inheritance 52-55
motor effect 358, 359
motor neurones 45, 46
mutations 57, 58
mutualism 121
myelin sheaths 44, 45

N

national grid 363
natural selection 61, 62
negative feedback 98, 105, 106
nervous system 44, 45
neurones 44-46
neurotransmitters 45, 46
neutralisation reactions 193, 196, 199, 200, 249
neutral wires 352
neutrons 146, 317, 320, 322
Newton's First Law 273
Newton's Second Law 273, 282
  investigating 276, 277
Newton's Third Law 274, 282
nitrifying bacteria 135
nitrogen cycle 134, 135
nitrogen-fixing bacteria 135
nitrogen oxides 258
noble gases 232
non-communicable diseases 71, 80, 81
non-contact forces 333
non-indigenous species 127

non-renewable energy resources 296, 298
nuclear equations 322
nuclear power 298
nuclei 17, 18
nucleotides 50
nucleus 316, 317, 320

O

obesity 80-82, 107
oestrogen 101, 103
ores 214
osmosis 33
  investigating 33, 34
ovaries 96, 100, 101
oxidation 202, 208, 211, 212

P

pancreas 96, 106
parallel circuits 345, 346
parasitism 121
pathogens 71, 72
  defences against 75
percentage masses 168
percentile charts 40
period 301
periodic table 150, 151
permanent magnets 357
pH 193-196
pH probes 380
phagocytes 115
phenotypes 52, 53, 57, 58
phloem 91
photosynthesis 87-89, 131
  investigating rate 89
physical changes 366
pipettes 379
pituitary gland 96, 98, 101
plant cells 18
plasma 116
plasmids 18, 68
platelets 116
plugs 352
plum-pudding model 316
pollutants 257, 258
pollution 122
polymers 164
populations 121-124
  estimating sizes 123
positrons 321, 322
potable water 133, 191
potential difference 337-340, 350
  in parallel 345
  in series 344
  mains electricity 352
potometers 94
power 331, 349, 350
power ratings 349
precipitation 132
precipitation reactions 198, 235, 239, 249

precision (of data) 7
preclinical testing 78
predation 122
pressure 368
progesterone 101, 103
prokaryotic cells 17
proteases 30
proteins 30
protists 65, 72
protons 317, 320
Punnett squares 53
purification of copper 206
purity 183, 191

Q

quadrats 123, 124

R

radiation 320
radioactive decay 320, 324
radio waves 309-311, 314
random errors 8
random sampling 123
range (of data) 9
rates of reaction 29, 235-240, 243-245
  calculating 240
ray diagrams 306
reaction profiles 245, 247, 248
reaction times 284
reactivity of metals 209, 210
reactivity series 208, 214
receptors 44, 46
recessive alleles 52, 53
recycling 217, 218
red blood cells 115, 116
redox reactions 211, 212, 230, 231
reducing energy transfers 294
reduction 202, 208, 211, 212, 214
reflection 306
reflexes 46
reforestation 128
refraction 306, 307
relative atomic masses 148, 149
relative formula masses 168
relay neurones 45, 46
renewable energy resources 296, 297
repeatability (of data) 6, 7
reproducibility (of data) 6, 7
resistance 337, 339, 341, 342
  in parallel 345, 346
  in series 344, 346
resistant organisms 62
resolution 7
  of microscopes 21
respiration 111-113
  investigating rate 113
restriction enzymes 68
resultant forces 273, 334

reverse osmosis 133
reversible reactions 221-223
R_f values 189, 190
ribosomes 17, 18
ripple tanks 303
risk assessments 142
risk factors for diseases 80, 81
root hair cells 91
ruler drop test 284

S

safety 8, 385
salts 193, 195, 196, 198-200
sample size 7
satellites 311
scalars 266
scale drawings 334, 335
scientific drawings 21
scientific method 2
secondary immune response 76, 77
selection pressures 61
selective breeding 66
sensory neurones 45, 46
sensory receptors 44
separating mixtures 184-186, 188-190
series circuits 344, 346
sex determination 54
sexual reproduction 19, 20, 48, 49
significant figures 9
simple distillation 184, 190
simple molecular substances 160, 161
smoking 80
solar power 296
solenoids 360
solids 179, 180
solubility 198
soluble salts 199, 200
sound waves 303
specialised cells 19, 20, 41, 42
specific heat capacity 370
specific immune response 75
specific latent heat 371
speed 266, 267
  of waves 302-304, 306
sperm cells 20, 48
standard form 24, 317
starch 28-30
states of matter 179-181, 366
state symbols 139
stem cells 41, 42
stimuli 44, 46
STIs (sexually transmitted infections) 73
stomata 92
stone tools 64
stopping distances 285
stratigraphy 64
strong acids 194
subcellular structures 17, 18
sulfur dioxide 257

Index

surface area to volume ratios 109, 110, 244
symbol equations 138, 139
synapses 45, 46
systematic errors 8
systems 289, 329

T

tangents 240, 270
target organs 96
temperature 312, 367
    of a gas 368
temperature-time graphs 372
testes 96
test for
    carbon dioxide 195
    chlorine 228
    hydrogen 195
    oxygen 259
thermal conductivity 294
thermal insulation 293, 294, 371
thermistors 337, 341, 342
thermometers 380
thinking distances 285, 286
three domain classification 65
thyroid gland 96, 98
thyroxine 98
tidal barrages 297
titrations 200
transects 124
transformers 363
translocation 91
transmission 306
transpiration 91-94, 132
    rate of 93, 94
transverse waves 302
trends in energy resources 299
tuberculosis 72
tumours 39
Turkana Boy (fossil) 63
type 1 diabetes 107
type 2 diabetes 107
typical speeds 267

U

ultraviolet radiation 309, 313, 314
uncertainties 15
uniform acceleration 269
uniform fields 356
units (S.I.) 12, 13, 24
Universal indicator 193, 380

V

vacuoles 18
validity (of data) 6
valves 117, 118
variables 6
variation 57, 58
vectors 266
    in disease 72
    in genetic engineering 68
veins 117
velocity 266, 268, 271, 273, 382
velocity-time graphs 271
viruses 71, 73
visible light 309, 313
voltage 337, 338
voltmeters 337, 340, 382

W

waist-to-hip ratios 82, 107
wasted energy 292, 293
water baths 383
water cycle 132, 133
water treatment 191
water uptake (plants) 92, 94
wave equation 302
wavefronts 306
wavelength 301
waves 301-315
    electromagnetic 309-314
    longitudinal 302
    ray diagrams 307
    reflection 306
    refraction 306, 307
    sound 303
    speed 302-304, 306
    transverse 302
weak acids 194
weight 278
white blood cells 75-77, 115, 116
wind power 296
work done 330, 331
    on a spring 376
World Health Organisation (WHO) 71

X

X chromosome 54
X-rays 309, 313, 314
xylem 91, 92

Y

Y chromosome 54

Z

zero errors 8
zygotes 48

Physics Equations Sheet

You'll Be Given Certain Equations in the Exams

In each physics paper you have to sit for your GCSE Combined Science, you'll be given an equations sheet listing some of the equations you might need to use. That means you don't have to learn them, but you still need to be able to pick out the correct equations to use and be really confident using them. The equations sheet won't give you any units for the equation quantities — so make sure you know them inside out.

The equations you'll be given in the exam are all on this page. You can use this page as a reference when you're doing the exam questions in each section, and the Practice Papers at the end of the book.

(final velocity)² − (initial velocity)² = 2 × acceleration × distance $v^2 - u^2 = 2 \times a \times x$

force = change in momentum ÷ time $F = \dfrac{(mv - mu)}{t}$

energy transferred = current × potential difference × time $E = I \times V \times t$

force on a conductor at right angles to a magnetic field carrying a current = magnetic flux density × current × length $F = B \times I \times l$

potential difference across primary coil × current in primary coil = potential difference across secondary coil × current in secondary coil $V_p \times I_p = V_s \times I_s$

change in thermal energy = mass × specific heat capacity × change in temperature $\Delta Q = m \times c \times \Delta \theta$

thermal energy for a change of state = mass × specific latent heat $Q = m \times L$

energy transferred in stretching = 0.5 × spring constant × (extension)² $E = \frac{1}{2} \times k \times x^2$